# Western Religion

# Religion and Reason 2

*Method and Theory*
*in the Study and Interpretation of Religion*



MOUTON · THE HAGUE · PARIS

# Western Religion

*A Country by Country Sociological Inquiry*

*edited by*

HANS MOL

*in collaboration with*

MARGARET HETHERTON and MARGARET HENTY

MOUTON · THE HAGUE · PARIS

Library of Congress Catalog Card Number: 73-152083

*Jacket design by Jurriaan Schrofer*



*Printed in the Netherlands*

# Introduction

I. Initially this volume was intended primarily for undergraduate students. It was planned to fill the gap left by the absence of any text book, English or otherwise on the Sociology of Religion in the various Western countries.[1] Initial discussions with prospective authors (primarily the members of the Committee on the Sociology of Religion of the International Sociological Association) indicated widespread support. There were very few refusals from among the list of desired contributors which were almost invariably the most prominent sociologists in the field in the various countries represented.

This book as it stands still meets the original purpose. It provides material which extends the students' horizons beyond the American or English speaking world. It will acquaint them with fascinating differences within Western civilization and in this way give them a bird's eye perspective on the religious situation in their own country – something which is all too often missing in sociology of religion courses. In terms of class or student projects the material also lends itself admirably to three types of essays: those comparing religious phenomena in different countries, those dealing with higher level generalizations or those using the bibliography as a guide to more detailed study.

Originally the book had the secondary purpose of encouraging creative interplay between theory and generalizations based on a wide range of hitherto unavailable cross-cultural empirical data. This was particularly important to the senior author at the time, who had just embarked on the first and large-scale 'Religion in Australia' survey at the Australian National

1. There is indeed *Le Bilan du Monde Encyclopedie Catholique du Monde Chrétien* [1964] but as this is almost exclusively concerned with general statistics, it is of little value to those who want a sociological description or guide to specific research projects. There are a number of bibliographies, including those edited by Carrier and Pin [1964] and Berkowitz and Johnson [1967] but these are not fully comprehensive and more importantly do not include annotations, evaluations or descriptions of findings. There are more complete accounts of specific countries in the various issues of *Social Compass* and *Archives de Sociologie des Religions*, but apart from the fact that many are not in English, they have been written for different purposes from widely varying orientations and do not adequately cover the international scene.

University. Where to begin, what to ask and how to interpret the data would obviously depend on as comprehensive a view as possible of the progress and sophistication of the sociology of religion in other countries.

It was this secondary purpose which almost became primary. When contributions began to flow in we realised that we had struck an unexpected hoard of untranslated research reports almost completely unknown in the English speaking world. Despite the efforts of the international (primarily European) journals, we became convinced that there was a need for sociologists in the Anglo-Saxon world to acquire greater appreciation of the empirical findings and theoretical concerns of colleagues in other countries. The point is well taken by Dr Laeyendecker who complains that Dutch work has not been given due prominence precisely because of the language barrier; the same could be said of a number of other countries represented here. It is thus hoped that this project may contribute substantially to the international feedback between sociologists.

Associated with this blockage of international communication is what may be called a tendency to ethnocentricity in the discipline. We have in mind here, the tendency to use explanatory schemes based on narrow national assumptions which need to be modified in view of cross-cultural findings. Evidence of such biases is not difficult to cull from the literature,[2] but perhaps we may illustrate the point from the 'Religion in Australia' survey.

Gerhard Lenski [1967, p. 225] recently suggested that the reason Catholics are less socially mobile than Protestants in the U.S.A., is that the former are more inclined to rate obedience ahead of intellectual independence. Now, Australian data supports the attitudinal difference between Catholics and Protestants, but not the difference in mobility. In other words, the cross-cultural comparison suggests that American differences in mobility need an additional explanation. Differential mobility patterns have also been linked

2. In American studies religious developments are frequently explained without looking beyond national boundaries to the more general global context. Thus W. W. Sweet [in McNeill, 1939, p. 382] attempts to explain revivalism in terms of the frontier influence in American Christianity rather than in terms of contemporary and similar European movements. Herberg [1955, p. 131] also tends to relate religious individualism only to the American frontier. Similar failures to look beyond national frontiers may be seen in recent bibliographies. Berkowitz and Johnson [1967, p. XII] exclude the majority of non-English references given here on the insulting basis that this would lead primarily to repetitiveness 'not an increase in the scope of the material studied'. A similar narrowness of selection is found in Johnson's *Religion and Occupational Behaviour* [1966]. A further fertile source for other examples of American provincialism in the sociology of religion are the justified complaints of French sociologists in their review of the American literature in *Archives de Sociologie des Religions*.

with the status conferring functions of church membership in America – functions which are not characteristic of the less mobile English society with its more privatized, compartmentalized religion. [Wilson, 1966, p. 107ff]. However, in Australia, while mobility patterns resemble American ones, the whole religious scene is reminiscent of England. Again, this suggests that an explanation which links differential mobility with presence or absence of status conferring functions of religion needs to be modified in a wider context. We thus hope that the variety of cross-cultural findings presented in this volume will be helpful in suggesting alternative and broader theories for the explanation of socio-religious phenomena.

We also hope that the book will be of value to the lay public and for those who have a non-professional interest in the social bases of religious phenomena in various countries. The book could, for example, be used quite effectively for briefing in organizations sending personnel to foreign countries.

When the following chapters were solicited authors were given complete independence in the selection of material, subject only to a general request to present a representative account of work done in their country and to follow a standardized scheme as far as possible. Within this schema there is an initial and necessarily brief historical section concerned with the origins of traditions and interests which are currently operative in different countries. Next follows a demographic section, basically a guide to the extent and structuring of religious pluralism.[3] The third section on religious beliefs and practices concerns that area normally subsumed under the secularization debate. Later sections concern the macro-social relationships between religious institutions and politics, class, economy, etc. Many chapters include a final section covering current research projects and areas of particular interest in different countries. Lastly, each chapter has a Bibliography, a comprehensive if introductory guide to the literature in the field in each country.

This framework, indicated in the text by the major headings, was suggested by the material known to exist, and adopted with the student rather than the professional sociologist in mind. It is intended as a guide to major areas of interest and an aid to cross-reference. All but a couple of authors have been able to utilize it but in so doing variety and freshness of approach have been partly sacrificed; in the summary historical sections, over-simplification is perhaps a besetting sin and, in general, conformity to the schema has influenced selection so that minor areas of significance in some countries have at times been included at the expense of more detailed treatment

3. The term is used here in Lenski's sense of those 'situations in which organized religious groups with incompatible beliefs and practices are obliged to coexist within the framework of the same community or society' [Lenski, 1965, p. 25].

of major areas. Most of these faults are inherent in the survey nature of this project and in the attempt to reach a dual audience with different needs. On balance we would argue that the disadvantages are outweighed by the advantages of facilitating a systematic approach to cross-cultural understanding of the sociology of religion, its data collections, theoretical orientations and substantive findings in various countries.

Finally, as responsibility for inclusion of articles, regulations as to length etc. remain with the editors a few words on the bases of selection. The decision to exclude the non-Christian, non-Western world was made regretfully. The book is already long; contributors would have been hard to find; comprehensiveness would have been impossible and we would have had to go outside the field of sociology for material. Within the Western Christian world it has been possible to be comprehensive. Western and Eastern Europe, and the old Colonies of large-scale settlement, the United States, Canada, Australia, New Zealand and South Africa have been included. With the exception of Portugal and Yugoslavia, which are represented by reprints of recent articles, and East Germany where a précis of a longer article has been used, all chapters have been submitted specifically for this project. The only major omissions are, Rumania and Latin America. Little sociological work has been done in the first one and it proved impossible at this stage to find contributors. For Latin-American countries it proved very difficult to get individual authors and we felt that the existence of Houtart and Pin's recent book [1965] is a partial justification for the omission.

The decision to be comprehensive has meant some unevenness of quality, an unevenness which reflects the differential development of the sociology of religion in various countries. To some extent this has been counteracted by allowing greater length to countries in which it is better established. Hence the long chapters from small countries like the Netherlands and Finland and the relative brevity of the Russian chapter.

II. The following chapters present a patchwork of varied developments. They do not pretend to be strictly definitive, but except in the odd case such as England where the author's individual achievements dominate, they may be taken as roughly representative of the state of sociology of religion in the different countries.

As the chapter headings indicate, the weight of emphasis has been on the collection of data concerning religiosity as associated with conventionally defined religious institutions. All chapters thus have some contribution to make to the debate on secularization but interest in some of the wider theoretical issues of the sociology is more limited. The spectrum in terms of the amount and type of data available, the level of analysis and theoretical development is a wide one, and reflects both the way in which sociology has become institutionalized and the kinds of facilities for data collection which exist in the different countries.

In the nations of traditional Catholic dominance, Italy, Spain, Portugal, France, Austria, Belgium and Eire the concerns of ecclesiastical bureaucrats have had a major role in the initiation of research; sociology tends to have strong connections with ecclesiastical or para-ecclesiastical institutions and to be dominated by the sociological approach pioneered by Gabriel le Bras in France. Yet within this group of countries there is considerable variation. A prodigious amount of data has been collected in France which ranks next to the U.S.A. in the number of recent publications in the field [Dobbelaere, 1968, p. 335]. At the other end of the scale are countries like Ireland (Èire) and Portugal where few studies have been done. In Italy and Spain there have been a vast number of local and regional studies often carried out by the clergy or lay groups, but reliability is uneven.

Interest in theoretical development in these countries is limited. Partly this arises from a certain pessimism about existing possibilities; this point of view is put by Professor Isambert in the French chapter:

> French sociologists – who know from Durkheim in another connection the dangers of a too rapidly established sociological theory of religion – are in no way anxious to formulate such a theory and are content for the moment with concentrating their efforts on conceptual rigour.

Partly it arises from the applied nature of the research and its concern with immediate pastoral problems. In some circles it is conventional to decry such research, yet while it is true that the lack of theoretical integration in research retards the development of the discipline and dissipates resources, it is also true that even when data collection has proceeded without theoretical guidelines, as most frequently happens in applied pastoral sociology, secondary analysis within theoretical frameworks may be possible. The Netherlands chapter provides a good example of this process. Indeed it is part of the rationale of this project that the compilation of cross-cultural data from various sources can contribute to the further growth of the discipline.

An equally large bloc is formed by the Communist countries. In general, census data on religion have not been collected in recent decades (or if available it has been suppressed as with the Russian census of 1937). The lack of basic data is supplemented by survey research of variable representativeness. While Bulgarian data here are based on a nation-wide survey with a sample of 45,000 people, Russia itself has only produced isolated small-scale studies. The other countries fall somewhere between the two extremes.

In these countries, with Poland a dominantly Catholic country providing a unique case, traditional religiosity tends to be studied primarily as a form of social deviance. The general background for these studies is the Marxist theory that theistic religiosity, as a form of consciousness, will retreat before scientific materialism as the socialist state is built. However, as the author of the Russian chapter notes, and as the chapters here indicate, there has been a move away from

> the assertion of dogmatic dialectical materialism... (in) the relatively recent attempt to develop the sociology of religion as an independent science, objectively grounded in concrete, verifiable experimentation.

This is a welcome trend as reliable data on the relevance of theistic religion in widely differing socio-political systems is important for the further development of sociological understanding. In this connection readers will find the comparison of secularization in Capitalist and Communist societies, which forms the theoretical framework of Dr Varga's chapter on Hungary, of particular interest.

In terms of sociographic data the Scandinavian countries are richly supplied by census records and church statistics. In Finland, for example, the official Lutheran Church has collected annual data in each parish for more than fifty years on church attendance, participation at Communion, Sunday School, parish meetings, etc. With a conformist tradition of extremely high formal membership in the established State Churches, and low rates of regular church participation, these countries offer an interesting comparative field for the study of religious pluralism and 'secularisation'. The Finnish chapter in particular offers a valuable theoretical basis for the analysis of these phenomena.

The eleven remaining countries represented here are less easily classified. None of the four ex-British colonies has a well-developed tradition of interest in the sociology of religion. All have census data on religious affiliation which has been used by contributors in the discussion of religious pluralism, and with the exception of Australia, ethnic, religious cleavages. The national survey on religious beliefs and practices which has just been conducted in Australia makes her something of an exception in this group. But in general these countries are characterized by an academic rather than a pastoral orientation towards the sociology of religion and chapters represent a reasonable degree of theoretical sophistication.

Of the discipline in England, David Martin recently wrote

> It is no exaggeration to say that hundreds of social scientists could be employed on these problems (concerning religion in Britain) and still leave the field unexhausted. As things are, some dozen or more expend their part-time energies in the sociology of religion, encountering the

> surprise of the sociological community and the suspicion of some sections of the churches [Martin, 1967, p. 117].

However, the English chapter contains some penetrating insights on the factors involved in rates of religious practice and on minority group religion. In Scotland the situation is worse. Dr Highet is the only professional sociologist involved in the field and his efforts have been directed mainly towards the collection of data concerning church membership.

The remaining chapters include Switzerland and West Germany, the U.S.A. and the Netherlands. The U.S.A. leads the whole field in number of publications, and degree of theoretical interest [Dobbelaere, 1968, p. 335]. Professor Moberg's chapter here presents an able summary of these developments. In the Netherlands, the sociology of religion has moved from a pastoral sociographic approach over the last two decades to an academically based theoretical interest. Again, Dr Laeyendecker's chapter provides one of the most stimulating chapters in this project and should be of particular value in increasing communication across language barriers.

Perhaps one of the disappointments of this project is the overwhelming concentration on the sociology of religious institutions defined in terms of every-day usage, and the dearth of work concerned with the generic phenomena of ultimate value orientations, their functions and relevance to the general social system. Glock and Stark's analysis [1965] of functionally alternative value orientations implies that the study of humanist and radical value orientations is a legitimate focus for the sociology of religion. Further, if these orientations are in fact functionally equivalent there will be implications for what Yinger calls the 'double root of religion – the fundamental individual and group needs' [Yinger, 1957, p. 16]. These may be summarized as individual needs for meaning in face of the ultimate questions of life, and group needs for shared belief and action patterns, the socially integrative mechanisms by which individual needs and desires are relativized and subordinated in terms of values which harmonise group life.

The question of identifying these value orientations, and the question of to what extent 'non-religious' value orientations fulfill 'religious' needs at various levels of the social system are questions hardly as yet established as part of the discipline. But if the sociology of religions is to grow theoretically it must be concerned with analytic rather than conventional-substantive definitions of its field of interest, and hence we feel it worthwhile to highlight here what is but a naissant concern in some chapters of this volume.

One of the many reasons for reluctance to admit these new concerns is no doubt that the challenging questions tend to have come from without the mainstream structural-functionalist orientation of the discipline. They have been put in such terms as redefining 'religion' or grasping meaning rather than 'sociologically relevant effect' [e.g. Vrijhof in Brothers (ed.), 1967, pp. 58–66]. Similarly Berger and Luckmann have argued that the theme of secularisation should be given up in the face of the historical evidence that ecclesiastical institutions have rarely monopolized 'religion' and in the face of contemporary trends – increasing privatization of religion, waning attachment of large numbers of people and weakened legitimating potential of ecclesiastical institutions. The central question of the discipline could then be defined as 'What are the characteristic legitimating processes actually operative in contemporary society' [Berger and Luckmann, 1963, p. 423]. While we do not wish to support the view that functionalism has little to offer in a more widely defined sociology of religion, nor the contention that secularization is a moribund issue, it seems clear that these new orientations pose questions of real importance.

We might have expected some systematic study of such issues in Communist countries, but as already indicated this is not so. Only Bulgaria, which has a project to study changes in the form of 'social consciousness' under the socialist régime, provides a possible exception. In non-Communist countries there is some evidence of interest. About half the chapters consider the relationship between church affiliation and voting patterns. Some of these data invite the kind of analysis Glock and Stark [1965] used to analyse the competing value orientations of radicalism and conventional religiosity. There are also passing references to quasi-religious forms in some chapters. However, the most significant study of this range of questions is in the area of defining societal overarching systems of values and their relationship to traditional Christianity – the phenomenon frequently called societal religion.

Societies which support religious pluralism seem to have spawned most interest in this topic. In America there is, as Dr Moberg points out

> a strong conviction on the part of many scholars that underlying the apparent diversity of American religion is a single basic American culture religion centred around 'the American Way of Life' as 'the operative faith' of the American people.

The Swiss chapter also has some suggestive insights on the process by which the societal value system has arisen there. It is seen to involve the parallel processes of increasing autonomy and restriction of the religious sphere proper, with the increasing proliferation of certain ethical principles now detached from the Christian dogma from which they were originally derived. Tentatively, and primarily supported by only one investigation, it is suggested that

> we are moving towards a post-Christian Humanism, a religious con-

> ception which has become devoid of its Christian substance in order to make way for an Eastern Mysticism, for religious syncretism, for a pronounced moralism.

In the English, Austrian and Danish chapters, there is also an attempt to define societal religion. The latter perhaps deserves special note as an example of important and slightly publicised work being done outside the English-speaking world. An interdisciplinary project is attempting to devise methods to describe 'the religion of the people'. The relationship between popular religiosity and more church-bound forms of piety, as well as such questions as attitudes towards the meaning of life and the idea of the 'holy' is being considered. Dr Thorgaard comments that it is hoped this project will contribute to 'current theoretical and methodological discussions, with special reference to the contributions already made by the structural-functionalist, Berger-Luckmann and Matthes-Rendtorff approaches'.

The question of societal religion is often presented as the reverse side of the secularization coin – to what extent does conventional religion still contribute to societal cohesion and value systems? It thus seems to form a bridge, if only at the total cultural level, between the questions outlined earlier and the more conventionally based sociology of religion.

At the present time the concept of societal religion perhaps raises more questions than it answers. There seems to be little study of the social structures in which it is embedded, or its articulation in individual roles. The assumption of a unitary societal system of values on the total cultural level and the assumption that it is 'religious' in the sense of providing individual and socially integrative functions, have hardly been investigated. Still, we direct the reader's attention to the discussion of societal religion in the following chapters, since this is an area which may lead to a widening of the analytic base of sociological theory of religion. Certainly it indicates a step in the direction of raising a series of questions concerning conventionally 'religious' and 'non-religious' value orientations and functions at all levels of the social system.

One final 'new' area in the sociology of religion deserves brief mention. This is the area of social change within religious institutions. The Dutch chapter contains an interesting theory of the relationship between structural change in the churches in response to the need to adapt to new social conditions and normative change. Here, as also in the Danish chapter, it is suggested that concern with secularization, measured in terms of decline in the traditional indices of church attachment, belief and practice, may obscure more fruitful study in the area of religious change. Both these chapters have important implications for further developments in the theoretical framework of current studies in the sociology of religion and should be perhaps related to recent articles of Parsons [1964], Bellah [1964] and Shiner [1967]. The evolutionary perspective of these articles implies positively functional aspects in the privatization or increasing differentiation of religion in society, aspects which tend to be neglected by traditional studies of secularization.

III. Earlier we suggested that this project provides both a wider range of cross-cultural data than is normally available to the English speaking student, and a counterpoise to narrow national biases in the explanation of phenomena. On these features rests the claim that the volume can encourage a wider and more creative interplay between generalization and theory which is the basis of sociological development. We would have liked to present the project as a contribution to the task of universalizing sociological theory, to specifying which theories hold in all societies, and which hold only under specific national conditions. Yet we must admit that such a sweeping claim is unrealistic in the present state of the discipline.

From a cross-cultural viewpoint, the data in the following chapters have marked deficiencies, if by cross-cultural study we mean the rigorous testing of theoretical hypotheses. The range and type of variables differ from country to country. Populations concerned vary from national samples to relatively small regional studies and techniques of measurement and investigation are likewise unstandardized. Any proposals made on the basis of such data must be highly tentative.

Then there are other problems of interpretation. Many of the authors here comment on the difficulty of interpreting the meaning of one indicator, church-going across denominational boundaries, e.g. between Protestants and Catholics, and the problem is of course magnified in the cross-cultural context. To what extent is the meaning of any indicator the same in different societies? In the U.S.A., for example, there is good evidence that people play 'musical church to a status striving tune' [Demerath, 1965, p. 22]: the same phenomenon is not evident in Australia. To what extent does church-membership merely provide for gregarious activity and to what extent does it involve subjective involvement in transcendent legitimations? A host of such questions suggest themselves. Some chapters take them up in the context of their own country, but any cross-cultural suggestions must be highly speculative, for to put the matter crudely, we cannot always be sure what our indices are measuring, or that they measure the same thing in different contexts.

To some extent this is merely an empirical problem – we need more data based on more discriminating indices. However, a more important stumbling block is in the area of conceptualization. There can be no rigour in hypothesis testing unless the link between concept and indices is tight. The problem is clearly seen in the loose use of concepts like 'religion', 'religiosity' and 'secularization' in this book. Current literature does reflect dissatisfaction with this state of affairs. We have already indicated something of the impact of Glock and Stark's attempt to define 'religion' in a way which accommodates non-theistic ultimate values. Their typology of the complex dimensions and sub-dimensions in the concept of theistic religiosity has also had widespread influence. Secularization, likewise, has been under fire. What are the empirical referents for 'sacred' and 'secular'? What are the dimensions involved here? To what extent are these interconnected? [Martin, 1965]. Is secularization a unitary process? These questions will have to be resolved on the level of concept formation and data well matched to the concepts before there can be any great advance in finding 'generic propositions applicable to all religions' [Yinger, 1957, p. 22].

In view of these difficulties our approach will be highly tentative and a little simplistic. As an exercise in the way this volume may be used we will select from various chapters significant theses, hypotheses and generalizations related to secularization in theistic religion, and where data from other countries seem to be at least roughly comparable, we will attempt to examine their wider validity. We do not pretend that this process is equivalent to scientific verification but we hope it will produce informed speculation which may later lead to rigorous investigation.

As a tentative framework of approach we propose to look at some questions which arise from the dual potential of religion to meet fundamental personal and societal needs. For the individual it is well established that religion can provide a context of meaning for life; it can fulfil a variety of needs which vary with social contexts (gregariousness, group identification, etc.) but universally it has particular relevance in providing integrative frameworks in those life situations in which powerlessness, contingency and meaninglessness would otherwise appear as overwhelming. For society, at least in Durkheimian terms, religion can function as a basis for societal cohesion and integration, by processes of symbolic legitimation and relativization or subordination of conflicting aims of individuals and sub-groups which may threaten cohesion.

However, the model of a tightly articulated, religious system positively functional at individual, sub-group and total societal levels is an ideal type. Counter tendencies and negative functions can occur within the model at all levels. Much of the literature in the field, and indeed many of the following chapters, could be read from the viewpoint of identifying these strains. Here however, we will focus on one particular type of dislocation, the possibility of separation between a) a context of meaning salient to individuals and b) the institutional perpetuation of an interpretation of reality. In the ideal model these aspects will be complementary and might be derived from a view of functional necessity. The individual has need of meaning in ultimate life problems (and derivatively in less critical life situations) but these meanings ideally should be shared, non-problematic and stable elements of his sociocultural environment, i.e. they must be institutionalised and supported by stable norms and sanctions which in turn may provide the Durkheimian basis for social cohesion. It is likely that once social differentiation proceeds to the point where there are specific religious institutions, there will be some lack of fit between these two aspects, either as part of a functional dilemma between meaningfulness and perpetuation of rigidified solutions to institutional problems [see O'Dea, 1966, pp. 92–97] or as the result of conflict with other social structures and legitimating apparatuses which make religious meanings more problematic.

In the following chapters the study of secularization can be viewed as a study in the dislocation of the dual function of religion. Three particular patterns emerge. The first, in societies with fairly uniform religious traditions derived from Protestant State Churches, is associated with an amorphous national consensus on religious matters and large-scale erosion of the individual meaning-giving function of religion. The second is associated with cleavage in traditionally Catholic states in which the upper classes appear to derive both meaning and integration from religion, while sections of the lower classes exhibit massive alienation and disbelief. The third pattern is associated with religious pluralism, the differentiation of various religious meaning contexts in a variety of religious institutions: denominations, sects, etc. Such differentiation in general seems to increase the capacity of religion to provide meaning to individuals in modern societies while providing problems for societal integration. The task here is to draw together the explanations offered for national patterns in different chapters and to discuss to what extent the frame of reference we have offered is a useful integrative model.

The term 'secularization' is only occasionally clearly defined in the following chapters but most use it in an operational way to refer to a decline in attachment to ecclesiastical institutions and/or their modes of interpreting reality. As mentioned previously the cross-cultural comparability of data is limited, by national variations in measurement techniques and the comprehensiveness of indices. Church identification, attendance, membership, and belief in God are the most common ones, but even these have not been measured in all countries. In countries like Finland (in which a new survey has used Glock and Stark's dimension of religiosity), the United States, and Australia, a whole host of variables have been considered. In other places: Scotland, Yugoslavia, South Africa, etc. indices of religiosity are extremely limited. Communist countries tend to stress attitudinal rather than behavioural variables.

The difficulties of measuring decline in a temporal sense are obvious; only a few countries (e.g. Finland) have reliable time sequence data and the difficulties in interpreting such data are considerable (as is discussed e.g. in the English and American chapters). However, most countries have analysed data in terms of current structural differentials, particularly occupation, age, sex, class, education, political affiliation, etc.

For the purpose of this exercise we first propose to take one of these structural differentials – urban rural differences – and one of the measures of secularization – regular church attendance. We have chosen regular church attendance because measurements are reported in most chapters and because it is likely to be a better indication of the meaning-giving function of religion than mere membership or stated belief. It is also clearly correlated with the socio-structural variable. Almost universally, church-going in rural areas is higher than in urban areas; in most cases the difference is quite marked.

Explanations offered here for this phenomenon tend to emphasize either normative, structural, or economic/technological factors. Although there is some overlap they may be summarized as follows:

1. Current religious forms are anachronistic; they are fitted to a traditional framework and unified value structure which is now passing; consequently high levels of attachment are to be found in those areas of society which have felt the impact of social change less. Hence the higher rates of attendance in rural areas (see for example, the chapters on Belgium, the Netherlands, Finland, Canada, Yugoslavia, Czechoslovakia, Bulgaria).
2. Social differentiation or the multiplication of functionally specialized units in modern technological societies diminishes the saliency and control of religion and increases secularization. In terms of saliency, the religious role becomes one of many competing roles: it tends to be compartmentalized in the private sphere to avoid conflict and its relationship to other, often highly specialised, roles is unclear. In addition, non-religious structures provide alternate means of fulfilling social functions previously met by religious organizations, thus further decreasing their saliency. Urban social systems are more highly differentiated than rural ones, hence the lower rate of church attendance. In terms of control, the multiplicity of role involvements often associated with spatial and social segmentation and mobility in highly differentiated social systems, weakens the normative reinforcement of religious institutions and of informal, familial or local socio-religious groups. In this pluralist situation the churches' legitimating apparatus may be made problematic by competing systems of norms leading to a general relativization of values. [See, for example, chapters on Finland, Austria, England, U.S.A., Hun-

gary, the Netherlands]. Again the explanatory relationship to the urban rural difference in church-going is clear.

3. The scientific, industrial and technological revolutions have contributed to man's power to control the environment. Associated with awareness of this power and the lessened play of contingency is a lessened recourse to the Divine to control or explain phenomena and a stress of this-worldly activity or satisfaction rather than other future worldly gains. The writers from Communist countries, Yugoslavia, Hungary, Czechoslovakia and Bulgaria use this theory in association with the general Marxist orientation to explain urban-rural differences. Rural dwellers are less closely associated with the new technological revolution and its associated this-worldly achievement-orientation and de-mystification: they thus retain a greater affinity to the old theistic modes of thought. [For a non-Marxist variant of this explanation see the chapter on England].

These three sets of propositions sum up the basic explanations offered in this volume for secularization as viewed in urban-rural differences in church-going. The first of them emphasizes normative integration and depends on postulating that a far more cohesive cultural pattern, which existed in the past, survives best in rural areas. To have much explanatory potential it must rely also on the second and possibly the third categories of explanation. It does in fact assume that the structurally given needs of urban and country dwellers differ because of social change and that rural communities provide more efficient social support for religious norms and sanctions.

There are also some problems with the third kind of explanation. Given the combination of transcendent motivations and a thoroughgoing this-worldly activity in the 'Protestant ethic' and the high rate of church-going in the industrialized technological society of the U.S.A. (45 per cent attended church in the survey week in 1967) it would seem that extended power over man's environment need not in itself lead to a decline in attachment to ecclesiastical institutions. In view of this one might argue that while economic and technological factors have an influence on religious change, their influence still seems to be mediated by structural and cultural factors, and particularly by the existing cultural interpretation of increasing control over the environment.

A second problem with the third kind of explanation is related to the above. As is pointed out in the English chapter, although science has undoubtedly limited the play of contingency *generally*

> each particular person still feels the threat of fell contingency, and to the extent that natural and political power is socialized, focussed and centralized may even feel less powerful than ever before.

Thus technological advances do not remove the needs with which religion may be functionally associated. The question which has to be asked is: under what conditions are secular rather than religious value orientations likely to arise in relation to these needs?

As it stands, the second theory which explains urban rural differences in terms of the structural impact on normative integration seems to have a more general explanatory potential. In passing, we might also note that this approach has some advantages in theoretical economy; secularization itself can be seen as also the product of a parallel process of differentiation in the religious sphere, according to the evolutionary perspective of recent work by Parsons [1963] and Bellah [1964].

However, let us look more closely at the extent to which the social differentiation theory explains the overall pattern of secularization in this volume, in particular whether there is always a linear relationship between societal differentiation and secularization. We will look first of all at intra-social urban-rural differences; and then at a general cross-cultural index of social differentiation.

The European Catholic countries provide the first stumbling block. Although it is true that in all these countries, except perhaps Portugal, rural church attendance tends to be higher on the national average than urban attendance, the picture is complicated by marked regional differences, which indicate that some rural areas have lower rates of church-going than urban areas in the same society. In Spain there are traditional areas of low rural attendance. In France, the rural areas of Brie and the North of Burgundy are classified as 'missionary areas' which are 'escaping ecclesiastical influence'; in Italy the lowest rates of practice occur in the economically very depressed rural areas. In each of these countries as well as in the Catholic countries of Belgium, Poland, and Austria, the authors caution against an over-easy assumption that industrialization or urbanization will necessarily lead to a drop in church attendance. Cases of the reverse, especially in the more newly established industrial areas, can always be cited. Moreover, as the authors of the Italian and Spanish chapters point out, the pockets of extremely low rural practice may be deeply rooted in historical traditions which pre-date industrialization. The relationship with societal differentiation is thus not unilinear within these countries.

In Portugal surveys demonstrate the existence of large non-practising rural zones in the South of the country, areas in which the level of practice is much lower than in the adjacent urban areas. Dr Querido has analysed historical, demographic and economic factors which are reflected in differences between the North and South in family structure and its economic base. Although it is not clear in absolute economic terms that the North has a higher standard of living than the South, the nature of land tenure, the instability of the family unit and seasonal unemployment in the South, have produced a 'rural sub-proletariat among which class consciousness can only grow at an increasing speed'. The author comments:

> We touch here upon the richest element for a sociological explanation of non-conformism among the Portuguese Catholics. A rising social class has the tendency to reject all the values of the society of which it forms a part and which it identifies with the values of the dominant class. If the total society is Catholic at least sociologically, then Catholicism is rejected.

In other words, class cleavages can help to explain secularization where antagonism is directed against the power of a class identified with religion. This factor can, although need not necessarily be, independent of urbanization and industrialization, and thus of social differentiation. The distribution of power in a society is clearly a variable to be included in any general model of the factors affecting secularization. Before looking for further variables however, let us apply a general cross-cultural test to the societal differentiation hypotheses.

We might look at this question by using Robert M. Marsh's [1967, pp. 33–37] *Index of Societal Differentiation*. This measures the number of structurally distinct and functionally specialized units in a society and was constructed as a basis for cross-societal study. Scores on this scale range from 0 for the least differentiated societies to 109 for the U.S.A. Virtually all the countries considered in this volume are included, with the Portuguese score of 29.6 being the lowest. Marsh considers the Index to have greatest validity when societies at opposite extremes are compared, the next highest validity when societies in an intermediate position are compared with either pole, and least validity when societies adjacent are compared. The scale is based on four distinct indicators: political integration, social stratification, percentage of males in non-agricultural occupations and gross energy consumption in megawatt-hours per capita for one year. Now if we assume that national levels of weekly church attendance are an approximate index of secularization we might expect, on the basis of the second explanatory framework that there would be a rough parallellism between high scores on the Marsh Index and low scores on church-going and vice versa.

This is *not* the case. The highest level of weekly attendance (90–96 per cent of the population) is in fact found in Ireland with a Marsh Index scale of 42.7. Poland, with an Index score of 45.8 also has high levels of attendance, 30–35 per cent attend in the cities and an average of 70–75 per cent in rural areas. The next highest weekly level of church attendance (44 per cent of the population) is in fact found in the United States, at the top of the scale, while a number of other differentiated societies such as Belgium (Marsh

Index Score 74.6) have relatively high levels of church attendance. Low levels of weekly attendance are found particularly in the Scandinavian countries with Marsh Index Scores in the middle range: Sweden 62.7, Denmark 55.7, Norway 55.2 and Finland 47.5.

Our test is patently too rough to suggest that the hypothesis concerning the effect of social differentiation can be rejected. It seems to be supported in many of the following chapters by detailed study of differential labels of secularization in different social categories. These include not only urban rural differences, but also differences within urban environments in terms of size, age and location; occupational differences, etc. However, the failure of our general test, together with anomalies and qualifications suggested by various authors suggest that one must expect a complex arrangement of variables for which the following chapters can be scrutinized.

We have already pointed out that power differences within societies exert an important influence in some countries. Another variable of particular relevance is the differential capacity of religious organizations within society to resist normatively disintegrating influences. The Dutch chapter, for example, provides a sensitive analysis of the large number of variables to be taken into account in explaining the higher resistance of Catholicism and neo-Calvinism to norm erosion. A somewhat similar analysis of Celtic minority religions is provided by the English chapter, and indeed much of the material in this volume concerning church-sect, denominational and minority group differences in rates of secularization is relevant to this problem. In Europe, particular regional differences have also led to the suggestion of a variety of other factors such as number and status of the clergy (Poland, the Netherlands) and the nature of historical traditions (Italy, the Netherlands, Spain).

A catalogue of variables suggested by different chapters cannot be fully detailed. However, before leaving the subject we must note one particular problem raised by the assertion that comparing norm systems in highly differentiated societies leads to a general relativization of values which in turn weakens the churches' legitimate apparatus. As the logical extreme of such relativization would be anomie, it might be counter-argued that this is a situation in which individuals experience a need for the general integrative value orientation which religion supplies. It might be further argued that in such a situation there are positively functional aspects of the relegation of religion to the private sphere with its associated inability to concretize normative attitudes in relation to a multiplicity of specialized roles and statuses. If religious values are sufficiently abstract, the likelihood of challenge is limited.

Perhaps here is a general dilemma for highly differentiated societies: on the one hand a value system of sufficient generality to achieve consensus may have to be so amorphous and diffuse that it can provide little meaning-giving security for the individual; on the other hand value systems which are sufficiently specific to be perceived as salient and normative by the individual may be disruptive on the societal level. Our quest for the variables which explain 'secularization' might be rephrased in terms of our initial model, as a quest for conditions and limits under which religious institutions fulfil dual personal and societal functions in modern societies.

The Finnish chapter links religious pluralism with social differentiation as one of these conditions. Dr Seppänen suggests that:

> In Finnish society the degree of religiosity is related to the pluralist character of the society on the one hand, and to conformist religious choices on the other. The more differentiated the social structure of a society and the more conformist the religious alternatives, the less satisfactory are the choices in face of the pluralist situation and the smaller is the likelihood of high religiosity. In terms of church attendance, Finland and the other Scandinavian societies with conformist religious traditions have exceptionally low participation in comparison with other Christian countries. The continuous secularization process accompanying modernisation and pluralisation of Finnish and other modern societies with comparatively few religious alternatives, also proves the validity of the hypothesis.

The general pattern of religiosity in the Scandinavian countries involves a very high formal membership of the Lutheran State Churches. The percentages of the adult population adhering in Sweden, Denmark, Norway and Finland are respectively 98.25, 95.0, 96.3 and 92.4 (Finland has a second established church, the Orthodox Church to which 1.4 per cent of the population belongs). These countries are also characterized by very high use of church facilities for the rites of passage; Baptism, Confirmation and burials. Levels of listening to religious broadcasts are perhaps the highest in the Western world, although this may be partly due to lack of competition from other programmes. However, despite a diffused cultural religiosity, average levels of attendance at Sunday Morning services of the State Church are uniformly low: 2.7 per cent of the population attend in Sweden and Finland, 2.8 per cent in Norway and for Denmark the figure ranges between the extremes of 1.7 and 4.2 per cent. Although the State Churches may provide a basis for an amorphous general consensus they seem to have little capacity to give meaningful experiences to adults.

The significance of the pluralism hypothesis is increased when we compare the situation in Finland and Denmark with that in Sweden and Norway. Despite the similarities in State Church membership ratios this obscures differences in the proportion of the population who also belong to the

Free Churches, and religious movements or lay associations within the National Church. The data given in the relevant chapters of this book appear to indicate that, especially in Sweden and Norway, the general level of church-going is considerably increased by attendance at such services. This suggests, at least if church-going can be considered as an index of providing meaningful experiences to the individual, that the Scandinavian countries with a more 'pluralist type' religious structure have been more successful on the individual level. This might then be compared with the highly pluralist religious structure of the United States where although only 64 per cent of the adult population were church members in 1965, the majority of these (44 per cent of the population) had been to church in the week preceding the national poll. This again indicates (providing our interpretation of the meaning of church-going is not too wide of the mark) that a pluralist structure has greater capacity to give meaningful experiences to the church members.

The much lower church membership of the United States as opposed to the Scandinavian countries raises another aspect of religious pluralism – the problem of providing an overarching set of values for society. High non-membership in ecclesiastical bodies as well as high church-going is often characteristic of religiously pluralist societies. The Netherlands chapter offers a suggestive hypothesis concerning non-affiliation. It is that the church membership to population ratio is crucial; when the vast majority belongs to one church a break with the church may be represented as a break with the national community, and hence powerful sanctions prevent religious disaffiliation. Except in the Catholic South in the Netherlands where the regional community is identified with Catholicism this sanction is weak – one possible explanation of the very high non-membership rate in Holland. By contrast, membership in the Scandinavian countries is high despite church taxes and despite the inability of the State Churches to provide meaningful individual experiences for the vast majority of the population. Can we then tentatively suggest that the non-pluralist religious situation there does make it easier to find a basis for societal consensus on certain values?

However, religious pluralism may also have dis-functional effects for societal integration by creating tensions between minority groups. In the Netherlands, for example, while vertical pluralism (organizational segmentation of education, politics, trade unions, and other associations along denominational lines) has provided remarkable cohesion within the Catholic and neo-Calvinist sections of society, it has also increased conflict between religiously defined sections of the population. Yet against this one must balance the fact that the emergence of class antagonisms in politics have been lessened by the confessional basis of political adherence.

The analysis of the negative and positive functions of religious pluralism particularly in relation to integration at various levels, is a complex matter considered in a number of chapters in this project. It is also closely linked with interest in the phenomena of societal religion as the overarching symbolic system of a society which integrates various pluralist religious orientations.

Nevertheless, if religious pluralism were the critical variable in providing more individuals with meaningful religious experiences, we would expect that the Catholic countries: Austria, Belgium, France, Italy, Spain, Portugal, Poland and Ireland would show a pattern similar to the Scandinavian countries. This is not the case. We have already noted the high attendance rates in Ireland (Eire) and Poland. Austria and Belgium fall in a middle category with 34.5 and 35.6 per cent respectively of the population attending weekly church. In France the proportion of regular attenders falls to 20 per cent. However, in France, Italy, Spain, Portugal regional or class differences in attendance rates are so great that it becomes less meaningful to talk of average attendance rates. It seems that under certain conditions a homogeneous Catholic society can provide for integration both on the personal and societal level; under other conditions large sections of the population are alienated from it, and it becomes an integrative force only for the upper strata in society. Religion can thus be associated as we saw in Portugal with power conflicts in society – the lower classes are alienated from religion which represents the societal values they reject.

One variable we have not considered so far is the ideal one. In the English chapter Dr Martin suggests that the cross-cultural pattern of secularization and integration may be organised in terms of religious attitudinal differences. He begins by classifying societies as Protestant or Catholic dominated. Catholic societies, he argues, are characterized by collective class antagonism which 'involve massive belief and practice on the one hand confronted by massive unbelief and vigorous alienation on the other'. Protestant societies are associated with patterns of 'individual striving' and 'limited institutionalized conflict within wider unities and tolerances', and may be divided into two sub-varieties: the pattern of American pluralism and the Protestant State Church pattern.

> In the former religion is vulgarised, and therefore remains popular... whereas in the latter, religion remains permanently allied to an élite culture. This culture becomes alien once industrialism breaks up the organic nature of society, but the consequent erosion of institutional participation is *not* accompanied by substantial unbelief. It is important that where Protestant dissent develops on any scale and moves in partial conjunction with political dissent the appearance of militant un-

belief in association with secular, political radicalism is particularly unlikely.

A final set of hypotheses, which might also account for the anomalous position of Ireland and Poland, state that subject nations will seek sources of religious differentiations or use already existing differences as a rallying point, and that minority groups will tend to have higher rates of practice than majorities especially when excluded from the upper levels of society.

The Martin scheme is primarily classificatory, yet in highlighting the association of Protestantism with 'individual striving' and Catholicism with collective loyalties, it implies a causal connection between ideal elements and patterns of secularization.

Empirically, with the exception of the 'alienated' lower classes of Southern Europe, it does seem true that Catholicism has had greater success in enforcing ecclesiastical norms of, for example, church attendance than Protestantism, and it is further likely that this success stems in some measure at least from the theological legitimation of salvation through the institutional structures of the Catholic Church and its clergy, rather than through individual striving. The explicit definition of Catholic norms, the authoritarian basis of its dogma, its hierarchical structure, its maintenance of a celibate priesthood and a variety of other cohesive mechanisms might also be suggested as relevant to success in norm enforcement. However, the contrast between Protestantism and Catholicism could be pushed too far. On the one hand dissenting Protestant groups frequently have considerable success in norm enforcement and the monolythic nature of Catholicism is likewise open to challenge.

The connection between religious ideology and the presence or absence of class antagonisms is more complex. In the discussion of moral norms and social legitimations in England, Dr Martin contrasts the creative, eclectic capacity of Protestantism with the legislative rigidity of Catholicism which creates crises of authority on social issues. However, it is quite clear that class differences in religiosity cannot be solely attributed to such a factor.

Historical reasons are frequently associated with the fact that in Anglo-American countries political or class cleavage does not rest on religious cleavage. In England political and religious freedoms were won separately and thus legitimate issues and parties connecting state and religion did not arise [Alford, 1963, pp. 50ff.]. In Europe, on the other hand, the Reformation pattern strengthened the church-state bond. Subsequent movements for political and social reforms had a potentially anti-religious focus – hence the marked anti-clericalism of the French Revolution or the Republican cause in the Spanish Civil War. Still, if the historical association of church and state were the sole explanation we would expect the Protestant Scandinavian countries to have a secularization pattern based on class cleavage. Although there are class differences in religiosity in these countries, the contrast is minimal when compared to the Southern European Catholic countries. We cannot exclude the possibility of an intrinsic difference between Protestant and Catholic influence. Catholicism seems to have a general affinity to rigid upper class legitimations of the *status quo*.

Some account should also be taken of the actual and perceived level of lower class social and economic deprivation. In one of the few cross-cultural studies in the sociology of religion Glock and Stark [1965, pp. 210–224] investigated lower-class religiosity. Their hypothesis that: 'To the degree to which men seek to alter existing stratification arrangements, they are likely to have turned away from the prevailing religious institutions of their societies', maintained its predictive value in a cross-cultural study of English, French, Netherlands, United States and Columbian data which correlated variables related to religious attitudes, beliefs and participation, with political party's memberships. They thus put forward two predictive generalizations: in any given political system leftists will be less supporters of religion than rightists and that the proportions supporting religion will systematically decrease from the right to the left of the political spectrum. Moreover, the wider the political spectrum the greater will be the differences between the religious involvement of the rightists and the leftists.

It is important to note that the variable in question here is radicalism not class; that we are concerned with conflicting ideologies. The explanatory power in relation to class differences seems to come from the assumption that although class differences in attitudes within parties are minimal (class and party are in fact controlled for in the analysis) [Glock and Stark, 1967, pp. 93–99] lower classes have the most to gain from changes in the existing stratification arrangements, and hence the ideological variable explains a good deal of the differences in class levels of religiosity.

In reference to the European Latin Catholic countries it would seem that here the lower classes do have a great deal to gain from a change in stratification arrangements. Whether or not a detailed historical and economic investigation would support the conclusion that the level of class inequality and the slow rate of economic and democratic reforms is influenced by the nature of Catholicism must remain an open question.

Despite these problems the Martin schema has some important advantages. In the first place, it forces us to ask questions about the impact on society of the 'ideal' element in religion, questions which have been largely disregarded since Weber. In the second place, it highlights the value of a cross-cultural approach, the kind of approach which we hope this volume will foster.

Two tendencies in the sociology of religion at the moment seem to hamper this development. The first is a propensity to ethnocentrism which fails to take account of wider exploratory schemes, or anomolous findings in different countries. The second is a reverse tendency to assume that certain social forces have universal effects. Thus in the majority of studies which have been done in the last three decades, religion has appeared as a dependent variable – dependent on the inexorably secularizing forces of modern highly differentiated technological societies. But, as Martin points out in relation to technology, and as we have tried to illustrate here from other material in this volume

> it is not clear whether these indirect consequences of science have the universal impact some might expect... This means therefore that it may be appropriate to abandon 'universal' processes and look more closely at all the differentia between societies.

It is to this task that this project is addressed.

Finally, a note about the division of labour among the editors. When it became obvious that the *Religion in Australia*-survey demanded the entire time of the senior author, he asked his research assistants at the time (Mrs Hetherton and Mrs Henty***) to continue the Western Religion project on their own. Mrs Henty took the administrative task upon her, carried out the correspondence and negotiated the translations. Both she and Mrs Hetherton did some editorial work, whereas the latter also concentrated on the theoretical implications of this first attempt at cross-national comparisons of the survey materials.

In conclusion, let us say that the editors of this volume, probably even more than the reader, are aware of the shortcomings of the project. But we have great hopes that in another five years it may be possible to embark on a similar venture, this time with a better budget, better translations, more incisive editorial work, more uniformity and clarity in the use of statistics, more comprehensive comparisons and above all, more sophisticated research in the sociology of religion especially in those countries where the discipline is decidedly underprivileged.

HANS MOL*
MARGARET HETHERTON**

* Hans (J.J.) Mol was born in Rozenburg, The Netherlands, in 1922. He was educated at the United Theological Faculty, Sydney, Australia, the Union Theological Seminary, New York, U.S.A. (B.D., 1955) and Columbia University, New York (M.A., 1956 and Ph.D., 1960). He has since worked as a Lecturer in Sociology, University of Canterbury, Christchurch, New Zealand, 1961–63, and as a Fellow in Sociology, The Australian National University, Canberra, Australia, 1963–70. He is now Professor in the Sociology of Religion, McMaster University, Hamilton,

Ont., Canada. He was Secretary-Treasurer of the Sociological Association of Australia and New Zealand from 1963 to 1969. He is now Secretary of the Sociology of Religion Committee of the International Sociological Association. His major works include *Churches and Immigrants*, 1961; *Race and Religion in New Zealand*, 1966; *The Breaking of Traditions*, 1968; *Christianity in Chains*, 1969, and *Religion in Australia*, 1971.

** Margaret Hetherton was born in Sydney, Australia in 1938. She has obtained degrees from the University of Sydney (B.A., 1960, and Diploma of Social Work, 1961) and the University of New South Wales (M.A., 1967). She is currently engaged in research leading to her Ph.D. at The Australian National University, Canberra Australia.

*** Margaret Henty was born in Canberra, Australia, in 1946. She obtained the B.A. degree of the Australian National University at Canberra in 1967. She was a Research Assistant in the Department of Sociology until the beginning of 1971.

REFERENCES

Alford, Robert R., *Party and Society. The Anglo-American Democracies.* Chicago, Rand McNally, 1963

Bellah, Robert N., 'Religious Evolution'. *American Sociological Review*, 29 (3), June 1964.

Berger, Peter L., and Luckman, Thomas, 'Sociology of Religion and Sociology of Knowledge'. *Sociology and Social Research*, 47 (4), July 1963.

Berkowitz, Morris I., and Johnson, J. Edmund, *Social Scientific Studies of Religion.* Pittsburg, University of Pittsburg Press, 1967.

Demerath, N. J. III, *Social Class in American Protestantism.* Chicago, Rand McNally, 1965.

Dobbelaere, K., 'Trend Report of the State of Sociology of Religion, 1965–1966'. *Social Compass*, 15 (5), 1968.

Glock, Charles Y., and Stark, Rodney, *Religion and Society in Tension.* Chicago, Rand McNally, 1965.

Herberg, W., *Protestant-Catholic-Jew.* New York, Doubleday, 1955.

Houtart, Francois, and Pin, Emile, *The Church and the Latin American Revolution.* New York, Sheed and Ward, 1965.

Johnson, Benton, *et al.*, *Religion and Occupational Behaviour.* Eugene, Center for Research in Occupational Planning, University of Oregon, 1966.

Laloux, J., '*Practique réligieuse et appartenance sociale*' [Religious Practice and Social Behaviour]. *Social Compass*, 14, 1967.

Lenski, Gerhard, 'Religious Pluralism in Theoretical Perspective'. *International Yearbook for the Sociology of Religion*, I, 1965.

—, 'Religious Impact on Secular Institutions' in Joan Brothers (ed.), *Readings in the Sociology of Religion.* Oxford, Pergamon Press, 1967.

Marsh, Robert M., *Comparative Sociology. A Codification of Cross-Societal Analyses.* New York, Harcourt Brace and World, 1967.

Martin, David, 'Towards Eliminating the Concept of Secularization' in David Gould (ed.), *Penguin Survey of the Social Sciences*. Harmondsworth, Penguin Books, 1965.
—, *A Sociology of English Religion*. London, S.C.M.Press, 1967.
McNeill, J. T., *et al.*, *Environmental Factors in American History*. Chicago, 1939.
O'Dea, Thomas F., *The Sociology of Religion*. Prentice Hall, N.J., 1966.
Parsons, Talcott, 'Christianity and Modern Industrial Society' in Louis Schneider (ed.), *Religion, Culture and Society. A Reader in the Sociology of Religion*. New York, John Wiley, 1964.
Shiner, Larry, 'The Meaning of Secularization'. *International Yearbook for the Sociology of Religion*, 3, 1967.
Vrijhof, P. H., 'What is the Sociology of Religion' in Joan Brothers (ed.), *Readings in the Sociology of Religion*. Oxford, Pergamon Press, 1967.
Wilson, Brian, *Religion in Secular Society*. London, Watts, 1966.
Yinger, J. Milton, *Religion, Society and the Individual*. New York, Macmillan, 1965.

HANS MOL*

# Australia

## HISTORICAL INTRODUCTION

The British settlement of Australia at the end of the eighteenth century did not depend as did some earlier colonial enterprises – those of Spain and Portugal for example – on religious legitimation. Authority was, from the beginning, independent of religious *fiat*.

However religion had a well recognized role. As a source of social control its usefulness was recognized by the early Governors of New South Wales. They saw that a semblance of moral unanimity, a self enforcement of norms and an unenforced acceptance of official rule would greatly ease the problem of controlling friction and disorder in what was essentially a large and uniquely isolated jail. When the jail gave way gradually to a colony of free settlers, when transportation of convicts ceased (in 1840 in New South Wales and later in the other colonies) religion continued to be seen as a source of social control. Particularly among those who were sensitive to the colonies' reputation for insobriety, prostitution and gambling, the clergy were welcomed as 'moral policemen'.

Yet if the role of religion seemed clear in the beginning, its imported institutional forms had to undergo some process of modification in the colonial milieu. This was particularly true in the area of church-state relations. The situation of religious pluralism which arose from placing sizeable minorities of Irish and Scots among the English deportees demanded a local solution. In so far as the Home Government thought about it at all, it thought in English terms with the Anglican Church as the established church [Gregory, 1960, p. 60]. After all Presbyterianism was established only in Scotland; Methodism had only just broken with Anglicanism (1794); Catholicism in Ireland was a source of rebellious strife and legal Catholic Emancipation was not to come until 1829. To the early Governors also 'religion' meant Anglicanism. Presbyterianism could be tolerated, but although the arrival of the first Irish Catholic convicts in 1791 caused some consternation, no real provision could be made for this group before 1820 when two perma-

* See p. 23 for particulars.

nent priests arrived. By this time Catholicism was established as a strong minority religion. In the 1828 Census it represented about thirty per cent of the population (11,236 in a total population of 36,589) [O'Farrell, 1968, p. 20] and as Table 1 shows it tends to have fluctuated around twenty-five per cent for the last century.

The first steps towards a solution were taken in 1825 when Catholic and Presbyterian chaplains were given allowances from colonial funds, although a disproportionate share still went to the Church of England. However, in 1836 a Church Act revised the unequal system by allocating colonial funds to supplement the voluntary contributions of the three denominations without discrimination. The system remained in spite of the Anglican Bishop Broughton's angry protests that it was morally wrong and socially dangerous for the State to support true and false doctrines alike. This pattern of multiple establishment was followed by the other, younger colonies. The grants to the churches were substantial. In 1841 about 8 per cent of the total estimated expenditure in N.S.W. went to the churches.

These were but first steps in the solution of the problem of religious pluralism. During the second half of the nineteenth century, beginning with South Australia in 1853 [Pike, 1957, p. 437] the various states abolished state aid to religion. State aid to denominational schools was likewise withdrawn in the various states between 1872 and 1895, and State education systems free, compulsory and secular, were set up.

Although a generalised *laisser-faire* attitude, secularism, voluntarism (attacks by believers on the debilitating influence of state support) and sectarianism (mutual suspicion between religious groups particularly between Catholic and Protestant) had some influence on this legislation, it is best seen as a response to the situation of religious pluralism

> as reform not inspired by any doctrinaire rejection of the value of religion nor by any desire to persecute the Church, Protestant or Roman Catholic, but rather by a determination to make the State, in action and in law, the symbol of a common citizenship [Gregory, 1960 p. 88].

When Federation came in 1901, Section 116 of the Constitution provided that:

> the Commonwealth shall not make any law for establishing any religion, or for prohibiting the free exercise of any religion, and no religious test shall be required for any office or public trust under the Commonwealth.

The society-integrating role of religion had been weakened by opposition between the various religious institutions. In such a situation other more favourably placed institutions were likely to become the carriers of a unifying symbolism. The abandonment of state aid also expressed, as it did in other countries, the ongoing and increasing differentiation between religious and political functions. Increasing acceptance of the polity entailed a decreasing necessity for religious and other legitimation.

This does not mean that religious differences have not upset the harmony of the polity. In the colonial period sectarian bitterness was frequently roused to public display and affected such issues as immigration quotas, public appointments and above all education. The Catholic decision to boycott the secular education system and build a parallel denominational system without state aid, undoubtedly strengthened the cohesion of the Catholic body but it also contributed to a fear of Catholicism that occasionally erupted into claims of Catholic political conspiracy. Earlier the Irish basis of Catholicism coloured these claims, for example in the alleged Fenian plot of 1868, and the anti-conscription campaign of 1916–17 led by the Catholic Bishop Mannix.

In this century a major locale for these conflicts has been the Labour Party, which lower social status predisposed Catholics to support. The conscription issue split the Labour Party and increased Catholic influence within it. In the mid-fifties it was to split on sectarian lines following 'exposés' of Catholic domination of the anti-Communist cells in the Trade Union wing. The results of this conflict are still evident in the Liberal/Country Parties' long tenure in Federal office.

Thus the importation of religious division made it necessary to work out a framework for religious pluralism in Australia. Liberal legislation in this area, as in others, for example, in the extension of the franchise, came in advance of changes in the Mother Country, but residues of the problem continue to exist.

Within the churches too, the accommodation of imported institutional forms to the local situation has caused strain. Particularly until World War II important appointments tended to be filled from Great Britain thus strengthening ties with the home country. In Catholicism there were marked conflicts between the English Benedictine Hierarchy and the Irish laity and priests in the last century. Current conflicts partly represent a reaction to Irish cultural dominance in Australian Catholicism.

## DENOMINATIONAL COMPOSITION

The numerical strength of the denominations in Australia roughly reflects the original migration patterns. The fact that the bulk of immigrants came originally from England and Wales followed by Ireland and Scotland, accounts for the greater strength of the Anglican Church, followed by the Catholic and then the Presbyterian Churches. Methodism, the major English alternative to Anglicanism, grew from half the size of Presbyterian-

*Table 1. Religious denomination in Australia**

| Denomination | 1851[a] | 1881 | 1901 | 1933 | 1947 | 1954 | 1961 | 1966 |
|---|---|---|---|---|---|---|---|---|
| Church of England | 175,643 (52.71) | 819,645 (38.36) | 1,497,576 (39.68) | 2,565,118 38.69) | 2,957,032 (39.01) | 3,408,850 (37.93) | 3,668,931 (34.91) | 3,877,459 (33.57) |
| Catholic[b] | 87,357 (26.18) | 516,503 (24.17) | 855,799 (22,68) | 1,300,908 (19.62) | 1,586,738 (20.94) | 2,060,986 (22.93) | 2,620,011 (24.93) | 3,036,126 (26.29) |
| Methodist | 18,768 (5.63) | 241,968 (11.32) | 504,101 (13.36) | 684,022 (10.31) | 871,425 (11,50) | 977,933 (10,88) | 1,076,395 (10,24) | 1,124,310 (9,73) |
| Presbyterian | 34,249 (10.28) | 246,666 (11.54) | 426,105 (11.29) | 713,229 (10,76) | 743,540 (9,81) | 870,242 (9.68) | 976,518 (9.29) | 1,043,570 (9,03) |
| Lutheran | | | 75,021 (1.99) | 60,803 ( .92) | 66,891 ( .88) | 116,178 (1.30) | 160,181 (1.52) | 177,324 (1.54) |
| Greek Orthodox | | | | | | 74,745 ( .83) | 154,924 (1.47) | 255,493 (2.21) |
| Baptist | | 47,242 (2.21) | 89,338 (2.37) | 105,874 (1.60) | 113,527 (1.50) | 127,444 (1.42) | 149,819 (1.43) | 165,488 (1.43) |
| Church of Christ | | | 24,192 ( .64) | 62,754 ( .95) | 71,771 ( .95) | 80,364 ( .89) | 95,641 ( .91) | 102,545 ( .89) |
| Congregational (or Independent) | | 50,140 (2.35) | 73,561 (1.95) | 65,202 ( .98) | 63,243 ( .83) | 69,452 ( .77) | 73,526 ( .70) | 76,588 ( .66) |
| Salvation Army | | | 31,100 ( .82) | 31,210 ( .47) | 37,572 ( .50) | 42,838 ( .48) | 51,084 ( .49) | 56,501 ( .49) |
| 7th Day Adventist | | | 3,332 ( .09) | 13,965 ( .21) | 17,550 ( .23) | 25,329 ( .28) | 31,626 ( .30) | 37,617 ( .33) |
| Brethren | | | | 10,043 ( .15) | 13,002 ( .17) | 16,404 ( .18) | 15,523 ( .15) | 15,516 ( .13) |
| Hebrew | 1,778 ( .53) | 8,815 ( .41) | 15,239 ( .40) | 23,553 ( .35) | 32,019 ( .42) | 48,436 (. 54) | 59,343 ( .56) | 63,271 ( .55) |
| Other religion or denomination | 15,402 (4.67) | 205,933 (9.64) | 115,467 (3.06) | 128,793 (1.96) | 153,896 (2.04) | 187,826 (2.09) | 234,184 (2.24) | 285,646 (2.47) |
| No religion | | | 6,779 ( .18) | 15,417 ( .23) | 26,328 ( .34) | 23,684 ( .26) | 37,550 ( .36) | 94,091 ( .81) |
| No reply | | | 56,191 (1.49) | 848,948[c] (12.80) | 824,824 (10.88) | 855,819 (9.54) | 1,102,930 (10.49) | 1,138,899 (9.86) |
| Total | 333,197 | 2,136,912 | 3,773,801 | 6,629,839 | 7,579,358 | 8,986,530 | 10,508,186 | 11,550,444 |

Source: Census data * Figures in brackets represent percentages; a. New South Wales, Victoria and Tasmania only;

ism in 1851 to establish its strength by 1881. Together these four denominations account for 80 per cent of the population; none of the smaller bodies include more than 2½ per cent.

Fluctuations in denominational strength can also be related to changes in migration patterns. The relative decrease in the number of Anglicans and corresponding rise in the number of Catholics between 1947 and 1954 can be related to the influx of three-quarters of a million Catholic immigrants largely from Europe. The flow of Anglicans from Great Britain in the same period was much less: they accounted for only 18.6 or 20.8 per cent of all settlers when their contribution to the total population of Australia was about double these figures. There is no reason to think that later migration has substantially changed this picture [Price 1957, 1963]. However migration patterns are not the only cause of change in denominational composition.

a) *Fertility*

If overseas data are regarded as a guide, then one would expect a higher fertility ratio among Catholics than among Protestants. Table 2 shows that this is in fact so, although the fertility rate has varied considerably from Census year to Census year and has in 1891, been lower than the rest of the population. It should be noted, however, that Catholic women have tended to marry later and less than the rest of the population, although by 1961 the number of married Catholic women per 100 Catholic women over the age of 15 was only 1.4 less than the rest of the population (64.3 per cent for Australia as a whole, compared with 62.9 per cent of Catholics). This means that until recently, Catholics have not perpetuated themselves any faster than other denominations.

*Table 2. Denominational fertility ratios*

| Census year | Ratio of 0–4 year old children per 100 married women | | | | |
|---|---|---|---|---|---|
| | Anglican | Catholic | Methodist | Presbyterian | Total |
| 1891 (NSW | 102.9 | 96.0 | 101.7 | 98.3 | 98.8 |
| 1901 (NSW) | 77.5 | 80.5 | 77.8 | 73.5 | 77.1 |
| 1911 | 72.4 | 75.7 | 69.7 | 68.4 | 71.6 |
| 1921 | 59.6 | 65.9 | 59.3 | 56.3 | 60.1 |
| 1933 | 40.8 | 51.7 | 39.5 | 38.2 | 44.0 |
| 1947 | 39.7 | 48.4 | 40.3 | 37.5 | 43.3 |
| 1961 | 41.6 | 60.4 | 42.7 | 42.5 | 47.3 |

Day [1965] found that residence affected fertility rates considerably. The fertility of metropolitan Catholics is consistently closer to that of metropolitan non-Catholics than to rural Catholics.

The 1961 Census shows an interesting phenomenon; that inter-faith marriages (i.e. Catholic-Protestant) have a lower fertility rate than in-marriages, both Catholic and Protestant. Since inter-faith marriages are increasing, fewer of these marriages are likely to have completed child bearing.

b) *Inter-faith marriages*

As in other Anglo-Saxon countries, Australians think of inter-faith marriages as Catholic-Protestant marriages. There are too few Jews in Australia to make Jewish-Gentile marriages at all common. At the 1961 Census, 2,465 or 8 per cent of all married Jews, were married to a Christian spouse.

Traditionally there has been hostility in the Catholic Church to inter-faith marriages and hence one would expect Australian Catholics to marry less outside their faith. This is not the case. In-marriage is greatest among Anglicans (80.09 per cent of Church of England wives are married to Church of England husbands) compared with Catholics (77.41 per cent), Methodists (73.17 per cent), and Presbyterians (71.49 per cent). In-marriage is partly a function of the numerical proportion in the population rather than denominational cohesion. However, if mate-selection was completely random, the total in-marriage rate would be 22.39 per cent, and not 78.92 per cent which it is. Another reason why in-marriage figures are so high may be that in a population of immigrants, one can expect the married couples from England, Eire and Scotland to be uniformily Anglican, Catholic and Presbyterian. In 1961, 83.07 per cent of the Australian population was Australian-born, and it is therefore unlikely that the proportion of married immigrants could account for the high in-marriage rate. It is true too, that in some marriages, one partner adopts the religion of the other. The extent of this has been measured in the 'Religion in Australia' survey of 4,201 persons throughout New South Wales, Victoria and Tasmania.[1] Five per cent of Anglicans (n=748) who answered the relevant question said they had changed their religion as a result of marriage. Only six per cent of Catholics (n=453) had changed as a result of marriage. The remarkable feature of these figures is, therefore, a) that denominational adherence is a redoubtable factor in mate selection before marriage and b) that in this regard, Catholics do not differ

1. This survey was carried out from 1966–69 by the author at The Australian National University. It is based on a .067 probability sample covering 68 per cent of the Australian population and comprising 4,201 people. It was published in 1971 by Nelson, Melbourne under the title: *Religion in Australia.*

much from Anglicans, although the former are supposed to be more loyal to their church.

c) *Sex differences*

There is some ground for the hypothesis that men feel less attached than women to their churches. There is, of course, evidence for this in other parts of the western world and Australia is no exception. Both the 1954 and the 1961 Censuses show that there were more than twice as many men than women in the small 'no religion' category. In the 1966 Census there was a sharp rise (from 37,550 in 1961 to 94,091 persons in 1966) of people who reported to have no religion, the rise being greater for women resulting in a decrease of the sex ratio in this category (see Table 3). In the larger category of those who gave 'no reply' to the Census question regarding religion, there was also an over-representation of males as Table 3 shows. Although this category includes people who may be religious, a sizeable percentage is likely to be formed by those who have no religious preference. The decreasing over-representation of males in the Orthodox religion is attributable to the evening of the ratio of male to female Greek immigrants.

*Table 3. Sex ratios (number of males per 100 females) for the major religious denominations*

| Religion | 1954 | 1961 | 1966 |
|---|---|---|---|
| Church of England | 100.56 | 100.02 | 99.06 |
| Catholic | 103.68 | 103.47 | 101.54 |
| Methodist | 95.85 | 96.28 | 95.22 |
| Presbyterian | 98.03 | 97.67 | 96.31 |
| Lutheran | 107.94 | 106.08 | 103.10 |
| Orthodox | 146.17 | 121.45 | 113.12 |
| Baptist | 89.10 | 90.05 | 89.27 |
| Church of Christ | 89.17 | 89.29 | 88.71 |
| Congregational | 87.99 | 89.29 | 88.26 |
| Salvation Army | 90.01 | 91.29 | 92.00 |
| 7th Day Adventist | 78.84 | 82.66 | 81.99 |
| Brethren | 84.46 | 92.31 | 91.98 |
| Hebrew | 102.77 | 99.32 | 97.91 |
| Other religion or denomination | 103.31 | 103.64 | 100.27 |
| No religion | 236.80 | 204.20 | 180.30 |
| No reply | 120.48 | 117.59 | 119.74 |

Source: Census material.

The differential effect of sex on religious affiliation is not just a present-day phenomenon. In 1901 the New South Wales Statistician showed that in a mixed marriage the children were more like to follow the mother's religious affiliation (65.88 per cent) than the father's (34.12 per cent). One of his tables surprisingly showed that this was also true for marriages where the father was Catholic.

d) *Inter-church relations*

In the twentieth century several attempts have been made to unite the major denominations. There have been discussions between the Presbyterian, Methodist and Congregational Churches since 1901, but all meetings have met with failure. The Church of England sent observers to the most recent committee meetings in 1957 and have expressed interest in union on several other occasions. However, all attempts to unite have so far failed in Australia. The former primate of the Church of England in Australia, Archbishop H. Gough feels that the laity is to blame. 'The leaders of the churches want unity. The majority of the lay people do not. They are the grass roots and you can't force the grass roots...' [*Sydney Morning Herald*, 16 October 1965, p. 16]. The more recent Gallup Polls contradict Dr Gough. According to a 1965 Poll, 70 per cent of respondents said that Catholic and Protestant Churches at least should try to unite, and of this majority, 76 per cent considered their uniting very important. Similar responses were obtained in two 1966 Polls. There was not much difference between denominations, but in all of them, more Catholics were union-minded.

In the 'Religion in Australia' survey, 21 per cent of respondents (n=1825) said that they did not want their denomination to merge with another. Another 15 per cent had no opinion or said they did not belong to a church. Thirty-seven per cent wanted complete merger, but 12 per cent wanted to exclude Catholics and 8 per cent to exclude one or more of the fringe sects. A further 6 per cent gave other replies.

Attitudes towards church union were not related to age, church-going, regular prayer habits or belief in God. There appeared to be a relationship between the traits of the 'authoritarian personality' [Adorno, *et al.*, 1950] and opposition to merger.

The survey findings suggest that peoples' attitudes towards merger have little to do with religion in general and religious belief in particular. This being so, the implication for ecclesiastical strategy are that theological arguments about the nature of the Church (and maybe the ministry) are likely to be a waste of time if one hopes to change the grass-roots attitudes to church union thereby [Mol, 1969b].

RELIGIOUS BELIEFS, PRACTICES, AND EXPERIENCES

Religiosity can be measured by several criteria. One can measure a person's proferred beliefs, his religious knowledge, his practices and his experiences. The 'Religion in Australia' survey measured all these factors to some extent. From the 'belief in God' question it could be ascertained that the majority of Australians believe in God in some form or another, as shown in Table 4. Eighty-four per cent of men and 92 per cent of women believe in some kind of God. Table 5 shows definition of the Church. Here the sex difference is

*Table 4. Religious beliefs of the Australian population*

| Belief in God | Cumulative percent | |
|---|---|---|
| | Males | Females |
| I know that God really exists and have no doubts about it | 43 | 55 |
| While I have doubts, I feel that I do believe in God | 63 | 76 |
| I find myself believing in God some of the time but not at other times | 69 | 83 |
| I don't believe in a personal God, but I do believe in a higher power of some kind | 84 | 92 |
| I don't know whether there is a God, and I don't believe there is any way to find out | 93 | 96 |
| Other | 100 | 100 |

again pronounced, with more women accepting the orthodox definition of the Church. These two belief questions indicate that the Australian population has on the whole, a positive regard for religion and the Church. Only 1 per cent of the sample thought that the church could be harmful to society.

An International Gallup Poll taken in the early 1950s, showed that 95 per cent of Australians said that they believed in God, but that only 63 per cent believed in life after death, which is equally important to a Christian [Oeser and Hammond, 1954]. An Australian Gallup Poll unearthed some interesting denominational differences on the subject of Hell. This Poll which was carried out in 1959 found that 27 per cent believed in a fiery Hell, but 54 per cent denied this, saying it was 'Hell on earth' or 'A state of mind'. Of Catholics, 62 per cent believed in a fiery Hell, but only 17 per cent of others believed in this. On the other hand, 11 per cent of Catholics said there was no Hell, compared with 28 per cent of the rest of the sample.

Religious knowledge was only questioned in one item of the 'Religion in

*Table 5. Definition of the church*

| Per cent who agrees that | Males (n=867) | Females (n=959) |
|---|---|---|
| The Church is appointed by God, it is the home and refuge of all mankind | 25 | 32 |
| The Church is the one sure foundation of civilized life; Every member of society should be educated in it and support it | 16 | 17 |
| On the whole the Church stands for the best in human life, in spite of shortcomings found in all human institutions | 35 | 35 |
| The usefulness of the Church is doubtful. It may do as much harm as good | 9 | 6 |
| The Church is not important today – it doesn't count | 4 | 1 |
| The Church is a stronghold of much that may be unwholesome and dangerous to human welfare | 1 | 1 |
| Other replies, or no answer | 10 | 7 |
| Total | 100 | 100 |

Australia' survey. Respondents were asked to agree or disagree with the statement that 'The book of Acts of the Apostles gives an account of Jesus' life on earth'. Of males, 16 per cent disagreed (correctly) and of females, 14 per cent disagreed. Nearly 50 per cent of each group said they were not sure. This knowledge was strongly related to religiosity; fo thosewho go to church regularly, pray daily and have no doubts about God's existence, 31 per cent correctly answered the question. Of those who do not attend church, do not pray daily and have doubts about God's existence, only 12 per cent were correct. From this evidence we cannot say that religious knowledge has been tested, for there were not enough questions asked, and the question which was asked may not be an adequate measure. It is notable that the differences between denominations were not significant. Of Anglicans, 14 per cent were correct, of Catholics, 12 per cent, Methodists, 15 per cent and Presbyterians 14 per cent.

Table 6 shows the extent of religious practice, both public and private, in

*Table 6. Religious practice by sex*

| Per cent who | Males | Females |
|---|---|---|
| Attends church usually or always (once a month or more) | 35 | 42 |
| Prays daily | 25 | 40 |

*Table 7. Religious practice by denomination*

| Per cent who | Anglican | Catholic | Methodist and Presbyterian | Total |
|---|---|---|---|---|
| Attends church usually or always | 20 (n=1625) | 70 (n=1114) | 36 (n=940) | 39 (n=4200) |
| prays daily | 25 (n=738) | 50 (n=407) | 28 (n=451) | 33 (n=1825) |

the 'Religion in Australia' survey. As is to be expected, women are more active than men. These figures are in keeping with the church attendance figures published by the Gallup Poll. These two sources also show that more Catholics attend church regularly than do Protestants (see Table 7), and more Catholics pray daily. The Protestant figures on church attendance may be slightly deflated as the numbers include children who usually attend Sunday school rather than church. The prayer question was only asked to adults.

From the information on three measures of religiosity, belief in God, regular church attendance and daily prayer, the sample was divided into six groups, ranging from very religious to agnostic or atheistic, in the hope that this could provide a predictor of various attitudes and experience. These six groups were:

1. 'orthodox believers' – those who believe in God without doubt, pray daily, and attend church regularly, (n=311);
2. 'public believers' – those who believe in God without doubt, do not pray daily and attend church regularly, (n=146);
3. 'private believers' – those who believe in God without doubt, pray daily and do not attend church regularly (n=177);
4. 'believing secularists' – those who believe in God without doubt, do not pray daily and do not attend church regularly (n=250);
5. 'vacillating secularists' – those who have doubts about God's existence or believe some of the time, do not pray daily and do not attend church regularly (n=364);
6. 'consistent secularists' – those who do not believe in a personal God, do not pray and do not attend church regularly (n=287).

Using this classification one could hypothesise that these groups would differ on religious experiences and moral attitudes. Table 8 shows this to be true for all religious experiences which were asked about, although in some

*Table 8. Religious experiences of the Australian population*

| Percentage who | Total population | 'Orthodox believers' | 'Public believers' | 'Private believers' | 'Believing secularists' | 'Vacillating secularists' | 'Consistent secularists' |
|---|---|---|---|---|---|---|---|
| Have had an experience of being in the presence of God | 48 | 84 | 67 | 74 | 45 | 30 | 10 |
| Have had an experience of being saved in Christ | 34 | 66 | 49 | 58 | 33 | 14 | 3 |
| Have had a feeling of being afraid of God | 22 | 33 | 31 | 29 | 15 | 25 | 7 |
| Have had a feeling of being punished by God | 27 | 40 | 32 | 35 | 19 | 27 | 11 |
| Have had a feeling of being tempted by the Devil | 35 | 65 | 49 | 38 | 30 | 25 | 11 |

of them the differences were not significant. Also it is notable that more private believers in some instances reported an experience than 'public believers', and in two instances that more 'vacillating secularists' reported experiences than did 'believing secularists'. In all instances the 'orthodox believers', the 'public believers' and the 'private believers' reported more religious experiences than the population average, and in all instances the 'orthodox believers' and 'consistent secularists' form the two extremes of the continuum.

Table 9 shows several attitudes of these six groups. It is interesting that religiosity is a better predictor of attitudes than denomination or belief alone. In all instances the 'orthodox believers' prove more morally conservative than the 'consistent secularists'. The two statements regarding feelings towards an Englishman and a Japanese reflect the fact that the 'orthodox believers' were more prepared to say they would feel friendly and at ease, while the 'consistent secularist' tended to adopt the more neutral 'would feel nothing either way', not a negative 'would feel unfriendly'. In general the consistent secularists chose neutral answers to all questions, suggesting that religious involvement is correlated with a clearer delineation of approved or disapproved conduct.

## RELIGION AND CLASS

Historical sources agree that whatever the situation at the moment, in the past Catholics and Methodists have been over represented among the lower classes. Even recently, the proportion of Catholics among business executives has been thought to be particularly small [Spann, 1961]. They are better represented in the public service but there not in the higher ranks, [Davies and Encel, 1965] and are under-represented among the academic staff of universities [Tien, 1965]. Methodists have been traditionally associated with the lower skilled occupation, shop-keepers, and, in South Australia with mining. Anglicans and Presbyterians are slightly over-represented in the upper classes, but are not exclusively represented there. Figures from the 1901 Census of New South Wales show roughly the same pattern, although surprisingly little variation between the different denominations.

Davies observed from the 1947 Census of Australia that in contrast to Britain and the United States the major Australian denominations had very similar occupational profiles [Davies, 1958]. Catholics had a greater percentage of labourers and a smaller percentage of craftsmen than the other denominations. However, they have a larger percentage of professionals and semi-professional adherents than Anglican and Methodists. They, with the Anglicans, also have a smaller proportion of adherents in rural occupations

*Table 9. Ethical values of the Australian population*

| Percentage who | Total population | 'Orthodox believers' | 'Public believers' | 'Private believers' | 'Believing secularists' | 'Vacillating secularists' | 'Consistent secularists' |
|---|---|---|---|---|---|---|---|
| Disapproved of the person who has a small job on the side and does not declare it for income tax purposes | 35 | 56 | 40 | 49 | 32 | 22 | 21 |
| Disapproved of the person who has sex relations before marriage | 63 | 90 | 72 | 82 | 66 | 54 | 27 |
| Disapproved of the person who has sex relations after marriage with someone other than husband or wife | 86 | 93 | 90 | 94 | 86 | 88 | 74 |
| Disapproves of the Catholic who uses the contraceptive pill | 20 | 48 | 27 | 28 | 12 | 10 | 6 |
| Admires the person who is very patriotic | 49 | 60 | 46 | 56 | 52 | 43 | 40 |
| Would feel friendly and at ease in the presence of an Englishman | 70 | 80 | 70 | 69 | 71 | 72 | 62 |
| Would feel friendly and at ease in the presence of a Japanese | 46 | 58 | 55 | 42 | 43 | 41 | 44 |

compared with Methodists and Presbyterians. But as a whole the occupational profiles are remarkably similar. It should not be said that there has been an occupational levelling since 1901, for the two Censuses may not be comparable, as the first was for a state and the second for a nation. In addition, Census definitions of different occupations have changed slightly, becoming more comprehensive and allowing the more specific categories to become submerged.

Census data also show (Table 10) that Catholics have always had a higher proportion of unemployed, especially in 1933 during the Depression. Anglicans, because of their size remain close to the national average while Methodists and Presbyterians show fewer unemployed.

*Table 10. Number of unemployed per 1,000 males in the workforce*

| Census | Anglican | Catholic | Methodist | Presbyterian | No religion | Total |
|---|---|---|---|---|---|---|
| 1961 | 37 | 54 | 26 | 28 | 62 | 42 |
| 1954 | 14 | 17 | 10 | 11 | 23 | 15 |
| 1947 | 28 | 32 | 21 | 22 | 47 | 28 |
| 1933 | 237 | 279 | 170 | 171 | 395 | 234 |
| 1921 | 85 | 115 | 61 | 69 | 156 | 86 |

Source: Census Bulletins.

There seem to be more differences in religiosity between the various social classes. Data from a survey on social class conducted in 1965 by Broom, Jones and Zubrzycki at the Australian National University, show that 76 per cent of Catholic respondents mainly male, in the work force, in the upper occupational bracket (n=120) had been to church in the preceding month, 57 per cent of the middle group (n=154) and 63 per cent of the lower (n=155) bracket. For non-Catholics the corresponding percentage were 36 per cent upper (n=498), 25 per cent middle (n=513) and 23 per cent lower (n=437).[2]

The Australian Survey Project of the Department of Political Science, Australian National University shows similar trends. This was carried out in 1967. In this survey 72 per cent of Catholic heads of households in the upper occupational bracket (n=67) went to church once a week or more, 48 per cent of the middle (n=79) and 47 per cent of the lower (n=107) brackets. For non-Catholics the corresponding percentages were 27 per

2. I should like to thank the authors for making these data available to me.

cent upper (n=261), 21 per cent middle (2=229) and 16 per cent lower (n=245).[3]

Other dimensions of religiosity do not show the same class differences, according to the 'Religion in Australia' survey. There are few differences in daily prayer, having had the experience of being in God's presence, a belief in God. Attendance at denominational schools was more common in the upper occupational groupings. This latter findings is not surprising as Protestant private schools are very expensive, and Catholic schools, although compulsory, still cost more than some lower income families can afford.

## RELIGION AND POLITICS

Protestants in Australia tend to prefer the coalition of the Liberal and Country Parties now in power; Catholics, on the other hand seem to favour the Australian Labor Party somewhat more. Although there was a split in the Australian Labor Party in the mid-fifties, resulting in what came to be called the 'Democratic Labor Party', and although this party was mainly the outcome of Catholic reaction to the extreme left-wing of the Labor Party, between 40 and 50 per cent of Catholics voters continued to prefer the Labor Party. Taking both Australian Labor Party and Democratic Labor Party together we find the following voting intentions of Catholics in the Federal Pre-Election Surveys from 1946 to 1961: 1946, 72 per cent, 1949, 73 per cent; 1951 68 per cent; 1954, 73.6 per cent; 1955, 66.5 per cent, 1958, 70.7 per cent; 1961, 64.3 per cent, 1966, 57.5 per cent [Spann, 1961].

Table 11 shows that other denominations are more inclined to favour the Liberal/Country Parties. Even holding social class constant, which was possible in the 'Religion in Australia' survey, the over representation of Catholics voting Labor is not entirely the result of Catholic over-representation in the working class. There is a tendency for church-going Catholics to be more conservative and to vote for the Liberal/Country Parties. [Mol, 1971].

Australians seem to feel on the whole that church leaders ought to refrain from giving political advice to their membership. When in 1960 the Gallup Poll asked whether the respondents felt that church leaders had the right to tell their members for whom *not* to vote, 71 per cent of Catholics, 94 per cent of Presbyterians, 94 per cent of Methodists, 96 per cent of Anglicans and 100 per cent of Baptists answered in the negative [*Sydney Sun*, 15 September 1960].

3. I should like to thank Dr D. Aitken and Mr M. J. Kahan of the Department of of Political Science, A.N.U. for making these data available.

*Table 11. Percentage of respondents by denomination and voting intention in the 1966 federal elections*

| Parties | Catholic | Church of England | Presbyterian | Methodist | Other Christian | Other |
|---|---|---|---|---|---|---|
| Australian Labor Party | 43.1 | 35.5 | 30.0 | 35.9 | 36.0 | 41.0 |
| Liberal/Country Parties | 33.1 | 55.8 | 59.7 | 56.7 | 48.1 | 34.3 |
| Democratic Labor Party | 14.4 | 2.3 | 2.1 | 2.8 | 5.3 | 2.3 |
| Independent and Don't know | 9.4 | 6.3 | 8.1 | 4.5 | 10.6 | 22.5 |
| Total | 100.0 | 100.0 | 100.0 | 100.0 | 100.0 | 100.0 |

Source: Gallup Poll.

RELIGION AND EDUCATION

In the nineteenth century the Bible-reading denominations such as the Presbyterians and the Methodists had a higher literacy rate than the Anglicans and particularly the Catholics. However at the present the intergenerational differences regarding levels of education are far greater than the denominational differences. As in the United States more Catholics are inclined than non-Catholics to agree that 'the most important thing for a child to learn is to obey rather than to think for himself': this holds true also when one compares Catholics and others in specific educational and age categories.

There seems to be little difference between the religious practice of those with high and low educational attainment. There is a slight tendency for more of those with tertiary education (38 per cent are regular, n=153), to attend church regularly than those who completed a secondary (33 per cent, n=614) or only a primary (33 per cent, n=1773) education, but the percentage of Australians who say that they pray daily (also 33 per cent, n=602) is almost the same for each of these categories. This also applies to religious experiences. (48 per cent of the sample claims to have had or thinks that it has had a 'feeling of being somehow in the presence of God' since childhood) and for the belief that God exists (49 per cent claims this belief and has no doubt about it), the percentage is approximately the same for all educational categories. While amount of education does not make much difference, whether or not one went to a denominational school *does* have an effect [Mol, 1968].

Those who have attended Catholic schools score more highly on the religious variables of the survey that the others. More of them go to church regularly, pray regularly, believe in God without doubt, are of the opinion that the church is appointed by God, and report having had religious experiences. Those Catholics who had had no Catholic-school education did not score as highly, but nevertheless, more highly than Protestants.

Catholics with at least some Catholic-school education tended to be more prudish than Catholics who had been to state schools or Protestants. More of them disapproved of the person who has had sex relations before marriage, and also of the fellow Catholic who uses the contraceptive pill.

The important difference between non-Catholics who have been to denominational schools and those who have not are generally unrelated to religious factors. The differences are either political (they would rather see the Liberal/Country Parties win), or educational (more than twice as many have completed at least a secondary education), or occupational (managerial or grazing circles).

In the above-mentioned survey it was also found that Catholics more than Protestants and Catholic-school Catholics more than state-school Catholics tended to have the majority of their closest friends in the local parish. Age (being over 40) strengthened the relationship between Catholic education and other factors such as friendships in the local church, disapproval of the person who has sex relations before marriage, and so on. Being under 40 weakens the pattern. Age had no effect on the relationship between Catholic-school education and church-going. However, it did on prayer; the younger people with Catholic-school education tended to pray as regularly (daily) as older people who had not the benefit of a Catholic-school education. This suggested that the more private, devotional habits and experiences were more common among older people, but that the more public religious practices were largely independent of age.

REFERENCES

Broom, Leonard and Glenn, Norvall D, 'Religious differences in reported attitudes and behaviour'. *Sociological Analysis*, 27 (4), Winter, 1966.

Broom, Leonard, Jones, F. Lancaster, and Zubrzycki, J., 'Social Stratification in Australia' in J. A. Jackson (ed.), *Social Stratification*. Cambridge, Cambridge University Press, Sociological Studies No. 1, 1968.

Day, Lincoln H, 'Family Size and Fertility' in Davies, A. F., and Encel,s. (eds.), *Australian Society*. Melbourne, Cheshire, 1955.

Lenski, Gerhard, *The Religious Factor*. New York, Doubleday, 1961.

BIBLIOGRAPHY

*Current Affairs Bulletin.* 22 (4), 16 June, 1968.

Davies, A. F., and Encel, S., (eds.), *Australian Society.* Melbourne, Cheshire, 1965.

Dent, Owen, 'The Utility of the Church-Sect Typology'. Unpublished Master's Thesis. Canberra, A.N.U.

Gregory, J. S., 'Church and State, and Education in Victoria to 1872', in French, E.L. (ed.), *Melbourne Studies in Education* 1958–1959. Melbourne, Melbourne University Press, 1960.

Hickman, David C. 'The Schools and Religious Orientation', unpublished Ph.D. thesis, Canberra, Australian National University, Australia.

Inglis, K. S., 'The Australian Catholic Community', in Mayer, H. (ed.), *Catholics and the Free Society, an Australian Symposium.* Melbourne, Cheshire, 1961.

—, 'Religious Behaviour' in Davies, A. F. and Encel, S. (eds.), *Australian Society.* Melbourne, Chesire, 1965.

Mol, J. J. (or Hans), 'The Social Relevance of the Australian Churches.' *Social Compass*, XIII (2), 1966.

—, *Religion in Australia.* Melbourne, Nelson, 1971.

—, 'A Collation of Data about Religion in Australia.' *Social Compass*, XIV (2), 1967.

—, 'The Effects of Denominational Schools in Australia.' *The Australian and New Zealand Journal of Sociology*, 4 (1), April, 1968.

—, *Christianity in Chains.* Melbourne, Nelson, 1969a.

—, 'The Merger Attempts of the Australian Churches.' *Ecumenical Review*, XXI, January, 1969b.

Oeser, O. A. and Hammond, S. B., *Social Structure and Personality in a City.* London, Routledge and Kegan Paul, 1954.

O'Farrell, P. J. 'A History of the N.S.W. Labour Movement 1880–1910 A Religious Interpretation.' *J. of Religious History*, 2 (2), December 1962.

—, *A History of the Australian Catholic Church.* Melbourne, Nelson, 1968.

Price, Charles A. 'The Integration of religious groups in Australia.' *International Migration*, 1, (3), 1963.

—, 'The Effects of Post-War Immigration on the Growth of Population, Ethnic Composition and Religious Structure of Australia.' *The Australian Quarterly*, XXIX (4), December, 1957.

Scott, Peter, 'The Population Structure of the Australian Cities.' *The Geographical Journal*, 131 (4), December, 1965.

Southall, Ivan (ed.), *The Challenge.* Melbourne, Lansdowne Press, 1966.

Spann, R. V., 'The Catholic Vote in Australia' in Mayer, H. (ed.), *Catholics and the Free Society. An Australian Symposium.* Melbourne, Cheshire, 1961.

Tien, H. Y., *Social Mobility and Controlled Fertility.* New Haven, College and University Press, 1965.

HUGO BOGENSBERGER*
PAUL ZULEHNER**

# Austria

## HISTORICAL INTRODUCTION

The establishment of a bishopric at Salzburg in the eighth century marks a turning point in the history of Christianity in Austria. The beginnings date back to the Roman Empire, but large migrations from the east disrupted early missionary effort and it was not until Charlemagne gradually established his ascendancy that vigorous Christian activity again became possible. The monks, who moulded church life from this period until the abolition of numerous monasteries under Joseph II were the main agents of cultural change. Yet, political and ecclesiastical consolidation of the border territory of the German Empire from Salzburg to Passau developed at a very slow pace. It was only in 1469 that a bishopric was established in Vienna. From then on a series of bishoprics grew up farther out at Gurk, Seckau and even at Brixen.

The common task of cultivating the land had led to a very close relationship between church and state. Bishops gained substantial positions in the realm. This historical and, at first, fruitful association underwent a severe crisis at the time of the Reformation. Growing political conflict between the dynasty and the feudal lords developed into a religious division between Catholic and Protestant factions. The result of this was that the reigning family and the Catholic Church became bound even more closely together. The crisis ended in a common religious and political victory for the Counter-Reformation and the Catholic dynasty. The ground was prepared once more for an exceedingly fruitful period in the history of Austria. Freed from political strife and strengthened internally by the religious restoration, Austria was able to cope successfully with its task as the bulwark of Europe against the Turks.

* Hugo Bogensberger was born in Sieghartskirchen, Austria, in 1929. He is currently Director of the Institute for Socio-Religious Research, Vienna.

** Paul Zulehner was born in Vienna, Austria in 1939. He is currently Vice-rector in the Seminary, Assistant at the Institute for Ethics and Social Sciences of the Theological Faculty at the University of Vienna. He is a committee member of the Institute for Socio-Religious Research.

Under Maria Theresia and her son Joseph II, however, the ambivalence of the tight bond between church and state became apparent. The enlightened police-state increasingly integrated the church into its system. In many ways the church became a police institution in the service of the state, and as such it went through an extensive organizational restructuring. Today the Austrian church bears the marks of these developments.

With the French and then the Industrial Revolutions, Austria also experienced a powerful politico-social upheaval. Society began to develop institutional forms independent of the church. Secularization, in the sense of the society coming of age, was hastened particularly by the liberal middle class (as in 1848) and the ensuing social democratic movement. The fundamental assertion was a demand for the separation of church and state; their alliance was seen as the basis of the existing social and political order and thus as a restraining influence on the newly developing society. The basic politico-cultural arguments of the nineteenth and twentieth centuries testify to the growing autonomy of institutions like schools, marriage and economy.

Moreover, this development has not so far been completed. The relationship of the church to the state and to individual social institutions has, however, undergone very significant changes in the last century. The church, which had previously formed an alliance with the reigning dynasty and later, after the fall of the Austro-Hungarian Monarchy in 1918, with the Christian Socialist party, has now renounced this political involvement and in so doing must give up some subsidiary functions which it had previously undertaken. At this stage, one cannot predict the eventual outcome in Austria of this reformation of religious institutions and the associated clarification of the true function of the church.

## DENOMINATIONAL STRUCTURE

The population of Austria is preponderantly Roman Catholic. Table 1 demonstrates that the social and cultural development of the last fifty years with the strong political caesuras of 1934 and 1938 has done little to alter this situation. Since 1910 the proportion of Catholics has decreased by 5 per cent in Austria. Unlike any other European country it has experienced a real increase (doubling) of the proportion of Protestant Christians but at the present level of 6 per cent they are still only a small part of the total population.

The increase in the number of Protestants is largely to be attributed to migration from Germany in 1938–45 and to the stream of refugees from Central and Southern Europe after the end of World War II. People also

*Table 1. Religious denominations in Austria*

| Denomination | 1961 N | 1910 % | 1934 % | 1951 % | 1961 % |
|---|---|---|---|---|---|
| Catholic including Roman and Greek Catholic, and Armenian Rite | 6,298,589 | 93.7 | 90.5 | 89.1 | 89.0 |
| Protestant A.B. and H.B.* | 438,663 | 3.1 | 4.4 | 6.2 | 6.2 |
| Old Catholic | 29,652 | 0.1 | 0.5 | 0.5 | 0.4 |
| Jewish | 9,049 | 2.9 | 2.8 | 0.2 | 0.2 |
| Other | 27,872 | 0.1 | 0.1 | 0.2 | 0.4 |
| No religious affiliation | 266,009 | 0.1 | 1.6 | 3.8 | 3.8 |
| Unknown | 3,973 | – | 0.1 | 0.0 | 0.0 |
| Total | 7,073,807 | 100.0 | 100.0 | 100.0 | 100.0 |

* A.B.: Union of the Churches of Augsburg (Lutheran)
H.B.: Helvetian Church (Reformed Calvinist)
Source: *Ergebnisse der Volkszählung* (1951 Census), 1951, p. 29, and *Volkszählungsergebnisse* (1961 Census), 1961.

changed their denomination on political grounds for example during the period of the corporate state based on Catholic ideology (1934–38), and in 1938 and after, as a result of the annexation of Austria by National-Socialist Germany. Avoidance of the indissolubility of Catholic marriage was also in many cases the reason for a change to Protestantism or Old-Catholicism. The movement out of the Church on political grounds in 1922–23, 1934 and 1938–39 was an expression of the increasing proportion of non-believers. Only a small proportion of those who left the Catholic Church in those years re-entered the Church after 1945.

*The Roman Catholic Church*

There are two ecclesiastical provinces in Austria: Vienna and Salzburg. The former, with the archdiocese of Vienna, embraces the suffragan bishoprics of Eisenstadt, St. Pölten and Linz. The second, with the archdiocese of Salzburg, embraces the suffragan bishoprics of Seckau-Graz, Gurk-Klagenfurt and the apostolic administration of Innsbruck-Feldkirch. A dense parish network embraces the whole territory of the Austrian state, and virtually all of the larger political communities have their own parish. The Catholics of the Byzantine (Greek) Rite are cared for by a central parish in Vienna, the Armenians by a Mechitarist congregation in Vienna.

*Table 2. Survey of Catholic organization 1957/60*

| Diocese | Numbers of | | | | | | |
|---|---|---|---|---|---|---|---|
| | Catholics[1] | Churches[2] | Deaneries | Parishes and Registrars | Catholics per Parish | Priests[3] | Catholics per priest |
| Archdiocese of Vienna | | | | | | | |
| *Urban* | 1,491,791 | 1,468 | 16 | 198 | 7,534 | 479 | 3,114 |
| *Rural* | 609,325 | | 38 | 437 | 1,394 | 524 | 1,162 |
| Diocese of Eisenstadt | 232,946 | 276 | 15 | 173 | 1,346 | 195 | 1,194 |
| Diocese of St. Pölten | 613,791 | 530[4] | 27 | 415 | 1,479 | 538 | 1,140 |
| Diocese of Linz | 1,053,700 | 683 | 35 | 465 | 2,266 | 720 | 1,463 |
| Archdiocese of Salzburg | 410,717 | 491 | 19 | 205 | 2,003 | 288 | 1,426 |
| Diocese of Graz-Seckau | 1,003,200 | 1,126 | 45 | 375 | 2,675 | 607 | 1,652 |
| Diocese of Gurk-Klagenfurt | 416,241 | 903 | 27 | 333 | 1,249 | 373 | 1,116 |
| Apostolic Administration of Innsbruck | 334,362 | | 14 | 250 | 1,337 | 323 | 1,035 |
| Apostolic Administration of Feldkirch | 199,909 | 627 | 6 | 129 | 1,549 | 171 | 1,155 |
| Total Austria | 6,365,909 | 6,104 | 242 | 2,980 | 2,136 | 4,220 | 1,508 |

Sources:
1. From church statistics 1957.
2. Diocesan directories.
3. I.K.S. Survey.
4. Assessment.

*The Protestant Church A.B. and H.B.*

These consist of a union of the Augsburg (Lutheran) and the Helvetian (Reformed Calvinist) Churches. The highest authority is the general synod and the high Church council A.B. and H.B. in Vienna. There are 153 Lutheran parishes dispersed throughout Austria. The traditional territories of the Austrian Protestants are the Alpine areas (Kärnten, Steiermark, Upper Austria) which were used as a retreat at the end of the Reformation and some areas of Burgenland, where (since they were under Hungarian rule until 1918) a larger number of Protestant communities were able to survive despite the Counter-Reformation. After World War II new Protestant communities grew up among the refugees who flowed into Salzburg and Upper Austria.

*The Old Catholic Church*

This church was founded in protest against the dogma of papal infallibility which was proclaimed at the first Vatican Council. It has been recognized officially in Austria since 1877. It has twelve parishes, six of which are in Vienna.

*Jewish Religious Community*

The number of Jews in Austria was drastically decreased by the persecution of the National Socialist régime, but communities currently exist in Vienna, Graz, Linz, Salzburg and Innsbruck.

*Other religious groups*

In addition to the four religious bodies mentioned above, the Greek Orthodox, Methodists, Mormons, Moravian Brethren and Muslims of the Hanefite Rite are legally recognized religious bodies at the present time. The Greek Oriental (Orthodox) Church in Vienna has two parishes, one Serbian, and one Rumanian, as well as a church for the Russian embassy. The Methodist Church has been active in Austria since 1871 and officially recognized since 1951; it has about 2,000 members and 10 ministers. The Church of Jesus Christ of the Latter Day Saints (Mormon) has been legally recognized since 1955 and has about 800 members in eight communities. The Moravian Brethren and Islam (the Hanifite Rite) were legally recognized in 1880. At present they do not have any congregations in Austria.

### RELIGIOUS PARTICIPATION AND BELIEFS

To begin with, data on various acts of identification with the church as an institution can be given. Practically all Catholics in Austria have their children baptized, send them to the religious instruction given in all state schools (primary school, six to ten years; high school, ten to fourteen years) and to confirmation and first communion. Church burial is also desired by almost all baptized Catholics. Although these practices are almost universally observed, there is as yet no way of telling whether they arise from general religiosity, or specific institutional attachments. Even church dues, which are levied directly by church authorities without the mediation of state offices and which were introduced in 1939 during the National Socialist régime, are paid by virtually all Catholics without legal action being necessary.

Other acts of identification like church wedding ceremonies or Easter duties are somewhat less widespread. The proportion of church wedding ceremonies in the whole of Austria since 1955 was between 74–79 per cent. Of course, non-church weddings include all cases of marriage after divorce where a church wedding is impossible; the proportion of church weddings for first marriages is 90 per cent and more. According to church statistics 30–40 per cent of Catholics fulfil their Easter duties, while participation in regular Sunday Mass sinks, on the average, to about a third.

Table 3, which is based on an enquiry among Catholic parents in the city of Salzburg is indicative of the highly differentiated pattern of church attendance.

*Table 3. Church attendance among Catholic parents in Salzburg (1966)*

| Extent of Church Attendance | n=258<br>% |
|---|---|
| Every Sunday | 28 |
| At least once a month | 19 |
| Only on major feasts | 27 |
| Even less often | 11 |
| Never | 15 |
| | 100 |

Source: I.K.S. Report No. 78a, Vienna, 1966.

The investigation of other criteria of religiosity and churchmindedness was only begun in Austria a few years ago. Investigations in various parts of

Austria [Schasching, 1962; Bogensberger, Cserjan and Vaskovics, 1966; Fischer and Holl, 1967; I.K.S., 1966, Part 1] indicate that the existence of a higher being is almost universally accepted. There is less conviction about the doctrinal definitions of the church than about general religious truths like the acceptance of the existence of a higher being. In the above mentioned investigation of Catholic parents it was found that 59 per cent held that Jesus is the son of God but only 35 per cent were convinced of a life after death; 79 per cent were uncertain about at least one in four of the beliefs questioned, i.e. they did not have orthodox opinions according to church standards.[1]

An investigation of the religious behaviour of industrial workers (the group with the smallest degree of religious participation) has, however, shown that, even among Catholics with a minimum of agreement concerning specific Christian religious truths, there is a strong informal religiosity in the family.

The fragmentary and diverse character of the acceptance of religious beliefs and religious practices indicates the presence of a highly differentiated church population. The problem of clarifying this ecclesiastical stratification is increasingly becoming a major topic of socio-religions research in Austria [Wössner, 1967]. At present it is not possible to set up a pattern of differentiated participation and identification of Catholics with the Church for the whole of Austria or even for larger socio-economically homogeneous regions. From eleven variables concerning religious attitudes and behaviour of Catholic parents in Salzburg,[2] one factor of church mindedness was extracted which made it possible to delineate three distinct subgroups: active church members (17 per cent), sympathetic towards the church (34 per cent), antipathetic towards the church (49 per cent).

1. The subjects raised were: the creation, life after death, the person of Christ, the origins of the Bible, the relationship of religion to the family.

2. The factor analysis was applied to the following variables:
1) Attitude towards life after death;
2) Attitude towards the person of Christ;
3) Attitude towards pre-marital sexual intercourse;
4) Attitude towards church weddings;
5) Church-attendance;
6) Educational goals of the parents (religious – non-religious);
7) Should the marriage partner of the child be believing and religious;
8) Method of bringing up children (religious – non-religious);
9) Frequency of conversations about religious questions;
10) Prayer with the children;
11) Possession of a Bible.

*Table 4. Attitude of Catholic parents towards church doctrines, norms and religious practice*

| | Category of Catholic parents who are: | | |
|---|---|---|---|
| | Active church members | Sympathetic towards the Church | Antipathetic towards the Church |
| | n=45 | n=88 | n=125 |
| | % | % | % |
| Believe definitely in life after death | 93 | 45 | 6 |
| Accept that Jesus is the son of God | 98 | 74 | 35 |
| Thoroughly oppose pre-marital sexual intercourse | 78 | 37 | 17 |
| Unconditionally favour church weddings | 96 | 87 | 35 |
| Think their child's marriage partner should be a believer in religion | 89 | 35 | 1 |
| Are regular church attenders | 96 | 32 | 1 |
| Pray with the children | 78 | 79 | 22 |
| Possess a Bible | 71 | 34 | 11 |

Source: I.K.S. Report 79a, Vienna, 1968, p. 26.

Table 4 shows the correlation of those categories and some of the individual variables used for their description.

In the 'active church members' category it is noteworthy that less than three-quarters possess a Bible and that only about 80 per cent pray with the children or 'thoroughly oppose' pre-marital sexual intercourse which, after all, is much less than the acceptance of doctrinal norms, religious practice, and observation of church rites. Apparently individual religious initiative (prayer with children) and moral dilemmas (the norm of sexual behaviour) present greater difficulties than agreement with the standards of belief and religious practice.

Within the group of those sympathizing with the church the degree of acceptance is much lower than in the group of the active church members in such categories as life after death, church attendance, moral distinction, bibles in the family, whereas when one examines religious acts which concern the children (prayer with children and a church wedding for the children) agreement with the orthodox position still remains high. Even with those antipathetic towards the church, the norms related to children produce the most positive responses; it is only in other fields (religiosity of marriage

*Table 5. Religious practice in Austrian dioceses 1958/60*

| Church district | Sunday Church attendance | | |
|---|---|---|---|
| | Catholic inhabitants | Total | % |
| Total Archdiocese Vienna | 2,057,570 | 411,775 | 23.5 |
| *Vienna-City* | (1,363,713) | (226,476) | (19.5) |
| *Vienna County* | | | |
| North | (291,745) | (100,473) | (40.5) |
| South | (402,112) | (84,826) | (24.8) |
| Diocese St. Pölten | 608,928 | 214,869 | 41.5 |
| Diocese Linz | 1,043,151 | 393,093 | 44.4 |
| Diocese Eisenstadt | 228,089 | 82,468 | 42.5 |
| Archdiocese Salzburg | 397,391 | 133,974 | 39.7 |
| Diocese Seckau | 986,771 | 257,268 | 30.7 |
| Diocese Gurk | 412,329 | 101,527 | 29.0 |
| Apostolic Administration of Innsbruck-Feldkirch *Innsbruck* | 319,930 | 146,684 | 54.0 |
| *Feldkirch* | 193,161 | 90,734 | 55.3 |
| Total Austria | 6,247,320 | 1,833,202 | 34.5 |

Source: Austrian church statistics 1957; Census of the City of Vienna 1958; Levy of I.K.S. 1955/60

partner, regular church attendance, opposition to premarital sexual intercourse), that agreement sinks to a minimum 1 to 17 per cent.

The churchmindedness of Catholics is strongly influenced by regional and social factors, such as the urban-rural division, size of community etc. On the whole, until now, all these factors have been measured by one criterion only, namely attendance at Sunday Mass.

Regional differences can be verified statistically by examining the varying numbers of Catholics in individual dioceses (which fluctuate from 81–96 per cent of the total population) or by considering the even greater variance in the figures for church attendance in different areas. These figures represent the ratio of those actually attending Mass to those obliged to do so (i.e. all Catholics minus 9 to 15 per cent excused because of sickness or age).

Church attendance in the cities and densely populated areas is considerably under 30 per cent, but the parishes within the cities often show marked variations. In Innsbruck, for example, church attendance varies from 19 to 76 per cent. Community size alone is not the deciding factor, for communities of extremely different sizes present practically the same figures: Vienna with over 1.6 million inhabitants has a church attendance of 19.5 per cent; Krems with about 20,000 inhabitants has 18.9 per cent, while in the industrial town of Neufeld with 2,500 inhabitants, 14.9 per cent are regular attenders.

Age and sex exert a clear influence on religious practice. A comparison of various church attendance census figures shows that the age groups can be enumerated in the following order, according to church attendance: 6–14 years; over 65 years; 14–25 years; 45–60 years; and finally, with the smallest attendance, 25–45 years. The high rate of attendance of children during their school years is explained by social pressures and hence the dropping off of religious practice on leaving school is not to be seen as a diminution of belief. Once the role expectation 'religion is for children only' has disappeared, the actual situation of the young person becomes apparent. In most cases he has not been subjected to a religious socialization within the family. Further specific research is needed to explain the increase in religious activity – growing religiosity and churchmindedness – in higher age groups. The differences in religious practice for particular age groups may be the expression of a change in religious behaviour for different generations, indicating that the people of the present and the future are less active religiously than those of the past.

Whether a person works or not, is at least as significant a variable in relation to religious practice as the occupation he has. In the overwhelming majority of parishes investigated, the rate of Sunday church attendance is higher among those not employed (children, housewives, pensioners) than among those who work. In the former group, school children have the highest rate (in 54 per cent of parishes) followed by recipients of old age pensions, pensioners and housewives. Among those employed the situation is more complex. In half the parishes investigated the classification of occupations according to proportional church attendance is: civil servants, salaried employees, self-employed and free-lance professions, workers. In 86 per cent of the communities investigated workers show the smallest proportion of church attenders while civil servants and the salaried employees (in about 66 per cent of cases) have the highest proportion.

Low church attendance by workers seems to be partly associated with degree of industrialization. The effect of industrialization appears independent of size of community. In communities where the proportion of the population engaged in industry and manufacture was over 65 per cent there was a correspondingly low figure for church attendance – 9–15 per cent. On the other hand, in agricultural areas the proportion attending mass was, as a rule, higher than average: in seventy-four agrarian communities of the archdiocese of Salzburg it averaged 46 per cent. In general, one can conclude from these figures that church attendance declines in proportion to the decrease in agriculture and increase in industry and trade. However, it should be remembered that there is a difference between old and new industrial areas. Areas which experienced early industrialization have a very small proportion of regular church-goers, whereas the proportion is relatively high in communities in which industrialization was completed late (e.g. Wörgl and Wattens in Tirol, Lend in Salzburg).

Community research in Krems, Salzburg and Eisenstadt established that increase in education is associated with an increase in church attendance. This is certain in the case of salaried employees and civil servants only.

From an historical perspective it is clear that political attitude plays a substantial role in Austria with regard to the intensity of religious practice. Because the role of political attitudes has not yet been examined sufficiently it is difficult to separate from other factors (e.g. occupational ones) but it can be assumed, or at least hypothesised, that the effect of political attitude is different now to thirty years ago. Certain relationships are also obvious. It can be established that the number of church attenders varies according to the political structure and that, in general, a higher proportion of church-goers accompanies a higher proportion of Ö.V.P. voters (the Conservative Party: *Österreichische Volkspartei*).

## THE FAMILY AND RELIGIOUS PRACTICE

Table 6, based on data from three cities, demonstrates a pattern of family conformity in religious practice: in the majority of families investigated either all the members of the family go to mass or (as in most cases) no-one does.

*Table 6. Catholic family church attendance*

| Number of family members attending Sunday Mass (excluding children under the age of seven not obliged to attend) | % of Families<br>Krems population c. 20,000 | Salzburg population c. 110,000 | Eisenstadt population c. 7,000 |
|---|---|---|---|
| All | 4 | 6 | 13 |
| Some | 20 | 19 | 34 |
| None | 76 | 75 | 53 |
| | 100 | 100 | 100 |

Sources: I.K.S. Reports No. 74, 77, 84, Vienna, 1965, pp. 27, 29, 30.

It should be pointed out that these data are based in each case on one isolated census of church attendance only; thus, there is a certain inaccuracy in the dividing line between regular and irregular church-goers.

Religious behaviour (judged by the indicator of fulfilment of the Sunday obligation to attend Sunday Mass) is thus influenced, in the majority of cases, by the other members of the family, above all by the parents. Strong conformity in family behaviour (66–81 per cent practising or non-practising) is only the case if one considers all Catholic families. However, if one considers only those families from which at least one person goes to Sunday Mass, then family uniformity seems not to be strong. In 40 per cent of this category, some members practise, but it is the school age children who practise in contrast to their non-practising parents and elder brothers and sisters. The behaviour of these children can hardly be considered as not conforming to family norms, since an investigation in Salzburg showed that three-quarters of Catholic parents require their school age children to attend Mass. Parents require this even when they themselves do not attend regularly (only 28 per cent indicated that they were regular church-goers).

An examination of the question of family conformity in religious practice in relation to varying size and composition of families as well as to the occupation of bread-winners showed that there is no significant deviation in family conformity as described above. The proportion of families in which no-one practises, irrespective of occupation, never sinks lower than 64 per cent; the proportion of fully practising families fluctuates between 0 and 7 per cent. The most significant variations as shown by the Krems study are the following. Families consisting of three generations have the largest proportion (31 per cent) of partially practising families. By contrast 91 per cent of young and fairly young married couples without children are non-practising. With an increasing number of children the proportion of partially practising families increases, which is, of course due to the practice of the children. The families of skilled workers have the greatest proportion (89 per cent) of non-practising families. The families of higher civil servants and salaried employees have the lowest. However, workers have a higher proportion of partially practising families (31 per cent) than do civil servants (15 per cent).

With a decreasing degree of urbanization and hence small community size, the proportion of families in which no-one practises decreases strongly, yet the proportion of fully-practising families does not increase in the same way. However, the proportion of partially-practising families does increase and, for the most part, this can be explained by the stronger tendency of non-practising parents in smaller communities to encourage their children to go to church. In addition, the socio-cultural system of the smaller communities still strongly encourages religious practice in children. In the city, family uniformity of practice (or non-practice) is greater because these influences encouraging religious activity in children are largely nonexistent.

The following generalizations can be made about the religious practice of children. Six to ten year old children all practise if their parents do; half of them when only one parent does, and about a quarter if both parents do not. The same can be said about ten to fourteen year olds, except that only a fifth practise if their parents do not. Among fourteen to eighteen year olds, in so far as they still live in their parents' house, less than a tenth participate if their parents do not go to Sunday church. Thus the majority of children and young people, as they grow older, follow the practice of their parents. Yet it is a fact that one in eight young people between the age of eighteen and twenty-five, who still live in their parents' house, go to church although their parents do not. Hence, while the influence of the family is certainly an important variable it is not completely determining in relation to church attendance. A distinct decline in religious practice occurs among young married couples. Among the eighteen to twentyfive year old married couples only 3 per cent practise their religion. Marriage leads to a lessening of the religious practice of both parties.

The significance of the family in religious socialization has been analysed in detail in a study in Salzburg. Particular religious socialization techniques, like religious instruction and children's participation at Mass still meet with very wide approval. But Table 7 also shows that parents have greater reservations about their own participation in the religious education of their children.

*Table 7. Parental participation in religious socialization of children*

| Behaviour or attitude of parents | % who agree n=258 |
|---|---|
| Consider religious instruction necessary | 95 |
| Require their school age children to go to church on Sunday | 75 |
| Pray with their children | 60 |
| Discuss religious questions with the children | 61 |

Source: I.K.S. report 78, 1968, Part II.

There are clear divergencies between parents' religious behaviour and the demands they place on their children. While most parents approve of religious instruction and regular church attendance for children, only 35 per cent explicitly affirmed that they wanted to bring up their children religiously.

The influence of the family on religious socialization is also shown by continuity in the family pattern of religious practice. In a succession of three generations (grandparents, parents, children) religious practice (church-going) in the majority of cases shows a certain inter-relationship [I.K.S., 1968]. The relationship between the aims of religious education and socializing techniques, on one hand, and its results, on the other, is clearly apparent. Yet it is also evident that the family is not exclusively responsible for the process of religious socialization.

## RELIGION, CHURCH AND SOCIAL RELATIONS IN METROPOLITAN AREAS

Within the framework of a socio-religious study of the social inter-relations of Catholic families in metropolitan areas some aspects of this question were investigated: in what way and to what degree religion and the church play a role in social relationships; what connections exist with the local ecclesiastical institution, the parish and church officials (priests and members of church organizations).

One of the questions – to what extent people were aware of the attitude of other members of their social group to religion and the church – revealed that in about every sixth case these attitudes were unknown. In half of the families, people thought they were the same as their own.

Both among neighbours and among acquaintances or relatives, religious topics are often discussed by only about 5 per cent. A third of families discuss them occasionally and 50–60 per cent almost never. Every fifth man and every fourth woman questioned held that it was important that new acquaintances hold a similar religious attitude to their own. To sum up, it can be said that in freely chosen social relationships among groups of acquaintances or neighbours, religious orientation plays no role in the vast majority of cases [Goddijn and Goddijn, 1963, p. 59].

One fifth of the families interviewed have social contact with members of church organizations; half have no such contact and, in a third of cases, it is not known. An examination of the relationship between frequency of church attendance and social contact with members of church organizations shows that, with decreasing frequency of church attendance, the proportion of families who have members of church organizations among their social contacts falls from 35 per cent (among regular church-goers) to 10 per cent. Even in 25 per cent of families where the wife is a regular church-goer, it is not known whether members of church organizations are among their social contacts. One would rather have assumed that this factor was of greater importance to regular church-goers.

The fact that nine-tenths of the families in this study know to which parish their residential area belongs indicates that the parish is still widely known as the basic structure for integration into the church. However, relationships to the parish priest exist to a much smaller degree. About one third of the families know their parish priest and have spoken to him; another quarter know him but have not yet spoken to him, and, for one third of Catholic families he is an unknown person. About 75 per cent of families have never yet been visited by a pastor or a priest in their homes, although the number anticipating or desiring a visit exceeds the number visited. More time spent by the priest visiting people in their homes should thus improve the relationships between families and the parish.

Although one family in eight participates in parish reunions, more than four fifths never participate. Decreasing attendance at the Sunday Mass means decreasing participation in parish organisations, but nevertheless, regular church-goers only represent half of those participating in parish activities. The situation with respect to people interested in contact with a priest is such that more than half of those questioned could not think of anything they would ask a priest about. Advice, help and comfort is first of all sought of relatives, then from acquaintances and friends. A certain readiness exists to meet in the home to discuss philosophical-religious questions, about one-third of families would accept an invitation to a religious discussion; older people are more willing to accept such invitations.

This study has shown that the social life of a family is orientated towards the town as a whole. The parish, as a local institution can only build on a very small portion of this social network as a means of beginning social contacts. Religion and church matters play only a small part in social relationships. Moreover, there is no objective neighbourhood basis for the parish in the sense of a clearly defined neighbourhood group which could be 'christianized'. Social relations, in all realms of social activity, are increasingly determined by sympathy and not on a basis of mutual help. Free choice has become more apparent. In the case of making social contact with church representatives, congeniality and the appropriateness of the situation are more crucial than the simple existence of the objective institution as such (i.e. the parish).

### THE IMAGE OF THE CHURCH

Evidence concerning the components of the church's image, is provided by a recent pilot study among young people [Fischer and Holl, 1967, pp. 321ff]. From 148 socio-psychological variables five main factors were derived: *religiosity*, *distance from the church as an organization*, *social contact*, *criticism of tradition*, and *function* (attitude to the church as an institution).

Most subjects gained a positive rating on *religiosity* (designated as a sort of behaviour syndrome derived from church attendance, contributions to charitable purposes, help for old people, verbal manifestation of religious belief etc.). *Religiosity* in this sense, however, does not involve agreement with all church values and norms. A religious person has a positive attitude towards the church, at least in so far as it serves the cause of religion.

Except for a relationship with the personality dimension of conservatism, no relationship between religiosity and other personality factors was found. The hypothesis that religiosity is only a need e.g. for timid or frustrated people can thus be rejected.

The variables which loaded most highly on the factor *distance from the church as an organization* (e.g. the church should preferably not seek contact with me, but rather wait till I need it; most of what the priest talks about is not important for practical life; the church only consists of priest and members of religious orders; the church is only the concern of those who live on it;) indicate that religious people can reject the church as a (bureaucratic) institution. Even the decision to participate in religious services depends only slightly on the attitude towards the church as an organization.

In the factor *social contacts* the attitudinal dimension showed itself to be related to the fact that the church is a system with extensive social interaction taking place within various sub-groups. Thus the expression 'friends', which appears in some variables, clearly refers to the specific ambiance of religious youth groups, in which everyone knows everyone else, where people meet one another frequently and where organised festivities, excursions and public holidays are spent together, resulting in a typical in-group atmosphere. The variable church attendance loaded 0.50 on both the factors, *social contact* and *religiosity*. The desire to make social contacts, provided they are in conformity with one's social standards, is thus as strong a motive for church attendance as religiosity.

Of the other attitudinal dimensions *criticism of tradition* and *function* (factors 6 and 9) appear particularly important. Criticism of tradition fits the general picture of the loading on factor 6 better than alternative interpretations, such as dogmatism or conflict with the church, since the teachings of the church (independently of religious significance) were seen as a part of the traditional system of Austrian cultural norms. Thus rejection of this culture is also expressed in rejection of church teachings. The factor *function* defines the attitude to the church as an institution. The linking of morality with the church also points out its function.

The authors are of the opinion that the importance of this study lies primarily in its theoretical implications. The specific empirical findings, which are limited by the fact that the subjects do not represent a representative random sample, are less significant than the exposure of five relevant and independent attitudinal dimensions towards religion and the church. Hypothetically, it can be assumed that the attitudinal dimensions are valid for the majority of Austrian Catholics. The *feeling of belonging to the church* is a factor of religiosity in the first instance, and a factor of distance from the church as an organization in the second. Further determinants are factors of function and social contact. It is an important finding that none of the questions bearing on the feeling of belonging had a loading on the criticism factor.

Like attitude towards the church, *attitude towards the clergy* is also multidimensional. In the first place, it is determined by distance, then less strongly by religiosity and social contact (for example, when the priest is a member of a small discussion group or an adviser). Church attendance also seems to be determined in a similar way by motives of religiosity and social contact. *Attitude towards church teaching* is also multidimensional and here the most important determinant is certainly religiosity.

If the hypothesis that these findings are valid for the whole of the male youth population in Austria is true, then the traditional image of the church in Austria can hardly be expected to change in the next twenty to thirty years. These findings show an astonishingly firm adherence to a traditional stereotype, which is accepted in the general community and rooted in historical assumptions. People adhere to a diffuse kind of religiosity. There is little noticeable increase of atheistic currents in the increasingly secularised culture. People hold themselves at a friendly distance from the existing church organization. The majority of Catholics take up stereotyped religious attitudes and modes of behaviour which are not determined by the pronouncements of the religious institutions, the church.

## SELECTED BIBLIOGRAPHY

Bargon, Nina Elisabeth, *Die Messfeier in der Gedankenwelt des Hauptschulkindes* [Mass and High-school-children]. Unpublished Theological Dissertation, Graz, 1964.

Bodzenta, Erich, 'Forschungen in Österreich' [Research in Austria]. *Social Compass*, 2 (4–5), 1959.

—, 'Versuch einer sozial-religiösen Typologie der katholischen Pfarre' [An Attempt at Socio-Religious Classification of the Catholic Parish], in: Schelsky, H.; Greiner F., and Goldschmidt, D. (eds.), *Soziologie der Kirchengemeinde* [Sociology of the Parish]. Stuttgart, Ferdinand Enke Verlag, 1960.

—, 'Die Kirche in modernen Stadtbild' [The Church in the Modern City]. *Österreichische Gemeindezeitung*, 1961/2.

—, *Die Katholiken im Österreich* [Catholics in Austria]. Vienna, Herder-Verlag, 1962a.

—, *Industriedorf im Wohlstand* [Prosperity and small-sized industrial villages]. Mainz, Matthias-Grunewald Verlag, 1962b.

Bodzenta, E.; Dellepoort, J. J., and Grond, L., 'Kirchliche Sozialforschung und Seelsorge. Berichte aus Österreich' [Socio-Religious Research and Pastoral Work of the Clergy. Report from Austria]. *Der Seelsorger* (Vienna), 26 (10/11), Special Issue, 1956.

Bodzenta, E.; Greinacher, N., and Grond, L. (eds.), *Regionalplanung in der Kirche* [Regional Planning in the Church]. Mainz, Matthias Grunewald Verlag, 1965.

Bogensberger, Hugo, 'Einstellungen zu religiösen Wahrheiten und religiös-kirchlichen Normen' [Attitudes to Religious Beliefs and Church Norms] in: *Kirche in der Stadt. I: Grundlagen und Analysen* [The Church in the City I: Principles and Analyses], edited by *Österr. Seelsorgeinstitut* [The Austrian Pastoral Institute].

Dellepoort, J., and Grond, L., 'Stand und Bedarf an Priestern in Österreich' [On Priests in Austria]. *Social Compass*, 4 (3/4), 1956.

Dittrich, Robert, 'Konfession und Geburtenproblem' [Denomination and Birth Control]. *Der Seelsorger* (Vienna), Special Issue, 1952.

Fischer, Gerhard H. and Holl, A., 'Kirche auf Distanz' [Estrangement from the Church]. *Der Seelsorger* (Vienna), 37 (5), 1967.

Fresner, Eduard, *Männliche Landjugend in der Steiermark* [Village Youths in Steiermark]. Unpublished Dissertation. Graz, 1967.

Freytag, Norbert, 'Sozialstruktur und religiöse Praxis in einer industriellen Mittelstadt' [Social Structure and Religious Practice in an Industrial Middle-Sized Town]. *I.C.A.R.E.S.* (Vienna), 1957.

Goddijn, W., and Goddijn, H. P. M., *Kirche als Institution* [The Church as an Institution]. Mainz, Matthias Grunewald Verlag, 1963 p. 73 ff.

Golomb, E., *Die steirische Priesterschaft* [The Priests in Styria]. Unpublished Dissertation. Graz, 1959.

Helczmanovski, H., 'Strukturplanung für ein Landgebiet' [Structural Planning for a Rural District] in: *Regionalplanung in der Kirche* [Regional Planning in the Church], edited by E. Bodzenta, N. Greinacher, L. Grond. Mainz, Matthias Grunewald Verlag, 1965.

Holl, A., 'Katholische Jugend' [Catholic Youth]. *Der Seelsorger* (Vienna), 32, 1962.

—, 'Sozialpsychologische Überlegungen zur religiösen Kommunikation' [Social Psychological Reflections on Religious Communication] in: *Kirche in der Stadt I: Grundlagen und Analysen* [The Church in the City I: Principles and Analyses], edited by *Österr. Seelsorgeinstitut*, [The Austrian Pastoral Institute]. Vienna, Herder-Verlag, 1967.

Institut für kirchliche Sozialforschung (I.K.S.), Wien [Institute for Socio-Religious Research, Vienna], *Zur Wiener Stadt- und Kirchenplanung* [Vienna Town Planning and Building of Churches]. Vienna, Report No. 10, 1953.

—, *Die Wiener Hochschulen* [The Vienna Universities]. Report No. 12, 1954.

—, *Religiöse Praxis in einer Grosstadtpfarre* [Religious Practice in a City Parish]. Report No. 25, 1957.

—, *Kirche am eisernen Vorhang, soziale Situation und religiöses Leben im Burgenland* [The Church next to the Iron Curtain, Social Situation and Religious Life in the Burgenland]. Report No. 35–38, 1958a.

—, *Innsbruck Heute* [Innsbruck Today]. Report No. 41–44, 1958b.

—, *Die katholischen Mittelschulen in Österreich* [Catholic Secondary Schools in Austria].

Report No. 48, 1959.
—, *Zur Situation der Kirche in Österreich* [On the Situation of the Church in Austria]. Report No. 50, 1960.
—, *Die Frauenorden und Kongregationen in Österreich* [Women's Orders and Congregations in Austria]. Report No. 63–66, 1961.
—, *Die Erzdiözese Wien in der Gegenwart* [The present situation of the Archdiocese of Vienna]. Report No. 67–69, 1961/63.
—, *Pfarr- und Kirchenplanung für Österreich* [Planning of Parishes and Building of Churches in Austria]. Report No. 71, 1962.
—, *Bevölkerungestruktur und religiöse Praxis in Krems* [The Social Stratification and Religious Practice in Krems]. Vienna, Report No. 73, 1963.
—, *Bevölkerungestruktur und religiöse Praxis in Krems: Familie und religiöse Praxis* [Social Stratification and Religious Practice in Krems: Family and Religious Practice]. Report No. 74, 1965.
—, *Religion und Familie. Part 1: Religiöse Einstellungen und Verhaltensweisen bei katholischen Familien* [Religion and Family. Part 1: Religious Attitudes and Behaviour of Catholic Families]. Report No. 78, 1966.
—, *Religion und Familie. Part 2: Die Funktion der Familie für die Tradierung religiöser Einstellungen und Verhaltensweisen* [Religion and Family. Part 2: The Role of the Family in the Religious Socialization]. Vienna, Report No. 79, 1968.
Jachym, F., and Dellepoort, J. (ed.), *Die europäische Priesterfrage* [Problems of the Priesthood in Europe]. Vienna, I.K.I.F.K.S., 1959.
Jaromir, R., *Bibel und Zeitgeist* [The Bible and the Spirit of our Time]. Vienna, 1959.
Klostermann, F.; Kriegl, H.; Mauer, O., and Weinzierl, E., *Kirche in Österreich 1918–1965* [The Church in Austria]. Vienna, Herder-Verlag, 1966.
Knoll, August M., *Christlich-soziale Bewegung in Österreich* [Social Christian Movement in Austria]. *Lexikon für Theologie und Kirche* [The Lexikon of Church and Theology]. Freiburg, Herder-Verlag, 1957.
—, *Gnade und Zins* [Grace and Interest]. *Jahrbuch der österr. Leogesellschaft* [The Year Book of the Austrian Leonine Society]. Vienna, 1934.
—, *Das Kapitalismusproblem in der modernen Soziologie* [The Problem of Capitalism in Modern Sociology]. Vienna, 1953.
Lindner, T.; Lentner, L., and Holl, A., *Priesterbild und Berufswahlmotive* [The Priest and the Choice of the Priesthood as a Vocation]. Vienna, Herder-Verlag, 1963.
Matzueller A., *Die Situation der Religion und der Kirche innerhalb der industriellen Arbeitswelt* [The Situation of Religion and the Church in the Industrial Civilization]. Unpublished Dissertation, Innsbruck, 1966.
*Österr. Seelsorgeinstitut* (Editor) [The Austrian Pastoral Institute], *Kirche in der Stadt I. Grundlagen und Analysen* [The Church in the City I. Principles and Analyses]. Vienna, 1967.
Rosenmayr, L., *Familienbeziehungen und Freizeitgewohnheiten jugendlicher Arbeiter* [Family Relationships and Leisure Habits of Young Workers]. Vienna, Verlag für Geschichte und Politik, 1963.
—, *Religiöse Praxis der Jungend* [Religious Practice of Youth]. *Der Seelsorger*, 35 (1), Vienna, 1965.
—, *Sociology in Austria.* Cologne, Hermann Bohlaus Verlag, 1966.

—, 'The Sociology of Religious Phenomena in Germany and Austria since Max Weber' *American Catholic Sociological Review*, 1954/6.

Rudolf, Karl, *Die Pfarre, Gestalt und Sendung* [The Parish, its Form and its Mission]. Vienna, Herder Verlag, 1954.

Schasching, Johannes, *Der Begriff des Religiösen in der Religions-soziologie* [The Concept of the Religious in the Sociology of Religion]. *Jahrbuch des Institutes für christliche Sozialwissenschaften der Westfälischen Wilhems-Universität* [The Year Book of the Institute for Christian Social Sciences of the Wilhelms University of Westphalia], edited by J. Höffner, Münster, Verlag Regensburg, 1962, S. 93.

—, *Kirche und industrielle Gesellschaft* [The Church and Industrial Society]. Vienna, Herder-Verlag, 1960.

—, *Soziologie der Pfarre* [Sociology of the Parish]. *Die Pfarre* [The Parish], edited by H. Rahner, Freiburg, Lambertus-Verlag, 1956.

Schiefer, Josef, *Christusbild und Christusglaube unserer Jugendlichen an berufsbildenden Schulen* [Christ and Belief in Christ Amongst our Youth in Technical Schools], unpublished Theological Dissertation. Graz, 1966.

Silberbauer, Gerhard, *Österreiche Katholiken und die Arbeiterfrage* [Austrian Catholics and the Problems of the Working Class]. Vienna-Graz, Styria, 1966.

Suk, Walter, *Das Bild einer Grosstadtpfarre* [The Parish of a Large City]. *Soziologie der Kirchengemeinde* [Sociology of the Church Community], edited by D. Goldschmidt, F. Greiner, and H. Schelsky, Stuttgart, Enke-Verlag, 1960.

Swoboda, Heinrich, *Grosstadtseelsorge* [The Pastoral Work of Priests in Big Cities]. Vienna, 1909.

Vaskovics, Laszlo, A., *Religiöse Praxis im Spannungsfeld familiärer Einflüsse* [Religious Practice and Family Influences]. *Der Seelsorger* (Vienna), 35, (6), 1965, pp. 388ff.

—, *Religionssoziologische Aspekte der Sozialisierung wertorientierter Verhaltensformen* [Socio-Religious Aspects of Socialization of Value Oriented Behaviour], in: *Internationales Jahrbuch der Religionssoziologie. 2: Theoretische Aspekte der Religionssoziologie* [The International Year Book for Sociology of Religion. 2: Theoretical Aspects of Religious Sociology of Religion], edited by J. Matthes, Köln-Opladen, Westdeutscher-Verlag, 1967.

Winter, E. K., *Probleme der Religionssoziologie* [Problems of Sociology of Religion]. *Zeitschrift für gesamte Staatswissenschaft*, 1931.

Zulehner, Paul, *Zur religiösen Situation in der Stadt* [On the Religious Situation in the Cities], in: *Kirche in der Stadt 1: Grundlagen und Analysen* (The Church in the City. 1: Principles and Analyses], edited by *Österr. Seelsorgeinstitut* [The Austrian Pastoral Institute], Vienna, Herder-Verlag, 1967a.

—, *Kirche und Austromarxismus* [Church and Marxism in Austria]. Vienna, Herder-Verlag, 1967.

FRANÇOIS HOUTART*

# Belgium

## HISTORICAL INTRODUCTION

Christianity was introduced into what is now Belgium during the Roman occupation. In the fourth century there were bishoprics in some Gallo-Roman towns (Tongres, Tournai), but the beginnings of Christianity were almost wiped out by the Frankish invasion and colonization.

It was not until the sixth and seventh centuries that the period of real expansion and consolidation began; bishoprics were established and the struggle against paganism and popular superstition was organised. The development of monasteries (thirty between 530 and 640) strengthened these foundations. The monasteries became active centres of faith and culture (Abbatial schools) and contributed to the Carolingian renaissance. However, both the renaissance and the progress of evangelization were hampered by the Norman raids beginning in 820 and intensifying in violence during the second half of the century.

In 959 when the Duchy of Germany was divided in two, the provinces of Belgium were incorporated together with Holland and Germany, into Lower Lotharingia. The tenth century saw the 'secularization' of the Church; bishops became temporal princes, and their nomination, for the most part, was the prerogative of laymen. Christianity became the state church. Nevertheless, this was a golden age for the Church, marked by the establishment of new religious orders.

The trend which had begun in the tenth century was accentuated in the

* François Houtart was born in Brussels, Belgium in 1925. He was ordained priest at Malines in 1949 and received his Licentiate in Political and Social Sciences from the University of Louvain. He has also studied sociology at Chicago and Indiana Universities. In 1956 he became Secretary General of the International Conference of Religious Sociology. Father Houtart is currently Director of the Center for Socio-Religious Research of Louvain, Secretary General of the International Federation of Institutions for Socio-Religious and Social Research (F.E.R.E.S.), and a Member of the Secretariat for non-believers in Rome. His major works include *The Church and the Latin American Revolution* (with Emile Pin), 1965.

following three centuries, but not without dissent. While emperors nominated bishops, investing them with the cross and the mitre, some bishops claimed the autonomy of spiritual power. During the Investiture disputes, the Imperial Church of Lotharingia sided with the Emperor, but rivalry among some abbeys and feudal lords damaged the imperial power; gradually the feudal lords began to interfere in the nomination of the bishops. At the same time convents and abbeys multiplied, the great religious orders were founded and the 'Beguines', – women who lived a communal life devoted to charitable works, but who did not take religious vows – emerged.

In the fourteenth and fifteenth centuries, through marriages and inheritance, the Dukes of Burgundy became overlords of all principalities, with the exception of Liège, in the present Bénélux region and Northern France. The Church was now closely united with the papacy, and the clergy exercised influence in politics. This period is also marked by the rise of mysticism with John Ruysbroeck, Thomas à Kempis and Denis Chartreus, and by the foundation of the University of Louvain, authorized by Pope Martin V in 1425.

The period from the sixteenth century to the French Revolution introduced marked changes. In 1482 the marriage between Mary of Burgundy and Maximilian of Austria brought the Provinces of Belgium under domination of the Hapsburgs. The Provinces thus became the principal battlefield of the wars between the French and the Hapsburgs. The advent of the Reformation, with its roots in the Humanism of the Renaissance (Erasmus) and the moral and institutional decay of the Church, brought about a political and religious split: the Peace of Westphalia in 1648, sealed the division between Calvinist Holland and the Catholic Pays Bas du Sud (the Spanish Netherlands) where the authorities prevented the spread of the Reformation. It was here that the Catholic revival had begun in 1559 with, in particular, the reform of the dioceses (the establishment of the archdiocese of Malines). The Jesuits, introduced in 1542, were among the main architects of the reform mainly through their teaching. Another important factor in the renewal of the Church was the stabilisation of relations between church and state: the Holy Seat preserved for itself the right to consecrate the bishops proposed by the state.

Originating in the work of a Belgian theologian (Janssens, Bishop of Ypres), Jansenism, despite its condemnation in 1642, spread rapidly. It was supported by some bishops but eventually, in 1715, the University of Louvain submitted to the Bull 'Unigenitus'.

In the eighteenth century, the Church suffered as the consequence of Hapsburg policy. Joseph II closed the convents and replaced the diocesan seminaries with general seminaries; he granted an edict of tolerance to Protestants and also abolished ecclesiastical jurisdiction in matters of marriage. This dictatorial reform stirred up, in 1789, the Belgian Revolution, which drove out the Austrians. The States of Brabant gained independence.

In 1794, the States were annexed by revolutionary France. The new authorities suppressed liberties and privileges, forbade public worship, confiscated church property and abolished religious orders. The University of Louvain was closed.

Belgium was attached to France from 1794 to 1814. In 1801, the Concordat re-established liberty of public worship, reorganized diocesan boundaries and gave the government the right to nominate bishops; in return the government agreed to pay salaries to the clergy (in exchange for confiscated property). Meanwhile, difficulties multiplied particularly in relation to the nomination of bishops and the Imperial Catechism. The authorities had to use force in Ghent and Tournai. A schismatic movement, called Stevenisme, opposed the Concordat, and was not reabsorbed again until 1958.

In 1815, the Treaty of Vienna reunited Holland and Belgium under the same crown. The government of Holland introduced the Basic Law which established the equality of all denominations under the jurisdiction of the State and aimed at the establishment of a national church independent of Rome. The Belgian Church united with the Liberals in opposition to the King. The Revolution which flared up in 1830 resulted in an overthrow of the Government of Holland on the 25th August.

In 1831, the Treaty of London assured the independence of Belgium. The new Constitution defined the permanent status of the Church: three official denominations were recognized and their clergy were to receive renumeration from the state. The same constitution also assured the freedom of education. The issue of education, however, was to contribute to future disagreements between church and state. The University of Louvain was reopened in 1835.

The Church in Belgium took an important part in the missionary movement. This activity was favoured by the colonial policy of the Government (establishment of the Scheutistes in the Congo, 1888). The publication of the encyclical *Rerum Novarum* led to a great social movement among Catholics (Congresses in Liège, 1886–87–90; the Malinese Congress, 1891) and contributed to the establishment of professional and social organizations. In the intellectual domain Cardinal Mercier, professor of Thomistic philosophy at Louvain (1882), led the revival of Thomistic Scholasticism. The same prelate, when he was archbishop of Malines, was, together with Lord Halifax, one of the pioneers of the ecumenical movement (talks in Malines, 1921–26). Another Belgian, Dom Lambert Beauduin, was among the first initiators of liturgical renewal and was very active in the ecumenical movement (Monastery of Chevetogne, and its review, *Irenikon*).

In 1926, Father Lebbe founded the *La Société des Auxiliares des Missions*

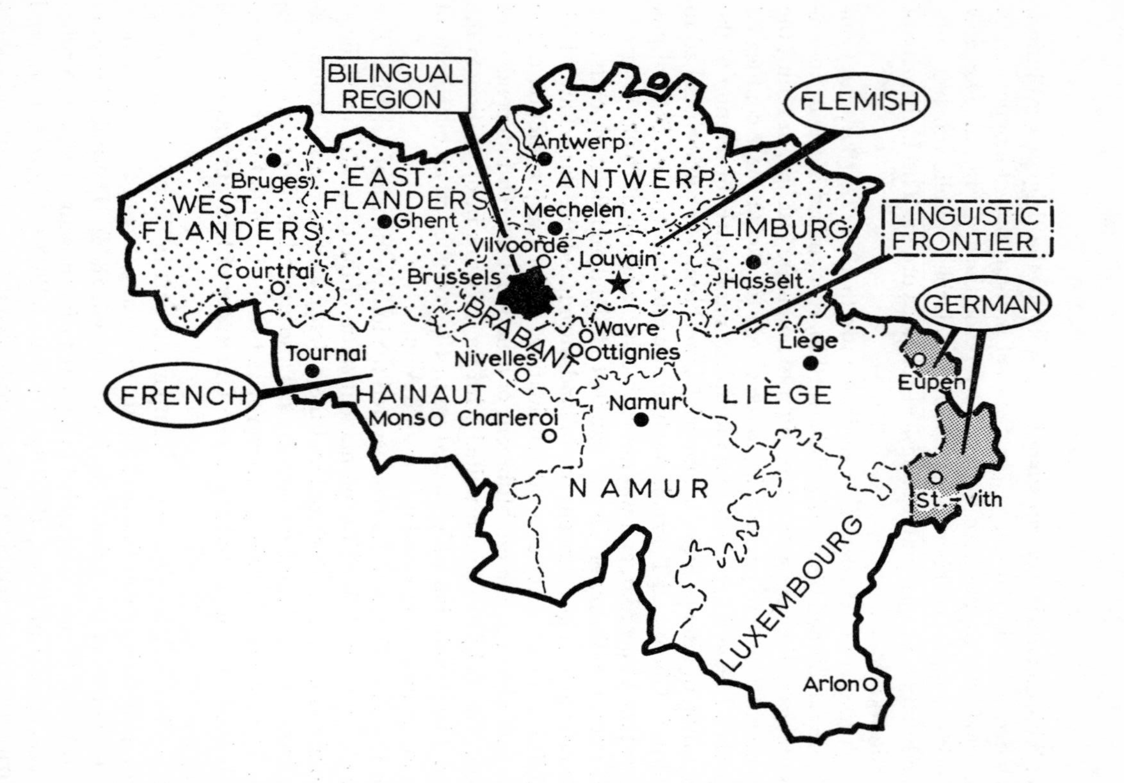


*Linguistic division of Belgium*

(The Auxiliary Missionary Society) and was largely responsible for the consecration of native bishops in China.

Father Cardijn, the founder of specialized Catholic Action, started *La Jeunesse Ouvrière Chrétienne* (Young Christian Workers' Movement) in 1925. The great pastoral and spiritual revival of the Catholic Church in Belgium, the rediscovery of the urgency of the missionary work, the reorganization of parishes and the liturgical renewal, owed much to this movement and the developments of the years 1940–44. The second Vatican Council has given this movement renewed vitality.

## DEMOGRAPHIC DATA

As 96 per cent of the Belgian population is baptized in the Catholic faith, general demographic data is applicable to Catholics. However, it is necessary to distinguish two cultural regions in the country: the Flemish region with its Dutch language, and the French speaking Walloon region. The capital city of Brussels straddles both regions and is bilingual. This division is not only linguistic; significant demographic, religious and political differences also exist. The following statistics and interpretations are based on regional data.

*Table 1. Population*

| Region | Population | |
|---|---|---|
| *Flanders* | | |
| Anvers | 1,506,627 | |
| East Flanders (Ghent) | 1,301,073 | |
| West Flanders (Bruges) | 1,636,670 | |
| Limburg | 631,326 | |
| Flemish Brabant (District of Louvain) | 378,844 | |
| Total | | 4,854,540 |
| *Wallonia* | | |
| Hainaut | 1,331,953 | |
| Liège | 1,017,875 | |
| Luxembourg | 220,315 | |
| Namur | 380,265 | |
| Walloon Brabant (District of Nivelles) | 223,087 | |
| Total | | 3,173,495 |
| *Brussels and Suburbs* | | 1,528,345 |
| Total | | 9,556,380 |

Source: I.N.S., 31 December 1966.

*Table 2. Demography and religious practice*

| Region | Population % | Practising Belgians % | Belgian parish priests % |
|---|---|---|---|
| Flanders | 50.8 | 56.0 | 53.5 |
| Wallonia | 33.0 | 24.0 | 41.5 |
| Brussels & Suburbs | 16.2 | 20.0 | 5.0 |

Source: I.N.S., 1966.

*Table 3. Births, deaths and marriages*

| Region | Births | Deaths | Marriages |
|---|---|---|---|
| Flanders | 88,172 | 56,773 | 40,080 |
| Wallonia | 46,768 | 44,069 | 21,290 |
| Brussels & Suburbs | 18,567 | 17,632 | 8,744 |

Source: I.N.S., 1966.

*Table 4. Fertility rates*

| Region | Births per 1,000 |
|---|---|
| Flanders | 18 |
| Wallonia | 14 |
| Brussels | 12 |
| Total Belgium | 16 |

Source: I.N.S., 1966.

*Table 5. Population increase*

| Region | Population | | Increase |
|---|---|---|---|
| | 1961 | 1966 | % |
| Flanders | 4,684,409 | 4,854,540 | 3.6 |
| Wallonia | 3,038,796 | 3,173,495 | 4.4 |
| Brussels & Suburbs | 1,439,536 | 1,528,345 | 6.1 |
| Total Belgium | 9,189,749 | 9,556,380 | 3.9 |

Source: I.N.S., 1966.

While the relatively high rate of growth of the Walloon region may be explained by the importance of foreign immigration, that of the Flemish region is due to a higher rate of natural increase. The rate of growth of the capital is inflated by large internal immigration.

*Table 6. Distribution by age and sex*

| % | 0 to 20 years Males | 0 to 20 years Females | 20 to 40 years Males | 20 to 40 years Females | 40 to 65 years Males | 40 to 65 years Females | 65 and over Males | 65 and over Females |
|---|---|---|---|---|---|---|---|---|
| Age group | 51.01 | 48.09 | 50.06 | 49.94 | 48.49 | 51.51 | 42.30 | 57.70 |
| Total population | 31.01 | 28.03 | 27.05 | 26.03 | 30.02 | 30.07 | 10.06 | 13.09 |
| Age group as % of total population | 30.05 | | 26.09 | | 30.05 | | 12.01 | |

Source: Population Census 1961.

THE PRACTICE OF RELIGION

The proportion of Belgians baptized in the Catholic Church varies from 80 per cent in the urban industrial districts to more than 90 per cent in the rural districts. Protestants comprise only 3–4 per cent of the population. For this reason the following short discussion considers only Catholics.

The following more detailed observations should be made. First, while the percentage of Sunday observance appears higher in Flanders than in Wallonia, the division according to the linguistic zones is not ideal. We find that the proportion of those practising is relatively low in Flemish Brabant and Antwerp and much higher in Luxembourg. Secondly, the practice of religion varies greatly in inverse ratio to the density of population (Liège, axe Mons-Charleroi, Brussels-Malines). However, one finds examples of the opposite case. The correlation is not perfect, but is highest between low religious practice, population density and industrialization. Thirdly, in the Walloon region, two factors have been responsible for the low proportion of those practising religion: the ageing of the population and the attractiveness of Brussels for the Walloon speaking population of Brabant.

*Table 7. Sunday observance, calculated from the number present at mass on third sunday of October 1966*

| Region | N | % | Practising population as % of total | % |
|---|---|---|---|---|
| *Flanders* | | | | |
| Antwerp | 504,235 | | 33.4 | |
| East Flanders (Ghent) | 555,451 | | 42.5 | |
| West Flanders (Bruges) | 543,267 | | 54.0 | 43.05 |
| Limburg | 540,000[1] | | 54.0 | |
| Total | 1,942,953 | 56.00 | | |
| *Wallonia* | | | | |
| Hainaut (Tournai) | 244,980 | | 18.03 | |
| Liège | 317,595[2] | | 31.00 | 27.08 |
| Namur-Luxembourg | 269,971 | | 46.00 | |
| Total | 832,546 | 24.00 | | |
| *Archdiocese of Malines-Brussels*[3] | | | | |
| | 694,514 | 20.00 | 34.08 | 34.08 |
| Total | 3,470,013 | 100.00 | 35.6 | |

1. Estimate based on the number of practising persons in Bruges: the actual number is probably greater.
2. Less the total for Limburg.
3. The total population of 1,992,139 in the diocese of Malines-Brussels includes the metropolitan area of Brussels and the province of Brabant.

## ECCLESIASTICAL AND SECULAR ORGANISATIONS

### *Youth Movements*

The Catholic Youth movement has two main orientations: the spiritual, embracing all social strata, for example the *Croisade Eucharistique* (the Eucharistic Crusade) and Catholic Action, specialised according to the social milieux and supervised by the Hierarchy. Catholic Action may or may not be attached to some specific social organization. In the first case the objectives are essentially apostolic as in: *Jeunesse Etudiante Catholique* (The Young Catholic Student's Association) in the private and public schools;

*Equipes Universitaires* (University Groups); *Jeunesse Indépendante* (Independant Youth Association); and *Jeunesse Rurale* (Country Youth Association). In the second case, where Catholic Action is integrated in a social movement its objectives concern both education and welfare. Such movements as *La Jeunesse Ouvrière Chrétienne* (Young Christian Workers' Association) and the branches of *La Jeunesse du Boerenbond* (Youth Branches of Boerenbond), fall into this category.

It is also necessary to distinguish educational movements such as the *Fédération Nationale des Patros* (National Federation of Guilds), social clubs for girls and boys from local parishes, or the *Fédération des Scouts et Guides Catholiques* (Catholic Federation of Scouts and Guides).

*Adult Movements*

Spiritual movements may be divided into those open to all ages, for example *Ligue du Sacré Coeur* (League of the Sacred Heart), *Congrégations Mariales* (Marian Clubs), *Apostolat de la Prière* (Apostolat of Prayer) and general Catholic Action, for example, *Légion de Marie* (Legion of Mary), *Action Catholique des Hommes* (Catholic Action for Men) – both parochial organizations.

Specialized Catholic Action again may be classified into organizations not integrated into a social movement, such as the Catholic Action groups of independant or rural social classes, and those which are attached to the *Mouvement Ouvrier Chrétien* (Christian Workers' Movement). The latter includes *Ligues Ouvrières Chrétiennes Féminines* (Leagues of Catholic Women Workers) and Catholic Action for male workers, which are organized as mass movements in Flanders, and as *Equipes Ouvrières* (Workers Groups) in the French speaking areas.

Family and professional movements are also part of Catholic Action. The Family Pastoral Centre was founded in 1959. Each diocese has a Commission for the Family Apostolate and Marriage Preparation Courses which prepare engaged couples for future responsibilities. Movements for the spiritual welfare of the Family include: *Equipes Notre Dame* (Marriage Groups), *Fraternités de Route* (Fraternities of adult boy-scouts) and *Foyers Compagnons de Saint François* (Companions of St. Francis).

The aim of professional movements is to study the social doctrine of the Church and apply its principles. The principal organizations are: U.N.I.A P.A.C. which unites employers and employees; *Société Médicale St. Luc* (Medical Society of St. Luke); *Société Sts. Côme et Damian* (Society of St. Cosmas and Damian) (for the pharmacists) and *Fédération des Instituteurs Chrétiens de Belgique* (Federation of Belgian Christian Teachers).

THE RELATIONSHIP BETWEEN CIVIL STATUS, OCCUPATION, RESIDENCE AND RELIGIOUS LIFE

The following data are based on a detailed survey of two Belgian industrial agglomerations, Charleroi in the Walloon region, and Ghent in the Flemish region:

*Table 8. Sunday observance and sex in the Charleroi area*

| | Population | Number practising | % of population | % of practising |
|---|---|---|---|---|
| Men | 83,841 | 11,306 | 13.49 | 39.19 |
| Women | 94,060 | 17,538 | 18.65 | 60.81 |
| Total | 177,901 | 28,844 | 16.21 | 100.00 |

Although in the general population women outnumber men in the ratio of 53/47, practising women outnumber practising men in the rates of 3/2. 31.4 per cent of those practising are under twenty years of age.

*Table 9. Religious practice and civil status in the Ghent area*

| Civil status | % of practising | |
|---|---|---|
| | Women (31.1) | Men (25.6) |
| Single | 47.2 | 38.3 |
| Married | 23.3 | 19.7 |
| Widowers/Widows | 22.5 | 17.0 |

There are 137 practising women per 100 men, while in the population as a whole the corresponding ratio is 112 women per 100 men.

The extent of religious practice is higher among persons with higher education, and accounts for the balance between men and women in this category. Among workers the picture is very different: for every 100 men aged over 20 years who practise there are 189 women. There is, therefore, a considerable number of families who are divided in terms of religious behaviour.

One should note that except among higher executives, the percentage of those practising in these occupational groups is generally lower than the

*Table 10. Religious practice and occupation in the Charleroi area*

| Social and occupational categories | Men | | Women | | Total | |
|---|---|---|---|---|---|---|
| | N | % | N | % | N | % |
| Managers and self employed | 357 | 31.96 | 760 | 68.04 | 1,117 | 100 |
| Persons with higher education | 1,381 | 49.06 | 1,034 | 50.94 | 2,815 | 100 |
| Clerks | 2,381 | 38.49 | 3,805 | 61.51 | 6,186 | 100 |
| Workers | 1,907 | 34.42 | 3,634 | 65.58 | 5,541 | 100 |
| Not elsewhere classified | 284 | 17.61 | 1,329 | 82.39 | 1,613 | 100 |
| Total | 6,310 | 36.53 | 10,962 | 63.47 | 17,272 | 100 |

*Table 11. Religous practice and occupation among males in the Ghent area*

| Social and occupational category | % of practising |
|---|---|
| Higher ranks | 44.9 |
| Lower ranks | 31.4 |
| Employees | 25.6 |
| Businessman, craftsmen | 20.3 |
| Workers | 10.2 |
| Total working population | 19.1 |

average for men in this area (25.6). In effect, the non-working part of the population, together with working women, has a higher rate of religious practice.

In terms of the working population only, it seems clear from these two studies that the categories in which the proportion of those practising is greatest is among the higher ranks. The lowest percentages found among the workers in the Ghent region and the business-men and self-employed in the region of Charleroi, closely approximates to that of the workers. The problem which faces the Church concerns its adjustment to the needs of the working world.

The table shows that the percentage of practising immigrants (9.58) is lower than amongst the native born (14.52). This difference is possibly due to the fact that there are fewer females than males in the immigrant popula-

*Table 12. Religious practice in the Charleroi area: aliens and Belgians*

| | Men | | Women | |
|---|---|---|---|---|
| | N | % | N | % |
| Immigrants | 20,235 | 58.12 | 14,573 | 41.88 |
| Total population | 93,109 | 47.48 | 102,983 | 52.52 |
| Immigrants practising | 1,336 | 6.75 | 1,970 | 13.25 |
| Native born practising | 11,533 | 12.39 | 17,794 | 17.28 |

tion. This cannot be without the influence on the behaviour of the immigrants. Furthermore, the index of superior religious practice for women stands at 200 compared with 139 for Belgian women; thus twice as many immigrant women as immigrant men practise their religion.

*Table 13. Religious practice in the Ghent area: aliens and Belgians*

| | % of practising | |
|---|---|---|
| | Men | Women |
| Immigrants | 39.2 | 42.8 |
| Total population | 33.8 | 38.4 |
| Practising immigrants | 27.7 | 32.5 |
| Native born practising | 21.9 | 27.1 |

By contrast here the percentage of practising immigrants is higher than native born thus contradicting suggestions that immigrants abandon their religion on arrival in urban areas. It is necessary to view this in the light of actual conditions of migration. Nowadays, the contrasts between the town and country are less marked as urban civilization extends beyond the confines of the town.

Marked differences in immigrant religious practice exist in these two cities. The higher proportion of practising women is much less marked in Ghent than Charleroi, even though the percentage of immigrant women is clearly the same. In so far as men are concerned, the proportion of practising immigrants is quite small in the region of Charleroi, in comparison to Ghent, although the proportion of immigrants is clearly higher in Charleroi.

THE INFLUENCE OF THE RELIGIOUS FACTOR ON VOTING BEHAVIOUR

A survey which was carried out in 1956 [Smet and Evalenko, 1956] was designed to throw light on the correlation between the proportion of those who go to church on Sundays and the electoral success of the *Parti Social Chrétien* (Social Christian Party). The hypotheses stated, that electoral support for Social Christians and Liberals came from employers and cadres, to whom could be added the small fraction of those practising among workers and employees.

*Table 14. Religious practise and voting (based on the average proportion of practising persons)*

| Political party* | % of practising | |
|---|---|---|
| | Walloon districts | Flemish districts** |
| P.S.C. 1950 | 0.93 | 0.73 |
| P.S.C. + P.L. 1950 | 0.92 | 0.81 |
| P.S.C. 1954 | 0.85 | 0.71 |
| P.S.C. + P.L. 1954 | 0.84 | 0.79 |

* P.S.C. = Parti Social Chrétien.
P.L. = Parti Liberal.
** The Flemish region includes the following provinces (administrative divisions): Antwerp, West Flanders, East Flanders, Limburg and Flemish Brabant. The Walloon region includes the provinces of Hainaut, Liège, Luxembourg, Namur and Walloon Brabant.

It is clear that these coefficients are higher in Walloon Region than in Flanders. In Wallonia this can be explained in terms of the almost perfect harmony between social structure, religious practice and political opinion. The proportion of practising workers is small, and moreover, the electoral figures as compared with those for social classes, indicate that very few workers vote for the P.S.C. or for the Liberal Party.

In Flanders, Sunday observance is considerably stronger among wage earners. Although we have established the correlation between religious practice and voting, the coefficients seem to be influenced by the class structure: people belonging to the working class vote for left-wing parties, even when they practise religion more or less regularly.

Table 14 illustrates another important regional difference. The addition of Liberal Party figures to those of the P.S.C. slightly weakens the correlation between religious practice and political affiliation in Wallonia. In Flanders the reverse is true. The correlation is considerably higher when the

Liberal Party is added. In fact, in the whole Flemish Region, the number of wage earners who practise religion, is so great that it exceeds the total number of employers and cadres.

The electoral rolls of voters with Catholic tendencies suffered fairly considerable losses in 1954. Some practising people voted for non-religious parties. In Flanders, however, the setback to the P.S.C. proportionate to its electors has been smaller than in Walloon; part of the losses of the P.S.C. have been recouped there by the Liberal Party, but in Wallonia the Liberal Party recovered only a minimal proportion of its electoral support.

Another method of analysis can be tried now: the following table, using the percentage of those practising among workers as a base, allows us to compare the influence of the employer-cadre vote, and the practising worker-employee vote in relation to both the P.S.C., and P.S.C. and Liberal Party.

*Table 15. Occupational states, religious practice and voting*

| Political party | Occupational category | % of practising | |
|---|---|---|---|
| | | Walloon districts | Flemish districts |
| P.S.C. | Practising employer + cadres + wage earners | | |
| | (base: average rate) | 0.91 | 0.71 |
| | (base: minimum rate) | 0.92 | 0.71 |
| P.S.C. + P.L. | Practising employers + cadres + wage earners | | |
| | (base: average rate) | 0.91 | 0.83 |
| | (base: minimum rate) | 0.94 | 0.83 |
| P.S.C. | Employers + cadres | 0.83 | 0.52 |
| P.S.C. + P.L. | Employers + cadres | 0.85 | 0.71 |

This table permits us to make several simple observations: the correlation between the P.S.C. and employers+cadres of 0.83 in Wallonia and 0.52 in Flanders, increases to 0.91 (or 0.92) and 0.71 respectively when we add to the employers and cadres the fraction of the workers considered as practising. With the inclusion of the Liberal Party the equivalent correlations rise from 0.85 and 0.71 to 0.91 (or 0.94) and 0.83.

Compared with the first method of analysis based on coefficients computed on the average rate of religious practice the second method enables us to clarify the factors which explain the voting pattern. The class structure is one factor for it is clear that employers and cadres are the principal supporters of the P.S.C. and the Liberal Party. However, wage-earners also provide a significant proportion of the vote particularly in Flanders. There the influence of religion amongst practising workers is sufficiently strong to counter-balance the influence of the class structure.

This study carried out in 1956, no longer applies to the current situation because of the evolution of the parties. The Liberal Party has accepted Catholic candidates and the political unity of Christians no longer exists, especially after the elections in 1968.

### CONCLUSIONS: THE BELGIAN 'CATHOLIC WORLD'

A study by C.R.I.S.P. from which much of the preceding material has been drawn is entitled *Structure and Evolution of the Belgian Catholic World*. The authors explain the title as follows:

> To speak of the 'Belgian Catholic World' is to recognise the existence of a distinct culture at the heart of Belgian society, which represents values and institutions different from other 'Worlds' and other 'spiritual families'. We use this term to aid our discussion, recognizing that it probably cannot be employed rigorously; the sociological concept which it suggests perhaps only represents a superficial unity which is challenged by some features of the times both internal and external.

We have already described several Christian organizations in Belgium – those which are subject to the Hierarchy. A complete listing would have been possible by including the Catholic education system (57% of school population), the charitable institutions and the hospitals, and by incorporating a varied collection of social organizations such as: *Movement Ouvrier Chrétien* (The Christian Workers' Movement); *Confédération des Syndicats Chrétiens* (The Federation of Christian Trade Unions) (54.7 per cent of workers, 57 per cent of employees and 48.6 per cent of Belgian civil servants in 1963); *Alliance Nationale des Mutualles Belges* (The National Union of Belgian Mutual Insurance Societies) (44.8 per cent of Belgians in 1966); *Fédération Nationale des Cooperatives Chrétiennes* (The National Federation of Christian Co-operatives) (116,000 members in 1963) and agricultural organizations such as *Boerenbond* in Flanders (270,173 members in 1964) and *Alliance Agricole Belge* (Belgian Agricultural Union) in Wallonia (25,000 members). All of these organizations have two branches (and sometimes two perspectives), Flemish and Walloon.

Such terminology seems to justify the expression *Belgian Catholic World*. Nevertheless, these powerful and varied Christian institutions are under vigorous questioning among Catholics themselves, particularly since the Council. The aims of the organizations themselves are changing from a strictly defensive attitude in matters of faith to an engagement with the contemporary world which seeks cooperation with non-Christians. They justify this in terms of the incarnation of Christian values. Debate on the value of these organisations takes place, not only among marginal Catholics, but on the official level itself. The Episcopate is seeking more effective pastoral structures.

The unity of the Catholic world would seem to have been seriously disturbed. Regionalism – the division between Flanders and Wallonia – is beginning to gain importance within the Church itself; the case of Louvain is a clear example of it. The Social Christian Party is less and less a factor in Catholic unity.

One does not see clearly how all of these points of issue will be transformed from the level of intellectual debate into effective action in social structures which are still predominantly conservative.

SELECTED BIBLIOGRAPHY

Centre de Recherche et d'Information Socio-Politique (C.R.I.S.P.), 'Structure et Evolution du Monde Catholique en Belgique' [Structure and Evolution of the Catholic World in Belgium]. *Courrier hebdomadaire*, 10 February, 1967.

Dingemans, L. and Remy, J., *Charleroi et son agglomération: Aspects sociologiques de la pratique religieuse* [Charleroi Conurbation: Sociological Aspects of Religious Practice], Vol. III. Sodegec et C.R.S.R., 1962.

Dobbelaere, K. *Sociologische analyse van de katholiciteit* [Sociological Analysis of Catholicism]. Antwerp, Standaard, 1966.

*Encyclopédie catholique du monde chrétien* [Catholic Encyclopedia of the Christian World]. Tournai, Casterman, 1964.

Houtart, F. *Les Paroisses de Bruxelles* [The Parishes of Brussels]. Brussels, 1954.

Houtart, F. and Dingemans, L. *Pastorale d'une région industrielle* [Pastoral Study of an Industrial Region]. Brussels-Paris, Ed. du C.E.P., 1964.

Institut National de la Statistique (I.N.S.), *Mouvement de la Population*, 1966.

Laloux, J. *Mettre l'Eglise en état de Mission* [To Prepare the Church for an Active Apostolate]. Brussels-Paris, Ed. du C.E.P., 1964.

Moreau, E. de, *Histoire de l'Eglise. Collection belge des manuels d'Histoire* [History of the Church. Belgian Collection of Historical Manuals]. Tournai, Casterman, 1941.

—, *Histoire de l'Eglise en Belgique* [History of the Church in Belgium]. Brussels, Ed. Universelles, 1949.

P.A.S.C.O. (University of Louvain), *Tussen Atheïst en gelovige* [Between Atheist and Believer]. Tielt-The Hague, Lannoo, 1965.

Piérard, L. *Histoire de la Belgique* [History of Belgium]. Paris, P.U.F., 1948.

Smet, Roger de, et Evalenko, R. *Les Elections Belges. Explication de la répartition des suffrages* [Belgian Elections. Explanation of the Voting Pattern]. Brussels, Institut Solvay, Université Libre de Bruxelles, 1956.

Van Houtte, J. *De Mispraktijk in de Gentse agglomeratie* [Mass Attendance in the Ghent Conurbation]. Sint-Niklaas Waas, Drukkerij Schneiders van Kerckhove, 1963.

JIVKO OCHAVKOV*

# Bulgaria

## HISTORICAL AND STATISTICAL INTRODUCTION

Profound social and economic changes have occurred in Bulgaria since the Communist victory of 9 September 1944. Before 1944, private property was the predominant element in the realms of industry, craftsmanship, agriculture and commerce. This is no longer so. According to official statistics for 1963, the socialist sector contributed 99.5 per cent of the national income; 99.3 per cent of industrial production, 99.5 per cent of agricultural production, and 99.9 per cent of retail trade. Private property now only exists as an infinitesimal remnant. In the rural areas in 1963 only 0.6 per cent of the total arable land was in private hands; 981 large, socialist, agricultural co-operatives and eighty-five state agricultural farms have superceded the more than a million private farmers of 1939.

In addition, Bulgaria has risen from a backward agricultural country to an advanced agricultural and industrial nation. Between 1939 and 1963 industrial production increased from 15 to 51 per cent of the national income. The rural population was reduced from 77.3 to 59.2 per cent of the total, yet the average increase in the absolute value of rural production in the period 1959–1963 compared with 1932–38 was about 79 per cent. Mechanization, hardly evident in 1939 when there were only 3,000 tractors in Bulgaria, accounted for 93.1 per cent of the work on co-operative farms.

The socialist reconstruction of the national economy has been accompanied by profound changes in the social structure. Classes and social groupings which characterized the old society based on the domination of private property over the means of production, no longer exist, save as an insignifi-

* Jivko Ochavkov was born in Debar, Bulgaria in 1913. He has worked as editor of the journal *Filosofska Misl* 1945–63, Professor in the State University of Sofia, 1948–54, head of the Historical Materialism section of the Institute of Philosophy to the Bulgarian Academy of Science, 1952–66, and is currently the Director of the Institute of Sociology to the Bulgarian Academy of Science. Major publications include *Vaznikvaneto na marksizma* [The Arising of Marxism], 1948, *Istoricheskiiat materializøm i sotsiologiiata* [Historical Materialism and Sociology], 1958 and *The Waning Process of Religion in Bulgaria*, a Sociological Survey, 1968.

cant residue. The essential difference has been the complete disappearance of the privileged classes and groups of exploiters, such as the industrialists, the Koulaks (large land holders), merchants, etc.

Current social structure is characterized by the existence of three social groups: the working class, bound to the socialist state property; the class of peasant co-operative workers, bound to the socialist co-operative property; and the group of clerical workers (including the intelligentsia) of which the majority are bound to the socialist state property. The social and economic relationships between these groups are those of men freed from all exploitation, governing the country and constructing a new society under the leadership of the working class.

Following these social and economic changes, the standard of living of the people has improved, and, in 1962, the real income of the population had practically doubled that of 1952. A cultural and educational revolution on a grand scale has simultaneously taken hold of the country.

The rapid change to which Bulgaria has been subject since 1944 offers a splendid field for the sociological study of the general structure of society and the relationships between the various sectors of social life. Official statistics provide a record of changes in the realms of economics, politics, education and social class structure, but not in the realm of social consciousness. As religion represents one of its most observable forms it was chosen as the focus of a pilot study, undertaken in 1962, by the sociologists of the 'Historical Materialism' Department of the Institute of Philosophy of the Bulgarian Academy of Sciences.[1]

This survey also offered an exceptional opportunity to verify, on a large scale, the Marxist-Leninist theoretical prediction that religion, in so far as it forms social consciousness, will disappear at a rate proportionate to the growth of communist society.

## RELIGIOUS PARTICIPATION AND BELIEFS

The following exposition is based on results obtained from the first of two questionnaires used in the survey.[2] A representative national sample of

1. This study was directed by the author. Approximately 200 scientific assistants, and 3,000 interviewers voluntarily took part and were directed by twelve sociologists, including the author: T. Stoïtchev, N. Mitov, V.Tzonev, S. Mihailov, N. Stéfanov, I. Popov, D. Troïanov, R. Vassilev, M. Draganov, R. Pecheva, Z. Staïkov.

2. Questionnaire 2 deals with religious practices, atheism and local traditions. Forms were completed by interviewers from data in official documents, from local courts, socio-cultural societies and from information given in interviews with qualified people. This information gave data on characteristics of different regions but was not representative for the country as a whole.

45,000 adults,[3] drawn by a multi-stage random sampling procedure yielded 42,664 valid questionnaires.[4]

Originally it was intended to interview subjects directly. However, a pre-survey indicated that this method was subject to various errors. Most of the subjects seemed confused and were hesitant to respond. Later, when verifying responses by comparing them with information from the respondents' friends and with official documents (population registers, etc.), it was evident that replies were often false. Some respondents tended to overstate (or understate) their incomes; some said they had higher educational qualifications than they did have; women generally said they were younger than they were. But most important of all, some of the less devout believers qualified as 'religious of category III' said they were unbelievers, and more important, certain unbelievers were reluctant to confess (or even hid) the fact that they had had a religious marriage ceremony or that they had had their children baptized or circumcised.

The explanation of this high false response rate is not to be found in the false propaganda that believers are persecuted in Bulgaria and that all religious groups are forced to meet in secret. In fact, Bulgarian citizens are absolutely free to profess the religion of their choice, to celebrate any religious ceremony, or to be atheists, and act accordingly. What is more, the Church receives regular subsidies from the State. It is true that atheism has been propagandized in our country but this has been done on an entirely scientific basis without hurting anybody's religious sentiments. It is also true that religious views are freely propagated, not only by the religious press but also through various ceremonies.

Certain non-practising believers, among those qualified as religious of category III, were prompted not to declare the religious views in order to differentiate themselves from overtly practising believers. Other respondents, believers and non-believers, hid their beliefs or practices for other reasons; conscious of the growing public opinion which tends more and more to judge believers as being culturally backward, these people refused to admit their beliefs or practices, as others refused, through shame, to give their true education, age, etc.

For the rest of the survey, the interview method was abandoned. The pre-survey having shown that, for the most part, respondents were most objective and exact in their answers when the questions asked did not affect them personally, it was decided to question people outside the sample, i.e. two or three witnesses brought together for each subject in the survey.

3. The age of majority in Bulgaria is 18.

4. J. Ochavkov, 1966. A detailed analysis of methodological considerations is given here.

Although authorized to do so for certain items, interviewers rarely saw the subject directly. Only to verify the responses to certain questions – for example, if the subject had icons in his house, or if his parents or spouse were believers – did the investigating commissioner visit the house of the subject.

A procedure of anonymous inquiring was also used to check response errors. In every locality in which it was possible to collect at least three fourths of the subjects in the sample, they were invited to come together and were given printed sheets with three questions and the different appropriate responses. By underlining one of these responses, each subject indicated his sex, whether or not he was 'religious', and whether he said the prayers of the household. The sheets were then placed, by the subject himself, in a ballot box to ensure anonymity. A total of 20,675 respondents gave their answers in this way. Where there was a marked discrepancy between response to these sheets and the questionnaire, new questionnaires were filled by new investigating commissioners for the respective persons. And on the basis of a final control about 2,000 clearly erroneous questionnaires were discarded.

The accuracy of sample can be seen by the similarity of sample data and official statistics as shown in Table 1.

*Table 1. Survey population data and official statistics*

| | Official data on the total population % | Data gained from the survey sample % | Difference % |
|---|---|---|---|
| Men | 49.46 | 48.97 | —0.49 |
| Women | 50.54 | 51.03 | +0.49 |
| Members of the Communist Party | 9.73 | 10.12 | +0.39 |
| Members of the National Front | 60.47 | 61.05 | +0.58 |

One of the main theoretical problems of this survey was the problem of defining the religious person. Criteria were established on the basis of the three principal structural elements of religion: religious ideology, religious psychology and religious practice. The process of the waning of religion in Bulgaria has led to a loosening of the connection between these various dimensions. Hence, for the purpose of the survey, it was deemed necessary to define as religious any person having, even to the least degree, some form of religious awareness (ideological or psychological) irrespective of whether or not he practised his religion.

Human consciousness is made objective through the spoken or written word and by action. As language sometimes serves to camouflage rather than to express thought, it could be said that action is the only adequate criterion. But, if acts such as attendance at church on ordinary religious days or saying the prayers of the household[5] can be regarded as manifestations of the religious consciousness of a subject, the same cannot be said for marriages, baptisms and religious funerals, which are significant as measures of the importance of religion in social life. In the survey those who participate only in the latter type of religious act without any other indication of religiosity have been classified as non-religious. However, one must definitely consider as religious those people who have expressed their religious awareness by spoken or written word, even if they do not attend church or if they do not say the prayers of the household. Equally, those who attend church or say the prayers of the home, without expressing their religious awareness by spoken or written word, must be classed as religious.

According to these criteria the survey found that in Bulgaria 35.51 per cent are religious and 64.44 per cent non-religious.[6] It is important to note that the anonymous inquiring technique confirmed the results of the study by questionnaire giving equivalent percentages of 33.06 and 62.12.[7]

The just adduced data justify the distinction between religious acts which manifest individual religiosity and those of a more social nature, such as marriages, baptisms and funerals, which are connected with critical events: birth, death and marriage, in the lives of individuals. Acts of the former type involve only a minority of the population, but the latter are the most enduring aspect of religion in Bulgarian society. The rate of participation varies, but it is significant that a large proportion of those defined as non-religious also take part.

In the case of marriage, this is largely to be explained by the influence of parents and spouses: 77.28 per cent of those who celebrated a religious marriage have religious parents, and 14.17 per cent of non-religious husbands have religious wives.[8]

Religious practice related to birth has been retained to an even greater extent. It is apparent that religious husbands and wives, and, even more their religious parents, have a greater possibility of using influence in the

5. These are set prayers which are said in the household

6. The maximum percentage error is 1.23 ( $\Delta = \pm 1.23$), this is to say that, among the adult population of the country, the religious are not less than 34.28 per cent and not more than 36.74 per cent.

7. The rate of non-response was 0.5 per cent with the questionnaire and 4.82 per cent with anonymous interviewing.

8. Only 1.88 per cent of non-religious wives have religious husbands.

*Table 2. Participation in religious activity*

| | Sample % | Religious category % | Non-religious % |
|---|---|---|---|
| Attend church | 21.57 | 60.77 | |
| *regularly* | ( 4.79) | 13.49 | |
| *irregularly* | (16.78) | | |
| Say the prayers of the household[a] | 17.39 | 52.59 | |
| Have an icon at home | 22.16 | 45.53 | |
| Celebrate the day of the dead[b] | 27.18 | 61.56 | |
| Married since 1945 with a religious as well as civil ceremony | 36.10 | 73.64 | 28.37 |
| Those who had their children, born after 1945, baptized or circumcised[c] | 52.42[d] | 72.44 | 43.76 |
| Those who have had relations buried at a religious ceremony since 1945 | 91.91 | | 70.98 |

a. Data from anonymous inquiring.

b. According to Orthodox custom in Bulgaria 'the day of the dead' (All Souls Day) is celebrated by going to the churchyards to say prayers for the dead and leave food on the graves.

c. If the daughters of Jews and Moslems who are neither baptized nor circumcised are excluded from the total of children born since 1945, the proportion of baptized and circumcised children is raised by almost 5 per cent. Also, 72.44 per cent o baptized or circumcised children have at least one religious parent and 43.76 per cent at least one non-religious parent.

d. This figure refers to the total population, not just those in the sample.

matter of baptism and circumcision than in religious marriages. They are able to take upon themselves the initiative for having children baptized or circumcised.

The most enduring practice has been that of religious burial; since 1945, 79.88 per cent of all burials in Bulgaria have been carried out after a religious ceremony. However, it must be emphasized that this depends also on the convictions of the deceased person.

The most important reason for the retention of these religious practices lies undoubtedly in the fact that efforts to substitute civil ceremonies, carrying at least the same spirit of solemnity, have not been sufficient. On the basis of the results of our study, a greater effort has been made in this direction during the past few years.

Table 2 also indicates that the category of people defined as religious is not homogeneous. For each of the first type of religious acts investigated, a considerable proportion (ranging from 38.44 per cent of those who do not celebrate the day of the dead, to 54.47 per cent of those who do not have a religious corner in their home) do not participate. The pattern seems to indicate that religious awareness varies and that its gradual weakening is characteristic of the transition from being religious to non-religious.

This problem has been specially examined in the course of the survey. The investigating commissioners classed the religious into three groups according to their degree of religiosity. In the first group are those people whose religious awareness, being psychological as well as ideological, is the strongest. It represents 16.23 per cent of the religious and 5.76 per cent of the total sample. Included here are all those people who attend church regularly and those who actively propagate and defend their religion (3.89 per cent of the religious), whether or not they attend church regularly, or at all. The religious of this group adhere to the concepts of the catechism and obey it in their daily life. For them religion is a matter of the deepest conviction.

In the second group are people who have a weaker religious awareness, which is psychological rather than ideological in character. Their religiosity is more or less passive; on principle they are tolerant towards atheism, and do not actively propagate or defend their religion. They are more numerous than the first group (40.52 per cent of the religious, 14.38 per cent of the whole of the respondents).

In the third group are those who have the weakest religious awareness, almost totally psychological. They are the most passive religious people, hesitant, but not yet entirely liberated from religion. They believe (unsystematically and without leaning on it in their daily lives) in at least 'some supernatural force'. In this group the signs of religious practice have not yet vanished entirely, but they are rare and usually tied to external motives (influence of parents, spouse, etc.). This group is the most numerous (42.33 per cent of the religious, 15.49 per cent of the total sample). None of those who attend church regularly are found in the second and third groups. On the other hand, some of those who attend irregularly or never are included (30.47 per cent of the religious of the second group and 58.28 per cent of the religious in the third group never attend church).

Of the religious, 75.25 per cent are Orthodox and 18.19 per cent are Moslems. This distribution is not very different from the traditional pattern in Bulgaria. The 1910 census found that, for the entire population (adults and children), 84.01 per cent were Orthodox, 13.88 per cent Moslem, and 2.11 per cent were members of other faiths; in 1934 the pattern had hardly altered (the respective percentages were 84.39, 13.51 and 2.10). The difference from our figures can be explained by the fact that the process of waning of religion has been more rapid among the Orthodox than it has among the

Moslems. It is clear, too, that the census calculation concerning the religious obtained only according to the official document on baptisms or circumcisions is inaccurate. Our study confirms this, since 20.48 per cent of respondents stated they were non-religious before 1945;[9] 43.25 per cent have thus become non-religious since 1945.

Thus it is apparent that religion has not yet vanished from Bulgaria. There is no doubt, however, that the waning process is going on, and that the Marxist hypothesis, according to which this waning cannot fail to be considerably amplified during the building up of a socialist society, has been confirmed by our enquiry. The principal elements of religion are fading, then disappearing in the following order: religious ideology; pure religious practice (prayers of the household, attendance at church); religious psychology; religious practice concerned with important events of an individual's life. Perhaps there is here a general law of the waning process of religion. It appears to be the inverse of religion's appearance in the history of man and its reproduction during the individual life span.

## RELATIONSHIP OF RELIGION TO AGE AND EDUCATION

Table 3 shows that younger people are less religious than older people. It is not a question of age as a biological phenomenon, but of age as affected by certain social influences which have made themselves felt and which have accumulated over time. If this were not so, one could conclude that religion will always exist, but in fact, religion has declined even among the aged, if at a lesser rate. It must be made clear that no one is ever religious at birth. One becomes religious by virtue of certain social conditions. It is when these conditions are born that religion is born too. And it will exist as long as those specific conditions exist, reproducing itself in every generation. The process of the waning of religion in our country has advanced a lot because the conditions propitious to the existence of religion are vanishing in the course of the building of the new society. The process has been realized along two lines: first by accelerated reducing of the reproduction of religion, that is, in the number of people who are becoming religious; and secondly, to the number of those, who, having been religious, are renouncing their faith. Our study shows clearly the existence of these two processes. According to the data shown in Table 3, 87.88 per cent of respondents between the ages of eighteen and twenty-three years are non-religious. It would be completely absurd to suggest that they had previously been religious and had since

9. Of the religious, 1.2 per cent did not indicate their faith. About 16 per cent of respondents who were non-religious before 1945 were adults at that time.

*Table 3. Religiosity by age among respondents*

| Age | Religious<br>% | Non-religious<br>% | No response<br>% | Total<br>% |
|---|---|---|---|---|
| 18–23 | 12.02 | 87.88 | 0.10 | 100 |
| 24–28 | 17.58 | 82.36 | 0.06 | 100 |
| 29–38 | 22.98 | 76.95 | 0.07 | 100 |
| 39–48 | 30.34 | 69.57 | 0.09 | 100 |
| 49–58 | 44.40 | 55.60 | – | 100 |
| 59–68 | 60.10 | 39.88 | 0.02 | 100 |
| 69 and over | 78.02 | 21.88 | 0.10 | 100 |

given up their religion; in fact they were children under the age of five by 9 September 1944, and have been socialized during the development of the socialist society, having experienced those social factors which are causing religion to fade. The fact that 12.02 per cent of them are religious shows, however, that the reproduction of religion continues. This first process is necessarily the fundamental cause of religious decline. The second type must not be neglected because it is under the influence of the religious that the reproduction of religion has been realized; 87.90 per cent of the religious have religious parents,[10] and 45.55 per cent have an icon corner in their home. The fact that only 5.99 per cent of the religious have non-religious parents shows that, outside the family circle and without its support, religious people exercise only a little influence in the reproduction of religion. As for the non-religious, 51.34 per cent have religious parents and 9.30 per cent have an icon corner in their home. This seems to prove that the social factors determining the fading of religion are much stronger than those which uphold its existence.

There is a real dependency between the decline of religiosity and the rising level of education. Better education assures a better knowledge of science. The following data illustrate the rising standard of education in Bulgaria: 3.71 per cent of respondents have completed some form of university or tertiary education (compared with 1.1 per cent in the 1934 census); 10.97 per cent have finished secondary school (3.7 per cent in 1934); 32.63 per cent have studied but not completed some secondary education or seven years of schooling (11.3 per cent in 1934). In 1962, 47.31 per cent of the population had finished at least primary school (i.e. seven years) compared with 16.1 per cent in 1934.

10. No response = 6.11 per cent.

*Table 4. Degree of education and religiosity*

| Degree of education | Religious % | Non-religious % | No response % | Total % |
|---|---|---|---|---|
| Illiterate and made literate | 81.06 | 18.94 | – | 100 |
| Elementary school (4 years) | | | | |
| a) not completed | 58.80 | 41.16 | 0.04 | 100 |
| b) completed | 45.92 | 54.04 | 0.04 | 100 |
| Primary school (7 years) | | | | |
| a) not completed | 34.85 | 65.08 | 0.07 | 100 |
| b) completed | 20.88 | 79.05 | 0.07 | 100 |
| Secondary school | | | | |
| a) not completed | 13.51 | 86.41 | 0.08 | 100 |
| b) completed | 10.10 | 89.80 | 0.10 | 100 |
| Tertiary education completed and higher completed or not completed | 7.75 | 92.19 | 0.06 | 100 |

Table 4 shows that the effect of education on declining religiosity is progressively magnified when the declining process of religiosity has begun in the course of the building of a new society. This is well illustrated by the fact that only an average of 16.86 per cent are religious among those who have finished at least primary school (i.e. seven years).

What we have just said about the relationship between religiosity and education is equally valid if one looks at the relationship between religion and self-education through the reading of newspapers, works of literature or scientific publications.

Table 5 indicates that not only do religious people read less secular literature, but their religiosity seems to be an obstacle to the development of their political, artistic and, above all, scientific culture. Among the religious respondents, 16.75 per cent read the basic religious works, 14.89 per cent read literary works and only 3.88 per cent read scientific works.

### RELATIONSHIP OF RELIGION TO SOCIAL AND ECONOMIC STRUCTURE

The old social and economic structure no longer exists in Bulgaria. Table 6 shows, however, that its influence has not yet disappeared completely. The Koulaks, the industrialists, the large merchants, the lesser merchants, and

*Table 5. Religiosity and personal culture*

| Those who read | Regularly % | Irregularly % | Not at all % | No response % | Total % |
|---|---|---|---|---|---|
| Newspapers | | | | | |
| Religious | 7.46 | 25.55 | 66.87 | 0.12 | 100 |
| Non-religious | 38.31 | 37.81 | 23.73 | 0.15 | 100 |
| Works of literature | | | | | |
| Religious | 2.55 | 12.34 | 84.94 | 0.17 | 100 |
| Non-religious | 19.33 | 35.05 | 45.43 | 0.19 | 100 |
| Scientific literature | | | | | |
| Religious | 0.65 | 3.23 | 95.93 | 0.19 | 100 |
| Non-religious | 9.32 | 17.69 | 72.71 | 0.28 | 100 |
| Basic religious works (the Bible or the Gospels, the Koran, the Talmud) | | | | | |
| Religious | 3.07 | 13.68 | 82.88 | 0.37 | 100 |
| Non-religious | 0.27 | 1.97 | 97.57 | 0.19 | 100 |

the better-off craftsmen used to belong to the dominant classes and groups; 56.38 per cent of them or their children are religious. At the other end of the scale, only 34.88 per cent are religious among the classes and groups who were

*Table 6. Social origin and religiosity of respondents*

| Social origin | Religious % | Non-religious % | No response % | Total % |
|---|---|---|---|---|
| Officials and clerks | 17.25 | 82.75 | – | 100 |
| Workers | 22.51 | 77.41 | 0.08 | 100 |
| Small craftsmen | 36.65 | 63.04 | 0.31 | 100 |
| Professionals | 37.14 | 62.86 | – | 100 |
| Better-off craftsmen | 37.25 | 62.53 | 0.22 | 100 |
| Poor peasants | 37.26 | 62.70 | 0.04 | 100 |
| Better-off peasants | 38.56 | 61.59 | 0.05 | 100 |
| Small merchants | 45.19 | 54.81 | – | 100 |
| Industrialists | 45.45 | 54.55 | – | 100 |
| Better-off merchants | 51.53 | 48.47 | – | 100 |
| Well-off craftsmen | 57.89 | 42.11 | – | 100 |
| Large merchants | 58.33 | 41.67 | – | 100 |
| Koulaks | 58.59 | 41.41 | – | 100 |
| Others and no-responses | 39.29 | 60.57 | 0.14 | 100 |

in fact unprivileged and oppressed: the workers, officials and clerks, the poor and better-off peasants, small craftsmen. Among those respondents who belonged, according to the old economic structure, to the social middle class – small merchants, better-off craftsmen and others – and among their children, 39.38 per cent are religious. In 1962 the three categories represented 1.93, 93.24 and 1.52 per cent, respectively, of the total population.

It must be pointed out that the influence of social origin on respondents' religiosity is not a reflection of the development of the new social and economic structure – rather it runs counter to the influence of this development. The data of Table 7 show the existence of a direct relationship between the actual social and economic situation of the respondents and their religiosity.

*Table 7. Actual social status and religiosity of respondents*

| Social status | Religious % | Non-religious % | No response % | Total % |
|---|---|---|---|---|
| Officials and clerks | 13.29 | 86.61 | 0.10 | 100 |
| Co-operative craftsmen | 20.48 | 79.52 | – | 100 |
| Workers | 24.42 | 75.53 | 0.05 | 100 |
| Co-operative farmers | 46.66 | 53.30 | 0.04 | 100 |
| Small merchants, craftsmen and other private individuals | 55.74 | 44.26 | – | 100 |
| Private farmers | 72.44 | 27.27 | 0.29 | 100 |
| No response | 45.68 | 54.32 | – | 100 |

The first four categories of Table 7 consist of those directly connected to the socialist means of production, among whom, the average percentage of religious people is 34.48. By contrast the next two categories consist of those who have generally risen from the old privileged groups. Here, the average proportion of religious people rises to 59.74. It is obvious that the waning process of religion has been more effective within the first cluster than within the second. This is most significant for the overall decline of religion in Bulgaria in view of the relative strength of the two clusters in the total population. The second represented, in 1962, 3.33 per cent of the adult population of the country, 5.61 per cent of the religious and 2.07 per cent of the non-religious. The corresponding percentages for the first cluster are 94.97, 92.19 and 96.49.

A comparison of corresponding social groups emphasises still further the determining role of the social and economic structure. The percentage of religious people among private farmers is much higher than among co-operative farmers[11] (72.44, 46.66); and among private craftsmen, much higher than among co-operative craftsmen (53.96, 20.43). Even more interesting are the differences in religiosity rates among the three principal social groups of socialist society: officials and clerks (including intelligentsia), workers and co-operative farmers. As shown in Table 7 the proportion of religious people in these social groups increases in that order.

The working class was one of the fundamental classes in the social and economic structure of the old régime. Deprived of the means of production, they were the most exploited and, naturally, the most interested in changing the social structure. They played a leading rôle in the socialist revolution. Directly tied to the superior form of socialist ownership, that of the State, and to industrial production, they have become, in the new society, the directing force in the State and that is why their social and political awareness is most advanced. It is this which explains why the religiosity rate of the workers is less than that of the co-operative farmers.

Peasants, in the old social and economic structure, were not a uniform class. The great majority of them were exploited and oppressed, but, their attachment to their private property, small as it was, prevented them from playing the same role as that of the working class in the socialist Revolution. The co-operative farmer class was born after the revolution but is connected with an inferior form of socialist property, co-operative property. And besides, agricultural production has not yet been liberated from the vagaries of nature. For these reasons, and others, the process of waning of religion is not so rapid among the farmers as among the workers.

The religiosity rate is lowest among clerks and officials (including intelligentsia). The essential reason for this difference lies in the fact that the latter are better educated and for the most part are connected with socialist state property.

The greater social mobility of the last few years has also affected the religious composition of these three social groups. Of our respondents, 3.28 per cent originated from the old group of clerical workers and 15.89 per cent are now clerical workers; 13.64 per cent have working class origins, and now 26.98 per cent are workers; 75.57 per cent have peasant origins (both poor and better-off peasants) and 51.04 per cent are now co-operative farmers. The principal trend seems to be the following: the poor and better-off peasants and in a still higher degree co-operative peasants, have become workers or officials; on their part, some workers have become officials. Social mobility

11. In 1963 there were 1,429,000 members in the 981 co-operative farms in Bulgaria. Each co-operative has an average of 1,455 members and covers 3,860 hectares of arable land. Each of the eighty-five state agricultural farms employ an average of 1,248 people and cover 4,100 hectares.

may be the passage of an adult from one social status to another, or the passage of children from the social status of parents to another. Peasants have become workers mainly by the first form of mobility and officials by the second. After 9 September 1944, and in the course of about twelve years, workers have become officials mainly by the first form of mobility; after that the second form dominates.

Young people are always less religious than adults; according to the results of our study, 3.23 per cent of the white-collar workers aged eighteen to twenty-three years, 9.40 per cent of the workers and 17.85 per cent of the co-operative farmers of the same age, were religious. It follows that those young people, who were farmers and have become workers, are more religious than those workers who have become officials. This is the same, moreover, for older persons. A comparison of social origin and current social status (Tables 6 and 7) shows that social mobility leads to a lessening of the number of religious among clerical workers, a slight rise among workers and a still greater rise among co-operative farmers. The percentage of religious people is lower in the urban population (25.65) than in the rural (41.56).

The improved status of women brought about by the economic and social changes of the new régime has also reduced the rate of religiosity. They are, by law, the equal of men and take part more and more actively in industry, and in social, political and cultural life. Among female subjects it was found that 7.73 per cent had been non-religious before 1945, but 20.12 per cent had become so since 1945. Before 1945, women represented 37.73 per cent of the non-religious population compared with 43.21 per cent in 1962. The percentage of religious among women (44.75) has always been higher than that of men. The percentage of women in the first, second and third categories of religiosity was 68.84, 67.77 and 60.20 respectively. Thus the social inequality of woman under the old régime still continues to weigh over her to some extent despite her new rights.

RELATION BETWEEN RELIGION AND POLITICS

Religiosity has been shown to be declining in all socialist countries. This process unfolds, however, in a specific manner in each country. The outstanding feature in Bulgaria has been its rapidity compared to that found in other socialist countries and particularly in those where the Catholic faith is dominant. Catholicism is fixed more firmly in peoples' conscience and in social practice than is the Orthodox faith. Nevertheless, the predominance of the Orthodox faith in Bulgaria, while it is of great importance, is not the sole determinant. Other factors have also favoured the quickening of the decline of religion: an ever increasing social and political awareness, an aspiration for more and more knowledge and a more active participation in social and political life. These progressive traditions have arisen under the influence of the Communist Party of Bulgaria. The National Front, made up of different parties and political organizations which were united in 1948 into one social and political organization, has played an important role. Table 8 on the relationship of religiosity to political affiliation shows that the largest proportion of the adult population belongs to the National Front, while lesser proportions belong to other political organizations independent of it. The fact that 69.04 per cent of the total population belongs to some political body can perhaps be regarded as a peculiarity of Bulgarian society. Such great membership could not have been possible without the progressive social and political traditions of the Bulgarian people.

*Table 8. Membership of political organisations and religiosity*

| Organization | Religious % | Non-religious % | No response % | Total for three categories % | Total adult population % |
|---|---|---|---|---|---|
| Communist Party of Bulgaria | – | 99.93 | 0.07 | 100 | 9.88 |
| Communist Youth League of Bulgaria | 5.66 | 94.26 | 0.08 | 100 | 8.99 |
| Bulgarian Agricultural Union | 30.04 | 69.96 | – | 100 | 2.51 |
| National Front | 39.76 | 60.18 | 0.06 | 100 | 61.05 |
| Total belonging to an organization | 30.97 | 68.04 | 0.07 | 100 | 69.04 |
| No organization | 56.19 | 43.78 | 0.08 | 100 | 30.96 |

This has contributed to the momentum of declining religiosity. It is clear that the rate of religiosity is substantially lower among those who belong to a political organization than among those who do not belong. However, it is also clear that political organizations have a minority of religious members. This percentage is as high as 39.76 for the National Front – higher than the total of religious people in the population (35.51). Hence the great majority of the religious in Bulgaria have an awareness of, and a progressive and socialist leaning towards, the social and political aspect. This was also verified by the following fact: 16.40 per cent of the active, militant members of the organizations of the National Front and 14.96 per cent of their leaders are religious. This indirectly confirms the previously stressed fact that only

16.23 per cent of the religious (5.76 per cent of the total sample) have an ideological religious conscience.

The waning process of religion as revealed by the survey is thus a complex process determined by a network of interacting factors – changes in the whole social structure; changes in the economic, social, political and cultural systems. While economic factors are thus not the sole determinant, they undoubtedly constitute the essential underlying factor. Although the material presented here represents only the most important findings of the survey and only a twentieth of the tables it is clear that the Marxist Leninist hypothesis has been substantiated. A further account of the survey can be found in the collective work, *Le processus de l'évanouissement de la religion en Bulgarie* [1968].

## SELECTED BIBLIOGRAPHY

Angelov, S., 'Khristilianstvoto i obshchestveniiat zhivot' [Christianity and Social Life]. *Juridicheski Pregled.* 1906.

Christov, P., *Tsurkvata i rabotnichestvo* [Church and the Working Class]. Sofia, 1929.

Draganov, M., 'Formiraneto na religiozni vazgledi u podrastvashchite pokoleniia v Bulgariia' [The Forming of Religious Conception in the Rising Generations in Bulgaria]. *Izvestiia na Instituta po filosofiia* (Proceedings of the Philosophical Institute, 10, 1965.

—, 'Bulgarkata i religioznite otzhivelitsi' [The Bulgarian Woman and Religious Remnants]. *Mladeszh,* 1, 1965.

—, 'Religioznata psikhika i neinoto preodoliavane v Bulgariia' [Religious Psychology and its Waning in Bulgaria]. *Novo Vreme.* 7, 1966.

Hadgijski, I., *Bit i dushevnost na bulgarskiia narod* [Popular Customs and State of Mind of the Bulgarian People], 1, 1940.

Mizov, N., '*Otnosno protsesa na preodoliaveneto na religiiata v Bulgariia*' [Something on the Waning Process of Religion in Bulgaria]. *Filosofska Misl,* 6, 1963.

—, *Islamt v Bulgariia* [Islam in Bulgaria]. Sofia, 1965.

—, 'Preodoliavaneto na religiiata i izmeneniiata na lichnostta u nas' [The Waning of Religion and Changes of Individuals in Bulgaria]. *Filosofska Misl,* 9, 1968.

—, *Zhivotot, praznitsite i religiiata* [Life, Holidays and Religion]. Sofia, 1964.

Ochavkov, J., 'Sotsiologichesko izsledvane na religioznostta na pulnoletnoto naselenie v Bulgariia' [Sociological Survey of Religiosity of the Adult Population of Bulgaria]. *Novo Vreme,* 5, 1964.

—, *Opyt sotsiologicheskogo issledovaniia religioznosti naseleniia v Bolgarii* [An attempt at a Sociological Survey of Religiosity of the Population in Bulgaria]. In the collection *Opyt i metodika konkretnykh sotsiologicheskikh issledovanii* [Attempts and Methods of Concrete Sociological Research]. Mysl (Moscow), 1965.

—, 'Problèmes méthodologiques d'une enquête sur la religiosité en Bulgarie' [Methodological problems of an enquiry on religiosity in Bulgaria]. *Archives de sociologie des religions,* Vol. 21, 1966.

—, 'Les résultats d'une étude sociologique de la religiosité en Bulgarie' [The results of a sociological study of religiosity in Bulgaria]. *Revue française de sociologie*, 7, 1966.
Ocharvov, J. (ed.), *Protses na preodoliavaneto na religiiata v Bulgariia – sotsiologichesko izsledvane* [The Waning Process of Religion in Bulgaria – A Sociological Survey]. Sofia, 1968.
Pecheva, R., *Religiia i bit* [Religion and Popular Customs]. Sofia, 1963.
Petrov, G., *Religiia i zhivot* [Religion and Life]. Sofia, 1926.
Stoitchev, T., *Sotsializm i religiia* [Socialism and Religion]. Sofia, 1965.
Trayanopolski, A., *Religiia i sotsiologia* [Religion and Sociology]. Sofia, 1936.
Velinov, P., '*Religiia i sotsiologiia*' [Religion and Sociology]. *Misl*, 4–5, 1898.

HAROLD FALLDING*

# Canada

## INTRODUCTION. MULTIPLE COMMUNITIES AND THEIR CHURCHES

Canada, as a nation, is an uneasy alliance of two communities and civilizations. Wishful thinking should not blind anyone to that. The Catholic French and Protestant British heritages are in an unstable marriage of convenience still. There are also, of course, minorities from other cultures than these. But whether the variety in an ethnic mixture assumes problem proportions is always a question of power. If one group is sufficiently ascendent to sponsor a government, the society is virtually 'theirs'. The minorities will go along with them unless, or until, they feel there is advantage in trying their separate strength. The British community has had that ascendence over the others, the French included, for a considerable period of Canada's history. It is now being challenged by the Quebec French, although only by this one group. The growth in economic and political influence of the French has led to a reassertion of their communal solidarity, as could be expected.

I cannot take that cramped perspective on modern religion that sees it as an 'individual matter' or 'private matter'. Modern or ancient, religion is overwhelmingly communal and collective – it is constitutive of society itself. The fabric of ties that we have in mind when we speak of 'society' has its toughest strands supplied by religion. The idea, for instance, that religion has been diminished and relegated to a private sphere through the separation of church and state, seems to invert the truth. Is it not rather the case that the state, as the technical manager of some of the community's mundane affairs, has been judged less communal than religion? Government can

* Harold Joseph Fallding was born in Cessnock, Australia, in 1923. Since completing his Ph.D. at The Australian National University in 1955, he has worked as Senior Research Fellow at the University of Sydney 1956–58, Senior Lecturer in Sociology at the University of New South Wales 1959–62, Visiting Associate Professor of Sociology, Rutgers, The State University, New Jersey, 1963–65. Since 1965 he has been Professor in the Department of Sociology and Anthropology at the University of Waterloo. Major works include *The Sociological Task*, 1968, 'The Family and the Idea of a Cardinal Role', *Human Relations*, 1961, 'Secularization and the Sacred and Profane', *Sociological Quarterly*, 1967, and numerous poems.

therefore be extruded out and given a separate compartment. By the same token, the one government can discharge the same specialized function for a number of communities simultaneously, as they seek to form a nation. But it still takes a religion for men to express their common commitment to that which is ultimate and all-embracing – and it is embracing enough, of course, to embrace the separated state. If there is a mosaic of diverse religious expressions in modern nations like Canada, it is not because religion is a 'private matter', but because many communities have settled or emerged there, each compelled to have its distinctive religious expression. It is only an 'individual matter' in the sense that the mobile individual may consequently have the option of choosing between alternatives.

It is in this kind of perspective, I believe, that the state of religion in Canada has to be analysed. The resurgence of French communalism alerts us to wait and see what religious expression it will generate. Right at its beginning, indeed, there was a reassertion of the Catholic laity, expressed as a fairly direct anti-clericalism. In any case, Canadian Catholicism has been recognized all along to have a unique character and vigour, and this can be attributed to its communal roots in Quebec.

Yet the fact that religion is a communal expression is precisely the thing that has made it problematic in the modern, mobile world. Its peculiar pitfalls now are that it can be anachronistic and divisive – the opposite of what it is supposed to be. No wonder it has come to seem a mockery to some of the children of its champions. People can find themselves living out some 'ism' or other that was really relevant to some community of another time and place. And by this very fact they can be thrown out of community with their neighbours. Only a sense of present community strong enough to override their traditional allegiances could give them a religious expression that is shared, contemporary and relevant.

Among a certain section of the Canadian people this happened. For here one of the first fruits of the ecumenical movement ripened – in the formation of the United Church of Canada. It is interesting that the community this church had for its base was the nation. It is not a national church in the sense of being an established or privileged church, but it *is* the church of a nation. And it seems inevitable that insofar as the diverse sections of Canadian society are drawn into a more tightly knit national effort, other religious differences will also fade and even disappear. The United Church of Canada, which absorbed the Methodists, Congregationalists and some of the Presbyterians in 1925, widened its embrace further in 1968 to absorb the church of the Evangelical United Brethren. Discussion for union between the United and Anglican churches has been underway since 1943, and many people expect that this union too will be consummated. In a document of 1966, *The Principles of Union Between the Anglican Church of Canada and the*

*United Church of Canada*, these churches announced that it was their plain intention to proceed to organic union.

There is also a definite thaw in Canada on the traditional distance between Protestant and Roman Catholic. At the local level now there are many confrontations.[1] Saint Michael's, the Roman Catholic College in the University of Toronto, set up a Centre of Ecumenical Studies and issues a journal, *The Ecumenist*. The mounting sense of unity was symbolized in the Christian Pavilion of the World Exposition in Montreal in 1967. Roman Catholics and Protestants participated in this together because, in the words of Father Jean Martucci, 'Sharing the same faith, the same hope and the same charity, they want to bear the same witness to Christ and his Gospel'. At first glance, religion in contemporary Canada presents a bewildering disarray. But order may come into our understanding of it once we discern the order being worked out in it. Canadian religion is the imported furniture of the people of many traditions who have to work out a new life together. Insofar as they do achieve one community they may be expected to make one church.

## HISTORICAL BACKGROUND, THE ORIGINAL PROBLEM: DIVERSITY

It was not as a missionary enterprise but a commercial one that Canada (as New France) was settled by westerners after 1534. Walsh [1968] and Wilson [1966] insist on this in their separate accounts of church growth in Canada – to which accounts the following synopsis adheres closely. From 1615 onwards, however, the Roman Catholic missionary enterprise that was encouraged by Champlain increasingly shaped Canadian life. The pattern of life set by it persisted in Quebec (also known earlier as Lower Canada) until the present century. It was, indeed, much more influential among white settlers than among the native Indians, who were resistant to evangelization. When New France came under continuing British rule in 1759, its Roman Catholic and French-speaking identity was already secure. The British who assumed control were overwhelmingly Protestant, but the toleration extended to the French gave full scope to their way of life. It was one characterized by sentimental attachment to the farm and local parish, and taking inspiration and guidance from the parish church, school and curé. In Gérin's [1898] account of the parish of Saint-Justin and Miner's [1938] account of

1. As this was being written, I was involved in the organization of a religious census of the city of Waterloo, Ontario. This was undertaken by the churches jointly. Catholics and Lutherans, Pentecostalists and Presbyterians, United Churchmen and Mennonites, amongst others, worked together in teams to collect information on the religious affiliation or preference of the city's population.

the parish of Saint-Denis, we have it vividly portrayed. In Quebec, church leadership preceded civil government as a stabilizing and integrating force, as Laval's career illustrates. As Vicar Apostolic in Canada and as Bishop of Quebec, his work between 1659 and 1684 had a lasting influence on the institutions of French Canada, and on education especially.

But early Canada was not Roman Catholic entirely. By Champlain's time the Calvinistic Huguenots were being made welcome and their dependability in business and administration taken advantage of, as Reaman's [1966] study shows. Yet when Champlain returned to Canada in 1633, after an interlude of British rule, any further transportation of the Protestants had been forbidden by Richelieu, and from that time this first phase of Protestant influence was in eclipse. Settlements elsewhere on the continent had Protestant populations, however. Sir Humphrey Gilbert, who was sent to Newfoundland in 1583, instituted public worship according to the Church of England. Settlers came to Nova Scotia (then Acadia) from Protestant Scotland, and subsequently moved to Newfoundland.

By the second half of the eighteenth century Anglicanism had taken root in Nova Scotia, Prince Edward Island and Cape Breton. An Anglican Bishop of Quebec, appointed in 1793, made contact the following year with Anglicans already operating in Ontario (then Upper Canada). Anglicanism went ahead quickly and from the beginning of the nineteenth century spread with the frontier population. Presbyterianism, likewise, increased with the British immigration, and came to rival Anglicanism in influence. Reformed Churchmen from Holland and Germany also came to Nova Scotia in 1750. At first the Calvinists were very divided among themselves. But it seems that one of the main constraints towards church unity in Canada soon put its yoke on them: the spectacle of a frontier society in moral chaos through lack of a spiritual ministry. The scattered population generated a demand for ministry that exceeded any single organization's ability to supply it. At the same time, the frontier situation made the imported distinctions of the separate church organizations redundant.

> The various Presbyterians soon discovered that frontier conditions did not encourage the luxury of old divisions. One of the factors in a quickly growing co-operation with others, and with each other, was the observation that morals had declined almost to paganism wherever no church or ministry existed. This was precisely what the Roman Catholics learned in Quebec when the supply of priests and services of worship fell short. The most cynical person cannot deny that the presentation of the claims of God, by whatever church, was indispensible for sturdy and responsible citizenship [Wilson, 1966, pp. 25–26].

Whereas the pioneer Anglicans and Presbyterians in Canada were mainly transplanted Britishers, Wilson identifies a secondary wave of early church activity in which the main membership and leadership came from the American colonies. This included the Congregationalists, Baptists, Methodists, Disciples of Christ and some others – although the British Wesleyans and certain Congregationalists make a partial exception. Also, in the mid-eighteenth century some German Lutheran immigrants came to Nova Scotia. But these virtually disappeared in time, largely due to their transference of loyalty to the Anglican church when the English language became dominant in their communities.

The United Empire Loyalists who came to Canada from the American colonies after the outbreak of the American Revolution in 1776, made the Anglo-Saxon, Protestant element numerically predominant in the country as a whole. The arrival of the Loyalists coincided with a certain amount of social disorder, especially on the frontier, and it was the itinerant Methodist preachers of Ontario (then Upper Canada) who responded to this challenge. As a result, an evangelistic Methodism became the dominant religious force in the early part of the nineteenth century. Even the staid critics of its enthusiasm had to concede its faithfulness:

> Here, without means of instruction, of social amusement, of healthy and innocent excitements, can we wonder that whisky and camp meetings assume their place, and 'season toil' which is unseasoned by anything better? Nothing, believe me, that you have heard or read of the frantic disorders of these Methodist love-feasts and camp-meetings in Upper Canada can exceed the truth; and yet it is no less a truth that the Methodists are in most parts the only religious teachers, and that without them the people were utterly abandoned [Clark, 1965, p. 169].

Thus S.D. Clark quotes Mrs. Jameson on the matter. It is Clark's thesis that the sectarian character of this early Methodism is what made it relevant to the rural frontier, but that it underwent a change to respectability that made it unresponsive to the urban workers at the end of the century. Then it was the Salvation Army that stepped into the breach: it became to the urban workers what Methodism had been to the rural immigrants earlier. The same kind of development is traced for another place and a still later time in W.E. Mann's *Sect, Cult and Church in Alberta* [1962]. He shows that in the western province of Alberta, between 1887 and 1947, and especially from 1930 on, sects and cults came to number almost fifty and grew at the expense of the more established churches. He says they were better attuned to the interests and needs of certain groups that were still mobile: immigrants from Europe, farmers moving from one part of the province to another, and the rapidly multiplying urban workers in the cities of Calgary and Edmonton. Conspicuous among these movements was that led by Aberhart. Aberhart fused fundamentalist religion with Social Credit political action and formed a Social Credit government in Alberta in 1935 which has remained in office ever since. E.C. Manning made a successor to Aberhart in both the religious and political aspects of his leadership. Premier of Alberta for twenty-five years, he retired at the end of 1968.[2]

However, before we turn our attention more completely to the west, we should note that the branches of the church we have identified in the east continued to grow – and others came in to make for still greater diversity. The Congregationalists, for instance, who settled first in the Maritimes from New England, spread across the country. But they never achieved a numerical strength in any way comparable to the Baptists, who came into Canada by the same kind of route. By the mid-nineteenth century the Baptists had 150 churches in Lower and Upper Canada, and they were responsible eventually for the development of two universities – Acadia and McMaster. Moravians coming from Michigan started a mission to Indians in Ontario in 1792, although this work was handed over to the Methodists in 1902. Around 1800, immigrating Pennsylvania Germans blazed a trail to Waterloo County and other places in Southern Ontario. Reaman [1957] has made a detailed study of the composition and various destinations of this migration. Ontario's original Mennonites and Lutherans were largely recruited from these people, and there were also Dunkards, Reformed Churchmen and Moravians amongst them. Along with the German people there came mi-

2. I interviewed Mr Manning during his last year of office as Premier, and while this chapter was being written. Mr Manning, as well as carrying his heavy public responsibilities, was then still active in a regular evangelical radio ministry that is non-denominational and that he has carried on for many years. The kind of connection that Mr Manning sees existing between religion and politics is interesting. There is not the remotest trace in it of any kind of theocracy, wherein belief and ethics are imposed on the general public. He insists that church and politics are separate and do not mix, and he denies that the political programme of his party is in any direct sense rooted in religious doctrine. He conceives religion as a personal spiritual experience, without which a person has neither the ability nor obligation to meet higher ethical standards. At the same time, he states that their religious conviction is what gave Aberhart and his followers the humanitarian concern that drove them, ultimately and almost unwillingly, to political action. The party has been called Social Credit because of a rather bizarre monetary policy it expounded during the depression, but this has definitely never been characteristic of it. It has taken whatever pragmatic steps seemed necessary to promote stability and wealth in Alberta, all with the object of securing maximum opportunity and fulfillment for the individual. To secure those benefits for the individual without making him dependent on a welfare state has been the keynote of the programme. How to do it for the future is the subject of Mr Manning's *White Paper on Human Resources Development* presented in 1967.

grating Pennsylvania Quakers and others besides. Two groups in the United States joined forces in 1946 to form the Evangelical United Brethren. Some brethren in this tradition, which was German originally, came to Ontario from Pennsylvania in 1812, and their church grew. Churches of Christ started in the Maritimes in 1810 and spread shortly after to Ontario. The Church of God was introduced into Ontario in 1888 and has spread across the country.

It was about the time the provinces joined in Confederation in 1867 that economic and population pressures made the opening of new territory in western Canada imperative. Roman Catholic orders were very active then on the frontier in ministering to the pioneers. Protestant missionaries, originally sent to the Indians and Eskimos, were also suitably placed to attend to newcomers. But the same kind of frontier problem that had been experienced in the east was magnified in the west. How to minister to so scattered a population? If the Roman Catholic response was to locate religious orders throughout the region, the Protestants judged that their answer lay in pooling resources. It was from the attempt to do this that the decisive impetus to church union in Canada came. Walsh points out that church union as a solution of western problems was first initiated by the Presbyterians – but it was in a rather curious way that it happened. The energetic missionary leader James Robertson 'had involved his church in so many and great responsibilities that his successors felt compelled to lessen some of their burden through co-operation with other churches' [Walsh, 1968, p. 273]. There was much discussion both between the churches involved and within them before union was agreed to, and in the end it split the Presbyterians, so that some remained outside. But before it ever came into being a united church in the west was virtually a fact, due to regional exigencies.

Yet we would be wrong to regard the settlement of the west as wholly an epic of church co-operation. I have already referred to Mann's observations on the appearance of sects and cults in Alberta; and it is a fact that the growth of unity among a group of like-minded churches was parallelled by a visible growth in diversity. The division between Catholic and Protestant was, if anything, probably heightened, due to competition for influence in the new territory. Indeed, it is almost certainly true that their separate numerical weakness in the national count, vis-a-vis the numerically strong Catholics, has supplied a second motive all along for the Protestant churches that joined in the quest for union. Then again, the frontier provided the opportunity for self-determination that certain utopian immigrants were seeking. There were, for instance, settlements in Manitoba of refugee Mennonites from Russia. Hutterites also settled there and in Alberta. And there were the colourful Russian Doukhobors, whose religion and ethics Herbison [1968] described. Coming to Saskatchewan in 1899, they moved still further to British Columbia when pressures to conformity again became intolerable. Depending exclusively on 'inner light' for guidance, they disdain the constraints of law and learning, a fact that has led to religiously sanctioned nudism, arson and school-evasion among the extremists.

We have passed in quick review but a sample of the developments that made the Canadian religious scene so much a patchwork. There has been no consideration of some of the smaller groups such as the Greek Orthodox and Jews. To complete the impression of diversity we should also remember the presence of the Indian and Eskimo, and their respective religious beliefs. The Indians have various and intricate beliefs but belief in a great benevolent spirit is commonly included amongst them. The Eskimo believe that nature is pervaded by efficacious spirit forces, for communication with which the shamans are specially endowed. Some of the Eskimo have been very responsive to Christian missions.

With this heritage of religious diversity, what can be said of religion at the present day?

## THE COMPOUNDING PROBLEM: MOBILITY

### *Denominational composition*

Table 1 gives the official figures from the Dominion Bureau of Statistics for the numbers adhering to different denominations in Canada as a whole, at three points in time. From this Table we may note that in 1961 Roman Catholics were approaching one-half the population of the country and, so far as single denominations go, far exceeded the size of any other one. The United Church, which was next in order of size, had fewer than half as many adherents. If we leave those classified as 'other' out of account, the portion of the whole contributed by all the Protestant churches taken together was only two percent greater than that contributed by the Roman Catholic church. One would not find such a concentration of Roman Catholics all across the nation, however. The high proportion of them in the national total is due to their great concentration in Quebec, where they make up nine-tenths of the population. Outside of Quebec the Roman Catholic fraction of the population averages about a third.

The table allows us to compare the denominations' rate of growth over the twenty-year period, 1941–1961. In this period, when the population of the country increased by more than half, there was no really spectacular shift in the percentage contributed by each denomination. But the percentage of Presbyterians and Anglicans perceptibly declined (by 2.7 per cent and 2 per cent respectively), that of Roman Catholics perceptibly grew (by 4 per cent).

*Table 1. Principal religious denominations of the population, census years 1941, 1951 and 1961*

| Religious denomination | 1941 N | 1951 N | 1961 N | 1961 % |
|---|---|---|---|---|
| Adventist | 18,485 | 21,398 | 25,999 | 0.1 |
| Anglican Church of Canada | 1,754,368 | 2,060,720 | 2,409,068 | 13.2 |
| Baptist | 484,465 | 519,585 | 593,553 | 3.3 |
| Greek Orthodox | 139,845 | 172,271 | 239,766 | 1.3 |
| Jehovah's Witnesses | 7,007 | 34,596 | 68,018 | 0.4 |
| Jewish | 168,585 | 204,836 | 254,368 | 1.4 |
| Lutheran | 401,836 | 444,923 | 662,744 | 3.6 |
| Mennonite[a] | 111,554 | 125,938 | 152,452 | 0.8 |
| Mormon | 25,328 | 32,888 | 50,016 | 0.3 |
| Pentecostal | 57,742 | 95,131 | 143,877 | 0.8 |
| Presbyterian | 830,597 | 781,747 | 818,558 | 4.5 |
| Roman Catholic | 4,806,431 | 6,069,496 | 8,342,826 | 45.7 |
| Salvation Army | 33,609 | 70,275 | 92,054 | 0.5 |
| Ukrainian (Greek) Catholic[b] | 185,948 | 191,051 | 189,653 | 1.0 |
| United Church of Canada | 2,208,658 | 2,867,271 | 3,664,008 | 20.1 |
| Other | 272,197 | 317,303 | 531,287 | 2.9 |
| Total | 11,506,655[c] | 14,009,429 | 18,238,247 | 100.0 |

a. Includes 'Hutterites'
b. Includes 'Other Greek Catholic'
c. Exclusive of Newfoundland

Source: *Canada Year Book, 1967. Official Statistical Annual of the Resources, History, Institutions and Social and Economic Conditions of Canada*, Dominion Bureau of Statistics, p. 199.

Although by 1961 their percentage of the total was still not significant, the membership of some of the smaller groups increased greatly in relation to their number in 1941. The Jehovah's Witnesses multiplied by nearly ten, the Pentecostalists by two and one-half, the Mormons by two.

*The church's influence: religion, politics and education*

More important than the numerical support given to denominations is the churches' political influence, the commitment of their memberships and the effectiveness of their ministry and witness. It is difficult to speak about these things for religion in Canada as a whole. Canadian religion still awaits the scientific investigation that workers like Stark and Glock [1968] have given to religion in the United States. One may glean insights from the sociological literature, and a certain amount can be learned from official church histories and from the studies undertaken by the *Centre de Recherches en Sociologie Religieuse* at Université Laval and by Stewart Crysdale when reporting to the Board of Evangelism and Social Service of the United Church of Canada. Yet those studies are denomination and action oriented.

As for political influence, no church in any province of Canada now is established or has privileges given it by law. The Anglican church in the Maritimes enjoyed certain privileges at first, like the receipt of property and the exclusive right to perform marriages, but such privileges were eventually denied it. Porter [1965] claims that the power triumphs of the church are most clearly seen in the struggle for the control of education. For the Catholic Church has always insisted on having control of the education given to its members and it has been successful in preserving this. Throughout Canada two networks of schools exist, public and 'separate', the former expressing the dominant religion of the province, whether this be Protestant or Catholic. Parents of children attending the 'separate' elementary schools may direct their school tax to the support of these schools exclusively. But the running of 'separate' schools has been an extremely costly enterprise and there is mounting anxiety about their future. Changes in the economy and government policies on capital financing of schools, constantly put them at a disadvantage.

*The challenge of secularization, urbanization and industrialization*

The evidence available shows an awareness in the church that the challenge before it now is distinctly different from that facing it during the days of migration and settlement. It is the secularization of an urban-based, industrial civilization that confronts it. Everyone is implicated in this civilization, for urban change brings a concomitant rural change. The church faces a population with loosening roots whose thought and action, careers and life styles are marked by an increasing rationality and self-determination, and therefore by status and life-phase differentiation. His denominational affiliation, incidentally, may put constraints on a person's ultimate location in this kind of milieu. For example, Porter [1965, pp. 98–103] uses data on median incomes in census tracts to show that higher incomes are differentially associated with Protestantism and lower incomes with Catholicism in five widely separated Canadian cities – in Halifax, Ottawa, Windsor, Winnipeg and Montreal. Porter [1965, pp. 91–98] also endorses the prevalent view that it is the (mainly Protestant) British who promoted the industrial development of Quebec. But the churches' problem is to so husband and deploy resources as to meet the changing needs of mobile people wherever they are located. It seems fair to say that the rate of change in this demand has itself proved disconcerting. In many places in the church there is a sense of ineptness and inadequacy – and humility, searching and concern. For, seemingly quite suddenly, it had become exceptionally hard to *reach* people, in two senses of the word. It was hard to reach them all practically, for they were in so many different life-situations. And it was hard to reach them theologically. For, whereas responsible pastors thought it mischievous to formulate the crisis clumsily by saying *God* is dead, they knew that a person's *image* of God dies when his experience widens. Generations who move from their social and intellectual origins are stranded till they find reformations of their faith.

Two popular books, *The Comfortable Pew* [Berton, 1965], and *Why the Sea is Boiling Hot*, [Berton, *et al.*, 1965], were actually commissioned by the Anglican and United churches respectively to vocalize popular criticisms of where the church is lagging. An accusing finger was pointed at things like lack of real communication with the people, being over-occupied with itself as a business, being out of step with the advances of science and rationalism, being paralysed by an ethical rigidity that precludes a more discriminating morality, particularly with regard to sex. The authors of *Crestwood Heights* [Seeley *et al.*, 1963] on the other hand, were not invited critics but wrote as sociological observers. Yet they were not disposed to give any flattering picture of the role of religion in a Canadian suburb. They see the modern citizen burdened with the task of discriminating for himself between ends and means in the mazes of secular society. Typically, they think, he has perpetrated an inversion of the traditional ends and means: success, health and happiness are his gods. Religion is the means, and it is good or bad for him and his children according to whether it furthers access to these. The school teachers and human relations experts are the high priests of the secular religion and they have, deviously, brought the church under their tutelage.

> Formerly the views of the church dominated the parent who in turn dominated the child and the teacher directly – and the child again indirectly through the teacher. The existing configuration would suggest that the teacher now influences child and parent, who mutually influence each other, and these, in turn, unite to influence the church. The school, supported by the human relations experts and their institutions, has largely replaced the church as an ideological source ... [Seeley *et al.*, 1963, p. 241].

Whyte [1968] has summarized the answers to questions on religion asked in Gallop Polls of the Canadian Institute of Public Opinion. He interprets them to show a decline in fundamentalist religion with urbanization and, more important, a feeling on the part of people in general that the church's influence in their lives is weakening with the growth of urbanization in the nation. One particular thing he draws attention to is a new rural predicament: migration to the city and the changing economic base of rural industry have made it impossible for the same small area to support a separate church and ministry.

The Laval research [Laval, Université, 1964–68] has tried to define the situation and attitudes of the people in Catholic Quebec, and the studies are occupied with the need to make many adaptations if spiritual instruction is to be effectual in the Catholic parish now. For, as Falardeau [1949; 1951] had pointed out, the 'parish' that persists as an urban district has been largely emptied of its former social functions: Hughes [1943] had described the beginning of that transformation in his study of the industrialization of a Quebec town. The Roman Catholic church has involved itself very directly with the welfare of the rural and urban worker for some time, of course, and not only in Quebec. The ideology of workers' co-operatives was introduced into Nova Scotia in the 1920's by way of the extension programme of St. Francis Xavier University at Antigonish. Fishing and industrial communities were shown how to solve their own problems through grass roots action. They were also encouraged to form producers' and consumers' co-operatives in the belief that this would put a brake on industrial monopolies. Father M.M. Coady [1939] has recorded some of these achievements. The Roman Catholic clergy in Quebec were undoubtedly too prone to equate virtue with ruralism and tradition, thereby lending insufficient help to their flock in the transition to industrialization. But that day has passed. A notorious incident in Canada is the resignation of Archbishop Charbonneau of Montreal after he had lost favour supporting strikers in 1949, and his stand is simply expressive of influential pro-labour sympathy within his church. Its expressions have not always been popular with workers in general, of course, insofar as it did promote independent Catholic unions at one stage, and it has slowed Quebec's integration into national and international unionism.

Crysdale [1965] made a national survey of the beliefs and social attitudes of the United Church people. This was mainly to test whether there was sufficient consolidation of opinion in that church to allow united action on social issues. It revealed a diversity in both theological and social outlook: the more urbanized the members the more liberal were they in both respects. Prior to this survey, Crysdale [1961] had written a review of the attitudes developed by the Canadian Protestant churches to the industrial struggle between capital and labour. He says they were slow at first to disengage any part of their sympathies from capital. But he considers there is evidence since 1919 that these churches have revolted against the self-sufficiency of the so-called 'Protestant ethic' that prevailed for two centuries. They now reject both the Lutheran dualistic ethic that separates the personal and social spheres and any pseudo-Calvinistic identification of righteousness with personal prosperity. They look for opportunities to influence public opinion and policy towards greater social justice. Subsequent to the national survey, Crysdale [1966] has written an account of the outreach efforts of some of the more innovating United Church congregations, as they try to adapt to change. Bridges have been built to the alienated youth in Toronto's Yorkville, to Negroes in Halifax, to the affluent at leisure in Banff – and so on.

Not least harrowing in the self-examination of the contemporary church is the realization of a prodigious ineptness and wastefulness in missionary endeavour. Zeal has scarcely been equalled by knowledge here. There was abundant zeal and, if Sweet [1947] is right, the Protestants' zeal for missions in North America sprang from the same fountainhead as the zeal for the social gospel and, for that matter, the zeal for all the other kinds of 'activism' that North America has seen in modern times. He traces all of it to the evangelist Jonathan Edwards and his preaching of an ethic of disinterested benevolence. A concern for missions, both at home and abroad, had always characterized the Roman Catholics. The Quebec Catholics have been exceptional among Catholics in the support given to missions. The Oblate Fathers, in the north-west and British Columbia, have been exceptional among missionaries in the effectiveness of their work – and was it because it was a principle with them to minister to material need as much as to spiritual? It was in the nineteenth century, however, that the Protestants' missionary societies burgeoned, serving both home and foreign fields. So far as the churches' mission to Canada's own people is concerned, there have been conspicuous successes – particularly in the *short run*. Names like Duncan, Bompas, Peck and Evans conjure up images of remarkable achievements. But it is the long run effects of missionary penetration that now so often seem disappointing. Some of them are quite contrary to those intended: vital people have been changed into demoralized and dependent wards. There is no choice but to recast the missionary enterprise entirely, as Melling [1967] points out, and in such a way as to integrate these people into the dominant community.

Clearly this is another day of humiliation for the church, and the crisis in Canada simply seems to reflect something much more widespread. The coincidence of a number of things has shaken the church into a new consciousness of relativity, and two things especially have been unsettling. First, rapidly growing knowledge has intensified both change itself and the *awareness* that time changes all things: parents and their own children will have to follow different ways. Even the span of living memory must henceforth countenance different beliefs and moralities as true and right, each for their time – even though the *criteria* of truth and right remain constant. Secondly, the eroding of the walls of isolation that is making one nation and, indeed, one world out of the people of different traditions, has forced an awareness that much that is distinctive in traditions is not relevant to the interaction of neighbours. If changes like these have been disconcerting at first, they are scarcely discouraging to the faithful who stay with them and agonize secretly. These people wrest opportunities from them for new strategies. Anyone who has his ear to the ground can hear in Canada's churches this formidable army gathering. What surprised them is that so much had to be conceded to relativism in an institution concerned with the absolute. It has been their painful lesson to learn that although religion is an engagement with the absolute there is nothing absolute in any of the means by which it is engaged.

SELECTED BIBLIOGRAPHY

Berton, Pierre, *The Comfortable Pew.* Toronto, McClelland and Stewart, 1965.
Berton, Pierre, *et al., Why the Sea is Boiling Hot.* Toronto, Ryerson Press, 1965.
Clark, S. D., *Church and Sect in Canada.* Toronto, University of Toronto Press, 1965.
Coady, Moses M., *Masters of their own Destiny. The story of the Antigonish Movement of Adult Education through Economic Cooperation.* New York-London, Harper, 1939.
Crysdale, Stewart, *The Industrial Struggle and Protestant Ethics in Canada: A Survey of Changing Power Structures and Christian Social Ethics.* Toronto, Ryerson Press, 1961.
–, *The Changing Church in Canada, Beliefs and Social Attitudes of United Church People.* Toronto, Board of Evangelism and Social Service, United Church of Canada, 1965.
—, *Churches Where the Action Is! Churches and People in Canadian Situations.* Toronto, Board of Evangelism and Social Service, United Church of Canada, 1966.
Falardeau, Jean-C., 'The Parish as an Institutional Type.' *Canadian Journal of Economics and Political Science*, XV, August, 1949.
—, 'Religious Sociology in Canada.' *Lumen Vitae*, VI, 1951.
Gérin, L., 'L'Habitant de Saint-Justin.' *Proceedings of the Royal Society of Canada*, IV, 1898.
Grant, John Webster (ed.), *The Churches and the Canadian Experience: A Faith and Order Study of the Christian Tradition.* Toronto, Ryerson Press, 1963.
Herbison, Hugh, 'Doukhobor Religion.' *Canadian Society, Sociological Perspectives* (3rd. ed.), edited by Blishen, Jones, Naegele and Porter. Toronto, Macmillan of Canada, 1968, pp.539–62.
Hughes, Everett-C., *French Canada in Transition.* Chicago, University of Chicago Press, 1943.
*Laval, Université, Centre de Recherches en Sociologie Religieuse: Study Series.*
(i) Routhier, Abbé François, *Etude Sur le Comte de Montmorency.* 1964.
(ii) Lapointe, Gérard, *La Côte de Beauport.* 1964.
(iii) Lapointe, Gérard, *Structures Sociales et Attitudes Religieuses.* 1967.

(iv) Lessard, Marc-A., *Le Comté de Portneuf.* 1967.
(v) Rouleau, Jean-Paul, *Chicoutimi.* 1968.
(vi) Delalande, P. Vianney, *Québec Métropolitain.* 1968.

Mann, W. E., *Sect, Cult and Church in Alberta.* Toronto, University of Toronto Press, 1962.

Melling, John, *Right to a Future: The Native Peoples of Canada.* Toronto, Anglican Church of Canada and United Church of Canada, 1967.

Miner, Horace, *Saint-Denis, A French Canadian Parish.* Chicago, University of Chicago Press, 1938.

Porter, John, *The Vertical Mosaic: An Analysis of Social Class and Power in Canada.* Toronto, University of Toronto Press, 1965.

Reaman, G. Elmore, *The Trail of the Black Walnut.* Toronto, McClelland & Stewart, 1957.

—, *The Trail of the Hugenots in Europe, the United States, South Africa and Canada.* Baltimore, Genealogical Publishing Company, 1966.

Seeley, John R., Sim, R. Alexander, and Loosley, Elizabeth W., *Crestwood Heights, A Study of the Culture of Suburban Life.* Toronto, University of Toronto Press, 1963.

Stark, Rodney and Glock, Charles Y., *American Piety: The Nature of Religious Commitment.* Berkeley, University of California Press, 1968.

Sweet, W. W., *The American Churches.* London, Epworth Press, 1947.

Walsh, H. H., *The Christian Church in Canada.* Toronto, Ryerson Press, 1968.

Whyte, Donald R., 'Religion and the Rural Church'. *Canadian Society, Sociological Perspectives* (3rd ed.), edited by Blishen *et al.* Toronto, Macmillan of Canada, 1968, pp. 574–589.

Wilson, Douglas J., *The Church Grows in Canada.* Toronto, Committee on Missionary Education, Canadian Council of Churches, 1966.

ERIKA KADLECOVÁ*

# Czechoslovakia

## HISTORICAL INTRODUCTION

Christianity was introduced into the court of the Great Moravian State in the ninth century from Byzantium, or more particularly from Salonica, and brought with it the Slavonic liturgy and a new script. After the fall of this state, Bohemia became the cultural and administrative centre, and gradually the Latin liturgy came to dominate. In 972 the first episcopate was founded in Bohemia and was elevated to an archbishopric in 1344.

The Church quickly acquired, not only immense importance as practically the sole bearer of contemporary education, but also outstanding political influence and enormous wealth. By the beginning of the fifteenth century it owned about one half of the total farming land in Bohemia – and it is needless to emphasise the significance of land in a feudal society. The prevalence of 'secular' over spiritual interests in the 'debased' feudalized Church drew the attack of a number of preachers and the Czech Reformation was born. It reached its peak in the appearance of the greatest phenomenon in Czech medieval spiritual history, John Hus. The burning of Hus at the Council in Constance in 1415, after his refusal to recant, aroused a storm of protest in Bohemia which eventually led to the Hussite revolution.

When the rebellious Czechs could not be subdued by crusading armies from all over Europe, the Ecclesiastical Council in Basle accepted their demands. The so-called 'Compactate' recognized a high degree of autonomy in the Bohemian, Moravian Church, communion under both species and sanctioned clerical reform which forbad priests to claim ownership of worldly possessions. This external victory led to a definite breach between the radical and moderate wing of the Hussites (Tabor and Prague) and to the defeat of the radical Taborites by the united forces of the Hussite right wing and Catholics.

After the Hussite Wars the Utraquists (Hussites) and a small minority of

* This article was written before October 1968, when Mrs. Kadlecová held both high academic and governmental positions. It has proved impossible to communicate with her since that time.

Catholics co-existed together. Thus while Europe was tormented by religious strife and wars the ideas of tolerance and freedom of worship triumphed in Bohemia and were incorporated in public records. However, disenchantment with the secularization of the official Utraquist Church, its compromises in foreign diplomacy and at home, led to the foundation of the Church of the Bohemian Brethren in 1467. This small, and throughout almost its whole existence, persecuted or just tolerated church, played an important role in the cultural and spiritual development of the nation. Inspired by the strong personality of Peter Chelcicky it strove to approach, in purity of morale and a strict orientation to the Holy Scripture, the example of the early Christians. The Kralice Bible which preserved the treasure of the Czech tongue, almost on the verge of extinction in subsequent centuries, came from this church.

The consolidation of European Catholicism by the Counter-Reformation brought a massive onslaught on the freedom and rights of the Utraquist Church and an attempt to champion the Catholic minority at its expense. The Utraquists scored one last victory when their freedom was solemnly proclaimed in Rudolf's 'Letter of Majesty' in 1609 which assured the free exercise of religion to all who professed the 'Confessio Bohemica'. However, the renewed onslaught of the Counter-Reformation provoked a revolt of the Czech Estates and after their defeat in 1620 a harsh stop was put to religious freedom. Re-Catholicization was carried out with cold brutality. While those of the nobility and burghers who refused to adopt the Catholic faith were free to leave the country, the poor had no such choice. Thus, the spiritual and political élite of the nation was either executed or exiled and its estates confiscated. Inside the country all books suspected of heresy were systematically burnt; for 160 years people accused of being secret Protestants were persecuted and tortured.

In 1781 Joseph II issued his Edict of Toleration which secured free exercise of religion to Lutherans and Calvinists. But it was too late. In the once 90 per cent Hussite Bohemia, only about 2 per cent took advantage of the proffered religious freedom. The continuity of religious life had been interrupted; Czech Protestantism had to start all over again. The fact that people remained in the Roman Church was no proof of the victory of Catholic doctrine; rather it expressed their indifference.

In the wake of the First World War, came a mass withdrawal from the Roman Church demonstrating indignation over the symbiosis of the Church and the hated Hapsburg monarchy. In the first post-war years 19 per cent of the populace left the Church in the Czech lands.[1] It is noteworthy that

1. Czechoslovakia is roughly divided into two parts: the Czech lands (the western part), inhabited predominantly by the Czechs, and Slovakia (the eastern part), inhabited by the Slovaks.

after this crisis the Church managed to consolidate. Catholicism, divested of its privileges and State support, made for the first time in centuries, a successful attempt to incorporate itself by virtue of its specific values, in the context of Czech thought and culture. This process was interrupted by the Second World War and then complicated by subsequent events.

The position of any social group in contemporary Czechoslovakia is primarily determined by the attitude it took towards Fascism and German occupation, in the years preceding the Second World War and during it, and towards the character of the subsequent Republic. Part of the clergy collaborated with the German Fascists and was thus co-responsible for their crimes. This was particularly marked in Slovakia where the puppet government appointed by Hitler had extensive support among the Catholic clergy. The Quisling President of the then existing Slovak State was also a Catholic priest. Nevertheless, the greater majority of believers and the clergy were against Fascism. They remained faithful to the nation and democratic ideas, and, together with Communists, filled the prisons and concentration camps. Thus the position of the Church after the liberation was, keeping in mind the dominating influence of the Communist Party, relatively more favourable than after 1918. There was no wholesale departure from the Church; there was neither reproach nor attack; the Government strove with all available means for a good mutual relationship. In 1945 Czechoslovakia was the only one of the Popular Democracies which immediately renewed diplomatic relations with the Vatican.

In the period between May 1945 and February 1948 a sharp class struggle flared up concerning the future development and character of the Republic. Should it become socialist, as the Communist Party advocated, or return to the pre-war capitalist bourgeois democratic republic? The Church hid neither its sympathies for the second alternative nor its support for the parties which resisted a socialist evolution. However, while it did not keep neutral, it equally did not violate the will of its faithful by unlawful means. Therefore, even at the moment when the question of power was decided in favour of a socialist development, during the decisive February events, the possibility of a non-antagonistic relationship between the new régime and the Church remained open.

Between February 1948 and the summer of 1949 protracted and at times hopeful negotiations were under way between the Government and the Church hierarchy. Ultimately the outcome was determined not alone by the attitude of the two parties but by the decisive intervention of the Vatican – at the time not inclined to a peaceful settlement. The *coup de grâce* was delivered by the Excommunication Decree of Pius XII, July 1949, by which Communists and readers of the Communist Press were expelled from the Church. In October 1949 Church Laws were enacted which globally regulated the rights and duties of the churches and the relationship between them and the State. Considered as the outcome of failed negotiations and as a unilateral formulation of legal relations which defined the vanquished party its place, rights and duties, it must be conceded that the laws were, by a long way, not as harsh as might have been expected.

The most notable provision was the setting up of a State Office for Church Affairs, today the Department for Church Affairs at the Ministry for Culture and Information. Its task was meant

> to ensure that Church and religious life should develop in concord with the Constitution and the principles of a Popular Democratic régime and thus to assure for each individual his constitutional right of freedom of worship, based on the principles of religious tolerance and equality of all denominations.

These Laws further state that the Government shall provide for the economic security of the churches and religious societies. The Government grants the clergy and personnel of religious societies a salary, i.e. basic salary, an allowance according to rank, and renumeration for extra activity, whereby the clergy remains in the employment of the Church and not in that of the State. For performing the function of a minister, State approval, tied to an oath of allegiance to the Republic, is required. Another provision for the economic protection of the churches stipulates that the State shall reimburse the deficit in the budget, allocated by the State.

That part of church property which represented means of production and hence could become a source of human exploitation, was secularized. This mainly affected land which, according to Czechoslovak law, could belong only to those who worked on it. Other church property was not nationalized and is still owned by the churches. Church property is under supervision as well as under protection of the State which guarantees that this property shall serve purposes of worship and also refunds all expenses needed for its maintenance.

The non-Catholic churches accepted the Laws without any further conflict. This is understandable since, only thanks to these Laws, did all churches in the country achieve complete equality. They also did not possess extensive lands, one of the basic problems in the negotiations with the Catholic Church. In addition, the non-Catholic churches acted from the beginning with a view to the internal situation in the country – the influence of the laity on church organizations enabled them to respect the attitude of believers. The enactment of the Church Laws meant another open clash with the Catholic hierarchy. This prevented a sensitive differentiation between indispensable interference in order to safeguard State sovereignty and interference crossing that borderline. It was all the more tragic that this clash occurred as the first symptoms of the Stalinist deformation appeared in Czechoslovakia.

At present the relationship between the churches and the State is on the surface consolidated, although there are still a number of unresolved problems. A prediction on the further development is beyond the scope of sociology.

## DEMOGRAPHIC DATA

Table 1 indicates the latest reliable statistics on church membership. There is no exact statistical data after the 1930 Census. In 1954 the registration of religious denominations was abolished. Church membership was not recorded in censuses in concord with the principle that religion is the citizen's private affair. Relevant data can be obtained only by sociological surveys, the latest of which was 1967.

*Table 1. Church membership in Czechoslovakia*

| | Czechoslovakia | | Czech lands | Slovakia |
|---|---|---|---|---|
| | 1930 % | 1967 % | 1967 % | 1967 % |
| Roman Catholics | 73.5 | 50.5 | 44.1 | 65.5 |
| Czechoslovak Church | 5.3 | 4.4 | 6.1 | 0.2 |
| Protestants | 7.7 | 7.4 | 2.6 | 18.8 |
| Orthodox | 1.0 | 0.6 | – | 1.9 |
| Greek Catholics | 4.0 | – | – | – |
| Other denominations | – | 1.1 | 0.8 | 1.7 |
| No denomination | 5.8 | 36.0 | 46.4 | 11.9 |

Contemporarily there are seventeen state approved churches and religious societies in Czechoslovakia and, in addition, there are others without state approval. As Table 1 shows, the Roman Catholic Church is the largest followed by the Czechoslovak Church. This was founded in 1920 as the peak of a reformist movement of Roman Catholic priests and laity which opposed some ecclesiastical dogmas, and advocated abolition of clerical celibacy and the introduction of a vernacular liturgy. It carries on the Hussite tradition. The Orthodox Church has most of its members in Slovakia and after the Second World War it was joined by the Greek-Catholic Church.

Of the Protestant Churches the most popular is the Slovak Protestant Church of the Augsburg Confession and the Protestant Church of the Czech Brethren. The latter is based on the tradition of the Czech Reformation, stemming particularly from Utraquism and the United Czech Brethren, Silesian Protestant Church, Reformed Christian Church in Slovakia, Protestant Methodist Church, United Baptist Brethren, the Religious Society of Czechoslovak Unitarians, Church of the Seventh Day Adventists, Old-catholic Church, Church of the New Apostles and the Christian Synods (Darbists).

The Jewish religious society which has been in existence since the tenth century is the only non-Christian denomination. During the German occupation 90 per cent of the people designated by Fascist legislation as Jews were murdered.

Table 1 also shows the considerable religious difference between the Czech and Slovak areas of Czechoslovakia. Whereas nearly half of the people in the Czech lands claim no denomination, only 11.9 per cent of the Slovaks have no religious affiliation. This difference is partly due to historical factors, but also reflects the more agricultural less industrialized socio-economic structure of Slovakia.

The churches have six publishing offices at their disposal which publish seventeen clerical journals and papers. Priests are trained in six theological faculties whose organization is similar to that of other colleges. Even before the Revolution there were no Church schools. Teaching of religion at State schools is voluntary. Classes of religion are attended by children whose parents sign an enrolment form.

## RELIGIOUS PARTICIPATION AND BELIEFS

Church membership does not necessarily correspond with religiosity. For various reasons someone who has lost faith may still belong to a church and, on the contrary, there may be deeply religious people with no denomination. From the aspect of influence of religion actual faith is more important than statistical data on church membership.

The first investigation of religiosity in post-war Czechoslovakia was performed by the Research Institute for Public Opinion in Prague in 1946 and 1947. It investigated only the Czech lands. No sociological surveys were made in the following years. The only recent investigation, and the only one which has been fully evaluated, is a survey on religiosity in the North-Moravian region in 1963.[2] This region has a population of 1,631,579,[3] is

2. The initial data on the basis of which the population sample was selected, was 1961 census data on the inhabitants of the North Moravian region classed according

the most industrialized region in Czechoslovakia and is second only to Southern Moravia with respect to magnitude of religiosity in the Czech lands. The investigation used a block of questions which had been put to respondents in 1946 in order to study in main outline at least, not only the state but also the movement of religiosity. Tables 2 and 3 illustrate the outcome of both investigations and the decline of religiosity in its individual components.

*Table 2. Religious belief and practice*

| Question | % Response | | | |
|---|---|---|---|---|
| | Yes | Doubtful | Never think about it | No |
| Do you believe in God? | | | | |
| 1946 | 64 | 16 | 8 | 12 |
| 1963 | 34 | 11 | 17 | 38 |
| Do you believe Christ was the embodiment of God? | | | | |
| 1946 | 33 | 18 | 11 | 37 |
| 1963 | 25 | 10 | 23 | 41 |
| Do you believe in post mortal life? | | | | |
| 1946 | 38 | 21 | 13 | 28 |
| 1963 | 24 | 9 | 18 | 49 |
| Do you go to church? | Regularly | Occasionally | On special occasions | |
| 1946 | 20 | 43 | 14* | 24 |
| 1963 | 13 | 21 | 15 | 51 |
| Do you pray in private? | | | | |
| 1946 | 28 | 28 | 14* | 29 |
| 1963 | 16 | 17 | 11 | 56 |

* The response category here was actually on big festivities.

to their economic and industrial vocation and according to the size of the district in which they resided. Abiding by the principle of random selection the sample was divided into relevant categories according to sex, age and education. The investigation was conducted in 54 places and covered 1,400 adults and 2,300 young people. For each community (town, village) a list was made showing how many citizens and of which type were to be questioned. Whenever possible we adopted the method of a random mechanical selection. If the size of the basic sample was too large for making lists of names we used the method of a two-phase selection, i.e. we first selected certain social units (apprentices homes, school classes, etc.) and, in the second phase of selection, individuals from these units.

3. The total population of Czechoslovakia is 13,745,577, divided between the Czech lands (Bohemia and Moravia) 9,571,531, and Slovakia 4,174,046.

*Table 3. Religious attitudes*

| Question | % Response Yes | No | Doubtful |
|---|---|---|---|
| Should a child have religious education? | | | |
| 1946 | 77 | 13 | 10 |
| 1963 | 32 | 49 | 18 |
| Are religious people generally more moral than the religiously indifferent or non-believers? | | | |
| 1946 | 33 | 30 | 37 |
| 1963 | 17 | 38 | 45 |
| Are religious people greater hypocrites? | | | |
| 1946 | 34 | 17 | 49 |
| 1963 | 32 | 9 | 59 |
| Do you feel distaste for members of some denominations?* | | | |
| 1946 | 33 | 67 | – |
| 1963 | 14 | 86 | – |

* The percentage of those who felt distaste for the following particular denominations in 1946 and 1963 respectively were: Catholics, 7.4, 3.8; Protestants 1.3, 0.07; Atheists 8.2, 1.7; Jews 15.9, 1.6. In 1963 3.3 per cent felt distaste for sectarians, and 3.2 per cent were not specific.

Although comparison is limited by the fact that the sample in the year 1963 was only one fifth of the sample used in 1946, certain general trends are clear. Firstly, there has been a sharp drop in religiosity ranging from almost one half with respect to belief in God to one quarter with respect to belief in Christ. The number of those advocating religious tuition for children shows an even sharper drop. Secondly, there has been a rise in conscious atheism. Thirdly, as decline in belief in God (a basic sign of non-conformist faith) [4] is substantially greater than decline in belief in Christ (a basic sign of conformist Christian faith), it appears that the firmly organized core of the complex of believers with a conformist faith is more resistant to change. Fourthly, a marked increase of mutual tolerance among individual denominations as well as between atheists and believers is evident. It should be

4. People with non-conformist faith do not conform to any of the religious creeds existing in Czechoslovakia, although they have some supernaturalist belief and, at least sometimes, visit a church. Conformist believers accept the fundamental beliefs of the Christian faith and fulfil at least some of their duties to their church.

noted that religiosity in North Moravia is high, above the average for the Czech lands; thus, it may be presumed that the actual drop in religiosity is larger than shown.

In the analysis of the 1963 survey, respondents were classified into three basic groups: atheists (A), believers (B), undefined (C). The atheist group comprised people whose answer to all questions relative to religion was emphatically negative. The believers group comprised people who fulfilled two conditions: they believed in the supernatural and derived from their faith certain practical conclusions in that they strove to establish contact with the supernatural. In order to be included in this category the respondents had to answer positively at least one of the following questions: Do you believe in God? Was Jesus Christ the embodiment of God? Do you believe in post mortal life? They also had to affirm one of the questions concerning religious practice: prayer in private, attendance at church service or

*Table 4. Levels of religiosity*

| Related indicators of religiosity | % of groups B and C |
|---|---|
| *Structure I* | |
| Church marriage | 81 |
| Marriage partner of the same faith | 81 |
| Baptized children | 83 |
| *Structure II* | |
| Concedes the existence of God | 45 |
| Prays in private, at least occasionally | 44 |
| Goes to church, at least on big festivities | 49 |
| *Structure III* | |
| Believes in God | 34 |
| Concedes that Christ was the embodiment of God | 35 |
| Concedes the existence of post mortal life | 33 |
| Prays in private, at least sometimes | 33 |
| Goes to church, at least sometimes | 34 |
| Thinks religious education for children essential | 32 |
| *Structure IV* | |
| Believes in Christ as the embodiment of God | 25 |
| Believes in eternal life | 24 |
| Receives the sacrament, at least sometimes | 24 |
| Reads religious texts, at least sometimes | 24 |
| Thinks it right to disseminate religion | 23 |

congregational meeting. The undefined group comprised people who were neither firm atheists nor firm believers. According to some basic indicators they had lost the character of a firm believer, according to others they still retained ideas or habits of a religious nature. According to these criteria 30 per cent of the adult populace in the North Moravian region are atheists, 30 per cent believers and 40 per cent undefined.

On the basis of various indicators an analysis of the internal structure of religiosity was attempted. Within the schema and limit permitted by a sociological investigation of this type, it was found that there are four cumulative structures or levels, each of which represents a correlation of specific religious concepts with practical action.

Although it was stated that at each level a connection between religious ideas and practical action was found, this does not apply to the first structure, the broadest and most common indicator. The ideological motive, the theoretical starting point for religious acts, has either become extinct or perhaps never existed. It is obvious that the form of religious act or adherence to the rite characteristic of the structure is not necessarily linked with real religiosity. It can be performed for reasons that have nothing to do with religion: the wish of relatives, tradition, attraction of the ceremony, ignorance of how to proceed otherwise, and equally superstition, or a vestige of magical ideas, i.e. an attempt to do everything in order not to defy fate and the dark powers. Hence, one cannot define people as religious because they participate in these acts, not even if the act was performed in the recent past. Naturally, one cannot regard as religious those who had performed these acts in the past but otherwise had lost contact with faith.

In Structure II, religious consciousness appears on the scene for the first time, if in a rudimentary form. Here, action is already mediated and supported by certain conceptions even if they are actually of a negative nature. One is not certain whether God exists and therefore acts, at least from time to time, as if He existed. One does not believe; one only concedes the possibility of God's existence theoretically. Motivation stems not so much from fear of a possible God but from need for a God. Faith has the function of a psychological insurance. It is not an organic part of the mind and life, but is artificially evoked in moments of crisis, tension, or emptiness. This is not an exceptional phenomenon, a psychological curiosity; it is manifest in 10 per cent of those interviewed and in one quarter of those who 'practise religion' to a more or lesser extent. Yet it seems that this structure is not yet a sufficient sign of religious life and thought. It represents both the extinction and discovery point of faith but in practical terms it implies relegation of religion to the back of the mind where it does not disturb and where it can always be retrieved for use.

Interesting in this structure is the relationship of the two components of religious activity. A greater percentage goes to church, at least on big festivities, than prays in private. From this derive several conclusions: the church and chapels of individual denominations are visited not only by fellow-believers but, at least occasionally, by those who have retained some faith however indefinite and even by those who have lost faith. Nearly one half of the population (49 per cent) goes to church or congregations at least on special occasions. The contact is a slight one, yet it has not been completely severed. The word, the rite, the atmosphere, may make an impression under favourable circumstances.

Private individual prayer is given up sooner than collective adoration. Common manifestation of faith, which may be only an outward gesture, might live on for a brief period in people who are parting with religion. This experience corrects somewhat a possible distrust of 'objective indices' of religiosity. But it likewise corrects the optimistic illusion in some clerical circles where it is thought that there is still a relatively large mass of the faithful who keep outside the church community for fear that they might encounter displeasure and misapprehension in their surroundings.

In Structure III for the first time faith appears as the basic motive for action. Here we can speak of believers, of religion in its totality. Religious action is no longer an ideologically unsupported defence reaction, but arises from a specific theoretical concept with which it is in full accord. Here faith in God arises clearly from concepts of Christian ideology. The connection with the basic article of Christian teaching – faith in Christ as the Saviour – is conclusive. Practically everybody who believes in God gives at least some credit to the doctrine about Christ. Related to the latter is faith in eternal life, which is accepted only as a possibility, a concession that something of the sort cannot be precluded. Faith is combined with action which no longer has the character of chance, emergency or exceptionality. The believer prays, at least sometimes, in private and sometimes attends common worship. It is symptomatic of people in this category that confidence in their own attitude, 'the certainty of faith' induces them to pass on their faith to their children. This characteristic was marked in our group and a typical sign of this structure.

In Structure IV the main pillar of belief is faith in Christ. This is definite Christian religion. From faith in the Saviour arises faith in eternal life. To common worship and private prayer is added another important component, taking the sacrament, at least occasionally – an act which is not linked merely with isolated profound changes in one's life. This indicator reflects not only the acceptance of a specific Christian doctrine, but also identification with a specific religious community and acceptance of its rites which means (irrespective of whether comprehended as a mystical or symbolical act) a separation from the irreverent mass and the recognition of membership in an exclusive, chosen, redeemed community. This aspect is also reflected in the new element that is added to this structure, i.e. activity directed inward and outward in the endeavour to deepen faith in oneself by reading and to disseminate it abroad.

Some indicators of religiosity are not mutually interconnected in such a conspicuous balance as outlined in the foregoing four structures. Yet their frequency is greater than the items in the fourth structure and hence they must enter into the latter two structures. These indicators are public witness of faith (29 per cent) and consideration of important life decisions from the religious angle at least sometimes (28 per cent). The latter indicator is particularly significant for it shows the crossing of religious thought into the profane sphere and the, at least proclamatory, subordination of vital decisions to religious norms.

One can generalise the above findings by stating that wherever faith in Jesus Christ appears as a firm subjective certainty, there appears, to a greater or lesser extent and more or less consequentially, all the other partial indicators of religiosity, studied in the investigation.

The structure of religiosity varies somewhat between Catholics and Protestants. In terms of the content of religious ideas Protestants outweigh Catholics in belief in God, whereas more Catholics believe in eternal life. Faith in Christ is equal in both confessions. Catholics have a more positive index in all basic signs of religious practice – church attendance, sacrament and private prayer, although the difference in individual prayer is so slight as to be almost negligible. Protestants show a marked distinction in their favour in two indicators – religious texts and consideration of vital steps from the religious aspect.

In order to understand the relative stability of various aspects of religious life, the categorically negative response to particular indicators was analysed in the undefined group (B). The order of items in Table 5 reveals the mode of gradual decline in religious faith.

The data in Table 5 yield the same conclusion as the previous discussion of religious structures: the most stable component in religious consciousness is faith in Christ. This is the essence: on its endurance religiosity rests or falls. With this faith are linked all other components.

Viewed from another angle, from the aspect of a decline in faith, the first signal is a slackening in the care for strengthening, deepening faith – the loss of interest in theological problems. This comprises not only reading religious books, but the Holy Scripture, prayers, the biographies of saints, etc. Another even more significant decline is heralded by a state in which religion ceases to be a compass in everyday life, where it forfeits its character as criterion of values, where the believer, without his being aware of it, is guided and directed by other than religious considerations.

*Table 5. Indicators of religiosity in the undefined group (B)*

| Those who | % of group B |
|---|---|
| Do not read religious literature | 38 |
| Have ceased considering vital steps from the religious angle | 31 |
| Do not confess their religious faith publicly | 14 |
| Have stopped taking the sacrament | 10 |
| Have not a marriage partner of the same faith | 8 |
| Though they believe in God do not believe in eternal life | 4 |
| Have not had a church marriage | 4 |
| Do not think religious education essential for children | 3 |
| Have stopped thinking of themselves as members of a church | 2 |
| Do not believe Christ was the embodiment of God, and hence have not had their children christened | 1 |

These two aspects which were apparent in wide circles of believers (more than one third in the first instance and nearly one third in the second) need not yet mean to the religious person a weakening in his religious ideas. The moment, however, in which faith becomes something of a burden, or at least a disadvantage in the eyes of others, implies already an involuntary shift to the critical attitude of his irreverent co-citizens. He does not identify himself with them but makes concessions which suggests at least that he prefers the quiet position of conformity to the mission as believer as witness.

Another statistically interesting indicator shows the neglect of the Christian's most important duty – active participation in sacrament. We are, of course, concerned with the sociological aspect of the ceremony as an integrating factor, and not with the theological aspect. It is interesting to note that 10 per cent of people who fail to adhere to this basic ritual act, which according to the teachings of all churches is the prerequisite of membership to a Christian community, still think of themselves as Christians despite the neglect of this duty. However, we must likewise appreciate the opposite aspect – i.e. that 90 per cent of believers take the sacrament, which fact testifies to a very strong internal link in Christianity.

Denomination exerts an influence on religiosity and its decline as is shown in Table 6.

Of the investigated denominations the Czechoslovak Church has the smallest percentage of true believers; 21 per cent true believers is an extremely low figure and signifies a sharp decline. Twenty per cent of members are only formally affiliated to the church and are conscious atheists. One may justly doubt that the small core of true believers will be capable of influencing the

*Table 6. Religiosity according to own and parental denominational membership*

| Denomination | Atheists % | Believers % | Undefined % |
|---|---|---|---|
| *Those who are:* | | | |
| Catholic | 8 | 55 | 37 |
| Protestant | 7 | 52 | 41 |
| Czechoslovak Church | 20 | 21 | 59 |
| No denomination | 62 | 2 | 36 |
| *Those of whom both parents were:* | | | |
| Catholic | 28 | 34 | 38 |
| Protestant | 18 | 39 | 43 |
| Czechoslovak Church | 40 | 9 | 51 |

undecided majority. The difference between Catholics and Protestants is statistically not significant. The degree of religiosity in people descendent from Czechoslovak Church parents intensifies the pattern of decline already apparent. Nine per cent of believers in the second generation is a figure which needs no commentary. A marked difference is shown with respect to Protestants and Catholics. Eighteen per cent of non-believing children in Protestant families means a substantial decline in religiosity, but this decline is not nearly as marked as that experienced in other denominations. The relative stability of Protestants is just as manifest here as in the figures given for the efflux from the church.

### RELIGION AND SOCIAL AND ECONOMIC FACTORS

Tables 7–10 summarise some of the most significant findings of the 1963 survey in this area.

These tables indicate that those groups of the population who represent the active core of society, whose activities are linked with progressive forms of production and who live in corresponding circumstances are losing interest in religion. Believers predominate in the older age groups whereas atheists predominate in the productive age group; believers are prevalent among women, atheists among men; believers have a majority in small communities, atheists in large towns; believers are more frequent in the agricultural population, atheists in occupations linked with the development of an industrial society. Among believers there exists a catastrophic shortage of intelligentsia and people with higher education which is a dangerous symptom for any ideological movement.

*Table 8. Degree of religiosity according to marital status and number of children*

| | Atheists % | Believers % | Undefined % |
|---|---|---|---|
| *Marital status* | | | |
| Single | 25 | 25 | 50 |
| Married | 32 | 31 | 37 |
| Widowed | 16 | 41 | 42 |
| Divorced | 23 | 27 | 50 |
| *Number of Children* | | | |
| None | 27 | 28 | 45 |
| One | 34 | 25 | 41 |
| Two | 34 | 30 | 36 |
| Three | 31 | 28 | 41 |
| Four | 27 | 47 | 26 |
| Five | 17 | 54 | 29 |
| More | 9 | 61 | 30 |

*Table 7. Degree of religiosity according to age and sex*

| | Atheists % | Believers % | Undefined % |
|---|---|---|---|
| *Age* | | | |
| 21–30 | 31 | 25 | 44 |
| 31–40 | 35 | 25 | 39 |
| 41–50 | 33 | 29 | 38 |
| 51–60 | 24 | 38 | 38 |
| 61 and over | 23 | 45 | 32 |
| *Sex* | | | |
| Men | 36 | 25 | 39 |
| Women | 24 | 37 | 40 |

*Table 9. Degree of religiosity according to urbanization, migration, and nationality*

| | Atheists % | Believers % | Undefined % |
|---|---|---|---|
| *Urbanization* | | | |
| Up to 2,000 inhabitants | 20 | 41 | 39 |
| 2,001–10,000 inhabitants | 26 | 34 | 39 |
| 10,001–50,000 inhabitants | 40 | 22 | 38 |
| More than 50,000 inhabitants | 46 | 13 | 42 |
| *Migration* | | | |
| Settled in the place in past 5 years | 41 | 17 | 41 |
| Settled in 1949–1957 | 45 | 17 | 39 |
| Settled in 1945–1948 | 42 | 20 | 38 |
| Old settlers | 21 | 39 | 39 |
| *Nationality* | | | |
| Czech | 31 | 29 | 39 |
| Pole | 9 | 75 | 16 |
| Slovak | 13 | 30 | 57 |

*Table 10. Degree of religiosity according to education and occupation*

| | Atheists % | Believers % | Undefined % |
|---|---|---|---|
| *Education* | | | |
| Basic | 24 | 35 | 42 |
| Secondary school | 35 | 31 | 34 |
| Medium specialized training | 43 | 20 | 36 |
| University | 62 | 6 | 32 |
| *Occupation* | | | |
| Worker | 24 | 30 | 46 |
| Employee | 40 | 21 | 39 |
| Intelligentsia | 51 | 15 | 34 |
| Housewife | 21 | 45 | 34 |
| Pensioner | 29 | 38 | 33 |
| Farmer | 7 | 73 | 20 |

CONCLUSION

From the basic data obtained in the investigation the following conclusions derive:

1. It must be recognized that religion still retains a relatively firm hold upon the masses and still remains an ideology whose influence should not be ignored. In Czechoslovakia religion is the only non-marxist ideology having a mass basis and at present it is still the most widespread ideology among the populace. It is tolerated by the Constitution; it has a well operating organizational basis and a highly skilled machinery. It is in legal contact with foreign church centres and believers, whose theoretical work it can use and modify for its own purposes. Freedom of religion is regarded as an elementary human right and hence it is protected by public opinion against any violent encroachment.
2. There is a marked shift of religion to the periphery of social processes. Religion still holds its position chiefly in those social groups and social spheres which are either becoming extinct or have as yet not undergone the radical transformation required by contemporary life.
3. No matter how critical and negative one's assessment of religion as such may be – the characteristics of believers as illustrated by the investigation is fundamentally positive. The core of believers is not recruited from members of the former ruling classes although many of these may tend to seek in the church a haven for their interests. The class profile of believers is dominated by farmers, workers and their wives. Deeper probing shows that in the majority, they are less skilled and less paid groups of workers who live in relatively difficult material circumstances, whose basic needs are not satisfied – creative work, lack of friendship, cultural life, a justified confidence in a better future. They are people with no position and no connection, they are not part of the élite of power or the élite of influence. They are the weak and poor of this society for whom and with whom a socialist society is being built. It would be absurd blindness to transfer the negative assessment of faith to the believers.
4. Inside religion an ideological and organizational relaxation is taking place. A major part of believers has become indifferent to the basic content of Christianity and has lost contact with church communities. In this country faith outside the church is, on the one hand, the result of historical developments (the interruption of the continuity of church religion which befell both branches of Christianity and resulted in a weakening of the tie between the people and organized forms of worship) and on the other hand, the product of a disintegration of traditional forms of Christianity in a modern society – individualization of faith, subjectivization of religious ideas. Though non-conformist faith may be strong and

deeply rooted in individuals, yet generally, it can be said that in modern society individual faith is less stable and less resistant to the pressure of reality which surrounds and corrodes it.

5. The fact that religion has ceased to be an ideology on which society is based, that it has been systematically ejected from the power-political sphere, signifies a lot. All external power and artificially maintained prestige has collapsed; gone is the idea that respectability of man is inseparably linked with some church, that non-appearance at church on Sundays is a social offence. However, all this affects the church only superficially – things have dropped away which only pretended to be religion, which donned the outer shell of faith but were no true faith. If the process stopped at this point it would represent a 'purge' benefitting religion.
   Religion, however, has been hit much deeper in its fundaments. The process of eliminating social conditions which generate religion as their essential image, has begun. The heavy losses suffered by religion in the past twenty years were primarily due to the loss of its integrating function. The political revolution which is chiefly responsible for these changes was, however, a single act and single and unrepeatable are its consequences. The consequences derived from this fact are today practically exhausted. It cannot be assumed that the retreat of religion will continue at the same pace or that it will be linear. Theoretically possible deviations and a temporary revival of the interest in religion in connection with the overall situation in our society must be recognized.
6. Though losing its integrating function, at the given stage of development religion still retains to a certain extent its compensating function. In it lies the objective basis and historical justification of its existence. In view of the fact that this function is no more linked with the integrating function – it has become independent and isolated – the phenomenon of religion is moving into the sphere of privacy.

The mission of religion as a compensatory ideology is not a peripheral, but an essential one. If there is a need for an ideology of compensation and if religion satisfies this need then, by virtue of this function, it is rooted in our contemporary society. The requirement for an illusory compensation cannot be eliminated by a single act – it will be a long, difficult process affecting the most fundamental spheres of social existence. Therefore, one must be prepared for a long co-existence of Marxism and religion not only on a world-wide scale but also inside a socialist society.

JØRGEN THORGAARD*

# Denmark

## HISTORICAL INTRODUCTION

Christian missionary activity had its beginnings in scattered places in Denmark in the eighth and ninth centuries. With support from the kings of the country, a general christianization commenced in the tenth century. The Roman Catholic Church enjoyed a religious monopoly for almost 600 years (although not without serious friction with royal authority). This monopoly was broken in 1536, when a Lutheran prince was elected King and the Lutheran 'state church' (statskirke) succeeded the Catholic.

With the liberal constitution of 1849, which abolished royal absolutism in favour of constitutional monarchy, Denmark, in principle, ceased to be a Christian state; it became denominationally indifferent, with complete religious freedom. The word 'state church' (statskirke) was replaced by the word 'national church' (folkekirke), and membership became non-compulsory (except for the Head of State, the King who must be a member of the 'evangelical-Lutheran' National Church). Being the church of the majority of the people, the national church is financially supported by the state, which at present pays one-third of its expenses, while two-thirds is provided for by the Church's own funds and by a special church tax. After 1849, continued liberal legislation contributed towards a significant democratisation and decentralisation.

Apart from the National Church, to which about 95 per cent of the population belongs, there are a number of numerically very small denominations, which account between them for about 3.8 per cent of the population.

The largest of them is the Catholic Church, which has about 25,000 members. Other denominations (Baptists, Methodists, etc.) have each a few thousand members.

* Jørgen Thorgaard was born in Hvidbjerg, Denmark in 1939. He is currently Head of the Cultural Editorial Staff of the Danish State Radio, Copenhagen. His major works include *Kirkeligheden i Aalborg Stift* [Church Participation in the Aalborg Diocese], 1967.

## RELIGIOUS PARTICIPATION AND BELIEFS

There have been surveys concerning religious beliefs in Denmark, but from a scientific point of view they have generally been wanting. According to an enquiry made in 1947 among a representative sample of those over eighteen years of age, 80 per cent replied yes to a question about the existence of God, whilst 55 per cent believed in an afterlife; 73 per cent held that God intervenes in human affairs.[1] Although these results were not established with the rigour which is nowadays required of enquiries in empirical sociology of religion, it would be difficult to escape the conclusion that there is a fairly solid belief in the existence of a supreme being. This belief is not expressed in external religious behaviour, about which we are considerably better-informed.

Church-attendance, a very important index of commitment to the church, has been surveyed with satisfactory scientific care in two important districts – important, because they probably represent the two extremes in Denmark with regard to religious activity. The districts are the capital city area (131 parishes in and around Copenhagen) and the Aalborg diocese (mainly the part of Jutland north of the Lim Fjord). For 1964, the average church-going figure in the capital city areas was estimated to be 1.7 per cent [Feldvoss, 1965–66, pp. 177–185].[2] For 1965 it was estimated to be 4.2 per cent for the North Jutland area [Feldvoss, 1967]. Accordingly, the church-going frequency for the whole of Denmark must be supposed to fluctuate between these two levels.

Church-going frequency has declined in the last forty years. An enquiry based on information from all parish clergy about church-going percentages in their parishes unequivocally shows a declining tendency.[3] Thus, in the Aalborg diocese, which has a higher church-going frequency than other dioceses, the average frequency decreased from 10.5 per cent in 1927 to 4.7 per cent in 1967 [I.D.K., 1967].

The number of church-goers is greater than might be suggested by the figures mentioned. One enquiry, based on information from a representative sample of the population [Kühl *et al.*, 1966], gave the following percentages for different categories: 31.4 claim that they never go to church; 30.5 say that they go at the major festivals; 25.0 say that they go 'now and then'; 5.3

1. *Dansk Gallup Institut* [Danish Gallup Institute] took this public opinion poll in April, 1947.

2. T. Feldvoss, 1967. Translator's note: The 'church year' in Denmark commences on the first Sunday in Advent.

3. See *Kirkelig Håndbog* edited by Nedergaard. Controls disclose that the percentages are exaggerated, but that the ratios between them are correct. See also Theirry [1954, pp. 18ff.].

go a couple of times a month, while 2.8 go once or more than once a week. (Controls show that the figures are exaggerated: Danes are prone to make an impression of being more religiously active than they actually are!) Presumably, figures from the Aalborg diocese are more reliable. There the part of the population which attends divine service at least once a month is calculated to be 13 per cent, whilst 57 per cent of the population of this diocese goes to church less than once a year [Thorgaard, 1967].

Religious broadcasts have a fairly large audience: 16–44 per cent listen to the daily morning devotional. (The figures give the extremes from the five main provinces of Denmark – interest declines with degree of urbanization). 13–44 per cent listen to the Sunday morning service, which is broadcast every Sunday, and 7–15 per cent of the population listen to a regular radio magazine on current religious affairs.

The frequency of baptism has been fairly constant during the last thirty years, with 90–99 per cent of the population having their children baptised (Copenhagen has the lowest rate; rural areas the highest). Similar values hold for confirmations. The figures for church weddings are smaller, but have risen in recent years. Almost all Danes have a church funeral. Communion statistics seem to show that communion frequency is increasing – although we do not know whether there are more communicants or whether people go to communion more frequently than they used to [Salomonsen, 1966]. Only somewhat more than 3 per cent of the population take part in parish activities other than worship. Two-thirds of these are of the age of fifty or more; on the other hand, there is no difference between the numbers of men and women [Kühl *et al.*, 1966, p. 71].

In all, the picture is one of very modest participation in church-worship, but also one of considerable use of the facilities of the church on the major occasions of life. This lack of homogeneity in using the church, which can be interpreted in more than one way, and which is, on the whole, similar to the situation in other Protestant areas of Northern Europe, has given the impetus to current behavioural-scientific research on the religiosity of the people of Denmark.

The widespread use of the facilities of the church in connection with the major junctures in life, and also the great willingness to continue to belong to the church (this is in many cases rather expensive: for most people, church tax amounts to 1 per cent of their income) should serve as a caution against hasty conclusions to the effect that the increasing decline of regular Sunday church-going expresses an increasing secularization. It is rather a question of a change in world-view and a change in the forms of piety. The church in Denmark is out of touch with this change both in form (liturgy) and in content (theology); it knows very little about – and is therefore unable to take into account – current modes of understanding of life.

RELIGIOUS BEHAVIOUR AND SOCIAL DATA

The Danish National Institute of Social Research found, in a painstaking investigation based on interviews, that high education tends towards a negative attitude to the church [Kühl *et al.*, 1966, pp. 63–71], while high social status in other respects tends towards a positive attitude. Church-going itself increases with age and decreases with the degree of urbanization. With regard to church-going there is no significant difference between men and women. In this investigation a particularly fruitful index of religious attitudes was introduced: people were asked whether they would join the national church if this were to become necessary.[4] Seventy–two per cent gave an affirmative answer. This shows a positive attitude to the church which cannot be inferred from the degree of actual participation in its activities. The most positive attitudes were found among executives and self-employed businessmen. Skilled workers and academics in the liberal professions were particularly negative to the idea of entry. This may be due to certain ideological traditions.

Obvious correlations between church-going frequency and the type of occupation were found in a comprehensive inquiry on the connection between church-going and social data in the Aalborg diocese [Thorgaard, 1967, pp. 56–113]. It appears that the farming milieu is by far the most favourable for traditional attachment to the church. In cities and suburbs, where urbanization and mobility are salient features, and where incomes are greater than in the countryside, the level of religious participation is low. The occupational group least attached to the church, both in rural and urban areas, is the working-class; if the occupational factor is kept constant, the self-employed are much more religiously active than the workers. This is also reflected in a corresponding connection between political radicalism and decreased church-going. Correspondingly the age factor plays an important part: in parishes with few old people (over 64) and few young people (under 15) the church-going percentage averaged 1.8; in parishes with many old and many young people it averaged 9.8. A number of these facts are connected with the spread of Indre Mission, an intra-church movement for spiritual revival. This has been influential, particularly in rural areas, and membership is often related to vertical mobility in non-rural occupations.

As this analysis is concerned only with a specific, normatively prescribed, kind of religious behaviour, it does not permit far-reaching conclusions. This enquiry does, however, throw some light on the connection between church-

4. Translator's note: Membership of the national church is by baptism, which the majority receive, and people who do not belong to it now, in many cases have had to take some active measure in order to leave it.

going and other objective indices: communion frequency, the composition of the parish council, church traditions and participation in parish council elections. There proved to be a fairly unmistakable connection between the church-going factor and these indices.

These data are too few and too unsystematic to permit any genuinely general conclusions. The results which they point towards do not, on the whole, deviate from results obtained by research in the sociology of religion elsewhere. It is interesting that people wish to belong to a church whose day-to-day activities attract them little. Study of this problem is one of the main issues in the sociology of religion in Denmark. In a popularized introduction to the sociology of religion P. Salomensen has suggested three hypotheses for a study of the ambivalent attitude of the average Dane to the National Church: firstly that he is personally indifferent to its present religious content, but is pushed into a nominally positive, but inactive relation to the national church by social pressures of tradition and convention (most often exercised in the form of family expectations); secondly that only in the National Church is he offered a canalization of his popular-religious sentiments (which are far from 'Evangelical-Lutheran'); thirdly that his 'image' of its doctrine and clergy is partly positive, partly negative, whereby his ambivalence becomes reinforced [Salomonsen, 1966, pp. 53–76].

## CURRENT RESEARCH

The problem of what are the underlying motives for a relationship to the Church in Denmark, as clearly ambivalent as is suggested by these data, confronts us with the very problem of understanding the actual character of the religious factor of those who are estranged members of the National Church.

A study project on methods, *An Investigation of Popular Religion in the Metropolis*, was initiated at Copenhagen University in 1964.[5] Its purpose is to 'devise methods for a description of the religion of the people of Denmark'. It is not yet completed. The project is interdisciplinary; it involves the co-operation of psychologists, sociologists, statisticians, historians of religion, and theologians. Some methods have been developed by the interdisciplinary study groups of *Nordisk Sommeruniversitet* (Nordic Summer University). The investigation is based on a structured interview instruction which does not prescribe any definite questions or formulations, but only what topics should be raised. The interviews, which last one to two hours, cover a whole range

5. The team which worked on the method studies was headed by P. Salomonsen who was appointed, in 1966, head of a new section in Copenhagen University for the sociology of religion, affiliated with the Institute of Danish Church History.

of matters, from general background data and religious behaviour, to more specific matters concerning the subject's attitude to the existence of God, the afterlife, the meaning of life, and the idea of the holy. The interviews are tape-recorded and are analysed according to the content of the *answers*, and not according to the *questions* asked.

*Content analysis* has shown, as a preliminary result, that the subjects (n= 125) use frequently occuring words in very different senses. This applies e.g. to words like 'Christian', 'religious', 'God', 'sin', etc. The analysis therefore points to a weakness in inquiries which presuppose a determinate usage primarily in, questionnaires with a predetermined range of answers. *Personality analysis* is done in accordance with an advanced statistical model designed by Professor Georg Rasch. The purpose of this method is to establish constant structures in a person's opinions and attitudes.

The completion of this project is expected shortly. It will then be possible to throw more light on the relationship between various forms of popular religiosity and more church-bound forms of piety. The possible connections between these two interpretations of human existence on the one hand, and psychological status and social behaviour on the other hand should then be clearer. An investigation of this kind is now being prepared; it is intended to be representative for the whole population of Denmark. Its purpose is not only descriptive-analytic; it is also hoped that it will constitute a contribution to current theoretical and methodological discussions, with special reference to the contributions already made by the structural-functionalist, the Berger-Luckmann, and the Matthes-Rendtorff approaches.

SELECTED BIBLIOGRAPHY

Feldvoss, T., 'Kirkebesøget i hovedstadsomradet i 1964' [Church-going in the Capital City Areas in 1964]. *Statistisk Månedsskrift* 8, 1965–66, pp. 177–185.

—, *Undersøgelse af kirkebesøget i Aalborg stift i kirkeåret 1965–66* [An Investigation of Church-going in the Aalborg Diocese in the Church Year 1965–66]. Copenhagen, 1967.

Institut for Dansk Kirkehistorie (I.D.K.), Department for the Sociology of Religion, *Kirkegangen i Aalborg stift 1927–1967* [Church-going in the Aalborg Diocese 1927–1967]. Copenhagen, 1967.

Kühl, P. H.; Koch-Nielsen, I., and Westergaard, K., *Fritidsvaner i Danmark med saerligt hensyn til radio og fjernsyn* [Leisure Time Activities in Denmark]. Copenhagen The Danish National Institute of Social Research, Publication 25, 1966.

Nedergaard, P. (ed.), *Kirkelig Håndbog* [Church Manual]. Copenhagen, published every four years.

—, 'En undersøgelse af Kirkegang' [An Inquiry into Churchgoing]. *Sociologiske Meddelelser*, Second Series 1, pp. 18ff.

Salomonsen, P., *Kirkelig adfaerd* [Religious Behaviour]. Copenhagen, 1966.
Thierry, P., 'En undersøgelse af Kirkegang' [An Inquiry into Churchgoing]. *Sociologiske Meddelelser*, Second Series 1, 1954.
Thorgaard, J., *Kirkeligkeden i Aalborg stift* [Church Participation in the Aalborg Diocese]. Copenhagen, 1967.

PAAVO SEPPÄNEN*

# Finland

Religion here is understood as a more or less coherent system of the value orientation concerning beliefs, practices, knowledge, experiences, and collectivities which are thought to be connected with the supernatural order of beings, forms, places, or other entities [cf. e.g. James, 1958, p. 42; Johnson, 1961, p. 392]. Describing the ways and the extent to which these value orientations are incorporated and manifested in Finland is one purpose of this paper; another, and more essential, is to make some proposals on interdependence between religion and other social entities.

## HISTORICAL INTRODUCTION

Historical events have influenced the type of religious collectivities and the characteristics of religion in Finland. Christian influences came to the country from the two great centres of the Christian world, Rome and Byzantium, in the tenth and eleventh centuries. After the Great Schism between the Byzantine and Roman Church, the peaceful period of conversion gave way to a period of crusades between 1150 and 1350. The great majority of the Finnish population was brought into contact with the Roman Church, whereas the influence of the Orthodox Church was limited to an eastern minority.

The Reformation brought a second major change in the type of Christiani-

* Paavo Seppänen was born in Savonlinna, Finland. He obtained his Ph.D. at the University of Helsinki in 1958. Since then he has been a Research Associate at the University of Helsinki, 1959–62, and Professor of Sociology at the University of Jyväskylä, 1962–64, the University of Tampere, 1964–68 the Finnish School of Economics 1967–68 and since 1969 Professor of Sociology, University of Helsinki. He was awarded an A.S.L.A.-Fulbright grant to study at Cornell University, Ithaca, N.Y., in 1958–59. His major works include *Muuttuva kulttuuri ja kirkollisuus* [Changing Culture and Church Involvement], Pieksämäki, 1962 and 'Muuttuva yhteisskunta' [Changing Society], *Sociologia*, 1965, The Role of Competitive Sports in Different Societies, Research Reports Institute of Sociology, University of Helsinki (Mimeo. No. 151), 1970.

ty in Finland. As a part of the state policy of Gustav the Vasa, king of Sweden and Finland, it was not based on any religious or social movement, and primarily reformed not religion itself, but the status of the church. The principle *Cuius regio eius religio* was induced. Royal power dominated the newly established Lutheran Church and a great proportion of the property, income and other privileges of the Catholic church were confiscated by the Crown in 1527. Yet many essential characteristics of that period of Catholicism were preserved in the forms and practices of religious life and vestiges remain even today.[1]

Accentuated conformity was perhaps the most dominant characteristic of religious life in the seventeenth and the beginning of the eighteenth centuries. Knowledge of the main tenets of Lutheran Christianity was required from everybody. Denominations other than Lutheran were considered illegitimate. The religious freedom admitted to the Orthodox minority in the peace treaty with Russia in 1617 was not respected and conversion of the minority to the Lutheran faith was a matter of policy. Even religious practices showed great conformity. Weekly church attendance was common, and ability to read was required from everybody who wanted to participate in Holy Communion,[2] which usually happened two or three times a year [Juva, 1955]. The comprehensive Church Law of 1686 and the so called Conventical Act of 1726, by which non-conformist religious meetings were forbidden, completed the pressure toward conformity.

Sweden-Finland ceased to be a great power during the first half of the eighteenth century. First reactions against religious conformity in Finland appeared about the same time. Several branches of the Pietist movement appeared first among the gentry, later among the peasantry and stressed the personal, rather than the collective aspects of religiosity. Usually these movements were controlled by local ministers and hence became part of ordinary ecclesiastical life.

A growing interest in secular affairs during the Enlightenment was the next great challenge to religion. After the Great French Revolution some alienation from religion appeared among an educated minority. Many priests were also influenced by the new ideas. However, to the ordinary

1. In those rural parishes of south-western Finland where Catholicism was effectively established during the Middle Ages, participation in Holy Communion at Easter time has continuously been significantly more frequent than in the rest of the country [Seppänen, 1962, pp. 19–20].

2. Ability to read was controlled by ministers in congregational meetings arranged once a year in each village. Even today this old tradition of annual congregational meetings is alive in most rural villages where participation ranges from 50 per cent downwards. The average in the whole country is around 10 per cent [Seppänen, 1962, p. 23].

laity and many of their priests this secular emphasis was too revolutionary. Several revivalist movements, more or less peasant phenomena, although frequently led by a representative of the clergy, marked the reaction.[3]

In spite of the fact that these movements were primarily a protest against increasing secularization in society, and particularly in the church, they remained a reaction within the church. This is characteristic of Finnish revivalism. At a time when revivalism in some other Protestant societies led to separatism and to new religious organizations, the church in Finland was able to assimilate those movements. It is not clear whether this was due to weaknesses in revivalism, or to the exceptionally strong position of the state church with its conformist tradition. There is an obvious parallel with the control exercised over dissenting tendencies within Catholic societies and in some American denominations.

The main revivalist movements are still alive in Finland and can be considered an essential part of religious tradition. The Evangelical Movement and Pietist Revivalism have spread almost throughout the country, whereas Laestadionism, originally a Lappish movement both in Sweden and Finland, has rallied support also in Northern Norway and numerous localities in the rest of Finland [Haavio, 1963, p. 214; 1965, pp. 23–85]. Yet, despite this the influence of these movements on the type and grade of general religious activity is minimal and is primarily limited to the traditional areas of affiliation or rather small groups of supporters in other localities.[4]

When Finland was incorporated within the Russian Empire as an autonomous Grand Duchy in 1809, the legal status of religious institutions in the country did not weaken. The Russian Tzar gave sanction to the inviolability of the Lutheran Church, and the status of the Greek Orthodox was improved and legalized. After municipalities were separated from the traditional parishes, a new church law for the Lutheran Church was passed in 1869. By this law the church was given extensive autonomy including a new right to enact laws concerning the church itself. The supreme administration of the church including the appointment of bishops as well as the final approval of laws passed by the Church Assembly, remained, however, in the hands of state authorities. This legalised bond between church and state based on

3. The most powerful of these movements were the Pietistic Revivalism of Savo and Ostrobothnia, led by peasant leaders, the Laestadionism of Lapland, the Evangelical Movement in the South-West of Finland and a less coherent movement of 'the Prayers' in separate places in Southern Finland.

4. An ecological analysis of two dioceses does not reveal any significant relationship between religious participation of the average population and the number of revivalist movements and their activity. However, a slight tendency toward greater activity among voluntary workers can be observed in those parishes in which revivalist movements are stronger than average [Niemi, 1966, pp. 111–112].

supreme authority of the state in church affairs and some privileges of the church, such as the ecclesiastical right to collect taxes, is still characteristic of the Lutheran and Orthodox Churches in Finland.

Much in the same way as the earlier pietist and revivalist movements were controlled, later religious protests have been controlled by the state and the state church. Although a special law gave other Protestants the right to found congregations in 1889, ordinary religious freedom was not established until the Act of 1922. All religious bodies except the Orthodox Church, which later received the status of the second state church, are still without the rights of the Lutheran Church. Other religious bodies have never been a real challenge to the conformist church.

### DEMOGRAPHIC DATA

The traditional tendency toward conformity and homogeneity is also revealed in the composition of the religious bodies of the country at the moment. About 92.4 per cent (i.e. 4,107,353) of the total population are members of the established Lutheran Church. The proportion of the other state church, the Orthodox Church, is about 1.4 per cent, and that of all the other registered denominations less than 0.7 per cent.[5] By far the largest, but at the same time rather heterogeneous minority, of 5.5 per cent, are those who are not members of any registered religious denominations but belong to the so-called civil register. A minority of them are members of some unregistered religious movements of which Pentecostalists, with an approximate membership of 28,000 or a little more than 0.6 per cent of the total population, are by far the largest [Haavio, 1965, pp. 145–152; Official Statistics of Finland VI C: 103, 163: 24, 120–21].

The denominations that are in the minority represent two different types. The members of some of them, particularly Jews, Roman Catholics, Mohammedans, and Anglicans, are primarily of foreign origin, whereas some others, such as Adventists, Free Church of Finland, Church of Jesus Christ, Jehova's Witnesses, Methodists, and Baptists, are supported by the native population.

The majority of denominations, apart from the Lutheran Church, primarily act in urban areas, particularly those denominations which are mainly supported by people of foreign origin. More than half the Catholics and Jews of the country live in Helsinki.

5. In 1960 these included Roman Catholics, 2,136 (0.05); Other Christians, 16,175 (0.36) – i.e. Free Church of Finland, Adventists, Methodists, Baptists, Church of Jesus Christ of the Latter Day Saints, Church of England, Jehovah's Witnesses and Non Christians (0.22) – i.e. Jews, Mohammedans. The figures in brackets refer to the percentage of the total population.

A secular protest appearing as withdrawal from the church, has for the most part been an urban phenomenon. Belonging to the civil register is, in bigger cities, four times as common as in the country. There is good reason to suggest that the more urbanized the social environment or the higher the division of labour in a society, the greater the likelihood of compensating for a conformist religious body by other bodies, religious or non-religious. This hypothesis is well supported also by ecological data [Niemi, 1966, pp. 111–112] and by time series statistics.

Table 1 indicates that the state churches, both the Lutheran and Orthodox, have lost rather than won support during the last fifty years, whereas the combined membership of other denominations and particularly the civil register have shown the opposite tendency. The pattern as well as the reasons for withdrawing from the Lutheran and the Orthodox Church, seem to be quite different. A relatively large number of the members of the Orthodox Church have scattered, in diaspora, and under these conditions the likelihood of being assimilated by the Lutheran majority, merely for practical reasons, is rather high. This type of withdrawal, caused primarily by the structural conditions of society, is a relatively steady and even phenomenon. On the other hand, there are great fluctuations between different periods of time in withdrawal from the Lutheran church. The first great wave occurred during the first half of the twenties immediately after the Act of Religious Liberty was passed. The second and considerably more powerful one followed World War II between 1945 and 1960. There are also two remarkable troughs. The first one began as early as the end of the twenties and reached its minimum during the war in 1941–1944, and the second, which is still

*Table 1. Withdrawal from the churches in Finland 1920–1959*

| | Excess of those who have withdrawn from: | | | | | |
|---|---|---|---|---|---|---|
| | The *Lutheran church* *for another denomination* over those who have joined it from other denominations | | The *Lutheran church* *for civil register* over those who have joined it from civil register | | The *Orthodox church* over those who have joined it | |
| | N | % | N | % | N | % |
| 1920–29 | 4,266 | 9.4 | 38,570 | 84.8 | 2,648 | 5.8 |
| 1930–39 | 399 | 1.7 | 19,904 | 86.5 | 2,730 | 11.8 |
| 1940–49 | 2,620 | 7.5 | 28,519 | 81.3 | 3,920 | 11.2 |
| 1950–59 | 6,545 | 4.3 | 143,487 | 93.7 | 3,176 | 2.0 |

Source: *Suomen evankelis-luterilainen kirkko*, Volumes 1918–1962. Official Statistics of the Lutheran church of Finland, published in five-year reports.

continuing, began with the new way of collecting church taxes in advance through payroll deductions made by employers every pay period.

The continuous growth of the civil register is the dominant pattern, the percentage rising from 0.0 in 1920 to 1.9 in 1940, 5.4 in 1960 and 5.5 in 1967. The correlation between the time series of withdrawal from the church and time itself is also as high as +.67. The correlation between time series of withdrawal from the church and the real national product per capita is equally high. Separation from the church has primarily been a secular movement, more toward the civil register than other religious denominations.

*Table 2. Proportion of population in civil register by sex, age and types of communities*

| | % Men | | | | | % Women | | | | |
|---|---|---|---|---|---|---|---|---|---|---|
| | 0–14 | 15–24 | 25–44 | 45–64 | 65+ | 0–14 | 15–24 | 25–44 | 45–64 | 65+ |
| Cities of more than 100,000 inhabitants | 9.1 | 11.6 | 26.4 | 23.9 | 12.2 | 8.8 | 5.9 | 9.8 | 10.9 | 5.3 |
| Other cities | 4.2 | 5.9 | 15.9 | 13.4 | 6.8 | 4.1 | 3.1 | 4.4 | 4.9 | 3.0 |
| Rural communities | 2.3 | 2.6 | 7.0 | 5.1 | 2.4 | 2.2 | 1.7 | 2.4 | 2.3 | 1.4 |

Table 2 indicates that the likelihood of compensating for the conformist church by other religious alternatives seems to be higher among women, whereas the tendency toward compensating by a secular alternative, the civil register, is primarily a movement of males.

Age is an additional variable explaining withdrawal and affiliation. However, its meaning seems to be different in the case of males and females, as it is different in the case of different denominations. Among traditional denominations, Roman Catholics, Jews, Methodists, Baptists, the Church of England, and the Free Church of Finland, as well as among sectarian and revivalist movements older age groups are over- and younger age groups under-represented. On the other hand, the more recently established bodies, Jehova's Witnesses and Mormons, especially the Mormons, show age groups considerably younger than the average.

Withdrawal from the church to the civil register was earlier revealed as a movement of males and an urban movement. Moreover, it is primarily a movement of city males at working age. As the Table 2 shows, it starts at the age of 15–24 and reaches its maximum at the age of 25–44 going down again in the age group of more than 65 years. With females, although the maximum is also at working age and minimum among those who are older than 65 years, the covariation with age is considerably lower and the maximum is reached at an older age than in the case of males. The difference of young adults at the age of 15–24 is, however, most interesting. At the same time when the proportion of young males in the civil register increases considerably compared with the corresponding proportion of children under 15, the proportion of young females at the age of 15–24 shows an opposite tendency. Although it is hard to find a good explanation for this phenomenon, it can be assumed that such institutionalized rituals as confirmation in teenage and church wedding some years later appeal, at least in our culture, more to girls than to boys. Whether this pattern depends more on psychic differences between males and females or differences in socialization remains unanswered.

Differences between sexes at working age of more than 25 years can be partly explained by church taxes which on an average exceed 1 per cent of total income. Single women are more often wage earners and tax payers than married women. They also compensate for the church by the civil register more often. In the case of men this difference is not to be found. Both single and married men are usually taxpayers and consequently no difference between them as to the membership in the civil register is to be observed [Seppänen, 1962, pp. 5–7]. Taxation is, however, probably only a releasing, intervening factor, which makes salient more profound factors.

One of these factors seems to be political affiliation combined with workers' position in society. The impact of radical socialist affiliation on separation from the church is especially apparent in the case of the Lutheran Church. Among people with bourgeois affiliation 91–92 per cent (urban and rural communities respectively) are members of the church. The corresponding percentages of Folk Democrats or Communists are 53 and 75 [Seppänen, 1962, p. 10]. Parallel to these findings are the relatively high ecological correlations between the proportion of those on the civil register and leftist, particularly Communist affiliation [Niemi, 1966, p. 111; Riihinen, 1965, pp. 226–227].

The tendency for religious and political institutions to be mutually supportive is characteristic of Finland. The bond between the Lutheran Church and the state is comparatively close. Bourgeois political affiliation and church membership are also closely related. The protest against the church has primarily been secular and socialist, appearing particularly among urban males with communist affiliation.

## RELIGIOUS PARTICIPATION AND BELIEFS

Even within a conformist Christian tradition such as is the case in Finland, several types of religious manifestations can be hypothesized. The following discussion is based primarily on the author's unpublished nation-wide survey which interviewed 910 married couples – husband belonging to the age group 34–38 years.[6]

*Religiosity according to own judgement*

Some consensus exists as to the more general areas in which religiosity ought to be manifested, thus a self-estimate is a simple, if rather ambiguous index of religiosity. Table 3 reveals that the great majority (about 90 per cent of all women and 72 per cent of all men) regard themselves as at least 'somewhat religious', whereas the proportion of those who consider themselves 'highly religious' is only about 5 per cent. Among women this proportion is, however, higher than the joint proportion of those who are 'somewhat adverse' and 'highly adverse', while the corresponding proportions among men are lower.

*Table 3. Religiosity of husbands and wives according to their own judgment, corresponding distribution of judgments of husbands and wives on their parents (N=910)*

| | Highly religious % | Somewhat religious % | Neither religious nor adverse % | Somewhat adverse % | Highly adverse % |
|---|---|---|---|---|---|
| Husband | 4.7 | 67.8 | 15.0 | 6.2 | 2.3 |
| Wife | 5.5 | 85.3 | 4.2 | 2.4 | 0.1 |
| Husband's father | 17.7 | 61.7 | 10.7 | 2.0 | 1.4 |
| Wife's father | 15.2 | 63.5 | 8.8 | 2.3 | 1.3 |
| Husband's mother | 27.1 | 61.4 | 5.2 | 0.7 | 0.2 |
| Wife's mother | 26.2 | 66.2 | 2.6 | 0.4 | 0.1 |

Differences between men and women are rather similar among both generations. Yet, differences between generations seem to be greater than differences between males and females of the same generation. This is particularly true of those who have been categorized 'highly religious'. Similar findings between age cohorts have been found in some other studies [e.g. Koskelainen, 1966a; Alapuro, 1967]. The difference between generations seems to be primarily in intensity, both religious and anti-religious; the present generation is less religiously involved, more agnostic. Though the great majority of

6. Unless otherwise stated the empirical data in the text and tables come from this survey.

the present generation, particularly women, still consider themselves religious at least to a certain degree, their religiosity is primarily of weaker intensity.

A second self-estimate of religiosity concerned women's own opinion of being Christian. Table 4 cross-tabulates the two self-estimates.

*Table 4. Women's own opinion of being christian by religiosity according to their own judgment*

| | % Regarding herself as: | | |
|---|---|---|---|
| | 'Highly religious' | 'Somewhat religious | 'Somewhat adverse' 'highly adverse' or 'neither religious nor adverse' |
| | N=52 | N=785 | N=63 |
| Does not strive to be Christian | – | 6 | 51 |
| Uncertain | 2 | 27 | 46 |
| Strives to be Christian | 98 | 67 | 3 |

Correlation between these two indices is high. Almost all of those who regard themselves as 'highly religious' also say that they strive to be Christian. On the other hand, among those who regard themselves as 'adverse' or 'neither religious nor adverse' the corresponding proportion is almost non-existent. Only two-thirds of the 'somewhat religious' say that they strive to be Christian. In a more concise sample from the Swedish speaking minority in Turku, the third largest city in Finland, about 75 per cent expressed a more or less positive attitude toward Christianity [Weckström, 1967, p. 9].

If the ideas of average people can be considered valid expressions of religiosity, then it can be said that the great majority of Finns are more or less religious.

*Religious beliefs*

The study of religious belief in Finland has been approached from the perspective of the doctrines of different religious bodies [Haavio, 1963, 1965; Koskelainen, 1966], and from the point of view of how people have accepted traditional doctrines: how they warrant the existence of the divine and define its character, what they understand by divine purpose and what they consider as proper conduct of man toward God and fellow man for the realization of divine purpose [Palo, 1952; Seppänen, 1962, 1966, 1968; Pyysalo, 1964; Siipi, 1965; Koskelainen, 1966, 1968; Haavio-Mannila and Suolinna, 1967; Kortekangas, 1967].

A majority of Finnish people seem to believe in God, although there is a significant difference between men and women. According to the author's survey 72 per cent of women believe that there is a God and only one God about whom Jesus Christ taught, whereas the corresponding proportion of men is only 46 per cent. There is, however, almost as large a percentage of men who believe in a 'superior essence who is variously called God or someone else'. The percentage of those who believe either in God or in a superior essence of another type – some kind of divinity – is 84 among men and 91 among women. In comparison with some American figures the Finnish ones are lower [Glock and Stark, 1965, p. 90].

Afterlife is another central characteristic of Christian faith. Although man's eternal fate is interpreted in several ways among Christian and even among Lutheran theologians, the ideas man has about afterlife can be considered an essential part of religious beliefs. Table 5 shows some Finnish data concerning those beliefs. Palo's data, which are based on a nation-wide sample of Finnish Gallup, are older and cover all age cohorts above 15, reveal that the majority of both men and women hold the traditional belief in man's dual fate, whereas the more recent sample of age cohorts around 35 gives considerably different findings. Anyway, it is obvious that the traditional conception of heaven and hell characterizes the religious belief of about one half of Finnish people. Gunnar Weckström's data from Turku also give support to this proposal. Fifty per cent of the total answered that they believe in afterlife [Weckström, 1967, p. 8].

*Table 5. Belief in afterlife according to two Finnish studies*

| Belief | % Men (Seppänen) N=910 | % Men (Palo) N=861 | % Women (Seppänen) N=910 | % Women (Palo) N=959 |
|---|---|---|---|---|
| That all men will be raised from the dead, some will inherit heaven, some others will be sentenced to hell | 35.4 | 54 | 45.1 | 63 |
| That nobody will be sentenced to hell but all will inherit heaven | 9.8 | 11 | 8.0 | 11 |

Additional source: Palo, 1952.

*Table 6. Opinion of Finnish women on items of religious beliefs (N=910)*

| | Fully agree % | Roughly agree % | Don't know % | Dis-agree % |
|---|---|---|---|---|
| Christ is the Son of God | 80 | 10 | 8 | 2 |
| By means of his death Jesus redeemed the sins of mankind | 63 | 19 | 15 | 3 |
| Resurrection of Christ really happened | 57 | 13 | 21 | 9 |
| Creation of the world happened as it is presented in the Bible | 57 | 16 | 21 | 6 |
| The Bible is the only real guide for life | 45 | 25 | 16 | 14 |

*Table 7. Beliefs of some Swedish speaking Finnish male workers (N=428)*

| | Yes % | Don't know % | No % |
|---|---|---|---|
| Do you believe that Christ is the Son of God? | 53 | 38 | 9 |
| Do you believe that God created the world? | 53 | 35 | 12 |
| Do you believe in the resurrection of Christ? | 49 | 40 | 11 |

Source: Grönblom, 1967.

Tables 6 and 7 present data on other beliefs and show that the majority has a tendency to believe in most of the tenets presented. The difference between men and women is, however, quite obvious. Although the sample of Swedish speaking workers is not very representative it can be proposed that men have a greater tendency to take a negative position or to take no position at all. A preference for an agnostic rather than an atheistic position also seems obvious.

*Religious knowledge*

The expectation that a person will be informed about his faith is common to all religions. Within the Lutheran tradition, teaching the main items of dogma and particularly the Gospel is given great emphasis. Consequently, it can be expected that knowledge of religious doctrine is one relevant component of religiosity.

It is, however, difficult to judge what kinds of knowledge ought to be considered as indicators of religious commitment. In Finland it has been studied simply by asking how much people know about some rather arbitrarily selected pieces of doctrine and scriptures. In his national survey Toivo Palo asked two different questions: 'What is the eighth commandment?' and 'What are the names of the Gospels?' The findings reveal that the majority of both men (50–60 per cent) and women (60–70 per cent) knew at least the name of one Gospel and 41 per cent of men and 52 per cent of women knew how the eighth commandment is worded [Palo, 1952, pp. 16–18, 131–132].

In the survey by the present author interviewees were given beginnings of some sentences from the Bible, from the Confession of Faith, and from the Lord's Prayer, and were asked to complete the sentences. Answers were categorized according to the degree of success. Cumulative distributions, which are given in Table 8, reveal that the majority was able to remember the particular items asked at least to some degree. There are, however, great differences between items. Those occurring frequently in service rituals were very commonly known word-for-word, whereas sentences from the Bible were known less accurately and less generally.

*Table 8. Cumulative distribution of some items of religious knowledge among Finnish women (N=910)*

| | Knew accurately<br>% | Knew accurately or approximately<br>% | At least fumbled after the right answer<br>% |
|---|---|---|---|
| 'It is easier for a camel...' | 34 | 45 | 54 |
| 'Blessed are the poor in spirit...' | 45 | 59 | 71 |
| 'Yea, though I walk...' | 48 | 54 | 62 |
| 'I believe in God...' | 91 | 93 | 95 |
| 'Our Father who...' | 94 | 95 | 96 |

In as far as the Confession of Faith and the Lord's Prayer may be considered as representative of religious faith then religious knowledge in Finland seems to be both widely and accurately accepted.

*Religious practice*

In the case of religious belief, the main emphasis has been on what people believe rather than its meaning. A parallel situation may prevail in the case of religious practices. All practising people are not necessarily religious; neither need non-practising people be non-religious. However, religious practices, such as church attendance, participation in Holy Communion, saying prayers etc. are a rather essential part of what is thought of as religiosity.

In Finland, the Lutheran Church has collected annual data in each parish for more than fifty years, on such activities as Holy Communion, church attendance, Sunday school attendance of children, participation in congregational meetings in rural parishes, the amount of offertory, etc. [*Suomen evankelis-luterilainen kirkko, 1908–1962,* 11 vols. (The Five Year Book of the Finnish Lutheran Church)]. Some of the data have been more thoroughly analysed [e.g. Seppänen, 1962; Niemi, 1966]. Also there are plenty of survey data concerning religious practice.

It seems necessary to distinguish participation in religious socialization which reflects parents' views on children's participation on the one hand, and adult participation in ordinary religious practices on the other.

According to church statistics participation in institutionalised socialization is a very common phenomenon. The percentage of those participating in Confirmation School – a more than two-century-old tradition – has continuously been more than 90 per cent of the age cohort of fifteen. Even though there has been a slightly decreasing tendency during the last decades, deviations from this conformist tradition have been rather rare. Participation in Sunday school is almost as common. Although there are no distributions for separate age groups it is possible to conclude from survey data that up to 80–90 per cent of all children have gone to Sunday school at least once. This is the only major religious activity which does not show a decreasing trend [Seppänen, 1962, pp. 15, 26–28]. Survey data on how parents socialize their children in religious activities, especially saying evening prayers, also shows both common and conformist conduct [Seppänen, 1968].

Religious participation among adults gives an essentially different picture. According to church statistics the average percentage of those attending Sunday services is 2.7 per cent among the total population and about 4 per cent among people older than 15. It varies from less than 1 per cent to about 15 per cent in different parishes. [e.g. Seppänen, 1962, p. 12; Haavio and Vikström, 1967, p. 4]. The trend is also slightly decreasing [Seppänen, 1962, pp. 11–13]. Various survey data [e.g. Palo, 1952, pp. 46–47, 145; Koskelainen, 1966b, p. 13; Haavio-Mannila and Suolinna, 1967, pp. 84–86; Weckström, 1967 pp. 3–23; Grönblom, 1967, p. 8], also give evidence of low attendance, which is especially characteristic of the Lutheran State Church. In Helsinki where the membership of the Lutheran Church is about 83 per cent of the total population, only 55.7 per cent of those attending church in the city attended Lutheran morning services. On the other hand, Adventists,

Pentecostals, Jehova's Witnesses, and Roman Catholics represent bodies with higher attendance [Koskelainen, 1966a, pp. 94–101]. In comparison with other countries, Finland, like her Scandinavian neighbours Sweden, Denmark, and Norway, belongs to the nations of exceptionally low church attendance [Seppänen, 1966, pp. 116–122].

Participation in Holy Communion and annual congregational meetings in rural parishes does not reveal any greater activity. Nationwide survey data from the year 1951 show that participation in Holy Communion during the year was 28 per cent among women and 17 per cent among men [Palo, 1952, p. 147]. Annual statistics available since 1912 give equal figures and reveal a decreasing trend. In 1912 there were fifty-five instances of participation in Holy Communion per 100 inhabitants older than fifteen years; in 1923 the corresponding figure was 33, in 1937, 23, and it is now about 20 [Seppänen, 1962, p. 12]. Because the proportion of those who partake in two or more communions a year is approximately 30 per cent of the total according to Palo's data, it is also possible to suggest that the proportion of annual communicants among the total population older than 15 years is less than 15 per cent or relatively low in comparison with some other countries, especially Catholic ones.

In addition, there is quite a lot of information about other religious practices in Finland. Table 9 indicates some of the author's survey findings.

The figures reveal that participation in religious activities as well as religiosity as a whole could be interpreted as either high or low depending on the criteria used. A very great majority of Finnish people are church members, attend church at least once in a few years, and say evening prayers at least now and then. On the other hand, only a very small minority attend church regularly, participate in Holy Communion, go to other types of religious meetings, ask the blessing at the meal regularly, say morning prayers regularly, read the Bible or other religious literature and ask the blessing before a personally important occasion. Evening prayers and active listening to religious services on the radio and TV are the only activities which show higher regular participation.

As a tentative conclusion on participation in religious activities in Finland two proposals shown in Table 10 can be given. Participation of children in religious activities – mostly religious socialization – is very high, both at the personal and institutional level. Involvement of adults, on the other hand, can be considered medium at the personal level but low at the institutional level. It is obvious that the conformist state church, with its power and comparatively good financial facilities, is rather effective as a socializing agent but its ability to give experiences important to the majority of people can be assumed rather negligible [see also Seppänen, 1966, pp. 121–135]. The importance of institutional activities arranged by the church in com-

*Table 9. Participation in different religious activities in Finland among married couples*

| | Cumulative % | |
|---|---|---|
| | Men N=910 | Women N=910 |
| Attends church *once a week* | 0.8 | 1.1 |
| Reads the Bible or some other religious book *regularly* | * | 2.2 |
| Attends church at least *once a month* | 3.4 | 6.6 |
| Participated in some religious occasion excluding Sunday services *during last week* | * | 7.0 |
| Says morning prayers *regularly* | * | 14.5 |
| Participated in some religious occasion excluding Sunday services *during the last three months* | * | 30.7 |
| Says morning prayers *at least now and then* | * | 40.7 |
| Reads the Bible or some other religious book *at least now and then* | * | 41.1 |
| Says evening prayers *regularly* | 16.5 | 44.7 |
| Attends Sunday services at least *twice a year* | 35.9 | 50.7 |
| *Usually* turns on the radio or TV in order to listen to the sermon | 31.7 | 51.5 |
| Asks the blessing before an important personal occasion *at least now and then* | * | 53.1 |
| Listens to the radio or TV sermon if the radio or TV happens to be on, but does not necessarily turn them on if they are off | 63.8 | 78.0 |
| Says evening prayers *at least now and then* | 75.6 | 85.3 |
| Belongs to the Lutheran church or some other denomination | 86.9 | 96.5 |

* Data not available.

*Table 10. Pattern of participation in religious activities among Finnish children and adults*

| | Personal level | Institutional level |
|---|---|---|
| Participation of children (participation in socialization) | High | High |
| Participation of adults | Medium | Low |

parison with personal ones seems to become less significant when people reach working age. This seems to be especially characteristic of men among whom any kind of religious activity – both institutional and personal – seems to be a minority matter.

*Religious experiences*

There has been a tendency to associate religious feelings with more extreme forms of religious experiences such as the conversion experience, talking in tongues, being visited by the Holy Spirit and the like. That there are more subtle and less public feelings which accompany religious belief and practice has also to be recognized. Faith, trust, and some kind of communion connote these types of feelings. The components which have been studied in Finland deal primarily with conversion experience, thanking God for something, experiences of being helped by God, and experiences of the grace of God. Table 11 reveals how common these experiences are.

*Table 11. Cumulative distribution of religious experiences among Finnish married couples – the ages of husbands between 34–38*

| | Cumulative % | |
|---|---|---|
| | Husband N=910 | Wife N=910 |
| Conversion experience | 2.3 | 3.5 |
| *Often* experienced the grace of God | * | 7.3 |
| *Often* experienced wish to confess sins to God | * | 8.8 |
| *Frequent* experience of being helped by God | 10.6 | 14.8 |
| *Often* experienced strong wish to thank God for something | * | 19.9 |
| Experienced the grace of God either *often or now and then* | * | 39.8 |
| Experienced conversion or development toward faith | 27.9 | 44.3 |
| Experienced wish to confess sins to God *often or now and then* | * | 47.8 |
| *Frequent or occasional* experience of being helped by God | 45.3 | 64.3 |
| Experienced a strong wish to thank God for something *often or now and then* | * | 72.0 |

* Data not available.

As in the case of religious practices, religious experiences can be considered either common or uncommon depending on the way they are defined. If regularity and involvement of the majority are required, then religious experiences among Finnish people, both men and women, are not common. If on the other hand, occasional experiences are included, then some kind of religious experience seems to reach the majority of all women and about half of men.

*Relationship between different components of religiosity*

Some American students of religion have also presupposed that there are different dimensions in religiosity [Fichter, 1951; Lenski, 1961; Glock and Stark, 1965] and this has also been expected in different Finnish studies [e.g. Seppänen, Koskelainen, Niemi, Pyysalo, Suolinna]. The data, however, do not support these assumptions. Although there are great differences in intensity between different variables describing religiosity, all these variables seem to correlate with each other. If correlations have not been found, the explanation has always been in the low reliability of the variable, not so much in the multi-dimensionality of religiosity. Table 12, which gives all correlations between separate variables among men in the author's survey, can be considered representative.

Instead of independent dimensions one can speak of separate nuances of religiosity. The most discernible nuances based on several factor analyses seem to be: (1) classical religiosity concerning beliefs, practices, experience, knowledge, and the consequences religion is considered to have; (2) fundamentalist shade of religiosity which emphasizes sin, conversion, and the like, and (3) church religiosity which values the church as a social institution [e.g. Seppänen, 1962, 1965, 1968; Koskelainen, 1966a, 1966b, 1968; Alapuro, 1967]. In addition, it is possible to distinguish as many minor nuances as one pleases.

Because most Finnish studies deal with random samples either on a nationwide or more local basis [e.g. Seppänen and Koskelainen] it is possible that high unidimensionality is due to the type of the sample, in which the proportion of the conformist majority is high and the proportion of those representing small religious minorities and possibly different dimensions of religiosity is low. Still, this is not the only explanation. Even in a sample of highly active members of different revivalist movements, sectarians, and devoted church believers no independent dimensions of religiosity were found [Pyysalo, 1964, pp. 247–267], although different shades or nuances of religiosity, such as fundamentalism, religious isolation, purity of doctrine and blameless way of life could be distinguished more clearly than among the average population.

*Table 12. Correlation matrix of different items of religiosity in a sample of Finnish men – age 34–38 years (N=910)*

| | 1 | 2 | 3 | 4 | 5 | 6 | 7 | 8 | 9 | 10 | 11 | 12 | 13 | 14 | 15 | 16 | 17 | 18 |
|---|---|---|---|---|---|---|---|---|---|---|---|---|---|---|---|---|---|---|
| 1 | | | | | | | | | | | | | | | | | | |
| 2 | 37 | | | | | | | | | | | | | | | | | |
| 3 | 30 | 40 | | | | | | | | | | | | | | | | |
| 4 | 40 | 48 | 35 | | | | | | | | | | | | | | | |
| 5 | 34 | 47 | 45 | 46 | | | | | | | | | | | | | | |
| 6 | 33 | 30 | 38 | 34 | 36 | | | | | | | | | | | | | |
| 7 | 27 | 36 | 40 | 37 | 34 | 43 | | | | | | | | | | | | |
| 8 | 27 | 36 | 39 | 33 | 45 | 32 | 39 | | | | | | | | | | | |
| 9 | 31 | 37 | 35 | 33 | 44 | 30 | 36 | 60 | | | | | | | | | | |
| 10 | 19 | 23 | 18 | 18 | 23 | 12 | 20 | 30 | 30 | | | | | | | | | |
| 11 | 22 | 27 | 29 | 26 | 31 | 22 | 32 | 53 | 51 | 34 | | | | | | | | |
| 12 | 22 | 27 | 27 | 27 | 29 | 20 | 27 | 48 | 46 | 40 | 60 | | | | | | | |
| 13 | 39 | 46 | 46 | 45 | 57 | 40 | 39 | 55 | 60 | 19 | 40 | 39 | | | | | | |
| 14 | 32 | 39 | 42 | 37 | 49 | 32 | 28 | 41 | 45 | 22 | 29 | 33 | 58 | | | | | |
| 15 | 39 | 41 | 43 | 43 | 57 | 37 | 34 | 45 | 50 | 18 | 33 | 32 | 67 | 62 | | | | |
| 16 | 39 | 43 | 34 | 46 | 47 | 31 | 36 | 40 | 40 | 29 | 36 | 35 | 49 | 39 | 49 | | | |
| 17 | 41 | 49 | 45 | 48 | 64 | 38 | 35 | 50 | 53 | 20 | 38 | 35 | 67 | 61 | 69 | 49 | | |
| 18 | 38 | 44 | 39 | 41 | 49 | 30 | 32 | 41 | 48 | 20 | 28 | 29 | 60 | 48 | 55 | 48 | 60 | |

Key:

1. Conversion experience or development to faith.
2. Experience of being helped by God.
3. Religiosity according to own judgment.
4. Saying evening prayers.
5. Belief in the existence of God.
6. Listening to church services on radio or TV.
7. Church attendance.
8. Attitude that the church is necessary in the modern world.
9. Attitude that the church is a constructive power in society.
10. Attitude that the church should be allowed to interfere in secular affairs.
11. Attitude that the church is not a political power.
12. Attitude that the church gives more to workers than the labour parties do.
13. Belief in the power of God's word.
14. Belief that the wonders of nature are creations of God.
15. Belief in salvation.
16. Belief in the Bible.
17. Belief in man's responsibility to God.
18. Belief in God as a solution to the problems of the world.

Unidimensionality of rather high grade need not, however, be characteristic of religiosity in each society. It may characterize only societies with a highly conformist religious tradition, whereas the assumption of multidimensionality made in several American studies [Fichter, 1951; Broen, 1957; Lenski, 1961; Glock and Stark, 1964] might be more clearly proved in societies of plural religious traditions.

## CONDITIONS ON WHICH RELIGIOSITY SEEMS TO DEPEND

The approach which emphasizes interdependence between social conditions and religiosity has characterized modern Finnish studies in the sociology of religion. This does not imply that more traditional psychological explanations of religiosity are necessarily invalid [Starbuck, 1899; James, 1902; Leuba 1912], but it does emphasize that the social conditioning of religious activity is a fundamental phenomenon. In the author's recent study more than one third of all interviewees consider Christian burial necessary although they do not believe in an afterlife. It is clear that the meaning of the ritual for these people can only be understood in terms of the social context. Hence current Finnish studies try to find out under which social conditions people have a tendency to seek refuge in religion, under which conditions religion is experienced as functional [e.g. Seppänen, 1962; Koskelainen, 1966, 1968; Niemi, 1966], and what are the effects of religion on conduct [e.g. Suolinna, 1968].

### *Socialization*

The central condition on which religiosity in Finland as in any society seems to depend is socialization [e.g. Argyle, 1958, pp. 39–46, 143–145]. According to social learning theory religious practices, beliefs, experiences, even consequential aspects of religiosity, are simply part of culture, and are systematically transmitted from generation to generation, in the same way as any other customs and beliefs.

There are three principal socializing agents of religion in Finland; family, church, and school. About 90 per cent of children have been taught at least evening prayer at home, according to the author's survey data. Religious instruction is part of the curriculum of elementary and secondary schools and a great majority of children are also sent to ecclesiastical Sunday schools; almost all go to confirmation school.

The survey data reveal that 62.5 per cent of the total, mentioned mother or father or both parents, when they were asked from whom they had primarily got the most valuable religious influences. Some ecclesiastical agents such as priests or youth leaders were mentioned in 16.7 per cent of cases and school teachers were the third group with 8.1 per cent of the total. The figures reveal the dominant role of the family in religious socialization. In addition Table 13 demonstrates that the intensity and quality of religiosity is highly correlated with parent's religiosity, despite the general decrease from generation to generation.

*Table 13. Correlations of various forms of religiosity and general religiosity of parents*

| | Analysis** of groups | | Analysis of individuals | |
|---|---|---|---|---|
| | Men N=30 | Women N=30 | Men N=910 | Women N=910 |
| Man's responsibility to God | .81 | * | .30 | * |
| Religiosity according to own opinion | .63 | .60 | .29 | .24 |
| Belief in God's existence | .81 | .63 | .29 | .17 |
| Church attendance | .62 | .80 | .23 | .22 |
| Belief in salvation | * | * | .27 | .23 |
| Belief that the creation of the world happened as said in the Bible | * | * | .26 | .21 |
| Belief in the Bible as the only real guide for life | * | * | .23 | .18 |
| Experience of being helped by God | .50 | .64 | .17 | .15 |
| Listening to the sermon on radio or TV | .57 | .49 | .20 | .19 |
| Saying evening prayers | .76 | .59 | * | .13 |
| Urging children to be quiet during the hours of Sunday service | .62 | .55 | .17 | .15 |
| Belief that it is necessary to be baptized by a Christian priest | .49 | .62 | .19 | .09 |

* Data not available.
** Correlations are based on group means. Groups were formed through cross-tabulation of the following independent variables: political affiliation, rural-urban dimensions, and type of socialization.

Research on the effects of religious socialization on everyday conduct of people has been started more recently. Kirsti Suolinna's preliminary observation made among Finnish and Swedish people on both sides of the border between Finland and Sweden in the valley of the River Tornio gives, however, a reason to suggest that religious socialization seems to have a highly restrictive influence on adolescent behaviour [Suolinna, 1968]. Similar observations were also made in a study of the cumulation of activities among Finnish youth. The range of activities is more restricted, yet not less active, among those who are active in religious associations than among those who are active in other types of organizations [Allardt, Jartti, Jyrkilä and Littunen, 1958, pp. 68–71]. Conformity exists both in types of religious collectivities and in patterns of religiosity. In addition, religion seems to have an even more restrictive influence in sexual behaviour than in socialization as a whole [Seppänen, 1962, 1965, 1968].

*The division of labour: urban-rural dimension*

Socialization is not, however, the only important factor on which religiosity depends; some social situations are structured more than others to produce or to preserve more positive or negative involvement in religion. In addition different quantitave nuances of religiosity are also socially conditioned. Analytically one may distinguish situations experienced individually and those people experience as social collectivities. Dependence of religiosity on both types of situations has been analysed in Finland,[7] although the present author has put main emphasis on the latter.

Different kinds of structural conditions may be described by such concepts as the division of labour, social stratification in relation to status differences, and social class with its connotation of conflict and power relations within society [e.g. Timasheff, Facey and Schlereth, 1959, pp. 244–263; Allardt, 1964, pp. 15–17, 1966; Dahrendorf, 1959, pp. 74–77, 237–238]. All these conditions can be considered central dimensions of modern industrial, pluralist societies. For operational purposes in the study of the present author, the division of labour dimension was replaced by the urban-rural variable, social stratification by the variable composed of different levels of education, and social class by the variable of class identification or class consciousness of the interviewees. Even if not optimal these operational variables proved to be fruitful in the empirical analysis itself.

In Finnish society the degree of religiosity is related to the pluralist character of the society on the one hand, and to conformist religious choices on the other [Seppänen, 1966, pp. 112–137]. The more differentiated the social structure of a society and the more conformist the religious alternatives, the less satisfactory are the choices in face of the pluralist situation and the smaller is the likelihood of high religiosity. In terms of church attendance,

7. Osmo Koskelainen has paid attention to more individualistic conditions people face. In addition Erik Allardt [1964a, pp. 194–214] has analysed structural conditions of religious decisions at the theoretical level applying his theory of solidarity as a function of social structure and pressure toward conformity.

Finland and the other Scandinavian societies with conformist religious traditions have exceptionally low participation in comparison with other Christian countries [Seppänen, 1966, pp. 116–125]. The continuous secularization process accompanying modernisation and pluralisation of Finnish and other modern societies with comparatively few religious alternatives, also proves the validity of the hypothesis. Covariance of secularization with the modernization process is very clearly marked in Finland [Seppänen, 1962, pp. 11–13; 1965, pp. 73–89].

However, our hypotheses can be further refined. One of the abiding propositions of sociology is that religion serves a central and crucial function in society supporting what has been variously called social integration, social solidarity, and social cohesion. If this assumption is valid, it is also evident that religious pressure toward solidarity, integrity or whatever else it may be called, is experienced in different ways in separate parts of a pluralist society. People living under certain social conditions may experience it positively, people under other conditions, negatively. At least two typical possibilities can be hypothesized; religion is connected with the value system of people in *traditional* occupations and it accords with those who hold actual *power* in a society. It has also been suggested that the former alternative is more characteristic of the sect than the church, whereas the latter is more obvious in the case of churches [see e.g. Troeltsch, 1931, p. 331; Pope, 1942; Yinger, 1957, pp. 125–155]. In accordance with these proposals it seems apparent that the religiosity of those who belong to the social section holding actual power in the society, in the centre rather than the periphery is likely to be *church-type religiosity*, whereas those belonging to traditional occupations and to the periphery have a propensity to emphasize *fundamental aspects of religiosity*.

Findings only partly presented here support these assumptions. As Tables 14–16 reveal, those nuances of religiosity which concern sin, traditional and restrictive sexual morals, more rigid norms of conduct, and rigidity in general, seem to be more characteristic of rural than urban people, whereas education and class identification explain variation in more institutional shades of religiosity.

All four analyses as well as several factor analyses which are not presented here give similar results. The more rural the conditions or the more traditional the occupations, the more likely is the religiosity of people to be characterised by fundamentalism, sin, strict norms of conduct and more restrictive socialization and moral codes. In addition, religious participation, which is less dependent on distances, also characterizes rural religiosity.

The analyses of groups give higher correlations than analyses at the individual level. Higher correlations are partly explained by the elimination of accidental or unique individual differences [e.g. Blalock, 1964, pp. 105–

*Table 14. Correlations of religiosity and the urban-rural dimension*

| | Analysis of groups | | Analysis of individuals | |
|---|---|---|---|---|
| | Male N=30 | Female N=30 | Male N=30 | Female N=30 |
| Listening to the sermon on radio or TV | .68 | .76 | .32 | .34 |
| Children urged to be quiet during the hours Sunday service is broadcast on radio or TV | .65 | .70 | .31 | .31 |
| The extent to which divorce is admissable | * | –.66 | * | –.29 |
| The index revealing the extent to which divorce, birth control, and re-marriage of the divorced are sins | * | .60 | * | .25 |
| Participation in religious occasions not arranged by the church | * | .65 | * | * |
| Belief in God's existence | .41 | .55 | .13 | .22 |
| Belief in salvation | * | * | .20 | .22 |
| Experienced conversion or development to Christian faith | .39 | .42 | .17 | .18 |

* Information not available.

107], partly by the fact that the average religiosity really depends on shared social situations.

*Social class and political affiliation*

Social class is usually considered one of the most important social factors on which man's behaviour depends. This proposal seems to be evident also in the case of religiosity. Class identification used as an operational equivalent in interviews. Empirically it proved to be a fruitful choice. It seems to be entirely independent of both religious socialization and the rural-urban dimension. But on the other hand it is, at least in Finland, highly correlated with political affiliation; identification with the working class and leftist political affiliation go together, as do identification with higher classes and bourgeois affiliation. The former could be called working class consciousness [Allardt, 1964, pp. 108–112] and the latter some kind of bourgeois consciousness.

Traditionally Finland has been and still is, a society where actual power is primarily, if not completely, in the hands of people with bourgeois affiliation and non-working class identification. It could be said that a kind of bourgeois hegemony has been prevailing in Finland. The position of the church with its conformist tradition also is highly dependent on the support of this section of the society [see e.g. Yinger, 1946]. Consequently, church policy in Finland has been in close accord with bourgeois politics. Under these circumstances it can be further hypothesized that religiosity, especially the aspect which emphasizes the church as a social institution or church religiosity depends on class identification or class consciousness.

Working class experience of the church is apparently less positive than that of people with bourgeois affiliation. The church not only passively supported bourgeois goals but also actively opposed the working class movement at the beginning of this century when Socialism effectively reached Finland [Soikkanen, 1961, pp. 140–160]. Working class attitudes were very much influenced by that conflict, as also by the comparatively close identification of priests with the Whites in the Finnish Civil War in 1918 and with bourgeois parties throughout the period of national independence since 1917.[8] Since World War II, while clerical support of bourgeois parties considerably decreased, it has not lost its essentially traditional character. The reaction of labour toward the church and the clergy has similarly not been neutral. The image of the church as a bourgeois agent is clearly expressed in the party programmes of both the Social Democrats and the Folk Democrats, although with diminishing bourgeois dominance among the clergy the Social Democrats have modified their tone [Seppänen, 1962, pp. 8–10].

Empirical findings clearly support the suggestion of close relationships between class identification and institutional shades of religiosity. All items, of which only few are presented in Table 15, reveal that the higher the strata identified with the greater is the likelihood of supporting the church, or vice versa, the lower the class identified with the greater the likelihood of alienation from the church. Dependency of religiosity on class identification is not, however, limited only to those items which concern attitudes toward the church and the central rituals of the church. Church attendance is considerably lower among the working class, workers experience the help of God less often than other classes, and even belief in the existence of God is lower among them. Social class and closely related political affiliation be-

8. Ninety-three per cent of the more than 500 priest candidates for the Diet between 1919–1966 have been on the ticket of bourgeois parties, and more than half of them have supported the conservative party. In the thirties when a Fascist party Isänmaallinen Kansanliike (I.K.L.) was legal 40 per cent of all priest candidates were nominated by this party [Koskiaho, 1966, p. 204].

*Table 15. Correlations of religiosity and class identification*

| | Analysis of groups | | Analysis of individuals | |
|---|---|---|---|---|
| | Male N=30 | Female N=30 | Male N=910 | Female N=910 |
| Considering the church a political institution | -.79 | -.48 | -.38 | -.28 |
| Holding the view that the church is obstructive to the efforts of the labour movement | -.80 | -.52 | -.32 | -.23 |
| Considering the church a constructive power in society | .73 | .48 | .29 | .19 |
| Church attendance | .62 | .46 | .23 | .19 |
| Experience of being helped by God | .66 | .33 | .18 | .12 |
| Religiosity according to self-estimate | .62 | .35 | .17 | .11 |
| Belief in God's existence | .64 | .01 | .16 | .07 |

long to those structural conditions on which religiosity in Finland primarily seems to depend. Additionally, it is interesting to observe that before Socialism was effectively introduced in Finland, low class position without class consciousness was not a sufficient condition to alienate workers from the church [Kortekangas, 1965]. Table 16 further supports the suggestion of high dependence of religiosity on political identification. Similar findings have since been made in other societies [Glock and Stark, 1965, pp. 210–226].

The dependence of religiosity on class and political identification is, however, lower among women than among men and there also seems to be a difference in the nuance of dependence. More personal aspects of religiosity such as belief in the existence of God do not correlate with class identification in the female group although they do in the male one. It would seem that class conditions have had a more profound influence on men's than on women's alienation from religion. Role differences may explain this phenomenon. Men work more often outside the home than women and consequently their experience of conformist and traditional religion has been in comparatively plural social situations, whereas the working roles of women as non-employed wives are more traditional and less differentiated. Additional support for the hypotheses that the experience of pluralist situations is the significant variable comes from the rather commonly observed higher similarity in religiosity of women and men in rural as opposed to urban

*Table 16. Dependency of shades of religiosity on political affiliation by type of community among Finnish men between 34–38 years (N=910)*

| | % With bourgeois affiliation | | With Social Democratic affiliation | | With Folk Democratic affiliation | |
|---|---|---|---|---|---|---|
| | Rural | Urban | Rural | Urban | Rural | Urban |
| Considers that it is important that a priest holds the burial service | 93 | 94 | 88 | 86 | 61 | 40 |
| Considers that it is important that a priest performs the wedding ceremonies | 92 | 88 | 82 | 76 | 50 | 30 |
| Says that his attitude to religion is positive | 90 | 81 | 76 | 70 | 50 | 31 |
| Attends church at least twice a year | 58 | 39 | 40 | 25 | 18 | 8 |
| Turns on the radio or TV in order to listen to the sermon | 50 | 19 | 31 | 21 | 27 | 11 |
| Experienced conversion or development to Christian faith | 41 | 30 | 21 | 20 | 14 | 11 |
| Believes that some will be saved and some others sentenced to hell | 48 | 26 | 34 | 18 | 11 | 3 |

Source: Seppänen, 1962, pp. 20–25.

situation. There are also some Finnish data which show that sexual differences in religiosity get greater after adolescence reaches its height somewhere between 25–45 and then get smaller, at first rather slowly, but after retirement quite rapidly [e.g. Palo, 1952; Seppänen, 1962]. But if the hypothesis is more generally valid, then there should also be differences between non-employed wives and wives working outside the home. On the basis of Finnish survey data this proposition has not been clearly supported [Seppänen, 1968].

Another and perhaps more evident alternative explanation is based on the division of roles between husband, task leader, and wife, emotional specialist, [Parsons and Bales, 1956; Zelditch Jr., 1956, pp. 307–351; Eskola, 1960, pp. 84–98; Sweetser, 1966; Stolte Heiskanen, 1968]. In her role the wife has to take care of religious socialization within the family. Though there are no specific data supporting the suggestion it seems likely that the wife's role contributes to the tendency to preserve the more personal nuances of religiosity despite the fact that, in general, low class position combined with comparatively strong class consciousness strongly increases the likelihood of alienation from the church.

*Education*

Education was assumed to be a dimension which describes the division of labour from a point of view different to the occupational and rural-urban dimensions. Because its correlations with some other indices of social status or vertical stratification are high [e.g. Rauhala, 1966], it can be considered as a variable describing not only education but also vertical stratification. This dimension is not, however, independent of the urban-rural dimension and of social class. In this particular study it fits somewhere between these two. Empirical correlations with the urban-rural dimension were about –.30 at the individual level and about –.55 at the group level, and those with class identification respectively about .35 and .65.

*Table 17. Correlations between religiosity and education*

| | Analysis of groups | | Analysis of individuals | |
|---|---|---|---|---|
| | Male N = 30 | Female N = 30 | Male N = 910 | Female N = 910 |
| Holding the view that the church should not interfere in secular affairs | –.67 | –.45 | –.23 | –.17 |
| Considering the church obstructive to the efforts of the labour movement | * | * | –.17 | –.19 |
| Considering that the church is a political institution | * | * | –.15 | –.17 |
| The degree to which birth control and is acceptable | * | * | * | .19 |
| The degree to which divorce is acceptable | * | .52 | * | .18 |
| The index showing the degree to which divorce, birth control, re-marriage of the divorced are sins | * * | –.43 | * | –.15 |
| Children urged to be quiet during the hours Sunday service is broadcast on radio or TV | –.24 | –.21 | –.15 | –.09 |

* Data not available.

Findings reveal at least one interesting fact; education has a tendency to preserve those shades of religiosity which can be considered highly institutional such as attitudes toward the church, but at the same time it has a tendency to alienate people from those shades which emphasize sin, restrictive norms of conduct, and the like. In addition, it is interesting that a great majority of the other shades of classical religiosity such as beliefs, most practices, personal experiences etc. seem to be completely independent of education. A further analysis concerning the role of education reveals, however, that when education is combined with high activity in reading books, then formal education also has an additional, yet rather slight tendency to lessen beliefs and practices.

### *Personal experiences*

In addition to shared social situations there are different kinds of situations which people experience mostly as individuals. The basic hypotheses concerning the influence of these experiences are connected with frustration. Finnish findings are still preliminary and mostly unpublished, but seem to suggest some dependence of religiosity on experiences such as the sudden death of a close relative, danger of death, nervous breakdown, and a sudden attack of disease [Koskelainen, 1968]. Little study has been done on the influence of individually experienced positive situations, although some scattered observations and findings concerning the dependence of certain shades of religiosity on comparatively high social position give support to this type of theoretical assumption.

## CONCLUSION

Finland can be considered a country of exceptionally conformist religious organizations and religiosity. Differences are more of degree than type. There is no evidence of multidimensionality of religiosity in the sense of different independent dimensions. However, different shades or nuances of religiosity may be distinguished: church religiosity: classical religiosity including traditional beliefs, practices, and experiences; and fundamentalist religiosity with its general rigidity and emphasis on sin, restrictive socialization and strict norms of conduct. As to the grade of religiosity, high church membership, high religious knowledge, and positive attitudes toward religion are characteristic of Finnish religiosity on the one hand, as are moderate level of belief and low participation in practices on the other.

Dependence of religiosity on some structural and ideological conditions in society is highly evident. Increasing pluralism in society combined with conformist religion is a general condition of secularization and alienation from the church and from the religion the church represents. The comparatively close relationship between the church, representing the conformist religious answer, and the bourgeois parties representing social classes in actual power is a central condition on which the relatively high alienation of workers from the church primarily seems to depend. Fundamentalist religious traditions represented primarily by revivalist movements have some support among the rural population but not among the urban and the educated part of the population.

SELECTED BIBLIOGRAPHY


Alapuro, Risto S., *Ikä ja arvot* [Age and Values], unpublished Master's thesis, The Department of Social Sciences, University of Helsinki, 1967.

Allardt, Erik, 'Uniformity and Variety as Conditions for Solidarity and Conflict'. Institute of Sociology, University of Helsinki, 1963 (Mimeo. 24).

—, 'Patterns of Class Conflict and Working Class Consciousness in Finnish Politics', in Erik Allardt and Yrjö Littunen (eds.), *Cleavages, Ideologies and Party Systems.* Transactions of The Westermarck-Society, Vol. X. Helsinki, 1964a.

—, *Yhteiskunnan rakenne ja sosiaalinen paine* [Social Structure and Pressure Toward Conformity]. Porvoo, WSOY, 1964b.

—, 'A Theory on Solidarity and Legitimacy Conflicts', in Goode, J. (ed), *The Dynamics of Modern Society.* New York, 1966.

—, 'Scandinavian Sociology,' *Social Science Information sur les Sciences Sociales,* VI, August, 1967.

Allardt, Erik, Pentti Jartti, Faina Jyrkilä and Yrjö Littunen, *Nuorison Harrastukset ja yhteisön rakenne* [Leisure-time Activities and The Structure of Society]. Porvoo, WSOY, 1958.

Broen, William E. Jr., 'A Factor-analytic Study of Religious Attitudes.' *Journal of Abnormal and Social Psychology,* 54 (1) 1967.

Eskola, Antti, 'Aviopuolisoiden valintaan vaikuttavat tekijät' [Some Factors Influencing the Differentiation of the Roles of Spouses]. *Väestöntutkimuksen vuosikirja* [Yearbook of Population Research in Finland, includes short English summaries]. VI, 1960.

Grönblom, Gunnar, *Inställning till religion och samhälle bland svenskspråkiga arbetare i Pargas* [Attitudes toward Religion and Society among the Swedish Speaking Workers in Parainen]. Institutet för Ekumenik och Socialetik vid Åbo akademi [The Institute of Ecumenics and Social Ethics] at the Abo Academy, 1967 (Mimeo. No. 3).

Haavio, Ari, *Evankelinen Liike* [The Evangelical Movement]. With a German summary 'Evangelische Bewegung'. Turku, 1963.

—, *Suomen uskonnolliset liikkeet* [Religious Movements in Finland]. Helsinki, WSOY, 1965.

Haavio, Ari, and Vikström John, *Gudstjänstmenighetens struktur i Finland* [The Structure of Ecclesiastical Participation in Finland]. Institutet för Ekumenik och Socialetik vid Åbo akademi [The Institute of Ecumenics and Social Ethics at the Abo Academy], 1967 (Mimeo. No. 4).
Haavio-Mannila, Elina, and Suolinna Kirsti, *Rajan vaikutus Tornionlaakson erilaistumiseen* [Border as a Differentiating Factor in the Tornio River Valley]. Institute of Sociology, University of Helsinki, 1967 (Mimeo. No. 86).
Juva, Mikko, *Varsinais-Suomen seurakuntaelämä puhdasoppisuuden hallitsemina vuosisatoina (1600–1808)* [Congregational Life in South-Western Finland during the Puritanistic Centuries 1600–1808]. Turku, 1955.
—, 'Protestiliikkeet Suomen kirkkohistoriassa' [Protest Movements in Finnish Church History]. *Teologinen Aikakauskirja* (4) 1962.
Kortekangas, Paavo, *Kaupunkilaiset ja kirkko* [Townspeople and the Church]. Porvoo, WSOY, 1967.
—, *Kirkko ja uskonnollinen elämä teollistuvassa yhteiskunnassa* [Church and Religious Life in Pre-industrial City 1855–1905]. Porvoo-Helsinki, WSOY, 1965.
Koskelainen, Osmo, *Uskonnosta ja uskonnollisuudesta Helsingissä* [On Religion and Religiosity in Helsinki]. Institute of Sociology, University of Helsinki, 1966a, (Mimeo. No. 61).
—, *Uskonnollisuudesta Helsingissä* [On Religiosity in Helsinki]. Institute of Sociology, University of Helsinki, 1966b, (Mimeo. No. 74).
—, *On Religiosity in Helsinki.* Unpublished manuscript, 1968.
Koskiaho, Tapio, 'Suomen evankelisluterilaisen kirkon papit kansanedustajaehdokkaina 1919–1966.' [The Priests of the Finnish Lutheran Church as Candidates for Diet 1919–1966]. *Politiikka, 8* (4), 1966.
Niemi, Ilppo, *Uskonnollinen toiminta undenaikaistuvassa yhteiskunnassa* [Religious Activity and Modernization]. Institute of Sociology, University of Helsinki, 1966. (Mimeo. No. 59).
Palo, Toivo, *Kansan käsitys kirkosta* [People's Opinion of the Church]. Pieksämäki, Suomen kirkon seurakuntatyön keskusliitto, 1952.
Pyysalo, Risto, *Maamme eräiden herätysliikkeiden ja niihin verrattavien osaryhmien uskonnollisen käyttäytymisen eroista* [On Differentiation of Religiosity among Finnish Revivalist and Other Religious Movements], Ph.D. dissertation. Helsinki, 1964.
Rauhala, Urho, *Suomalaisen yhteiskunnan sosiaalinen kerrostuneisuus* [The Social Stratification of Finnish Society]. With English summary. Helsinki, WSOY, 1966.
Riihinen, Olavi, *Teollistuvan yhteiskunnan alueellinen erilaistuneisuus* [The Inner Differentiation of a Society in the Process of Industrialization]. Helsinki, WSOY, 1965.
Seppänen, Paavo, *Muuttuva kulttuuri ja kirkollisuus* [Changing Culture and Church Involvement]. Pieksämäki, Suomen kirkon sisälähetysseura, 1962.
(Also in Swedish under the title: *Den Nutida kulturen och kyrkligheten*).
—, 'Muuttuva yhteiskunta' [Changing Society]. *Sociologia* 2, 1965.
—, 'Religious Solidarity as a Function of Social Structure and Socialization.' *Temenos*, II, 1966.
—, *On Religiosity in Finland.* Unpublished manuscript, 1968.
Siipi, Jouko, *Luopumisen aika* [Time for Leaving the Church]. Hämeenlinna, Arvi A. Karisto, 1965.

Soikkanen, Hannu, *Sosialismin tulo Suomeen* [Advent of Socialism in Finland]. Helsinki, WSOY, 1961.
Stolte Heiskanen, Veronica, *Community Structure and Kinship Ties; Extended Family Relations in Three Finnish Communes*. Unpublished manuscript, 1968.
Suolinna, Kirsti, *Functions of Religiosity*. Unpublished manuscript, 1968.
Sweetser, Dorian Apple, 'The Effect of Industrializaton on Inter-generational Solidarity.' *Rural Sociology*, 31 (2), June 1966.
Waris, Heikki, 'Social Institutions in Finland', in Rose, A.M. (ed.), *Institutions of Advanced Societies*. Minneapolis, University of Minnesota Press, 1958.
Weckström, Gunnar, *Religiöst beteende och religiösa åsikter inom Åbo svenska församling* [Religious Behaviour and Religious Attitudes Within the Swedish Lutheran Congregation in Turku]. Institutet för Ekumenik och Socialetik vid Abo akademi [The Institute of Ecumenics and social Ethics, at the Abo Academy], 1967 (Mimeo. No. 2).

REFERENCES NOT SPECIFIC TO FINLAND

Argyle, Michael, *Religious Behaviour*. London, Routledge and Kegan Paul, 1958.
Blalock, Herbert M., *Causal Inferences in Nonexperimental Research*. Durham, 1964.
Dahrendorf, Ralf, *Class and Class Conflict in an Industrial Society*. London, Routledge and Kegan Paul, 1959; Stanford (Cal.), Stanford University Press, 1959.
Fichter, Joseph H., *Dynamics of a City Church: Southern Parish*. Chicago, University of Chicago Press, 1951.
Glock, Charles Y., and Stark, Rodney M., *Religion and Society in Tension*. Chicago, Rand McNally, 1965.
James, William, *The Varieties of Religious Experience*. New York, Longmans, 1902.
Johnson, Harry M., *Sociology: A Systematic Introduction*. London, Routledge and Kegan Paul, 1961.
Lenski, Gerhard, *The Religious Factor*. Garden City, Doubleday, 1961.
Leuba, J. H., *A Psychological Study of Religion*. New York, Macmillan, 1912.
Parsons, T., and Bales, Robert F., (eds.), *Family, Socialization and Interaction Process*. Glencoe (Ill.), Free Press, 1955.
Pope, Liston, *Millhands and Preachers*. New Haven, Yale University Press, 1942.
Starbuck, E. D., *The Psychology of Religion*. New York, Charles Scribner's Sons, 1899.
Timasheff, Nicholas S.; Facey, Paul W., and Schlereth, John C., *General Sociology*. Millwaukee, 1959.
Troeltsch, Ernst, *The Social Teaching of the Christian Churches*. New York, Macmillan, 1931.
Yinger, J. Milton, *Religion in the Struggle for Power*, Durham, Duke University Press, 1946.
—, *Religion, Society and the Individual*. New York, Macmillan, 1957.
Zelditsch, Morris, Jr., 'Role Differentiation in the Nuclear Family: A Comparative Study in Family', in: Parsons, T., and Bales, Robert F. (eds.), *Family Socialization and Interaction Process*. Glencoe (Ill.), Free Press, 1955.

FRANÇOIS A. ISAMBERT*

# France

The development of the sociology of religion in France has been determined, as in several Latin countries, by two dominating facts. On the one hand, the overwhelming majority of the French are of Catholic origin; on the other hand, a large proportion do not practise their religion of origin. Hence participation or non-participation in religious life, largely dominated by Catholicism, is more significant than the distribution of the population between various faiths. In any case this distribution is difficult to assess with strict accuracy since the state census has no question on religious affiliation and religious bodies do not enumerate their members. Investigations have to be based on estimates which themselves rely on different criteria in relation to different faiths.

## HISTORICAL BACKGROUND

Without going back to the formation of the Frankish kingdom, created through the good-will of the bishops, it should be said that the religious question in France has acquired over a long period a dramatic aura, for it has been concerned with stamping out heresies, or participating in the Crusades.

The Reformation divided France into two. The relative liberalism of the Edict of Nantes (1598) did not lessen the division, and the following century, until its revocation, was something of an armed peace. During this period and up to the middle of the eighteenth century, the Catholic Church asserted its domination in a climate of repression, in which the Protestants were not the only victims. Voltaire was to stigmatize this oppression in his writings. At this time, Protestantism, decimated, took on a solidarity typical of any

* François A. Isambert was born in Koblentz, Germany, in 1924, of French parents. He holds the degrees of *Agrégé de Philosophie* and *Docteur ès Lettres*. He was successively Assistant-Professor at the *Sorbonne* (Paris), researcher at the *Centre national de la recherche scientifique*, Professor at the universities of Lille and Nanterre. He is currently Professor at the *Ecole pratique des Hautes Etudes* (Economic and Social Department), Paris, where he teaches Sociology of Religion.

persecuted group. This is still evident today in the solidarity of the Huguenot descendants, even when they have given up all forms of religious practice. At the same time a current of anti-clericalism (against ecclesiastical fanaticism) became an ideological rallying point.

The French Revolution was not at first anti-clerical, but was unable to absorb the foreign structure of the Catholic Church, even the group who had adopted the Civil Constitution of the Clergy. For several years, all religions were abolished. Catholicism in the nineteenth century was still haunted by this spectre. With the Restoration in 1815, the Church again took on a repressive aspect, but only in its writings and official statements. Catholicism and the spirit of the French Revolution appeared somewhat antagonistic, the first appearing inseparable from royalty while the Republic seemed to be anti-clerical, or at least secular, which is to say, totally separated from the Church. In 1905, the Church became a restricted body through its separation from the State. In the debates leading up to this, the school system took a central position, for both Church and State sought to take, or keep, it for itself.

One should definitely not forget the tradition of liberal Catholicism which appeared in 1830 with Lamennais and Lacordaire, and then with Ozanam. This tradition was later claimed by the followers of the Catholic socialists. It must be said that this was for a long time an extreme minority position. It should not be confused with a certain opposition to the Vatican which arose from the Gallican tradition established by the Episcopate in the *Ancien Régime*. This is found again in the middle of the nineteenth century with Monseigneur Dupanloup who was otherwise socially conservative. Such men as Montalembert also appeared conservative, or later Albert de Mun and La Tour, who were also founders of the *cercles ouvriers* (workers groups). During the second half of the nineteenth century, it is notable that the most popular Catholic writer was Louis Veuillot, who attacked with equal fury both anticlericals and the Christian Democrats.

For its own part, anti-clericalism took a step forward among teachers, with the foundation of the *Ligne de l'Enseignement (1864)*, and also in the socialist movement. A polarization occurred which is still shown in political life, on the one hand between the priest and the teacher, and on the other hand between the 'whites' and the 'reds'. We can see that these opposing factions are still apparent in religious and electoral statistics, where the 'left' is the least practising.

### DENOMINATIONAL STRUCTURE

For Catholicism, baptism indicates the limits of affiliation. In 1958, it was calculated that 91.5 per cent of all children born were baptized. Canon Boulard, who made the calculation, estimates that, in view of the relative stability of customary religious behaviour, this proportion allows us to estimate fairly precisely the proportion of baptized French Catholics. To the approximately 46,000,000 Catholics so enumerated must be added 800,000 Protestants, 500,000 Jews, 300,000 Moslems, 150,000 Orthodox and approximately 100,000 members of various sects [Le Bras *et al.*, 1966; Boulard, 1954]. This would leave about 5 per cent who belong to no religion.

These calculations indicate a definite increase in the last ten years in the number of Jews and Moslems, because of immigration. On the other hand, the long term tendency of Protestants seems to be towards diminution. Denominationally Protestants are divided more or less as follows: Calvinist Reformed Churches: *l'Eglise Réformée de France* (The Reformed Church of France), *l'Eglise réformée évangéliste indépendante* (The Independent Evangelist Reformed Church), *l'Eglise réformée d'Alsace et de Lorraine* (The Reformed Church of Alsace and Lorraine), 500,000 members; the Lutheran Churches, principally *l'Eglise de la confession d'Augsbourg d'Alsace et de Lorraine* (the Church of the Augsburg Confession of Alsace and Lorraine) 250,000; and smaller denominations including the Baptist Churches with 12,000 members. The sects seem to have undergone considerable enlargement since the last war. The most numerous are *les Pentecôtistes* (the Pentecostalists) 35,000; *les Darbystes* (the Darbysts) 20,000; *les Néo-apostoliques* (the Neo-Apostolics) 15,000; *les témoins de Jehovah* (the Jehovah's Witnesses) 13,000; and *les Amis de l'Homme* (the Friends of Man) 10,000.

If the Catholics are in the majority everywhere (although with varying rates of practice) the other faiths are concentrated in well-defined areas. Protestantism has three strongholds: Alsace (about 240,000), the old 'desert' areas, a place of refuge from the persecutions around the valley of the Rhône (120,000), and the Parisian area (more than 75,000). Their concentration in the latter area seems to be a consequence of the general concentration of the population, together with the existence in Paris of an influential but not numerous core of Protestants. On the other hand, in Alsace and the 'desert' country Protestants represent a sizeable proportion of the population (28 per cent in the Department of the Lower-Rhine, 9.5 per cent in the Upper Rhine; 17 per cent in the Gard, 9 per cent in the Drôme, 8 per cent in the Lozère). Traditional but secondary centres of influence like Montbelliard and La Rochelle have lesser numbers: 37,000 in the Department of Doubs and 34,000 in the Departments of Deux-Sèvres and the Charente-Maritime respectively. To sum up, the localisation of French Protestantism stems both from historical influences and from the attraction exerted by the capital.

Until a recent date there was a similar pattern with Judaism. About half of the Jews reside in the Parisian agglomeration and yet Alsace is a traditionally favoured locale for Jewish communities. Finally, since the Middle Ages the Midi of France has been the site of numerous synagogues. But the immigration which followed the events in North Africa upset this pattern of distribution. Refugees flooded into Marseilles and the Jewish community grew to 160,000 people. However, above all 'the new feature is the dispersal of Judaism throughout the national territory' [Le Bras *et al.*, 1966, p. 704].

Islam must be included among the religions of some importance in France. Unfortunately the number of Moslems and their distribution is not at all accurately known. The figure given above, a very rough approximation, and the actual number, is subject to important fluctuations. The established Muslim part of the population is quite small. The fluctuations concern the workers coming from North Africa (principally Algeria, and also Morocco and Tunisia), who often leave their family in the country of origin and return there after some years.

The case of the Orthodox, in which the data are almost as inaccurate is a little different. Here it is principally a question of Russian refugees or descendants of refugees from the 1917 Revolution, to whom have been added people from the popular democracies who have come to join them.

The result of all this is that Catholicism, easily in the majority, almost exclusively dominates the religious life of France. However, two factors contribute to modify this situation somewhat. Protestantism, like Judaism, has given France influential political leaders and heads of industrial, commercial and financial undertakings as well as intellectuals of the first rank. On the other hand, the ecumenical tendencies which basically characterize Catholicism lead, in France, to Protestantism and Judaism taking a large part in activities such as those of *Centre Catholique des Intellectuels Français* (Catholic Centre of French Intellectuals). The importance of these two faiths is thus not exactly in proportion to their numerical strength. Nevertheless, in view of the small numbers of non-Catholics and the very imperfect state of sociological knowledge concerning them, we will have to concentrate almost solely on Catholicism to characterize the religious life of the French.

## RELIGIOUS PARTICIPATION

As G. Le Bras has noted, one cannot calculate the number of Catholics without clarifying whether one is talking about *active members* of the Church or simply those who are *enrolled* in certain registers. More precisely, the degree of practice indicates the extent to which one belongs to the Church. The largest number, that of the baptized, comprises a proportion of the French population variously estimated at between 89 and 94 per cent.

But the number of adults who received the Easter Eucharist is estimated at only 30 per cent (this second criterion being traditionally that by which the Church numbers the *faithful*). A much larger proportion marries in church and has a religious funeral; on the other hand, the number who regularly attend weekly Mass is certainly very much smaller.

The absence of more exact figures in this matter is quite surprising. Despite the impressive number of investigations into the practice of religion in the whole of France, no single systematic survey allows us to calculate an overall figure which is absolutely accurate. However, we possess an investigation carried out in 1952 in which 37 per cent of the subjects interrogated (all baptized, and so representing 33 per cent of the French population) said that they attended Sunday Mass 'regularly'. Now it is known that in this type of research there is a general tendency for people to over-evaluate their own behaviour, and so to interpret the regularity of their own practice in a rather generous manner. If one compares this percentage with the 46 per cent who stated that they partook of the Easter Sacrament, one can estimate that the number of French adults who actually attend Sunday Mass regularly is a little more than 20 per cent.

On the other hand, we possess differential data which are much richer. By collecting exclusively rural information, starting with local boundaries and progressively extending his exploration, Canon Boulard was able to establish maps [Boulard, 1954] dividing France into three zone-categories: a) where the majority practise, b) where a minority practise, and c) 'missionary country' where at least 20 per cent of the children are not catechized. It is immediately obvious that in the West, Bretagne together with the forestlands; in the East, Alsace and Lorraine together with Franche-Comté; and lastly the Massif Central, especially in the South-Eastern corner, make up the three great masses of practising Catholics. A part of the Norman coast, French Flanders, the Basque country together with Béarn and part of the Alps must be added to this. On the other hand, not only the Parisian basin but a huge diagonal strip running S.W.-N.E. marks out the zone in which practice is weakest, with – not counting the towns – two blocs in particular escaping ecclesiastical influence, one corresponding to Brie and the North of Burgundy, the other approximately to the Department of Creuse.

The data concerning towns present far less regional variation. What is most striking is the parallelism between the scale of practice and social stratification. The strongest difference is that which contrasts the working class with other social categories, including employees, as shown by Table 1.

On the other hand, it is among the upper ranks, the business executives and the liberal professions, that one finds the highest rate of practice. Yet, if the most highly thought of social positions tend in general to be the most strongly practising, it is sometimes by wealth and sometimes by the degree of

*Table 1. Attendance at Sunday Mass by social strata in selected French cities*

| | % Attending Sunday Mass | | | | | | |
|---|---|---|---|---|---|---|---|
| | Manual labourers | | White collar workers | | Others | | Total rate |
| | M | W | M | W | M | W | |
| Toulouse (1933) | 2.1 | 6.6 | 22.0 | | 11.7 | | 13.5 |
| Saint-Laurent (1950) | 1.7 | | 6.3 | | 6.2 | | 10.0 |
| Saint Hyppolyte (1951) | 1.25 | 6.0 | | 7.0 | | 17.0 | 6.0 |
| Paris (diocese 1954) | 1.7 | 2.8 | 5.9 | 9.5 | 11.3 | 13.8 | 15 to 16 |
| Bordeaux (town) (1955) | 5.8 | | 14.7 | | 9.5 | | 16.8 |
| (suburb) | 3.8 | | 10.2 | | 7.2 | | |

Source: *Cahiers Internationaux de Sociologie*, Vol. 25, 1958, p. 118.

education that the difference is most marked.

Leaving the practice of Mass for a more customary form, funeral rites, we find again, in Paris at least, a dichotomy between the working class, which is much weaker in its observances, and the rest of the population. The map of Catholic funerals follows very nearly inversely that of the working-class population.

The few investigations which have been carried out into Protestantism, particularly in Alsace, disclose analogous facts. Thus in Strasbourg, of 100 Protestants of the working class, five take part in worship; of 100 middle class Protestants, 30 take part, while there is an estimate of 40 per cent in the upper classes [Coutrot and Dreyfus, 1963, p. 113].

Finally, we may enquire into the evolving course of religious practice in France. It is known that in Paris Catholic funerals represented 74 per cent of the yearly total and at the present moment are again very close to this percentage, after a downward fluctuation never below 63 per cent from 1900 to 1925. There is therefore a very great stability, with reversal of the wave of anti-clericalism at the beginning of the century. As far as mass observance goes, the data deal with too short a period to allow the identification of trends. At the very most one can draw on a certain number of records which suggest a drop in practice in rural zones in the course of industrialization, while one may presume a rise in certain urban sectors. Certain rural localities in which the degree of practice was formerly very low have witnessed a spectacular rise since the beginning of the century at the same time as a new industry was being established (for example Bois-d'Amont in the Jura, pointed out by Ligier). But these are exceptions.

## RELIGION AND POLITICS

As we have seen since the French Revolution, and up until the Second World War, Catholicism has tended to polarise political life – the partisans of the political conquests of the Revolution appearing as unyielding adversaries of the Church and vice-versa. At the present time one can still adduce as evidence certain correspondences between the map of Catholic practice and the maps of the right-wing electorate. On the other hand, Protestant areas, including Alsace until the German conquest of 1870, are traditionally left-wing. On the whole, Communism has taken root in the non-practising zones and certain Protestant regions of the Midi, and the M.R.P. (*Mouvement Republicain Populaire* a party not exclusively Catholic) has found favourable ground where practice is strongest. Gaullism, which has composite electoral support and has taken a large number of voters from the M.R.P., has itself developed more easily in Catholic regions. In Alsace Catholics and Protestants are found in great numbers under the sign of the Cross of Lorraine.

Finally, the polarization of political opinion around the priest and the schoolmaster remains a reality in certain areas. However, both of these two influential figures are losing their prestige or, at least, their political influence. Conversely, the diversity of the parties in France gives Catholics the opportunity of multiple choice, and the lesson of relativism that they draw from this sometimes leads them to cross the limits laid down, explicitly or implicitly, by their pastors. In the survey already referred to, 40 per cent of the Communist electors said they were Catholics, and 13 per cent said they observed certain rites (that is, they were practising Catholics who at least received Easter communion). Comparable figures of 66 per cent and 31 per cent were found in the S.F.I.O. (Section Française de l'Internationale Ouvrière). Formerly the flag-bearer of anti-clericalism, the radical party, no longer seems to fulfill this function in the minds of its voters.

The absence, in France, of a 'Catholic Party' partly explains this diversity. Doubtless it is fully explained by the popularization of the distinction between the *spiritual* and the *temporal*, which generally implies the separation of church and state. Certainly, this separation is inoperative on two points: the question of schools and that of Communism. The parties which support State aid to private schools have benefitted on various occasions by the often explicit support of the Catholic hierarchy, and the association of parents of students of Catholic schools has played an important political role in certain dioceses like that of Luçon. But 'free' (i.e. not state controlled) education interests only a limited section of Catholic opinion. The other section takes advantage of state education which respects the beliefs of the pupils and often provides teaching of superior quality. As for the condemnation of Communism by the Church (not a specifically French phenomenon) it has become paradoxically linked in France to a certain rehabilitation of socialism among Catholics: the line of demarcation is being displaced towards the left; to vote radical or socialist is not considered by Catholic opinion on the whole as an act hostile to the Church.

Nevertheless, it would be an exaggeration to say that the religious and political attitudes of French Catholics are independent. One finds political non-conformity on both the *progressiste* and *integriste* wings. The former, the product of the common fighting in the Liberation, emphasized the convergences between Christianity and Communism from the point of view of the pressing needs of social justice. It has been crippled as much by condemnations of ecclesiastical origin as by the growing number of refusals, among 'progressivist Christians', to follow the Communist Party in its attitude towards the U.S.S.R., notably during the invasion of Hungary. At the present moment the main legacy of 'progressivist' Christianity has been inherited by the non-Communist extreme left (in particular the P.S.U.: Parti Socialiste Unifié).

As for the Catholic extreme right, it underwent a spectacular revival at the time of the Algerian war, embodying the objectives of the struggle against Communism, against Islam, and against the 'abandonment' of old French possessions. But, between the two, there is a great 'centrist' mass which appears, on the whole, favourable to social reform although at the same time suspicious of gaining power by political coalitions such as the *Front Populaire* (Popular Front) with Communists. Until the advent of Gaullism its line of conduct was mainly that of 'social Catholicism' which, though a minority viewpoint before the war, has come to be the outlook of a majority of French Catholics. Its most characteristic means of expression was the M.R.P. Today, the rallying of a great part of this mass to Gaullism does not foreshadow the future. Now after the death of General de Gaulle, it is quite possible that a new centrist re-grouping will take place, with a fairly strong Catholic colouring, or that Gaullism itself will become more classically oriented to the right.

## THE SOCIOLOGY OF RELIGION IN FRANCE

The sociology of religion is well established in France. With Auguste Comte it held a prominent position. It was to achieve full growth in Durkheim's *Elementary Forms of Religious Life* and in the work of Lucien Lévy-Bruhl. However, these were investigations into the social essence of religion in general, based, in Durkheim and Lévy-Bruhl, as in Marcel Mauss, on archaic religions.

It was Gabriel Le Bras who, in 1931, was to make an appeal for historical and sociological investigation into religious practice in France. Although little attention was paid to it at the time, except by a few historians, Canon Boulard was to be inspired to carry out his surveys into religious practice in the French country areas. Then a few young sociologists supported by a growing number of clergy threw themselves into the study of the practice of Catholicism in the towns. At the present moment there is no diocese in France which has escaped the vigilant eye of Canon Boulard and his collaborators. Certain surveys are simply administrative and arise out of the Bishop's pastoral visit. Others consist of questionnaires filled out by the parish priests, which make it possible to establish the degree of practice among Catholics of various ages, sexes and professions. Still others (in the towns) are directed at the laity themselves and constitute a proper census in which everyone has to fill out a form which records the principal social characteristics. Such work is most meaningful in a church where practice is codified and where members can be classified as those who fulfil the minimum prescriptions, those who do less (the irregular) and those who do more (the devout). However, it does not lose its significance where the prescriptions are more flexible, as F. G. Dreyfus has demonstrated for Alsacian Lutheranism.

Nonetheless, if practice is an objective indicator of integration into a church, it only directly demonstrates the 'ritualistic' dimension of the phenomenon [Glock, 1959]. Thus since 1949 opinion-surveys have comprised a series of questions on the beliefs of the French population. In short, to take up the above distinction, the 'ideological dimension' was also explored. Secondary analysis of the surveys of the French Institute of Public Opinion regrouped the answers to particular questions concerning belief in God, the resurrection of the body, the divinity of Jesus Christ, etc. [Martins, 1961]. It then became evident that these indicators were firmly correlated with the previous ones and that the two dimensions – if one keeps to the dogmatic points which are the objects of catechist teaching – in fact formed only one. It was evident that 'religious conformity' without giving a pejorative connotation to the term, was in fact the focal point of a vast area of sociology in France, although viewed from several points of view.

On the other hand, if for the majority of the French population the alternatives are Catholic conformity or detachment from all organized religion, the study of non-conformity was to be of primary importance for H. Desroche and J. Séguy. Henry Desroche raised the question in 1956 in the second issue of the journal *Archives de Sociologie des Religions*, which also devoted its fourth and fifth issues (1957 and 1958) entirely to Messianism and Millenarianism.

For a long time religious non-conformity was studied almost exclusively outside the dominant church, that is, the Catholic Church. But Catholicism had witnessed, in less than a century, at least two notable non-conformist currents: Modernism and Progressivism. The credit goes to Emile Poulat for having undertaken a socio-historical study of the first, and for having studied with remarkable penetration a phenomenon closely connected with the second – the worker-priests. More recently, the crisis of the clergy and the range of attitudes towards the role of the priest were the object of several studies, some of which are still in progress, in the *Centre d'Etudes Socio-Religieuses de Lille* (Center for Socio-Religious Studies, Lille) which is under the direction of Canon Verscheure.

To sum up the course of the sociology of religion in France, let us say that after the great classics there was a wave of sociology of Catholicism which made quite exceptional progress taking practice as its main object and then extending into the field of religious attitudes. In the meantime, other researchers were studying other dimensions of religious life in the area of non-conformity. The sociology of Catholicism found an organ of co-ordination in the *Centre Catholique de Sociologie religieuse* (the Catholic Centre of Religious Sociology) while the *Groupe de Sociologie des Religions du Centre National de la Recherche Scientifique* (Group for the Sociology of Religion of the National Centre of Scientific Research) and the *Ecole pratique des Hautes Etudes* (School of Advanced Applied Studies) without neglecting the sociology of Catholicism, looked more in the direction of non-conformity, at least through its journal, *Archives de Sociologie des Religions*. One should also call attention to the existence of *Centre protestant de sociologie religieuse* (Protestant Centre of Religious Sociology). These various institutions collaborate whenever the occasion arises.

At the present moment new fringe factors are being explored, in particular secularized rites and the political expression of religious attitudes. This concern with investigating border-line cases no doubt goes hand in hand with an implicit desire to formulate a sociological theory of religion in the modern world, which is free of adherence to any kind of theology. But this is particularly difficult at a time when theology itself is seeking in sociology lessons which would enable it to emerge into the light of day. It is easy to understand that French sociologists – who know from Durkheim in another connection the dangers of a too rapidly established sociological theory of religion – are in no way anxious to formulate such a theory and are content for the moment with concentrating their efforts on conceptual rigour. Stimulated by the work of the phenomenologists, but also scornful of the excessive notional abundance of their work, they are returning to a humble but necessary attempt at redefinition, after investigations, of the concepts of festival, ritual, myth, the sacred, secularization, etc.

SELECTED BIBLIOGRAPHY

*General works*

Le Bras, G., *et al.* 'La vie religieuse', [Religious Life] in *Panorama de la France* [Panorama of France]. Paris, La documentation française, 1966.

Coutrot, A., and Dreyfus, F., *Les forces religieuses dans la Société française* [Religious Forces in French Society]. Paris, Armand Colin, 1965.

*Encyclopédie catholique du monde chrétien* [Catholic Encyclopaedia of the Christian World], Vol. II, 2nd. edition. Tournai, Casterman, 1964.

Isambert, F. A., *Christianisme et classe ouvrière* [Christianity and the Working Class]. Tournai, Casterman, 1961.

*Catholicism*

Boulard, F., *Premiers itinéraires en sociologie religieuse* [Basic Outlines in Religious Sociology]. Paris, Ed. Ouvrières, 1954.

Dansette, A., *Histoire religieuse de la France* [Religious History of France]. 2 vols. Paris, Flammarion, 1953–1956.

—, *Destin du catholicisme français (1926–1956)* [The Course of French Catholicism (1926–1956]. Paris, Flammarion, 1957.

Duroselle, J. B., *Les débuts du catholicisme social en France* [The Beginning of Social Catholicism in France]. Paris, P.U.F., 1951.

—, 'La France est-elle encore catholique?' [Is France Still Catholic?]. *Sondages*, 4, 1952.

Le Bras, G., *Etudes de sociologie religieuse* [Studies in Religious Sociology]. 2 vols. Paris, P.U.F., 1953–1956.

Mury, G., *Essor ou déclin du catholicisme français* [Progress or Decline in French Catholicism]. Paris, Ed. Sociale, 1960.

Pin, E., *Pratique religieuse et classes sociales* [Religious Practice and Social Classes]. Paris, Spes, 1956.

*Protestantism*

Leonard, F. G., *Le protestant français* [The French Protestant]. Paris, P.U.F., 1953.

—, *Histoire du protestantisme* [History of Protestantism]. Paris, P.U.F., 1963.

Lestringant, P., *Visages du protestantisme français* [Aspects of French Protestantism]. Cahiers du réveil, Tournai, 1959.
Mehl, R., *Traité de sociologie du protestantisme* [Treatise on the Sociology of Protestantism]. Neuchâtel, Delachaux et Nestlé, 1965.
Stephan, R., *Histoire du protestantisme français* [History of French Protestantism]. Paris, Club des Libraires Français, 1961.

*Judaism*

Aubery, Pierre, *Milieux juifs de la France contemporaine* [Jewish Spheres in Contemporary France]. Paris, Beauchesne, 1956.
Berg. R., *et al. Guide juif de France* [Directory of French Judaism]. Paris, Migdal, 1968.
Blumenkranz, B., *Juifs et chrétiens dans le monde occidental, 430–1096* [Jews and Christians in the Western World, 430–1096]. Etudes Juives, No. 2. Paris-The Hague, Mouton, 1960.
—, *Bibliographie des juifs en France* [Bibliography of the Jews in France]. Paris, Centre d'Etudes Juives, 1961.
Rabi, *Anatomie du judaïsme français* [Anatomy of French Judaism]. Paris, Ed. de Minuit, 1962.
Robbin, M., *Les juifs de Paris; Démographie, économie, culture* [The Jews of Paris; Demography, Economics, Culture]. Paris, Picard, 1962.
Roland, Ch., *Du Ghetto à l'Occident; Deux générations yiddiches en France* [From the Ghetto to the Occident; Two Yiddish Generations in France]. Paris, Ed. de Minuit, 1962.

*Sects*

Chery, M. C., *L'offensive des sectes* [The Offensive of the Sects]. Paris, Ed. du Cerf, 1954.
Seguy, J., *Les sectes protestantes dans la France contemporaine* [Protestant Sects in Contemporary France]. Paris, Beauchesne, 1956.

*Other works*

Desroche, H. C., *Socialisme et sociologie religieuse* [Socialism and Religious Sociology]. Paris, Ed. Cujas, 1965.
—, 'Approches du non-conformisme Français' [Directions in French Non-Conformity]. *Archives de Sociologie des Religions*, (2), 1956.
Isambert, F., 'La sociologie religieuse en France' [Religious Sociology in France]. *Revue de l'Enseignement supérieur*, (1–2), 1955.
Maitre, J., 'Les sondages sur les attitudes religieuses des français' [Surveys on the religious attitudes of the French]. *Revue française de sociologie*, (I–VI), 1961.
Martins, A., '*Analyse hiérarchique des attitudes religieuses*' [Rank Order Analysis of Religious Attitudes]. *Archives de Sociologie des Religions*, 11, 1961.

Poulat, E., *Histoire, dogme et critique dans la crise moderniste* [History, Dogma and Criticism in the Modernist Crisis]. Tournai, Casterman, 1962.

OTHER REFERENCES NOT SPECIFIC TO FRANCE

Glock, C., 'The Religious Revival in America', in J. Zahn (ed.), *Religion and the Face of America*, University of California, 1959.

GÜNTER KEHRER*

# Germany: Federal Republic

## HISTORICAL INTRODUCTION

To understand the history of tensions between Emperor and Pope in the Middle Ages, one must go back to the actual situation in what was later to be the German state during its period of Christianization. Within the Roman province, Germania, the boundaries of which were formed roughly by the Main and the Rhein, there was no movement towards Christianization which could have gripped the indigenous Germanic inhabitants. The few Christian settlements – especially along the Mosel – were probably peopled exclusively by Romans and oriental immigrants. Apart from the effects of Irish-Scottish monks (e.g. Boniface) the Christianization of the area later to become the German state, was carried out at the same time as the eastern and northern expansion and consolidation of Merowingian and later Frankish rule. This attained a decisive stage in the political and religious subjection of the Saxons to the Frankish empire under Charles the Great (Charlemagne). In practice this resulted in the formation of a type of State Church, in which the ruler had a decisive influence upon the organization of the Church. The Emperor was the protector of the Church. This line of thought was also continued under the Saxon rulers: through granting land to the bishops they were brought into a feudal system of loyalty to their overlords.

Open conflict between the Emperor and the Pope became unavoidable when after the Cluniac reform movement the papacy emphasized its independance and then conversely strove for supremacy in political matters. Not the least inflammable of the issues was who possessed the right to invest

* Günter Kehrer was born in Frankfurt in 1939. He studied Sociology, Psychology and Statistics at the University of Frankfurt, 1960–62 and studied Sociology, Social History and Social Ethics at the University of Tübingen 1962–65, obtaining his doctorate in 1965. Since 1966 he has been lecturer in the Sociology of Religion at the University of Tübingen and Assistant at the *Institut für christliche Gesellschaftslehre* of the University of Tübingen. Major publications include *Das religiöse Bewusstsein des Industriearbeiters* [The Religious Consciousness of the Industrial Worker], 1967, and *Religionssoziologie* [The Sociology of Religion], 1968.

bishops. The majority of bishops supported the imperial claim, whilst the monasteries which had been influenced by the reform movement often took the side of the papacy. As the German emperors were not able, in the long run, to institute successfully a central administration over the area of Germany, the conflict remained unresolved and further allowed that the secular and religious princes (though legally subservient to the Emperor) gained an increase in sovereignty in their own areas. This left the unity of the Empire standing only as a symbol. In the slowly forming 'territorial states' the papal Church on the other hand, gained an influence which had been hitherto impossible in the German Empire.

The Reformation belongs to this period. It was originally conceived of by Luther as an internal church reform movement but very soon took on political dimensions. The *Reichsacht* against Luther was in fact frustrated by the intervention of the Saxonian prince. From then on Luther enjoyed the patronage of powerful territorial princes: out of a theologically legitimated reform grew a movement in which the protagonists' political and religious motives became inextricably entwined. Especially in the free state towns the new belief rapidly gained ground. Already at the *Reichstagen* (state parliaments) of 1526 and 1529 in Speyer, it had become evident that it was no longer possible to stem the tide of the Reformation. Despite several military victories of the Catholic Emperor Charles V against the Protestant princes united in the *Schmalkaldischen Bund*, 1555 brought the Augsburg religious freedom pact, sanctioning the religious dualism of the state: every prince determined which belief was to be valid in his territory *(cuius regio, eius religio)*. After the final disintegration of every hope of retaining religious unity through internal Church reform, the question arose for the Reformers, on what basis should the reformed dioceses be organised? With the break-up of the old church hierarchy only the feudal authority of the secular princes remained as a stabilizing factor, especially since the organization of the new church was threatened by radical chiliastical movements. Despite the originally democratic idea of Luther, that each community was to choose its own pastor, the emergency solution was that the church was placed under the guidance of the secular princes. Thus the foundations were laid for an actual state-church in the protestant territories. The ruler of the land became *summus episcopus*. Not least, this coincided with the tendency in the slowly forming territorial states, not to recognize any legitimate opposing authority. Until 1570 about 70 per cent of the German state was evangelical (Protestant). Transformed internally through the reform Council of Trent (1545–1563), the Catholic Church in Germany began the counter Reformation from 1570 onwards, which newly laid down the final form of religious relations in Germany. Once again in 1648, at the Peace of Westphalia a definition was given of the religious situation: the year 1624 was taken as the decisive *annus discretionis* for the (religious) recognition of each area. Apart from the differentiations in the Protestant camp which are of little import for the situation nowadays, there was a confrontation of purely Catholic states and purely Protestant states. The mass aggregation, which can be seen from any map showing religious affiliation, of Catholics in the west and south of Germany (with the exception of Württemberg) and the concentration of Protestantism in the north and east (with the exception of Silesia, which was owned by Austria until 1756) resulted from the political and religious disputes of the sixteenth and seventeenth centuries. The religious homogeneity of the territorial states (with the exception of an expanding Prussia) remained intact until the official end of the Holy Roman Empire's German nation in 1805. Only the dissolution of many small states and their incorporation in the union of Rhenish states under Napoleon, brought with it a religious heterogeneity of the territorial states, whose enlightened, absolutist rulers however had no interest in religious uniformity any longer. The principle of the feudal church organization in the initially Protestant states remained – if in modified form – until the end of the German monarchy in 1918. Despite the federal structure of the German Empire from 1871 to 1918, Prussia's ruling position which made its King the Emperor of Germany remained unchallenged. For the German Catholics this meant the psychological knowledge of being a minority, which was highlighted by the quantitatively small proportion of Catholics in the total population (approximately 35 per cent); this poses relevant consequences for the political life even of the present day. After 1918 the formal structure of the evangelical churches had to change, as with the fall of the monarchy the *summus episcopus* of the Lutheran and United churches disappeared. Legally the state churches remained independent of one another – a condition which guarantees the 27 still existing evangelical churches their existence as corporations within official law. In the years 1933 to 1945 the National Socialist régime attempted to produce uniformity among the churches, which in the case of the Catholic Church failed because of its independence of the state, whilst in the evangelical churches only a theologically legitimated countermovement *(Bekennende Kirche)* disrupted complete uniformity. The unity of the evangelical churches which was re-introduced after 1945 as the general union of the E.K.D. *(Evangelischen Kirchen in Deutschland)* has nowadays become a fiction because of the division of Germany. The same holds true for the united German bishops conference of the Catholic Church.

DEMOGRAPHIC DATA

To understand the denominational composition of the West German population it is necessary to know distributions of membership as well as historical data. According to the constitution of the Federal Republic, no established state church exists, and this is also true for the states. However, the major churches are not associations but rather corporations within official law and as such have the right to tax members, and obtain financial assistance from the state. In practice this means that every church member has to pay 8 to 10 per cent of his income tax to the state finance bureaus, who in turn pass the money to the church administrations. Any religious or secular organisation can become a corporation within official law, as long as its members and its internal structure give proof that it is not merely a short-lived organization. Beside the twenty West German Landeskirchen and the Catholic Church, the relatively small Early Catholic Church, the Jewish cultural community and several independent religious groups are corporations within official law. Recruitment of members to the two large denominations does not result from any outside membership drive: religious status is almost exclusively a matter of inherited status, which is already determined at birth. It is not sociologically meaningful for a Protestant which Landeskirche he belongs to, but it is the broad differentiation between Catholic and Protestant which forms the relevant religious dichotomization of West German society. Thus it is incorrect to speak of the evangelical Landeskirchen as denominations; it would be more apt to dub the Catholic and evangelical Churches as Volks (Popular) churches. At the 1961 census the following religious distribution of the population of the Federal Republic (including West Berlin) was found. Of the population of 56,100,000, 50.5 per cent belonged to the E.K.D. covering the united evangelical churches, 0.6 per cent to the independent evangelical churches (Methodists, Baptists, etc.), 44.1 per cent to the Roman Catholic Church, 0.1 per cent to various eastern orthodox churches, 0.04 per cent to various world religions (e.g. Islam, Buddhism), 2.8 per cent had no religious affiliation, 0.7 per cent of the population gave no answer. In the preceding census of 1950, exact figures are given only for the Roman Catholic Church. In 1950, 44.3 per cent of the population was Catholic [S.J.B.D., 1967, p. 42; 1961, p. 49]. A longterm shift of the denominational composition of the population through change of religion is unlikely, although since 1968 the number of people leaving the great churches grows continually (1970 about 200.000 Protestants and Catholics), while the number of people entering the churches decreases (1970 less than 30.000). The causes for these fluctuations are unknown until now. [Kehrer, 1970]. Thus overall the picture is one of static equilibrium between the two major churches, which together encompass 95 per cent of the German population. The other religious groups hardly count.

This stable religious duality is only valid for the overall federal area. Within the separate states the situation is fundamentally different: the northern state of Schleswig-Holstein in 1961 showed a proportion of nearly 88 per cent Protestants, whilst to the west, the Saar recorded 74 per cent Catholic. The other nine states are somewhere between these two extremes, and only Baden-Württemberg, Rheinland-Pfalz and Nordrhein-Westfalen have a similar distribution to that of the whole federal area [S.J.B.D., 1967, p. 42]. These states were administrative creations after 1945. Not even the increased horizontal mobility after 1944, brought about far-reaching denominational intermingling in the cities. In the country areas, even today, practically homogeneous denominational zones are not rare. Of the seventeen country districts in the government seat of Südwürttemberg-Hohenzollern, ten have a Catholic population of more than 80 per cent and three have a Protestant population of similar magnitude. In an overview of the socio-religious situation in the Federal Republic it must always be taken into account that the religious factor is different among the various states. As it is permissible to ask religious affiliation in the census of the Federal Republic, different data emerge for sociographically oriented sociology of religion: data which is continuously being analysed by the statistical bureaus of both major churches [cf. *Kirchliche Jahrbücher* (evgl.), *Kirchliche Handbücher* (kath.), *Statistische Berichte der Evangelischen Kirche in Deutschland* (S.B.E.K.D.)]

The relatively strong religious homogeneity of the smaller sociographical entities is of fundamental importance to the question of religious intermarriage. Despite the undisputed lessening of social control, which forms the basis of such marriages, there has been, since 1954, no noticeably steep increase. Protestant-Catholic mixed marriages rose from the 1954 percentage of 20.8 of all marriages to 23.4 per cent in 1965 [S.B.E.K.D., No. 251]; which though continuous, is an exceedingly slow increase. But with more specific calculations, in which so-called conuptial indices are used (i.e. the relationship of the number of actual mixed marriages is raised to that of probable mixed marriages), one finds that the number of mixed marriages always remains below the expected frequency. This may be partly explained by the limited sample used as the basis for calculations which cancels out the factor of different regional distributions. One can correctly state that up until now the marriage pattern is primarily one of religious endogamy. Various explanations of this can be offered: 1) the churches exert a social control which forces religious endogamy. 2) The marriage market is religiously homogeneous even without church control. 3) Before marriage one partner is converted, resulting in a statistically homogeneous marriage. This final explanation can be discarded at once: even if all changes from the

Protestant to the Catholic Church and vice versa resulted from this motive; in 1957 for example, only about 3 per cent of all marriages would have been involved. Thus only possibilities 1) and 2) remain as explanations, which combined give an index of the interweaving of social and religious factors in German society. The tendency – even if slight – towards an increase in the number of mixed marriages, appears to indicate that this interweaving is not becoming solidified, but is, on the contrary, beginning to break up. Investigations into the motives behind religiously homogeneous and religiously heterogeneous marriages are not available in Germany, so that beyond the demographic data one can only speculate.

A further field, which is often investigated in Germany is the birth-rate of different denominations [Burger, 1964, pp. 105ff.]. Although official birth records classify live births according to the denomination of the father and the mother, these data are too sociologically undifferentiated to afford further sociological analysis. As a minimum prerequisite, figures would have to be calculated on the basis of the relationship between those born and the number of marriages, differentiated according to denomination of the marriage partners and whether the mother is of child-bearing age. It might then become apparent that the higher Catholic birth-rate which is apparent by rough calculation, is due to a statistical artifact. In 1965 [S.J.B.D., 1967, p. 54], 48 per cent of all legitimate live births were to Roman Catholic mothers. If one assumes that the age range and the distribution of the sexes is the same for Catholics and Protestants and that at the same time there is no difference between the denominations in the numbers of marriages and the average age of marrying, then this would indicate a higher birth-rate for Catholics, which could be accounted for by the religious factor. However, one cannot make these assumptions. It is equally difficult to isolate other social factors which might determine the birth-rate; social class, occupation, urban-rural residence. Consequently one can only recognize that Catholics have a higher birth-rate and express the wish for more detailed investigations which satisfy sociological criteria.

Among the denominational controversies, the problem of divorce is dominant. In 1965 45 per cent of all dissolved marriages were homogeneously Protestant, 22 per cent Catholic and just on 23 per cent Protestant-Catholic marriages [S.J.B.D., 1967, p. 59]. As there is no information as to the denominational structure of total marriages in the population, one can only speculate about this. If one takes into account that more than 66 per cent of all divorces occur in the first ten years of marriage, it is possible to say with all due caution that Protestant marriages show a higher probability for divorce than Catholic ones, whilst religious inter-marriages contribute under certain circumstances divorce figures proportional to their numbers. More specific investigations could show that religious influence on divorce figures is negatively correlated with the population density. This leads to the conclusion that the social control of the Catholic Church through its strict divorce laws is still only efficient in country areas. Apart from that it must be kept in mind that civil divorce is only one of the possibilities for disintegration of a marriage. American studies show that the number of divorces and cases of wilful desertion are negatively correlated for Catholics and Protestants.

All the results which indicate different demographic features for Catholics and Protestants lead to the question of whether there is a true dependent relationship where the religious factor functions as an independent variable, or whether a spurious correlation may exist. Even if, as in the case of higher fertility rates or divorce, there is a theological cause, this does not mean that there is nothing else relevant from the social context. This is shown in one area where there is little religious influence: internal migration between the various states in Germany which have previously shown a religious homogeneity has not led to general denominational heterogeneity, but has rather tended to stabilize the denominational *status quo* [S.B.E.K.D., Nos. 280, 284, 285]. An explanation of this phenomenon is not possible on the basis of existing data, for it does not concern any sociological predictions. With some caution one can guess that there are differentiated patterns of social attitudes in Germany, which are either caused by religion or at least correspond with religious affiliation and often unconsciously result in a special tendency for migrating groups to remain cohesive. In general it may be stated that the interesting field of demography is used very little in sociology. This is all the more astonishing as it was demographic studies which at the beginning of the century gave an impetus for the fruitful development of religious sociology.

## RELIGIOUS PARTICIPATION AND BELIEFS

From statistical analysis West Germany is shown as a society where the population is organized almost totally into one or other of the two major churches. Membership in either the evangelical or Catholic church is a matter of unquestioned, inherited social status, which is as noteworthy as the nationality with which one is born. The social basis of this popular church membership is baptism, which in West Germany is practised nearly exclusively as infant baptism (within the first three months of the child's life). As – with the exception of the years between 1933–45 – no decrease in baptisms can be discerned, automatic recruiting for the churches is ensured and also the long-term numerical relationship of one church to another. The motives behind parental actions in having their children baptized are virtually unknown. Direct social motivation is not likely, as the baptismal service is becoming increasingly private and is seen as a special event for the participation of the immediate family. A minor study – not representative – showed that Protestant industrial workers did not regard baptism as necessary because of social pressure, but rather because membership of a church could bring with it positive social consequences [Kehrer, 1968, p. 150]. One may well suppose that the churches in the eyes of their members are not so much voluntary organizations, but are seen rather as quasi-state administrations, for which the concept of 'member' is not applicable in a strict sense. The structure of church organizations further supports this attitude. The minister in his parish is largely independent of support from parish members. He has attained an education equivalent to that of a civil servant at a state university, is payed by a central administration, which also finances the investiture of the parish.

Whilst almost all members of the church are baptized and have church burials, church weddings are showing a slight decreasing trend. In 1890 nearly 100 per cent of all Protestant couples were married within the Church. By 1933 the proportion had decreased steadily to 88 per cent, by 1939 it was just over 60 per cent, but since the end of World War II it has once again risen to over 80 per cent. Apart from low numbers caused by the National Socialist régime, the rate appears to have stabilized for religiously homogeneous marriages at about 85 per cent. The reasons for church weddings are very complex. Firstly, although civil marriages have been obligatory in Germany for the past 90 years, they have never attained the ceremonial status of church weddings. Also marriage is one of the few events in the life of a person which even today in West Germany is celebrated with a certain amount of display, and some rituals (white dress for the bride) are still retained. On the other hand, a church wedding is connected with a certain amount of financial expenditure – against which the churches protest in vain – and is consequently rejected by some young couples in straitened financial positions. In addition, not marrying within the church does not prevent the baptism of any children from that marriage. Finally one might add that church rites, as they are seen by the general population, are not religious practices, so much as quasi-governmental administrative acts.

A completely different picture presents itself when one looks at participation of the general population in regular ritual and non-ritual functions of the churches. The real or presumed secularization, which theologians believe is taking place, does not concern itself least with the small number of church members at divine service and other church functions. Following the development in France by G. le Bras and F. Boulard of '*sociologie religieuse*', investigations were also undertaken in the 1950's in Germany which attempted to discover the *practique religieuse* of mainly the Catholic population. The main method used was counting the various attendances at Mass. This method was largely taken over from France [Greinacher, 1955]. Although in present-day religious sociology the question of religious participation is only minor, it is necessary for a complete picture of the religious situation in the Federal Republic to form an impression which allows a more differentiated idea of religious organization than that obtained purely from demographic statistical data. According to the results of opinion-research, we know that 27 per cent of the total population state they go regularly to divine service, 29 per cent state they seldom go and 20 per cent state that they never go [J.M., 1947–1955; 1956, p. 11]. All the same these findings are not so straight-forward, as Reigrotzki [1956] was able to show that Catholics understand only attendance at Mass every Sunday as being regular attendance, whilst Protestants who go to divine service once a month consider themselves regular attenders. Even if one disregards these differences, there still remains the fact that education, urban-rural differentiation, age and sex correlate with frequency of church attendance. As a rough generalization one can say: 1) Women attend church more often than men (23 per cent of the men call themselves regular church attenders compared with 33 per cent of the women; 24 per cent of the men never go to divine service compared with only 12 per cent of the women). 2) The most frequent attendance is shown by the age group over 60, the least frequent by those aged between 30 and 45 [Reigrotzki, 1956, pp. 20ff was able to show that this applied particularly to Catholic men, but was not so apparent with Protestants and women]. 3) Whilst Reigrotzki came to the conclusion that men who had matriculated went to church on the average more frequently than those who had finished primary school or lower secondary school levels, the Institute for Demoscopy indicated rather a reverse relationship. As Reigrotzki's study was planned with sociological differentiation, the results under the circumstances are more reliable. In any case it is certain that level of school attainment and attendance at divine service are correlated positively rather than negatively. 4) As expected, frequency of attendance at divine service and population of the parish are negatively correlated. This latter result contradicts our third conclusion. It is certain that fewer academics live in rural regions than in urban regions. If both relationships were equally strong, they would have to cancel each other out, or at least cause a differentiation of the individual correlations. Unfortunately we do not possess any material which gives more than two factor relationships. In order to do this, either questioned samples would have to be large enough for the groups to remain of sufficient size, or comparative rural-urban studies would have to be carried out, which would have to contain far more material than is obtainable from the statistical bureaus. The disadvantage of the school of *sociologie religieuse* in its restriction on *practique religieuse* is most noticeable in that it overlooks the whole field of attitudes and the complexity of social factors. The determination of correlations alone defines the research subject. To then give a 'sociological' explanation, 'sociologists' of religion often make use of social preconceptions: that age is related to religious inclination, that women are more religiously disposed, that urbanization leads to secularization, etc. The 'value' of such phenomena need not be discussed. The interesting question, of whether the higher rate of religious participation in older people is due to attitudes obtained during the socialization process or on the other hand is part of the socio-cultural defined role of old people, can not be correctly answered at present; even if the implied correlation in the second relationship would seem to indicate that this may be correct. The sociologically relevant question should be: what social function does divine service have in the social system of the community, and in the social system of the family? The pastoral tendency of German church sociology after 1950 however has prevented this question becoming central. With the theologically based concept of a separation (diastasis) between church and society, which is now being increasingly criticised by religious sociology [Matthes, 1964] and the tendency to see sociology as an instrument for increased efficiency in handling church matters, it was not possible to view forms of religious participation as social actions. Thus although the *sociologie religieuse* has resulted in a series of sociographical results, it has not contributed significantly to any deeper understanding of sociological knowledge. A few years ago, an experiment was undertaken to analyse the frequency of church attendance of different groups with the help of a questionnaire borrowed from research into stereotypes – 'how nations see each other'. Peter-Habermann [1967] was able to show that the images held by the 'church-goer' were largely those characteristics which indicated an inability to 'overcome the problems of living', and consequently one cannot identify the majority of the population with the church-going population. Even if Peter-Habermann's study cannot be regarded as representative, her results do largely concur with other qualitative studies [Kehrer, 1966]. Furthermore it supports the formulation emerging from another investigation in Reutlingen (Württemberg), that the religious are on the fringe of overall society [Goldschmidt *et al.*, 1960, p. 130]. With all due caution, one can say that there is a difference between nominal church membership and participation in church rituals, which is dependent on many factors in the social structure and on the cultural patterns of West German society. In this context it must be kept in mind also that often traditional cultural patterns shape the outward appearance of a religion over the centuries, so that differences appear between parishes, making it doubtful whether, in a strict sociological sense, one can speak of a single characteristic of church membership. In the framework of the parish – the only social area where a differentiation of the membership role can be investigated – it is possible, according to Luckmann, to distinguish four different forms of membership: a) the leaders, b) those who are active in church functions, c) those who attend community worship, and d) those who are on the parish fringe [Goldschmidt *et al.*, 1960, p. 130]. Together these four categories form the church community. To determine the categories, three variables are used: ritual participation (e.g. attendance at divine service), non-ritual participation (e.g: participation in church affairs), and subjective identification. The above model of the differentiated membership role appears because of the decline in manifestation of the variables from the first to the fourth category. The model itself is a modified adaptation of Fichter's [1958] classification, which was very skillfully applied to the conditions of German Protestantism. Köster [1960] published the results of an investigation which concentrated on a sociological analysis of the leadership level and the active core of a north German parish. From this it becomes clear that the active core of a parish is 1) socially very narrow, i.e. composed of only few social strata, in which the traditional middleclass occupations especially attain a prominent place, 2) the beliefs of these groups of people, in no way coincide with theological doctrine. Thus this investigation also confirms the supposition that to be religiously active stems from diverse social motives. The predominance of the middle classes in the active parish has already been demonstrated from differentiated figures of attendance at Mass for Catholics [Greinacher, 1963] and seen within the framework of community studies on Protestants [Bismarck, 1954; Pflaum, 1954]. Thus in six selected German towns, for every 100 Catholic workers, at the most 24 attend Mass, whilst in the same towns, of 100 officials, 50 or more consistently attend Mass (except Munich with 33 per cent). Naturally this finding again correlates with the connection between income and Mass attendance. Manual workers for the most part take the least part in the life of the parish. As in Germany there are no noteworthy sects which could provide a religious equivalent for the working class, the basic religious needs – insofar as these can be at all assumed – of the workers have to be satisfied outside organised religious bodies. One can assume that at least until 1933 this function was fulfilled in part by the political and union organizations of the working class which to a certain extent developed ritual forms. The situation outlined earlier of the evangelical churches before 1918, allowed these to become a conservative element in the social structure of a monarchical society which the workers saw as the ally of feudal and bourgeois opposition. The situation of Catholicism was somewhat different, as it found itself in the position of a social minority and therefore developed stronger tendencies towards comprehensive socio-religious socialization, which was expressed in, among other things, the existence up until 1933 of fairly strong Catholic unions. Still, not even the Catholic Church could prevent large groups of the working class developing into 'dormant Catholics'. The causal chain of these historical conditions is still noticeable today, especially as the most enduring attitudes towards church and religion are obtained through the child socialization process.

Recently, several investigations on the religious beliefs of the West German population were published [Kehrer, 1966, Harenberg, 1968; Wölber, 1959], which follow the forgotten tradition established in the studies of Rade, Levenstein, Dehn and Piechowski. These new investigations attempt to overcome the narrow beginning made by the *pratique religieuse* type of restricted church sociology. They encounter the special problem that systems of modern theological belief are so varied that a direct confrontation with the people's view of the world is impossible. However, all the investigations showed that there is a large discrepancy between the theological understanding of the belief and the church on the one hand and on the other their social interpretation. Even the faithful, measured in terms of action criteria, do not appear to be in a position to understand the theological meaning. Overall the picture appears to be one of distanced well-meaning towards the church, which is connected with a widespread rejection of the traditional content of Christian belief (e.g. the divinity of Jesus Christ, the Resurrection, etc.). Most widespread is belief in God, but it does not reach the extent which Herberg [1955] reports for the U.S.A. Exact figures are here purposely absent, as the only representative investigation into belief in God did not put the question in such a way as to be reliable. However, the finding that a virulent antipathy to the church does not exist may be taken as certain. The basis of concurrence nevertheless, should be seen more in terms of moral than of religious conviction. It must always be kept in mind that in Germany in the last 400 years the question of religious affiliation was not subject to individual decision (nor is it nowadays), and that churches are not primarily experienced in face-to-face contact, but are seen rather as large administrative concerns which manifest themselves at a community level through an official who originally also commanded political resources. The religious revival, which occurred in Germany also after 1945, was not so much concerned with a revived belief as with an upward revaluation of the churches, which had emerged relatively uncompromised from the National Socialist state.

## SOCIAL CORRELATES OF RELIGION

The different denominational recruiting of relevant social groups in Germany at the beginning of the twentieth century gave the impetus for the most important contribution which German sociology made to religious sociology. As is well known, Max Weber, in his study *The Protestant Ethic and the Spirit of Capitalism* began with a presentation of the educational and material differences between Catholics and Protestants in Baden. Although similar connections had already been recognised by the philosophers of the Enlightenment, it was Weber who for the first time interpreted these connections in a historically causal sense. Although the critique by K. Samuelsson [1964] of Weber's data has made it clear to even the most partisan defenders of the Weber-thesis that the roughly calculated figures on which Weber based his theory should be interpreted differently, the overall result shows that often denominational differences match other social differences. It is the task of sociology to make clear, whether here in fact it is a case of religiously caused social differences, or if it is not much more a case of mutual third factors which act as causal agents. As in the second section where we indicated the possible connection between demographic structure of the population and its religious composition, we will attempt now to describe the results of German religious sociology, insofar as it is concerned with the sociologically explicable relationship between social and religious structures. The separation of this section from the second one on demography is naturally artificial, as the so-called natural structuring of the population does not remain uninfluenced by social phenomena either.

The problem under consideration can best be attacked by way of differentiated sociological investigations, as for example in the model study by G. Lenski *The Religious Factor* [1961]. A comparable investigation does not exist in Germany. E. Reigrotzki's *Social Interweavings in the Federal Republic* [1956] could be named, although it has the disadvantage (a weakness which is insurmountable in the sociology of religion) that instead of putting forth a precise question at the beginning of his material, Reigrotzki attempts to show generally the connections between religious, political and leisure-time activities. Other investigations, which are cited below pose a precise religious sociological problem, but are nevertheless often based on official statistics which are again not sufficiently differentiated to prevent any possibility of spurious correlation. To explain the connections between social structures and religious factors, it is often necessary to take a path of informed sociological supposition as it would be frivolous to attempt the exact testing of hypotheses on the basis of the fragmentary materials available. Three areas, which have been relatively better researched, will be dealt with 1) denomination and education; 2) denomination and social stratification (occupation); 3) denomination and voting behaviour. Since the appearance of Weber's work, the cliché about the inferior education standards of the Catholics compared with that of the Protestants has become the subject matter of often irrational controversies between the denominations. As this question lends itself well to statistical investigation one can, for instance, work on the basis of the number of pupils in different types of schools. This can be followed up through official statistics which publish regularly the denominational composition of students. For the non-German reader we must point out that the German school system has three levels. Following a primary school which is obligatory for all children for four years (ages 6 to 10), one can then either, a) continue at primary school for what is nowadays a further 5 years or b) attend a secondary school for 6 years, or c) attend a grammar school for 9 years (various small modifications among the states need to be considered). A change from one type of school to another is unusual. University education requires as a prerequisite the successful completion of a grammar school education. Erlinghagen [1965] published all the available data he could find, which show that the Catholic population in the Federal Republic is not as well educated. The weakness of these data lies in that in each case figures are calculated on the proportion of Catholics attending the different types of schools and the proportion of Catholics in the population. These figures are valid only on the assumption that Catholics and Protestants are quite identically distributed along social levels, regions, etc. One can safely say that this assumption is false. Some other data can be cited to show the Catholic educational deficiency: in 1963 77 per cent of the Munich population was Catholic and 23 per cent was Protestant. In the primary schools, the proportion of Catholic to Protestant pupils was very nearly identical. In the grammar schools, 53 per cent of the pupils were Catholic and 42 per cent were Protestant [Erlinghagen, 1965, p. 48]. In 1955–56, 56.5 per cent of the students at universities and other tertiary institutes were Protestant and 39.5 per cent were Catholic, but the denominational structure of the population at that time (1955) showed 51.2 per cent Protestants and 45.2 per cent Catholics. But also within student groups there are considerable differences: thus the proportion of Catholic students in the scientific-technical and medical faculties is very small, whilst in the arts disciplines the contrast is less pronounced. These data are of interest not only to politicians in charge of cultural affairs but are also relevant to the sociologist, as formal education is becoming increasingly the institutionalized channel of social mobility. Educational discrepancies perpetuate themselves in social categories. Even if we can be sure that different educational levels between denominations have not increased during the last fifty years but rather decreased, the discrepancies are today still large enough so that one can speak of considerable inequality in opportunity for Catholics compared with Protestants. Apart from the Weber thesis, we have no way of explaining this phenomenon. However, before one sees the above examples of data as a confirmation of the Weber hypothesis, it would be necessary to refine the methods of investigation to the extent that they attain statistical reliability. Firstly one would have to make sure that the Catholic deficiency in education is independent of social class, and if it were feasible, investigations into the socialisation atmosphere of the family would be necessary, as according to current sociological knowledge it is here that conscious attitudes which are likely to determine later behaviour are formed. However, according to other investigations it is thought that differential attendance at school is a variable dependent on social class. As even nowadays the German school system is in practice a class system in that the decision as to which type of school a child will attend is mainly dependent on the family's status, the differences in school attendance due to different classes are higher than that caused by the respective denominations. Six per cent of all students at German universities come from working-class families, whilst nearly 45 per cent of the population are manual workers.

The relevant question here is the one of the relationship between denomination and social class. The investigation carried out by Janowitz [1958] in West Germany showed that 34 per cent of those questioned among the upper middle-class were Catholic and 66 per cent Protestant. Even if the upper boundary of the middle-class as defined by Janowitz is very questionable, the overall result is reliable. Other investigations [Scheuch and Rüschemayer, 1960] show that there is no relationship between social class and denomination. This contradiction can probably be explained by the fact that Janowitz based his findings on a random sample of the total population of West Germany, whilst Scheuch and Rüschemeyer restricted their investigation to Cologne, a predominantly Catholic city. This would appear to indicate that class models are dependent on the geographical area in which they occur. Occupational groups among the upper middle-class are urban occupations, and more Protestants live in urban regions than Catholics, however, in a predominantly Catholic city, Catholics would have had the opportunity to penetrate all areas equally. Naturally this result indicates a social fact which requires sociological explanation but also an historical explanation. In this case, two historical happenings stand out: 1) it was the free cities of the empire which in the sixteenth century quickly became Protestant (a verification of the 'Marxist' explanation of the Weber thesis as put forward by Birnbaum [1953]), 2) the later ruling power of Germany, Prussia, was Protestant. These two factors taken together could under certain circumstances explain adequately why a class model standing for the whole of West Germany should find itself with an excessive proportion of Protestants in the upper middle-class, whilst the same phenomenon does not occur in the originally Catholic town of Cologne. In contrast to the Warner approach to social class it is more meaningful in the case of Germany to see occupation as being the most relevant criterion of social class. If one concentrates in the first place on the social *élites* (which are part of the upper class without question), glaring inequalities in the denominational composition of these *élites* become apparent. Zapf has exhaustively investigated the composition of the *élites* in Germany. Thus in 1965, of 78 high-ranking generals in the West German army, 78 per cent were Protestant and 18 per cent were Catholic. In 1951 of 153 professors at the University of Freiburg (in predominantly Catholic south Baden) only 12 per cent were Catholic. Of 997 higher public servants in 1950, 26 per cent were Catholic and 68 per cent were Protestant [Zapf, 1965; 1966]; Similar figures can be found among the business *élite*. These figures are particularly surprising, as the C.D.U. (Christian Democratic Union) has been predominantly in power since 1949 and this party cannot be accused of anti-Catholic bias. The only possible explanation lies in that there is very little occupational mobility in Germany, i.e. the *élite* have tended to remain the same. Because the administrative-*élite* had been mainly formed by Prussians up until 1945, its Protestant image is understandable. The almost complete religious closure of rank among the *élite* is only very superficially caused by religion, and is more the result of specific political-historical conditions.

We possess considerably more exact results for the voting behaviour of the two major denominations. But here also, to understand an initially confusing situation, it is necessary to cast a glance at political history. The formation of the German state in 1871 with the exclusion of Austria, made the German Catholics a minority group; the psychological pressure of this position was strengthened by the abortive *Kulturkampf* waged by Bismarck against the Catholic Church. The formation of the 'Centre Party' of German Catholics created a political 'pillar of strength' for the German Catholics, which certainly had no equivalent on the side of the Protestants. Until 1933 the Centre was the Catholic party, regardless of social class, whilst the bourgeois Protestants had the choice of liberals or conservatives. Then in 1945 followed the formation of the supra-denominational C.D.U. *Christlich-Demokratische Union*, Christian-Democratic Union). This party is still functioning today and it appears to be a successor of the old Centre Party and at the same time forms a replacement for the no longer existing conservative parties, which up until 1933 were predominantly Protestant. The second major party of the Federal Republic, the S.P.D. (*Sozialdemokratische Partei Deutschlands*, Social Democratic Party of Germany) was until 1933 traditionally the political representative of the working-class. Since 1957 however, one can see a drift to the right, as the middle classes have increasingly joined it. Liberalism is represented by the F.D.P. (*Freie Demokratische Partei*, Free Democratic Party); this party is – as is traditional German liberalism generally – predominantly Protestant in image. One can see that in the federal elections, predominantly Catholic areas (Bavaria, south Baden, the Saar, the Rheinland) vote mainly for the C.D.U., whilst the Protestant areas (Schleswig-Holstein, Hamburg, North Hessen) are not united in their voting. Thus in strongly Protestant Schleswig-Holstein, the C.D.U. has a majority, whilst the S.P.D. dominates in North Hessen. The following hypothesis is offered as explanation: for Catholics, religion plays a more important part in voting behaviour than for Protestants, for which social class plays a determining role. In predominantly rural Protestant areas, which before 1933 voted for the Conservatives, the C.D.U. became the successor of the conservative parties (e.g.: Schleswig-Holstein), whilst in strongly industrialized Protestant regions, the old loyalty to the working-man's party (S.P.D.) remains intact (e.g. North-Hessen). In contrast, the Catholic population tends only in urban areas (e.g. Munich, Cologne) to vote for the S.P.D. Liberalism (F.D.P.) recruits its support from small independent businessmen (in North-Württemberg also from Protestant farmers); it is almost exclusively supported by Protestant voters. This also applies to the in 1966–69 strengthened nationalism, N.D.P. (*National demokratische Partei Deutschland*, National Democratic Party of Germany), which is strong especially in the former strongholds of the F.D.P. It has been pointed out by Lipset that German fascism was the political radicalization of the liberal voters.

In contrast to, for example, the Netherlands, a differentiated picture arises in Germany of voting behaviour. At least three factors have to be taken into account: social class, urban-rural differentiation and religion. Already Reigrotzki [1956] and more recently E. Blankenburg [1967] have pointed out that there is a fourth variable which should not be underestimated: the extent to which the individual is bound to the church, measurable by religious participation. It appears certain that with increasing religious participation in either denomination, the proportion of C.D.U. supporters rises, whilst even non-practising Catholics vote significantly more frequently for the S.P.D. All the same – as has already been shown – religious participation is dependent on social structure and on urban-rural differentiation. Thus here again is shown that in a sociological sense few relevant relationships can be put forward on the sole basis of simple statistical facts, i.e. of membership in one or the other of the two churches, as religious status, being inherited, is in fact taken out of the range of individual decision. To obtain better results from the field of voting behaviour, it would be necessary to do either long-term panel studies, or very differentiated regionally defined analyses. The material we have now is too narrow to support the formation of sociological theory.

## THE FUNCTIONS OF ORGANIZED RELIGION

L. von Wiese defined churches as 'establishments for the collective care of religious needs'. The results, mentioned in part (c), mean either, that the religious needs have strayed far from the church or that the churches fulfil functions in West German society which can only in a mediated sense be traced back to religious needs. One of the most important problems of German religious sociology is to analyse which functions the churches fulfil in a society, the members of which, although almost all belonging to either one or the other of the major denominations, participate only peripherally in these organizations. To fulfil this task even superficially, one has first to take into account that the church organizations are present at the parish level only to a small degree, so that in fact to begin with the sociology of the parish yields only little relevant sociological material. By virtue of the quasi-governmental administrative structure of the churches and their affiliated organizations (here one can mention especially charitable organizations which often reach beyond the borders of regionally autonomous churches), the churches, as involved in political decision-making, are an important factor in the political life of the Federal Republic. This can be shown without much trouble at various levels: education, welfare-policy, mass media.

*Table 1. Public and private primary schools in eight states according to denominational character (1961 and 1963)*

| States | | Protestant schools % | Catholic schools % | Non-denominational State schools % |
|---|---|---|---|---|
| Schleswig-Holstein | 1961 | – | 0.1 | 99.9 |
| | 1963 | 0.1 | 0.1 | 99.9 |
| Lower Saxony | 1961 | 11.6 | 7.6 | 80.8 |
| | 1963 | 11.8 | 7.8 | 80.3 |
| North Rhine Westphalia | 1961 | 28.4 | 57.3 | 14.3 |
| | 1963 | 28.5 | 57.2 | 14.3 |
| Hessen | 1961 | – | – | 100.0 |
| | 1963 | – | – | 100.0 |
| Rheinland-Pfalz | 1961 | 25.2 | 48.8 | 26.0 |
| | 1963 | 25.1 | 48.7 | 26.2 |
| Baden-Württemberg | 1961 | 7.9 | 16.6 | 75.5 |
| | 1963 | 7.9 | 16.6 | 75.5 |
| Bavaria | 1961 | 22.1 | 74.4 | 3.5 |
| | 1963 | 21.7 | 74.3 | 3.9 |
| The Saar | 1961 | 28.7 | 71.3 | – |
| | 1963 | 28.9 | 71.1 | – |

Source: S.B.E.K.D., No. 249.

There are very few schools in the Federal Republic which are directly supported by the churches. The overwhelming majority of schools are under the control of the state governments, however the organization of primary schools in several states is not denominationally neutral.

In the states of Bremen, Hamburg and West Berlin, there are practically no denominational primary schools. The very disparate picture conveyed by the Table is caused mainly by the cultural levels of the states which have completely different ways of dealing with the problems of denominational schools. Thus in the Saar the norm is the denominational school, other schools can only be set up at the behest of a certain number of parents. In Hessen it is the exact opposite. Denominational schools are in fact state schools which strive to attain denominational homogeneity. Teacher training in these states is partly or wholly carried out at denominational teacher training colleges. It is of the greatest sociological interest that even in the denominationally homogeneous regions, there is a tendency for the parents, if asked, to vote for non-denominational state schools and that the problem of schools coming under denominational control was until recently a widespread taboo in political battles. At the same time it has been possible in recent years to see a tendency to get away from the denominational element in school life (as for example in Baden-Württemberg and Bavaria – in contrast to Lower Saxony). The training of teachers at denominationally segregated institutions is regulated by governmental contracts between the state and the churches. Whether the goal which the apologists for denominational schools put forward is attained, namely that of religious unity of instruction be presented so that thereby personality can be built up, integrated around a religious centre, has never been seriously investigaged. The observation that areas with a high proportion of denominational schools show on the average a low percentage of the population attending grammar schools and universities says little if taken in isolation, as these areas are at the same time predominantly agricultural. Equally unexplained is whether the existence of denominational schools leads to a hardening of denominational differences and thus finally to the formation of two large religious sub-groups in West German society. Here again it is necessary to take into account that the child's introduction into primary school is largely an administrative act, which in practice takes place without the considered decision of the parents. This is because in many communities there is only a denominational school or a non-denominational school. It can hardly be expected for many parents to decide on an application for the erection of another type of school, considering the completely authoritarian attitude in regard to schools. Whether the primary schools of a state are organized along denominational lines or otherwise depends primarily on the agreement between government and church, and here the party composition of the parliament is decisive. *Cum grano salis* one can maintain, that publicly the denominational schools are defended only by the highest among the Catholic hierarchy, whilst the *élite* of the Protestant tends verbally to support non-denominational state schools. The problem of denominational schools is a good example of Riesman's theory on vetogroups which hand out political decisions without having to explain which collective interests the groups actually represent. A further firm anchorage of the churches in education is the existence of religious instruction (with denominational variations) at all state schools (with the exception of the state of Bremen). This connection between state authority in schools and church controlled instruction in the beliefs of both churches, supports the already often formulated hypothesis, that the churches in West Germany are administrative in character.

In the region of welfare policy, the churches are winning increased influence. Matthes was able to show how through use of an ideological concept of pluralism, both the major church welfare-organizations were able to attain to a position in general welfare – policy which had not been envisaged in the original conception by parliament [1964; 1965–8 (1), pp. 43ff]. As church welfare does not grow from parish life, but is rather administered by its own bureaucratic organizations, the latter do not serve to revive parish life, but rather strengthen the administrative character of the churches. In 1965, the Protestant welfare organization by itself supported nearly 54,000 hospital beds and about 63,000 places at old peoples' homes. The parallel Catholic organization (Caritas) even exceeds these figures. Thus in the area of social welfare, the churches carry out a considerable part in the integration of West German society; it must still be kept in mind that state and church institutions differ very little either in their structure or in their estimation of what cultural role they play. The trend towards denominationalizing social welfare will not, according to what one can predict, lead to the results known from the Netherlands, but rather to a development similar to that described by Herberg in the U.S.A. i.e. the development of a common ethical creed, in the framework of which the social positions of the churches can be consolidated without a denominational dichotomization of society ensuing.

The mass media of radio and television are not privately owned in the Federal Republic. However, one cannot correctly say that radio and television are state owned, as the individual stations are largely autonomous and are financed through a tax on each receiver as well as income from advertising. Control of the stations is exercised by a television advisory council composed of representatives of various organizations; besides representatives from both the churches, there are also union and political party members, etc. This practice – which came into existence after 1945 – has two effects: firstly it prevents the formation of denominational or politically-dominated stations, secondly the final transmitted programme is a compromise between equally strong veto-groups. Virulent religious conflict is prevented from the start through the toning down of possible conflicts drawn from public discussion. Not having investigated whether in fact a pluralistic society exists in the Federal Republic, important control mechanisms in the mass media were so instituted as if this pluralism existed in practice. The same applies for a majority of 'advisors' who serve in an advisory capacity to the holders of political decision-making positions. As it is only very seldom that the existence of these veto-groups comes to light, they are to a great extent beyond the mainstream of criticism. For the churches this means that they can often present their not clearly legitimated interests without the active participation of their members. This lack of activity in turn contributes to the lessening of religious participation as cause of cohesion. The small amount of participation of church members in the life of their churches is reflected in the strategy of the church bureaucracies to control possible social conflicts through compromise with state and government organs before such conflicts can become socially virulent.

## CONCLUSION

German religious sociology, which since the work of Max Weber and E. Troeltsch was until 1933 strongly oriented towards phenomenology and history, and included also the non-Christian religions in its universal outlook has been, since 1945, conducted only by G. Mensching [1947; 1959] on this basis. In contrast there has been since 1950 a noticeably strong leaning towards the concrete problems of the two major churches which led to a sociology of the parish, very restricted in its theoretical basis. Having become church sociology, religious sociology largely came to take on the function of a science auxiliary to pastoral theology. Since then loud criticism on the part of all religious sociologists have deplored this development. By 1958, D. Goldschmidt [1959] suggested that the field of the sociology of religion should be considerably extended in the direction of a sociology of valuative belief-systems, within which framework research into ideology and investigations of social stereotypes would have a place. T. Luckmann [1965] who was influenced by the Durkheimian concept of religion, decided there was a need to distinguish between the unique social form of religion within the church organization and the amorphous religion of modern society. He can see instances of a non-church formulated religion, including the cultivation of privacy, of the family, which are largely separated from the normal materially-oriented social sphere of the individual. On the other hand, G. Kehrer [1968] represents the view that the social understanding of the churches which has been reduced to ethical principles and which in turn does not need the participation of the church members, is the civil religion of modern society, a thesis obviously inspired by W. Herberg. In 1964, J. Matthes pointed out [1964] that it was necessary for the sociology of religion to view the churches within the framework of an analysis of modern society. These new theoretical perspectives which are not completely disparate among themselves put forward theories which until the present have not been validated by empirical research. The basis of such empirical research would have to be closely associated with sociological theory and take into account especially the cultural sustems of modern society. These reflections, consciously oriented towards the tradition of the sociology of religion (Durkheim, Weber), are a way for the latter to become free of its isolation in West Germany.

## BIBLIOGRAPHY

This bibliography is in no way exhaustive. Basically those works are mentioned which contain material on the socio-religious situation in the Federal Republic, or those which are representative of the position of German sociology of religion after 1945.

Bismarck, K. von, 'Gesellschaftliche Struktur der christlichen Gemeinde' [Social Structure of the Christian Community], in: *Evangelisches Soziallexikon*. Stuttgart, 1954.

Blankenburg, E., *Kirchliche Bindung und Wahlverhalten* [Connection with the Church and Voting Behaviour]. Olten, 1967.

Burger, A., *Religionszugehörigkeit und soziales Verhalten* [Religious Affiliation and Social Behaviour]. Göttingen, 1964.

Dittrich, R., *Konfession und Geburtenproblem* [Denomination and Birth-problem]. Vienna, 1951.

Erlinghagen, K., *Katholisches Bildungsdefizit* [Catholic Educational Deficiency]. Freiburg, 1965.

Fichter, J., *Soziologie der Pfarrgruppen* [Sociology of Pastoral Groups], Münster, 1958.

Freytag, J., *Die Kirchengemeinde in soziologischer Sicht* [A Sociological View of the Church Community]. Hamburg, 1959.

Fürstenberg, F., '*Kirchenreform und Gesellschaftsstruktur*' [The form of the Church and Social Structure]. *Revue d'Histoire et de Philosophie Religieuse*, 1961.

—, 'Soziologische Strukturprobleme der Kirchengemeinde' [Problems of Sociological Structure in the Church Community]. *Zeitschrift für evangelische Ethik*, 9, 1963.

—, (ed.), *Religionssoziologie* [Sociology of Religion]. Soziologische Texte Bd. 19 [Sociological texts, Vol. 19]. Neuwied – Berlin, 1964.

Goldschmidt, D., *Zur Religionssoziologie in der Bundesrepublik Deutschland* [The Sociology of Religion in the Federal Republic of Germany]. *Archives de Sociologie des Religions*, 8, 1959.

—, Greiner, F., and Schelsky, H., (eds.), *Soziologie der Kirchengemeinde* [Sociology of the Church Community]. Stuttgart, 1960.

—, and Matthes, J. 'Probleme der Religionssoziologie' [Problems in the Sociology of Religion]. *Kölner Zeitschrift für Soziologie und Sozialpsychologie*, VI, 1962.

Greinacher, N., 'Evolution de la pratique religieuse après la guerre' [Evolution of Religions Practice after the War]. *Social Compass*, 4 (5), 1963.

—, *Soziologie der Pfarrei. Wege zur Untersuchung* [Sociology of the Parish. Ways of Investigations]. Colmar-Freiburg, 1955.

Harenberg, W., *Was glauben die Deutschen?* [What do the Germans believe in?]. Munich, 1968.

*Jahrbuch der öffentlichen Meinung 1947–1955* (J.M.) [Yearbook of Public Opinion 1945–1955]. Allensbach, 1956.

Janowitz, M., 'Soziale Schichtung und soziale Mobilität in Westdeutschland' [Social Ranking and Social Mobility in Western Germany]. *Kölner Zeitschrift für Soziologie und Sozialpsychologie*, (10), 1958.

*Kirchliche Jahrbücher (evgl.)* [Church Yearbooks (Protestant)]. Gütersloh.

*Kirchliche Handbücher* (kath.) [Church Handbooks (Catholic)]. Köln.

Kehrer, G., *Das religiöse Bewusstsein des Industriearbeiters. Eine empirische Studie* [The Religious Consciousness of the Industrial Worker. An Empirical Study]. München 1966.

—, *Religionssoziologie* [Religious Sociology]. Sammlung Göschen Bd. 1228. Berlin, 1968.

—, 'Kirchenaustritte in Deutschland' [Leaving the Churches in Germany]. I.D.O.C.-International, 1970, 5.

Köster, R., 'Die Kirchentreuen. Bericht über eine Untersuchung in einer evangelisch-lutherischen Gemeinde Norddeutschlands [The Faithful. Results into Research on an Evangelical Lutheran Community in the North of Germany] in: Goldschmidt, D., Greiner, F., and Schelsky, H. (eds.), *Soziologie der Kirchengemeinde* [Sociology of Church Community]. Stuttgart, 1960.

Lohse, J. M., *Kirche ohne Kontakte* [Church without Contacts]. Stuttgart, 1967.

Luckmann, T., *Das Problem der Religion in der modernen Gesellschaft* [ The Problem of Religion in Modern Society]. Freiburg, 1963.

Matthes, J. (ed.), *Internationales Jahrbuch für Religionssoziologie* [International Yearbook of Religious Sociology]. Bd. 1–4. Cologne and Opladen, 1965–1968.

—, *Gesellschaftliche Konzeptionen im Sozialhilferecht* [Social Conceptions in Social Welfare Law]. Stuttgart, 1959.

—, *Die Emigration der Kirche aus der Gesellschaft* [The Emigration of the Church out of Society]. Hamburg, 1964.

—, *Religion und Gesellschaft*, [Religion and Society]. Hamburg, 1967.

*Statistische Berichte der Evangelischen Kirche in Deutschland* (S.B.E.K.D.) [Statistical Reports of the Evangelical Church in Germany], edited by *Kirchenkanzlei der E.K.D.* [The Church Office of the E.K.D.]. No. 1ff. Special No. 249, 251, 280, 284, 285. Hannover.

*Statistisches Jahrbüch für die Bundesrepublik Deutschland* [S.J.B.D.]. [Statistical Yearbook for the Federal Republic of Germany]. Stuttgart and Münich, 1961 and 1967.

Wölber, H.-O., *Religion ohne Entscheidung. Volkskirche am Beispiel der jungen Generation*

[Religion Without Decision. Popular Church from the Example of the Younger Generation]. Göttingen, 1959.

Wurzbacher, G. *et al.*, *Der Pfarrer in der modernen Gesellschaft* [The Pastor in Modern Society]. Hamburg, 1958.

Zapf, W., *Wandlungen der deutschen Elite* [Changes in the German Elite]. Munich, 1965.

—, (ed.), *Beiträge und Analyse der deutschen Oberschicht* [Contributions and Analysis of the German Upper Class]. Munich, 1966.

Mensching, G., *Die Religion* [Religion]. Stuttgart, 1959.

—, *Soziologie der Religion* [Sociology of Religion]. Bonn, 1947.

Müller-Armack, A., *Religion und Wirtschaft* [Religion and the Economy]. Stuttgart, 1959.

Peter-Habermann, I., *Kirchgänger-Image und Kirchgangsfrequenz* [Image of the Churchgoer and Frequency of Attendance]. Meisenheim am Glan, 1967.

Pflaum, R., [Mayntz), 'Die Bindung der Bevölkerung an die Kirche' [The Tie of the Population to the Church], in: Wurzbacher, G. (ed.), *Das Dorf im Spannungsfeld industrieller Entwicklung* [The Village in the Tension Field of Industrial Development]. (ed.), Stuttgart, 1954.

Reigrotzki, E., *Soziale Verflechtungen in der Bundesrepublik* [Social Interwovenness in the Federal Republic]. Tübingen, 1956.

Scheuch, E. K., and Rüschemeyer, D., 'Scaling Social Status in Western Germany.' *British Journal of Sociology*, 1960.

Schreuder, O., *Kirche im Vorort* [The Church in the Suburb]. Freiburg, 1962.

REFERENCES NOT SPECIFIC TO GERMANY

Birnbaum, N., 'Conflicting interpretations of the rise of Capitalism.' *British Journal of Sociology*, 4, 1953.

Herberg, W., *Protestant – Catholic – Jew*. New York, Doubleday, 1955.

Lenski, Gerhard, *The Religious Factor*. New York, Doubleday, 1961.

Samuelsson, K., *Religion and Economic Action*. New York, Harper and Row, 1964.

BERNARD WILHELM*

# Germany: Democratic Republic

## INTRODUCTION

October 7th, 1969, was the twentieth anniversary of the German Democratic Republic. With the Soviet occupation of the immediate post-war period, this marks almost a quarter-century of communist rule in Eastern Germany. All areas of social life – the economy, culture, the arts, sciences, law, etc. – have been influenced and restructured by the régime of the S.E.D. (Socialist Unity Party). One exception remains. The Party was not able to bring the churches under complete control, but instead had to endeavour to relegate the churches to the fringes of public life. The churches remain outside direct state control, and their administration can, within certain limits, continue to operate independently. As a matter of fact, the churches are the only mass organizations which continue to function on a non-socialist basis, in spite of the desires of the Party.

The continued existence of the churches in the D.D.R. is not directly endangered. However, the range of their activities has been reduced, with a very few exceptions, to the conduct of worship services only. Much more important for their future than direct pressure against them by the communist authorities is the process of secularization within the developing socialist society, and the cumulative effect of decades of communist indoctrination, counterbalancing and reducing the rôle which the churches formerly had in the social life of the people.

The decline in membership in the churches is evident in the 1964 census, the results of which were published in the autumn of 1968. Of the approximately 17,000,000 inhabitants of the D.D.R., 31.86 per cent are without religious affiliation (as compared with 8 per cent in the 1950 census), 59.35 per cent are members of Protestant churches (80 per cent in 1950), and 8.1

* Bernhard Wilhelm was born in Berlin in 1925. He was educated in Political Science at the Free University Berlin, and Loyola University, Los Angeles. He holds the position of Director of Research at the *Centre de Recherches et d'Etude des Institutions Religieuses*, Geneva, Switzerland. He is author of numerous articles and studies on international relations and on religion in Eastern Europe and the U.S.S.R.

per cent are Catholics (11 per cent in 1950). The question of the causes of this decline naturally arises. Generally speaking, approximately one-fourth of the decline may be ascribed to flight to the West, and the great bulk of the remainder is due to the process of secularization (cf. the comparable phenomenon in many Western countries), with only a small part attributable to atheist propaganda.

This pattern of decline is corroborated by statistics concerning baptism, weddings, and funerals. According to census figures which appear to be, on the whole, reliable, there is a downward trend in the popularity of these ceremonies – and in fact, enquiries made by the churches would suggest a more radical decline than that noted by the census.

In general, the membership of the churches can be divided into three categories: 1) convinced believers, the 'hard core' of church attenders, 2) traditional, or habitual believers, and 3) waverers, or 'certificate Christians' as they are called in the D.D.R., tend to be more stubborn in their practice of religion and the pattern of decline is not so marked, but the Catholic churches also have lost members because of the *Republik Flucht* (flight to the West). Generally speaking, the churches are living a ghetto existence, with stronger internal life, more exemplary behaviour, and better inter-Christian relations than are observable in many countries with more relaxed religious conditions. The churches are striving to preserve the substance of the faith unchanged, and to date, at least, seem to be succeeding rather well despite adverse conditions.

The Protestant churches of East Germany will be dealt with in greater detail than the Roman Catholic church. More information is available on the Protestant churches and in them the efforts of the D.D.R. government to undermine religion and the churches are more in evidence. It seems that Protestantism with its geographic and regional particularism and the resulting dissipation of its strength, presents an excellent target for attack by the Communist régime of East Germany.

## DENOMINATIONAL STRUCTURE

By far the greatest percentage of the Protestant population belongs to one of the eight regional churches found in East Germany. These churches reflect the differences of their founders (Luther, Zwingli or Calvin) so that, despite numerous attempts at unification in the past they are still divided on matters of liturgy and do not possess any unified church leadership. This centuries-old division has caused a permanent weakening of the churches. Although it seemed for a long time that the stress and confusion caused by the war and its aftermath might bring Christians closer together, the movements which tried to reappraise traditional interpretations of religion and belief, particularly in the Federal Republic, have caused the churches to become further split. As well as their confessional divisions, they are now divided along intellectual lines. The East German government has taken advantage of the disunity and disarray of the West German churches in its antireligious propaganda and its efforts to make the East German churches cut all ties with the churches of Western Germany.

The Protestant territorial churches include the four United Churches: a) the Protestant Church of Berlin-Brandenburg, b) the Protestant regional Church of Greifswald (until 28.3.1968 the Protestant Church of Pommerania), c) the Protestant Church of Görlitz (until 23.3.1968 the Protestant Church of Silesia), d) the Protestant Church of the Province of Saxony; the Protestant Church of the Union, i.e. the Protestant Territorial Church of Anhalt; and the three Protestant-Lutheran Churches: a) the Protestant-Lutheran Territorial Church of Saxony, b) the Protestant-Lutheran Church in Thuringia, and c) the Protestant-Lutheran Territorial Church of Mecklenburg.

These eight churches embrace about 271 church districts and more than 6,700 parishes. All eight regional churches were formal members of the E.K.D. *(Evangelische Kirche Deutschlands)* until 1968. The four United Churches and the Church of the Union of Anhalt belonged to the Protestant Church of the Union *(Evangelische Kirche der Union:* E.K.U.*)* and the three Protestant-Lutheran churches were members of the United Protestant-Lutheran Church of Germany *(Vereinigte Evangelisch-Lutherischen Kirche im Deutschland:* V.E.L.K.D.*)* until 1968. These associations were administrative organizations and did not presuppose unity of creed. They used to meet in West Germany and sent representatives to the all-German synod. In recent years it has become increasingly difficult and often impossible for representatives from the East German member churches to obtain permission to attend meetings. In fact, the question of the withdrawal of the East German member churches fron the all-German associations is a key one in the policy of the Pankow government toward the churches. Supporters of withdrawal claim that the unity of the Protestant churches is being used as an instrument of the cold war and that the churches of East Germany can have nothing in common with the West German churches and their support of the militaristic policy of the Federal Republic and N.A.T.O. Government propaganda constantly impresses on East German Christians and their leaders that only 'unpatriotic' people could still feel any affinities with the churches in West Germany.

Part of the movement towards establishing independence among the churches in the D.D.R. is the formation of the Association of Protestant Clergy in the German Democratic Republic *(Bund Evangelischer Pfarrer in der*

*Deutschen Demokratischen Republik)*. This Association was established on the 1st July 1958 with open State direction and support, both material and ideological. Within a year of its foundation, the Association counted 170 members scattered throughout East Germany, who were all active in the territorial churches.

The membership of the Association is made up exclusively of Protestant pastors and ministers. It publishes a monthly paper, the *Evangelische Pfarrerblatt*, in which, together with questions of organisation and similar matters, spiritual instructions in a 'progressive spirit' are given. The Association is financed by the National Front.

The Association represents an alliance of the Protestant ministers who stand in open opposition to the Protestant church leadership – and less on religious grounds than on political ones. It forms, within the regional churches of East Germany and therefore within the D.D.R., a kind of minister-faction which is loyal to the Pankow régime and which supports East German socialism and all it entails – including the destruction of the consciousness of German unity and the establishment of a 'State Church'.

As an instrument of propaganda, the Association possesses a significance which its relative smallness belies. At present, membership is about 300. However, the figures are rising and, with present trends among the younger generation of clergy, they may be expected to continue to do so. Furthermore, its influence is increasing considerably. It has members on almost all state and civic committees and the territorial churches will increasingly find themselves compelled to appoint members of the Association to leading positions.

Two Protestant churches of a special character are the Moravian Brethren (*Herrnhuter Brüdergemeinde*) and the Union of Protestant Reformed Churches of Germany *(der Bund Evangelisch-Reformierter Kirchen Deutschlands)*.

Originally a refuge for persecuted 'Bohemian brothers', the Community of the Moravian Brethren was founded by the Austrian Count Nikolaus Ludwig Zinzendorf (1700–1760) in 1722 on the Zinzendorf lands at Herrnhut. They call themselves a Protestant Free Church and are formally members of the E.K.U. The members are not politically prominent in East Germany. Despite their historical background and international connections,[1] they seem to be one of the few religious communities left relatively undisturbed by the Pankow government.

The Protestant Free (Non-Conformist) Churches are the Episcopal

1. At present the Moravian Brethren have twenty-three bishops and 493 pastors who preside over six autonomous provinces in the European continent, Great Britain, North America, South America, South West Africa and the U.S.S.R. The seat of the Brethren is at the place of origin, Herrnhut.

Methodist Church and the Union of Protestant Free Church Congregations *(der Bund Evangelisch-Freikirchlicher Gemeinden)* (Baptist Union) which combined in 1968 in accordance with the world-wide agreement of 1966 as 'the Protestant-Methodist Church of the D.D.R.' *(Evangelische-Methodistische Kirche)*; the Mormons; the Association of German Mennonite congregations; the Seventh-Day Adventists; and the Quakers. The last three can be disregarded as religious minorities of little significance.

The Methodist church in East Germany has in its service about 100 pastors, twenty-four parish-nurses, and about 1,800 lay helpers in parish work and religious instruction. In Erzgebirge, Voigtland and Thüringia alone, which are the stronghold of the Methodist church in East Germany, there are 273 meeting halls with ninety-three officiating pastors and about 700 voluntary helpers. The Church publishes a bi-monthly paper, *Die Friedensglocke*, which has been licensed since 1945.

The Methodist Church in East Germany, despite its affiliation with the American mother church, is considered thoroughly 'loyal' to the Pankow government. One reason for this is that church leaders lay stress on the 'social responsibility of the Methodist tradition' and refer to the influence of the Methodist Church on the development of the trade-union movement and the Labor party in Great Britain. All leading bishops support the D.D.R. government and a considerable percentage of church members (including clergy) are active in public life. For these reasons, the Methodist Church has little to fear from pressures from the State.

Although there are 33,430 Mormons in the German-speaking world (including Austria and Switzerland) and 22,500 in the Federal Republic, only 4,703 live in the D.D.R. where their religious centre is Dresden. Mormon believers in the D.D.R. were not affected by the persecutions of 1950–53 when many East Germans were arrested for religious activities. There is little information about them and they seem to be regarded as a religious minority of little importance since outwardly they appear loyal to the government.

The situation of the Roman Catholic Church in East Germany (numbering about 1.3 million) is quite different to that of the Protestant territorial churches. In the first place, it is part of a world body and therefore cannot be accused of narrow nationalism as are the regional churches over their membership in the united Protestant associations of Germany. Furthermore, it is a church *en bloc*, a homogeneous unity with a unified leadership. Changes in administrative boundaries do not affect this external and internal solidarity. Its doctrine cannot be tampered with, nor is it subject to a popular vote or to opportunism. The clergy in East Germany have not been intimidated by pressures brought to bear on them by the Government and still present a united front. Finally, because of the minority situation of

Catholics in East Germany, practising church members form a tightly-knit body. The pro-government *Begegnungskatholiken* (Encounter Catholics) have not made any significant impact.

In the light of these points, Ulbricht's offer to make an agreement with the Holy See represents a confession by the D.D.R. government of its tacit recognition of the inner strength and endurance of the Roman Catholic Church. The Roman Catholic Church can therefore expect to be left in peace for a time, at least until the eight East German regional churches withdraw from the all-German organisations. When this happens, it will provide the D.D.R. government with an excuse to create new bishoprics within the state boundaries of the Democratic Republic. This would in no way be disadvantageous to the Church as it would allow for the formation of strong centres of belief. In fact, here the interest of the Roman Catholic Church and the Government coincide.

The Jewish community in East Germany numbers about 1,300 people, of whom almost 850, i.e. over half, live in East Berlin. In the whole of the Democratic Republic there are eight independent communities (in East Berlin, Dresden, Halle an der Saale, Leipzig, Karl-Marx-Stadt, Magdeburg and Schwerin) which are united in the 'Union of Jewish Communities in the D.D.R.'

Every Jew born prior to 6 May 1945 is considered a victim of Fascism in the D.D.R., whether they were living at the time in the then Third Reich or had emigrated. It seemed natural that the Jews who remigrated would find a new homeland in the D.D.R., but this has not been the case. Jewish property was taken over as 'state property' by the D.D.R. government after the division of Germany. No restitutions have since been paid to the Jews and difficulties have been put in the way of any enquiries concerning former property. The position of Jews in the D.D.R. is then economically and politically weak. All contact between the East and West German Jewish communities is viewed with suspicion. Permission was not even granted for co-operation over the preparation of material for the Eichmann trial.

After the Slansky Trial in Russia in 1952 a period of pressure and arrests of Jews began in the D.D.R. which ended only with the death of Stalin. Since then, the Government has provided money for the upkeep and administration of old-ages homes, hospitals and also for the care of Jewish cemeteries. For considerations of propaganda despite the accusations it levels against them, the Government is at present prepared to tolerate the Jews. The present Jewish community, weakened by old age, resignation and hardship and deprived of economic or political power cannot be expected to put up much opposition. The Jewish problem is viewed as one of generation which will eventually solve itself since there is no growth of orthodoxy in the coming generation.

The Russian Orthodox Church consists of four parishes under the supervision of the Exarch for Central Europe appointed by the Moscow Patriarch. It is not politically prominent and although it has a certain tourist attraction it is not taken very seriously by the State and Party. Unlike the 'Russian Orthodox Church Abroad' in West Germany its members are not recruited from White Russians. They are therefore not hostile to the D.D.R. government, nor do they desire any connections with the Russian Orthodox Church in West Germany.

The Jehovah's Witnesses have, since 1949, been forbidden by law but the ban has merely driven them underground and made them more zealous than ever.

## RELIGIOUS PARTICIPATION

The general pattern in the D.D.R. is one of declining religious participation. The present church membership of 10,091,907 Protestants and 1,375,237 Roman Catholics represents a marked reduction in the number of Christians due to flight to the West and withdrawal from the churches. The number of clergy is most inadequate; there are 7,800 clergy (6,000 Protestant ministers[2] or curates and about 1,500 priests) who are aided by about 5,500 catechists.

In assessing the significance of these figures it should be remembered that the majority of church members are merely nominal adherents. There are no figures which reveal the level of personal Christian commitment. However, some conclusions about the level of religious participation and the factors involved in its decline can be drawn form the available statistics and reports of some of the Protestant regional churches.

In the district of the regional church of Saxony only 1,060 parishes out of 1,800 (with 2,300 congregations) have their own minister or are visited by

2. An acute shortage of clergy exists in the regional churches of East Germany and, since 1954, the number of divinity students has been constantly decreasing. Some measures have been adopted to help overcome this. For example, an Upper Seminary has been opened in Potsdam-Hermannswerder, open to divinity students of either sex, where the course is only four years. In the Thüringian regional church an honorary office of lector has been created to supply someone to read a sermon, written by the pastor, to the assembled congregation at services where the pastor himself cannot be present. This idea has been adopted by other regional churches who have learned from experience that when services occur infrequently owing to lack of ministers, attendance drops more quickly than when a service takes place every Sunday. The very fact that this office has been found necessary is, however, in itself an indication of the dearth of ministers and divinity students.

one. Decline in religious participation is illustrated by the number of children receiving the sacraments. In Leipzig in 1949, 5,700 children received Baptism; in 1960 only 1,400. In 1949 the number of those confirmed was 6,200; during the priod 1954–1958 the number declined to 3,500; in 1959 only 840 children received Confirmation. Moreover, according to a report of 15 November 1966 by the regional bishop, only 50 per cent of the children baptized in 1959/60, in the district of the regional church had been instructed in Christian doctrine when they began school. In Karl-Marx-Stadt the percentage was 11.5, in Leipzig 11.8. Among children, then, there is a considerable gap between the number receiving Baptism and the number receiving religious instruction.

The inadequacy in the number of clergy plays a part in the development of this apathy towards the church. However, the reason lies much more in a change of attitude among the people. Typical of this change is the situation described by Superintendent Böhm, one of the seven provosts of the regional church of Saxony, in his report on Wittenberg:

> Secularization has reached such a degree that even the Christian overtones in customs and habits have disappeared in all but the so-called Christian families... The People's church has died out here. All in all, in the greater number of communities the stagnation of church life is unmistakable.

Böhm described as a typical example a parish in an industrial area which, in 1950, counted 7,000 members. In 1965 only 3,500 were registered as 'approachable'. In 1965 there were only fifteen Baptisms, as against 100 in 1950. In the same period the number of church weddings had dropped from forty to four; the number of people receiving Confirmation from 100 to fourteen; the average number of school-children taking religious instruction (in a total of 800) from 300 to eighty. In a second example Böhm described the different picture that emerged in four small rural parishes, without in any way minimising the seriousness of the overall situation.

Rural parishes have, in general, greater religious participation. In the regional church of Berlin-Brandenburg in November 1964, the General Superintendent of Cottbus, stated in a report:

> While on the one hand many small village parishes still maintain today an intact church life in the tradition of the people's churches, in other places the process of secularization is so advanced that in fact only tiny parish communities still exist.

In the parishes of the big cities the process of disintegration is much further advanced. For example, in East Berlin the number of people receiving religious instruction dropped by as much as 57 per cent in the period from 1960 to 1963.

In the smallest regional church, that of Anhalt in 1966, only 96 of its 133 parishes had a minister. The number of church members following the reduction caused by flight to the West or people leaving the church, declined from 423,000 in 1954, to 260,000 in 1963. In the same period the number of those attending church services declined from 700,000 to 350,000, i.e. by almost half. The situation regarding baptisms, church weddings and religious instruction is as follows: in 1954 there were 2,100 church weddings, 5,700 Baptisms and 23,000 attending religious instruction. In 1963 the comparable figures were: 860, 2,400, and 11,000. These figures do not cover developments over the last five years but it can be concluded from the statements of leading church representatives that the declining trend is continuing.

These rather scattered data indicate the general pattern of decline in religious participation in East Germany. The shortage of clergy is a serious problem and it is also clear that a decisive factor in people's faith is the zeal of individual members of the clergy. Where this is lacking, the cohesion of the parish is seriously weakened. Small rural parishes have the strongest cohesiveness, yet while many sociological, geographic and other differences exist between parishes these are not really significant in the present decline of religious life.

One can only evaluate East German Christians as follows: the older, tradition-bound generation is usually deeply religious. The middle-aged generation, out of force of habit, has no desire to actually cut itself off from the churches. In fact, it still feels some attachement to them, yet is not prepared to make a stand for religious beliefs which are seeming less and less real. The youthful generation, who pass through an intensively atheistic schooling, cannot be expected to produce Christians with strong, inner convictions. This development is carefully noted by the D.D.R. government and the mode of its campaign against religion accurately reflects its estimation of the strength and significance of the churches.

### *Withdrawal from the churches*

While the decision whether or not to belong to a church is free and is guaranteed in the Constitution, pressures are exerted, especially on German youth not to participate in a church. Normally the child's parents have control over his religion and education until he is fourteen. At the end of his fourteenth year, the child is considered religiously mature and makes his own decision about religion – even if it is contrary to the will of those in charge of his education. This decision is made at a time when he is being prepared for the Youth Consecration Ceremony *(Jugendweihe)* and is most strongly under the influence of the socialist teachings connected with this ceremony. Other examples of pressures against religion are: difficulties in finding employment of one's choice, and enforced withdrawals from the church.

In 1965 the leadership of the National People's Army ordered a campaign to urge individual soldiers to renounce religion. This led to heavy conflicts of conscience and unrest among the troops, especially as any discussion with each other over the matter was strictly forbidden. On the other hand, there have been cases where the courage of individual recruits in openly declaring their religious beliefs has been recognized by the leader of their unit and special arrangements have been made to enable them to attend church services once a month.

The D.D.R. government views public withdrawal from the churches as recognition of the government. Renunciation of religion is a necessary condition for appointment to the higher and more authoritative ranks in the Party and State (no active officers in the N.V.A. belong to a church). Following a decree of 13 July 1950, withdrawal from a church is declared before the court in the town where the person concerned lives. The D.D.R. government have made the formalities as simple as possible. Registrars are also empowered to publicly attest the declarations of individuals and such declarations are immediately valid.

Whether the churches will ever be in the position to stem the tide of withdrawal which is encouraged by the régime remains to be seen. In Roman Catholic areas and among some of the Free Churches the Government's desired end is not being reached. In view of the strong spirituality and staunch religious attitudes of Christians in these areas this is not surprising. Among the Protestant churches, on the other hand, as a result of the wavering attitudes of church leaders, the present trend can at least be expected to continue.

## RELIGION AND THE POLITICAL GOVERNMENT

### *The administration of the churches*

The Communist Party, the State and the Churches have parallel administrative organs on four levels: national, district, county and local. The Christian Work Groups, which also operate on most levels, form a special organizational structure to ensure co-operation on all levels between the political and religious administrative machinery.

The Party does not have a direct hand in church affairs, nor does it need to since the S.E.D. (Sozialistische Einheitspartei Deutschlands: the Socialist Unity Party), The State party, controls every aspect of society and politics. The body responsible for policy toward the churches is the Central Comittee of S.E.D. The leading advisory body is the Department for Church Affairs. Under this department there exist corresponding departments in the 15 district branches of S.E.D. These departments at the district level control reports on church matters sent up from the district and city branches of S.E.D. These reports are usually drawn up by one man who works in close association with the expert on cultural affairs.

The whole arrangement of departments and reports is strictly subject – in accordance with the vertical principle of leadership – to instructions and inspections from superior organizations. The schema thus ensures first-class information both over individual members of the clergy and over the behaviour and mood of the laity. It further ensures unified procedure and despatch in the carrying out of instructions.

In Eastern Germany there exists a unique form of organization, the 'Christian Work Circles' which are, ostensibly, independent of the State and Party apparatuses. These groups claim to be above party or faction allegiances. There are no conditions of membership but members call themselves Christians and are formal members of a church or religious community. They take it upon themselves to be as good Christians as citizens and, precisely from a sense of Christian responsibility to play an active part in social and political events.

The activities of the groups on the whole parallel the endeavours of the Association of Protestant Clergy and the *Begegnungs-katholiken* (Encounter Catholics). The aim of the groups is to procure for the government, if required, enthusiastic consent to political measures on a broad 'Christian' basis and to give the impression that the Christians of East Germany are seeking, through these groups, to reach an understanding with the régime which they cannot reach through the hierarchy.

The groups are composed of both clergy and laity, although it is significant that up to 1968 no Catholic priests are among their members. It is also noteworthy that some of the Protestant clergy who work with them do not belong to the Association of Protestant Clergy in the D.D.R. These groups produce publications which endorse the stand of the D.D.R. government on political questions and attack the policies of the West, especially those of the Federal Republic and the U.S.A. Theology is enlisted in support of propaganda with the aid of biblical quotations. The similarity and timing of these publications with actions of the State and Party apparatuses show that the groups work in close collaboration with the Party and State. Also, since the circles do not have the status of a union, they must be financially supported from outside. The connecting link between these groups and the Party and

State is, in fact, the National Front, which not only supplies funds but also gives the directions.

The circles are organised on strict lines. The head body is the Christian Working Circle in the National Council of the National Front. Below this are Christian working circles in the district committees of the National Front. There are no groups at local levels. This vertical organization corresponds with the organizational scheme of the Party and State apparatuses.

An important point is that members of the circles come from the people and therefore in arguments over policy toward the churches it can be, and is, argued that the laity are in opposition to the Church leadership. This line of argument, as is shown in the statements of influential State officials, is becoming increasingly significant.

The administration of the churches is thus arranged in such a way that each church organization faces a corrective at the ideological, state and propaganda levels. Any church organization has to contend with three cadres who are not only encouraged and protected by the State but also have at their disposal the network of mass communications (parades, demonstrations, press, radio and televison).

*The policy of the government toward the churches*

*General policy.* There can be no doubt that the eventual object of the policy of the D.D.R. government toward the churches is the liquidation of religion and the abolition of the churches since an axiom of the Communist world and social order is the denial of the supernatural and therefore the denial of the existence of God. The attainment of this object, according to Communist teachings, is largely a generation problem. Therefore the younger generation in Communist countries are systematically educated to see their life's aim in the mastery of technology and material things.

Meanwhile it is certain that the D.D.R. government wants to come to an arrangement with the East German churches of all denominations and is producing a great deal of propaganda advocating co-existence between Christians and Marxists in the Democratic Republic. However, for such co-existence it lays down the following conditions. With regard to the Protestant churches it demands: abandonment of the concept of unity with the churches of West Germany; withdrawal from the all-German associations (V.E.L.K. and E.K.D.); support for the policy of the Pankow Government; active participation of the churches in civic and political life and the founding of an independent East German Church Union having no ties, spiritual or organizational, with the territorial churches of the Federal Republic. With regard to the Roman Catholic Church the government demands: recognition of the Democratic Republic of Germany as an independent German state by the Holy See; participation by clergy and laity in civic and political life and acceptance of the political, social and cultural goals of the Democratic Republic. There is no demand that ties with Rome should be cut but, as far as possible, the State is to have a say in the appointment of East German bishops. New bishoprics free of all connections with West German bishoprics are to be set up.

In accordance with the Leninist theory of the 'transition from quantity to quality', the D.D.R. government has changed its tactics toward religion. The error tactics of 1958–9 have been carefully smoothed over and the struggle against religion has been shifted from the street to the writing-desk. The form is now much less harsh, but the situation is no less critical.

*The place of the churches in East German Law*

Codified law defining the status of churches and religious groups in East Germany and the rights of the churches and their individual members only exists in the Constitution of 7 October, 1949. It has been dropped from the Constitution of the D.D.R. which came into force on 9 April, 1968. Special laws for religion and religious bodies, such as exist in other communist-ruled countries, do not exist in the German Democratic Republic. Matters deeply affecting the churches, such as the education of youth, can be altered or regulated quite arbitrarily and with little warning as most church matters are dealt with by the administration – usually by the state organs at the middle levels (provincial and district administrations).

Under the Constitution of 1968 the rights of the churches and religious associations have been whittled away. They are no longer automatically recognized as corporations under public law. Although the forthcoming Code of Civil Law of the D.D.R. will make it possible for them to be so recognized the decision will be left to the discretion of the state organizations at the middle levels. This will enable decisions to be made pragmatically. In individual cases the principle (still guaranteed under the old Constitution) of the independence of the churches and their legal rights will be open to possible abuse.

By denying the churches recognition as corporations under public law the state creates legally ownerless property which it can lawfully take over. The churches of East Germany are still big landholders. Church property amounts to about 260,000 hectares, of which some 200,000 belong to the Protestant church. This land was not touched in the land reform programme. Although the churches were forced to lease large tracts to agricultural co-operatives they retained ownership. The new Constitution provides an opportunity for this 'omission' to be corrected.

The present legal position of the churches is such that they are not only open to manipulation from without but also from within by those who wish to pave the way for the creation of a State Church in the D.D.R. and otherwise follow the path which the Party and State wish the churches to follow.

*Policy towards church taxes*

The Constitution of 1949 guaranteed the levying of church taxes, one of the chief sources of income of the East German churches, and, from 1945–50, the amount was credited to the churches from amounts deducted from wages. The individual's tax assessment is decided on the basis of income in accordance with strict regulations by the churches themselves quite independently of the government. In the Free Churches and the Sects, people willingly state their income and the Roman Catholic church has not had many difficulties in this respect. In the Protestant territorial churches, however, where 40 per cent of church members are exempt from taxes due to old age or ill health, the remaining able-bodied group, in receipt of an income, are often unwilling to give a reliable estimate of their income. The only way the churches can obtain reliable income figures is through the State Fiscal Office, but this office refuses to provide the necessary information. Hence the churches are forced to fall back on old, out-of-date records still in their possession and estimates are often in error. This causes hardship, injustice and discontent and has caused many people to leave the church. Moreover since 1956,[3] the churches have had no way of enforcing payment of church taxes. They are entirely dependent on the willingness and honesty of their members, and have suffered considerable financial loss as a result.[4]

*Policy towards the clergy*

State policy towards the churches is reflected in the decreased attractiveness of the ministry as a career, and in the subsequent decline in the numbers of clerical students in East Germany since 1954.[5] Moreover a significant trend

3. Originally the churches had legal powers to enforce the payment of their taxes. In 1952 this was amended so that the churches could only enforce payment through the courts. In 1956, however, the Ministry of Justice declared that official assistance to the churches in this matter was not to continue.

4. The following two examples indicate the current financial problem. In the regional church of Mecklenburg in 1966, out of a church membership of 1.1 million, only about 5,000,000 marks was received in church tax. The Mecklenburg regional church, it must be added, has the lowest percentage of withdrawals and is in a relatively favourable situation. In January 1968, the Görlitz regional church revealed that it has no hope of ever again reaching the total of church tax collected in 1964.

5. The life of members of the clergy of the regional church in East Germany is

in the training of the new generation of Protestant clergy is that their teachers are coming more and more from the generation of academics who unconditionally support the government. These teachers are typical of the generation of Protestant theologians who, in the conflict between Christian service and political ambition, have opted for the politics of the day.

By contrast, Roman Catholic seminarians pass through institutions owned by the Church and where the choice of lecturers is free from political considerations. This means that the new generation of Roman Catholic priests have a more unified training and more basic grounding in theology. They present a much more united front and their spiritual and intellectual presence is much stronger and more impressive than that of the Protestant younger generation of clergy. This is due not only to their strict spiritual and moral discipline but also to the fact that Catholic seminarians do not study under the political pressures which are constantly exerted on their Protestant counterparts.

*Policy towards the charitable institutions of the Protestant Church*

In East Germany the Protestant churches run fifty-three hospitals and sanitoria, sixty-two homes for the physically and mentally handicapped and also old-age homes, infirmaries, kindergartens, creches and municipal welfare centres. About 16,000 people work in these institutions. Each year this diaconal work undergoes further restriction by the State. Eventually, the entire care of healthy children is to be taken out of the hands of the churches and controlled entirely by the State, leaving only the care of children who are ill or handicapped to the Churches.

## CONCLUSION

Since 1960 the D.D.R. leadership consider the various religious denomina-

---

beset with difficulties. They have to work in atheistic surroundings among members of an indifferent parish; they live in uncertainty over what financial means will be available to them each month for the upkeep of their, usually large, families; they are universally overworked because of the shortage of clergy and they know that there is only a slight possibility of a younger minister replacing them when they become too old to continue their work. Furthermore, they must be prepared to adapt to the exigencies of the State regarding political and civic life without ever receiving any real backing and support from the church hierarchy. For these reasons, the divinity student in East Grmany goes about his studies in a more serious frame of mind than his West German counterpart. Many would-be students draw back altogether.

tions less dangerous than formerly, for their influence has been reduced to a minimum. The most important factors of mass-manipulation – education, mass-organizations, mass-media, etc. – were already oriented in an anti-religious direction.

The government, however, continues its atheist propaganda but refrains from the more extreme anti-religious activities. The hope of the régime is that the people will gradually become more and more alienated from religion. The leadership of the S.E.D. realized that an open struggle with the churches would be more harmful to their future policies than the subtle, patient measures now in force. 'Enlightenment campaigns' and harsh actions would only stiffen the reactions and emotions of the faithful. This does not exclude actions by which active Christians are discriminated against in education and in their professional careers.

In the long-term planning of the Communist régime there is an awareness that better results can be obtained by using a limited atheistic propaganda, intensified non-religious education and by encouraging the process of secularization. This method promises more success for the régime than open persecution. The churches in the D.D.R. as compared with other socialist states were never openly persecuted, but these more 'refined' methods have resulted in substantial reduction of the influence of all denominations in the society of the D.D.R.

DAVID MARTIN*

# Great Britain: England

The main part of the discussion which follows attempts to develop and relate certain theses bearing on religious institutions and beliefs in industrial Christian societies, with special reference to England. Initially it indicates very briefly certain processes which are more or less general to all these societies and probably to non-Christian societies as well. There follow three inter-related theses which attempt between them to account for the specific pattern of belief and practice found in England and to a lesser extent the United Kingdom. However, before proceeding with this general theme, it seems appropriate to summarize certain English data in a form comparable to other chapters in the collection.

## DENOMINATIONAL COMPOSITION

Obviously constituency figures, those figures derived from all those who, when asked their religion by pollster, army corporal or hospital attendant reply Catholic, Church of England or whatever it may be, will differ according to the total geographical area under consideration or the extent to which children and adolescents are included. Most of the studies on which these following remarks are based exclude Northern Ireland; all exclude Eire.

Those who identify themselves as Church of England make up two-thirds of the English population, or a significantly smaller fraction if Wales and Scotland are included. The Free Church constituency for the whole country stands at about 11 per cent. Roman Catholic identification reaches roughly the same order of magnitude. The Church of Scotland is of course the majority church in Scotland, but taking Britain as a whole it too has a constituency of somewhat under one person in ten. Thus, these four groupings ac-

* David Martin was born in Mortlake, England, in 1929. He is currently Reader in Sociology at The London School of Economics, having previously been a Lecturer there, and Lecturer at Sheffield University. His publications include *Pacifism: An Historical and Sociological Study*, 1965, *A Sociology of English Religion*, 1967 and *A Sociological Yearbook of Religion in Britain* (editor), 1968, 1969, 1970.

count for the great bulk of denominational identification, leaving only something under one-tenth unaccounted for.

Of this tenth, about half, possibly a little more, account themselves as not having any religious label. A further one per cent of the whole population is Jewish. This leaves 4 per cent to be divided among the sects, Eastern Orthodoxy and non-Christian religions. The Muslims, Hindus and various Orthodox Communions must each number about 200,000: together 1 per cent. The Orthodox are largely Greek (Cypriot) but there are Russian, Serbian and Armenian Churches also. Between 1 and 2 per cent can be attributed to the small sects (Witnesses, Mormons, Pentecostalists, Christadelphians, Gospel Halls, Brethren of various kinds and so on). This is the kind of maximum figure which emerges if one takes an average based on comparisons of local surveys.

Changes in the relative numerical strength of religious bodies as well as the overall decline in religious participation are reflected in data concerning various types of membership. In the Church of England, Baptisms stood at 650 per thousand live births in 1902, rose to 717 in 1927 and then dropped (especially from 1935 to 1940) until in 1960 they numbered 554. Confirmations fell from 42.8 per thousand in the 12–20 age group in 1911, to 34.2 in 1960. Marriages have fallen from 698 per thousand in 1899 to 474 in 1962, compared with rises in Roman Catholic and civil ceremonies, which in 1962 stood at 123 and 296 per thousand respectively. The peak for 'other religious ceremonies' for marriage ran from 1874 to 1924, since when they have shared the Anglican decline. In 1962 they stood at 102 per thousand. Other declines are noticeable in Easter day communicants, falling from 98 per thousand (of people over 15) in 1911 to 69 in 1962, and in electoral rolls, falling from 152 per thousand of the appropriate section of the population in 1927 to 81 in 1964 [Paul, 1964; Neuss, 1966].

Part of the decline in the proportionate number of Anglicans particularly in cities like Liverpool and more recently London is due to the effect of Catholic migration from Ireland and the continent. In 1851 Roman Catholics in England and Wales comprised 4.5 to 5 per cent of the population, nearly half of whom were Irish-born. By 1911 the percentage lay between 6 and 7. According to the Newman Demographic Survey this rose to 10.7 in 1951 and 12.2 in 1961. It is from 1910 that all the indices turn upward and they have continued to do so ever since. The proportion of Catholic marriages rose from 4.1 per cent in 1908 to 5.2 per cent in 1919 to 12.3 per cent in 1962; the baptismal birth ratio was 7.7 per cent in 1911, 9.2 per cent in 1924 and 16.1 per cent in 1963. It should be noted that Catholic increases, apart from migration, are largely through marriage and a somewhat higher birth rate. Though those self-identified as Catholics are some 11 per cent of the population, Catholic births stand at 16 per cent, reflecting a youthful age structure as well as a high fertility.

The Free Churches present a picture of continuous erosion. Initially they seem to have maintained themselves while the Church of England began to decline, but once their own decline set in, notably after the 1906 peak, it was quite rapid. Moreover the loss of influence is greater than it appears since the category of 'adherents' is believed to have dropped from 40 per cent to 10 per cent. Figures given by Christopher Driver indicate the extent of the loss [Driver, 1963]. From 1910 to 1966 Methodists in Britain declined from 1,168,415 members to just over 700,000. Over the same period Baptists in Britain declined from just under 400,000 to 280,000 and Congregationalists in England and Wales from 456,613 to about 200,000. Thus although about 11 per cent are self-identified as Nonconformist, of whom perhaps 8 per cent are Methodist, membership of the three major denominations (Methodist, Congregationalist, Baptist) is only somewhat over a million: under 3 per cent of the adult population. It is important that the age structure of Nonconformity is biased towards the higher age ranges, that the Sunday Schools have experienced steady erosion since World War I and that there is a marked female preponderance. One also suspects that Nonconformists may be concentrated in status groups with low fertility.

Some further evidence suggests that the overall balance within Nonconformity has shifted towards the fringe sects, especially the Pentecostals. However, the smaller bodies like the Unitarians, the Presbyterian Church of England, the Salvation Army and the Society of Friends, have all experienced some element of decline as well: between them they number some quarter of a million members. One must also include the Calvinistic Methodist Church with some 130,000 members, the majority of whom are in Wales.

## RELIGIOUS BELIEFS AND PRACTICE

In contemporary England religious *belief* of a rather amorphous kind is very widely disseminated, whereas religious *practice*, Anglican or dissenting, is low and anyway disproportionately middle class. Just how amorphous this belief is, can be gauged from comparing a total of 85 to 90 per cent believing in God and calling themselves 'Christian' with a total of 50 per cent believing in the life to come, almost the lowest for any nominally Christian country [cf. Public Opinion Quarterly 1964–65; Gallup Poll Summary, 1957 ... privately circulated]. Moreover the interpretation of the word 'Christian' brings it very close to the concept of 'decency'. A further important point concerns the way in which religious belief and practice are only loosely related [Mass Observation, 1948], so that many of those who practise are fairly unorthodox, while surprising reserves of religiosity (particularly as regards private prayer) exist among those who never attend church [cf.

Argyle, 1959]. So we have a situation where the majority of the nation approves of 'Christianity' and with it religious education in schools and all the paraphernalia of the Establishment (coronation included) because being 'Christian' means accepting there must be 'something' and 'doing as you would be done by'.

With respect to practice, however, some six out of every ten adults act on the assumption that you can be a good 'Christian' and live a decent life without going to church. As for the rest, 15 per cent are present on a Sunday, 20 per cent every two Sundays. Some quarter of the population attend ordinary services once a month, and some two-fifths or more attend at least once a year. By ordinary services one includes events like harvest festival and Remembrance Day which draw unusual numbers, but not rites of passage. The rites of passage are interesting simply because they partly cross the class and status barrier [Kaim-Caundle, 1959 for an interesting local study]. Over 90 per cent are buried with religious rites, some 80 per cent are baptized and some 70 per cent married in church, – though only about 24 per cent receive Anglican Confirmation [Basic data are to be found in Paul, 1964; Church Information Office, 1959, 1962, 1966; *Church of England Year Book*, 1969].[1]

There are, however, considerable denominational regional and other variations in the extent of religious participation. Of those who can be regarded as part of the Catholic community in England and Wales, some two million attend Sunday Mass, just over four out of ten. Some six out of ten claim to attend Mass most Sundays while seven to eight are present for their Easter and Christmas duties. This, of course, contrasts dramatically with Anglican laxity; only about one in thirteen Anglicans is present at Sunday service. Of the total Free Church community just under a quarter is to be found in chapel each Sunday, while something under 40 per cent attend at least once a month and under 60 per cent 'now and again'. Indeed less than 30 per cent of those calling themselves Nonconformist are entirely outside their churches' ministrations, compared with 40 per cent of Anglicans and 20 per cent of Roman Catholics.

The areas where practice is least, particularly as regards the Church of England, are undoubtedly new housing estates [Mogey, 1956, pp. 145–147] and old-established working-class areas in large cities. Here Anglican Sunday practice may vary between 0.5 and 2.5 per cent but there is usually a fair-sized Catholic population in such places which pulls up the overall

1. As regards Confirmation, Catholic and Dissenting ceremonies are not really parallel to the Anglican rite so they are omitted. Alarms about Confirmation have been much exaggerated. Most of the so-called loss was related to the declining birth rate 1947–51 [Martin 1967].

average. Not only is the Sunday attendance very low but the proportion of those never attending is much higher.[2]

Smaller-sized working-class towns are likely to achieve around 7 to 8 per cent attendance per week; if they rise higher, it usually indicates a substantial Catholic population. Market and country towns, even when based on industry, seem to have higher percentages: 15 in Banbury, 12.5 in Derby, 17.5 in Glossop. Yet High Wycombe has only 10 per cent conceivably because the Catholic population appears unusually small [Stacey, 1960; Cauter and Downham, 1954; Birch, 1959].

Suburbs also appear to be places of relatively high practice, and they are the only areas outside traditional market towns or country districts where Anglicanism recovers some of its dominance. Woodford for example achieves 15 per cent practice, and in the course of a month 34 per cent of the middle class and 17 per cent of the working class are found in church [Willmott and Young, 1960]. It seems that in a socially varied area working-class practice may not be quite as low as where the class affiliation is entirely monochrome.

Patterns of observance within England are plainly connected with complex variables relating to region, class and size of town. Gorer [1955] in his study shows a series of clear connections, even when the distribution of the Catholic population is allowed for. Thus cities over a million have a lower practice than those over one hundred thousand and the number rises again for towns under ten thousand. The north is more practising than the south, and the south-west more practising than the south-east. The upper middle class is more practising than the lower middle class, and a large gap yawns between the lower middle and the working class. Presumably one aspect of this class differential is the increase in practice with each rise in educational level.

## THE PATTERN OF SECULARIZATION

Three theses are expounded below but may be stated baldly without delay. The first classifies societies in terms of Protestant or Catholic dominance and associates with Protestantism and Catholicism certain patterns of individual striving or collective class antagonism respectively. These patterns are in

2. Thus in Dagenham some 83 per cent 'never went' [Willmott, 1963]. In Bethnal Green only 13 per cent attended in the course of a month, which probably means that three-quarters never go to church at all [Young and Willmott 1962]. In the Metropolitan Borough studied by Mass Observation 18 per cent attended during a month, but the number of those never darkening the church door was still 60 per cent [Mass Observation 1948].

turn associated with the appearance either of massive fissures based on class or a limited institutionalized conflict within wider unities and tolerances. From these two patterns certain consequences flow for the ideological formation of the intelligentsia, for the process of moral change and for the development of social legitimations. In the Catholic pattern these consequences involve massive belief and practice on the one hand confronted by massive unbelief and vigorous alienation on the other.

The second thesis separates out two sub-varieties within Protestantism: the pattern of American pluralism, and the pattern of Protestant state-churches (Anglican, Lutheran or Calvinist) with or without substantial Protestant dissent. In the former, religion is vulgarized and therefore, remains popular – in the proper sense of vulgarization and popularity – whereas in the latter, religion remains permanently allied to an *élite* culture. This culture becomes alien once industrialism breaks up the organic nature of society, but the consequent erosion of institutional participation is *not* accompanied by substantial unbelief. It is important that where Protestant dissent develops on any scale and moves in partial conjunction with political dissent the appearance of militant unbelief in association with secular political radicalism is particularly unlikely. This, of course, has been the English situation.[3]

The third thesis is in two sections, and states, firstly, that in a general way a nation denied self-determination by another dominating society will either seek sources of religious differentiation, or use the pre-existing religious difference as a rallying point. All the Celtic cultures in Britain evidence this, including Cornwall. The thesis states, secondly, that minorities as such tend to have higher levels of practice than majorities, and particularly so when they are excluded from the upper echelons. Not only do such minorities develop internal cohesion but may join up with political dissidents to make common cause against the dominant *élite*. Thus high practice and political radicalism have been characteristic of Catholic minorities, not only in England, but in the British Commonwealth and, (to some extent), America. Paradoxically this further contributes to the stable pattern of limited social conflict in Protestant societies by preventing any conflict *à l'outrance* with religion *as such* on the part of political rebels, as well as simultaneously ameliorating the violence of the protest. The Catholic contribution to unionism is notable in Britain as in the United States.

3. In Calvinist societies this dissent tends to be to the theological right and liberalization occurs *within* the main Calvinist body; in Lutheran societies dissent is a minor phenomenon and is inclined to pietism.

*Religion and industrial society*

Before organizing the English material within these three theses, the universal, or near universal, processes which occur in industrial society with respect to religion may be economically stated. The first general process involves a vast acceleration of social differentiation and augmentation whereby institutional religion ceases to be the hub of life and becomes a compartment, while the religious role of given persons become just one role among many others played in a wide variety of contexts. Religion becomes an 'interest' and the Churches come to provide the 'religious variety of club for the clubbable classes'. Moreover each non-religious segment throws up problems so specific and technical that it is not easy to see how highly general religious norms can be applied to them. It may be remarked that this 'loss of functions' need not necessarily be regarded as secularization. A similar loss has occurred in relation to the family and just as some sociologists argue that the family can now fulfil its specific function more perfectly, so it may be that religion becomes truly itself when relieved of welfare, or education or the need to legitimise the state.[4] The difficulty is that 'true' religion is then associated with comparative impotence just as 'diluted' religion was once associated with power.

The second general process is the direct impact of science. Presumably science augments the manipulative attitude towards the natural environment and also towards the social environment. Moreover the old rituals designed to conjure responses from nature or society are downgraded. Of course, this can be overstated. Our ancestors never thought rituals a substitute for pragmatic action; rogationtide accompanied sowing. But doubtless the *general* sense of human power is increased: the play of contingency is restricted, and the overwhelming sense of divine limits, which afflicted previous generations is much diminished.

At the same time this sense of unbounded power, and this restriction of contingency is *merely* general: each particular person still feels the threat of fell contingency, and to the extent that natural and political power is socialized, focused and centralized, may even feel less powerful than ever before. The scientific achievement creates its pessimisms as well as its optimisms, notably of course in relation to nuclear warfare. It is worth noting that the scientific threat, operating in the context of a pre-existing liberal optimism, has particular impact in the growth of peace movements with religious overtones in both Britain and America. Science also coexists with superstitions, beliefs in fate, magic, talismans and pre-Christian religion, as well as

4. It is interesting that this problem of specific role is paralleled in the academic field by the situation of philosophy.

with potent social myths. Maybe the lack of individual power contributes to the massive survival of beliefs in fate, in luck, in a universal moral balance and in superstitions of every kind [Gorer, 1965, partially documents this point].

One further possible impact of science must be considered in relation to the points about division of labour and specialization referred to above. Scientific achievement is now so specialized that the scientist is far less capable of making sophisticated judgements on belief systems, religious or otherwise, than the generally 'informed' humanist. Moreover, his activities are so technical that even if they did have deleterious implications for religion these would not seep through to society in general. What seeps through to society simply has to be bastardized and magicked out of all recognition. Hence the impact of science in this sphere is almost nil. Science has become as compartmentalized as religion.

But there remain the indirect consequences of science through its enormous impact on society, part of which is the process of segmentation already mentioned. Beyond this there are complex processes of social mobility which tended to erode familial and local ties and indeed continuity as such. The erosion of continuity in itself necessarily includes religion. Moreover, the increased speed of erosion and change, together with the variety of available roles and milieux radically relativizes perspectives. Eternal norms limp lamely after new situations, and securities of every kind are threatened. Technical change also, in particular car and television, – provides potent rivals to churches. Modern man is either mobile in his car or immobile in front of his television set.

Nevertheless it is not clear whether these indirect consequences of science have the universal impact one might expect, since after all the United States exemplifies these tendencies in their most developed form and nevertheless has flourishing religious institutions. This means, therefore, that it may be appropriate to abandon 'universal' processes, and look more closely at all the differentia between societies, in so far as they can be explained in the three theses stated at the outset.

### *Conflict and the Protestant and Catholic patterns*

The first thesis, contrasting the Protestant pattern of muted conflict and individual striving, with the Catholic pattern of massive conflict between religion and secular collectivities, can now be discussed in relation to three crucial areas: the intelligentsia, changing moral norms, and legitimations. Naturally the almost exclusive focus will be on the Protestant pattern as realized in England.

As regards the intelligentsia there are two aspects which are worthy of comment. First, the most important aspect of English intellectuals is their capacity to absorb new ideologies within Christian categories. New knowledge like that of the higher criticism or of the physical sciences after the mid-nineteenth century, tends to be reinterpreted without causing widespread collapse of faith. New ideologies, liberalism, democratic socialism, existentialism, take on a variegated Christian colouring. Intellectuals select those aspects of Christianity which are closest to their intellectual attitudes, whether they involve world-weary pessimism, medieval nostalgia or the utopian optimism of a Kingdom of God on earth.

All the same the intelligentsia contains almost the only significant group of explicit agnostics and atheists in England. Indeed one finds an echo of the French Catholic pattern in that there is a comparative polarization of belief and unbelief amongst intellectuals. Thus both regular practice and atheism are much augmented as compared with the rest of the population [Brothers, 1964]. Of course, this partly reflects the middle class character of the intellectual stratum. These atheistic tendencies of middle class intellectuals are reflected in the almost uniformly middle class and intellectual character of the humanist societies. Many humanists identify Christianity with a whole social establishment which is resistant to the forces of liberalization and with a commercial middle class which values money more than brains or even loves a lord more than it respects ability.

It is now appropriate to turn to the discussion of moral norms, in particular the issues raised by progressives and embodied in their various crusades. The progressive crusades, especially *C.N.D.*, are bound up very much with the development of moral norms. However, it is important to recognize that in Protestant societies these norms can take their point of reference either from Christian bases or from humanist ones – and so doing *can* arrive at broadly similar conclusions. The difference between this style and the Catholic style is broadly the difference between French cathedrals and English cathedrals: one is an act of rational vertical organization, the other a process of horizontal accretion. Where Catholicism attempts to legislate, Protestantism hands the problems over to the individual conscience in relation to social developments.

It is true, of course, that the Anglican Church sometimes speaks in the Catholic manner, but the fundamental Protestantism of English society assures that the Anglican voice is barely heard when it speaks. By the same token no crisis of faith results should the Anglican voice retract its words. This Laodicean apathy applies whether the voice is 'progressive' or 'regressive', sophisticated or naive: the fact that recent pronouncements are often both sophisticated and progressive makes no difference. No crisis of faith can result either way.

The quite different situation of Catholics in England, and elsewhere over questions like birth control, and divorce is obvious: for them teaching over moral norms can create a crisis of faith [cf. Spencer 1966; Gallup Poll, March 1967]. So far as the Free Churches are concerned, they appear more responsive to new situations, but in the public mind they are associated with teetotalism and the rejection of gambling. The former attitude is much relaxed while the latter is maintained. But few people in the Free Churches and nobody in the public at large feels religion as such to be implicated in the refusal or acceptance of alcohol [See Rodd, 1967 and 1968 for local Methodist and other denominations' attitudes to this and a whole range of social questions].

I have so far discussed the problems of moral change and development in terms of my contrast between Catholic and Protestant. There are certain aspects which do not fall into this contrast. For example, one influential segment of opinion, notably composed of the older style of evangelical and traditionalist Catholic, concerns itself with maintaining some ascetic norms, particularly with respect to sexual behaviour and drug addiction, and generally accuses the wider society of moral decay.

Another group consisting of existentialists, of various progressives and of new Catholics, focuses attention on the general problem of norms in a changing society, as well as sometimes taking up rigorist attitudes on issues like peace and war, colour, Rhodesia, freedom of expression and so on. Cross-cutting this division between traditionalist and progressives is another division between those who adhere to the 'folk-Church-concept', whereby ecclesiastical institutions attempt to bolster Christian norms for society in general – at the expense of dilution – and the 'elect minority' (or 'humble minority') concept, whereby Christians accept these norms only for themselves. As a matter of fact, the progressives, to the extent that they hold rigorist notions about (say) divorce tend to restrict their provenance to the group of committed Christians, but in so far as they make pronouncements on colour, colonialism etc., talk in terms of the whole society.

In considering legitimations, two points are out-standing: first they reinforce one another rather than compete, and, second, they exhibit not only a contrast between but a curious mingling of Protestant and Catholic motifs. As regards the slow accretion of mutually supporting legitimations one can show the manner in which the concrete symbol of the Crown, and the verbal symbol of the word 'Christian' co-exist with the mythology of popular rule through the ballot box and the individual rights of every free-born Englishman. It is interesting to note that even J.S. Mill called the ballot 'the eucharist of democracy'. As regards 'Crown' and 'Christianity', there is an almost universal agreement to accept both and therefore not to involve either explicitly in divisive and party political issues, although the Conservative Party used to make some implicit use of the monarchy and

Christianity in its propaganda.[5] In fact, they can only be explicitly utilised by either side in relation to *external* threats. The Rhodesian crisis provided an instructive example. The Labour Prime Minister did not scruple to invoke the Queen against the rebellious settlers, knowing full well the aura of the monarchy with Labour supporters. Moreover the attempt of Lord Salisbury to link the settlers' cause with the burden of bearing 'White Christian Civilization' was firmly quashed by none else than the Archbishop of Canterbury, urging vigorous action against the colonialist regime.

The mingling and overlapping of Catholic and Protestant motifs is particularly striking. Thus the individual is defended by a Protestant suspicion of all institutional encroachment, whether by the Church, bureaucracy, or Trade Union. Again there is a very Protestant fear of dogmatism in religion and in politics, allied with some mild respect for Church and clergy, mainly on the grounds that they perform good works through a vast network of charitable organizations, – as indeed they do. This is probably why the Church functionaries are more popular than government functionaries, or even doctors: a popularity they find difficult to believe [cf. A.B.C.T.V. 1965 for tables concerning the clergy]. But the Catholic aspect is equally evident in the enormous enthusiasm for medieval rituals like the Coronation and royal weddings, as well as for a whole complex of emotions associated with Christmas, the Gothic, the English countryside, craftsmen, boys voices and the sturdy Church tower or spire rising romantically over the market town. The English do not go very much to Church, but they like to have it there. It is part of the legitimate order; it proves that 'God's in his heaven, all's right with the world'.

### *Religion and the élite culture*

I now turn to the second thesis concerning the effects of maintaining an *élite* culture in association with the English Church. The argument is that on the one hand the Protestantism of England has prevented any massive confrontation of religion with secular radicalism, while on the other hand the retention of *élite* forms and conventions has prevented that necessary vulgarization which enabled American religion to suffuse the culture as a whole. Once the organic unities of English life were broken by the industrial revolution, working class life evolved its own cultural forms far removed from the gentry style permeating the upper echelons, and by extension, the

5. Christianity was certainly invoked to a minor extent in the beginning of the present century. An example can be found in Fenner Brockway's 'Bermondsey Story', [1949] where the local Conservative party is described as accusing the local I.L.P. of atheism and secularism – a foolish charge at that period, which the I.L.P. easily rebutted with a list of Christian activists in its ranks.

English Church. So, although the mildly reactionary and occasionally reformist attitude of Anglicanism played rather a minor role in alienating the working classes, the cultural gap widened beyond repair.

Dissent might conceivably have filled this gap, but the contrast between short-term hedonism in the majority of the working class and the pattern of religious enthusiasm and personal asceticism found amongst most dissenters, prevented any large scale absorption of the workers into the dissenting fold. The overlap between dissent and the working class merely resulted in a dissenting contribution to labour leadership, particularly, of course, in Wales. Otherwise dissenters tended to receive earthly rewards for religious discipline and moved towards the middle class or at any rate the lower middle class.

The result, as previously demonstrated, is that in contemporary England religious *belief* of a rather amorphous kind is very widely disseminated, whereas religious *practice*, Anglican or dissenting, is low and anyway disproportionately middle class. The distinction between middle and working class is indicated by the way in which Church attendance runs parallel to participation in voluntary associations as such [cf. Stark, 1964 for an alternative viewpoint]. Middle class patterns turn around voluntary associations, amongst which the churches are partly included, whereas working class patterns turn either around kinship or the public house, plus cinemas, sports outings – and television in the home. The point about television is quite important because there is a segment of the working classes which achieves some passive participation in institutional religion through radio and television [Cauter and Downham, 1954; Silvey 1955; A.B.C.T.V., 1965. See also the Files of the B.B.C. Audience Research].

*Religion and minorities*

We come finally now to the third thesis. The two parts of the thesis with respect to the cohesion of sub-cultures and of minority groups overlap each other, depending on the definitions used. There is no necessary connection between them, since clearly the cohesion of a sectarian minority like the Brethren is quite different from that of the Irish Roman Catholics in England. Setting both together is a marriage of convenience rather than necessity. Furthermore, the task of stating the thesis so that the two aspects are fully differentiated and all relevant qualifications stated would be a matter for a book not a few paragraphs. Plainly with respect to relevant qualifications these would include such complex matters as the interaction of social mobility, (of an individualistic or group variety), with group sub-cultural solidarity, and the further interaction between both these elements and the values of the group, particularly with respect to striving and educational attainment. Additional complications arise from a consideration of the values of the group in relation to acceptable degrees of practice. One obviously cannot ignore the importance assigned by Catholics to regular Sunday Mass.

As far as the national sub-cultures of Wales, Ireland and Scotland are concerned one need do little more than note that they each have a higher level of weekly religious practice than England; perhaps 90 per cent in the case of Eire and some 25 per cent amongst the rest. Of course this is partly due to the factor of remoteness which assisted the survival of sub-cultures in the first place and the lesser degree of industrialization which is found in less accessible areas. It is in such areas that one locates the last bastions of majority practice in the United Kingdom.

Of course it has been the immigrations, notably over the past century and a half, from the sub-cultures which have provided the minorities in England itself, excluding the indigenous and purely religious minorities of Free Churchmen and Sectarians. It will be useful to discuss the largely migrant minorities first, beginning with the Roman Catholics. Like almost all the religious minorities in England, the Roman Catholics are found in the large towns [cf. *Youth and Religion*; Gay, in Martin 1968 for regional distribution of Catholics]. Originally they favoured Liverpool; more recently they have increased notably in London and Birmingham. This has various consequences, so that the urban-rural differences in practice for all Churches taken *together* are partly obscured in towns where Catholics exist in large numbers.[6] It also means that a localized concentration of the Catholic population assists an efficient provision of churches. Moreover these churches have increased in number to meet successive waves of migration: the Irish in the mid-nineteenth and mid-twentieth century, the Poles, Hungarians and Italians, mainly since 1940. This expansion creates confidence. The problem of redundancy and redeployment affecting the English Church barely arises, especially since the immigrants once arrived are mostly working class and therefore much less geographically mobile than practising Anglicans [cf. Glass, 1970, re Catholic social mobility in London].[7]

The largely one-class character of Catholicism also increases homogeneity and militates against socially divisive influences; the Catholic gentry exists, of course, but it is minute. In particular Catholic priests are not invariably middle class and university trained in the way that most Anglican priests have been – at least until very recently.[8] Hence localised concentrations of

6. The Church of England most perfectly exemplifies the diminution of practice from village to large industrial complex. Easter Communions are some 16 per cent in Herefordshire, and under 1 per cent in some areas of East London.

7. Glass shows in this that upward mobility for Catholics is limited and downward mobility is high.

8. There has been some difficulty in the recruitment of Anglican ordinands since 1964. There is an increasing tendency in any case to take older men and the propor-

Catholics and partial homogeneity as regards class, ally with embattled minority status and the Roman Catholic valuation of institutional practice to produce the weekly attendance at mass of some four out of ten, which is in dramatic contrast to the Anglican proportion of one in thirteen. The proportion of baptised Catholics at Mass in the course of a year is perhaps over 75 per cent, which contrasts again, though less strikingly, with an Anglican proportion of those baptised amounting to some 40 per cent.

It is an interesting question why the other Celtic migrants in England do not adhere to high levels of practice but gradually conform to the dominant apathy – just as Bretons conform to the irreligious atmosphere of Paris. Doubtless this is partly because they are closer to English Protestantism than the Irish, notably of course to the Free Churches. At any rate the Churches of the Welsh and Scots Diaspora are small; the Presbyterian Church of England numbers only some 75,000. This suggests that Scots and Welsh are absorbed into English Protestantism, perhaps the Free Churches in particular, so that the Baptists gain from the Welsh and the Congregationalists from the Presbyterians.[9] If so this makes the previously discussed decline of the Free Churches in terms of the English population more striking.

The Free Churches remain of course more practising than Anglicans. To some extent their erosion reflects characteristics in direct contrast to those of Roman Catholicism. The Free Churches are found in the smaller towns and the suburbs and in some rural areas: they therefore have problems of maintaining *élan* in relation to a scattered constituency and also problems of deployment [Methodist Conference, 1958]. Moreover they value education and striving which in turn makes for social and geographical mobility and erodes both local roots and cohesion, as well as giving practising Free Churchmen a somewhat lower middle class character [Glass, 1970]. This depends on area: in the south-east where Free Churchmen are relatively infrequent they are socially indistinguishable from Anglicans; in the north (the reference is largely to Methodism) they retain a working class segment, perhaps partly derived from the Primitives. To the extent that they penetrate deeply into the middle class they often either succumb to Anglicanism or to theological liberalism. In the middle class proper some of the *raison d'être* of non-conformity rooted in social as well as theological antagonism,

---

tion of graduates has fallen. There is some dissatisfaction with the parochial ministry, especially among theological radicals who prefer the growing specialist ministries and want in addition a radical social commitment. The radicals have probably gained at the expense of the 'Catholics' [Coxon, 1967; Martin 1968].

9. As is well known, a merger is now proposed of the two churches, perhaps under the title of 'The Reformed Church'.

appears less meaningful, and the symbolic maintenance of this difference in, for example, teetotalism, feels somewhat exaggerated.[10]

This point about liberalism is worth consideration because it is probably correct to say that Free Churches resist erosion to the extent that they are low in the scale of status and have a large evangelical component. In England the Free Churches can be set on a very crude continuum running from the Quakers, Unitarians and Congregationalists as the highest in status, and most liberalised, to the Baptists as the lowest in status and least liberalised, with the Methodists somewhere in between. It looks as if the Congregationalists and Unitarians have suffered most severely and the Baptists least. Certainly the evangelicals in all Free Churches and in the Anglican Church create patterns of relatively exclusive association which persist even in the university milieu: the evangelical Inter-Varsity Fellowship is notably cohesive compared with the Student Christian Movement. Indeed the evangelicals rival the Roman Catholics in their ability to create the kind of ghetto mentality which preserves them against the corrosions of the wider society. Their stubborn resilience is a notable feature of recent years, particularly perhaps within Anglicanism.

By contrast the Jews often lack a ghetto-mentality, particularly perhaps in the large upper middle class of Jewry in North London. Jews are the only group whom one might expect to resemble the Catholics in stressing separatist education, but this has not been pursued on a large scale. British Jewry, somewhat less than half a million, consisting mostly of the descendants of the Eastern European Diaspora in the 1890's and those who migrated in the thirties from Germany, has avoided separatism and has paid the penalty of partial absorption. This absorption assists and is assisted by social mobility. At any rate intermarriage is such that Jewry may be substantially reduced in a generation or so. The high rate of recruitment to universities, notably London, results in a large number for whom Jewry is largely an ethnic category, and it is doubtless among these that the left-wing attitudes of the *deracine* intellectual find fruitful soil. Maybe this process is accelerated by the fact that religious Jewry (unlike the situation in the U.S.A.) is largely Orthodox: the Liberal and Reform Congregations in Britain are relatively small.

10. The north-south difference in Methodism may be partly a social class difference, partly a difference in degree of evangelical orthodoxy. Parts of northern Methodism are strongly evangelical, highly localized in feeling and somewhat separate from the bureaucratic superstructure, whereas south-eastern Methodism does not exhibit these characteristics to the same extent and is socially almost indistinguishable from the Anglican Church. These differences are symbolised in widely differing attitudes to the current proposals for Anglican-Methodist unity [cf. Martin 1969, articles by M. Hill and B. Turner].

The remaining minorities are largely non-Christian. They resemble the Catholics in being concentrated in particular areas of the working class districts of large towns. This is equally true for the two minorities which do happen to be Christian: the Orthodox, and the West Indians. The West Indians are a special case in that they alone explicitly desire social assimilation, and yet find English religious forms so cold and unfamiliar that substantial numbers turn to Pentecostalism. The desire for assimilation is notably less strong among Pakistanis, and other Muslims groups, and among Sikhs: together, these probably total well over a quarter of a million. Many of them come to England with at least the intention of returning [Butterworth in Martin 1969].

The Pentecostalist tendencies among West Indians introduce the question of the self-defined sectarian minority. Whether Pentecostalists are sectarians or the extreme wing of evangelicalism is a moot point [Wilson, 1961]. At any rate they have expanded rapidly of recent years. In so doing they may have benefited from the social elevation of the Salvation Army. It seems that evangelical penetration of the working class tends to take a new form in each generation – from Methodism to the Salvation Army to the Pentecostalists. The evangelised group then cuts itself off from the working class by differential mobility and then becomes partially liberalized. At any rate the other evangelical bodies, not only the Salvation Army but the 'Free Gospel Halls' have lost ground, partly to Pentecostals, and partly to genuine sectarians like the Ubiquitous Witnesses and latterly the Mormons. An exception to the point made above about liberalisation in association with mobility is provided by the Brethren (about 80,000), especially those of the Exclusive persuasion (about 30,000) [Wilson, 1967 discusses recent fissions in relation to attempts at extreme isolation]. Many Brethren achieve wealth through Puritan virtue but are so efficiently insulated that the outside world barely penetrates. This applies equally to Scots fisherfolk and business men. Indeed internal fission in favour of greater asceticism and exclusiveness is more likely than liberalisation.

### '*Secularization*'

Finally we come to some comments about the religious situation in Britain generally, notably with reference to 'secularization', using secularization as a term to cover belief, practice, and attitude [cf. Wilson 1966 for a rather different emphasis]. Obviously there has been a decline since the Religious Census of March 1851 when some seven out of twelve of those adults able to attend Church did in fact do so. The decline is clear for Protestantism, especially for the Free Churches. Roman Catholic losses have been less great and in any case masked by increase from migrations. Yet there are two qualifications worth making: one with respect to practice, the other with respect to attitude. As regards practice the extent of occasional practice has already been noted: up to 45 per cent in the course of a year, excluding rites of passage. We also know that emptier churches can reflect not so much cessation of practice as less *frequent* practice and a form of practice which is confined to particular points in the life cycle, like adolescence and the post forty years. This 'occasional conformity' ought not to be interpreted as a total cessation of church-going habit.

As regards attitude one must remember that we have exchanged a Laodicean eighteenth century church aiming at inclusion and comprehension for a more activist Anglicanism somewhat puzzled as to whether or not it should 'spew' the church of the Laodicean out of its mouth.[11] There is evidence that the broad mass of the English have been neither cold nor hot for a very long time. We need not go back to Pelagius, though he would hardly be disappointed with some aspects of English religion were his spirit to return. But we can reasonably go back to Schleiermacher, who commented on English indifferentism as long ago as 1798. And Jonathan Swift made identical comments ninety years previously – comments which make one wonder how far culture can be secularized without really ever having been thoroughly Christianized.

> 'For the rest, it may perhaps admit a controversy, whether the banishing all notions of religion whatsoever would be inconvenient for the vulgar. Not that I am in the least of opinion with those who hold religion to have been the invention of politicians, to keep the lower part of the world in awe by the fear of invisible powers; unless mankind were then very different from what it is now; for I look upon the mass or body of our people here in England to be as Free-thinkers, that is to say, as staunch unbelievers, as any of the highest rank. But I conceive some scattered notions about a superior power to be of singular use for the common people, as furnishing excellent materials to keep children quiet when they grow peevish, and providing topics of amusement in a tedious winter night.'

11. There is currently some debate as to whether the English Church should continue as a '*Volks-Kirche*'. This debate comes almost entirely from the most activist members of the Church; the *Volk* are content with things as they are.

SELECTED BIBLIOGRAPHY*

A.B.C. Television, *Television and Religion*. London, University of London Press, 1965.
Argyle, Michael, *Religious Behaviour*. London, Routledge and Kegan Paul, 1959.
Booth, C., 'Life and Labour of the People in London.' Third Series. *Religious Influences*, 7 vols. London, Macmillan, 1902–3, especially Vol. 7.
Brothers, J., 'Recent Developments in the Sociology of Religion in England and Wales.' *Social Compass*, 11 (3–4), 1964.
—, 'Religion in the British Universities.' *Archives de Sociologie des Religions*, 18, July-December, 1964.
Busia, K. A., *Urban Churches in Britain*. London, Lutterworth, 1966.
Calley, M. J. C., *God's People*. Oxford, Oxford University Press, 1965.
Clark, D., *Survey of Anglicans and Methodists in Four Towns*. London, Epworth, 1965.
Coxon, A. P. M., 'Patterns of Occupational Recruitment: The Anglican Ministry.' *Sociology*, January 1967.
Driver, C., 'The Non-conformist Conscience.' *New Society*, 27 June 1963.
Glass, D. V., 'Aspects of Social Status.' *Third London Survey*. London, Weidenfeld and Nicholson, 1970.
Isichei, E. A., 'From Sect to Denomination among British Quakers.' *British Journal of Sociology*, 15 (3), 1964.
Kaim-Caundle, P. R., *Religion in Billingham*. Billingham, Billingham Community Organization, 1959.
Kiev, A., 'Psychotherapeutic Aspects of Pentecostal Sects Among West Indian Immigrants to England.' *British Journal of Sociology*, 15 (2), 1964.
Loukes, H., *Teenage Religion*. London, S.C.M. Press, 1961.
Martin, D. A., 'The Denomination.' *British Journal of Sociology*, 13 (2), 1962.
—; Jackson, J. A., and Moore, R., 'Papers on the Sociology of Religion.' Originally given at the British Association. September 1965; published in *Advancement of Science*, June, 1966.
— (ed.), *A Yearbook of the Sociology of Religion in Britain*, No. 1. London, S.C.M. Press, 1968.
— (ed.), *A Yearbook of the Sociology of Religion in Britain*, No. 2. London, S.C.M. Press, 1969.
—, *A Sociology of Religion in Britain*. London, S.C.M. Press, 1967.
Mass Observation, *Puzzled People*. London, Gollancz, 1948.
Paul, L., *The Deployment and Payment of the Clergy*. London, Church Information Office, 1964.
Pickering, W. S. F., (ed.) *Anglican-Methodist Relations*. London, Darton, Longman and Todd, 1961.
Rees, A., and Davies, E. (eds.), *Welsh Rural Communities*. Cardiff, University of Wales Press, 1960.

* Extensive bibliographies are provided in my studies *A Sociology of English Religion*. London, S.C.M. Press, 1967 and D. Martin (ed.), *A Sociological Yearbook of Religion in Britain*, No. 3, London, S.C.M. Press, 1970 (compiled and annotated by R. Coles).

Rodd, C. S., *A Comparison of Attitudes to Social Questions between three Church Groups and a Control Group of Non-church-goers*. Birmingham, M. Soc. Sc. Thesis, 1967.
Rowntree, B. S. and Lavers, B. R., *English Life and Leisure*. London, Longmans, 1951.
Silvey, R. J., *Religious Broadcasts and the Public*. London, B.B.C., 1955.
Stark, R., 'Class, Radicalism and Religious Involvement.' *American Sociological Review*, 29 (5), October 1964.
Thompson, R. H. T., *The Church's Understanding of Itself*. London, S.C.M. Press, 1957.
Walters, G. (ed.), *Religion in Technological Society*. Bath, Bath Technological University Press, 1968.
Ward, C. K., *Priest and People*. Liverpool, Liverpool University Press, 1961.
Wilson, B. R., *Religion in Secular Society*. London, Watts, 1966.
—, *Sects and Society*. London, Heinemann, 1961.
— (ed.), *Patterns of Setlarianism Ideology and Organization*. London, Heinemann, 1967.

*Note*. Important historical interpretations are to be found in:
A. MacIntyre, *Secularization and Moral Change*, 1967.
D. H. McLeod, *Churches in Metropolitan London 1885–1914*. Ph. D. thesis Cambridge 1971 (showing the conventional character of Victorian religion).
K. Thomas, *Religion and the Decline of Magic*, 1970 (showing religious indifference in the 16th and 17th centuries).

JOHN HIGHET*

# Great Britain: Scotland

Though a small nation,[1] and one without political sovereignty, Scotland has much of interest to offer the sociologist of religion.

She is one of the few countries in the world (perhaps the only one) with a national church which is established yet free. Though she has thirty or so Christian denominations she has one church[2] (the national church – the Church of Scotland) which enjoys a much more prominent position within her boundaries than is the case with a single church in most other countries. From her went out men who greatly contributed to the spread of Presbyterianism as one of the world's ecclesiastical polities (as well as spreading both Christianity and education to many areas of the globe). Her history illustrates church people's penchant for schism-forming and yet also presents to the world a classic achievement in reunion several decades in advance of

* John Highet was born in Glasgow, Scotland in 1918. For many years he was a lecturer in Applied Sociology at the University of Glasgow, and he now holds the position of Head of the School of Social Studies at the Robert Gordon's Institute of Technology, Aberdeen. He has been a member of several Church Committees at General Assembly and Presbytery level, and was a member of a Scottish Advisory Council on Education. His publications include articles on education and youth, as well as the books *The Churches in Scotland Today*, 1950 and *The Scottish Churches*, 1960.

1. The author would like to emphasize that Scotland is a nation sociologically distinct from the nations of England and Wales, although the three together form a political entity called Britain. Scholars and others often confuse the adjective 'British' which applies to all three with the adjective 'English' which applies to only one [e.g. Wilson 1966, Martin, 1967]. Scotland has legal and educational systems distinct from those of England – plus-Wales, and unlike Wales has a separate national Church.

2. The word 'denomination' is used in a general sense to stand for a fellowship of Christian believers however organised, of whatever size, and whatever their beliefs. The term 'church' is here virtually interchangeable with 'denomination' except that as synonymous with 'denomination' the word has an initial capital while 'church' with a lower-case 'c' stands for the local, individual congregation (and, on occasion, for the building which houses them). Entanglement in the three-fold typology so dear to theoretical sociologists of religion. 'church, denomination, and sect', has been deliberately avoided here.

the contemporary vogue of ecumenicalism. And though by some indices she is currently 'secularized' she retains sufficient features of being a society where religion still matters for her to be worth looking at by today's debaters of the 'secularization thesis'.

## HISTORICAL INTRODUCTION AND THE DENOMINATIONAL SPECTRUM

For more than four centuries Scotland has been predominantly Protestant and her Protestants have been and are overwhelmingly Presbyterians, distributed (though very unevenly) over five denominations.[3] These five, with, in brackets, the latest available indices of their numerical following,[4] are: the Church of Scotland (1,233,808 in 1966): the Reformed Presbyterian Church (617, estimated, in 1959); the Free Presbyterian Church (650 full communicants plus 4,100 'official' adherents, estimated, in 1959); the Free Church of Scotland (1957 estimate: 5,909 full communicants plus 18,377 official adherents); and the United Free Church (20,396 in 1966).

The Church of Scotland is a Church 'established yet free'. It is Established in that it is in historical continuity with the Church of Scotland which was reformed in 1560, whose liberties were ratified by Act of the Scottish Parliament in 1652, and for whose continuance provision was made by the Act for Securing the Protestant Religion and Presbyterian Church Government (November, 1706). This Act was a 'fundamental and essential condition' of the Treaty of Union between England and Scotland (1707) and the Sovereign of the United Kingdom still promises to 'inviolably maintain' the religious settlement then established.

However, though thus 'by law established', the Church of Scotland is equally 'by law made free of the State'. According to the Constitution of the Church of Scotland in Matters Spiritual, accepted by the British Parliament's Church of Scotland Act (1921) the State, with certain safeguards, recognizes the Church's 'right and power subject to no civil authority to legislate and to adjudicate finally, in all matters of doctrine, worship, government and discipline in the Church'.

Though a national and established Church the Church of Scotland is thus

3. Until recently there were six: in 1956 the then United Original Secession Church joined with the Church of Scotland or, in the case of a minority of its membership, with other Presbyterian Churches.

4. Scotland has no official (or even semi-official) Census of Religious Bodies, and these data are the product of special enquiries by the author. Elsewhere [Highet, 1954; 1958; 1960] detailed analyses of church membership and attendance (including comparative data for England and Wales) have been published. Later figures have been specially calculated by the author for the purpose of this chapter.

in no sense a 'State Church', as is Britain's other Established Church, the Church of England, in which the Sovereign is the official head, making appointments to high office, and in which the Prayer Book, for example, can be changed only by Act of Parliament.

The Reformed Presbyterians of today are the descendants of those among the Societies of the Dissenting Covenanters (the 'Cameronians', called so after their leader, Richard Cameron, who died in 1680) who did not follow their fellows in entering in 1689–90 the Church of Scotland of the Reformation Settlement. The Free Presbyterian Church came into existence in 1893, formed by a group within the then Free Church who dissented from the latter's Declaratory Act of 1892 on the ground that thereby the Free Church had 'destroyed the integrity of the Confession of Faith as understood by the Disruption Fathers and their predecessors'. This Church thus claims, as against the present Free Church, to be the true heir of the 'Chalmers Free Church', or, more correctly, the Free Church of Scotland constituted at the Disruption of 1843.

This Disruption was the product of more than a century's difficulty in Church- State relations. In violation of the Act of Security and in breach of treaty the English passed the Patronage Act in 1712, which gave lay patrons the right to place a minister in a charge, if necessary against the wishes of the congregation. Further, in other ways the State showed an increasing tendency after 1707 to encroach upon the Church's autonomy in matters spiritual and ecclesiastical. In an effort to redress these injustices, the General Assembly of the Church of Scotland passed the Veto Act in 1835, reaffirming its opposition to patronage, and seven years later, when this Act was judged incompetent by the law courts, pressed the Claim of Right, which argued for the spiritual independence of the Church. The State rejected the claim; and on the first day of the General Assembly of 1843 about one-third of the Church of Scotland's ministers and possibly up to one-half of its membership, led by David Welsh and Thomas Chalmers, walked out of the Assembly Hall to gather in another place and constitute themselves the Church of Scotland *Free*.

The surprising thing is not that so many broke away but that so many stayed, though for 'non-disrupting' ministers at least one consideration was no doubt (understandably enough, though groundless in the event) uncertainty as to their future, should they follow Welsh and Chalmers.[5]

5. It is so *very* difficult to summarize Scotland's church history in a few sentences, but in that history is the theme of Church-State relations writ large, and a resolving of that problem for the world, let alone sociologists of religion, to ponder as a model. Here too are illustrations of the need for smaller groups to maintain vigilance against larger, even where their position seems secured by legislation. And the effects of the

Itself a victim of a breakaway in 1893 (as we have seen) the Free Church eventually rejoined the Established Church by two steps. In 1900 a majority joined with another breakaway body, the United Presbyterian Church to form the (original) United Free Church, which returned to the Church of Scotland in 1929. These unions thus in time brought the majority of Presbyterians back into one ecclesiastical stream. A main factor in making this possible was the British Parliament's Patronage Act of 1874 which abolished patronage and so removed the issue which had been at the centre of the earlier disputes. Despite this, however, there were still some who stood apart: those not joining the 1900 union continued the Free Church, and those dissenting from the 1929 union constituted themselves the United Free Church (Continuing). In 1934 the terminal word was dropped from the title. It is the descendants of these minorities who make up the Free Church and the United Free Church of today.

For long after the Reformation Roman Catholicism was disestablished and proscribed: it was not until the early nineteenth century that the Roman Catholic Emancipation Act abolished the penal statutes and secured toleration for Catholics. Almost fifty years later, in 1878, the Roman Catholic hierarchy was re-established. This Church grew on successive waves of Irish immigrants and the fecundity of these newcomers and their descendants: alone of the Scottish Churches its numerical strength increases almost in step with the birth rate of its community, which is higher than that of the non-Roman-Catholic section of the population – 'almost' because it is admitted that leakage does take place and that some Catholics baptized as infants 'lapse' when they reach adulthood. In recent years the Roman Catholic population – an estimated total which includes all who have been baptized (at however tender an age) – has been growing steadily. In 1966 it was 827,410 (as compared with, for example, 787,170 in 1959). Adjusted so as to be comparable with the membership of other Churches, the 1966 official total becomes 545,267 as the estimated number of adult Roman Catholics.

The Scottish Episcopal Church is the country's other representative of episcopacy, claiming direct descent from the pre-Reformation episcopacy. It is in full communion with the Church of England, the Church of Ireland, the Church in Wales, and the overseas members of the Anglican Communion, and is the parent of the Protestant Episcopal Church in the United States. At the end of 1966 its communicants numbered 53,793 (56,118 in 1959) and there were 93,951 (106,478 in 1959) in the category officially described as 'persons definitely attached'. This category includes, in addition to communicants, baptised infants and persons not communicants who

---

Disruption on Scottish society – in the spheres of education and poor relief, to mention two – were wide and deep [Reid, 1960; Burleigh, 1960].

may worship fairly regularly. Neither figure is strictly comparable with, say, the Church of Scotland membership total, and a figure somewhere between the two would be tolerably applicable. (See also Highet, 1960, Appendix B).

Congregationalism emerged with Presbyterianism at the Reformation as an alternative ecclesiastical polity but is similar to the latter in doctrinal position. Today's Congregational Union of Scotland (28,502 members in 1967 as compared with 34,495 in 1959) dates from 1896, when a union took place between the then Congregational Union and the Evangelical Union.

Slightly older, the Baptist Union of Scotland (founded in 1869; 1966 membership 18,279; 1959 membership 20,139) offers another example of independency as a Church polity. In all branches the Brethren movement – the ('open') Assemblies of Christian ('Plymouth') Brethren and the groups of 'exclusive' Assemblies – may number about 35,000 members, while other independent churches are the Churches of Christ (1,620 in 1959), the Churches of God (about 1,500), and the Unitarians (565 in 1959).

Methodism has never been strong in Scotland (where it is non-episcopal): it may be too akin to the country's native and nationally characteristic Presbyterianism to have been able to make the sort of impact there which it has made in England, the U.S.A., and other English-speaking countries. At the end of December, 1966, there were 11,819 members in the Scottish Synod (13,378 in 1958).

There remain to be mentioned a number of smaller religious bodies and their estimated membership (as of 1959 unless otherwise stated): the Pentecostal Churches – the Assemblies of God (c. 1,000), Elim Foursquare Gospel Alliance (c. 1,000), and the Apostolic Church (c. 1,500); the Jehovah's Witnesses ('active ministers' now probably well over 3,000); the Mormons (784 in 1959 but now perhaps 10,000); and Spiritualist groups: Spiritualists' National Union (2,776), the Greater World Christian Spiritualists' League (2,700 earlier in the fifties) and an unknown number of independent Spiritualist centres carried on by individuals. Even smaller bodies are: the Seventh Day Adventists (c. 500); Church of the Nazarene (c. 1,500 including recognized adherents); The New Church (or the Church of the New Jerusalem) (380); the Christadelphians (c. 400); the Society of Friends (333 in 1958); Christian Science (publication of membership statistics is not allowed, but there are less than twenty churches in Scotland). There is also the Salvation Army. It keeps its membership secret but it is active in Scotland both in social welfare and evangelism and in holding conferences; we can only say that indications suggest it is not without real support.* The Greek Orthodox Church; the Liberal Catholic Church about which information is lacking; a small company of Christian Jews numbering perhaps a few hun-

* Of these bodies, the Elim Foursquare Gospel Alliance, the Jehovahas Witnesses and, above all, the Mormons, seem to be the ones growing most rapidly.

dred; and a miscellaneous assembly of mission hall and gospel hall groups and similar gatherings, of various sizes, which meet quietly in places up and down the country, and about whom information is scant, complete the denominational spectrum.

Setting aside (as already covered in the foregoing figures) those members of mission and gospel hall groups who are also officially members of churches, we would probably not be far out in assessing the 'unattached' following of these groups at about 10,000.

No-one knows the precise number of non-Christian worshippers in the land. There may be 20,000-plus Jews, a majority of whom (leaders of the Jewish community think) practise their religion. The non-white population, though growing, is still relatively small. No exact statistics are available but the total is unlikely to exceed 10,000 and may be a few thousand less than that. Some Muslims and Hindus are devout, but spokesmen for these communities state that many have jettisoned observances required by their faith in regard to prayer, fasting, and diet. Devotees of Buddhism may number a hundred or two, most of whom are likely to be students. Relationships between these minorities and the rest of the population are on the whole harmonious.

## RELIGIOUS PARTICIPATION AND BELIEFS

Table 1 gives the overall membership picture of the country's adult population ('adult population' – because the overwhelming majority of the persons enumerated are adults and the figures exclude children).

As Table 1 is now somewhat out of date, the author has ascertained the latest available figures for as many churches as was possible by a moderate expenditure of time and labour. These are set out in Table 1a. However, the reader should bear in mind that it does not purport to rest on the same foundation of extensive enquiry as Table 1.

These data show that between 1959 and 1966 (to which date the majority of the newer figures relate) several Churches have lost ground. The Church of Scotland is down by 81,658, while the other Presbyterian bodies, as a group, have probably had a net loss of somewhat less than 4,000. This would make the combined Presbyterian membership in the region of 1,283,800. Among the group of Other Non-Roman-Catholic Churches, ascertained official figures show the following reductions: Scottish Episcopal Church (communicants), 2,325; Congregational Union, 5,993; Baptist Union, 1,960; and the Methodists, 1,559. There are, however, the gains made by some of the 'new' and highly evangelical bodies. I have no exact figures of their current membership, but indications suggest that these gains may be

*Table 1. Main denominational groupings of Christian Church adult membership in Scotland, 1959/8*: Firm but minimum index***

| Denominational groupings | Membership | % adult population 1959 | % total membership |
|---|---|---|---|
| Presbyterian | 1,369,140 | 39.1 | 66.1 |
| Other Non-Roman-Catholic Churches | 170,710 | 4.9 | 8.3 |
| *Total* Non-Roman-Catholic | 1,539,850 | 44.0 | 74.4 |
| Roman Catholic (est. adults) | 530,550 | 15.0 | 25.6 |
| *Total* (minimum index) | 2,070,400 | 59.0 | 100.0 |

* This table and Table 2 to follow, are dated '1959/8' to indicate that while most constituent data relate to 1959 a few are for 1958. To write '1958–59' would suggest reference is in each case to a continuous period bridging part of these two calendar years, which is not the case.

** All figures are rounded off.

Source: Highet, 1960, p. 55.

*Table 1a. Main denominational groupings of Christian Church membership in Scotland, 1966** (Based on known or estimated changes since 1959 to supplement Table 1)

| Denomination or Denominational grouping | Membership | % adult population 1966 | % total membership |
|---|---|---|---|
| Church of Scotland | 1,233,808 | 36.1 | 61.7 |
| Other Presbyterian Churches (est.) | 50,000 | 1.5 | 2.5 |
| *Total* Presbyterian (est.) | 1,283,800 | 37.6 | 64.2 |
| Other Non-Roman-Catholic Churches (est.) | 172,000 | 5.0 | 8.6 |
| *Est. Total* Protestant or Non-Roman-Catholic | 1,455,800 | 42.6 | 72.8 |
| Roman Catholic (est. adults) | 545,200 | 15.9 | 27.2 |
| *Total* (minimum index) | 2,001,000 | 58.5 | 100.0 |

* All figures but those of Church of Scotland membership are rounded off.

sufficient to offset the above losses and leave a net increase bringing the total for this category to about 172,000. If so, this would make the total Protestant or non-Roman-Catholic membership 1,445,800. The estimated Roman

Catholic adult population has risen by 14,717 to 545,267, bringing the total membership of the Churches included in the above computations to an estimated 2,001,000.

The caveat must at once be entered that from the point of view of international comparisons both the 1959 59 per cent and the 1966 58.5 per cent are 'firm but minimum indices' [Highet, 1960]. Either represents that section of the population who have satisfied the varying conditions for full or official membership as laid down by the bodies to which they are attached or – in the case of the Roman Catholic Church – for the most part are known to parish priests as those to whom he has responsibility and who ought to be attending mass. The total for either year necessarily leaves out of account those who are members of religious groups not making their membership known or for whom (for some reason) no information about extent of following is available. Further, except in a few cases where adherents form an officially recognized category, our total (whichever one we go by) excludes adherents in the looser sense of those who may attend services of worship and take some part in congregational life but who, for reasons of their own, have not publicly taken vows or otherwise committed themselves in the way they would have to do to be accepted as full members. Anyone who has any knowledge of Scottish religious life knows that there are such people, especially in the North-West of the country; it is only their exact number about which there is doubt.

It is important to stress that our total is a minimum measure of the population's attachment to the country's Christian Churches because for some other countries much is made of the findings of 'religious censuses' suggesting very high proportions of the population 'claiming religious affiliation', and to say the least, it is doubtful if in all these cases the 'affiliation' thus claimed bears any resemblance to the type of association represented by the full or official membership which in the main is the basis of our figures or even by unofficial 'adherence' of the kind just described. If we had membership figures for all religious bodies in Scotland, including mission and gospel hall groups, our membership percentage would naturally be higher.[6] If we knew how many 'adherents' there were, the measure of attachment of one order or another would be higher still. If we knew how many of those still not enumerated would in answer to an opinion-poll-type question about 'belonging to a Church', say they 'belonged' even if this meant no more than (for instance) that they were taken as children to a church by their parents, but had never been back since, the measure of affiliation of some kind would be greater again. It is idle to speculate where, by the questionable but

6. The author estimates that these might raise the 1959 percentage from 59 to 60 [Highet, 1960].

fashionable yardstick of pollsters' concept of 'belonging', Scotland would be placed in some international 'league-table'; what is important is that, taking the Scottish 1966 percentage here offered, this is a minimum measure based on the yardstick of vows publicly taken and of acceptance of commitment, either entered into as a conscious step or (lapsed and apostate Roman Catholics aside) voluntarily honoured as an inheritance from unconscious involvement through infant baptism.

Some years ago the author investigated, on this basis, the extent of church membership in England and Wales, and found that in 1951 only about 23 per cent of the adult population there were church members, and only 10 per cent were members of the Anglican communion. Insofar as the situation there may have changed in the interval, the trend is more likely to have been in a downward than an upward direction. Relatively to adult population, then, church membership in Scotland is about two and a half times what it is in England-plus-Wales, while the Church of Scotland, with more than one-third of the country's adult population in membership of it, and with a more-than-sixty-per-cent share of total membership, is a national Church to a far greater extent than is the Church of England, since the Anglican community in England and Wales can claim only a little more than 40 per cent of total church membership in these two communities taken together.

These differences between Scotland and England are frequently obscured. The caveats we have just been entering about pollsters' ideas concerning what constitutes 'church membership' are again relevant. English sociologists of religion have preferred the use of survey findings to the exercise of bringing the author's 1951 enquiry up to date, with the result that we find them talking about a huge percentage of the population of England, sometimes in the 90's, as church members. It has also been misleadingly reported that 64–70 per cent of the population are 'members' of the Church of England [Social Surveys, 1964, pp. 11, 19].

Another misleading practice is the habit of expressing, say, Church of Scotland membership as a percentage not of the population of Scotland but of the population of Britain as a whole [Martin, 1967, p. 36]. This seriously understates the higher proportion of church members in the Scottish population, and hides or masks significant comparisons with England.

The post-1959 trends reflected in Table 1a affect the positions of two of the main denominational groupings relative to each other more than they affect the general picture or the comparison with England and Wales. The adult Roman Catholics have increased, now representing almost 16 per cent of the adult population and about 27 per cent of total membership as computed. Even so, Presbyterianism despite some losses is still the country's chief religion and the Church of Scotland its leading denomination. The relative position of those Churches which are neither Presbyterian nor

Roman Catholic, is much as it was seven years ago: they represent 5.0 per cent of the adult population now as compared with 4.9 per cent previously. Within this category, however, the position of one of the constituent sub-groups has improved relative to the other sub-groups. This is how the 1966 '5.0 per cent' is made up (with the 1959 figures in brackets): Scottish Episcopal Church (communicants), 1.6 per cent of the adult population (1.6); the Independent Churches, 2.4 (2.5); Methodists, 0.3 (0.4); the Pentecostalists 0.1 (0.1), and 'Others' – including the Mormons and the Jehovah's Witnesses, for example, – 0.6 (0.3).

Table 2 summarizes the result of a special survey of church attendance in Scotland carried out by the author. This again is a minimum index since it excludes missions, the Salvation Army, the Christian Scientists, and other groups [Highet, 1960, p. 60].

*Table 2. Estimated Christian Church attendance by adult 'oncers', Scotland, 1959/8: minimum index**

| Denominational grouping | Estimated attendance at one Sunday service at least | Percentage of adult population 1959 | Percentage of church membership |
|---|---|---|---|
| Presbyterian | 472,160 | 13.5 | 22.8 |
| Other Non-Roman-Catholic Churches | 104,540 | 3.0 | 5.0 |
| *Total* Non-Roman-Catholic | 576,700 | 16.5 | 27.8 |
| Roman Catholic | 334,300 | 9.6 | 16.1 |
| *Total* (minimum index) | 911,000 | 26.0 | 44.0 |

* All figures are rounded off.
Source: Highet, 1960, p. 60.

How the general picture may have changed, no-one knows. One hears conflicting reports – of diminishing attendance level and enthusiasm in some places, but in others of packed services with the church very much a 'going concern' (often where, as in smaller towns, the local community has clearly-defined boundaries and indigenous leadership, and the church *can be* 'the parish church'). What is unlikely to have changed is the better attendance record, relative to their following, of some of the smaller 'older' Churches and some of the newer Churches, and the comparatively poor attendance performance of the members of the national Church, of whom two out of three are not taking up their seats in their pews with any regularity. There may also have been an extension of the practice of discontinuing evening services or of holding joint evening services with neighbouring congregations.

The Church of Scotland holds communion periodically throughout the year, and an interesting statistic which it reports annually is that of the number 'communicating at least once a year'. In both 1966 and 1965 this amounted to 71 per cent of the membership. In 1947, 72.7 per cent communicated at least once, while 69.5 per cent did so in 1956. The level has not, then, varied so very much over the past 20 years.

### *Youth attendance*

Though for various reasons the least tractable of ecclesiastical statistics,[7] figures of Sunday School and Bible Class membership in most Churches show a downward trend. The progressive decline in the attendance of boys and girls starting just after the age of ten and steepening markedly during the years of adolescence has been demonstrated [Gray and Sutherland, 1960]. A common reason for leaving was the unsuitability of the lessons. Sunday School teachers were often young and lacking in experience and parents' irregular attendance at church also had an effect. Nevertheless some churches report growing Sunday School support and other youth-oriented bodies such as the Scripture Union Inter-School Fellowship and the Inter-Varsity fellowships of Evangelical Unions could recently show evidence of expansion.

### *Marriages*

Over the past twenty-five years there has been a decrease in the percentage of Scottish marriages solemnized by a minister of religion and a corresponding increase in the percentage of civil marriages. From 11.3 in 1941 the latter has risen, more or less steadily, to 24.5 in 1966. Of the total of ecclesiastical marriages, over two-thirds (68.3 per cent in 1965, the latest year for which the percentage distribution is available) were solemnized by a minister of the Church of Scotland, 21.4 per cent were Roman Catholic marriages, 2.7 were in the Scottish Episcopal Church, 2.2 were Congregational Union and 1.1 were Baptist Union marriages.

From figures of ecclesiastical marriages some people purport to find that 'secularization' is less or (as the case may be) more rife than alleged, but it is very questionable if such conclusions stand up. So much depends on the

7. Since they vary so much in their age-band references – and for this reason are not translatable into percentages of age-groups – there is little point in giving the actual figures here.

varying practice of Churches and of individual ministers within them. In the Church of Scotland, for example, non-members are not obliged to become members as a condition of the solemnization, though individual ministers might encourage this. Hence in the case of a non-member bridegroom who agrees to a church wedding because he knows his church-member bride wishes it, it may mean little else than a concession to his loved one. Does this add anything at all to the 'non-secularity' evidenced by the fact that his bride is a member? On the other hand, if both partners are members of a Church, a church wedding adds nothing to the contribution the couple are already making, as church members, to 'non-secularity'. It is only from the number of church weddings involving two non-members, and the trend in these cases over the years, that one can draw conclusions about the continuing esteem, or growing lack of esteem, in which a church wedding as a 'rite of passage' is held. And such data are just what we are seldom if ever offered. Thus, ecclesiastical marriage can never, as an index, be a substitute for membership (or some other yardstick of affiliation and 'involvement') since what conclusions you can draw from them depend on knowing the membership status of the partners.

*Baptisms*

Similarly, lacking membership data, some commentators on other countries make much of figures of baptisms. For the Scottish Churches as a whole, no baptism figures exist. But we do not need these instead of membership data, and in any case they would be of limited value. However, taking the two largest Churches, we can note that in 1966 42,461 infant baptisms were performed in the Church of Scotland and 22,583 in the Roman Catholic Church[8] – roughly 44 per cent and 23.4 per cent, respectively, of the number of births that year.

The caveats applied to making deductions from church weddings data apply again in the case of baptisms, since again much depends on the requirements laid down by the different Churches and (sometimes) by individual ministers, and the information available (at least in Scotland) says nothing about whether, in particular cases of non-Roman-Catholic baptisms, both parents are full members or only one is. It is tempting to argue that, since baptisms in the above two Churches alone account for about 67 percent of all births, and inclusion of baptisms celebrated in the other Churches covered by our membership tables would bring the proportion even more in excess of the membership-to-adult-proportion of 58.5:100, then some parents have their children baptized although not church members. But

8. Supplied to the author by the Roman Catholic authorities.

the two terms of the equation are not comparable, since our membership figures are not broken down for the child-bearing age-groups, since (too) there are two adults to each infant, and since (further) a woman *could* have more than one child baptized in a given calendar year.

In any case, new Church of Scotland regulations which came into force in 1963 require that at least one parent be a baptized person and preferably both be baptized persons. This does not in itself give them the status of communicant members (which is the Church of Scotland criterion of what constitutes full and official membership and is the basis of its membership figure), but they would in most cases be expected to become so.[9] Until we know how many parents not members up to the time of the birth of their babies became so in order to have the babies baptized we can say nothing about the 'anti-secularization' influence of baptism, and the contribution such parents make to 'non-secularity' would then be reflected in the figures for communicant membership. Baptism data in themselves provide no measure of trends in secularization or its opposite which are not provided by membership figures, and in any case the plotting of historical trends is complicated in the case of the Church of Scotland by the regulations operating in and since 1963.

A recent enquiry into what baptism means to church members throws an original light on this subject.[10] The majority of respondents had been baptized as infants. Almost three-quarters of them said that the fact that they had been baptized was important to them, the most frequently-stated reason being (among Church of Scotland, Scripture Union, and University respondents) that baptism was seen 'as an entry to the Church, the fellowship of the Church being the significant thing'. Among Baptists, however, the reason gaining most 'votes' was 'baptism seen as a confession of discipleship', with 'seen as obedience to a command of Christ' next and 'seen as symbolic of one or more Christian truths' third. Whatever their denomination, the majority of those baptized later in life did not wish that they had been baptized as children, and a fair number were glad that they were not.

9. Parents not baptized as children would have to go through the ceremony of adult baptism to become communicant members; they would, obviously, have to do this to meet the prior condition that they be themselves baptized persons even if it were not insisted upon that they be communicant members.

10. The enquiry was carried out by the Rev. Philip Petty of the Church of Scotland by questionnaire circulated through the agency of some ministers, two university chaplains, and other intermediaries to church members, students, and participants in a Scripture Union conference. Mr. Petty does not claim necessarily to have reached a representative sample, but his findings (though not yet fully processed) are of interest and throw an original light on this subject.

### *Evangelistic activities and church extension*

A great deal of evangelistic activity of various kinds – mass rallies, local missions, parish 'visitation', the 'house church', Kirk Week, Industrial Chaplaincies, seaside services, by the printed word and by radio and television – has been engaged in since the war by a number of Scottish Churches, though there appears to have been a diminution in recent years in the intensity of efforts to 'bring in the unchurched masses' by the mass meeting and concentrated campaign approaches. A main reason for this may be that the fruits of these activities scarcely seem to justify the time, money and energy expended on them – as certainly seemed to follow from the assessment of their efficacy which the author attempted [Highet, 1960]. Even the superbly organised and widely publicised Billy Graham All-Scotland Crusade of 1955, centred on the city of Glasgow, appeared from the author's Glasgow Church Attendance Census to have but moderate impact, with about half of the 10,575 'gained attenders' seeming to have been lost to the Churches a year after the Crusade ended. It may well be, however, that the Churches have to engage periodically in activities of this kind if only as a 'holding operation' or to keep the move away in some sort of check.

Most of the larger Churches have been following a church extension programme and founding new churches in the post-war housing development areas and in the New Towns. Some of these are the liveliest and best-attending congregations anywhere in the country.

### *Beliefs and attitudes*

Little can be said authoritatively about the beliefs and attitudes of Scots churchfolk, because the Gallup-type polls that have recently provided English commentators with information about religious beliefs and attitudes either do not include Scotland in their interviewing or, if they cover a few Scottish respondents, do not analyse their replies separately. They are therefore unhelpful so far as Scotland is concerned, and unfortunately Scotsmen themselves have done little in this sphere.

## SEX AND SOCIAL CLASS COMPOSITION, AND GEOGRAPHICAL DISTRIBUTION

As is the case elsewhere, in almost all of Scotland's Churches women outnumber men both on membership rolls and at services of worship to an extent not explained by female/male ratios in the population; and Protestant Church membership in the main reflects lower-middle-class/upper-working-class positions [Highet 1960]. The Scottish Episcopal Church is customarily thought of as recruited chiefly from the middle-class. No doubt at one time its rural churches did have, and perhaps today still have, a disproportionate representation of the Scottish landed gentry and aristocracy. To these people, anglicised in manners and tastes and in other ways through their education (usually in England) at 'public schools' (in the English sense of the term), it doubtless seems fitting to be in 'the English Church[11]'. But the general membership today is much more varied in social status background than many people think. Thirty-nine congregations of this Church took part in the author's national sample survey [Highet, 1960] and of these 7 were described as a middle-class, 15 as lower middle-class/upper working-class, 8 as working-class, and 7 as 'mixed'. Heavily concentrated as it is in industrial areas, the Roman Catholic Church is predominantly working-class, but in some dioceses its population is more evenly distributed over the social classes and it should not be thought that, even in urban industrial centres, it is entirely without a professional, middle-class strain.

With the exception of the Brethren, who appear to be more representative than most bodies of the social classes, the Independent Churches are mainly upper-working-class or lower-middle-class – if anything leaning more to the former. The majority of Scottish Methodists are working-class, as are most Elim followers, most Jehovah's Witnesses, most Mormons, most members of the Nazarene Church, and (indications suggest) most of those attending mission and gospel hall gatherings. Scottish Adventists, however, are predominantly a middle-class group. It is noteworthy that, with the few exceptions stated, the 'newer' Churches find most of their support among the working-class – a commentary on the (admitted) failure of the older Protestant Churches to make much impact on this sector.

Fulfilling its obligation to provide a church in every parish, the Church of Scotland is in that sense as well as others the national Church. As mentioned, the Roman Catholic Church draws most of its population from the urban industrialized centres but its parishes are widely scattered throughout the country, and there are pockets of 'native Scottish Catholicism' in the West Highlands and Islands.[12] The traditional stronghold of the Scottish Episcopal Church is the East, North-East and Perthshire, it is relatively weak in Central and South-West Scotland and has but the flimsiest of holds in the West and North-West, though it has a footing in Appin and Glencoe. By contrast the Free Church, for example, until recently had most of its fol-

11. The Scottish Episcopal Church is at pains to point out that it is not 'the English Church in Scotland' but is indigenous, with a tradition; but there is no doubt this is how it appears to many.

12. The term 'native Scottish Catholicism' is used merely as a shorthand way of distinguishing these from their co-religionists on Clydeside and in other urban areas of Central Scotland who are of predominantly Irish origin.

lowing in the North and North-West, but recent population movement has set it well on its way to being, on balance, an urban Lowland Church, as the United Free Church has always been. The 'open' Brethren are strongest in the cities, in Ayrshire, Lanarkshire, and in the Moray Firth area, in which regions strong assemblies have been set up among the mining and fishing communities. The Assemblies of God find support in East Coast fishing villages and are also to be found in the Clydeside towns. The six congregations in 1959 of the Mormon Church were located in the four cities of Glasgow, Edinburgh, Dundee and Aberdeen (one in each) and in the large burghs of Airdrie and Paisley.

A recent enquiry into recruitment to the ministry provides interesting details of the social background of recruits [Thomson, 1967]. Since 1950 the areas providing most candidates for the ministry were not the rich agricultural areas and not the wealthy residential suburbs, but rather the industrial belt and the medium-sized industrial towns; in particular, the Highlands and Islands, which used to produce a fairly steady flow, have recently provided few recruits. Secondly, recruits now come less from the schools catering for the sons of professional men than from those catering for the sons of men in business and industry. Thirdly, examination of a sample of 100 boys and men training or intending to train for the ministry showed that at least 14 came from homes of skilled and unskilled manual workers, while the fathers of others represent a wide range of non-professional occupations (e.g., engineers, commercial travellers, clerks, shopkeepers, and so on); only 8 were the sons of ministers, and three professions – law, medicine and teaching – provided only 4 out of the 100. Fourthly, almost two-thirds of the 100 have entered, or will enter, on their studies not direct from school but after a period in employment of various kinds. These men, as Thomson comments, will bring to their ministry some experience of the daily life and work of business and industry and other spheres, and he adds that it is doubtful if the ministry in Scotland has ever had such a rich background from which to draw.[13]

THE CHURCHES AND PUBLIC ISSUES

The Presbyterian Churches in particular, though some of the non-Presbyterian non-Roman-Catholic Churches also, regularly make their positions clear on social, moral, political and economic problems through the resolu-

13. This background has been further enriched by recent revolutionary changes: in 1966 women were admitted to the eldership of the Church of Scotland and in 1968 to the ministry.

tions ('deliverances') of their supreme courts in annual assembly or through official publications.[14]

An outstanding example of an official committee pronouncing on current public issues is the Church and Nation Committee of the Church of Scotland. The range of its concern may be judged from this selection of topics covered in its report to the 1967 General Assembly: International Interests; African and Commonwealth Interests; Industrial and Economic Interests (e.g., housing, the economic situation, the Government's prices and incomes policy, planning and freedom); Social Interests (violence among juveniles, immigration, road safety); Church Interests (e.g., humanism, mixed marriages); Scottish Interests,[15] (e.g. local government, Scotland in Europe); and, (through a sub-committee on the mass media) standards of television programmes, the decrease in the number of British newspapers, reviews, and reputable magazines.[16]

A notable feature of Scottish life is the space given to Church news by the press. Several newspapers have 'Church correspondents' or otherwise run regular Church articles. The newspaper with the largest circulation in the country – the *Scottish Daily Express* – gives wide 'coverage' to Church news and views and takes a strong editorial position on many issues, such as the Bishops in Presbytery debate in 1957, as they arise.

## INTER-CHURCH RELATIONS

Apart from practical co-operation between the Churches in, for example, mass evangelistic activity (which many would argue is the only realistic kind of church unity) there have also been formal ecumenical discussions. Church

14. The Scottish hierarchy of the Roman Catholic Church do not make pronouncements on specifically Scottish matters, and on wider matters their position is of course that of the Vatican.

15. In connection with which (to give one instance) the General Assembly 'recognized the need for the Scottish people to take real responsibility for their country in future'. At several recent meetings, indeed, the General Assembly have shown themselves markedly sympathetic to the idea that Scotland should have more control of her own affairs, and in 1948 and subsequent occasions came out in favour of a greater measure of devolution by the British Parliament of legislative and administrative power in Scottish matters.

16. As the author suggested elsewhere [Highet, 1966] the awareness by the Church of Scotland (through committees such as this one) of sociological trends and problems to some extent makes up for its failure to operate (or encourage and assist some independent group to operate) a centre of research and teaching in the sociology of religion such as some other Western societies are running. There is also a lack of a really adequate conference centre.

of England-Church of Scotland negotiations have aroused heated debate, especially on the 'Bishops in Presbytery' issue which came particularly to the fore in the ill-starred Joint Report of 1957 [Highet 1960, pp. 153–159; Henderson, 1967].

As for steps towards unity among the Churches within Scotland, negotiations are proceeding between the Church of Scotland and the Congregational Union of Scotland and have reached the stage of consideration by the two sides of a 'Draft Basis and Plan of Union'. Progress in talks between the Church of Scotland and the Scottish Synod of the Methodist Church will have to await the outcome of the negotiations at present taking place between the Methodist Church and the Church of England. Meantime the Scottish Synod and the Church of Scotland are continuing their practical co-operation in mission, and some are making little secret of the fact that were the Scottish Synod free to decide its own policy, few insurmountable obstacles would be found to union between it and Scotland's national Church.

In general, relationships among the Churches in Scotland – not excluding those between the national Church and the Church of Rome – are good and are becoming better.

The problem of mixed marriages is a major stumbling block in relations between the Roman Catholic Church and (in particular) the Church of Scotland. The Catholic Church refuses to recognize as valid a mixed marriage celebrated before a minister of the Reformed Church and also insists, despite the recent somewhat modified 'New Instruction', that offspring of the marriage be baptized and reared in the Roman Catholic faith. In 1967, the General Assembly of the national Church recommended its ministers not to participate in Catholic marriage services where mixed marriages are involved (Church of Scotland, 1967, p. 181).

The number of such mixed marriages is not known, but it is clear to ministers and social workers that Catholic demands are the main source of tension in such cross-faith marriages: the community in general does little to exacerbate the strain such a couple may undergo, and this applies also to other cross-denominational marriages (on the whole infrequent) and to the very few cross-colour marriages that take place.

Some ministers report cases where the Catholic in a mixed marriage has become a Protestant, but indications suggest that the 'traffic of conversion' associated with such marriages is more often in the other direction. Since in any case the children of a mixed marriage will be baptized as Roman Catholics, some say that mixed marriages make a contribution to the rising Roman Catholic population, though this would seem to rest on the assumption that the Catholic partner, if not marrying a Protestant, would not have married, and had children by, a co-religionist.

## CONCLUSION

For a country to have (by our 'firm but minimum index') only 58.5–60 per cent of its adult population as Church members may not speak much for 'the state of religion' within it. Further, this level has been declining. Moreover, the level of regular church attendance – certainly that of the followers of the national Church – is scarcely impressive. Again, despite much endeavour, little headway has been made in 'bringing back (or in) the unchurched "masses".' What, then, are we to say about Scottish society from the point of view of its religious state? Is it a secular society?

There is no question that the forces working elsewhere towards 'dechurching'[17] have been operating in Scotland also: indeed, since they seem to work very strongly in the country that is neighbour to her, it would be surprising if she did not feel some impact from this. But in the lack of general agreement as to which level of church membership represents for a society the dividing line between being secular and being 'religious', it is open to one to suggest that, with a majority still in full, official membership of her Churches despite 'dechurching' influence, Scotland is not secularized.

This, though, is only one criterion: after all, the United States would seem to have a higher level of church membership (though it is by no means certain that the two sets of figures are strictly comparable) yet it has been described as a secular society [Wilson, 1966]. From here on, however, it is largely a matter of subjective evaluations of attitudes and other indices. (I have explained why I do not regard ecclesiastical marriages and baptisms and the trends they reveal as adding to the secularization debate what is not already contributed by membership data.) The foregoing sections have brought out some features not, perhaps, widely shared – for example, press 'coverage' of the Churches, the public's awareness of the Churches as a part of the society's fabric, the way in which ecclesiastical issues can still fire the churchman and interest the non-member.

It is, at the end of the day, largely a matter of atmosphere; and that Scotland's cultural atmosphere is still that of a religious – specifically of a largely Presbyterian – society, no-one who knows the country can seriously doubt. True, these things are difficult to pin down in words, in the space that remains, for those who have no acquaintance with them – though one can convey something (even if but negatively) by mentioning the contrast between the 'feel' of Scotland and the 'feel' of England.

Much, too, depends on what one expects the life of the Christian to be like in Western society of the mid-twentieth century. As Western culture and

17. I have not said, 'towards secularization', in order not to beg the question. Bu- the forces here in mind are those customarily pointed to as chief contributors to 'set cularization'.

economy are, the best which the best-intentioned and most committed Christian can do is live a severely modified version of the faith, for which I would suggest the term *para-Christianity*. This term should not imply quasi- or pseudo-Christianity – self-deception or hypocrisy. By this pragmatic if not idealistic criterion, the religiosity, the non-secularity, of the smaller country is still detectable in its cultural air as the smell of the Atlantic and the North Sea can be sniffed in its winds. And if this still does not help very much let me try to get over the point by repeating the story of the Scots scientist who was 'ranting and raving' against the 'Bishops in Presbytery' proposals. 'Why are *you* so worked up?' asked his friend. 'I thought you were an atheist?' 'So I am,' replied the scientist, 'but I'm a *Presbyterian* atheist'.

Well, no doubt the story is not true. But a good deal of the Scottish ethos is summed up in the fact that it so very easily could be.

ACKNOWLEDGEMENTS

For their comments on this chapter in typescript and assistance in other ways the author wishes to thank the late Rev. Professor Ian Henderson, M. A., D. D., Professor of Systematic Theology at the University of Glasgow; and recently Moderator of the Church of Scotland Presbytery of Glasgow, the Rev. Andrew Herron, B.D., LL.B., Clerk of the said Presbytery; and the late Mr J. M. Reid for commenting on this chapter in typescript and for assistance in other ways.

REFERENCES NOT SPECIFIC TO SCOTLAND

Martin, D., *A Sociology of English Religion*. London, S.C.M. Press. 1967.

Social Surveys (Gallup Poll) Ltd., *Television and Religion*. London, University of London Press, 1964.

Wilson, Bryan R., *Religion in a Secular Society*. London, Watts, 1966.

SELECTED BIBLIOGRAPHY

Compiling this bibliography is not a very congenial task, since there are few works in the field of the sociology of religion in Scotland other than the author's. There do exist a number of publications, mostly in booklet, pamphlet, or report form, which deal with aspects of the Churches' situation in society, notable among these being the annual Report of the Church and Nation Committee to the General Assembly of the Church of Scotland. Though in a very broad sense these touch on topics which might be regarded as within the compass of sociology, they are not specifically on sociological subjects nor sociological in their approach. This being so, there is little point in listing them here, the more so as they are surveyed in the 1964 article by the author.

There is also a fair corpus on Scottish ecclesiastical history but again few of these, apart from those mentioned here, take a social history approach.

Burleigh, J. H. S., *A Church History of Scotland*. London, O.U.P., 1960.

Cox, J. T., *Practice and Procedure in the Church of Scotland*. Edinburgh, Blackwood, 3rd edition, 1945.

Gray, J., and Sutherland, J., *A Survey of Sunday Schools and Bible Classes in the Church of Scotland*. Edinburgh, Church of Scotland Youth Committee, 1960.

Henderson, I., *Power Without Glory: A Study in Ecumenical Politics*. London, Hutchinson, 1967.

Highet, J., *The Churches in Scotland Today*. Glasgow, Jackson, 1950.

—, *Social Investigation of the Church: a study of recent enquiries*. Oxford, Church Union Summer School of Sociology, July, 1952 (unpublished).

—, 'The Churches', in Cairncross, A. K. (ed.), *The Scottish Economy*. Cambridge, Cambridge University Press, 1954a.

—, 'Scottish Religious Adherence.' *British Journal of Sociology*, IV, (2), 1954b.

—, 'The Churches' in Cunnison, J. and Gilfillan, J. B. S. (eds.), *The City of Glasgow*. A volume in the series 'The Third Statistical Account of Scotland'. Glasgow, Collins 1958.

—, 'The Protestant Churches in Scotland.' *Archives de Sociologie des Religions*. (8), July-December, 1959.

—, *The Scottish Churches: a Review of their State 400 years after the Reformation*, London, Skeffington, 1960.

—, 'Church-going in Scotland'. *New Society*, (65), 26 December 1963.

—, 'Review of Scottish socio-religious Literature.' *Social Compass*, XI (3–4), 1964.

—, 'Is Scotland Christian?.' *Glasgow Herald*, 11 October 1965.

—, 'Trend Report on the sociology of religion in Scotland.' *Social Compass*, XIII (4), 1966.

—, *Making Sense of Religious Statistics*.' University of Birmingham, Queen's College, January 1966 (unpublished).

MacLaren, A. A., 'Presbyterianism and the Working Class in a Mid-Nineteenth Century City.' *Scottish Historical Review*, XLVI, October 1967.

Mechie, S., *The Church and Scottish Social Development 1780–1870*. London, Oxford University Press, 1960.

Pryde, G. S. (ed.). *The Treaty of Union of Scotland and England 1707*. Edinburgh, Nelson, 1950.

Reid, J. M., *Scotland Past and Present*. London, Oxford University Press, 1959.

—, *Kirk and Nation*. London, Skeffington, 1960.

Robertson, D. R., *Church and Class in Scotland*. Unpublished Ph. D. Thesis. Edinburgh University, 1966.

Thomson, D. P., *Tomorrow's Ministers*. Crieff (Scotland), St. Ninian's Centre, 1967.

DEMOSTHENES SAVRAMIS*

# Greece

When one analyses the role of traditional values in contemporary Greek society, one soon discovers that these values are largely of religious origin. It is almost impossible to understand either the uniqueness of contemporary Greek culture or the structure of contemporary Greek society without the religious factor. Max Weber's assertion that 'in general modern man is incapable of appreciating the great significance which religious consciousness has had for the life-style, and culture, and the characteristics of a people', is particularly valid of Eastern Europe, and more concretely for those countries and cultures which developed exclusively under the influence of orthodox religiosity.

Unfortunately, a sociological investigation of the Orthodox realm of influence has hardly been undertaken. After Greece's liberation from Turkish domination three factors struggled for influence upon formation of the newly developing Greek culture. These were: 1) the classical element, 2) the Byzantine factor, i.e., Orthodoxy, and 3) Western systems of thought and styles of life. From the mixture of the classical element with the Byzantine i.e., the orthodox element, emerged a Graeco-Christian ideology, which proved stronger than all Western influence.

We hear much nowadays about the uniqueness of the Greek-Orthodox Church in comparison with the churches of the West. Let us see whether maybe the Orthodox doctrine of man (anthropology) has something to do with this uniqueness. According to this doctrine, man's sin has not totally corrupted him, and consequently the Eastern Church assumes that man is capable of self-renewal, self-transfiguration, self-completion, indeed of self-deification. There is a strong emphasis on the love of God. On this basis, one might expect Orthodox man to be endowed with enthusiasm and a feeling

* Demosthenes Savramis was born in Piraeus, Greece, in 1925. He has a Ph.D. in Sociology (Bonn, 1956) and a Th.D. (Athens, 1962). Since 1968 he is professor in the Sociology of Religion in Cologne. This essay is based on extensive research by the author, which results are to appear in a comprehensive work entitled *The Sociology of the Greek-Orthodox Church*. However, until this study is published, various material is scattered in the works of the author, mentioned in the Bibliography at the end of this chapter.

of certainty. After all he is co-worker in the ordering of the world. Since the divine attributes of reason, of freedom, and of love, have been weakened by sin, but have not been made impotent, he should be in a better position to develop these attributes than one who sees man as utterly depraved because of sin.

Why did such an optimistic anthropology not become the carrier of economic, cultural and political development in the Orthodox countries? The answer may lie in the observation that Orthodox anthropology allows for two possibilities. On the one hand man participates in the renewal of the individual and society on the basis of God's will, i.e., his Christianity becomes oriented towards social action; on the other hand, man seeks to attain completeness only for himself in isolation, and this leads to a passive, asocial or even anti-social Christianity. Athanasius the Great expressed this latter orientation when he said, 'God became man, so that we too could become gods'. The elevation of man into the divine sphere and his spiritual-mystical union with God is only a short step to other-worldly asceticism and world-denial.

The church of Greece today is the outcome of the second choice. The Eastern Church opted for a one-sided spiritualism at the expense of a possible renewal of the world.

The Eastern Church's decision for the wholly other, at the expense of the mundane favoured emotional religiosity at the expense of any rational religiosity. Hence the two separate spheres in Greek Orthodoxy – the sphere of clericalism, of monasticism, of sacraments and liturgy, and the sphere of secular activity.

Life's greatest ideal for Orthodox man – redemption from transitoriness – finds its clearest expression on Mt. Athos. While in the West active monastic asceticism found in Calvinism a supporter of Christian asceticism in its inner-worldly form, in the Eastern Church an active monastic asceticism was replaced on Mt. Athos by an asocial, or rather anti-social, passive, asceticism. Here then Christian asceticism disappeared behind the gates of the monasteries, and became totally lost from the point of view of a real social impact. It was not able to provide a vocational ethos and a guiding principle for a Christian life-style in the world. In place of a religious valuation of commerce (the West) we have a religious justification of inactivity (the East). The synthesis, 'prayer and work', the origin of which is to be located in the Eastern Church's active monastic asceticism, was on Mt. Athos, adapted to the requirements of passive asceticism and proclaimed in a new form as 'prayer and rest'. Orthodox man is devoid of, among other things, a rational objectivation of the profit motive as well as of a systematic, rational inner-worldly vocational ethic. Examples of this are the complete lack of an industrial social policy, and the many difficulties which are encountered in the attempt to organize a professional civil service. Nepotism dominates the scene and makes civil servants dependent upon persons and politics. The fact that a Sociology of Religion is next to unknown in Greece is partially responsible for the circumstance that the majority of Greek scholars has located the causes of Greece's social and economic backwardness in external historical-political circumstances.

Another consequence of the Greek Orthodox ethos is a completely different evaluation of the virtues. In contrast to the West the Eastern mind considers the passive virtues, such as endurance, acceptance, humility, sacrifice and especially suffering, as leading to salvation.

Greece remains an interesting example of a country which, though it is a part of highly developed and industrialized Europe, possesses a social system strongly dominated by religious and national elements which unite against all those forces demanding a transvaluation of values.

The military coup in April, 1967 underscored the fact that Church and society in Greece are practically separate worlds, united by common, especially national interests. Those officers, who allegedly fomented the revolution in order to protect these interests found revolution within the Church necessary, in order to ensure that the latter would be a worthy carrier of their Graeco-Christian ideology. Thus, the church could then be called upon to support their contention that the April revolution was a sacred affair. A church which was not a worthy representative of the Graeco-Christian culture was of no practical use for the leaders of the revolution. The prestige of the Church of Greece needed to be improved; this was accomplished by elevating one of the ablest persons of the Church to Archbishop of Athens and all of Greece. The April uprising once again supports the truth that the Church of Greece is able to maintain an unchanged existence simply because she can be conformed to the structure of whatever social order may exist at any one time.

Seen in this way, the Greek Church's contemporary attitude is the continuation of the utopian conception of a Graeco-Christian culture. The union of Emperor and patriarch, of altar and throne. It has been, and still is, the expectation of Greece's masters and upper social strata that the Church is there to support the existing order. This traditionalism inevitably favours those forces which are willing to bow to it, regardless of whether they serve the well-being of Greece, its society, and above all its people, or whether they exploit and tyrannize them.

BIBLIOGRAPHY

*Books*

*Aus der neugriechischen Theologie* [Contemporary Greek Theology]. Würzburg, 1961*.

*Zur Soziologie des byzantinischen Mönchtums* [The Sociology of Byzantine Monasticism]. Leyden-Cologne 1962.

*Ökumenische Probleme in der neugriechischen Theologie* [Ecumenical Problems in Contemporary Greek Theology]. Leyden-Cologne, 1964.*

*Die soziale Stellung des Priesters in Griechenland* [The Social Status of the Priest in Greece]. Leyden, 1968.

*Articles*

'Die griechisch-orthodoxe Kirche und die soziale Frage' [The Greek-Orthodox Church and the Social Question]. *Ostkirchliche Studien*, 7 (1958), pp. 66–84.

'Die Möglichkeit einer orthodoxen Sozialethik' [The Possibility of an Orthodox Social Ethic]. *Contemporary Greek Theology* (Wurzburg), 1961.

'Der universale Charakter der Orthodoxie' [The Universal Character of Orthodoxy]. *Ostkirchliche Studien*, 11 (1962), pp. 14–26.

'Drei Jahre Innere Mission der Kirche Griechenlands 1958–1960' [Three Years of the Greek Church's Home Mission 1958–1960]. *Kyrios* 2 (1962), pp. 26–35.

'Max Webers Beitrag zum besseren Verständnis der ostkirchlichen außerweltlichen Askese' [Max Weber's contribution to a Better Understanding of the Orthodox Church's Other-Worldly Asceticism]. *Kölner Zeitschrift für Soziologie und Sozialpsychologie*, 15 (Supplement 7, 1963), pp. 334–358. Also in: *Max Weber zum Gedächtnis*, ed. by Rene König und Johannes Winckelmann. Köln – Opladen, 1963.

'Die Sozialethische Sendung der orthodoxen Kirche' [The Social-Ethical Mission of the Orthodox Church]. *Die neue Ordnung*, 17 (1963), pp. 131–136.

'Christlicher Glaube und soziale Wirklichkeit in Griechenland' [Christian Faith and Social Reality in Greece] pp. 126–132, in: Klaus von Bismarck and Walter Dirks (eds.), *Christlicher Glaube und Ideologie*. Stuttgart, 1964. See the expanded version of this article in *Kyrios*, 4 (1964), pp. 137–150.

'*Ora et labora* bei Basilios dem Grossen' [*Ora et labora* in Basilius the Great]. *Mittellateinisches Jarbuch* 2 (1965), pp. 22–37 *(Festschrift für Karl Langosch)*. Also in *Kyrios*, 6 (1966), pp. 129–149.

'Der Beitrag der Laien für die ökumenische Öffnung der griechisch-orthodoxen Kirche' [The Laiety's Contribution toward an Ecumenical Opening in the Greek-Orthodox Church]. *Ostkirchliche Studien*, 15 (1966), pp. 308–327.

'Der Priester im Rahmen der neugriechischen Gesellschaft' [The Priest in the Context of Contemporary Greek Society]. *Kyrios*, 7 (1967), pp. 31–40.

'Das Apostelkollegium' [The Apostolic Council]. *Kyrios*, 7 (1967), pp. 252–255.

'Das Konzildekret über das Apostolat der Laien unter Berücksichtigung der Stellung der Laien in der Griechisch-orthodoxen Kirche' [The Apostolic Council's edict concerning the Apostolate of the Laity in the light of the Position of the Laiety in

* Extensive Bibliographies concerned with the theme of the Greek-Orthodox Church can be found in this book.

the Greek-Orthodox Church]. *Stimmen der Orthodoxie zu Grundfragen des II. Vaticanums* (Vienna-Freiburg-Basel), 1969 pp. 291–318.

'Die religiösen Grundlagen der neugriechischen Gesellschaft' [The Religious Foundations of Contemporary Greek Society], pp. 64–87 in: *Die verhinderte Demokratie:* Modell Griechenland. Frankfurt am Main, Suhrkamp, 1969.

'Wesen und Eigenart der griechisch-orthodoxen Kirche im Verhältnis zu westlichen Kirchen' [Nature and Peculiarity of the Greek-Orthodox Church in its Relation with Western Churches]. *Kyrios*, 9 (1969), pp. 42–57.

'Altar und Thron' [Altar and Throne]. *Wort und Wahrheit*, 25 (July/August 1970), pp. 317–330.

'Basilius der Grosse als Vermittler zwischen Himmel und Erde' [Basilius the Great as Intermediary between Heaven and Earth]. *Kyrios*, 10 (1970), pp. 65–75.

*See also:*

*Rapports des recherches sur la sociologie religieuse on Grèce* [Research Reports of religious Sociologie in Greece], presented by the 'Centre National des Recherches Sociales (EKKE)', Sophocleous, Athens at the XIth Conference for Sociology of Religion, 20-23 September 1971, Opatija, Yugoslavia.

IVAN VARGA*

# Hungary

## INTRODUCTION

Nowadays it is a platitude in the sociology of religion that a large-scale and rapid secularization process is taking place all over the modern world, especially in the industrially developed or developing countries. This fact is acknowledged by sociologists of religion, regardless of their ideological standpoint. The differences between them are not in recognizing this fact, but rather in interpreting its causes. There is also a consensus in acknowledging that secularization cannot be measured simply by the declared membership of particular churches or by the numbers of churchgoers.

However, in modern societies – be they capitalist or socialist – there are also less apparent processes. Sociological investigations show that these are increasingly gaining in importance. We refer, first of all, to the fact that the doctrines, commandments, precepts of religion have a constantly weakening impact on modes of thought and consequently on behaviour. We do not have in mind here the complete disappearance of belief in God; we are referring to other phenomena, for example that even church-goers are less and less directed in their everyday life and activity by the norms and prescriptions of religious morals; they do not set a high value to the dogmas of their particular religion; often disagree with the social doctrine implied in the view of history represented by the various churches, etc. In these cases conformism and the bonds of tradition are conspicuous components of religiosity, and this is accompanied by a formalization of the relationship with the supernatural.

* Ivan Varga was born in 1931 in Budapest, Hungary. He obtained his Ph.D. in Philosophy in the Institute of Philosophy, Hungarian Academy of Sciences. From 1963 to 1968 he was a Research Fellow of the Sociological Research Group in the same Academy. He is currently senior lecturer in sociology, University of Dar es Salaam, Tanzania. He is a member of the International Advisory Board of the Yugoslav philosophical review, *Praxis* and vice-secretary of the Research Committee of the Sociology of Religion, International Sociological Association. Major works include 'Teilhard, Marx et le progrès social' [Teilhard, Marx and social progress] in *Europe*, 1965, and 'La sécularisation de la jeunesse Hongroise' [The Secularisation of Hungarian Youth] in *Archives de sociologie des religions*.

Thus, we define secularization most generally, as the totality of all processes manifesting themselves in the increase of indifference toward religion, in the decrease and expiration of the influence of religion and in a conscious or unconscious growth of the mundane and materialist elements in behaviour and thought. While we agree with Hegel in acknowledging the anti-dialectic character of all definitions inasmuch as they fix a moment of the ever-changing and manifold reality, we think it important to give at least an instrumental definition in order to clarify our position with respect to the meaning of the idea under discussion.

Empirical data must always be placed in a theoretical framework in order for it to be meaningful. The data below are presented before my theoretical section in order that this chapter conform with the others in this book. However, on no account should they be interpreted without reference to the theoretical section which follows.

## SURVEY RESULTS

Hungary is an example of a country where socialist transformation has greatly changed the face of the society. These changes have not exclusively embraced the economic infrastructure and former social relationships, but effected equally institutions and social consciousness. All these transformations were reflected in the situation of the churches and in the decline of religiosity.

Unfortunately, there are hardly any data which could serve as a basis for comparison with the pre-war situation. The Constitution declares the principle of a secular State (i.e. the separation of church and state), thus we have no data available on religious or denominational affiliation. On the other hand, in pre-war Hungary, the sociology of religion did not exist at all, and after World War II the influence of the Stalinist version of dogmatic Marxism hampered the development of sociology – including research. Only from the early 1960's has sociology developed as a science and as an analysis of the existing social relationships. The sociology of religion was a part of this development, although the lack of previous research and traditions has seriously handicapped its evolution and restricted its scope. However, a number of research projects have already been done, mainly focussed on the problems connected with the religiosity of Hungarian youth.

A larger international comparative research survey has been carried on during 1967. This embraced pupils of the senior classes (17 years old students) of secondary schools in three capitals: Prague, Warsaw and Budapest. The size of the sample in each capital was between 700 and 1,000. The Hungarian section of the research had a sample of 724. The data we shall refer to are the results of this investigation.

On the basis of previous research as well as of a theoretical analysis we have set up a five-scale typology of religiosity the categories of which are as follows:

1. *Traditional religiosity.* In this category we included those who believe in the traditional systems of religious dogma, comply with the commands of the church, consider religious morals as being uniquely valid and authentic, believe in the transcendental sanctions of morals and comply with the requirements of religious practice in terms of church attendance, keeping fasts, making confession, partaking of the Lord's Supper, etc.

2. *Non-traditional religiosity.* Here we included those who believe in God or in a supernatural being, a Creator of the Universe, regardless of whether or not they believe that this God or supernatural being actually interferes in the course of the world and universe. It is notable that among the persons classified here a fair number hold (though not in a clear-cut manner) deistic and pantheistic views which might be interpreted – especially in the broader actual social context – as a step toward the decreasing of religiosity. This view seems to be confirmed by findings on opinions about the supernatural or mundane nature of morals. These people are especially undecided about the problem of whether guarantees or sanctions of morality are of a transcendent character. They differ from the first category also by complying irregularly or not at all or by mere conformity – under pressure from familial or environmental expectations – with the requirements of religious practice (church attendance, etc.) Their belief in God might even be accompanied by a distinct anti-church attitude. Among urban youth especially a layer can be found which, on the basis of a vague belief in God, creates for itself a kind of 'private morality' being a specific mixture of religious and worldly views.

3. *Religious indifference.* In this category we classified all those who are generally disinterested in religion. Their thinking shows traces of the influence of religious morals but this is due mainly to conformism and tradition or, sometimes, to a lack of sufficient deliberation. They either do not or only sporadically meet the requirements of religious practice. When they do practice it is mainly under pressure from their environment; when freed from their traditional background they frequently cease to practice altogether. Young people who have moved into the city provide a typical example; when visiting their mother-village they are influenced by their family and social surroundings and participate in the Sunday service by habit; but once they return to the city, where the traditional environment ceases to exert an influence, they discontinue church attendance.

Persons belonging to this group are, however, generally characterized by an indifference not only towards religion and related problems but towards problems of world-view *(Weltanschauung)* as well. Their interest is predominantly oriented towards the material aspects of life or, in the field of culture, they tend toward a value-neutral orientation, i.e. the formal 'purely aesthetic' side of cultural phenomena. The investigation found, too, that the members of this group are less interested in social problems or in the problems of their narrower community; their participation in community affairs is less active than those who are ideologically committed, irrespective of the direction of their commitment.

The existence of this group raises serious problems of methodological order, namely, should socio-religious research remain exclusively within the dimension of religion? A Marxist – or atheist oriented – sociology of religion might attach positive values to this phenomenon but would still remain on the surface and hence would be incapable of revealing relevant facts about the motivations or deeper content of religiosity, or non-religiosity; in order to do this, the sociology of religion has to trespass its own borders.

4. *Non-believers.* This group includes all those who do not believe in the existence of God or a supernatural being and, consequently, do not participate voluntarily in any form of religious practice. This, however, does not exclude the possibility that they would not refuse to participate in some religious activities or to get married in church under pressure from their environment – mostly from their family. Guarantees of morals as well as sanctions in observing moral norms are sought by them in this world exclusively. Their conviction is more or less conscious although coupled with various philosophical and ideological elements.

5. *Conscious atheists relying upon ideological bases, mostly upon Marxist philosophy.* Persons belonging to this group differ primarily from those ranked in the former group by supporting the refutation of any religious belief with a certain philosophical-ideological point of view. The social role of religion and of the churches is evaluated by them on a similar basis. They categorically refuse to participate in any form of religious activity.

Although this classification serves as a convenient framework for typology, it is not sufficiently detailed for a more refined analysis. Therefore the international comparative research adopted a more detailed division. This contains a five-scale classification of *religious thinking*, as follows:

1. Religious thinking
2. Categorically atheist thinking
3. Inconsequently atheist thinking
4. Undecided thinking
5. Traditionally religious thinking (sub-group of 1)

*Religious behaviour* has been classified into two groups:

1. Practising religion
2. Non-practising religion

From the combination of both factors (i.e. thinking and behaviour) we obtain the following complex scale:

1. Religious
2. Atheist
3. Irresolute, with a tendency toward religion
4. Irresolute, with a tendency toward atheism

The two typologies by and large are equivalent. The latter, however, is more detailed, and serves as a mean of further classification and comparison. It exposes, for example, a divergence between religious thinking and religious behaviour, as shown in Tables 1 and 2.

*Table 1. Distribution of the sample of Hungarian youth according to religious thinking*

| Classification | % |
|---|---|
| Religious | 14.0 |
| Categorically atheist | 42.5 |
| Inconsequently atheist | 14.5 |
| Undecided | 26.5 |
| Traditionally religious | 2.5 |

*Table 2. Distribution of the sample of Hungarian youth according to religious behaviour*

| Classification | % |
|---|---|
| Practising | 60.2 |
| Non-practising | 39.8 |

Comparison of Tables 1 and 2 shows that there are numerous young people who in their thinking have abandoned religion, but nonetheless take part in various activities connected with religion. The motivations for such participation were given by about 75 per cent, at least as one motivation, the wish of the parents, i.e. the larger family. The impact of the family and, more generally, of traditions and expectations of the environment is clearly shown by the distribution of answers to the question: 'Do you want a church wedding?' Thirty-seven per cent replied that they did want a church wedding, 33 per cent replied no, and 30 per cent were undecided.

But when we consider the answers of those who said they wanted a church wedding or were undecided, the motivations clearly show that only a minority wants to have it because of religious conviction (Table 3).

*Table 3. Reasons for wanting a church wedding*

| Reason | % |
|---|---|
| 1. Because only that marriage is proper which is blessed by the church | 27.0 |
| 2. Because I should obey the wish of my parents or my fiancé(e) | 15.0 |
| 3. I should decide so if my fiancé(e) wanted it | 13.0 |
| 4. Because I should otherwise be discredited in my surroundings, family, etc. | 0.6 |
| 5. Because other people do so | 11.0 |
| 6. Because it is more beautiful and ceremonious | 25.0 |
| 7. No response | 18.4 |

The impact of the social surrounding on consciousness is shown also by the data of Table 4 indicating pluralism of values on the one hand, and a tendency of detachment from religious values on the other. The question asked was 'What do you think about the relation between science and religion?'

*Table 4. Opinions about the relationship between science and religion*

| Opinions | Religious respondents % | Atheist respondents % | Irresolute tending towards religion % | Irresolute tending towards atheism % | Total % |
|---|---|---|---|---|---|
| The two do not disturb each other | 30 | 16 | 42 | 28 | 28 |
| The two are incompatible | 10 | 66 | 18 | 43 | 39 |
| The two complete each other | 48 | 6 | 25 | 13 | 19 |
| 'Do not know', 'don't care', etc. | 12 | 12 | 15 | 16 | 14 |
| Total | 100 | 100 | 100 | 100 | 100 |

We see that the ruling world view *(Weltanschauung)* has a fairly strong impact on the thinking of those who belong to the religious category but has more impact on the irresolute, tending toward religion category. The effect of the social surrounding becomes even clearer when we consider the views of the respondents on the questions of political nature. Of the total sample, 74.3 per cent belonged to the C.Y.L. (Communist Youth League), 6.1 per cent did not belong and 19.6 per cent said that they belonged but were not active.

These data are not of great importance in themselves when the monopo-

*Table 5. Religious beliefs by C.Y.L. membership*

| Classification | Members % | Non-members % | Inactive members % |
|---|---|---|---|
| Religious* | 12.2 | 19.6 | 19.9 |
| Categorically atheist | 47.8 | 30.2 | 33.7 |
| Inconsequently atheist | 13.2 | 8.0 | 17.3 |
| Undecided | 24.6 | 27.4 | 23.7 |
| Traditionally religious | 2.2 | 14.8 | 5.4 |
| Total | 100.0 | 100.0 | 100.0 |

* According to the Statute of the C.Y.L. believers can also be members of the League.

listic position of the C.Y.L. is taken into account, for it is the only youth association in Hungary. However, it is significant that a considerable proportion of the religious youth do not regard their religious beliefs as incompatible with the social and political ideas represented by the C.Y.L. (Apart from the fact that we cannot rule out a certain degree of careerism on this high percentage of C.Y.L. members, the figures nevertheless indicate the existence of a syncretic consciousness – which is prevailing in the existing socialist societies).

Whereas the above tables reveal a fairly significant difference in *religious thinking* between members of the C.Y.L. and youth outside the League, there is hardly any cleavage between the two groups in respect to *religious behaviour* (Table 6).

*Table 6. Religious practices by C.Y.L. membership*

| Practices | Members % | Non-members % | Inactive members % |
|---|---|---|---|
| Practising religion | 60.8 | 69.3 | 67.1 |
| Non-practising religion | 39.2 | 30.7 | 32.9 |

Although the members of the C.Y.L. – excluding non-active ones – are slightly less religious in their behaviour, the picture is rather similar for all the three categories, indicative of a gap between consciousness and practical behaviour. Certainly, since the sample was composed mostly of 17 years old secondary school pupils, we may attribute a great deal of influence to the parent's attitude. (And indeed, 63.8 per cent of the respondents' fathers and 68.5 per cent of their mothers are overtly or to a certain degree religious, the remainder being non-religious or not known).

Belief and behaviour taken together show a rather important difference (Table 7). One may draw the conclusion from this combined table that, in

*Table 7. Religious classification by C.Y.L. membership*

| Classification | Members<br>% | Non-members<br>% | Inactive members<br>% |
|---|---|---|---|
| Religious | 13.1 | 36.4 | 24.8 |
| Atheist | 36.9 | 24.6 | 31.2 |
| Irresolute, tending towards religion | 25.3 | 26.8 | 22.3 |
| Irresolute, tending towards atheism | 24.7 | 12.2 | 21.7 |
| Total | 100.0 | 100.0 | 100.0 |

spite of similar behaviour, socio-political affiliation and/or conviction does have an impact on the relation with religion. (This statement has been corroborated by all cross-tabulations with political affiliation). The impact is, however, not only the effect of personal political affiliation but – as one might conclude from Table 8 – also by the change of the broader social and political set-up.

Most naturally, attitude toward religion does determine the nature of answers given to these questions but even considering this, it is all the more remarkable that more than half of the religious youth answered the first one affirmatively, and respectively said 'no' to the question about religion and morals.

When we want to approach from another point of view the question whether religion represents a determining force upon the values and behaviour of young people under changed, and still changing, conditions, it seems to us that the most appropriate way is to scrutinize the relationship between religious and moral views. The general conclusion one arrives at here is that there is an ever growing separation of moral and religious views, more exactly: that a constantly growing number of religious people either consciously or almost spontaneously separate the two domains from each other. A very characteristic distribution of answers is displayed in the second section of Table 8.

These data are all the more impressive since the opinion still holds rather strongly among the older generations that religion – or, at least, religious instruction – is a guarantee of the morality of their children. (This has been

*Table 8. Attitudes of C.Y.L. members towards selected problems*

| Question | Alternatives | Religious % | Atheist % | Irresolute tending towards religion % | Irresolute tending towards atheism % |
|---|---|---|---|---|---|
| Should the Churches accept the social changes realised in Hungary after World War II? | Yes | 56.2 | 85.8 | 67.0 | 74.6 |
| | No | 30.7 | 4.1 | 14.3 | 7.1 |
| | No response | 13.1 | 10.1 | 18.7 | 18.4 |
| Are, to your mind, believers more moral than those who are indifferent towards religion or atheist | Yes | 27.6 | 1.9 | 15.8 | 5.9 |
| | No | 53.3 | 81.9 | 60.2 | 75.9 |
| | Not in general | 17.5 | 5.7 | 14.0 | 9.2 |
| | Non-believers more moral | 0.0 | 2.9 | 2.3 | 0.0 |
| | I cannot judge | 1.6 | 7.6 | 7.7 | 9.0 |

a prevailing argument in favour of enrolling one's child in religious instruction; in Hungary the schools being run by the state the teaching of religion is not compulsory but only on the special request of parents). We may, further, conclude that the above-mentioned separation of religion from morals is a widespread process. On the other hand, although this has to be further investigated in more detail, it seems to us that so-called 'private' morals, i.e. individualised and differing from canonised morals, which are essentially are secularized or at least based on a deistic-pantheistic view, are forging ahead.

And, finally, we should like to indicate the failure of one hypothesis, rather commonly accepted in socio-religious research carried out in East European countries. This is that our investigation showed the presupposition that girls are more religious than boys to be false. Although this conjecture holds true among the older generations and, among the youth in some provincial parts of Hungary, our investigations clearly revealed that such a hypothesis is untenable in the context of secondary school students in the capital (and, as some investigations have shown, in provincial towns the situation is the same). True, girls yields more to tradions and to pressures coming from the paternal home in their behaviour but there is hardly any significant difference between boys and girls in their religious thinking and religiosity. The corresponding data are in Table 9.

*Table 9. Sex distribution of belief, practice and classification*

| Classification according to | | Boys % | Girls % |
|---|---|---|---|
| Belief | Religious | 14.7 | 13.3 |
| | Categorically atheist | 39.6 | 45.8 |
| | Inconsequently atheist | 14.1 | 14.7 |
| | Undecided | 29.1 | 22.9 |
| | Traditionally religious | 2.5 | 3.3 |
| | Total | 100.0 | 100.0 |
| Practice | Practising | 57.2 | 62.6 |
| | Non-practising | 52.8 | 37.4 |
| | Total | 100.0 | 100.0 |
| Religiosity (Belief and Practice) | Religious | 13.5 | 15.4 |
| | Atheist | 40.2 | 34.2 |
| | Irresolute tending towards religion | 29.8 | 22.6 |
| | Irresolute tending towards atheism | 16.5 | 27.8 |
| | Total | 100.0 | 100.0 |

But 43.5 per cent of mothers and only 25.9 per cent of fathers of respondents were overtly religious (i.e. excluding the 'not very religious category' which was added to this number previously, and hence the difference) which seems to reinforce the correctness of our hypothesis concerning the older generations.

### THEORETICAL SECTION

In the vulgar popularised Marxist literature one often finds the idea that secularization begins only in socialism and is a necessary precondition of a higher level of socialist – i.e. of communist – society. On the basis of the actual historical process we have to refute these ideas, for we cannot assert that throughout history – from slavery to the socialist revolutions – a religious reflection of the world has been exclusively and unequivocally characteristic of all human thought. For example, let us refer to the growth and development of the classical, renaissance and bourgeois materialism, atheism and religious scepticism. On the other hand, it is obvious that up until the development of capitalist, or bourgeois, society the idea of transcendence has been present – with very few exceptions – in the widespread conceptions related to the essence and movement of the world.

The radical change begins with the firm establishment of capitalist production relations, and the flourishing of bourgeois society when the relationships of earlier societies were revolutionised, also with respect to secularization.

The causes seem to lie in the very nature of the capitalist mode of production. Without attempting an analysis of this we intend to take into account the following main factors.

Firstly, capitalist production introduces in a continually expanding way relationships of commodities and money. Consequently a dependence mediated by the market replaces direct personal dependence. At the same time as such instrumental relationships spread, social relationships take a reificated form and these forms turn – as forms independent of their creators – against their creators.

Secondly, natural limits do not restrain the growth of capitalist production (as earlier, for example, in feudalism where it was largely limited by the productive force of the soil), thus a new relationship with nature is formed. Capitalist production requires a tremendous development of basic and applied natural sciences which, in turn, enhance the rationalist knowledge of nature as well as the transformation of nature according to a knowledge of natural laws.

Both factors lead to a high degree of rationalization of the economy and through it of social life and thought. (Let us refer to Max Weber's idea about the disenchantment of the world). Indeed, the assertion of rationality resulting from the elementary needs of the economy is an extremely important element of secularization.

In addition to the above-mentioned factors, we have to take into consideration two further ones: as a result of accelerating growth, industry is capable of providing masses of consumer goods for the population, and the increase of mass-consumption is its vital interest; furthermore, the acceleration of industrial development has enormously increased social mobility.

Taken together, the enumerated factors encourage the establishment of that form of manipulation which stimulates extreme acquisitiveness. With the shortening of working hours and ubiquitous extension of means of communication and transport (especially private vehicles) leisure time increases and its forms become more diverse. At the same time – similarly as a result of manipulation – mass-culture and a manipulated form of leisure spending developed.

Consequent upon all these changes, one could query whether the alienation present in all class societies should manifest itself necessarily only in its religious form. To our mind this is not accounted for by anything. On the contrary, the mass-scale secularization taking place in bourgeois society is partially based on the fact that by industrial development and the manipulation of society, religious forms of alienation are not the only ones which are in the foreground and dominate social thought.

Thus, the very structure of capitalist society puts an end to relationships of domination and subjugation based on personal dependence and replaces them by reificated relationships. This bears on religiosity in that, unlike the former situation, the transcendency is not manifested in a personal form, i.e., people do not necessarily deduce their social dependence from a personal God. (We should like, nonetheless, to emphasise that this is not an absolute and straight-forward process but rather a tendency, which is the deepest core of the secularization process developing within capitalist society).

We must emphasise another factor developed by capitalist society, namely, pluralism. Modern society realised – not without conflict – the co-existence of various ethnic, religious, ideological groups, etc. Because these groups carry different ideologies, specific ideologies – especially religious ones – lose their monopolistic position in a given society. Thus, religion as an institutionalized ideology has to stand beside other institutionalized ideologies (e.g. political ones), and in addition, the various forms of manipulation of society consciously increase the tendency to diminish interest in ideological issues. As a result, the masses pay attention mainly to their immediate material situation and tend to be disinterested in their social relationships, in the broader connections and perspectives of their society.

There is, however, another tendency which, in order to complete the picture, should be at least mentioned. The point in question is that the working classes are increasingly organizing themselves in order to defend their vital interests. This is, from the point of view of our study, a conscious social activity aimed at the realisation of a pre-established goal. (We refrain ourselves from analysing the extent and intensity of this activity in different countries. Acknowledging both differences, we only intend to mention the presence of this activity as an inherent feature of bourgeois society). But all kinds of conscious activities do increase man's belief in his own power, capacities and possibilities. In other words, they constitute a factor increasing the process of secularization. This activity finds in Marxism a materialist philosophy and ideology which emanates in society and thus exerts an influence leading toward the enforcement of secular tendencies.

Nevertheless, we cannot assert that in bourgeois society other forms of alienation completely supersede the religious form of alienation. This is even less so since in this society man's dependence remains, as well as the relationships of rule and submission and social relationships remain hidden and intransparent (in a certain sense even more intransparent than in previous societies for it is much more difficult to discover the relations of dependence behind the relations of things), thus religion continues to play its role put forth in the above expounded frame of reference.

The changes brought about by the emergence of bourgeois society, especially by its industrial phase, caused a change in the function of the churches.

We cannot, however, give a detailed discussion of this, instead we would rather analyse some aspects of the changes in the content of religiosity.

From the subjective angle, from the angle of the individual, one could ask: what is the sense in modern society of belonging to a church; what is the relationship between church-bound religiosity and the life of the individual, or his inner life – i.e. to his intellectual and emotional world?

We might say that until the dawn of modern times subjective religiosity by and large coincided with the institutionally formed system of meaning and action bound to the church. However, together with the decomposition of feudal society, and even more with the emergence of capitalist society, the situation has been changed. Ideologies – religious, political, etc. – have been specialised and specialized institutions have appeared to impart these ideologies (e.g. political parties as carriers of political ideologies). Thus, a sort of 'range', '*assortiment*' has appeared before the individual. As a result (at least partially), the individual does not turn to the religious ideology as represented by the churches in every sphere and area of his life, but he resorts to other institutions according to his particular problem.

Moreover, and this might be even more important, the different institutionalized ideologies set out different norms (e.g. the norm of Christian humility and love, with the promise of an other-worldly salvation on one hand and the norm of the fight for national, economic, social liberation, for humanization of the real, earthly conditions of life, on the other). These norms are frequently controversial and conflicting. Hence, the individual increasingly relativizes the institutionally proclaimed religion, i.e. turns to it only when he has the need to do so. We might as well say that in his economic activity – during the, say eight hours of his working day – the individual is guided by the norms and requirements of the economy (e.g. those of economic success or of the ethics of the businessman, etc.), in his political activity by the political norms, i.e. by the norms of political life and by the requirements by parties of their members, etc.

Thus, religion is driven back in many respects to the domain of private life and increasingly loses its compulsory validity. When this process takes place under such circumstances that it cannot be replaced by a world-view which is capable of presenting a harmonious, more or less coherent view of nature, society and knowledge, then this relativized religion (or, more precisely, the so-called religious need) seeks new ways out, new solutions.

This again leads us to the problem of the emergence of so-called quasi- or surrogate-religions *(Ersatzreligionen)* or substitutes for religion. We call them so because they are not religions in the established sense of the word: they do not postulate a transcendent being or force which determines the fate of the world or their own, individual destiny. Rather, they attribute an illusory, in fact non-existent, force to real objects, viz. relations of men and objects, of men and men. Merely as an illustration we mention some of such surrogates: scientism and the myth of the omnipotence of technics, the star-cult and the cult of sex idols, the reactionary Führer-myth and the so-called cult of personality, nationalism and racialism, etc.

All of these surrogate-religions have this in common: while remaining on the level of immanence they do not seek the solution to real problems in the development of personality or conscious social activity. Instead, the object of their cult becomes the guide of behaviour (as in the case of the star-cult) or an irrational, mystic power is attributed to it (e.g. the myth of the omnipotence of technics or the cult of the personality).

Some rationalist thinkers [e.g. Gerhard Szczesny in his book *The Future of Unbelief*] explain the rise of such surrogate-religions by saying that human thought did not succeed in reducing the deepest moving forces, the most important factors of man's life and thinking to causal bases.

No doubt adialectic thinking is also a factor in the rise of these surrogate-religions. Nonertheless, to our mind, this phenomenon, too, needs an explanation. The causes lay even deeper and are to be sought first of all in social conditions.

There is always the possibility that the needs which brought religious ideas into being will emerge in this surrogate form while human activity is incapable of evolving on a wide range, while man is not consciously able to shape his social relationships and individual living conditions, and while there is no rationalist, materialist world view to sustain any attempts to do this. Although externally these ideas actually differ from religious ones, from an epistemological point of view and with regard to their social functions they display traits analogous to religious ideology.

In the preceding pages we attempted to describe in a very sketchy way the processes leading to, and reinforcing, actual trends in modern society. Up to now we have concentrated on bourgeois society. We intend, however, to focus our attention on the problems of secularization in a society which is consciously attempting to build social relationships upon a new basis and the ruling ideology of which is a materialist one.

By way of a preliminary, we must say that the above-mentioned traits and characteristics of the secularization process are valid for socialist societies since they are found there. However, we intend to point out specific differences which distinguish this process in this new society.

As is well known, Marx regarded socialist society as being a transitional stage between the capitalist and the developed communist phases of society development. That means that socialist society is Janus-faced: its institutions as well as its social consciousness comprise traits of bourgeois society and traits of a future, developed classless society.

A consequence of this transitional character of the socialist society is that those institutions which have not been developed by socialism subsist within it but function, or at least tend, to destroy their own existence. Let us take as an example the role of the state. The state as a product of the division of labour and of class society is a power separated from the members of society, but necessarily subsists in socialism. Nonetheless, one of the main functions of the socialist state is to be instrumental in drawing the members of society into the controlling and executive work of the organs of power. Thus, the state promotes its own withering away. (This and similar processes are to be understood only as trends containing manifold contradictions, e.g. contrary to the general tendency, the socialist state still remains an institution independent of, and opposed to, the individual who can hardly exert an influence over it, hence the state continues to be an alienated form. Despite all efforts of the statist bureaucracy, which strives for maintaining its relatively independent – and also privileged – position and thus contributes to the persistence of the alienated position of the state, the structure of socialist society, taken as a whole, counteracts these attempts in the long run).

This double-faced situation holds true for religion as well. The basic trend in socialist societies is, in this respect, towards secularization. Contrary to some accusations and assumptions, secularization is not primarily a consequence of religious persecution or restriction of church activity, and not even a primary consequence of a widespread cultural and ideological impact but is first of all the product of objective social conditions.

Without any attempt to deny that the socialist state applied – sometimes justified, sometimes not – restrictive measures against the churches, we nevertheless maintain that the churches and, more generally religion, perform basically a dysfunction in relation to the total society. They can be considered functional only in relation to religious communities but not to global society. We cannot go here into details but refer the reader to the social doctrine of the Catholic church which subsumes private property under the natural law, i.e. considers it as being of divine nature. This is obviously in contradiction with the existing relations of property.

Another characteristic point of the secularization process – closely related to the dysfunctional role of religion and the churches – in European socialist countries lies in the following. The main moving force of secularization in these countries is the rapid transformation of society into an industrial one. However, the industrialization process has been, and is understood to be a concomitant of a socialist transformation of the society. Thus, speaking of the industrialization process in European socialist countries, we always bear it in mind as an extremely complex social process accompanied by a high degree of social mobility. On the other hand, this complex and rapid industrialization process has created *en masse* a pluralism of norms and value-systems in culture and social consciousness.

Now, as far as religion is concerned by this process, it has failed completely to participate in the industrial and social transformation and has remained beyond its framework. As a consequence, religion has fallen into the background – objectively as well as in the every-day thoughts of people. Of course, this relegation is not to be conceived in the sense that people have lost their faith but rather in the sense that religious belief and morals have ceased to be – at least for the majority – the force determining their practical behaviour. In order to illustrate this statement let us refer to the well-known fact that religious people's behaviour in their place of work is regulated by the norms accepted there, or, as members of a formal or informal group (e.g. trade unions) the valid norms accepted there direct their behaviour.

To return to our original point, the problem is whether there are any differences (so-called specific traits) in secularization between bourgeois and socialist societies.

As to the distinctive features of socialist society, especially in its higher phase, we have seen, and I am sure the reader knows about it, that taken *in abstracto* and following logical considerations, this society has a fairly open and smooth development toward a complete secularization. In fact the picture presents itself in another light – especially when the time and space element is taken into account.

The past development of these societies was not free from social upheavals, shocks or, at least, sudden and deep changes. These were basically necessary since they reflected the profound changes in social relationships. Nonetheless the changes have been accompanied by unnecessary harassments, zigzags in the pursued political 'line' which, together with abrupt changes in the conditions of large segments of society, created a situation in which the only stable point seemed to be an Archimedian one, i.e. outside, and we may say above, this earth. This state of mind gave impetus toward religiosity even among those strata which previously practised religion as an act imposed upon them by social norms. Although religious feelings as such were not reinforced, the position of the churches was during a particular (rather early) period of development in the socialist transformation. (Here I refer to the Hungarian experience, most familiar to me, although I cannot rule out the possibility of a more or less similar evolution in the majority of East European socialist countries). With the creation of a one-party system (or, more precisely, with the aboliton of opposition parties, for in some socialist countries other parties than the Communist have remained), those elements which were adverse to the system rallied around the churches – mostly around the Catholic church – in order to express their opposing political feelings. Similarly, one can observe that with a transitional, temporary, deterioration of the political and/or economic situation participation in religious activities or church manifestations noticeably increases. Furthermore, as a reaction to an enforced but inapt indoctrination a certain vivified interest in religion became observable, especially among young intellectuals and students.

Notwithstanding these facts and phenomena, the general social climate, if we are entitled to use this expression, decidedly favours the process of secularization. As the state is non-religious, the educational system (with the exception of schools maintained by the churches) provides a scientific and materialist view of nature and society. Immensely accelerated social mobility, in conjunction with the rapid industrialization and urbanization processes, creates other types of social and moral problems as well as value orientations which are mostly beyond the competence or purview of the churches. This, together with the fact that a large segment of the population, mainly youth, has been freed from the environmental pressure of the traditionally more religious small village communities, creates a further impulse toward the abandonment of religion. Finally, the general trend of the spiritual and cultural life of the whole country, similarly, has a tremendous impact on the process of secularization.

## CONCLUSION

We are fully aware that the given data corroborate only fragmentarily our theoretical statements about the main tendencies and characteristics of the secularization process in a changing society. Being unable to publish all of the findings of even this particular investigation, we hope, nevertheless, that they exemplify in broad detail a process already well apparent and rapidly progressing. Further investigations could – and should – give more insight into various aspects of the secularization process. Although, as stated, we do not share the rather widely held idea that secularization is a kind of precondition for the further development of the socialist society, for we consider it a vulgarization of Marxism, in any case more sophisticated investigations into this field could make us better understand the transformation of consciousness and values in a society which, albeit has distinct features, is still *in statu nascendi*.

## SELECTED BIBLIOGRAPHY

The author wishes to apologize for the short bibliography listed. Very little has been published on the sociology of religion in Hungary, and the author was unable to compile his bibliography in Hungary where library facilities are more extensive. He would like to thank the editors for their efforts to find some publications related to the topic.

'L'Eglise de Hongrie sous le régime communiste' [The Church in Hungary under the Communist régime]. *Informations Catholiques Internationales*, 36, 1956.

*Die Lage der Katholischen Kirche in Ungarn im Jahre 1960* [The Situation of the Catholic Church in Hungary in the year 1960]. Vienna, Ungarisches Katholische Institut für Kirchliche Sozialforschung, 1960.

*Beiträge zur Lage der Katholischen Kirche in Ungarn im Jahre 1961* [Contribution on the Situation of the Catholic Church in Hungary in 1961]. Vienna, Ungarisches Katholische Institut für Kirchliche Sozialforschung, 1962.

Káldi, G., 'Die Kirche in Ungarn. Entwicklung und heutige Situation der kirchlichen Verhältnisse in Ungarn' [The Church in Hungary. Development and actual situation of Ecclesiastical Conditions in Hungary]. *Social Compass*, 4, 1957.

Varga, Ivan, '*Soziologische Untersuchungen der Religiosität der Jugend*' [Sociological Investigations on the Religiosity of Youth]. in: Olof Klohr (ed.), *Religion und Atheismus heute*. O-Berlin, V.E.B. Deutscher Verlag der Wissenschaften, 1966.

—, 'La sécularisation de la jeunesse hongroise' [The Secularization of Hungarian Youth]. *Archives de Sociologie des Religions*, 23, 1967.

—, 'Ifjúság, vallásosság, szekularizáció' [Youth, religiosity, secularization]. *Világosság*, 2, 1968.

REFERENCES NOT MENTIONED IN SELECTED BIBLIOGRAPHY

Szczesny, G., *The Future of Unbelief*, New York, George Braziller, 1961.

CONOR K. WARD*

# Ireland

## HISTORICAL INTRODUCTION

Christianity came to Ireland in the fifth century and rapidly replaced the variety of celtic religions which appear to have existed closely linked with the small clans and kingdoms of the political structure. In the next five centuries the Irish Church was both stubbornly independent and closely associated with Rome and developments on the continent of Europe. The twelfth century saw a Norman invasion claiming a religious mandate from Rome as well as a civil justification and the Irish Church was strongly influenced by the English Church from then until the sixteenth century. When the reformation break with Rome came in England in the sixteenth century the Irish Church remained loyal to Rome. In the following two centuries efforts to coerce the Irish to abandon Roman Catholicism were continuous and vehement, but were almost completely unsuccessful. The members of other Christian churches resulted almost entirely from their assignment to confiscated lands notably in Ulster, in the North East, but also throughout all except the Western quarter following the Cromwellian Wars. In the late eighteenth century many Catholics and some Protestant Dissenters came closer together in abortive republican rebellion. In the last years of the eighteenth century there was a gradual repeal of the penal laws which had persecuted, impoverished and disenfrancised the Catholics. In 1829 the last of these laws was removed from the statute book and in 1869 the Church of Ireland was disestablished and disendowed.

* Conor K. Ward was born in 1930 in Dublin, Eire and obtained degrees from the National University of Ireland (B.A. 1950), the Pontifical Urban University, Rome (B.D. 1952, M.A. 1954) and the University of Liverpool (Ph.D. 1959). He is currently College Lecturer in Social Science, University College, Dublin. His major publications include *Priests and People*, 1961; *Manpower in a developing community*, 1967, and *New Homes for Old*, 1969.

## DENOMINATIONAL STRUCTURE

Politically, Ireland is now divided into the Republic of Ireland (population 1966, 2,884,002) and Northern Ireland (population 1966, 1,484,770) which is part of the United Kingdom. In the religious sphere Ireland is regarded as a unit by almost all the religious groups including the Roman Catholic Church, the Church of Ireland, the Presbyterians, the Methodists, and the Hebrew Congregations, who between them embrace amost the entire population.[1] In the Irish censuses, and in the official statutory collection of vital statistics, religious affiliation is among the data obtained.[2] General over-all demographic information concerning religious groups is, therefore, easily available [e.g. *Enc. Cath.*, 1964, Vol 11, pp. 498–502].

For the many parts of the Republic of Ireland which are almost one hundred per cent Catholic detailed information is easily deduced from official statistics. The most religiously heterogeneous population in the Republic is in the city of Dublin and the surrounding districts. However, in the diocese of Dublin Catholics still constitute approximately 90 per cent of the population. For this area special analyses of the census data provide the information required for educational planning and voluntary social services provision which are organised almost entirely on a denominational basis. In the Republic of Ireland, according to the 1961 Census, 94.3 per cent of the population are Catholics. [See also *Herder Corr.* 1965, pp. 199–200].

Northern Ireland has 498,031 Catholics (34.9 per cent), 413,006 Presbyterians (29 per cent), 334,584 Church of Ireland members (24.2 per cent), 71,912 Methodists (5 per cent) and 97,929 others [1961 Census; Blanchard, 1963].

## RELIGIOUS PARTICIPATION AND BELIEFS

Few surveys dealing directly with patterns of religious behaviour and attitudes have been completed in Ireland. A very considerable amount of research is, however, currently under way and empirical data are increasingly becoming available, especially with regard to the Roman Catholics. General surveys of community patterns and social relations frequently provide some information on religion in contemporary Ireland.

1. Thus in *Encyclopédie catholique du monde chrétien* general data regarding Northern Ireland are found under *Royaume-Uni*, while religious data are found under *Irlande.*

2. In Northern Ireland religion may be omitted when completing the Census form, but only 2 per cent availed themselves of this option in 1957. The question on religion was not included in the 1966 Censuses.

## SURVEYS OF CHURCH ATTENDANCE AND COMMITMENT

Most pastors of Irish churches organise a parish census based on house-to-house visiting by the clergy. The results are not generally available, however, and there is no published empirically-based estimate of proportions of Sunday church-goers and Paschal Communicants. These categories are generally said to contain about 90 per cent of the Catholics in cities, and even higher percentage of Catholics in rural areas and a not much smaller percentage of other Christians for whom Sunday church attendance is less obligatory. The estimate for urban areas as a whole can only be described as an informed guess, but it is being confirmed in general by surveys as they gradually become available. Thus an interview survey with a random sample of 360 sixteen to twenty-one year olds in a depressed central area of Dublin City produced the following pictures of young female and young male Roman Catholics. Among the girls over two-thirds prayed every day, nine tenths had made their Paschal Communion, four-fifths went to Confession and Communion at least monthly, just over one-third went to Mass more often than every Sunday and Holy Day and ninety-five per cent went to Mass at least every Sunday. Among the boys and men a little over one-third prayed daily, three-quarters had made their Paschal Communion, slightly less than a half went to Confession at least once a month, one-eighth went to Mass more often than every Sunday and Holy Day and eighty-five per cent of the 16–18 year olds and seventy five per cent of the 19–21 year olds went to Mass at least every Sunday. Seventy per cent of those of both sexes who went to Mass weekly gave reasons based on belief, devotion and that it was normal behaviour for a Catholic. One-tenth of those under eighteen said that they went because they were made to go and a quarter of those over eighteen said that they went to Mass on Sunday from habit. There was some ambivalence with regard to the clergy: two-thirds of the girls said priests do good work for youth and four-fifths said that they understand young people, yet one-third said that it is difficult to talk to priests in Confession, while among the men the proportions were a half saying that priests do good work for young people and two-thirds that they understand young people, but two-thirds said that it is difficult to talk to priests in Confession. All except four per cent of parents of the teenagers of the area were said to be weekly Church-goers [O'Donohue 1969]. Similar results for adults were obtained in the course of a survey of family and kinship links in four different suburban areas of Dublin [Ward 1969].

The estimate that almost one hundred per cent of Catholics in rural areas go to church each Sunday is based on the clergy's conviction that little is unknown to neighbours and priests in a rural area. In fact, one of the few surveys carried out in this field revealed that approximately 96 per cent of the Catholics of the villages and rural areas studied were weekly or more frequent Mass-goers [Lewis, 1963, pp. 74–75]. An American anthropologist [Gallagher, 1969] reached a similar conclusion in a re-study of the rural community made famous by the classical Arensberg and Kimball studies in 1931–32. A picture of uniform religious adherence is also provided by another American anthropologist [Messenger, 1966, p. 25] with, however, some reservations about commitment. Two large-scale national sample surveys in the Republic have reported 95 per cent of all Catholics saying that they attend Mass each Sunday and in a national sample survey in Northern Ireland 75 per cent said that they were very or fairly religious.

A survey of fifteen to twenty year olds in the North of Ireland [Bleakley, 1964, p. 13] provided the following figures for the attendance at Sunday School, Bible Class, Morning or Evening Service of 300 school-boys and girls of different churches. In the countryside 95 per cent attend 'nearly always', 2 and 3 per cent attend respectively 'fairly often' and 'occasionally or never'. In the city the percentage of those attending 'nearly always' falls to 70, with 15 per cent in both of the other categories.[3]

Data on the practice of young workers obtained in the same survey, though not definitive because of limitations of sample selection, suggested a rapid fall-off after leaving school to a level of little less than half becoming irregular attenders.

An interview survey of the meaning of church-membership for a random sample of university students in Dublin has provided a great deal of information about patterns of behaviour and attitudes [O'Doherty, 1969]. On three central indices of practice which were obligatory for Roman Catholics (Mass attendance, Paschal Communion and Friday abstinence from meat) 84 per cent were conforming to the regulations of their church. Half of the sample were men and two-thirds of those not conforming were men – 22 per cent of the men interviewed said that they had not been to the Sacraments in the previous few years. Similarly more men than women said they did not accept one or more of the teachings of their church: 44 per cent of the men and 18 per cent of the women. Seventy-six per cent of the women students and 42 per cent of the men attended church more frequently than obliged to by the rules of the church. Eighty-one per cent of those interviewed thought that a particular responsibility to the community follows from the acceptance of Christianity. Similar results were obtained in a survey among

3. Bleakley did not analyse his data by denomination. Denominational differences are probably the source of the difference between Bleakley's percentage of Church-goers in Northern Ireland where Catholics are a minority and the estimates of 90 per cent attendance for *Catholics* derived from other sources.

engineering students [Anvil, 1968, pp. 38–39] and a questionnaire survey of a random sample of 263 second year students in University College, Dublin, showed general adherence to the norms of their Church by almost 90 per cent of the men and all except two per cent of the girls [Power, 1969]. As in the case of O'Doherty's study, Power found that three quarters of the girls and almost half of the men took part in religious services more often than the obligatory minimum of attendance at Mass each Sunday.

STUDIES OF RELIGIOUS PERSONNEL

The number of priests working in Ireland has increased steadily over the last hundred years rising from 3,061 in 1871 to 5,745 in 1961, an increase of 87 per cent. The increase was greatest between 1937 and 1961 when it was 50 per cent. During the period 1871 to 1961 the population of Ireland dropped by 23 per cent, so the number of Catholics per priest fell from 1,356 in 1871 to 558 in 1961. The ratio for the other Christian Churches is approximately half that for Catholics.

Large numbers of Irish priests go abroad each year immediately after ordination to missionary areas and to other English-speaking countries. During the period 1956–60 a total of 1,960 Catholic priests were ordained in Ireland of whom 1,338 or 65 per cent were working outside Ireland when a survey was undertaken in 1962 [Newman, 1963].

In 1965 there were almost exactly the same number of Irish priests working in Ireland and working outside Ireland – approximately six and a hal thousand. About two-thirds of those working outside Ireland were in English-speaking countries (4,368). Table 1 shows the location of Irish priests overseas in 1965.

*Table 1. Irish priests overseas 1965*

| Area | Number of priests |
|---|---|
| Australia and New Zealand | 764 |
| England, Scotland and Wales | 1,261 |
| South Africa | 97 |
| United States and Canada | 1,537 |
| Unclassified, distributed over the above areas | 709 |
| 'Mission areas' of Africa | 1,443 |
| 'Mission areas' of Asia and Oceania | 651 |
| 'Mission areas' of Latin America | 210 |
| | 6,672 |

Source: *Statistical analysis of Irish missionary personnel*, 1965.

The outward orientation of Irish Catholicism has been a feature of the last thirty years – paralleling the high emigration from the country during the period [*Herder Corr.*, 1967, pp. 204–212].

Data on numbers becoming priests and entering religious communities is a central theme of applied sociology of religion in Ireland and is the field in which most research has been done with regard to the Roman Catholic Church. Dr Jeremiah Newman, the professor of Sociology in the National Catholic Seminary, Maynooth who has carried out a number of surveys has summarized the position as follows: 'Ordinations (to the priesthood) in the country reached a peak of 447 in 1960 but dropped in 1961 to 397 and in, 1962 to 376. Since then there has been a slight upward trend to 404 in 1963 409 in 1964 and 412 in 1965. During the past year or so the intake into the major seminaries for secular clergy has, at least in a number of instances, fallen somewhat, although as yet not to any degree such as would cause unease.' [Newman, 1962, pp. 65–91; see also 1967, pp. 441–442; 1968, pp. 237–249]. A survey completed recently by the Conference of Major Religious Superiors shows the number entering clerical institutes went down from 279 in 1961 to 189 in 1965 and entry to brotherhoods attached to clerical institutes was 40 in 1961 and 22 in 1965. The entry figures for institutes of brothers have remained fairly steady, although dropping from 211 in 1961 to 180 in 1965 [Noonan, 1967, pp. 126–128].

Between 1956 and 1960 3,180 began the programme leading to the priesthood out of a total of 24,339 Catholic boys reaching the educational entry level in Ireland as a whole. The entry figure represents 12½ per cent of the total number. Professor Newman says that the proportion of those who begin the programme and go on to the end is estimated to have fallen from approximately 65 per cent in 1961 to approximately 50 per cent in 1967 [Newman, 1967]. In 1967 the Hierarchy of Ireland asked three Irish sociologists to undertake a survey in depth of the position with regard to the supply of priests and religious.

Information regarding vocations to religious sisterhoods was assembled in 1967 by the *Pro Mundi Vita* Information Centre which, with the co-operation of the Conference of Major Religious Superiors of Ireland and of the Missionary Service Centre at Dublin, was able to collect the relevant statistics. The pattern of development between 1958 and 1964 is shown in Table 2.

*Table 2. Development in the number of sisters belonging to Irish provinces (1958–64)*

| Sisters | 1958 | 1964 | 1964 (index 100=1958) |
|---|---|---|---|
| With perpetual vows | 8,611 | 9,301 | 108 |
| With temporary vows | 957 | 961 | 100 |
| Novices | 574 | 541 | 94 |
| Total | 10,142 | 10,803 | 106 |

Source: *Pro Mundi Vita*, 18, 1967, pp. 22–23.

In the same survey Table 3 gives the annual entries into the novitiate, the number of first departures for the missions or to English-speaking areas with citizens of Irish descent (mainly Great Britain, U.S.A., Canada and Australia).

*Table 3. Entries into the novitiate and first departures for the missions in the period 1958–1964*

| Year | 1958 | 1959 | 1960 | 1961 | 1962 | 1963 | 1964 |
|---|---|---|---|---|---|---|---|
| Number of entries* | 404 | 380 | 406 | 442 | 414 | 401 | 412 |
| First departure to the missions | 111 | 116 | 145 | 147 | 185 | 206 | 150 |
| First departure to 'English-speaking areas' | 47 | 56 | 65 | 52 | 59 | 42 | 71 |

* One congregation noted the number of postulants instead of novices.

RELIGION AND SOCIETY

Until recently religion was regarded as a unifying influence for those of the same religion and as a divisive factor at national level [Harris, 1961, pp. 137–49]. There is evidence that religious divisions are currently still a source of antagonism [Jenkins, 1968[4]; Jones, 1956, pp. 167–189; 1960, pp. 172–206] and the relics of the past remain in more or less segregated housing and political party loyalties in Northern Ireland [*Belfast Telegraph* National Opinion Survey, December, 1967]. The catalytic influence of religion in

4. Jenkins, reporting the results of his research, writes: 'To the west of Lough Neagh in Northern Ireland there is a small market town... Outwardly it appears to be a peaceful, integrated community but in fact it is split into two hostile communities which are segregated, polarised from each other and whose relations are characterised by a mixture of rank conflict and value conflict'.

community activity is reflected in general sociological surveys, which have found religion a central theme in discussions of contemporary issues and ministers of religion in important roles in the Irish social system [e.g. Ward, 1967; Kelly, 1968, Froyen, 1967; Harris, 1961].

## PROSPECT

In recent years sociologists of religion have tended to suggest that progress in socio-religious research will be by comparative studies of religious groups, and Christian sociologists have emphasised analyses of discernible differences in patterns of behaviour and attitudes between Christians of varying fervour and commitment. There appears to be ample opportunity in Ireland for sociological studies of these kinds. Such studies would appear to be particularly interesting where uniform practice must surely cloak differences in attitude and opinion. The resulting precision and clearer definitions would help too in the understanding of anomalies sometimes found in Ireland and among Irish emigrants elsewhere. It seems likely that current stereotypes of the Irish Catholic would not survive empirical investigation. Limited research already completed suggests that very many ordinary Irish Catholics are articulate, educated and intellectually committed to a mature apostolic faith. There is evidence too that there are those who are disinterested, and those who are alienated. Further research is needed to provide an increasingly accurate, objective, systematic account of religion in Ireland. It is particularly important in a country which is undergoing rapid social change. Socio-religious research in Ireland is likely to take the form of general sociological study of community life. It is unlikely to be the sociology of religion in the sense of the study of the sacred set over against the secular, but rather in the sense that the sacred permeates the secular, and religion as a relationship with God which affects every aspects of life, and is, in fact, ordinary everyday life. The sociological study of the community life of committed Christians might be the most useful contribution of Irishmen to the sociology of religion.

## BIBLIOGRAPHY

*Anvil*, 'Survey Report'. February 1968.

*Belfast Telegraph*, 'National Opinion Survey'. December 1967.

Blanchard, J., *The Church in Contemporary Ireland*. Dublin, Clonmore and Reynolds, 1963.

Bleakley, D., *Young Ulster and Religion in the Sixties*. Belfast, Christian Youth Committee, 1964.

*Encyclopédie catholique du monde crétien* [Catholic Encyclopedia of the Christian World]. Tournai, Casterman, 1964.

Froyen, V. A., *Social Life in a Rural Parish in Western Ireland.* Unpublished thesis. Minneapolis, University of Minnesota, 1967.

Gallagher, A. Jr., *A re-study of the Arensberg and Kimball Irish Community.* Research in progress (1969).

Harris, R., 'The Selection of Leaders in Ballybeg, Northern Ireland.' *The Sociological Review*, N.S. IX (2), 1961.

*Herder Correspondence.* 'Protestants in the Irish Republic.' II (7), 1965.

—, 'The Modern Irish Missionary Movement.' IV (7–8), 1967.

Jenkins, R., *Conflict and Polarization.* The British Sociological Association Conference, 1968.

Jones, E., 'The Distribution of and Segregation of Roman Catholics in Belfast'. *The Sociological Review*, N.S. IV (2), 1956

—, *A Social Geography of Belfast.* London, Oxford University Press, 1960.

Kelly, S., *Teaching in the City.* Dublin, Gill and Macmillan, 1969.

Lewis, F., *The Motives for Attending Holy Mass.* Unpublished Doctoral Thesis. Rome, St. Thomas Aquinas University, 1963.

Messenger, J.C., 'Man of Aran Revisited.' *University Review*, III (9), 1966.

Newman, J., 'Priestly Vocations in Ireland', in: Jachim, F., and Dellepoort, J. *Die Europäische Priesterfrage* [The European Pastoral Problem], Vienna, I.K.I.F.K.S., 1959'

—, 'The Priests of Ireland: A Socio-religious Survey. II: Patterns of Vocations.' *The Irish Ecclesiastical Record*, 5th Series, XCVIII (2), 1962.

—, *Socio-religious Survey of the Number and Distribution of the Clergy in Ireland.* Maynooth, 1963a.

—, 'The Sources of Priestly Vocations in Ireland'. *Seminarium*, 15th Year, N.S., III (1), 1963b.

—, '*Relazione sulla situazione delle vocazioni in Irlanda*' [Account of the State of Vocations in Ireland]. *Seminarium*, VII (2), 1967.

Noonan, F., 'Religious Vocations'. *Christus Rex: Journal of Sociology*, XXI (2), 1967

O'Doherty, K., *The Meaning of Church Membership.* Dublin, M. Soc. Sc. thesis, 1969.

O'Donohue, D., *A Survey of Attitudes and Values of Young People in Dublin.* Research in progress – a special analysis was made for the purposes of this article (1969).

Power, B., *A Survey of Religious Attitudes and Behaviour of Students.* Research in progress – a special analysis was made for the purposes of this article (1969).

*Pro Mundi Vita*, 18, 1967.

*Statistical Analysis of Irish Missionary Personnel.* Dublin, Missionary Service Centre, 1965.

Ward, C. K., *Priests and People.* Liverpool, Liverpool University Press, 1961, 1965.

—, *Manpower in a Developing Community.* Dublin, An Roinn Soathair, 1967.

—, *A Survey of Family and Kinship Contact at Christmas-time.* Research in progress – a special analysis was made for the purposes of this article (1969).

—, *New Homes for Old*, Dublin, I.N.P.C., 1969.

SABINO ACQUAVIVA*

# Italy

## HISTORICAL INTRODUCTION

The initial spread of Christianity in Italy and the formation of a Christian society there produced certain characteristics which distinguish Italy from other European countries. Even today these characteristics are of some importance. At least four factors are significant.

Firstly, the continuity between Christianity and pre-existing paganism was considerable. The high level of civilization in the pre-Christian society made it impossible for Christianity to become a complete substitute. Its structure had to adapt in both spirit and essence to the pre-existing situation; the Roman-pagan civilization in the midst of the Italic peoples was too strong to be annihilated all at once. Even today there are survivals of the earlier culture. The sanctuary *Monte Vergine* near Naples, previously a place of pagan pilgrimage whose origin is hidden in the distant past, is still an important centre of worship. The flourishing religion of the Osci (a group of Italic pre-Roman peoples who inhabited Compania probably 3,000 years ago) is evident in Greek Neapolis, and is still alive among present-day Neapolitans who retain many of its characteristics.

Due to the almost uninterrupted continuity of this high level of civilization from the first millenium before Christ, through the Roman and Byzantine

* Sabino Acquaviva was born in Padua, Italy, in 1927. Since 1959 he has been Professor of Sociology in the Faculty of Political Science at the University of Padua, and since 1964 has taught as well at the University Institute of Social Sciences in Trento. In 1957 he founded the journal *Sociologia Religiosa* of which he is still director. He is co-director of *Cultura e Politica* and a member of the management committee of *Sociologia*. Since 1961 he has been an honorary member of the D.K.T. Honour Social Sciences Society for distinguished work, and is the Society's 'Chancellor for Italy'. He has contributed articles to the *Enciclopedia Italiana* (1960 edition), *Enciclopedia filosofica* (1967 edition), *Enciclopedia dell'Ateismo* (1967 edition). His major books include *Sociologia Dinamica* [Dynamic Sociology], 1957; *Automazione e Nuova Classe* [Automation and New Class], 1958; *L'Eclissi del Sacro nella Società Industriale* [The Eclipse of the Sacred in Industrial Society], 1961, 1966², 1971³ and *La Scelta Illusoria* [The Deceptive Choice], 1965.

epochs, the Middle Ages, and the Renaissance to modern times, the peninsula offers ample opportunity for a deep, vast and valuable study in the field of religious sociology. It is sufficient to consider that in certain areas we can follow the evolution of the spirit *(tonus)* of religion and tradition in ethnic groups for a period of three millenniums.

Secondly, Christianity in Italy was an event centred in Rome and hence Latin in depth. It spread from Rome principally during the last quarter of the second century, when the Romans were beginning to replace Greek by Latin. However, the 'great propagation' in Italy began during the fourth century when all cities of some importance became bishoprics. Paganism ceased to exist as an organized religion between the fifth and sixth century. From the very beginning the characteristics of Christianity are therefore bound to Roman supremacy – a supremacy which penetrates deeply into history.

Thirdly, the major struggles of Roman Christianity in Italy were, on the one hand, against the Greek and hence Byzantine element (i.e. the Church using Greek rites) and on the other hand, against Islam; Protestantism was always a side issue. Especially in the south, ecclesiastical organization and cultural and spiritual attitudes were strongly influenced by this situation. After 1100 the religious structure in Italy became almost entirely Catholic, and remained so almost to this day. The survival of Greek rites was negligible; Islam became extinct; the spread of Protestantism was always limited, and even today Protestants number less than 100,000 in a population exceeding 53,000,000 (1966).

Fourthly, this situation gave rise to a capillary organization centred in Rome, with a large number of bishops and archbishops; one of the functions of this organization being the world-wide political administration of the Catholic Church.

These four points also illuminate the historical impact of the current religious situation in Italy, and explain, at least in part, its origin and development in time. Without reference to these aspects it is difficult to understand, at least on an historical level, why Catholicism assumed a monolithic structure in Italy – a country which, unlike Spain (at least in its northern regions) is very involved in the events of Central Europe.

## DENOMINATIONAL STRUCTURE

It would be appropriate at this point to proceed to a comparative analysis of the various religions existing in the peninsula, their structure and membership, the variations in fertility ratios in relation to type of religion, mixed marriages, sex and age differences, etc. This is not only impossible, but would be of little significance in Italy. Religious uniformity allows for little sociological significance to be attached to the development of the Protestant churches and sects. Furthermore, for reasons too lengthy to be discussed here, there is very little reliable information for analysis.

Members of the older Protestant sects in Italy, such as the *Valdesi*, are still in the majority. Of about 100,000 Protestants perhaps 80,000 are *Valdesi*. There is also a fairly wide diffusion of Protestant sects, such as the Pentecostalists, especially in the south and, more precisely, in the poorer parts of the peninsula. For these there are no reliable statistics.

The development of Protestantism in Italy is, in many ways, analogous to the Latin American pattern. It is likewise confined almost exclusively to depressed areas in Italy, the South. Furthermore, it is more often found in areas where Marxism is wide-spread. In fact, the conflict (nevertheless diminishing and at times almost non-existent) between the Catholic Church and Communism has prompted, and is still prompting many who have Communist political tendencies, to solve the conflict between religion and politics by choosing Protestantism.

In the North there is a 'practised' Protestantism, followed by many who, formally declare themselves Catholics, but in practice reject the church's dogmas and regulations. They have recourse to Catholicism only on major occasions such as marriage, and mainly as a tribute to custom. These people would probably adhere, at least in part, to a Protestant ecclesiastical organization were they to find themselves in a country where such an organization existed. On these matters, however, information is insufficient to provide exact figures.

Considerable information does, however, exist in relation to Catholicism. However, it is only recently that a series of investigations has been undertaken and they are less extensive than those of other countries such as France, Belgium, Holland and even Germany.

## RELIGIOUS PRACTICE AND BELIEFS AMONG CATHOLICS

As an initial general guide, the Doxa enquiry of 26 February 1962 [Universita di Padova, 1962] may be used. It concluded with the observation that 53 per cent of adult Italians 'go to church'. The majority do not thus necessarily assist at the religious service – the Catholic Mass. Further details from this study are given in Table 1 which indicates that on the whole the general pattern found in Italy is not dissimilar to that found in other countries.

Perhaps the most complete and reliable investigation is that conducted fifteen years ago by Aldo Leoni [1952] in the Mantova region (population 370,869). The investigation showed that 37 per cent of the total population

*Table 1. Church-going by sex, class and population density (in %)*

| | Church-going | |
|---|---|---|
| | Have been to church | Have not been to church |
| Men | 45 | 55 |
| Women | 61 | 49 |
| *Total* | 53 | 47 |
| Upper Middle Class | | |
| Men | 45 | 55 |
| Women | 62 | 38 |
| *Total* | 52 | 48 |
| Lower Middle Class | | |
| Men | 45 | 55 |
| Women | 59 | 41 |
| *Total* | 53 | 47 |
| Lower Class | | |
| Men | 43 | 57 |
| Women | 62 | 38 |
| *Total* | 54 | 46 |
| Districts with population: | | |
| less than 10,000 | 60 | 40 |
| 10,000–50,000 | 53 | 47 |
| More than 50,000 | 43 | 57 |

Source: Università di Padova, 1962.

of those obliged to practise 'were practising religion', i.e. attended Mass on Sundays. (This refers to rural parishes). However, religious practice oscillated between an average of 47 per cent in the Upper Mantovan Region and an average of 26 per cent in the Lower Mantovan Region. The equivalent percentages for Easter Duty fulfillment were 69 and 51. Between 1880 and 1882, a period for which the first useful information was obtained, practice oscillated between 82.3 per cent in the upper and 77.6 per cent in the lower areas. Between that period and 1952, practice in the city of Mantova dropped from 61 to 35 per cent.

Observations conducted by the author in the Alessandria region indicate that 48.3 per cent (110,532) fulfilled their Easter Duty [Acquaviva, 1957, pp. 141–147], and in Rovigo 73.9 per cent (of 201,317 obliged to do so) fulfilled it [Acquaviva, 1958a, pp. 139–147]. The author's partial study of the Padova region indicated that between 98.8 and 50 per cent fulfilled their Easter Duty, while a co-ordinated study of the whole diocese gave a figure of 78.8 per cent (of 704,608 obliged to practise) [Acquaviva, 1956b, pp. 495–502; 1956a, pp. 140–153]. In the diocese of Vieste and Manfredonia Easter Duty oscillated between 78.5 and 30 per cent [Acquaviva, 1958b, pp. 145–146].

The results of the investigation in the diocese of Volterra concerning the frequency of Sunday Mass attendance are very interesting. These show that practice in the whole diocese oscillates between a maximum of 48.29 per cent and a minimum of 9.63 per cent; in the town it is 20.77 per cent (of 10,314 obliged to go) and in the entire diocese 21.58 per cent (of 109,604 obliged to go) [Bagnoli, 1952, pp. 122–127, 401–104].

Other local studies worthy of mention have been conducted in Turin,[1] Rome,[2] Milano,[3] Gallarate,[4] Siena,[5] Poggetti,[6] Cesta,[7] San Donato,[8] a

1. In Turin 34 per cent practised (enquiry of 24th February 1952); this percentage was estimated from a sample consisting of about 38 per cent of the whole population of the urban centre. The percentage of religious practice in the diocese (the city excluded) was 58, also estimated from a sample of 38 per cent of the entire population [Leoni, 1953. pp. 705–725]. A second enquiry in Turin, undertaken on 25 May 1952, revealed the following results. City: from a sample of 298,695 inhabitants, the equivalent of 42 per cent of the entire population, 33 percent were found to frequent Sunday Mass. Diocese, excluding the city: out of 82,287 inhabitants, the equivalent of 27 per cent of the entire population (city excluded of course), 50.4 per cent were found to frequent Sunday Mass. With regard to the problem of religious practice in the region of Turin see also the recent enquiry [Università di Torino, 1956].

2. In Rome, 10 per cent of men, and between 25 and 30 per cent of both sexes frequent Sunday Mass [Droulers and Rimioldi, 1957. See also Censi, 1953; Donini, 1961, pp. 101–142; 1962, pp. 9–172].

3. In Milano, in September 1949, the frequency of attendance at Sunday Mass was 20 per cent. An enquiry undertaken in 1950 revealed a frequency of between 14 and 35 per cent, which seems to conform, more or less, to the previous findings. Thirty-eight per cent of the entire population fulfil the Easter Duty [Leoni, 1953, p. 714].

4. At Gallarate 62.3 per cent of the adult population attend Sunday Mass and 77 per cent fulfil Easter Duty [Leoni, 1953, p. 713].

5. For the agricultural parishes studied the percentage is, on an average, 33.7 per cent [VV.AA. 1957a p. 212].

6. For the town of Poggetti (Maremma Toscana), the religious practice among women was 20 per cent and that among men 0 per cent. These figures are comparable with (and in fact worse than) those found in the region of Volterra [VV.AA, 1957b, p. 8].

7. For Cesta, situated 24 Km. from Ferrara, religious practice is found to be about 20 per cent [VV.AA. 1957b, p. 32].

8. A maximum practice was found of about 47.2 per cent among both sexes: 27.5 per cent for men and 65.4 per cent for women [Milani, 1958].

*Table 2. Summary of results of various investigations and religious practice (going to*

| | Census Year | Number of parishes in 1963 | Number of parishes studied | Population (in thousands) | Population studied (in thousands) | Total number vicarages | Vicara numb studie in 196 |
|---|---|---|---|---|---|---|---|
| Milano | 1950/55 | 977 | 330 | 3.750 | 330 | Urb. | 2 |
| Torino | 1952 | 357 | 122 | 1.550 | 269 | Urb. | 2 |
| Firenze | 1959/60 | 488 | 5 | 980 | 25 | 38 | 23 |
| Bologna | 1959 | 454 | 148 | 830 | 564 | 53 | 16 |
| Padova | 1963 | 459 | 459 | 830 | 830 | 19 | 19 |
| Livorno | 1962 | 45 | 26 | 200 | 15 | 5 | 2 |
| La Spezia | 1960 | 187 | 4 | 240 | 8 | 19 | 2 |
| Ancona | 1963 | 46 | 46 | 130 | 130 | 6 | 6 |
| Pisa | 1964 | 163 | 163 | 270 | 270 | 22 | 22 |
| Lucca | 1961 | 257 | 29 | 250 | 99 | 15 | 3 |
| Alessandria | 1957 | 64 | 64 | 138 | 138 | 12 | 12 |
| Apuania | 1962 | 215 | 45 | 200 | 104 | 17 | 4 |
| Molfetta | 1959 | 21 | 21 | 86 | 59 | Urb. | 2 |
| Mantova | 1948 | 161 | 161 | 371 | 371 | 28 | 28 |
| Rovigo e Adria | 1958 | 110 | 110 | 278 | 278 | 17 | 17 |
| Massa Carrara | 1958 | 37 | 7 | 120 | 33 | 3 | 3 |
| Vieste e Man. | 1958 | 32 | 8 | 116 | 38 | 5 | 5 |
| Cortona | 1964 | 52 | 18 | 30 | 30 | 9 | 9 |
| Trieste | 1962 | 38 | 38 | 284 | 284 | 5 | 5 |
| S. Miniato | 1961 | 106 | 6 | 140 | 26 | 7 | 5 |
| Sansepolcro | 1965 | 136 | 136 | 350 | 350 | 9 | 9 |
| Pescia | 1962 | 46 | 5 | 46 | 14 | 1 | 1 |
| Prato | 1966 | 54 | 54 | 143 | 143 | 2 | 2 |
| Volterra | 1952 | 106 | 106 | 112 | 100 | 16 | 16 |
| Bergamo | 1963 | 106 | 26 | 630 | 100 | 16 | 16 |
| Modena | 1963 | 198 | 198 | 340 | 340 | 31 | 31 |
| Verona | 1962 | 354 | 254 | 670 | 670 | 47 | 47 |
| Lodi | 1962/22 | 254 | 254 | 208 | 208 | 25 | 25 |
| Osimo | 1965 | 40 | 40 | 60 | 60 | 5 | 5 |
| Imola | 1961 | 133 | 133 | 130 | 130 | 23 | 23 |
| Nardo | 1961 | 32 | 32 | 153 | 153 | 7 | 7 |
| Acireale | 1963 | 102 | 102 | 164 | 164 | 18 | 18 |
| Palermo | 1962 | 130 | 130 | 800 | 587 | 17 | 17 |
| Ivrea | 1961 | 146 | 146 | 172 | 172 | 28 | 26 |
| Noto | 1964 | 73 | 73 | 190 | 190 | – | – |
| Calabria (Tot.) | 1958 | – | – | – | – | – | – |
| Sassari | 1966 | 46(°) | 46 | 162 | 162 | 5 | 5 |
| Siracusa | 1966 | 60(°) | 60 | 260 | 260 | 6 | 6 |

* The term 'Devout' stands for those who participate continuously in the spiritual life of the community, even during the week.

*Mass every Sunday) in Italian dioceses**

| elay in ptism | Religious function | Sunday Holy Communions % | Followers | | | | Easter Holy Communions % | Separatists |
|---|---|---|---|---|---|---|---|---|
| | | | Men | Women | Total | Devout | | |
| – | – | – | – | – | 20 | – | – | – |
| – | – | – | – | – | 42 | – | – | – |
| – | 2 | – | 25 | 32 | 25 | – | 6 | 4 |
| – | – | – | 24 | 34 | 30 | (5) | 63 | 8 |
| – | – | – | 54 | 83 | – | – | 91 | – |
| 16 | – | 5 | – | – | 22 | – | 37 | – |
| 10 | 3 | – | 39 | 49 | 42 | (7) | – | 3 |
| – | – | 6 | 16 | 29 | 26 | (7) | – | 4 |
| 16 | 3 | 7 | 20 | 29 | 28 | (6) | 30 | 5 |
| – | – | – | – | – | 46 | (7) | 65 | 2 |
| – | – | – | – | – | – | – | 48 | – |
| 15 | – | 5 | 24 | 43 | 37 | (7) | 40 | 4 |
| – | – | – | 23 | 44 | 32 | – | – | – |
| – | 6 | 7 | 27 | 46 | 37 | (7) | 60 | 2 |
| – | – | – | – | – | 52 | – | 75 | – |
| – | 1 | 1 | 5 | 18 | 26 | (2) | 35 | 4 |
| – | – | – | – | – | 15 | – | – | – |
| 15 | 3 | 6 | 40 | 55 | 49 | (7) | 58 | 3 |
| – | – | – | – | – | 18 | (5) | – | 2 |
| – | 2 | – | 20 | 33 | 26 | (5) | 43 | 3 |
| – | – | – | 38 | 58 | 50 | (5) | 57 | 9 |
| 8 | 2 | 2 | 20 | 36 | 32 | (7) | 61 | 5 |
| – | – | – | 36 | 48 | 43 | (7) | 50 | – |
| – | – | 5 | – | – | 21 | (6) | 40 | – |
| – | – | 13 | 59 | 71 | 63 | – | – | – |
| – | – | – | 20 | 28 | 25 | – | – | – |
| – | – | – | – | – | – | – | 58 | – |
| – | – | – | – | – | – | – | 68 | – |
| – | – | – | 48 | 60 | 54 | (12) | 65 | 4 |
| – | – | – | – | – | 45 | – | – | – |
| – | – | – | – | – | 41 | – | – | – |
| – | – | – | – | – | 48 | – | – | – |
| – | – | – | 22 | – | 38 | – | – | – |
| – | – | – | – | – | 38 | – | 67 | – |
| – | – | – | 25 | 50 | 40 | – | – | – |
| – | – | – | 51 | 66 | 58 | – | – | – |
| – | – | – | 23 | 48 | 36 | – | – | – |
| – | – | – | – | – | 20 | (4) | 21 | – |

The term 'Separatists' stands for those who in all respects are not believers and who do not participate in the life of the Catholic Church, even if baptised.

sample of Genova [Cavalli, 1958, pp. 21–22], Treviso,[9] Ascoli Piceno,[10] and other centres.[11] All these studies lead us to the conclusion that the course of religious practise in Italy is similar to that in other Catholic countries.[12] There are also certain analogous characteristics.[13] Practice is decreasing with

9. For thirteen parishes the average regular observance of Sunday Mass was 84 per cent, the average irregular observance was 8.4 per cent, whilst an average of 2.9 per cent of Catholics did not go to Church at all [C.D.P.L., 1962].

10. At Ascoli Piceno the percentage of practising Catholics seems to be about 64 per cent [Riccitelli, 1962].

11. Among the other enquiries mention should be made of those undertaken by P. Toldo (already many in number) in the diocese of Bologna. For the city of Bologna the average practice was found to be 30.16 per cent of the total Catholic population [Toldo, 1962a]. V. Tomeo [1963, pp. 23–32] has also investigated two parishes in the province of Forli and two in the province of Lombardia.

12. We will not stop to consider other studies; instead we refer the reader again to two recent books of Silvano Burgalassi [1967a, 1967b] who, in attempting to form a complete picture, draws on investigations conducted on Cremona, Pistoia, Bergamo, Lucca, Treviso, Massa, Firenze, Rome, Olbia, Nuoro, Naples, Palermo, Fermo, Larino, Teramo, Matera, Monopoli, Irsina, Siracusa, Messina, Patti, Pozzuoli, Sorrento, Nola, Crotone, Imola, Forlì, Rimini, Reggio Emilia, Parma etc., The majority of these studies give a picture of religious practice which is more or less obscure and imprecise, and often not very reliable. The recent attempt by the review Vita [*La Pratica Religiosa in Italia*, 1966] to give a synthetic summary of religious practice in Italy is undoubtedly premature. However, we feel it is also premature to attempt to form even a regional picture (for single regions only) of religiosity itself with the facts we have available. One would run the risk of making such obvious errors that one would be well advised to renounce the undertaking. Even the information available to the ecclesiastic authorities, which furthermore is not known to the public or even the experts, does not appear to be much more reliable. More reliable are the results of a study (of wide interest) on Calabria [Seronde *et al.*, 1960].

13. On the general state of religious practice in Italy our own study [Acquaviva, and that of Burgalassi, 1967a, 1967b, with his extensive bibliographies] should be consulted.

A complete picture of religious practice among Italian people up to 1953 is offered in the study by A. Leoni [1953]. This study is based, to a great extent, on the Doxa enquiry of 1953 [See also, although already antiquated, *Associazione dei Liberi Credenti* 1916; Venturi, 1908, preface].

On the problem of vocations the studies are fairly vast and detailed;this question has been dealt with competently above all by Silvano Burgalassi [1967a, 1967b] and Aldo Leoni [1958]. The studies by E. Falconi [1956; 1960] are also interesting and informative.

14. Quirino Principe of the Centre of studies in religious sociology in Padova has collected data on the decline in religious practice since about 1700 [Principe, 1959]. His figures indicate that for the period 1744–53, 99.57 per cent practised in the urban

time[14] and also in proportion to increases in the number of inhabitants in population centres. The rate of practice of the working class is smaller than among other classes.

Table 2 presents a summary of the most precise statistics available. It is based on a synthesis of Silvano Burgalassi [1967a], the abovementioned studies and still others. In an attempt to give a resumé of the whole Italian situation the results of these studies have been drawn together and presented analytically although it is recognized that the different investigations have been carried out with varying degrees of precision and are thus of variable reliability.

The following tables attempt to analyse the question more deeply, to see if one can identify some of the variables which determine religious practice. Table 3 shows the distribution of religious practice in the urban areas of the cities analysed. As one can see, the separatists are still few in number – only 3 per cent.

*Table 3. Religious practice in urban areas – General*

| Cities | Separatists | Initiated (Baptism, religious marriage & funeral) | Observers of Mass (M) | Observers of Easter | Devout (D) (More than Sunday worship) | Practising (M + D) |
|---|---|---|---|---|---|---|
| N | % | % | % | % | % | % |
| 44 | 3 | 61 | 28 | 50 | 8 | 36 |

centres of Padova, and 99.91 per cent in the surrounding countryside. For more detailed information on this subject I recommend the study of Q. Principe [1959].

With regard to the situation in Italy as a whole, Burgalassi [1964: 147–69] makes the following observations: 'the conclusions of major importance which result from our research are the following two: 1) that we are witnessing a 'gradual tendency' towards the elimination or reduction of de-formism, i.e. Easter Holy Communion versus attendance at Sunday Mass, in the sense that it is increasingly true that those who observe Easter are exclusively those who attend Sunday Mass; 2) that we are witnessing another 'general tendency': it is increasingly true that those who observe the faith are tending towards a more complete and deep attitude towards religion, and are therefore tending to become 'devout'.

Both of these tendencies are a direct consequence of the decline of 'traditions' in favour of a strong sense of 'conviction' which seems to be found among an increasingly large number of the laity.

Furthermore a third consequence of what has been mentioned above can be identified: younger groups frequent the sacraments most often, whilst older groups often remain anchored to the old tradition of receiving Holy Communion only once a year – at Easter.'

Further, as Table 4 indicates, religious practice on the whole decreases with the increase in urban population, and is least on the outskirts of densely populated areas.

*Table 4. Religious practice as a function of the density of the urban population*

| City (Inhabitants) | Cases examined N | Religious practice in the centre of the city % | Religious practice in the outskirts of the city % | Difference % |
|---|---|---|---|---|
| More than 300,000 | 6 | 27 | 16 | –11 |
| Between 100,000 and 300,000 | 8 | 33 | 18 | –15 |
| Between 50,000 and 100,000 | 9 | 33 | 29 | – 4 |
| Less than 50,000 | 21 | 72 | 25 | –47 |
| Total and average practice | 44 | 45 | 24 | –21 |

There is some difference between areas which are predominantly urban and those which are predominantly agricultural in nature. However, this difference, as can be seen in Table 5, is not as great as one might expect.

*Table 5. Religious practice and rural urban differences*

| Dioceses | Rural vicariates studied in relation to the cities on which they are centred | Frequency of attendance to Sunday Mass | | | Frequency of observance of Easter Holy Communion | | |
|---|---|---|---|---|---|---|---|
| | | City | Country | Difference | City | Country | Difference |
| N | | % | % | % | % | % | % |
| 22 | About 90 | 36 | 41 | +5 | 50 | 58 | +8 |

Burgalassi [1967b] found that, among the samples analysed, religious practice is one and a half times more frequent among women than men. Table 6 presents some of his results.

*Table 6. Religious practice and sex (in %)*

| Sex | Total urban districts | Centre of the cities | Outskirts of the cities | Mixed vicariates | Rural vicariates |
|---|---|---|---|---|---|
| Males (M) | 25 | 29 | 18 | 27 | 24 |
| Females (F) | 40 | 47 | 30 | 43 | 43 |
| Ratio (F/M) | 1.60 | 1.62 | 1.67 | 1.60 | 1.80 |

Source: Burgalassi, 1967b.

RELIGION AND HISTORICAL FACTORS

The current distribution of religious practice in Italy (and its evolution) is a function of a series of factors to which separate consideration should be given.

At the beginning of this chapter the point was made that there are many historical factors which throw light on the religious scene in contemporary Italy. Actually in any situation, if one reduces sociological research to a study of social structure one is bound to achieve a result which is insufficient and incomplete. This is particularly true in Italy where considerable distortions of reality can arise. Ethnological, political and cultural differences between various regions are so deeply rooted that any research which does not consider them of major importance cannot be reliable. Some consideration of the formation and evolution of the various regions in Italy will make this point clear.

On traversing the mouth of the Po, the main Italian river, one crosses an ancient frontier, which has been a political boundary for over 1,000 years and which became an administrative boundary only ninety-four years ago.[15] At Ferrara, a few kilometres south of the frontier, there were, for centuries, bloody wars against the Papal States. The Dukes of Este, the lords of the region south of the river, were known through the centuries as enemies of the clergy and the church. Even in the fourteenth century the phenomenon of illegitimacy was so widespread that Hercules I of Este, was jokingly

15. Nor should one forget that at the dawn of history the frontier between the ethnic regions of Etrusca and Paleoveneta was in this region. It was also the frontier between Venice and Aemilia in the Imperial epoch, and between the 'bizantini' and the 'longobardi' in the late Middle Ages. Thus, except for a few interruptions, it is a frontier which remained unchanged for several millennia.

nicknamed 'the father of the country' due to the great number of his illegitimate offspring.[16]

At the present time, while on the other side of the Po the rate of religious practice rises as high as 85 per cent to 90 per cent, on the south side religious practice among men can be as low as 0 to 5 per cent, and the frequency of funerals without a religious service ranges from 60 to 70 per cent. One can easily conclude that the irreligion found in the provinces of Romagna and Ferrara is a historical one, rooted in the past. Hence any attempt at an interpretation based solely on the study of current social structure – the agricultural proletariat, urbanism, Marxism, etc. – would be inappropriate. The fact that the two regions have been divided by a frontier and have followed two different and continually divergent political systems for a thousand years, largely if not completely explains the religious difference.

Such a history of ancient divisions – centuries or thousand year old frontiers – is characteristic of nearly all the Italian regions; for a countless number of centuries, for example, whoever crossed the Appennines between Bologna and Firenza and between Genova and Milano, paid customs.

And the racial differences? What Italian citizen does not know that the Latin language has not by any means ethnically unified the peoples who occupied the peninsula before Rome? It is sufficient to note that the ancient ethnic, linguistic, political and cultural frontiers existing between the lands occupied by the Italic, Gallic or Gallic-Celtic peoples are still today the boundaries between the territories inhabited by peoples speaking the Gallic-Italic dialects (Piemonte, Lombardia, Emilia, Romagna, etc.), and those speaking the Italic dialects.

Numerous observations might be added on the psychology of the people, the changes they underwent when crossing ancient frontiers, these chains of mountains and these rivers, these environments which are frequently bound to religion or to enemies of the church, as we have seen in relations between particular regions and the Papal States. However, what has been said should be sufficient; to delve more deeply into the question would mean to embark upon considerations too analytic for the scope of this study.

Fundamental to the sociological and religious study of Italian society is the more recent impact of the industrial revolution. Although late with respect to Northern and Central Europe and above all North America, it has permeated the peninsula since 1950 with an intensity which once would have been difficult to foresee. Vast transformations have followed this development; millions of Italians moved from agriculture to industry and tertiary activities, from south to north, from country to city. Radical changes

16. Hercules I of Este is well known as the originator of the first plan of European urban development, thus creating in Ferrara the so-called 'Herculean addition'.

occurred in personal needs and religious interest, as in basic personality, cultural level, degree of education, etc. Political and economic interests were transformed, as also were religious systems, in their basic structure.

Such an evolution means, as the sociologist realizes, a religious crisis. This crisis has been far-reaching and deep, and has reduced the religious condition of numerous regions in Italy to a state similar to France, where religion is in a poor state. Virtually nothing is known of this phenomenon – the spread of secularization and irreligion – on the surge of the industrial revolution. Very little has been done by way of an exhaustive study of Italian society in the socio-religious field: this is a grave matter because, obviously, in such a structural transformation we watch the extinction of an extremely interesting phenomenon. We will not be able to study it in the future.

In conclusion then, because both the statistics derived from particular studies and the synthesis of those given above are tied to the rapid development of Italy in recent years, they are consistent with the findings referring to other countries. On the other hand, they are also tied firmly to historical circumstances typical of Italy. For example, as we have seen it is impossible to state for the peninsula as a whole that religious practice in the country is more frequent than in the city. In what was the republic of Venice this at least, generally speaking, is true but in the region of Emilia, in what was the Duchy of Ferrara, for historical reasons, the situation is completely the reverse.

Moreover, it is not true that religious practice is more frequent in the less developed agricultural areas. On the contrary, in Italy, even if, roughly speaking, it appears that religious practice in the city is less frequent than that in the country, it has also been observed that *in the less densely populated areas and in those regions where agriculture and industry are well integrated, religious practice is much more frequent than in those areas which are predominantly low income agricultural areas.*

Having made this point it appears we can also defend the view that, due to certain historical factors and the under-development of some regions, especially in the southern part of the peninsula, the greatest damage to religious practice in Italy was done in the past. This happened especially in the first part of the last century and to a great extent before the industrial revolution. Certainly, industrialization, with large-scale internal migration and the rapid pace of economic development, has exerted an influence since about 1950. But this influence is less than one would conclude from a superficial analysis which did not take into consideration historical factors and some correlations of a different nature.

RELIGION AND POLITICS

One ought not to believe that the current influence exerted by the political factor, whilst being, without doubt, of considerable importance, is as obvious as some appear to believe. Burgalassi [1961, 1964, 1965] has tried to establish the correlations between religious practice and other parameters among which are votes for the Catholic party *Democrazia Christiana* (Christian Democrats) and the Italian Communist Party, currently the two strongest political parties. Table 7 combines the results.

*Table 7. Religious practice and votes for the Catholic or Communist Parties by region (in %)**

| Region | % of people practising | | | | | | | | | |
|---|---|---|---|---|---|---|---|---|---|---|
| | 0–9 | 10–19 | 20–29 | 30–39 | 40–49 | 50–59 | 60–69 | 70–79 | 80–89 | Average |
| | Votes for the Christian Democrats | | | | | | | | | |
| North Italy | – | – | 40 | 51 | 59 | 75 | 85 | 96 | 87 | 60 |
| Central Italy | – | 15 | 24 | 29 | 34 | 49 | 44 | 50 | – | 26 |
| South Italy | – | 20 | 25 | 35 | 44 | 37 | 48 | – | – | 30 |
| National average | – | (11) | 29 | 38 | 45 | 53 | 59 | (78) | (87) | 38/40 |
| | Votes for the Communist Party | | | | | | | | | |
| North Italy | 85 | 69 | 59 | 49 | 43 | – | – | – | – | 30 |
| Central Italy | 51 | 48 | 43 | 28 | 21 | 21 | 21 | – | – | 28 |
| South Italy | 39 | 34 | 32 | 28 | 29 | – | – | – | – | 30 |
| National average | 58 | 50 | 44 | 35 | 31 | (21) | (21) | – | – | 38/40 |

* The percentages in brackets are not fully representative due to the lack of complete information.
Source: Burgalassi, 1967.

Table 8 shows the results of a correlation of religious practice with other factors such as urbanism, altitude of the region and level of income and education.

It is clear that correlations do exist, but they are certainly not of the macroscopic order some scholars have suggested. The factors of which we have spoken above, including the historical ones, help weaken the correlations. For example, many have attributed the considerable decline in religious practice to the spread of Communism. *To a certain extent* this is valid but the

*Table 8. Correlation matrix of religious practice and other factors: urbanism, altitude of the region, income and education levels*

| Region | Christian Democrats | Italian Communist Party | Urbanism U | Altitude of region A | Income I | Education E |
|---|---|---|---|---|---|---|
| North | + 0.028 | – 0.026 | + 0,014 | + 0.016 | – 0.174 | + 0.300 |
| | | | U | + 0.03 | – 0.02 | + 0.450 |
| | | | | A | – 0.010 | + 0.086 |
| | | | | | I | + 0.605 |
| | | | | | | E |
| Centre | + 0.380 | – 0.068 | – 0,017 | – 0.013 | – 0.257 | – 0.031 |
| | | | U | + 0.009 | + 0.013 | – 0.002 |
| | | | | A | + 0.072 | + 0.002 |
| | | | | | I | + 0.006 |
| | | | | | | E |
| South | + 0.064 | – 0.00096 | + 0.190 | + 0.023 | – 0.012 | + 0.121 |
| | | | U | 0 | + 0.004 | + 0.011 |
| | | | | A | + 0.0036 | – 0.125 |
| | | | | | I | + 0.173 |
| | | | | | | E |

converse process is even more valid. The extension of the Socialist and later the Communist vote is helped, and in the past was greatly helped by the *already existing* infrequent religious practice, which was determined among other things by the factors previously mentioned.

## CONCLUSION

As already stated, despite the statistics and information which we have been able to gather in these pages, we are far from being able to offer an exhaustive and precise picture of religious practice in Italy. Due to the lack of sufficient investigations and the limited quality of the techniques employed, the available information is somewhat approximate.

However, despite the limitations of the means at our disposal we hope to have offered an approximate model to orientate the reader to the state of religious society in Italy. Many characteristics are quite similar to those of other Western countries; religious practice has evolved according to certain definite patterns, among which are its greater decline in the working classes than the bourgeoisie and in large cities rather than in small ones. This evolution is deeply bound up with the influence of historical factors, particularly those operating since the eighteenth century.

## SELECTED BIBLIOGRAPHY

Acquaviva, S. S., 'Alcune note introduttive al problema dello stato della pratica religiosa nella regione di Alessandria' [A Few Introductory Notes on the Problem of the State of Religious Practice in the Region of Alessandria]. *Sociologia religiosa*, I, (1), 1957.

Bellomia, S., *La Sicilia: area religiosamente depressa*? [Sicily, A Religiously Depressed Area?]. Rome, The Gregorian Pontifical University (multi-copied), 1964–65.

Bolzon, O., *Inchiesta religioso-sociale eseguita nelle Foranie di Cornuda e Montebelluna* [A Socio-Religious Enquiry Conducted in Vicarages of Cornuda and Montebelluna] (multi-copied). 1958.

Bonicelli, G., 'La prima inchiesta sulla religiosità del Veneto' [The First Enquiry on the Religious Practice in the Region of Veneto]. *Il Regno*, V (12), 1962.

Braga, E., 'Risultati di un rilievo statistico sulla Messa festiva in Jesi' [Results of a Statistical Study on Participation in Mass on Festive Days in Jesi]. *Uff. Cat. Dioces.* (multi-copied) 1964; and in *Aggiornamenti sociali*, XVII (6), 1966.

Burgalassi, S., 'La religiosità urbana in Italia in base a recenti statistiche' [Religious Practice in Urban Italy based on Recent Statistics]. *Architettura e Liturgia* (Assisi), 1965.

—, '*La situazione religiosa in Italia*' [The Religious Situation in Italy] in J. Labbens, (ed), *La sociologia religiosa* [Religious Sociology]. Rome Ed. Paoline, 1961.

—, *Il Comportamento religioso degli Italiani* [The Religious Behaviour of Italians]. Firenze, Vallecchi, 1967a.

—, *Italiani in Chiesa* [Italians in Church]. Brescia, Morcelliana, 1967b.

Cafiero, F., Brunori, G., 'La borgata Giordani in Roma' [The Giordani Borough in Rome]. *Orientamenti sociali*, VII (2), 1951.

Barli, C., 'La frequenza alla Messa in Italia' [Attendance at Mass in Italy]. *La Misura*, II (2), 1960.

Cassin, E., 'La vie religieuse de la Calabre' [Religious Life in Calabria]. in: Seronde, A. M. *et al.*, *La Calabre* [Calabria]. Paris, A. Colin, 1960.

Censi, M. A., 'Una indagine campione in una parrocchia urbana; Studio sulla par rocchia SS Maria. Immacolata del Quartiere Romano Tiburtino' [A Sample Study in an Urban Parish; Study of the Parish of Mary the Immaculate in the Romano Tiburtino]. *Orientamenti sociali*, 23 (11), 1953.

—, 'L'étude écologique d'une paroisse des faubourgs de Rome' [An Ecological Study of a Parish on the Outskirts of Rome], in: *Paroisses Urbaines, Paroisses Rurales* [Urban Parishes, Rural Parishes]. Tournai, Casterman, 1958.

Comelli, O., 'La rilevazione più completa sulla pratica religiosa di una città [The

Most Complete Exposition of Religious Practice in a City]. *Il Regno*, IV (1), 1961.

Contiguglia, 'Una tipica parrocchia siciliana, Tortorici' [A Typical Sicilian Parish, Tortorici]. *Studi sociali*, (5), 1964.

D'Ascenzi, G., '*La situazione religiosa nelle campagne italiane*' [The Religious Situation in the Italian Countryside]. *Orientamenti sociali*, 27 (11), 1957.

Dell'Ana, P., 'Indagine sui partecipanti alla Messa festiva nella diocesi di Nardò (Lecce)' [Enquiry into Attendance at Mass on Festive Days in the Diocese of Nardò (Lecce)]. *Boll. ufficiale diocesano* (7–10), 1961.

Del Vescovo, M., 'La presenza dei fedeli alla Messa festiva nella diocesi di Molfetta' [The Attendance of the Faithful at Mass on Festive Days in the Diocese of Molfetta]. *Tempi nostri*, (35–36), 1959.

De Michelis, C., *Elementi per uno studio della pratica religiosa in Italia* [Material for a Study of Religious Practice in Italy]. Rome, The Gregorian Pontifical University (multi-copied), 1965.

Donini, A., 'Practica y Actitudes religiosas (nella Parrocchia di S. Maria alle Fornaci (Roma)' [Religious Practices and Activities in the Parish of S. Maria at Fornaci, Rome]. *Sociologia religiosa*, V (7), 1961 and VI (8), 1962.

Droulers P., and Rimoldi, A., 'La Sociologia religiosa in Italia' [The Sociology of Religion in Italy]. *La Civiltà Cattolica*, (2–3), 1952.

*La Practica Religiosa in Italia* (Religious Practice in Italy) *Vita*, (4), 1966.

Leoni, A., 'Elementi di spiegazione sociologica e geografia nella pratica religiosa nella diocesi di Mantova' [Explanatory Sociological and Geographical Notes on the Religious Practice in the Diocese of Mantova]. *Realt sociale d'oggi*, VI (1), Milano, 1951.

—, *Sociologia e geografia religiosa di una diocesi; Saggio sulla pratica religiosa nella Diocesi di Mantova* [Religious Sociology and Geography of a Diocese; Study of Religious Practice in the Diocese of Mantova]. The Gregorian Pontifical University, Rome, 1952.

—, 'La pratica religiosa in cifre' [Religious Practice in Statistics]. *Iniziativa*, (6), 1955.

Manzini, G. M., 'Sondaggio sui messalizzanti a Villa del Conte (Prov. e diocesi di Padova)' [Research on Sunday Mass Attendance at Villa del Conte (Province and Diocese of Padova]. *Sociologia religiosa*, VIII (11–12), 1964.

Martina, A., 'Ricerche socio-religiose nel Lazio' [Socio-Religious Research in Lazio]. *Leonianum Anagninum*, XXXV (1–3), 1959.

Massucco Costa, A., 'La comunità cattolico-valdese di Torre Pellice' [The Catholic-Valdese Community of Torre Pellice]. *International Review of Community Development*, 13–14, 1965.

Miegge, A., 'La diffusion de protestantisme dans les zones sous-dévélopés de l'Italie méridionale' [The Spread of Protestantism in the Under-Developed Areas of Southern Italy]. *Archives de Sociologie des Religions*, (8), 1959.

Modugno, R., *Ricerca socio-religiosa in Lavello (Potenza)* [Socio-Religious Research in Lavello, Potenza]. (multi-copied), 1956.

Pellicciari, G., 'La parrocchia di Rescaldina (Milano)' [The Parish of Rescaldina, Milano], in: Pizzorno, A. (ed.), *Comunità e razionalizzazione* [Community and Rationalization]. International Congress on Technological Progress and Italian Society, 1961.

Petralia, G., 'Appunti per una inchiesta sulla situazione religiosa di Palermo' [Notes for an Enquiry on the Religious Situation in Palermo]. *Politica e Cultura*, (5), 1958.

Pizzoli, R., 'La parrocchia di Tuenno' [The Parish of Tuenno]. *Lettera di sociologia religiosa*, II (3), 1962.

Principe, Q., 'Diocesi di Padova, Pratica religiosa (1744–1753)' [Diocese of Padova, Religious Practice (1744–1753)]. *Sociologia religiosa*, III. (3–4), 1959.

Reschiglian, M., 'La pratica religiosa in un'area rurale (Lion-Albignasego-Padova)' [Religious Practice in a Rural Area (Lion-Albignasego)]. *Sociologia religiosa*, IV (5–6), 1960.

Riccitelli, B., 'Frequenza alla messa festiva in Ascoli Piceno' [Attendance at Mass in Ascoli Piceno]. *Centro catt. dioc.*, (12), 1962.

Rimoldi, A., 'La pratica religiosa nella diocesi di Volterra' [Religious Practice in the Diocese of Volterra]. *Orientamenti pastorali*, (1), 1953.

*Sociologia religiosa* [Religious Sociology] III (3), 1959. Documents section. This provides a bibliography of many local studies.

Toldo, A., '*I tre vicariati di S. Giorgio di Piano, Minerbio e S. Pietro in Casale*' [The three Vicariates of S. Giorgio di Piano, Minerbio and S. Pietro in Casale]. Bologna, I.S.A.B. (Istituto Statistico dell Archidiocesi Bolognese), 1959a.

—, 'Rilevazione sulla frequenza della messa domenicale' [Observations on the Attendance at Sunday Mass]. *Chiesa e Quartiere*, (12), 1959b.

—, *I tre vicariati di Bazzano (e dintorni), Monte S. Pietro e Savigno* [The Three Vicariates of Bazzano (and Neighbourhoods) Monte S. Pietro and Savigno]. Bologna, I.S.A.B., 1960.

—, *I due vicariati di Loiano e Vado* [The Two Vicariates of Loiano and Vado]. Bologna, I.S.A.B., 1961.

—, *I due vicariati Castel S. Pietro Terme e Ozzano Emilia* [The Two Vicariates of Castel S. Pietro and Ozzano Emilia]. Bologna, I.S.A.B., 1962b.

—, *Annuario dell'Archidiocesi di Bologna*' [Annual of the Arch-diocese of Bologna]. Bologna, U.T.O.A., 1963a.

—, *Il vicariato di Cento* [The Vicariate of Cento]. Bologna, I.S.A.B., 1963b.

—, *I due vicariati di Castelfranco Emiliano e S. Giovanni in Persiceto* [The Two Vicariates of Castelfranco Emiliano and S. Giovanni in Persiceto]. Bologna, I. S. A. B., 1964.

—, *Il vicariato di Budrio* [The Vicariate of Budrio]. Bologna, I.S.A.B., 1966.

Vitrotti, G., 'Indagine psicosociale su una comunità mista (cattolico-valdese) nel Piemonte' [A Psycho-Sociological Enquiry on a Mixed Community (Catholic-Valdese) in Piemonte]. *Rivista di psicologia sociale*, IV, 1957.

Vogt, E., *Inchiesta sul rione di Castro Pretorio* [Enquiry into the Castro Pretorio Quarter]. Rome, University Pro Deo, 1958.

Wang Chi Yuan, L., *Socio-religiosa observatio parochiae S. Benedicti urbis Romae* [Socio-Religious Study of the Parish of S. Benedicti in the City of Rome]. Hong Kong, Pontif. Atheneam Internationale Angelicum, 1961.

Zingaro, R., 'La pratica religiosa di Andria (braccianti)' [Religious Practice in Andria (day-labourers)], in: Labbens, J. (ed), *La sociologia religiosa* [Religious Sociology], Rome, Paoline, 1961.

Zoccali, V., '*Vita sociale e religiosa in un centro calabrese di recente industrializzazione (Crotone)*' [Social and Religious Life in a Recently Industrialised Town (Crotone) of Calabria]. Conv. Documents of the A.C.L.I. Association, *La chiesa ed i lavoratori dell' industria* [The Church and Industrial Labourers]

REFERENCES NOT SUPPLIED IN THE SELECTED BIBLIOGRAPHY

A.C.I., *L'anima religiosa del mondo d'oggi* [The Religious Soul in the World Today] Rome, 1957.

Acquaviva, S. S., 'Un primo contributo alla sociologia storico-religiosa del Padovano' [A First Contribution to the Historical-Religious Sociology of 'Padovano']. *Studia Patavina*, III (1), 1956a.

—, 'Appunti metodologici per la preparazione di una ricerca sociologico-religiosa su un'area sufficientemente estesa' [Notes on Methods used for the Preparation of Sociological-Religious Research in a Sufficiently Vast Area]. *Studia Patavina*, III (3), 1956b.

—, 'Dati sociologico-religiosi della regione polesana' [Sociological-Religious Information on the 'polesana' region] *Sociologia Religiosa*, II (2), 1958a.

—, 'Vieste e Manfredonia' [Vieste and Manfredonia]. *Sociologia religiosa, II* (2), 1958b.

—, 'Sociologie religieuse et sociologie des religions en Italie' [Religious Sociology and Sociology of the Religions in Italy]. *Archives de Sociologie des Religions*, (12), 1961.

*Associazione dei Liberi Credenti* [Free Believers Association] *La coscienza religiosa in Italia alla vigilia della grande guerra* [The Religious Conscience in Italy on the Eve of the Great War] Preface by Romolo Murri. Firenze, 1916.

Bagnoli, A., 'Insegnamento di una statistica e rilievo statistico sulla frequenza alla messa' [A Statistical Exposition and Statistical Notes on the Frequency of Attendance at Mass]. *Bollettino diocesano di Volterra*, XXXII, 1952.

Burgalassi, S., 'Sintesi religiosa d'Italia' [Religious Synthesis in Italy]. *Il Regno, III* (5), 1960.

—, 'Aspetti e tendenze sociologiche in Italia: l'eucarestia e i fedeli [Sociological Aspects and Tendencies in Italy: The Holy Eucharist and the Faithful]. *Studi di Sociologia*, II (4), 1964.

—, 'Le publicazioni italiane di sociologia religiosa' [The Italian Publications on Religious Sociology]. *Lettera di sociologia religiosa*, 1–2, 1965.

Cavalli, L., *Quartiere operaio* [Labourer Quarters]. Genova, Official Studies in Sociology and Labour, 1958.

C.D.P.L., *Settimana diocesana di aggiornamento, pastorale* [A Work Devoted by the Diocese to the Up-dating of Pastoral Matters]. Treviso, 1962.

Falconi, C., *La Chiesa e le organizzazioni cattoliche in Italia* ]*1945–1955)* [The Church and Catholic Organizations in Italy (1945–1955)]. Torino, Einaudi, 1956.

—, '*La Chiesa e le organizzazioni cattoliche in Europa*' [The Church and Catholic Organizations in Europe]. Milano, Comunità, 1960.

Leoni, A., 'La situazione religiosa in Italia' [The Religious Situation in Italy]. *Realtà sociale d'oggi*, VIII (11–12,) 1953.

—, *Aggiornamento o processo di adeguamento degli Istituti religiosi femminili alle esigenza della società italiana* [Up-dating or Process of Adapting the Religious Institutions for Women to the Requirements of the Italian Society]. Rome, Supplement A.L.A. under the patronage of the *Sacra Congr. de Rel.* 1958.

Milani, L. M., *Esperienze pastorali* [Pastoral Experiences]. Firenze, Lib. ed. Fiorentina 1958.

*Notiziario Passionista*, 'Le inchieste del notiziario passionista' [The Investigations of the 'Notiziario passionista'], [Passionist Congregation of the Holy Cross and Passion of Christ – instituted by St. Paul of the Holy Cross in 1737]. Supplement to the *Notiziario Passionista*, 4, 1957.

Seronde, A. M. et al., *La Calabre, Une région sous-développé de l'Europe méditerranéenne* [Calabria, An Under-developed Region of Mediterranean]. An Enquiry directed by Jean Meyriat. Paris, A. Colin, 1960.

Toldo, P., 'Pratica religiosa e atteggiamento politico a Bologna' [Religious Practice and Political Attitudes in Bologna]. *Questitalia*, (56–57), 1962a.

Tomeo, V., '*La parrocchia nel suo contesto sociale*' [The Parish in its Social Context]. *Il Paradosso*, June-December, 1963.

Università di Padova, *L'Inchiesta Doxa* [The Doxa Enquiry]. Bulletin 3–4, February, 1962.

University of Torino, *Ricerche sulla zona di Torino-Lucento. Appunti e premesse per lo studio sociologico di una zona periferica di un grande centro urbano* [Research on the Torino-Lucento Region. Notes and Premises for a Sociological Study of a Peripheral Region of a Large Urban Centre]. Torino, Institute of Political Science in the University of Torino, 1956.

Venturi, P. Tacchi, *Stato della religione in Italia alla metà del secolo XVI* [The State of Religion in Italy During the Middle of the Sixteenth Century]. Rome-Milano, 1908.

LEO LAEYENDECKER*

# The Netherlands

## INTRODUCTION

It is said that where three Dutchmen are together they will found a church. The proverb has some truth. Sharp religious cleavages and debate on religious problems have been characteristic of the Netherlands since the Reformation and manifest themselves with unexpected vehemence.[1] Holland has never witnessed the general religious indifference found in many neighbouring countries (Scandinavia, France, England); church and religion belong to the most important moulding forces which have given the whole pattern of Dutch social life a characteristic stamp. Nowhere in the surrounding European countries is vertical pluralism [Matthes, 1965; Moberg, 1962] (organizational segmentation along denominational boundaries) or the high rate of formal non-membership in the church (a paradoxical indicator of religious involvement) more striking. The latter is related to interesting developments within Dutch Catholicism since the Second Vatican Council, developments which will exert a great influence on the social situation.

For the sociology of religion the Netherlands is thus a particularly interesting field – one moreover, in which investigation is facilitated by the small scale of the society. It is due to linguistic barriers only that the prominent place of Dutch work in the sociology of religion is not recognized [W. Goddijn, 1960; Laeyendecker, 1967a] and a great number of publications are virtually unknown outside Holland.[2]

* Leo Laeyendecker was born in Utrecht, Netherlands, in 1930. He studied philosophy and theology 1950–58, social sciences in Amsterdam 1958–64. He is currently Reader in Sociology at the University of Amsterdam. His doctorate was granted from the same university in 1967. His contribution, originally written in Dutch and translated on responsibility of the editor, dates from 1968 and describes tendencies which have not changed but accelerated since.

1. That was apparent from the different reactions from the Protestant side when Princess Irene was converted to Roman Catholicism.

2. Much has been gained from making *Social Compass* an international journal. It is

Especially in its initial phase, which continued beyond the end of World War II, the sociology of religion was characterised by the tradition of the sociographical school of Steinmetz – by a rigorously descriptive orientation and a copious use of census data [van Doorn, 1965, p. 73]. It is only in recent years that the lack of theoretical development has been counterbalanced, and a *rapprochement* has been sought with the theoretical framework of general sociology [H. Goddijn, 1958; Laeyendecker, 1967b; Schreuder, 1962].

With this trend, the discipline has found a modest place in some universities, and research facilities have improved. The move away from the post-war location in religious institutions [3] with their concentration on ecclesiastical problems, coincided paradoxically with a growing interest for the sociology of religion in ecclesiastical circles. [4] However, in the process, relations between sociology and the churches may again be deteriorating.

The emphasis on questions of ecclesiastical policy has left its mark on accumulated research findings. The subjects which have attracted most attention in Dutch research are not necessarily the most important and the manner in which they have been treated is not necessarily the most productive. But in the following discussion of this research [5] we will try to correct these deficiences.

## HISTORICAL INTRODUCTION AND DENOMINATIONAL SPECTRUM

Catholicism dominated the Christian scene in the Netherlands until the Reformation, when Calvinism became the prevailing force. The rise of Calvinism is related to the whole political and social situation in the sixteenth century [Ellemers, 1967]. At that time Europe was characterized by far-reaching structural and cultural changes: the spread of modern capitalism, economic crises, changes in the system of social stratification and rising nationalism. A strong feeling of discontent was alive in Holland. It mani-

published in The Netherlands, and is the means of spreading outside its borders many articles written by Dutchmen.

3. The Sociological Institute of the Netherlands Reformed Church was established in 1945, the Catholic Social Ecclesiastical Institute in 1946 and the neo-Calvinist Sociological Institute in 1954.

4. The short-circuits were sometimes painfully obvious. On the one side, the churches expect too much from the sociologists (for example, for solutions of their problems); on the other hand, they disapprove of the way in which the sociologists form and approach their problems. It is significant that the Netherlands Reformed Church closed down the Sociological Institute in 1968.

5. The responsibility for these comments is taken entirely by the writer of this article.

fested itself in protests and insurrections against the Spanish monarchs Charles V and Philip II, and also against the powerful Catholic Church. Resistance was suppressed but discontent prevailed among all levels from the nobility, to the depressed lower classes [Kuttner, 1949].

The climate was therefore ripe for a protest movement but for this, a general ideology was still lacking. Erasmian Humanism as well as incidental religious protest movements (such as Anabaptism) were too narrowly tied to certain social strata. Calvinism, however, succeeded in appealing to a range of interests and attracted the lower classes, and the lower nobility. After 1566 it began to appeal to the significant merchant class. This group regarded Catholicism as a greater threat to economic freedom than Calvinism,[6] it is the group which was the centre of the struggle against Spain and from which emerged the religious leaders required by the new movement. In William of Orange a charismatic leader was found and so a national war started, which lasted for eighty years. He was converted to Calvinism in 1573, and his early military victories against the Spanish gradually brought the northern part of the Netherlands to the side of the insurgents. Although at this time not more than 5 per cent of the population was Calvinist, the success of the political movement strengthened the new religion, particularly among the merchants.

That Catholicism remained a strong minority is not only the result of the relative tolerance of the Calvinists but also of the locally differentiated resistance of Catholicism itself. Even today the South of Holland (with the exception of the south-western province of Zealand) is almost totally Catholic. This area remained under Spanish rule until the peace of Munster in 1648, allowing Catholicism to recuperate and reorganize itself in such a way that even after incorporation in the Netherlands Calvinism was not able to achieve any successes. However, even in the northern areas wholly Catholic enclaves remained. This has been variously attributed to the qualities of the Catholic clergy in these places [Fruin, 1901], the efficiency of the Catholic ecclesiastical organization [Rogier, 1945–47], and limitations in the force with which Calvinism could impose and maintain itself [Geyl, 1960; Banning, 1953–62; Kruijt, 1948; Visser, 1957]. These factors influenced the pattern of denominational distribution in Holland today and form a continuing focus for historical-sociological investigations.

The Synod of Dordrecht in 1618 marked a confrontation between the merchant-based liberal (Remonstrant) and rigorous, theocratic, intolerant (Counter-remonstrant) currents in Calvinism. Although victory went to the latter, economic interest guaranteed that the influence of strict observance

6. In general the Catholic beliefs offered little room for economic developments, by the unyielding attitude towards the embargo on interest, among other things.

was held within bounds, and hence also provided that non-conformists (Remonstrants, Mennonites and Catholics) gained some latitude, although limited. Between 1651 when Calvinism became the state religion and 1795 when its special privileges were abolished during the French Occupation, orthodox intolerance continued to be counterbalanced to some extent by those of liberal persuasion. These two currents within Protestantism in Holland are still present; they have in the course of time strongly influenced the ecclesiastical pattern. Especially in the nineteenth century divisions among the strict Calvinists led to break-away groups, the majority of which combined in 1892 as the *Gereformeerde* (neo-Calvinist) Churches of Holland.

Together with a number of smaller groups which sprang from it, the neo-Calvinist Church represents 8 or 9 per cent of the population. It must be considered as a reaction, called forth or supported by certain social causes, against a steadily increasing theological liberalism within the church of the Reformation, called since 1816 the *Hervormde* (Dutch Reformed) Church. Until the beginning of the nineteenth century the Dutch Reformed Church contained almost 60 per cent of the population. Since then its membership has sharply decreased, until in 1960 it comprised slightly more than 28 per cent of the population.

Catholicism has always constituted a considerable minority, although its size has fluctuated from a high of about 47 per cent in 1656 to a low of at most 34 per cent in 1726 after losses in the provinces of Holland, Utrecht and Gelderland. Until the middle of the nineteenth century the percentage increased again to more than 38, but then decreased again to 35 in 1909. Since then it has risen to 40.4 per cent in 1960 to become the largest single denomination. Growth, however, has not followed the same pattern in all parts of the country [de Kok, 1964]. Due to its strong organization Catholicism has exerted an influence in socio-economic life out of proportion to its numerical strength: this is particularly true of the situation since 1853, when restrictions against free organization of the Roman Catholics were exempted.

Thus the three main religious persuasions, Catholicism, Liberal Protestantism and Orthodox Protestantism (the latter both embodied in a variety of churches) have fluctuated in strength. Moreover, their interrelationships have been of great importance. Catholic hegemony disappeared in the sixteenth century and by the middle of the seventeenth century Calvinism had become the state religion. Yet tensions within Calvinism put a break on religious intolerance; Catholics remained a significant minority.

In the beginning of the twentieth century Catholicism and Protestantism co-operated on the political level against Liberalism in their struggle for equal rights of denominational education. However, vertical pluralism and the pattern of separation and approach, to be considered later, make the pattern of current denominational interrelationships a complex one.

RELIGIOUS PARTICIPATION AND BELIEFS

On the basis of available figures it can be said, that, until the last quarter of the last century, religion and church coincided – with very few exceptions, every Dutchman belonged formally to a church community. Speaking about religion then is speaking about churches; through the churches religion exerts a great influence on social life. Lacking investigations which go beyond the collection and interpretation of statistical data it is not possible to decide how far personal religious beliefs, attitudes and customs were in accord with the official ecclesiastical framework. It is quite possible that church-membership could not be taken as a guarantee of the presence of religious convictions and practices. The converse is however no problem, for the simple reason that almost everybody was a member of a church.

That one cannot draw conclusions about personal religious experience too quickly from broad statistics has become very evident from modern investigations [Köster, 1959; Rendtorff, 1958; Dobbelaere, 1966]. These differentiate with greater justification between the different motivations of formal membership and participation. The understanding has been growing that there are several variants within the categories of membership and non-membership which are not necessarily parallel to gradations in religious experience and conviction.

The changes which have taken place since the last quarter of the nineteenth century in the position of the churches within Dutch society cannot, as will become apparent below, be equated just with changes in the significance of religion. Such changes, however, form a good point of departure for the following considerations.

*Church membership*

Table 1 demonstrates that the rate of non-affiliation has risen considerably since the middle of the last century, although, at the present time, it is rising at a decreasing rate. The increase in non-attachment has, however, always been greater than the increase in the total Dutch population for the same period.[7] In interpreting Table 1 it is essential to understand the nature of the census definition of 'no church affiliation'. The category includes both those who lack formal membership requirements (Baptism, Confirmation, etc.) and those who indicate in the census reply that they do not wish to be considered (any more) as belonging to a church. Thus inclusion in this category does not imply irreligiosity or that such people never attend

7. The results of the censuses are published in the publications of the *Centraal Bureau voor de Statistiek* (Central Bureau of Statistics).

*Table 1. Church affiliation as percentages of the total population*

| | Catholic | Calvinist | | Other* | No church affiliation | Inter-censal increase in non-affiliation |
|---|---|---|---|---|---|---|
| | | Hervormd | Gereformeerd | | | |
| 1859 | 37.1 | 54.6 | | 8.2 | 0.1 | |
| 1869 | 36.5 | 54.6 | | 8.8 | 0.1 | |
| 1879 | 35.9 | 54.5 | | 9.3 | 0.3 | 205.4 |
| 1889 | 35.4 | 48.7 | 4.0 | 10.4 | 1.5 | 414.4 |
| 1899 | 35.1 | 48.6 | 8.2 | 5.8 | 2.3 | 42.1 |
| 1909 | 35.0 | 44.3 | 9.4 | 6.3 | 5.0 | 152.6 |
| 1920 | 35.6 | 41.3 | 9.1 | 6.2 | 7.8 | 83.4 |
| 1930 | 36.4 | 34.5 | 8.7 | 6.0 | 14.4 | 114.5 |
| 1947 | 38.5 | 31.1 | 9.7 | 3.7 | 17.0 | 43.4 |
| 1960 | 40.4 | 28.3 | 9.3 | 3.6 | 18.4 | 28.1 |

* These other groups include Lutherans, Mennonites and Jews.
Source: Census data.

church services. Similarly formal membership does not imply active participation or religiosity. Information concerning this cannot be obtained from census data. On the other hand, detailed investigations which take these questions into consideration can never reach the whole population. Nor is it likely that the statistics give the total number of non-adherents. Yet with all their inherent limitations, census data are nevertheless valuable.

There are striking differences in regional and occupational patterns of non-membership. In dealing with this we will limit ourselves to the 1960 Census.[8] Far above the national average of non-membership are both the northern provinces (29 and 24 per cent) and both the western and strongly urbanized provinces (36 and 23 per cent). A very small percentage of non-adherents is found in both the southern Catholic provinces (less than 2 per cent). The other provinces lie to a greater or lesser extent below the national average. The highest percentages of non-adherence are not found in the largest cities; Amsterdam, Rotterdam, The Hague, Utrecht (respectively 48, 34, 30 and 21 per cent) but in the industrial district west of Amsterdam (from 50 to 55.7 per cent). In the agrarian north there are also many very small communities with a percentage of non-adherence above 40 per cent.

The distribution of non-adherence amongst occupational categories is

8. It is little use comparing growth percentages because the absolute initial figures for those outside the church compared with the total Netherlands population is so small.

similarly irregular. The intellectuals, and the liberal professions, have a percentage of non-adherence which is significantly higher than the national average and similar to the workers and the new middle class (clerical workers, civil servants, etc.). As against this, farmers, businessmen and the old middle class (retail traders, artisans, etc.) have a percentage of non-adherence which is lower than the national average.

It is astonishing and moreover to be regretted that in Holland little research has been done into factors which have influenced the development of non-adherence. The first important religio-sociological study in Holland dealt with this problem, but it has prompted comparatively little afterthought. [Kraemer, 1960; Kruijt, 1933; Staverman, 1954] However, several minor studies throw some light on the problem. Another one is in preparation, but has not been published yet.

The most important factor seems to be the inadequate response of the churches to the pauperising of a great proportion of the Dutch population [Kruijt, 1933, chap. 6.] in the middle of last century. The churches offered many a helping hand individually, but ignored the need for structural change and indeed, supported the *status quo* when the rising tide of Socialism attempted to inaugurate structural changes in the socio-economic situation. Life was made miserable in the churches for the few clergymen who zealously advocated the rights of the workers. Hence, the workers became alienated from the churches and found in the messianic Socialist creed a new and inspiring gospel. The social struggle became for the workers also a struggle against the conservative churches.

Against this background it is remarkable that the first appearance of mass non-adherence was in the agrarian north. However, labour relations in the large-scale agricultural undertakings were not dissimilar to those experienced by an industrial proletariat. The churches condemned labour opposition to these conditions. Non-adherence was strong here and strengthened by the periodic agrarian crises, for example in the years between 1880 and 1895 and the years between 1918 and 1930. Even now there are still villages with the Communist majority (a unique phenomenon in the Netherlands) [Hofstee, 1938; Staverman, 1954].

Motives for church membership suggest another factor. Recent research indicates that purely social motives can be determinants. Church-going provided opportunity for contacts, for gathering and spreading news and it had, in the days of sabbatarianism, recreational value. Again, charitable work – relief of individual social want – was the churches' preserve. With the development of the press, social clubs (non-religious), and the secularising of charities these incentives lost strength. Decreased membership may be seen as a response to loss of social function of the churches, although objections to the use of this term have been raised [Matthes, 1964].

Industrialization naturally brought about a migration process: towns rapidly increased in size and population. Non-adherence was marked in these population centres. Social need was generally stronger there than in the country and erosion of the old culture patterns, of which the churches were part, weakened the normative sanctions against non-membership [Groenman, 1952]. The developing modern scientific world image did not fit well with world images preached by the churches [Kruijt, 1933, chap. 8; Nijk, 1968].

In general one can speak of the break-down of a traditional living framework with which the churches had completely identified themselves. They were unable to accommodate to the new developments. Their organisations could barely cope with the effects of migration and urbanisation[9] and their sanctions and norms bore witness to a social reality which was being increasingly undermined. The churches lost relevance even to their members, in particular they lost strength in the occupational categories which did not resist change in the traditional pattern of life – the workers, professionals and new middle class [Smits, 1952, p. 104].

On the other hand the question rises which denominations were affected most by the development of non-adherence. It is difficult to pin-point the exact number of losses but it is clear that the Dutch Reformed Church suffered the greatest losses and the Roman Catholic Church appeared strengthened. However, the difference is exaggerated by differences in the birth rates for the two denominations.[10] Whereas the Dutch population has increased approximately 124 per cent in the last sixty years (1899–1960) the increase in the Dutch Reformed Church over that period amounts to hardly 30 per cent; the Roman Catholic and Neo-Calvinist churches have increased by about 160 per cent.

Without going into all kinds of statistical details, it can be supposed that the factors influencing the Dutch Reformed Church (increase, regional and social spread) are similar to those involved in the general development of non-adherence. This is noticeable both quantitatively and also in the one-sided social composition of the Dutch Reformed Church. Recruitment is becoming increasingly restricted to members of the middle classes [Vermooten, 1960, p. 120]. Farmers and agricultural workers are over-represented and the intellectual and higher professional categories are under-represented (compared to their proportion in the total population).

In the Catholic Church labourers equal or slightly exceed the national proportion. As is the case among the neo-Calvinists, the intellectual and

9. They were too strongly bound to their geographical structure (church and pastoral work were tied to one place).

10. Some have tried to calculate the actual loss from the larger denominations but arrive at radically different results [Smits, 1952, p. 104].

higher professional categories are under-represented [Kuiper, 1953; 1964]. However, this is caused by somewhat different factors as will be shown later, and the arrears are now clearly being made up. Although the Catholic Church has lost many members to non-adherence her losses in the various social categories are lower than in the Dutch Reformed Church.

It is remarkable that the percentage of non-adherents is greater in the Netherlands than in the neighbouring West-European countries (Germany, Switzerland, Ireland and the Scandinavian countries), in which the census estimate of non-membership is rarely above 5 per cent. The explanation cannot be that the factors stimulating non-adherence are unique to the Netherlands, or that the degree of de-christianization is greater in the Netherlands than, for instance, in the Scandinavian countries, or that statistics relating to a formal church membership have no value whatsoever. In all these countries the church is going through a phase of general change marked by strongly diminished participation and, in the Netherlands, also[11] by increased formal non-adherence. Staverman's opinion, [1954, pp. 41–49] that the ratio of church members to the total population is an important factor in this change is plausible. Wherever the church and national community are identified a formal break with the church can also be experienced as a break with the community. Wherever the strong tie is missing, non-adherence is unchecked.

This tie is not very strong in the Netherlands, which historically has been strongly regionally differentiated. The two southern, nearly completely Roman Catholic, provinces provide an exception but there non-adherence was lower than 2 per cent in 1960. The Dutch Reformed Church, which of old claimed, with Government support, to be the national church,[12] has been exposed to great tensions in the last century; wherever the discontent with the church looked for an outlet and found it, a formal break occurred. This explanation of the underlying bases of change is only just plausible, but if it is tenable, there still remains the question of the form in which the general change in the position of the churches in society will manifest itself – in non-adherence or other developments.

### *Future developments*

As Table 1 showed, the average rate of increase in non-adherence has been retarded in recent decades. However, this cannot be interpreted in a facile way as optimistic for the churches. The occupational categories in which adherence is strongest are the traditional occupations of diminishing im-

11. Also, but not exclusively, as will be seen from what follows.
12. The authorities took drastic action against those who separated in 1834.

portance and influence in society. In the intellectual, higher professsions and the new middle classes, non-adherence is above the national average. Further, there are important differences in the age composition of church members and non-members. The percentage of 0–29 year olds in the Netherlands is 52, in the Dutch Reformed Church 46, in the Roman Catholic Church 57, and among the non-adherents 51.

The higher proportion of young people among Catholics is due to their traditionally high birth-rate. However, this is decreasing rapidly and is steadily approaching the mean national birth-rate. In the long run the growth of non-adherence will thus at least keep pace with the growth of the Catholic Church, but will very soon overtake that of the Dutch Reformed Church. Moreover, while the churches can probably only rely on their own natural growth, non-adherence will also increase from church desertions.

Even if one accepts a retardation in the process, increase in non-adherence will probably remain more rapid than that of adherence. How much more rapid is difficult to predict quantitatively on the basis of available data. Moreover, it has to be emphasized that this formal non-adherence is only one indication of the altered position of the churches in the Dutch society and might not even be the most reliable. The relativity of census data is demonstrated by comparison with a mass-survey carried out in 1966 by a market- and opinion-research organisation for a national Dutch magazine [*God in Nederland*, 1967].

To the question'Do you belong to a denomination or religious grouping?' 33 per cent of those questioned (of 19 years and older) answered negatively which seems to be in contrast to the conclusion noted above that there is a retarded increase in non-adherence. It is difficult to compare this survey with the census findings. The circumstances were not the same. Moreover, non-adherence is interpreted more widely in the census, and response is affected by the official nature of census enquiries. Probably private investigation gives more accurate results. This is supported by the results of an opinion survey undertaken in 1947, some months after the census, which asked a question identical to that used in the census. 17.3 per cent of the population were non-adherents according to the census, but this increased to 27 per cent in the survey. On this basis 30 per cent could be expected to be non-adherent by 1966 [Dekker, 1967, p. 281]. Hence the 1966 survey seems to provide a more accurate assessment than the 1960 census. In any case, it is clear that the churches mean little to the 14 per cent who are adherents in the census and non-adherents in the survey.

*Church participation*

Participation is not easy to assess, since total figures for the whole of the

Netherlands are lacking. Some, but definitely not all denominations keep up to date records but these are sometimes only estimates of the local ministers and in any case show only the objectively observable forms of participation (going to church, receiving communion, club life within the church, etc.). The real meaning of what the church stands for in the life of the church members is much harder to assess. Surveys, like the 1966 one, in which acceptance of certain Christian dogmatic and moral positions was investigated, produce not much more than data on verbal attitudes – and in the Netherlands people are not very inclined to talk openly about these things. Nevertheless, the data, however limited, still provide some important indications.

Catholic data are the most comprehensive and objective. Sunday Mass and Easter duties are, moreover, more or less compulsory. If these are not maintained it indicates at least an aloofness towards the church in its current institutional form [Steeman, 1967]. In an enumeration of the people going to Sunday Mass in January 1966, 64.4 per cent of Dutch Catholics above the age of seven years (for whom this is compulsory) appeared to have fulfilled their Sunday duty. In the big cities this percentage was the lowest (Rotterdam 34.2, Amsterdam 39,4. The Hague 39.8); in the rural municipalities it was highest exactly in those parts where the Catholics form a very small minority (the non-adherent North).[13] Wherever one can make comparisons with previous enumerations, a gradual but strong decline in Sunday Mass attendance is evident. In so far as the data are reliable, one can also conclude that labourers constitute the lowest percentage attending.

As far as Easter duties are concerned (going to Mass and receiving the Eucharist) the national percentage of those fulfilling their duties is higher than the above (86.8 per cent on the 1st January, 1965). This time it is not the non-Catholic North which has the highest rate but the homogeneous Catholic South (more than 92 per cent).

The Dutch Reformed Church does not make these practices obligatory, hence one can expect the number of people going to church to be less and this is confirmed by data on Amsterdam [Vermooten, 1960, p. 238]. A survey there indicated that in 1957 the total number of people going to church weekly was about 4 to 5 per cent of all adherents, and 20 per cent of the total number of church members (who have proclaimed a profession of faith and are accepted as members). In 1955 only 21.1 per cent of the total number of adherents, by birth or Baptism, were professing members. The 1966 survey also shows a clear decline in church-going – 40 per cent of the people questioned said that they went to church less than formerly. Figures

13. This is the interesting fact that Catholics stick more closely to the church in those areas where they form a minority [W. Goddijn, 1957].

for Utrecht in 1957 are slightly higher than those in Amsterdam and about as high as in the Hague [Banning, 1953–62, Vol. VII]. The Hague figure is much higher for the neo-Calvinists.

Among the neo-Calvinists other data show that about 80 per cent attend Sunday church regularly. It appears that this religious grouping still offers strong resistance to changes, which are now under way in other denominations. But even here a turning point is noticeable in resistance to the tradition of having a second divine service on Sunday.[14]

It is thus abundantly clear that the old pattern of church-going is declining; the need for it has been reduced. The traditional forms in which the culture of the church was passed on have a more limited function. This has important implications for normative integration and, although less is known about it, assimilation of the system of values.

The weakening of the churches' normative control is indicated by a variety of data. The decline in the numbers fulfilling the Easter duties implies an attitude of nonchalance towards church norms. Among Roman Catholics there is a growing number of marriages with non-Catholics [van Leeuwen, 1953; 1959; 1968]. There is also evidence of weakening adherence to the Catholic norms of sexual conduct particularly in regard to methods of birth-control and pre-marital sexual intercourse.[15]

Although the 1966 survey cannot be compared with earlier investigations, it provides indications of diminished identification with the denominations. One-third of respondents felt the churches should not give compulsory prescriptions about birth control. (This was about equal for Protestants and Catholics). On the question as to whether one had to obey all the prescriptions of one's church, the percentage giving an unqualified positive response was for Catholics, Reformed and neo-Calvinists: 49, 41 and 66 respectively. One can safely say that, at least in the case of Catholics, this represents a change from the situation before and just after World War II. Comparable data derive from the question as to how one would react if a son or daughter chose another denomination. Among Catholics, Reformed and Calvinists the percentages of those who would have no objections was respectively; 22, 29 and 8. The respective percentages of those who would resist was 23, 16 and 25. Here again comparison with earlier years is not possible. However, we are inclined to interpret these findings as indicative of diminished identification with the denominations.

The problem, experienced by both Catholics and Protestants of recruiting

14. Information from Dr G. Dekker, former director of the *Gereformeerd Sociologisch Instituut*.

15. This is apparent from an increasing number of publications in the field of marriage experience and marriage morals. For a small investigation see *Katholiek Archief*, XX, 1965, 1084–1089.

people to the ministry points in the same direction. Ordinations to the Catholic priesthood have not kept pace with the growth of the Catholic population; moreover they are lagging at an increasing rate. The obvious shortage of priests will increase as the priesthood increasingly appears outmoded [Poeisz, 1967]. This problem is also reflected in the decreased number of applicants for study for the priesthood, increased drop-outs during training [Dellepoort, 1955; Poeisz, 1963], estimated at 20 per cent between 1955–1960 [*Katholiek Archief*, 1968, 378–379], and the so-called phenomenon of so-called 'defection' which has reached considerable proportions in the Netherlands. In 1966 and 1967 respectively 60 and 145 priests left the priesthood –0.5 and 1 per cent respectively. Conservative estimates (i.e. based on current needs) of the shortage of ministers in the Dutch Reformed and neo-Calvinist churches, estimate that between 1970–1980 the shortage will amount to 27 per cent of the number needed [Passenier, 1961].

Apart from the fact that slowed-down recruiting for leading positions may have consequences for the survival of the churches as institutions, it is often also considered as an expression of a diminished religious vitality. This may be most aptly applied to the position in Catholic regular orders which also have great difficulties in recruitment. The average age of members is increasing rapidly and various solutions are discussed, e.g. continence or discontinence. It is evident that the traditional ideal of the cloister had hardly any attraction for young Catholics. The number of releases from vows is substantial, though difficult to verify because of the reticence[16] of the different religious communities [Baan, 1965; Dellepoort, 1955; H. Goddijn, 1960].

Only general conclusions can be drawn from these scattered and disorderly data which offer little that is new to the average Dutchman: the churches in their traditional form have considerably lost significance for their members. Participation has decreased as has identification with the church; less influence is conceded to the church with respect to private life, and normative integration has become weaker. Moreover, the pattern of expectation has changed: an aspect which is considered more fully later.

## RELIGION AND SOCIETY: VERTICAL PLURALISM

Dutch society is remarkable for its organisation along denominational lines, the so-called *verzuiling* (vertical pluralism). This phenomenon began to develop in the second half of the nineteenth century [Kruijt and W. Goddijn,

16. An investigaton was completed very recently by the Institute for Applied Sociology at Nijmegen; it could not be used for this article. It confirms the pessimistic forecasts.

1962]. This is essentially bound up with the development of the phenomenon of organization which became possible only after industrialization began and the isolation of the local communities was broken under the influence of improved communications and by migration. The efforts of Catholics to become emancipated, (after the restoration of the episcopal hierarchy in 1853) and the revival of orthodox Calvinism which was concerned with strengthening the internal organization rather than developing a theocratic form of government, also had a strong influence on this process. In addition, it may be seen as a striving for emancipation, especially among the 'unimportant people'.

In their fight to have church schools put on an equal footing with those of the state, Protestants and Catholics had a common rival (among others) in Socialism, which also used sound organization in its struggle for emancipation.

Without going further into the many possible shades of difference within the concept *verzuiling* (vertical pluralism), [Kruijt and W. Goddijn, 1962, pp. 76ff.] it can be broadly established that there are three pillars *(zuilen)*: the Catholic (which represents one church), the Protestant (in which various Protestant churches have a part), and the neutral, the others.

It is desirable to distinguish between church (organizational) and denominational (socio-religious) connections, which need not be identical *per se*. Two possibilities exist: the leadership of the church may exert a powerful influence on the organizations which form the 'pillars', or these organizations may only be established on certain denominational principles. In that case the leaders of the church as an organisation are prevented from exercising any power. In actual fact, however, it is often a question of a mixture of the two.

Vertical pluralism is not equally strong in all sections of the community. Education is probably the most rigorously 'pillarized' area. About 90 per cent of both Catholic and neo-Calvinist parents chose (in 1959) the education provided by their own denominations. The trade unions are only slightly less 'pillarized'. In 1959, 84 per cent of the Catholics and 95 per cent of the neo-Calvinists supported their own political parties, respectively K.V.P. (Catholic People's Party) and A.R.P. (Anti-Revolutionary Party). Associations of various kinds ranked much lower (average 70 per cent), with marked individual variations, independent of the professed aims or policies of the associations. It must be kept in mind that almost every adult citizen must make a choice where education and politics are concerned, but that far from everyone is a member of an association. Moreover, where the differentiating factors operate, the percentages of the 'pillarized' organizations (within the total number of organizations in those sectors) vary greatly. Within the limited scope of our study, we cannot penetrate more deeply.

The process of vertical pluralization intensified, especially in the third decade of this century, and after World War II. The number of denominational organizations grew. Before 1950/60 there were scarcely any opposite trends in evidence. The Socialist Party's attempt to win over members, or at any rate, votes from other 'pillars' succeeded only with respect to the Dutch Reformed Church, but failed for the most part with the Catholics and the neo-Calvinists. In 1962 it could be demonstrated that the tendency towards increasing vertical pluralism in the sphere of organization was still much stronger than the new reverse tendency [Kruijt and W. Goddijn, 1962, p. 88]. Particularly in the domain of education vertical pluralism continued to increase, though in the political sphere a slight reversal was evident. A change was apparent also in the views of the higher intellectual stratum, but in the face of inertia in the whole institutional-organizational pattern only very slow disintegration of the pillarised structures could be expected.

*Table 2. Survey findings on attitudes to vertical pluralism, 1966*

| Those who | % of Total population | % of Catholics | % of Dutch Reformed Church | % of Gereformeerden (Neo-Calvinists) |
|---|---|---|---|---|
| Chose an elementary school whose teaching was based on particular religious principles | 56 | 86 | 54 | 96 |
| Thought that politics and religion must be kept apart | 58 | 52 | 54 | 13 |
| Thought that the following organisations must be based on religious principles: | | | | |
| Youth clubs | 56 | 66 | 67 | 93 |
| Trade Unions | 31 | 40 | 33 | 79 |
| Sports clubs | 22 | 27 | 21 | 61 |
| Radio programme associations | 40 | 49 | 48 | 87 |

Source: *God in Nederland* (God in the Netherlands), 1967, pp. 237–238.

Table 2 provides new information on attitudes to vertical pluralism. In the sphere of education, opinions are still clearly in favour of vertical pluralism. Even among those who had been brought up within a church, but who indicated to have no present religious affiliation, 18 per cent chose a school whose teaching was based on religious principle. With regard to higher education, the evolution appears to have gone further, although precise information is not available. We can see an indication of the trend in the fact that the Catholic University has established a commission to consider its doctrinal foundations; something similar can also be found at the (Calvinist) Free University at Amsterdam.[17] On the political level it would seem that the position is much more fluid, and as is to be expected, the results concerning associations are different and more varied. We cannot conclude, however, that striking changes have taken place in recent years, at least until 1968.

We pointed out above that the choice made on a denominational basis did not necessarily mean membership of the churches themselves. The figures given in Table 2 are related to denominational background, not to church membership. We can examine whether and to what extent the church leaders have a formal say in the vertically plural organizations, but we cannot easily check how much influence the churches exert via their preaching and pastoral work. It is probable – there are a number of indications – that the influence of the church has diminished to a greater extent than has the influence of religion. This would seem to signify a weakening of the position of the churches, which is not yet the same as a weakening of religion. We must now examine this point more closely.

## RELIGION AND THE CHURCH

### *The growing discrepancy between religion and the church organisation*

The facts we have so far discussed all point in the direction of a changed and weakened position of the churches in everyday life. They appear to mean less and less to the ordinary person. This loss of meaning is expressed in its most acute form by means of a break with the church, formal withdrawal, and less obviously by a lessened participation in church life. Further, although the churches have lost influence at the organizational level, vertical pluralism still has a strong denominational basis, but the churches as organizations have less formal influence on it.

The question is whether these tendencies provide a basis for conclusive judgments about the significance of religion in the Netherlands, and the life of the inhabitants. The 1966 enquiry provides us with a quantity of interesting information. Of those questioned, 89 per cent were of the opinion that

17. This is established mainly because of the insistence of students, many of whom hold themselves apart from the churches. A non significant percentage can genuinely be regarded as outside the church.

one can be a believer without ever going to church. Of the Catholics, 86 per cent thought in this way, of the Dutch Reformed Church 92 per cent, of the neo-Calvinists 76 per cent, and of those not brought up with a religion, 93 per cent. In addition, 71 per cent felt that Christianity should be propagated over the entire world (the respective percentages for the above categories were: 82, 98, 38). Only 4 per cent did not believe in a god or a higher power, and 13 per cent did not know if a god or a higher power existed. More than 50 per cent of the non-church members or 'dechurched people' believed in a god or a higher power. Of those now outside the church, 12 per cent of those brought up without religion and 28 per cent of those brought up within the church believed in a life after death. In the same categories, 23 and 27 per cent respectively regarded the Bible as the Word of God. For 24 per cent of the men and 32 per cent of the woman who never go to church, faith *(geloof)* had a specific meaning.

It is clear that there is no question of complete absence of faith *(geloof)* among the people outside the church. What is more remarkable is that within the category of church membership there is a far-from-unanimous answer to the question whether there is a God who concerns himself personally with each human being. Among the Catholics and Dutch Reformed Church it was 'only' a little more than 60 per cent, while 35 per cent of the Catholics acknowledged only that there is 'something like a higher power that rules our lives'. Of the Catholics 20 per cent and of the Dutch Reformed Church 18 per cent did not believe in a life after death; fewer than 75 per cent believed in an after-life. Only 64 per cent of the Catholics and 75 per cent of the Dutch Reformed Church regarded the Bible as the Word of God. For 10 per cent of the Catholics and 17 per cent of the Dutch Reformed Church faith had no significance in every-day life. This is also true for 8 per cent of the men who never go to church.

Without asserting that faith and church meant the same thing in the past – that is certainly not the case – it has become clear that religion and church have grown apart. Faith, for many who are not members of a church, still has a meaning, and conversely, membership of a church is no guarantee that genuine belief is present. It is not easy to interpret this development. Many see this phenomenon as a process of decay in religion, proceeding along a number of independent lines, and passing through different phases. More than 60 per cent of those questioned (from all churches) believed that the influence of religion on everyday life is fading, and only a slightly smaller percentage considered this an unfavourable phenomenon. Without excluding this possibility, although its interpretation in the light of diverse secularization theories is no simple task [Nijk, 1968; Vrijhof, 1964] we must nevertheless pay serious attention to a lively discomfort with the current form and activity of the churches.

During the discussion concerning non-church affiliation or dechurchment it was remarked that its rapid increase in the beginning of the twentieth century was especially connected with the collapse of the traditional framework of everyday life, and every-day life with which the churches had identified themselves. They, the churches, had no adequate answer to the new developments which appeared in the community. We can point to a similar situation at the present time: further developments are appearing on a large scale, and the churches are once again proving inadequate. These problems are of a different nature to the earlier ones, and those at the beginning of the century; today's problems are world problems – war and peace, atomic weapons, underdeveloped countries. Yet the churches still confine themselves almost completely to a concern with our inner lives, which concern is irrelevant to world problems [*Terzake*, 1967, pp. 146–173]. Some people are of the opinion that discontent with the churches expresses itself, not so much in increasing withdrawal, as in reduced participation in the life of the church [Swanborn, 1963, p. 5]. If this is so, the question arises as to which factors are influential in this shift. It would otherwise be no more than an intrusion in the European pattern. It is not, however, at all certain that this assumption is defensible. In the period of the rapid growth of non-church affiliation, the process may have manifested itself swiftly and violently, yet in the course of years may have continued at a much slower speed. Diminished participation is very likely to evolve in the long run into complete withdrawal. However, the possibility is not excluded that, within the churches, a different view of non-participation and diminished normative integration is developing. What earlier, through intense self-consciousness of the churches led to sharp sanctions and a resultant withdrawal, now receives far more acceptance within the churches which, forced by circumstances, make an adjustment. Moreover, they have at their command fewer and fewer opportunities for authoritative action. The following section examines this assumption more closely.

*Reactions and developments within the churches*

On the one side we can discern a purely defensive reaction; intransigent resistance to any change in the traditional pattern. This resulted mostly in an introversion in isolation. Until 1954 at least this was the official policy of the Catholic Church, as illustrated by a sensational episcopal declaration of that year, which forcefully recommended isolation [*De Katholiek...*, 1954]. It still continues among the neo-Calvinists and is based on the doctrine of 'antithesis' preached by A. Kuyper [Dengerink, 1948]. Among the Dutch Reformed Church it is less obvious but within that church there is a wide spectrum of opinion, which ranges from open liberal views to extremely conservative ones. This defensive reaction seems to be a rear-guard battle: it offers few prospects. Probably only those who feel at home within archaic structures and concepts remain associated – those who cannot respond to a creative and contemporary policy in the churches.

On the other hand we can observe various manifestations of a striving towards renewal and adjustment. This striving is naturally stimulated by the ever more obvious symptoms of crisis but it is also affected by an internal dynamic and logic – radical measures are needed to implement reforms on even a modest scale and this creates further tensions and impetus to change. A number of inter-merging phases can be distinguished [Laeyendecker, 1967a].

The most important tendencies in the first phase which began prior to World War II were the endeavour to present the old unaltered religious heritage in a new guise, and, as a rule, a rather negative appreciation of the development of the modern society [Dippel, 1947; Couwenberg, 1957]. Religious sociology, of the sort practised by G. Le Bras, provided a more responsible method of diagnosing the situation [Banning, 1953–62, 1960; Kruijt, 1960; Reuvekamp, 1945; Smits, 1952; Zwanikken, 1959; Dronkers, 1962; van de Ende, 1961; W. Goddijn, 1960; Hoekendijk, 1964; de Jong, 1953; van Leeuwen and Stoop, 1956; Smits, 1963; Stoop, 1953; Thung, 1965]. Yet investigations were mostly within a very modest compass, and seldom went further than the counting of church-goers and correlations between sex, age, class and social status. Though broadly-based and skilled, religious sociology had little influence, and was even rejected by some. Confronted with disconcerting facts, the church tried to find links with such areas of living as work, recreation, mass media, etc., which largely circumscribe the daily lives of modern man. Most striking was the attempt to form viable communities of church congregations. New methods were necessary: a different kind of preaching, new liturgical forms, a more systematic approach on a personal level and concomitant changes of orientation in the training of the clergy (less abstract theology was taught and more factual information concerning the areas in which they work after their training were included).

The attempt to form viable congregational communities heralds the transition to the second phase of renewal and adjustment. Since non-church affiliation and lessened participation seemed to be more strongly established in the bigger cities, an attempt was made to combat what seemed to sociologists and others to be essentially urban characteristics of increased loneliness and rootlessness. By creating small, conveniently arranged church groups people could find a church community in which they felt at home [Kuiters, 1950; van Leeuwen, 1954]. Formed on a basis of geography or social compatibility these groups were intended to give people the security which would enable them to withstand the effects of the 'damaging' factors in modern society. With this purpose in mind, smaller parishes and compatible congregations were planned. Small churches were considered to be ideal; social contacts after church services were encouraged, and in addition, participation in conducting services was promoted.

These were not the only new methods used: improved methods of organization were at issue. Pastoral work had previously been organized almost entirely upon a geographical basis – a basis supported by Canon Law and theological considerations. An organizational reconstruction took place as far as was possible within the limits of this framework, yet gradually extended beyond it. The reconstruction was, in fact, an accomodation to social developments which had been incorrectly assessed. The ideology of increasing loneliness slowly lost its influence, and the value of a mobile urban pattern of living received increased consideration. Partly because it had produced poor results the ideal of the small congregation gradually lost its popularity and thus other forms were sought which fundamentally affected the autonomy of the local congregation [van de Ende, 1963; Heukels, 1963; Jansen, 1962; Kraemer, 1965; Laeyendecker, 1965; Schreuder, 1965; Thung, 1965b]. A general disposition towards doing things on a larger scale also made its influence felt in the organization of the churches [W. Goddijn, 1958; Schreuder, 1965a; *Terzake*, 1968], This demanded further changes in the areas of authority occupied by the lower officials – changes which could be achieved only with difficulty.

These developments did not take place in all the churches in the same manner and to the same degree. What we have described was especially true of the Catholic Church, but problems of the same sort also played a role within the larger Protestant churches [Vermooten, 1960; Vrijhof in Banning, 1953–62, Vol. VII, pp. 110–168]. In all churches the inevitable consequence which arose from the search for new methods was the need to reorganize church structure. The role of office-bearers and the laity also needed redefinition.

The number of clergy has steadily declined over the years necessitating a more efficient use of personnel, which is clearly bound up with the changes in church organization. It was argued that the clergy should adhere more closely to the demands of their function and profession. This had a far-reaching influence on clerical education, and on the framework of co-operation and authority.[18] In conjunction with the demand for integration of

18. In recent years the diverse forms of training for the priesthood have been co-ordinated. Originally, each diocese and each regular Order had its own form of training; a situation which was inefficient both economically and in the provision of personnel, and which also affected the quality of training for the worse. The number of training centres has now been reduced to six: two Catholic Theological Colleges,

laymen at new levels of spiritual leadership it necessitated an examination of the position of the clergy within the churches. The status of the laity in the church has slowly improved and at the same time it was recognized more and more, that the clergy had become isolated from society. In comparison the laity have greater contact and hence, carrying the gospel to the society and putting it into practice, are pre-eminently the tasks of laymen [Hoekendijk, 1964]. Once lay competency to make judgments is recognised, acceptance of their right to participate in ordinary congregational affairs is a question of time. This leads to the search for methods and forms which will guarantee the right of the layman to have a voice in church affairs.[19] Thus a different view of the structure of authority is required.

The process by which a new need springs from the impetus to create a new organisational framework (as a consequence of the new methods) is clear from these examples. The new need is for reconsideration and changes in theological viewpoints which lie at the base of the existing structure and which are an impediment in certain respects to the necessary renovations. In other words, this third phase concerns the creation within the churches themselves, of 'theological space' for ecclesiastical innovations.

Alterations in theological thinking have also been encouraged in another way. We have already mentioned the problem of the identification of the churches with the traditional social framework and their difficulty in finding a relevant approach to new, world problems. Their system of values and norms and their religious doctrine and moral standards were typical products of a by-gone system of community living. Within the churches, although very slowly, members have become conscious of the need to analyse the relationship between theology and society in order to arrive at a balanced vision of the relativity of theological points of view [Laeyendecker, 1967b, c]. Such a vision is essential for a continuous adjustment to new social developments.

This phase develops slowly because within the churches there is strong resistance. It is founded on fear of undermining the authority of Christian truth. Only a minority realize that in these fast-moving times theological pauses are scarcely possible. To facilitate a permanent flexibility these people feel called to make a constant examination, in the light of the Gospel, of the

one in Amsterdam and one in Utrecht; two centres in the South (Eindhoven and Heerlen) and two theological faculties, one at the Catholic University at Nijmegen, and the other at the School of Economics at Tilburg. It is possible that six is still too many, the future will decide. The quality of the training is, at any rate, improved.

19. The rights of the laity to make demands has been established by the Pastoral Council, in which representatives of the entire Netherlands Catholic ecclesiastical province meet, together with the bishops. For information concerning the organization and progress of this Council, see *Katholiek Archief*, 1966–1970.

concrete reality in which we live. It seems, however, that although the majority of church members can comprehend that the unrest within the churches is unavoidable, they are eager to return as quickly as possible to a situation with fixed points of orientation. It is therefore also possible, but not to be verified empirically, that church members are estranged from the church precisely because of the lack of fixed and trusted precepts; the church no longer offers them the certainty that they need.

Taking all this into consideration it is clear that the claims of the churches are certainly less absolute. They no longer set themselves up so readily as the only legitimate institutionalization of religion; they recognise that they have failed in many respects, and from this admission, have reached a more positive understanding of the people outside their sphere of influence.[20] All this leads to allowing more room for individual variations in religious experience; the churches are becoming increasingly pluriform on a number of different levels. Whether, and to what degree this is connected to the reduced growth of non-church affiliation or 'dechurchment' cannot be verified empirically. The hypothesis, however, seems extremely plausible.

### *Influence of the empirical sciences*

The empirical sciences have furnished an important contribution to these processes within the churches. In the first place, they have provided, and continue to provide an adequate basis of knowledge about the society which previously the churches woefully lacked. On this level, their usefulness was fairly easily recognized, and as long as they had no pretensions to anything deeper, co-operation was possible. Directly after World War II religious institutions for social research were established.[21] However, it may not be concluded that their work was universally appreciated. Strong opposition, particularly effective through informal relationships, remains in existence.[22]

Sociologists, in particular, have contributed to the consideration of the framework of organization, but their relationship with the churches is more difficult. On the one hand, in trying to achieve a more adequate and consequently revised formulation of the real problems, sociologists have not always remained within the area of influence allotted to them by the theologians and church leaders. On the other hand, the latter sometimes cherished unrealistic expectations of sociology which led to some disappointment.

20. This is evident from the boom which concepts such as church-outside-the-church, etc., are undergoing in present-day theological literature.

21. See Note 8.

22. The Sociological Institute of the Dutch Reformed Church obtained an official status because it was recorded in the church order of 1951. This was far from universally accepted as a step forward. In 1968 it was dissolved (as an economy measure!).

Now, however, as the approach of the sociology of knowledge to theological promises gains impetus the critical point in the mutual relationship seems to have been reached. Developments cannot yet be predicted. Yet it is certain that the pretensions of the theologians even in their own estimation [Kooistra, 1955; Lammers, 1957; Laeyendecker, 1967c; de Loor, 1965, 1967; Schillebeeckx, 1962; Schreuder, 1964] (theology as queen of the sciences) have been reduced and that their influence in the church, already impaired by the use of a language that was unintelligible to the majority, is waning rapidly. Moreover, it is now recognized, at least in principle, that education to a modest level in the empirical sciences is necessary for future clergymen, though the plans for the realization of these ideas are practically everywhere still in their infancy.[23] However, a modest optimism seems warranted.

## INTER-CHURCH RELATIONSHIPS

So far we have chiefly concentrated our attention upon the position of the churches in general, and have only, when it became necessary, differentiated between a few of the larger denominations. We must now turn to a brief consideration of relationships between the churches, as the complex of interchurch relationships has had a wide influence on Dutch society.

We have already noted that the numerical strength of the different denominations in relation to each other has undergone important changes. The pronounced Protestant majority at the turn of the century has now disappeared, smaller groups have declined, while Catholics and the non-affiliated category have grown. We have also pointed out that the churches, in varying measure, have lost to non-church affiliation, but that differential birth-rates have also played a part. We shall amplify our remarks on both these points.

It is not easy to pin-point the factors that are of importance concerning our first point. One cannot really assume that the factors which work in favour of non-church affiliation (dechurchment) have affected the different denominations in unequal measure. These factors were universal social forces, although they could have affected the different churches at different rates. In addition the degree of geographical and social isolation associated with rural-urban differences and the modern-dynamic pattern of culture (to be discussed below) could have played a part. However, here we will concentrate on differential resistance within the churches.

23. This concerns specially the theological training institutes, mentioned in Note 18. A sociological training is provided within the theological faculties at both Leiden and Nijmegen.

From the middle of the nineteenth century, the Catholic Church has distinguished itself by a strongly pronounced effort towards emancipation. As previously noted, she had been relegated to a minority-position ever since the Reformation. For a long time the two southern Catholic provinces were regarded as second-class provinces and were economically exploited; poverty and under-development were proverbial in these areas [van Heek, 1954, pp. 120ff.]. Official positions were not open to Catholics; they were poor, and even in 1900 only 1.5 per cent of the student body was Catholic [Verweij-Jonker, 1962, p. 107]. Emancipation leading to full citizenship in the Dutch community for Catholic members began with the founding of the Catholic press [Verweij-Jonker, 1962, p. 111]. Shortly after the episcopal hierarchy was restored in 1853 Catholicism became conscious of its potential. Emphasis was laid by the Catholic leaders on unity, on united action, and on the pooling of resources. In 1883 the platform for a Catholic political party was drawn up, and an extensive organizing body gradually came into existence. In addition to the permanent place that Catholicism thus achieved in the Netherlands, the Roman Catholic State Party has taken a central position in the relationships between the political parties since the introduction of universal suffrage. These developments promoted a strong feeling of group-solidarity, powerful social control, strong normative integration and, as a result, cultural isolation. All outside influences which could have had a disintegrating effect on Catholic unity were energetically resisted. This striving for emancipation coincided with an intense experience of Catholic faith, strong participation in church affairs, implicit obedience to the church authorities, and gradually, when emancipation began to bear fruit, with an unmistakable sense of triumph [Rogier and de Roeij, 1953, p. 809]. The factors which contributed to dechurchment, (non-church affiliation) achieved very little hold on this Catholicism-on-the-march.

The neo-Calvinist section of the community representing the strict side of Calvinism set itself apart to a greater or lesser degree from the Dutch Reformed Church in which liberalizing influences were not unusual. They were the 'unimportant people', who were very conscious of their religious calling, and under the leadership of A. Kuyper, strove for emancipation, their efforts directed in the first instance towards a system of protestant education of their own. They also developed a view of society, aiming at autonomous development of all sub-sectors which obtained strong support by certain theological principles, the so-called *souvereiniteit in eigen kring*. They were the first in the Netherlands to establish a political party (1878), (The Antirevolutionary Party) and already by 1880 had founded their own university [Verweij-Jonker, 1962, p. 115]. They also were characterized by a strong group-solidarity, powerful social control and cultural isolation. Here also were strong internal forces, as is clear from the above-mentioned facts, and persisting up to the present day, opposing the disintegrating forces which came from outside.

The Dutch Reformed Church has exhibited all the advantages and disadvantages of a majority group. There was a much more limited need for efficient organization, because the ecclesiastical organization was grafted on to the political organization, and also because there was no need to press for emancipation. From the time of the Reformation, she had been exposed to internal tensions concerned with theological currents. In the seventeenth, eighteenth and nineteenth centuries, liberal theology steadily increased its influence [Hofstee, 1938; Staverman, 1954; Vermooten, 1960; Weiler, 1962]. The integrating force of common convictions plus a clear aim towards worthy objects was absent; on the contrary, there was an inner divergence which in the nineteenth century unmistakably came into the open with, among other things, the separation of the neo-Calvinist groups. The internal resistance to dissolving influences was weak. Once the dynamics of dissolution had been set in motion, it moved inexorably to its logical conclusion. Certain social categories of people disappeared, the Netherlands Reformed Church shrank to a church of middle-class people and farmers, and it had, and still has, a diminished appeal to other social classes. The national percentage formed by her adherents was halved between 1869 and 1960.

Against this background one must also consider the differential birth-rate statistics which naturally form an important determinant in the development of the quantitative ratios.

In the Roman Catholic Church, rigid ideas concerning the morality of marriage exists. Until recently, every form of birth control except complete continence was rejected. The periodic continence has only been accepted as permissible within the framework of morality for a few decades. This rejection of birth-control, supported by a long ethical tradition, was given a special significance within the struggle for emancipation.

The birth-rate of the Catholics far exceeds the birth-rate of other groups. Up to 1947 the average number of living births per 100 first marriages of Catholics exceeded that of the neo-Calvinists by 13.6 per cent, that of the Dutch Reformed Church by 44.6 per cent and that of those outside the church by 63.2 per cent [van Heek, 1954, p. 51]. This noticeable difference is attributed by some sociologists [van Heek, 1954, p. 116; Poeisz, 1965] to the frontier mentality which marks Dutch Catholicism, the religious *élan*, coupled with a high level of ambition, favourable future expectations, and in addition, though independent of the previously-mentioned factors, a rigid adherence to a norm. The high birth-rate – higher than that of other Dutch churches and Catholics outside the borders of the Netherlands (Germany and Belgium) – is thus seen as a means of giving emancipation a quantitative basis.

Others credit this 'religious' factor with much less influence. They emphasize the development of a modern-dynamic pattern of culture [Hofstee, 1962] distinguished by a willing acceptance of change, a receptive attitude towards outside influences – towards education, information, and the weakening of traditional ties. This acceptance of change (via a changed attitude towards medical care) promotes a different attitude towards birth and death. Hence, since 1880 there has been a reduction in births and deaths. The modern-dynamic pattern of culture seems to have spread through the Netherlands from the north-west to the south-east. Denominational differences appear as a secondary factor expressed particularly in differential resistance to this modern-dynamic pattern. The relatively high birth-rate among the neo-Calvinists could also be explored by the argument.

Although debate on this problem has quietened, there is no clear unanimity.[24] What is clear is that Catholics and neo-Calvinists owe at least the maintenance of their numerical strength to their relatively high birth-rates. They could perhaps have increased their strength still more if it had not been for the fact that dechurchment had also affected these groups, albeit much later than the Dutch Reformed Church. In so far as the relatively higher birth-rate masked the loss of members, it must be admitted that this effect will become steadily less, since the birth-rates of both Catholics and neo-Calvinists are falling. In our opinion, this is bound up with an opening up of these closed groups, a completion of the emancipation, a greater inner differentiation, and a lessening influence of ecclesiastical authorities. In other words, the same social factors are now starting to work in the opposite direction.

It probably does not require demonstration that these quantitative relationships reflect the attitudes that the churches assume towards each other. Before we examine this further we shall summarize several other aspects of these three most important groups.

## EDUCATION, CULTURE AND POLITICS

Several times we have pointed out the differences in social composition between the large denominations, so that further reference is unnecessary, except concerning the extent of education and intellectual development. Certainly since 1923, when the Catholic university was founded, a gradual change has taken place in the depressed educational situation of Catholics. It is remarkable though that they have not shown, then or now, equal in-

24. See *Mens en Maatschappij*, 38 (1963), pp. 81–134; 257–277 for several discussions.

terest in all branches of study, being farthest behind in the exact sciences and very involved in the humanities and social sciences. The same is true of the neo-Calvinists. This can be ascribed to the influence of the spiritual climate within the church groups, but there could also be chance factors at work [Hofstra, 1967, pp. 158–161; Hooijdonk, 1965; Matthijssen, 1958]. Important changes in position have taken place in the last thirty years. The percentages of Catholics among academics rose from 15 to 23, and also among the neo-Calvinists from 4 to 7. It is evident that the leeway has not been made up (the percentages of Catholics and neo-Calvinists in the population are 40.4 and 9.3), but it will probably continue to reduce. Changes in position bring with them a relative lowering of the number of academics among the liberal Protestants and secular groups, so that in the domain of higher education a levelling-out is slowly taking place.

This development is, on the one side, to be seen as a phase in the emancipation process, but the fact that is was not until the third decade of this century that it really got under way indicates that there was inside Catholicism (and inside the neo-Calvinist groups), strong resistance to modern scientific knowledge. Emancipation and strong group solidarity had also led to such an extreme cultural isolation that one can quite correctly speak of a Catholic ghetto,[25] that is, however, now being broken down at an increasing speed.[26]

A somewhat similar situation is found among the neo-Calvinists. Their marked upward mobility from the ranks of the 'unimportant people' was supported by their own university (1880). However, the university does not pursue scientific knowledge to any great degree. We find the neo-Calvinists chiefly in professions that they value relatively highly [Kuiper, 1964, p. 422] especially those connected with authority and power. The Free Calvinist university occupies an advanced position in the whole process of development within the neo-Calvinist section of the community. There is an intense divergence of opinion between the university and the reactionary element, which is represented in the university by the controlling positions, indicating that *this* emancipation is not proceeding without difficulties.

The attitude to culture in the broad sense is reserved in the extreme among the neo-Calvinists, and only gradual change is taking place.[27] Certainly

25. This became a popular war-cry in the programmatic literature concerning the situation in the Roman Catholic Church. It had deep roots; cf. Rogier and de Rooy [1953].

26. This is clearly a reaction-phenomenon; the speed of the break-down is understandable from the extreme isolation of the Catholic minority in the past. See also Abbink [1963].

27. See, for instance, the *Rapport film- en bioscoopvraagstuk* by the General Assembly of the Calvinist Reformed Church in 1957.

the stricter groups among them, though not very great in numbers, hold a negative attitude towards the development of technology and science, and diverse forms of cultural amusements. This is rooted on the one hand, and in our opinion the most strongly, in theological concepts which in their turn are clearly influenced by the social situation of the neo-Calvinists; on the other hand, it is part of their desire (and need) to maintain their own subculture.

With the Catholics, this rejection was much less powerful in terms of principle, but they also were apprehensive of the disintegrating influences which could originate in modern culture and penetrate the closed group-life of the Catholics. However, the increasing influence of the mass media, greater access to culture, and the weakened internal situation of this church doomed the resistance to failure.

The discussion of vertical pluralism has already indicated that political connections in the Netherlands were (and are) strongly influenced by denominational-religious relationships. The first political party founded on a confessional basis was the Anti-Revolutionary Party, which was established in 1878 upon strict Calvinist principles. In 1883 a Catholic Party followed. The Socialist Party was not formed until ten years later [Verweij-Jonker, 1962, p. 115]. In 1895 a split occurred in the Calvinist party which led to a second Protestant party, the Christian Historical Union, which was less strictly Calvinist.

This confessional basis of political parties with orientations based on religious principles, and others on denominational unity, obscured socio-economic divergencies within the parties. The Right and Left were brought together and the class struggle in these circles mitigated to an important degree [Kruijt and Goddijn, 1962, p. 102]. Rivalry between the Socialist Party and the denominational parties was expressed in the choice between loyalty to socio-economic equals and the bond of the religious group. Only among liberal protestants could one be, at one and the same time, a member of the church and a member of a Leftish party, but this was of limited significance to the Left because there were few working-class people among the Unitarians.

The Catholic Party acquired the function of a centre, not only by uniting the Left and (mainly) the Right, but also because it was not possible to form a government without it. The protestant parties usually attached themselves to this group. Combinations were attempted alternately with the Left and Right, according to whichever objects were being pursued at the time. Except for a short period after World War II the denominational parties have supported the Right. This tendency was undoubtedly strengthened by the internal organization of these parties. In this manner, the denominational parties have dominated the political image of the Netherlands.

After World War II the old Socialist Party, now called the *Partij van de Arbeid* (the Labour Party) tried to effect a break-through. They were successful only with the Dutch Reformed Church. In addition, there were both Catholic and Protestant sections in the Labour Party, but they did not have much influence upon the actual political ratios, which were extremely stable for a long time. In 1918 the Catholic Party numbered 30 per cent, in 1933 28 per cent and in 1963 32 per cent of the electorate. All the Protestant parties together, in the same years, numbered 22, 28 and 20.5 per cent, while Socialism (excluding Communism) fluctuated around 30 per cent.

At the present time, the integrating forces in the churches are weakened and connection between denominational principles and concrete political programmes has become blurred, so it becomes increasingly difficult to keep people of diverging socio-economic views in the one denominational party. Within the Catholic People's Party, a Leftish minority which works towards co-operation with the socialists can be clearly distinguished, and a similar group exists among the Anti-Revolutionaries. The majority in both of these parties, and certainly the majority of the Christian Historical Union, are oriented towards the Right, and aim at co-operation with the conservative Liberal Party. A few very small strictly orthodox Calvinist parties stand clearly on the Right in the field of political influence.

The position of the denominational parties, particularly the Catholics, is greatly weakened at the present time. The latter's national percentage has been diminishing rapidly for a number of years. In the 1967 parliamentary elections the Catholic Party received only 26.5 per cent of the votes. The total of the Protestant parties was still 20.9 per cent, slightly more than in 1963, but it must be kept in mind that this proportion forms the hard core of electors whose vote is governed by confessional bonds. Roughly half of them belong to the neo-Calvinist group. It can be expected that even within this group political contrasts will become more and more conspicuous. As it is improbable that all the parties will develop in the same direction, this could begin to influence the established pattern of co-operation between the Christian parties. At the moment a large section of the three big Christian parties is working towards closer organizational co-operation for progressive political action.[28] Those who are further to the Left are dissatisfied with this plan and have little faith in this kind of progressive leadership. After the last elections, a small group of radicals split off from the Catholic Party (1968). This group has noticeably played down its Christian basis for a

28. One does not think immediately of a large C.D.U. but close to it. However, there exist groups in all parties which are on the one hand against co-operation and amalgamation, yet on the other hand are against a consistent progressive policy.

vaguely defined 'Christian inspiration'. It wants to pursue a progressive policy in co-operation with all who are of a like mind.[29].

Some examination of voting patterns is in progress but there is little examination, in the narrower sense, of the relationship between religion and politics in the Netherlands. However, from the one study concerned with investigating the relationship between Protestantism and a progressive attitude [Hoogerwerff, 1965], it has emerged that Protestants are less often progressive than Catholics and those outside the churches with respect to social politics. This must in part be explained by their relatively high incomes, but also by the relatively cut-off position of orthodox Protestantism. Much investigation must still be done in this field before accurate information is available about the relationships between religion and politics.

## SEPARATION AND APPROACH

We have already noted that after the Reformation relationships between the churches of the Netherlands were often very difficult. Even today this is clearly evident [W. Goddijn, 1957].

With the Catholic reaction to discrimination both defensive secrecy (inversion) and religious stimulation, cultivation of their own religious convictions and piety, began to flourish vigorously [van Heek, 1954, p. 123; Rogier and de Rooij, 1953, p. 207]. For obvious reasons, Catholics sought alternatives to economic and professional discrimination, they went into trade and prospered mightily. It was only much later, in the eighteenth and nineteenth centuries, that the close group-organization of the Roman Catholic Church in the Netherlands developed.

This discrimination, which lasted formally until 1796 when the privileges enjoyed by the Calvinists were abolished, but which actually lasted much longer, has resulted in a noticeable backwardness among Catholics in the Dutch community; which has only gradually diminished, and, in our opinion has not yet disappeared in all sections of society. It has also formed the basis for an intricate complex of beliefs, prejudices and mutual distrust, that in its turn is either maintained or intensified by the practices emanating from it. The after-effects of the historical majority-minority relationship were perceptible long after official parity was established [W. Goddijn, 1957, p. 62].

In the Protestant section of the population, violent emotions rose to the surface when the Catholic episcopal hierarchy was restored. Although complicated by political opposition to a liberal-progressive government, the Protestant fear of a restoration of Catholic power was evident. In a later

29. In April, 1968, this party was christened the *Politieke Partij Radicalen* (Radical Political Party). Twenty per cent of its members were Protestant, the rest were mostly Catholics. This party is firmly left-wing.

phase, this fear was fed by the increasing emancipation of the Catholics, their close group-organisation, and their relatively high birth-rate, as a result of which many Protestants, right up to the 1950's, feared a future majority of Catholics in the Netherlands.[30] In particular, Catholics were upbraided for their obedience to a foreign law-giver which obedience must incapacitate them as patriots.

When emancipation began to bear fruit, the Catholic reaction expressed itself in an aggressive jubilance. Past backwardness was interpreted as the product of lasting neglect, and a future Catholic Netherlands was painted in vivid colours. This did nothing to reduce the Protestant alarm. National history written from a Catholic or Protestant viewpoint illustrates all the mechanisms of group-judgment, group-image, fixed ideas and prejudice [W. Goddijn, 1957; Weima, 1963]. It is understandable that these are deeply rooted and resistant to change.

Within Protestantism there have also been areas of conflict between the Dutch Reformed Church and the splintergroups that established the neo-Calvinist churches in 1892. The Dutch Reformed Church, with the support of the civil authorities, took drastic action against the dissenters of 1834. Dissenters looking for the freedom which was denied them in their own land, were encouraged by those who had gone earlier, [van Hinte, 1928; Prakke, 1948] to emigrate to the U.S.A. However, relationships among the Protestant groups have at no time been as bad as those between Protestants and Catholics. The comparatively small numbers of neo-Calvinists was probably a mitigating factor.

It would be going too far outside the scope of this project to examine all aspects of these inter-church relationships. However, it is interesting to mention some of the data produced by the 1966 investigations which concerns the popular image of the large churches. The majority of respondents regarded the Dutch Reformed Church as progressive, trustworthy and tolerant; the Catholics as progressive, tolerant, militant and hypocritical; and the neo-Calvinists as stodgy, stiff and hypocritical.

For some years past, the relationships between the churches have shown improvement. The increase in the general cultural level, as described in an earlier paragraph is partly the cause. The churches have all been driven to adopting a defensive attitude towards the rest of the world, they experience the same problems, and seek support among themselves. Theological thinking has become less absolute, and the relativity of fundamental theological principles has also received attention. It is clear that prejudices are fewer, images favourable, and willingness to co-operate, especially at an

30. The Protestant Professor Miskotte wrote in 1947 that, sooner or later, there will be only one dilemma, to leave the country or defend it. Quoted by van Heek [1954, p. 151].

organizational level, greater. Political co-operation between Protestant and Catholic parties has played a part and currently ecumenism is passing through a boom period. However, the step from verbal support to genuine activity is not always easy to take; an ecumenical impasse may form when historico-sociological factors which are only slowly losing their influence, are not taken sufficiently into account.

Within this process of approach, attention must be given to the *connubium*, the right to inter-marry. In several studies, the development of the 'mixed marriage' has been examined [van Leeuwen, 1959; Dekker, 1965]. There seems to have been generally an increase over a long period (from 1900 onward), but in more recent years a stabilization, or even a decrease. Though in earlier years only the negative aspects of the mixed marriage were emphasized, it is possible that in the present favourable ecumenical climate too little attention is payed to them. The pastoral responsibility of the churches is certainly strongly emphasized with regard to mixed marriages. The still-not-sufficiently-relaxed attitude of the Catholic Church in the Netherlands is nevertheless a manifest symptom of a changed climate. What impression the church-blessed mixed marriage will make on the actual inter-denominational attitudes cannot be predicted with certainty, nor must we forget that the marriage of church members with people outside the churches will probably provide an even greater problem.

## BIBLIOGRAPHY

Abbink, G. A. M., 'De priester binnen de eigen evolutie in Nederland' [The Priest within the Catholic Evolution in the Netherlands]. *Tijdschrift voor Theologie* [*Journal of Theology*], V, 1963.

Baan, M. A., *De Nederlandse Minderbroedersprovincie sinds 1853* [The Dutch Province of the Franciscans since 1853]. Assen, Van Gorcum, 1965.

Bachiene, W. A., *Kerkelijke geographie der Vereenigde Nederlanden* [Ecclesiastical Geography of the United Netherlands]. Amsterdam, 1768.

Baijer, A. E., and Koebben, A. J. F., '*Leiders en volgelingen in een religieuze groep*' [Leaders and Adherents in a Religious Group], in: Mulder, M. (ed.), *Mensen, groepen en organisaties* [People, Groups and Organizations]. Vol. I. Assen, van Gorcum, 1963.

Banning, W., *et al.*, *Sociologie en kerk* [Sociology and Church]. The Hague, 1951.

Banning, W., (ed.), *Handboek der pastorale sociologie* [Handbook of Pastoral Sociology]. 7 vols. The Hague, 1953–1962.

Beins, E., 'Die Wirtschaftsethik der calvinistischen Kirche der Niederlände 1565–1650' [The Ethics of Economics of the Calvinistic Churches of the Netherlands 1565–1650]. in: *Nederlands Archief voor Kerkgeschiedenis*, 1931, pp. 81–156.

Dekker, G., *Het kerkelijk gemengde huwelijk in Nederland* [Mixed Marriages Solemnized in Church in the Netherlands]. Meppel, J. A. Boom, 1965.

—, 'De kerk in de branding' [The Church in Rough Sea (Breakers)], in: *God in Nederland* [God in the Netherlands]. Amsterdam, Van Ditmar, 1967.

Dellepoort, J. J., *De priesterroepingen in Nederland* [The Call to the Priesthood in the Netherlands]. The Hague, 1955.

Dengerink, J. D., *Critisch-historisch onderzoek naar de sociologische ontwikkeling van het beginsel der 'souvereiniteit in eigen kring' in de 19e en 20e eeuw* [Critical-Historical Examination of the Sociological Development of the Principle 'Sovereignty in your own Sphere' in the nineteenth and twentieth centuries]. Kampen, Kok, 1948.

Doorn, J. A. A. van, 'De emancipatie der Nederlandse Rooms-Katholieken in de sociologische literatuur' [The Emancipation of Dutch Roman Catholics in Sociological Literature]. *Sociological Guide*, 5, 1958.

—, *Beeld en betekenis van de Nederlandse sociologie* [Image and Significance of Dutch Sociology]. Utrecht, 1965.

Dronkers, A., 'De kerk en het nieuwe psychologische klimaat der moderne massamedia' [The Church and the New Psychological Climate of Modern Mass Media]. *Wending*, 17, 1962.

Egberink, L., 'La paroisse; quelques aspects des recherches' [The Parish, some Aspects of Research]. *Social Compass*, 6, 1958.

Ellemers, J. E., 'The Revolt of the Netherlands. The Part Played by Religion in the Process of Nation Building.' *Social Compass*, 14, 1967.

Ende, W. M. I., van de, 'The Personal and the Functional Element in Pastoral Care.' *Social Compass*, 8, 1961.

—, 'Veranderingen in de stedelijke parochie' [Changes in City Parishes]. *Sociale Wetenschappen* [Social Sciences], 6, 1963.

—, 'Afscheid van een binnengroep: verandering in de kerk' [Farewell to an In-group: Change in the Church]. *Sociale Wetenschappen*, 9, 1966.

Fruin, R., *De wederopluiking van het katholicisme in Noord-Nederland, omstreeks den aanvang der XVIIe eeuw* [The Revival of Catholicism in the Northern Netherlands, about the beginning of the Seventeenth Century], in *Verspreide Geschriften*, III, The Hague, 1901.

Geyl, P., 'De protestantisering van Noord-Nederland' [The Protestantizing of the Northern Netherlands]. *Noord en Zuid, eenheid en tweeheid in de Lage Landen* [North and South, Unity and Duality in the Low Countries]. Utrecht–Antwerpen, 1960.

*God in Nederland. Statistisch onderzoek naar godsdienst en kerkelijkheid* [God in the Netherlands. Statistical Investigation of Religion and Church Attendance]. Amsterdam, Van Ditmar, 1967.

Goddijn, H. P. M., 'La portée et le développement de la théorie en sociologie réligieuse' [Trend and Development of Theory in Religious Sociology]. *Social Compass*, 6, 1958.

—, 'The Sociology of Religious Orders and Congregations.' *Social Compass*, 7, 1960.

—, 'The Monastic Community Life in our Times.' *Social Compass*, 12, 1965.

Goddijn, H. P. M. and Goddijn, W., *De kerk van morgen* [The Church of To-morrow]. Roermond – Maaseik, Romen & Zn., 1966a.

—, *Sociologie van kerk en godsdienst* [Sociology of Church and Religion]. Utrecht – Antwerpen, Spectrum, 1966b.

Goddijn, W., *Katholieke minderheid en protestantse dominant*. Assen, 1957.

—, 'Fonction du doyenné' [The Function of Deanship]. *Social Compass*, 6, 1958.
—, 'Catholic Minorities and Social Integration.' *Social Compass*, 7, 1960a.
—, 'Propaganda and the Continuity of Religious Groups'. *Social Compass*, 7, 1960b.
—, 'The Sociology of Religion and Socio-Religious Research in the Netherlands.' *Social Compass*, 7, 1960c.
—, 'Pluralisme réligieux et chrétienté' [Religious Pluralism and Christianity]. *Social Compass*, 10, 1963.
—, 'Le rôle du prêtre dans l'église et la société' [The role of the Priest in Church and Society]. *Social Compass*, 12, 1965.
Godefroy, J., and Thoen, C., 'Criminaliteit en moraliteit onder katholieken' [Criminality and Morality among Catholics]. *Social Compass*, 1, 1963.
Gorkum, P. H. van. *Kerk en voorlichting* [Church and Enlightenment]. Kampen, Kok 1962.
Heek, F. van, *Het geboorteniveau der Nederlandse rooms-katholieken* [The Birth-Rate of Dutch Roman Catholics]. Leiden, 1954.
Heukels, J. M., '*Een wijkgemeente in de grote stad*' (A Suburban Congregation in the Large City]. Utrecht, University of Utrecht, Sociological Institute, Rapport No. 10 (Mimeo.), 1963.
Hinte, J. van, *Nederlanders in Amerika* [The Dutch in America]. Groningen, 1928.
Hoekendijk, J. C., *De kerk binnenste buiten* [The Church Inside Out]. Amsterdam, 1964.
Hoeven, A. ter, 'Een vergeten hoofdstuk over de religieuze praktijk in Tilburg' [A Forgotten Chapter concerning Religious Practices in Tilburg]. *Sociological Guide*, 4, 1957.
Hofstee, E. W., *Het Oldambt*. Groningen, 1938.
—, '*De groei van de Nederlandse bevolking*' [The Growth of the Dutch Population], in: den Hollander, A. N. J., *et al.* (eds.), *Drift en Koers*. Assen, 1961.
Hofstra, S., 'De nieuwe religieuze beweging in ons land' [The New Religious Movements in our Country]. *Mens en Maatschappij* [Man and Society], 3, 1927.
—, 'Die gegenwärtige Situation der niederländische Soziologie' [The Current Situation in Dutch Sociology], in: Eisermann, G. (ed.), *Die gegenwärtige Situation der Soziologie* [The Current Situation in Sociology]. Stuttgart, 1967.
Hoogerwerff, A., *Protestantisme en progressiviteit* [Protestantism and Progressiveness]. Meppel, Boom, 1965.
Hooijdonk, P. van, 'Intellectuele emancipatie van de Nederlandse katholieken in de laatste jaren' [Intellectual Emancipation of Dutch Catholics in Recent Years]. *Sociale Wetenschappen* [Social Sciences], 8, 1965.
Impeta, C. N., *Kaart van kerkelijk Nederland* [Map of Church-going Netherlands]. Kampen, Kok, 1961.
Jansen, E. P., *De wijkgemeente in wording* [The Genesis of a Suburban Congregation]. Utrecht, University of Utrecht, Sociological Institute, Rapport No. 5 (Mimeo.), 1962.
Jong, P. de, 'De predikant ten plattelande en in de stad' [The Preacher in the Country and in the City]. *Sociological Bulletin*, 7, 1953.
—, 'De ademhaling der N.H. Kerk gedurende de 20ste eeuw in een zich verstedelijkend Nederland' [The vicissitudes of the Dutch Reformed Church during the

Twentieth Century in the increasingly urbanised Netherlands]. *Sociological Bulletin*, 14, 1960.
—, 'De kerk en het woelige kwartaal van 1903' [The Church and the Turbulent Three Months of 1903]. *Sociological Bulletin*, 18, 1964.
Jukema, J., *kerkelijk leven in de Noordoost polder* [Church Life in the North-east Polder]. Zwolle, 1959.
*De Katholiek in het openbare leven van deze tijd: Bisschoppelijk Mandement* [The Catholic in Public Life at the Present Time; Episcopal Mandatory Letter]. Utrecht, 1954.
Kemenade, J. A., van, *De katholieken en hun onderwijs* [The Catholics and their Education]. Meppel, Boom, 1968.
Kempe, G. Th., *Criminaliteit en kerkgenootschap* [Criminality and Religious Denomination]. Nijmegen, 1938.
Kloos, P. M., 'Traditionele onkerkelijkheid in Drenthe' [Traditional Secularism in Drenthe]. *Mens en Maatschappij* [Man and Society], 36, 1961.
Kok, J. A. de, *Nederland op de breuklijn Rome-Reformatie* [The Netherlands on the Dividing-line Rome-Reformation]. Assen, 1964.
Kooistra, K., *De gereformeerde theoloog en de sociologie* [The Calvinistic Reformed Theologian and Sociology]. Franeker, 1955.
Kraemer, P. E., 'Enkele Haagse buitenkerkelijke religieuze groeperingen in cijfers' [Statistics of Several Religious Groups Outside the Churches in the Hague]. *Sociological Bulletin*. 6, 1952.
—, '*Oorzaken van onkerkelijkheid in enkele hoofdlijnen geschetst*' [Causes of Dechurchment Broadly Sketched]. *Sociological Bulletin*, 14, 1960.
—, 'Secularisatie en kerkstructuren' [Secularization and the Structure of the Churches]. *Sociological Bulletin*, 18, 1964.
Kraemer, P. E., *et al.*, *Gemeente in meervoud* [Congregation in Plural Form]. Amsterdam 1965.
Kruijt, J. P., '*De onkerkelijkheid in Nederland*' [Non-Church Affiliation in The Netherlands]. Groningen, 1933.
—, 'Mentaliteitsverschillen in ons volk in verband met godsdienstige verschillen' [Differences in Mentality in our People in connection with Religious Differences]. *Mens en Maatschappij* [Man and Society], 18, 1943.
—, 'Rooms-Katholieken en Protestanten in Nederland' [Roman Catholics and Protestants in The Netherlands]. *Sociological Bulletin*, 1, 1947.
—, 'Verklaringen van de geografische verbreiding der kerkelijke gezindten in ons land' [Elucidations of the Geographical Expansion of the Religious Denominations in our Land]. *Sociological Bulletin*, 2, 1948.
—, 'Levensbeschouwing en groepssolidariteit in Nederland' [Outlook on Life and Group Solidarity in The Netherlands]. *Sociologisch Jaarboek* [Sociological Yearbook], 11, 1957.
—, 'The Influence of Denominationalism on Social Life and Organizational Pattern.' *Archives de Sociologie des Réligions*, 4 (8), 1959.
—, 'Die Erforschung der Protestantische Kirchengemeinde in den Niederländen' [The Investigations of the Protestant Church Congregations in the Netherlands]. in: Goldschmidt, D., Greiner, F., and Schelsky, H. (eds.), *Soziologie der Kirchengemeinde* [Sociology of Church Congregations], Stuttgart, 1960.

Kruijt, J. P. and Goddijn, W., 'Cloisonnement et décloisonnement culturels comme processus sociologiques' [Pillarization and de-pillarization as a Sociological Process]. *Social Compass*, 9, 1962.

K.S.K.I. (Katholiek Sociaal Kerkelijk Instituut), *Diaspora in beweging* [Diaspora in Change]. Rapport 309. The Hague, 1967.

Kuiper, G., 'Beroep en kerkgenootschap' [Professions and Church Affiliation]. *Mens en Maatschappij* [Man and Society], 28, 1953.

—, 'Beroep en kerkgenootschap opnieuw bezien' [Professions and Church Affiliation Reviewed]. *Mens en Maatschappij*, 39, 1964.

Kuiters, R., *Onze parochiestructuur, een belemmering voor de zielzorg?* [Our Parish Structure, a Hindrance to Pastoral Work?]. Laren, 1951.

Kuttner, E., *Het hongerjaar 1566* [1566, a Year of Hunger]. Amsterdam, 1949.

Laan, H. C., *De rooms-katholieke kerkorganisatie in Nederland* [The Roman Catholic Church Organization in The Netherlands]. Utrecht, 1967.

Laeyendecker, L., 'Reflecties op het begrip 'gemeenschap' in verband met de zielzorg' [Reflections on the Concept 'Community' in Connection with Pastoral Work]. *Theologie en zielzorg* [Theology and Pastoral Work], 61, 1965.

—, 'The Development of Sociology of Religion in The Netherlands since 1960.' *Social Compass*, 14, 1967a.

—, *Religie en conflict* [Religion and Conflict]. Meppel, 1967b.

—, 'Theologie en maatschappij [Theology and the Community]. *Vox Theologica* (The Voice of Theology), 37, 1967c.

—, 'Het priesterambt als een professie?' [The Priestly Office as a Profession?]. *Mens en Maatschappij* [Man and Society], 43, 1968.

Lammers, C. J., 'Over theologen en sociologie' [Concerning Theologians and Sociology]. *Sociological Guide*, 4, 1957.

Leent, J. A. A. van, 'The Sociology of Parish and Congregation.' *Social Compass*, 7, 1961.

Leeuwen, B. van, 'Echtscheidingen van katholieken in Nederland' [Catholic Divorces in the Netherlands]. *Social Compass*, 2, 1953a.

—, 'De groei van de Nederlandse bisdommen' [The Growth of the Dutch Dioceses]. *Social Compass*, 1, 1953b.

—, 'De structuur van de zielzorg sociologisch gezien' [The Structure of Pastoral Work, seen Sociologically]. *Levende Zielzorg* [Living Pastoral Work], Utrecht, 1954.

—, *Het gemengde huwelijk* [The Mixed Marriage]. Assen, 1959.

—, 'Echtscheidingen van katholieken in Nederland' [Catholic Divorces in The Netherlands]. *Katholiek Archief* [Catholic Archives], 23, 1968.

Leeuwen, B. van and Stoop, W., 'Traditionele en moderne vormen van zielzorg in Nederland' [Traditional and Modern Forms of Pastoral Work in The Netherlands]. *Social Compass*, 4, 1956.

Loor, H. D. de, *De kerk en het moderne platteland* [The Church and Rural Areas of Today]. The Hague, 1963.

—, 'Coöperatie en interrelatie van sociologie en theologie' [The Co-operation and Inter-relation of Sociology and Theology]. *De Heerbaan* [The High Road], 18, (2), 1965.

—, 'Soziologie und Theologie' [Sociology and Theology]. *Zeitschrift für evangelische Ethik* [Journal of Evangelical Ethics], 11, 1967.

Matthijssen, M. J. A. M., *De intellectuele emancipatie der katholieken* [The Intellectual Emancipation of Catholics]. Assen, 1958.

Nagel, W. H., 'Criminality and Religion.' *Social Compass*, 8, 1961.

Nijk, A. J., *Secularisatie* (Secularization.) Rotterdam, 1968.

Passenier, J., 'De behoefte aan theologen tot 1980' [The Need for Theologians up to 1980]. *Sociological Bulletin*, 15, 1961.

Poeisz, J. J., 'The Pastoral Significance of Catholic Associations,' *Social Compass*, 6, 1958.

—, 'Déterminants sociaux des inscritions dans les séminaires et des ordinations des nouveaux prêtres aux Pays Bas' [The Social Determinants behind the Numbers entering Seminaries and the Ordinations of New Priests in The Netherlands]. *Social Compass*, 10, 1963.

—, 'Gruppenisolierung, Kirchlichkeit und Religiosität: das niederländische Beispiel' [Group-isolation, Church Life, and Religiosity: the Dutch Example]. *International Yearbook for the Sociology of Religion*, I, edited by J. Matthes, Köln-Opladen, 1965.

—, 'The Parishes of the Dutch Church Province, 1.1.1966.' *Social Compass*, 14, 1967a.

—, 'The Priests of the Dutch Church Province, Number and Functions.' *Social Compass*, 14, 1967b.

Ponsioen, J. A., 'Godsdienst en groepssolidariteit' [Religion and Group-solidarity]. *Sociological Yearbook*, 11, 1957.

—, 'Sociologische beschouwingen naar aanleiding van de veranderingen in de Nederlandse kerkprovincie na de tweede wereldoorlog' [Sociological Views with Reference to the Changes in the Dutch Church Province since the Second World War]. *Annalen van het Thijmgenootschap* [Annals of the Thijm Association], 54, 1966.

Prakke, H. J., *Drenthe in Michigan*. Assen, 1948.

Reuvekamp, G. J., *St. Martinus, Tongelre: sociografie ener parochie* [St. Martinus, Tongelre: the sociography of a parish]. Assen, 1945.

Riemersma, J. C., *Religious Factors in Early Dutch Capitalism*. 's-Gravenhage, 1967.

Rogier, L. J., *Geschiedenis van het katholicisme in Noord-Nederland in de 16e en 17e eeuw* [History of Catholicism in the Northern Netherlands in the Sixteenth and Seventeenth Centuries], Amsterdam, Elsevier, 1945–1947.

Rogier, L. J. and Rooij, N. de, *In vrijheid herboren* [Born Again in Freedom]. The Hague 1953.

Schillebeeckx, E., 'Theologische reflecties op godsdienstsociologische duidingen in verband met het ongeloof' [Theological Reflections Concerning Religious-sociological Interpretations in connection with Unbelief]. *Tijdschrift voor Theologie* [Journal of Theology], II, 1962.

Schlichting, L. G. A., *Over godsdienst en politiek* [Concerning Religion and Politics]. Assen, 1967.

Schreuder, O., 'Le caractère professionel du sacerdoce' [The Professional Character of the Priesthood]. *Social Compass*, 10, 1963.

—, 'Church and Sociology.' *Social Compass*, 11, 1964.

—, 'De parochie in discussie' [Discussing the Parish]. *De nieuwe mens* [The New Man] 16, 1965a.

—, 'Priesterbeelden' [Images of the Priest]. *Tijdschrift voor Theologie* [Journal of Theology], V, 1965b.

—, *Gestaltwandel der Kirche* [The Changing Form of the Church]. Olten, 1967.

Smits, P., *Kerk en stad* [Church and the City]. The Hague, 1952.

Smits, P., *et al'*, *De kerk en het nieuwe weekend* [The Church and the New Weekend]. Assen, 1963.

Staverman, M., *Buitenkerkelijkheid in Friesland* [Secularism in Friesland]. Assen, 1954.

Steeman, Th., 'L'église d'aujourd'hui: une exploration de la Hollande catholique en 1966' [The Church of Today: an Exploration of Catholic Holland in 1966]. *Social Compass*, 14, 1967.

Stoop, W., 'Enkele beschouwingen over de aanpassing van de zielzorg aan de noden van onze tijd' [Some Remarks Concerning the Adaptation of Pastoral Work to the Needs of our Time]. *Social Compass*, 1, 1953.

Straver, C. J., *Massacommunicatie en godsdienstige beïnvloeding* [Mass Communications and Religious Influence]. Hilversum, 1967.

Suverein, W. J. P., 'Onderzoek naar de beroepsklassen in het Nederlandse volk en in de verschillende kerkgenootschappen' [Investigation of the Classes of Employment to be found among the People of The Netherlands, and among the Different Denominations]. *Sociological Bulletin*, 5, 1951.

Swanborn, P. G., 'Cijfers, cijfers...' [Figures, Figures...]. *Sociological Bulletin*, 17, (1), 1963.

Swanborn, P. G., *et al.*, *Kerk en stedelijk perspectief* [The Church in Urban Perspective]. The Hague, 1965.

*Terzake, Gesprekken van sociologen en theologen over kerkvernieuwing: I, Presentie en pretentie; II. Over schaalvergroting* [Discussions between Sociologists and Theologians concerning Church Renewal: I. Presence and Pretence; II. Concerning an Increase in the Scale]. Utrecht-Baarn, I. 1967; II: 1968.

Thung, Mady A., 'Sociologische opmerkingen bij het begrip "functie van de kerk"' [Sociological Remarks Concerning the Concept 'Function of the Church']. *Sociological Bulletin*, 10, 1956.

—, *Werken op Zondag: een onderzoek naar de meningen van ploegenarbeiders* [Working on Sunday: Investigating the Opinions of Shift-workers]. The Hague, 1962.

—, 'Reclame, publiciteit en vormingswerk van kerken' [Advertising, Publicity and Education by the Churches]. *Wending*, 20, 1965a.

—, 'De verhouding van functionele en categoriale gemeenten' [The Proportion of Functional and Categorial Congregations]. *De Heerbaan*, 18 (2), 1965b.

Vermooten, W. H., 'De situatie in de godsdienstsociologie' [The Situation in the Sociology of Religion]. *Mens en Maatschappij* [Man and Society], 22, 1947.

—, *Hervormd Amsterdam en zijn maatschappelijke achtergronden in de 19e en 20e eeuw* [Netherlands Reformed Amsterdam and its Social Background in the Nineteenth and Twentieth Centuries]. *Handboek der pastorale sociologie* [Handbook of Pastoral Sociology], Vol. IV. The Hague, 1960.

Vermooten, W. H. and Vries, W. de., *Godsdienst en maatschappij* [Religion and Community]. The Hague, 1950.

Verweij-Jonker, H., 'De emancipatiebewegingen' [The Emancipation Movements]. in: Hollander A. N. J. den, *et al.* (eds.), *Drift en koers*. Assen, 1961.

Visser, J., 'De plaatselijke verspreiding der katholieken in Friesland tot het begin der 19e eeuw' [The Local Distribution of Catholics in Friesland up to the beginning of the Nineteenth Century]. *Social Compass*, 5, 1967.

Vrijhof, P. H., 'Opleiding en afkomst der grotestadspredikanten en theologische studenten' [Education and Background of Preachers in the big cities and of Theological Students]. *Sociological Bulletin*, 1, 1947.

—, 'De sociale afkomst van de predikanten der N.H. Kerk' [The Social Background of the Preachers of The Dutch Reformed Church]. *Sociological Bulletin*, 2, 1948a.

—, 'De sociale structuur van de kerkelijke colleges in de N.H. Kerk' [The Social Structure of the Church Colleges in The Dutch Reformed Church]. *Sociological Bulletin*, 2, 1948b.

—, 'Sociale aspecten van de oecumenische situatie, met name in Nederland' [Social Aspects of the Ecumenical Situation, with Reference to The Netherlands]. *Sociological Bulletin*, 13, 1959.

—, 'Some Remarks Concerning the Parish as a Social Problem and as a Topic for Social Research in The Netherlands after 1945.' *Archives de sociologie des religions*, 4, (8), 1959.

—, 'Was ist Religionssoziologie' [What is the Sociology of Religion], in: Goldschmidt, D., and Matthes, J. (eds.), *Probleme der Religionssoziologie* [Problems of the Sociology of Religion]. 1962.

—, 'Secularisatie in sociologisch perspectief' [Secularization in Sociological Perspective]. *Sociological Bulletin*, 18, 1964.

—, 'De religieuze personalisatie als centraal probleem voor de godsdienstsociologie' [Religious Personalization as the Central Problem for the Sociology of Religion]. *Sociale Wetenschappen* [Social Sciences], 8, 1965.

Warners, Christine M., 'De huisgemeente' [The House Church]. *Sociological Bulletin*, 16, 1960.

Weiler, A. G., *et al.*, *Geschiedenis van de kerk van Nederland* [History of the Church in The Netherlands]. Utrecht – Antwerpen, Spectrum, 1962.

Weima, J., *Psychologie van het anti-papisme* [The Psychology of Anti-Papism]. Hilversum, 1963.

Wertheim, W. F., and Vreede-de Stuers, C., 'The Development of Non-Western Sociology of Religion in The Netherlands since 1945.' *Social Compass*, 12, 1965.

Winkeler, H., 'Towards a Typology of Religious Personality Structures among Non Church-going Catholic Workers.' *Social Compass*, 12, 1965.

Zeegers, H. H., and Godefrey, J., 'Rookgordijn om het kindertal' [Smoke Screen Round the Number of Children]. *Social Compass*, 1, (1), 1953.

Zwanikken, W. A. C., 'Parochiesociogrammen en de methode van zelfonderzoek' [Parish Sociograms and the Method of Self-Examination]. *Sociale Wetenschappen* [Social Sciences]. 3, 1959.

# New Zealand

When André Siegfried visited New Zealand in 1904, he found that no tradition remained so strong as the religious one. This was not necessarily a compliment. It could mean, as in fact it did, that although New Zealand was acquiring an identity of its own, in religious affairs it remained true to the old world. The religious buildings are in the same style as those in the mother country; and the ministers preach on the same lines [Siegfried, 1914, p. 310].

Of course this was to be expected. Any culture pattern which relates the sacred is by definition more stable and more resistant to change. This is as true for the primitive tribe as it was for European immigrants in the U.S.A. [Mol, 1961] and for British immigrants to New Zealand in the last century. Of all adjustments which migrants have to make in a new environment, the religious ones require most effort and time.

My first task is then to describe this stable pattern in its many facets. Having done this, we can attempt to appraise its present vitality and role and from this can make some comment on what may be to come.

## HISTORICAL INTRODUCTION

Although organized settlement did not begin in New Zealand until 1840, there were by that time a number of Maoris who professed to be Christian. The impetus to missionary activity had come from the Church Missionary Society, an evangelical body formed in 1799 – a product of the late eighteenth century religious revival in Britain. Two tradesmen missionaries (a rope-maker and a carpenter) joined the chaplain of the convict colony of New South Wales, the Reverend Samuel Marsden, and formed the nucleus of the first band of missionaries who landed in New Zealand in 1814. Marsden purchased land from the Maori chiefs, converted some and interested others. The energy and boundless enthusiasm with which Marsden directed the work of his followers was, however, somewhat marred by his inability to appreciate those elements of Maori culture which seemed to be inimical to evangelical middle-class British Christian thought.

Unfortunately for the early missionaries, traders and whalers had about as much contact with the Maoris as the missionaries themselves, and the Maoris, who were frequently engaged in wars with neighbouring tribes, showed a clear preference for the guns of the traders and whalers to the crafts and creeds of the Christians. Since the missionaries required a complete understanding of the catechism and a general profession of Christian faith, conversions were understandably slow, and it was not until 1825 that real progress in baptisms was made. Thereafter conversion became more widespread, and among the salutary effects of the proselytising were the emancipation of tribal slaves and the abandonment of cannibalism.

Between 1830 and 1860 the influence of the Church Missionary Society's numerous activities in New Zealand expanded, as did the influence of the Methodist missions; the Roman Catholic mission, established in 1838 under French sponsorship, at first claimed large numbers of conversions, but these statistics were later revised, and the Catholic missionary influence proved to be relatively modest in actual fact. Through schools, hospitals and chapels the Maoris were presented with middle-class morals and manners and the cultural expressions of European society. These they largely eschewed, so that after about 1860 the influence of the missionaries upon Maori and hence on New Zealand culture in general diminished; politically, however, the missionaries prepared the Maori for British annexation of New Zealand.

The first settlement in New Zealand intending to colonise the islands was established at Port Nicholson (Wellington) in 1840. By 1848 a group of Presbyterians had founded their own settlement at Otago and in 1850 a number of Anglicans established themselves at Canterbury. In a pattern reminiscent of events in the United States, these early settlers then established regions of religious influence and forms of worship that have been maintained to the present day.

## DENOMINATIONAL STRUCTURE

The denominational figures of the various censuses accurately reflect the influx and comparative strength of regional migrations. The absence of large-scale migration from continental Europe is visible in the numerical insignificance of Lutheranism. However, the prominence of migration from England is shown by the fact that throughout the history of New Zealand the Anglican and Methodist denominations constituted almost without exception the majority of the population (see Table 1).

Sometimes the original patterns of migration are still visible in the proportional distribution of denominations. The 1961 census figures show that close to half the population of Otago and Southland are Presbyterian, al-

*Table 1. Religious denominations in New Zealand (ex-Maoris), 1851–1961**

| Denomination | 1851 | 1881 | 1911 | 1951 | 1961 |
|---|---|---|---|---|---|
| Church of England | 14,179 | 203,333 | 411,689 | 703,637 | 829,175 |
| | (53.09) | (41.50) | (40.82) | (38.58) | (36.88) |
| Presbyterian | 4,124 | 113,108 | 234,662 | 443,976 | 535.512 |
| | (15.44) | (23.09) | (23.27) | (24.34) | (23.82) |
| Roman Catholic | 3,472 | 68,984 | 140,523 | 247,597 | 335,442 |
| | (13.00) | (14.08) | (13.94) | (13.58) | (14.92) |
| Methodist | 2,755 | 46,657 | 94.827 | 147,548 | 161,227 |
| | (10.31) | (9.53) | (9.40) | (8.09) | (7.17) |
| Baptist | 400 | 11,476 | 20,042 | 31,449 | 40,510 |
| | (1.50) | (2.34) | (1.99) | (1.72) | (1.80) |
| Brethren | – | 1,967 | 7,865 | 20,871 | 24,197 |
| | – | (0.40) | (0.78) | (1.14) | (1.08) |
| Mormon | – | 271 | 365 | 1,859 | 5,799 |
| | – | (0.05) | (0.04) | (0.10) | (0.26) |
| Salvation Army | – | – | 9,707 | 13,485 | 15,301 |
| | – | – | (0.96) | (0.73) | (0.68) |
| Church of Christ | – | 2,873 | 9,187 | 11,937 | 10,307 |
| | – | (0.59) | (0.91) | (0.65) | (0.46) |
| Congregationalist | – | 6,699 | 8,756 | 6,768 | 9,041 |
| | – | (1.37) | (0.87) | (0.37) | (0.40) |
| Seventh Day Adventist | – | – | 1,113 | 5,849 | 7,598 |
| | – | – | (0.11) | (0.32) | (0.34) |
| Jehovah's Witnesses | – | – | 39 | 1,540 | 5,010 |
| | – | – | – | (0.08) | (0.22) |
| Lutherans[a] | | 5,773 | 4,477 | 3,309 | 4,817 |
| | | (1.18) | (0.44) | (0.18) | (0.21) |
| Jews | 65 | 1,536 | 2,128 | 3,661 | 41031 |
| | (0.24) | (0.31) | (0.21) | (0.20) | (0.18) |
| Others[b] | 1,712 | 10,490 | 16,961 | 36,840 | 54,370 |
| | (6.41) | (2.14) | (1.69) | (2.02) | (2.42) |
| No religion | – | 2,788 | 10,222 | 20,559 | 23,319 |
| | – | (0.57) | (1.01) | (1.13) | (1.04) |
| Object to state | – | 13,978 | 35,905 | 122,911 | 182,242 |
| | | (2.85) | (3.56) | (6.74) | (8.11) |
| Total | 26,707 | 489,933 | 1,008,468 | 1,823,796 | 2,247,898 |
| | (100) | (100) | (100) | (100) | (100) |

* Figures in brackets represent percentages. Source: Census data.
a. 1851: not specified. b. 1851: includes unspecified.

though not even a quarter of the total New Zealand population belongs to that denomination. This reflects the concentration of the Scots in these southern parts of the South Island ever since 1848 when the first ship arrived. Scottish migration has meant that Presbyterians have been relatively stronger than in other countries with a predominant Anglo-Saxon pattern of migration – Canada, Australia and the United States of America. A similar over-representation of Catholics on the West Coast of the South Island also originated in the attraction of the mining fields for the Irish, many of whom came to these areas via Australia. However, with only 15.1 per cent of the total New Zealand population Catholics are relatively less numerous in New Zealand than in other countries of large-scale immigration.

On the other hand, migration patterns are not always responsible for overrepresentation of denominations in certain geographical areas. The Church of England has 48.0 per cent of the population of the East Coast (North Island) statistical area, although only 34.6 per cent of the total New Zealand population; Methodism has 11.8 per cent of the Taranaki area (West Coast of the North Island), but only 7 per cent of the total. The 1837 arrangement between Anglicans and Methodists to concentrate their Maori mission work in the East and West coasts respectively partly explains this uneven denominational distribution.

Throughout New Zealand history the relative denominational proportions have not varied a great deal. The slow decline of Anglican, Presbyterian and Methodist proportions and the slow increase of Catholic proportions in the non-Maori population over the last forty years are most probably due to different fertility ratios. There does not seem to have been a disproportional influx of Catholic migrants from overseas apart from approximately 10,000 Dutch Catholics who have entered the country since World War II. However, this amounts to only 8 per cent of the Catholic increase from 1945–1961 and a closer look at the Catholic birthrate is therefore warranted. Particularly in the most recent census (1961) the ratio of 0–4 year old children to women of the age of 15–40 was much higher for Catholics than for the total population as Table 2 shows. One can therefore expect this trend of Catholic increase to continue.

The Catholic position on birth control is one important reason for the higher Catholic fertility. However, there are other factors: Table 2 shows clearly that the economic depression of the 1930's had quite an impact on the fertility rates of all denominations (including Catholics). The fact that Catholics tend to be over-represented in the lower classe in New Zealand which traditionally have a higher fertility rate may also contribute to the difference. On the other hand, Catholics tend to be slightly more urbanised and have a higher percentage in the 'never-married' class; these factors in turn lower the ratio.

*Table 2. Fertility ratios for selected denominations (number of 0–4 year old children per 100 women aged 15–40)*

| Denomination | 1921 | 1936 | 1945 | 1961 |
|---|---|---|---|---|
| Church of England | 52.16 | 37.55 | 48.61 | 69.31 |
| Prebyterian | 52.45 | 39.35 | 49.79 | 69.97 |
| Methodist | 49.94 | 37.68 | 52.03 | 68.52 |
| Catholic | 53.22 | 42.10 | 52.60 | 88.74 |
| Total population | 52.46 | 39.36 | 50.88 | 74.34 |

Source: Census, 1961.

Since the Catholic Church strongly opposes divorce and since Catholic divorce rates in the United States are lower – lower than those of Protestants, inter-faith marriages and marriages in which neither partner has a religious affiliation [Moberg, 1962] – one would expect lower Catholic divorce rates in New Zealand. This is not what the statistics show. In a pioneering study of the field A. J. Nixon [1954] found that there was no striking disproportion between Catholics and non-Catholics among divorced females at the 1945 Census and that this was not due to the avoidance of remarriage by divorced Catholics. Nixon calculated (presumably also from the 1945 census figures) that the number of divorced women per 100 married women in the same religious groups was 2.41 for Anglicans, 1,55 for Catholics, 1.27 for Methodists and 1.20 for Presbyterians). We can bring this information up-to-date by calculating the 1961 ratios: 2.01 for Anglicans, 1.50 for Catholics, 1.46 for Methodists and 1.34 for Presbyterians. Although the range for denominational differences has become considerably smaller since 1945, the rank order between the denominations has remained the same.

There could be manifold reasons for the discrepancies between American and New Zealand findings. Nixon found that there was in New Zealand 'a fairly marked inverse relation between the ranks of divorce frequency and social status' and Catholics in New Zealand are over-represented in the lower classes. Another important explanation not mentioned in the Nixon study may be the high proportion of inter-faith marriages. Church records in New Zealand show that approximately one half of the marriages celebrated in Catholic churches are mixed marriages [O'Neill, 1951, p. 13]. It is very likely that the female Catholic divorced-married ratio in New Zealand would be much smaller than 1.5 per cent if the mixed marriages could be excluded. Similarly it could be reasoned as Nixon does that 'if one were to make a division between devout and non-devout members of whatever church, it is likely that significant differences in divorce frequency would be found'. This factor of devoutness or 'interiorized faith' is crucial for religious research, but there is no New Zealand project as yet which measures this factor and relates it to other social phenomena. The high Anglican divorce rate is probably related to the fact that the Church of England more than any other denomination has a very high percentage of nominal members, for whom the strict divorce regulations are not imperative and for whom religion is not meaningful as a uniting tie in marriage.

New Zealand is also part of the general Anglo-Saxon pattern with respect to sex ratios in religious affairs. At the 1961 Census the ratios ranged from 160 women to every 100 men listed as Christian Scientist to only 30 women to every 100 men returned as Atheist, with the Methodist 108, Presbyterian and Anglican 103 and Catholics 102 females for each 100 males.

## RELIGIOUS BELIEFS AND PRACTICES

As yet there are no quantitative data on religious beliefs of the New Zealand population. The available data on church attendance are an inadequate measure of belief, as the motives for attending church each Sunday vary between denominations and between individuals. Yet it is, if nothing else, an indication of the degree to which members meet the expectations of their particular denomination. One can safely say that the influence of a church on the beliefs and attitudes of those who never participate in church activities is small indeed.

From 1874 to 1926, a Census of Places of Worship was collected from church officials. This gave information on the number of people in church districts who attended services. By totalling the number of people who attended services in each of the four major denominations, and dividing these by the number belonging to each denomination according to the Census of the year, one can obtain a rough estimate of church attendance, as shown in Table 3.

Although there is a rough consistency in church attendance for each denomination, the data should be treated with caution. It is possible that not all clergy returned the form; some may have overestimated, and there may be inconsistencies in the inclusion or exclusion of occasional church-goers, children, and those who attended more than one Sunday service. To obviate this last possibility, church officials were also asked in 1916 and 1926 to indicate the number present at the service with the largest attendance. Table 4 shows that the figures obtained from this question substantially decrease the percentage of church attenders. Of course these figures underestimate the active members of each church, as those who worshipped on the Sunday but not at the largest service were not counted.

*Table 3. Attendance at church services in New Zealand by denominations 1874–1926*

| Year of Census | % of members attending Church of England | Presbyterian | Methodist | Roman Catholic |
|---|---|---|---|---|
| 1874 | 15.66 | 25.58 | 59.52 | 27.17 |
| 1878 | 16.41 | 26.91 | 60.24 | 22.96 |
| 1881 | 15.89 | 25.86 | 51.29 | 28.12 |
| 1886 | 17.38 | 30.41 | 52.69 | 32.17 |
| 1891 | 14.70 | 28.83 | 54.63 | 34.98 |
| 1896 | 17.01 | 30.48 | 56.03 | 36.52 |
| 1906 | 17.66 | 25.56 | 46.53 | 32.69 |
| 1911 | 12.94 | 23.55 | 48.61 | 34.26 |
| 1921 | 23.32 | 35.88 | 59.14 | 56.37 |
| 1926 | 25.30 | 34.72 | 50.76 | 52.95 |

Source: Census data.

*Table 4. Attendance at the largest-attended service on the day by denomination 1916–1926*

| Year of Census | % of members attending Church of England | Presbyterian | Methodist | Roman Catholic |
|---|---|---|---|---|
| 1916 | 11.97 | 23.32 | 39.58 | 35.56 |
| 1921 | 11.18 | 20.14 | 35.88 | 35.86 |
| 1926 | 10.60 | 19.52 | 28.32 | 31.87 |

Source: Census data.

More recent and more accurate surveys of church attendance confirm that the Church of England suffers most from merely nominal adherence. The *New Zealand Herald* survey of church attendance on Sunday July 17th, 1949 in Auckland city showed that approximately 4 per cent of Anglicans, 32 per cent of Presbyterians 26 per cent of Methodists and 75 per cent of Catholics worshipped that day [O'Neill, 1951]. A Christchurch survey in 1962 found that in a sample of 988 randomly chosen inhabitants, 11 per cent of Anglicans, 18 per cent of Presbyterians, 25 per cent of Methodists and 68 per cent of Catholics had been to church on the previous Sunday [Mol, 1962]. Even allowing for a considerable margin of error in all these figures, the low Catholic percentages in Tables 3 and 4 remains very puzzling. We know from similar statistics in Australia and the United States that Catholic attendance is at present hardly ever below 60 per cent. Comparing the different surveys and opinion polls of weekly church attendance in other Anglo-Saxon countries, it is generally true to say that in all these countries Catholic attendance is uniformly high (60–70 per cent), but that with the exception of the United States where one in three attends church, at the most one in five Protestants in Australia, England and New Zealand worships weekly.

Differences between the sexes are pronounced with regard to frequency of worship. In the Christchurch survey, the attendance ratio of females over 20 per 100 males over 20 was 133 for Anglicans, 142 for Presbyterians, 125 for Methodists and 105 for Catholics [Mol, 1962]. In the same survey single people over 20 proved to be about twice as active in church as married people. It was also found that after the age of 14 in the non-Catholic denominations, church activity declined rapidly until the middle twenties when the percentage of Church-goers in the total population remained at a constantly low level. This is a rather important finding because it indicates that in Protestantism children are expected to attend church and Sunday school, but that religious activities and adult behaviour are dissociated. This religious passivity of meaningful adults (e.g. parents) determines the New Zealand child's values and aspirations much more than the values communicated in sermons and Sunday school lessons.

## RELIGION AND SOCIAL CLASS

There are indications that the main New Zealand denominations are not randomly distributed over the population. Reeves has an interesting observation on this point:

> In proportion to their numbers the Scots are more prominent than other races in politics, commerce, finance, sheep farming and the work of education. Among the eighty European members of the New Zealand House of representatives there has seldom been more than one Smith, Brown or Jones and hardly ever a single Robinson; but the number of McKenzies has often been three. The Irish do not crowd into the towns, or attempt to capture the municipal machinery, as in America, nor are they a source of political unrest or corruption. Their church's antagonism to the National Education system has excluded many able Catholics from public life. Some 2,400 Jews live in the towns, and seem more numerous and prominent in the north than in the south. They belong to the middle class; many are wealthy. These are often

> charitable and public spirited, and active in municipal rather than in parliamentary life [Reeves, 1924, p. 363].

The different occupational distribution of Catholics in New Zealand has also been noted by Nixon who attempted to find evidence for his thesis that Catholics are more prone to divorce because they are over-represented in the lower classes.

> ...Catholics, being 13.5 per cent of the community, comprised only 10.9 per cent of the farming population, 11.1 per cent of those in medical and hygienic services, 12.4 per cent of those in education, religion, arts and sciences, 10.2 per cent of those in finance, banking and insurance. On the other hand, they comprised 18.1 per cent of those in the liquor trade, 20.1 per cent of those in hotel work, 17.3 per cent of those in fishing and trapping, 16.5 per cent of those in forestry, 15.1 per cent of those not adequately describing their occupations, 15 per cent of those in sport and entertainment... [Nixon, 1954].

The Christchurch survey found similar disproportions. In this study the category 'professions' was sufficiently broad to include not only lawyers, architects and executives, but also teachers, large farmers etc. Of the 403 Anglicans of the sample, 19 per cent belonged to this category, of the 241 Presbyterians 22 per cent, the 105 Methodists 16 per cent and the 143 Catholics 6 per cent [Mol, 1962]. It is likely that the heavy under-representation of Catholics and the slighter under-representation of Methodists in the New Zealand professions would apply to the entire population. The Christchurch data are certainly in line with both observations and findings of Australia, Great Britain and the U.S.A. with the exception that in the United States the Methodists and the national percentage of professionals are about the same. Blaikie [1969] on the other hand found in his sample of a Christchurch suburb (St. Albans) that there was no significant difference between the various denominations. However, his sample may have been unrepresentative. The discrepancy may also have been caused by difference in operational definition of occupation.

What rationale lies behind these denominational discrepancies? At least in New Zealand it does not appear that the Irish Catholics had less access to positions of honour, wealth and status. It may be that the New Zealand figures could be at least partially explained in terms of the relative absence amongst Catholics of certain values which are functional from the institutional religious point of view, but disfunctional from the point of view of the secular society. Gerhard Lenski, who did a large-scale research project on religion in Detroit, found that there were important value differences between the Catholic, Protestant and Jewish interviewees. On the basis of his data he distinguishes between intellectual heteronomy (obedience to the dictates of others) and intellectual autonomy (thinking for oneself). He says:

> Upper-middle-class Detroiters are far more likely than lower-working-class Detroiters to value intellectual autonomy above heteronomy, and within all of the class levels, Jews and white Protestants are more likely than Catholics to do this [Lenski, 1961].

However, the above paragraph should not be interpreted to mean that the access to desirable positions was not occasionally hindered by inter-faith rivalry. The open antagonism in the early days of the colony to the Catholic Bishop Pompallier is a case in point [Moran, 1894]. Another later example was the virulent Protestant Political Association which was formed towards the close of the reign of the Catholic Prime Minister, Sir Joseph Ward 'to discredit Sir Joseph and his Government on religious grounds' [Lee, 1938]. On the other hand compared with the American anxiety regarding the religion of their presidents the New Zealanders seem to have generally shown less undue concern: '...the prime ministers accurately depict the relative strength of New Zealand's sectarian divisions. Nine of the eleven were Protestants; two (Ward and Savage) were Catholics. Vogel, who belongs to the older period is the only Jew ever to have been premier' [Lipson, 1948, p. 293]. For a few years in the early 1960s, the leader of the Labour Party in New Zealand was Nordmeyer, a Presbyterian minister.

The religious institutions in New Zealand are generally held in high respect by the entire population. Even the large numbers of those who keep away from the churches still vaguely assume their special sacred position in society. Those who are not involved in the life of the churches are often apologetic about their lack of religious concern and hardly ever antagonistic. This is reflected in the esteem with which the clergy is held. In a large sample of people who were asked to grade thirty occupations socially, the Nonconformist minister was ranked fifth behind doctors, country solicitors, company directors and business managers. However, significantly, the semi-skilled and unskilled classes gave the Nonconformist minister a lower rating than the higher classes. He also received a higher rating from females than from males [Congalton, 1954].

In other studies which Congalton conducted in Australia a distinction was made between 'Clergyman with university degree', 'Clergyman with some university training', 'Clergyman with no university training' [Congalton, 1963]. It is beyond doubt that as in Australia, a university degree increases the status of a minister in New Zealand. However, whether he has a university education or not largely depends on the requirements of his denomination. In a study of all active parish ministers (ninety) of the Anglican, Baptist, Church of Chirst, Congregational, Methodist and Presbyterian church in the Christchurch area, Richard Thompson discovered that degrees were held by 75 per cent of the Presbyterian and 67 per cent of the Congregational, 49 per cent of the Anglican, 44 per cent of the Methodist and 10 per cent of the Baptist Ministers [Thompson, 1957]. Thompson also went into the home background of these ministers and he noticed that 'an unusually large number of Methodist ministers came from the homes of skilled workers (40 per cent) Presbyterian ministers from farms (29 per cent) Baptists from professional homes (30 per cent) and Anglicans from vicarages (23 per cent)' [Thompson, 1951]. Some of these findings (e.g. the ones regarding the university degrees of ministers) are likely to be approximately true for the whole of New Zealand; on the other hand it is likely that the professional home background of Baptist ministers is the exception rather than the rule.

A study has been done in New Zealand relating religion and social class with delinquency. O'Neill's [1951] analysis of a sample of New Zealand delinquency cases (age 7 to 17 inclusive) during 1949–1951 showed that 19.8 per cent of the deliquents were Catholics, although the proportion of Catholics in the total New Zealand population according to the 1945 census was only 13.45 per cent. Even after age was controlled (the proportion of Catholics in the age group 5–15 years in 1945 was 15.72 per cent) Catholics were still over-represented. However, if we accept attendance at Catholic schools as a measure of the hold of the church on the membership, (to send their children to Catholic schools is a matter of serious obligaton for Catholic parents in New Zealand) then the majority of families from which these delinquents came can be classified as marginal members. (The 64 per cent of the Catholic children at Catholic schools provided only 33.6 per cent of the Catholic delinquents, while the 36 per cent State schools provided 66.4 per cent of the delinquents' [O'Neill, 1951].

## RELIGION AND POLITICS

No work has been done to date on the voting patterns or other political behaviour of the various denominational groups. The effect of religious institutions has been ambiguous. On the one hand, there is no historical evidence that any of the churches as organizations have been responsible for the specific measures of advanced social legislation. But then on the other hand there have been many clergymen both Catholic and Nonconformist who have been very prominent in political radicalism [Lee, 1938]. The factory Act of 1890 and 1894 which limited sweated labour was largely the result of the humanitarian crusading by ministers [McLintock, 1949]. More intangible of course has been the influence of Christian laymen on the political climate of opinion.

### THE FUTURE

Although there is a dearth of sociological studies in New Zealand and the time is hardly ripe for a full appraisal of the vitality and function of religion, there are a number of concrete indications in the present which will inevitably have a bearing on the future.

We started out by mentioning the tenacity of religious patterns. This means that we can expect slight rather than drastic changes. We can also expect that the historical capacity for self-vitalization in Christianity may make a fool of any prophet of doom of whom there have been a considerable number both inside and outside the churches in the last few centuries. This is particularly true in New Zealand where the religious situation does not seem to have changed much. There appears to be in every generation a core of church members who will perpetuate and consolidate the religious function of interpreting life from the point of view of a specific undiluted Christianity. However, this does not mean that there are no acute danger signals in some of the New Zealand religious institutions or indeed in the entire Western world of which it is so much a part.

One of these danger signals from the point of view of traditional Christianity is that the actual religion of the New Zealanders (here now defined as the areas in life which are 'sacred', in which one has a large emotional investment and for which one is an unwitting missionary) has increasingly less to do with the professed religion of the churches. The framework of meaning which motivates even the average churchgoer seems to be informed by the secular values of scientific humanism or materialism rather than Christian salvation. This alienation from historic Christianity runs parallel to the erosion of functions of the traditional religious institutions. The more specialised and diversified societies become, the more former religious tasks (such as science, medicine, philanthropy, psychological care and even ethics) are taken over by non-religious organizations. Many churchgoers continue their churchgoing habits because they feel under obligation or because religion in some vague way decorates life for them.

Another danger signal is not only the erosion of the traditional Christian belief-system but also the lack of loyalty of Protestants to their churches. The percentage of those who state to have no religion or object to stating their religion in the New Zealand census has increased from 2.94 per cent in 1901 to 9.15 per cent in 1961.

Although our Table 3 seems to indicate an increase in church attendance, the more reliable recent investigations seem to show that at the most one fifth of the adult Protestant population goes to church regularly. It is interesting that particularly the younger generation in the major Protestant churches is intent upon making religion more relevant to daily life. The question is whether increased social relevance will also increase membership loyalty. The actual problem of the major New Zealand Protestant denominations (and for that matter, their overseas counterparts) is their amorphous social structure: the membership does not feel bound by the norms and this dilemma cannot be solved by programmes of social action only. This problem is of course much less acute in Catholicism and the sects and one can therefore expect a very slow increase in both numbers and influence of these religious organizations at the expense of the decent-middle-class churches in the years to come.

At the same time, this lack of cohesion in the major Protestant denominations is also an indication of the essential Protestant tone of New Zealand society. The alliance of culture and religious institutions can indeed be regarded as indicative of strength: the churches are socially thoroughly respectable; their pronouncements on national ethics whether or not well informed are taken seriously although not necessarily implemented. However, the alliance has other weaknesses which are a consequence of amorphous and secularizing tendencies: the churches will generally be in the rearguard rather than the vanguard of social change. This is not necessarily because of ecclesiastical conservatism, but because an independent controversial and progressive policy may further weaken the tenuous hold on the membership. The option of decreasing one's involvement in a religious institution is more easily taken when there are no sanctions against such a move. Where such social sanctions and/or individual guilt feelings regarding apostasy exist, the church can follow a more independent, maybe even vanguard line of action.

This is evident in the area of race relations in New Zealand [Mol, 1966]. The hold of the major Protestant denominations on both Pakeha (white European) and Maori (Polynesian) members, as expressed in church attendance figures is rather weak. The Maoris in particular do not feel at home at the more formal Pakeha services and if they go to church at all tend to frequent special Maori services. Integration policies of the major Protestant denominations (and there is much pressure towards such policies) inevitably flounder on the fact that the membership does not want integration and gets away with not wanting it. However, the Catholic and particularly the Mormon hold on membership is such that these denominations can much more successfully implement such a policy and overcome initial antagonisms. They can do this mainly because a decrease in religious involvement has inevitable repercussions (through conscience or through the opinion of those fellow church members for whom one cares) which the membership will want to avoid. And so both races learn naturally to worship together and get used to it. One can therefore expect in the future a continuation of successful integration policies in the more cohesive bodies, such as Catholicism and the sects and lesser success in the more amorphous churches until integration in other social areas becomes an accomplished fact.

The current varied positions of the New Zealand churches on an amorphous-cohesive scale also affects their capacity to break through the inevitable embeddedness of class and culture. The amorphous churches will generally have to accept the *status quo* as it has developed through the like-seek-like motivation in the local congregations. This segregation becomes then automatically reinforced because those who are 'unlike' feel free to drop out. However, the cohesive churches will be more capable of breaking through this crustlike mundane pattern by their capacity to make the religious norm more central. Still as far as the centrality of a more purely religious norm is concerned Catholicism and the sects have their own problems. The satisfaction of the mere performance (church-going) in Catholicism or the ritualised 'hail-fellow-well-met'-ness as a substitute for Christian love in the sects also constitute danger signals. They only differ in kind from the ones of the less cohesive churches.

However true all this may be on the level of institutional posture and relations, the future influence of Christianity in New Zealand also heavily depends on the very intimate encounter of persons at work, recreation or at home. Churchgoers are judged by their fellow citizen on whether their Christian commitment makes a consistent difference. If it actually does, the church-goer does not preach 'at' them and does not appear better than they are, this is all the better for the esteem in which the churches are held. Even so: the translation of this esteem into active church participation is the exception rather than the rule in a secular society where at least the majority of males tend to associate religion with 'sissyness'.

## REFERENCES AND SELECTED BIBLIOGRAPHY

Argyle, Michael, *Religious Behaviour*. London, Routledge and Kegan Paul, 1961.

Blaikie, Norman W. H., 'Religion, Social Status and Community Involvement: A Study in Christchurch.' *Australian and New Zealand Journal of Sociology*, 5, (1), 1969.

Congalton, A. A., 'Social Grading of Occupations in New Zealand.' *British Journal of Sociology*, 4, 1954.

—, *Occupational Status in Australia*. Sydney, University of New South Wales. Studies in Sociology, No. 3. 1963.

Elder, J. R., *The History of the Presbyterian Church in New Zealand: 1840–1940*. Christchurch, 1940.
Harré, John, 'To be or not to be.' *Landfall*, March 1966.
Latourette, Kenneth Scott, 'The Great Century.' *History of the Expansion of Christianity* 5.
Lee, John A., *Socialism in New Zealand*. London, T. Werner Laurie, 1938.
Lenski, Gerhard, *The Religious Factor*. New York, Doubleday, 1961.
Lipson, Leslie, *The Politics of Equality*. Chicago, University of Chicago Press, 1948.
Moberg, David O., *The Church as a Social Institution*. Englewood Cliffs, Prentice-Hall, 1962.
McLintock, A. H., *The History of Otago*. Otago, Otago Centennial Historical Publications, 1949.
Mol, J. J., *Churches and Immigrants*. The Hague, Research Groups for European Migration Problems, 1961.
—, *Church-Attendance in Christchurch, New Zealand*. Canterbury University, Research Project 4 of the Department of Psychology and Sociology, 1962.
—, *Religion and Race in New Zealand*. Christchurch, National Council of Churches, 1966.
Moran, Patrick Francis, *History of the Catholic Church in Australasia*. Sydney, Oceanic Publishing Co., 1894.
Nixon, A. J., *Divorce in New Zealand*. Auckland, Auckland University College, Bulletin 46, Sociology Series 1, 1954.
Oliver, W. H., 'Christianity Among the New Zealanders.' *Landfall*, March 1966.
O'Neil, D. P., *Catholics and Delinquency*. Unpublished Master's Thesis. Victoria University, 1951.
Reed, A. H., *The Story of Canterbury*. Wellington, Reed, 1949.
Reeves, W. P., *The Long White Cloud*. London, Allen and Unwin, 1924.
Siegfried, André, *Democracy in New Zealand*. London, George Bell, 1914.
Sinclair, Keith, *A History of New Zealand*. Harmondsworth, Middlesex, Penguin Books, 1959.
Thompson, Richard H. T., *Training for the Ministry*. Christchurch, University of Canterbury, 1957.
Thompson, Richard H. T., and Couch, Moke, 'Maoris and the Urban Churches. Part 1.' *New Zealand Theological Review*, 2, (1), Spring, 1966.
—, 'Maoris and the Urban Churches. Part II: Colloquium.' *New Zealand Theological Review*, 2 (2), May 1967.

EDVARD D. VOGT*

# Norway

## HISTORICAL INTRODUCTION

There is a profound continuity, both in the faith of the people and in the institutions, territorial divisions, etc. between the Medieval Catholic Church in Norway, and the modern Lutheran Norwegian Church. Many phenomena today are virtually unchanged and can only be explained by reference to the factors that caused them in the Middle Ages. The centenaries of the great events in the history of the medieval church are celebrated today with great popular participation and without any consideration of the Reformation as a break with an alien past. The Gregorian, the Lutheran and the Haugian reform movements did not so much represent ruptures with the past, but new syntheses between a deeper tradition and the necessities of new cultural and social situations. This sense of unity with the past may be due to the homogeneity of the population, the slowness of the changes in economic and political structures, and the slow geographical and social mobility. It is only in the last few decades that the rate of change, in particular the exodus of the rural population into the towns and into new occupations, has increased to an extent that severely threatens the continuity of religious traditions.

The Haugian reform movement was started by the peasant's son Hans Nielsen Hauge, when he challenged the clergy's monopoly of religious leadership in the last decade of the eighteenth century. It is characterized by the development of a personally conscious and committed religiosity in the common people, and the concomitant development of a powerful network of voluntary lay organizations for home and foreign mission.

* Edward D. Vogt was born in Kristiansand, Norway, in 1923, and has been a political prisoner of the Nazis, National Secretary of the Norwegian Young Liberals, municipal councillor, director of a Sociological Institute in Rome, Research Fellow at the University of Bergen. He is a secular Catholic priest and a 'consultore' of the Vatican Secretariate for Non-Believers. He holds degrees from universities in Oslo and Rome, and has published ten books and longer research reports, and about twenty articles in scientific reviews. He is co-editor of *Revista di Sociologia*, *Sociologia Internationalis*, and *Concilium.*

Some of the dynamism of this movement was no doubt derived from the social class tension between the clergy, as part of the ruling élite, and the rural and urban lower classes, that gradually emerged as self-confident partners in the political and economic system. At the same time the feeling of a direct, personal religious calling and responsibility may often have been the point of departure for economic and political entrepreneurial ventures. Hauge himself became a successful merchant and industrialist in one period of his life, and his movement has been suggested as a confirmation of Max Weber's thesis [Jonassen, 1947; Flint, 1964].

## DENOMINATIONAL STRUCTURE

The Norwegian population of 3.8 million was, in relation to religion in the 1960 Census, divided into three groups: the members of the State-sponsored Norwegian Church (96.3 per cent), the members of other religious bodies (3.15 per cent), and those who are not members of any religious body (0.6 per cent).

### *The Norwegian Church*

An outsider observing the passionate debates and the complicated manoeuverings for positions between the many sharply divided groupings within the Norwegian Church, might believe it to be on the point of breaking up into a group continuing the State church system and a group constituting a free church, into a clerical-sacramental church and a lay-revivalist church, into a liberal church and an orthodox church. This impression would be wrong. These divisions are real enough but they criss-cross rather than run parallel, and the result is a church with high cohesion, far higher, incidentally, than the Churches of Sweden and Denmark, where the divisions may tend of fortify each other.

The composite, pluralist, multi-tiered system of the Norwegian church is difficult to describe in terms of the usual model – a hierarchical pyramid or concentric expanding circle that may possibly serve in the description of some other churches. A better model may be an elipsis, with two centres, the one clerical-governmental and the other lay-associational. These are not in dichotomic opposition to each other, but complementary so that each position within the system has a positive relation to both centres, although with the preponderance of one of them. Clericalism and anti-clericalism are virtually non-existent. The mighty General Secretaries of the lay associations are often ordained ministers. Those who clamour most for independence from state control are the same or the associates of those who staff the state and municipal control organs, like the present Minister of Church Affairs, Mr Bondevik. The liberal theologians are often traditionalists in liturgy, church government and in relation to the sacraments.

The financing of the Norwegian Church is divided almost equally between the Government and the Municipalities, on the one hand, and voluntary contributions on the other. Governmental contributions (in 1965 about 6.5 million dollars) go mainly to wages and pensions of the about 1,050 state-appointed clergy. Municipal contributions (of about the same amount) go mainly to the construction and maintenance of the church buildings and to the lay functionaries. The money collected by voluntary associations amounts to about 4.5 million dollars for the foreign missions, about 2.5 million dollars for parish work and about 6 million dollars a year for the operation of the lay home mission associations and their youth and social work. Thus the composite annual 'budget' of the Norwegian Church should amount to about 26 million dollars, or about 7.5 dollars per member, and 0.3 per cent of the Gross National Product. Seventeen per cent of the total goes to the foreign missions.

The cost of the extensive religious instruction in the schools, and the running of the University Faculty of Theology is not included in these figures, but with more than ten per cent of the class time dedicated to religion in the nine first grades, and extensive programmes also in the secondary schools and other educational programmes, this represents a considerable subsidy.

### *Church organizational structures*

A classification of the great multitude and variety of organizations and organs would have to consider variations along three main dimensions: territorial-communal or functional-specialised; clerical dominated or lay dominated; state controlled or private-associational. This would leave us with a matrix of eight combinations as a basic typology, if, that is, a dichotomic separating point could be established on each of the three dimensions. For our descriptive purpose here, this would seem too elaborate, and we will concentrate the description on the two most important 'boxes': 1) the territorial-communal-clerical-state controlled structures, and 2) the functional-lay-associational structures. Some structures of the other six types will be mentioned in connection with the basic type to which they are closest.

With regard to the first 'box', the nine dioceses and the 586 parishes into which the country is divided, each enjoy a certain autonomy within the framework of the laws legislated by the Storting and the governmental or departmental decrees and instructions. The clergy is appointed with tenure by the Government. However, local bodies are first consulted: for the parish clergy, the Parish Council and for the appointment of bishops, all the Parish Councils of the diocese, the clergy of the diocese, and the bishops and theological professors.

The older rural parishes are usually divided into two or three sub-parishes with their own churches, units that before the Reformation were often parishes with resident priests. If the parish priest is alone, he will celebrate the 11 a.m. Sunday High Mass, which is usually the only official service, in each of these churches on subsequent Sundays. If he has a 'personal' assistant, they will take turns. Sometimes a 'resident' assistant priest will be nominated to one of the sub-parishes, when it becomes sufficiently populous.

The parish priest of the cathedral parish is called *Domprost* and he is the Vicar General of the Bishop and the Dean of the surrounding parishes. The other parishes are grouped together in Deaneries of from two to eleven parishes with a Dean elected by and among the parish priests.

In each sub-parish, *Sogn*, there is a varying number of semi-clerical employees, of whom the *klokker*, or bellringer, has both liturgical and administrative functions as well as a part in other of the parish priest's functions, like religious instruction. Traditionally a trusted man in the village, working on a part-time basis, he has had an important function in mediating between the people and the priest who comes from outside. The priest stays in the parish only for a limited period (on an average maybe six years). Previously he represented a different social class and culture, and was maybe also Danish born. Now when the clergy is recruited from all classes and many parishioners have an education equal to the priest's this function is less important. The current tendency is to make the *klokker* as parish administrator into a full-time professional career. Hence he will now more rarely be appointed from the ranks of the parishioners.

For those church members (more than 75 per cent) who are not regularly involved in the lay associations, the 'church' is simply the parish and the diocese. Interaction with it is through the actions and words of the parish priest, or the *klokker*, at the Sunday services or when the member or his relatives and friends go through the rites of Baptism, confirmation, marriage and burial.

The Parish Council decides on the use of the parish church and other buildings and thus has extensive control of pastoral activities. It is elected in open elections, but usually only about ten per cent of parish members participate. As the lay associations form the only voting blocks, they are regularly able to staff the Council with their own members.

A number of specialized institutions have developed in the last few decades as auxiliaries to the territorial-clerical system. They represent the voluntary initiative of concerned laity mostly of the urban, professional class which falls outside the sphere of influence of the traditional lay associations. As the purpose is to involve people directly in the clerical-territorial church, these efforts have generally been met with suspicion and resistance from the lay associations.

Among the most important institutions are the *Institute for Congregational Activities*, which furthers socio-religious research, parish evangelical missions, and experiments in new structures and activities. An *Institute for Christian Education* has modernized books and other means of religious instruction. It has also altered the basic routines of pre-confirmation classes in schools and parishes. Other new agencies are a nation-wide *Family Counselling Service*, Church Academies, organizations for encounters of church people and intellectuals, an institution for *Development and Emergency Aid*, an *Institute for Ecumenical Activities*, and a *Christian Film Institute*.

With regard to the second 'box', the voluntary lay associations are, according to their programme, specialized agencies of the church for home and foreign mission. They are, however, also territorially organized mass movements, with a strong sense of brotherhood, and a great variety of services and works for and by the members. From the viewpoint of their members they may often tend to become the equivalent of sects. In the first decades of this century, when the clerical-state structures appeared to have fallen prey to an unorthodox liberal theology this tendency was particularly pronounced. As a counter-measure the lay associations established their own free Theological Faculty, which was then recognized by the State as equivalent to the University Faculty. Since then it has educated two-thirds of the present-day clergy – a clergy often recruited from the ranks of the associations and endowed with an orthodoxy and a piety acceptable to them. With this clergy in the parishes and often as bishops, with their lay members in command of the various parish and other councils, and indeed with the same clergy in important positions in the lay associations themselves, the danger of a schism has passed.

The twenty-five associations for foreign missions support more than 900 missionaries and a great multitude of institutions in Asia, Africa and Latin America. There are also fifteen major associations for home mission in Norway (and for the seamen abroad). These forty associations have about 35,000 local affiliate associations. This means that there would be about 60–70 associations in the average parish, but in practice the number is reduced as many mission circles, ladies' associations, etc. serve as the local affiliates for more than one of the national associations. However, the fact remains that the number of organizations and activities is very large, particularly considering that, apart from the youth activities which include more than half the young people, only about 10–25 per cent of adults are involved directly as members (see Table 8).

The two largest home mission associations are *Det Norske Lutherske Indremisjonsselskap* (The Norwegian Lutheran Home Mission Society) and *Vestlandske Indremisjonsforbund* (Western Norway Home Mission League). The former, founded in 1868, is based in Oslo, with 2,880 local associations and about 230 employees. The latter, based in Bergen, dominates Western Norway. It is divided into fourteen districts with 1,400 local associations and prayer houses in most of the parishes. Apart from the technical personnel in its schools, printing operations, etc. it has fifty salaried officials and preachers. In the last decade both organizations have seen a significant expansion in youth work, with large youth camp facilities created in virtually all districts. The *Sunday School Movement* gives grade school children religious instruction additional to that given in school. Classes are given by 9,300 voluntary laymen and women who teach about 180,000 children enrolled each year in 3,200 Sunday schools. With about 60,000 children born a year this would indicate that the majority of children are reached by the system.

The *Seamen's Church* is another fully voluntary movement. In thirty-one of the world's major ports it has establishments staffed by priests and lay assistants, thus reaching virtually all of the 40,000 Norwegians sailing the seven seas.

### *Categories of members*

A full typology of the members of the Norwegian Church would take the form of a matrix with at least the following three dimensions: 1) a clerical-lay dimension, 2) a dimension from the most active and frequent participation to the most passive and infrequent form of membership, and 3) a parish-association dimension distinguishing among members who gravitate to one or other of these two centres of activities.

Here we will content ourselves with some comments on the clergy. Some statistics on the various forms of lay participation will be given later.

There are 1,044 positions for ordained ministers in the state system. Another 160 theological graduates, most of them ordained, are working in the various voluntary home mission associations, and about 230 are employed in the secondary schools as teachers, mainly of religion. About 180 graduates of the two theological faculties are working in or for the foreign missions. Most of the other 7–800 foreign missionaries are graduates of mission seminaries, of which the most important is situated in Stavanger.

Apart from these, there are about 1,000 laymen with full-time appointments in the State Church system, as administrators in the Ministry of Church Affairs (which forms the minor part of the Ministry of Church and Education), as *klokker* and janitors, organists and social workers. In the voluntary associations there may be about 400 more or less full-time lay organisers and evangelists.

The more than a thousand wives of the bishops, parish priests and other clergy normally fulfil important pastoral functions, with particular responsibilities for the women and their organisations, for church social work, etc.

A small number of women are graduates of Theology and some of them have for long had full ministerial appointments as chaplains to hospitals and female prisons. Only one has so far served as parish priest, and this case generated great opposition within the lay associations as guardians of the traditions. In contrast to Denmark and Sweden, there is in Norway no High Church party among the non-associational church members, and the reaction outside the Lay associations has been rather positive and often even enthusiastic to the ordination of women.

Some information on the social background of the clergy will help clarify their role in the Norwegian Church and society. In the first centuries after the Reformation the clergy was to a large extent self-recruited, or recruited from other families of the small élite of Royal officials and wealthy merchants. Through the patronage of some parish priest a few sons of peasants might be sent to Copenhagen for theological studies. This was indeed virtually their only possibility of upward mobility into the élite, within which their sons again might freely choose other careers. It was, however, common for at least one of a priest's sons to become a priest, and at least one daughter to marry a priest.

The priests[1] and their families on the church farm in the centre of the parish fulfilled (and still fulfil) an important social function as mediators between the urban, European, academic civilization and the local, native culture. They organised the beginning school system and, having until recently had to draw their main income from the church farm, they even pioneered modern agriculture, earning in the eighteenth century the nickname 'Potato-priests'. Romantically identifying with the past glories of the Norwegian kingdom and sponsoring the just grievances of the people against the bureaucracy in Copenhagen, they became, with their relatives in other élite positions, the leaders of the national awakening, that led to the free constitution of 1814 and full national independence in 1905.

Of the priests graduating between 1801 and 1910 45.7 per cent had fathers who were priests and other Royal officials, the rate decreasing from 63 per cent in the beginning of the period to 36 per cent in its last decade. Of these officials nearly three-quarters were priests, their percentage of the total

1. This term renders their status as ordained 'men of God' better than the term 'minister'. The Norwegian word is *Prest* and the people often call them 'Father'.

number of fathers decreasing from 45 to 21. Well-to-do urban merchants accounted for 11.6 per cent of the fathers; 14.3 per cent were smaller merchants and other independent citizens, 11.3 per cent were functionaries, 14.7 per cent farmers (a proportion that increased from 3.7 per cent in 1801–20 to 28 per cent in 1881–1900) and 2.4 per cent were from the working class. This latter figure actually decreased from 5 per cent to one per cent between the first and the last decade of the nineteenth century [Mannsaaker, 1954, p. 198].

Of the fathers of the theology graduates between 1950 and 1955, 14.6 per cent were priests, another 10 per cent were graduates of other university faculties, 6.3 per cent were teachers in the elementary school (without a University degree), 11.2 were merchants, 15.7 lower management, 14.1 farmers, 6.8 artisans, 11.7 workers, and 9.8 per cent had unknown occupations [Pollan, 1962, pp. 83–98].

*The Dissenting Churches*

The twenty odd recognized religious bodies 'dissenting' from the Norwegian church contained, as previously stated, only 3.15 per cent of the Norwegian population in 1960. The small number of dissenters imposes the stigma of deviation upon them, especially upon the children and especially in the smaller, more intensely orthodox Lutheran communities. Although there is no significant legal discrimination against the dissenters, social pressure is sufficiently strong to make the rate of departure from the sects, especially in the second and third generations, far larger than the number of adult converts, except for a few sects like the Pentecostalists and the Jehova's Witness-

*Table 1. Norwegians 'Dissenting' from the Norwegian church*

| | 1950 | 1960 |
|---|---|---|
| Roman Catholics | 4,753 | 7,875 |
| Methodists | 11,570 | 11,196 |
| Baptists | 8,964 | 9,315 |
| Adventists | 5,440 | 5,272 |
| Free Lutheran Churches | 17,319 | 16,773 |
| Pentecostals | 30,036 | 34,122 |
| Other religious groups* | 23,247 | |
| No religious membership | 21,985 | 22,345 |
| Total | 123,314 | 134,500 |

* Among the 'Other religious groups' there were in 1960: 4,188 Jehova's Witnesses, 1,548 Anglicans, 1,241 Mormons, 365 Greek Orthodox, and 841 Judaic religion.
Source: *Folketellingen* (Census), 1950, pp. 34–35; 1960, pp. 30–31.

es. The Salvation Army is not considered a 'dissenting religious body' in terms of Norwegian law and statistics. It functions sociologically as a Lay association and most of its officers and followers regard themselves as members of the Norwegian Church.

*Table 2. Male/female and rural urban proportions in the main dissenting bodies in 1950 (in %)*

| | Men | | Women | |
|---|---|---|---|---|
| | Rural | Urban | Rural | Urban |
| Roman Catholics | 2.5 | 5.9 | 1.7 | 6.5 |
| Methodists | 4.9 | 14.0 | 5.7 | 15.6 |
| Baptists | 7.3 | 5.4 | 8.6 | 6.9 |
| Adventists | 3.6 | 3.8 | 4.5 | 5.7 |
| Free Lutheran Churches | 20.4 | 16.1 | 18.8 | 15.4 |
| Pentecostals | 27.1 | 14.0 | 32.9 | 18.4 |
| Other religious groups | 14.4 | 14.9 | 14.4 | 15.6 |
| No religious membership | 19.8 | 25.9 | 13.4 | 14.9 |
| Total | 100.0 | 100.0 | 100.0 | 100.0 |
| N | 33,797 | 22,668 | 37,272 | 29,577 |

Source: *Folketellingen* (Census), 1950, pp. 34–35; 1960, pp. 30–31.

The Roman Catholic Church is in a particular situation among the dissenting churches, both because of the heavy proportion of foreigners among its leaders and members, and because it is the principal target of prejudice. Among the about 8,000 Catholics there are more than 400 nuns mostly from Germany and Holland, running twenty-one hospitals and a number of schools, three Bishops and about sixty priests, only fifteen of them Norwegian born [Vogt, 1962].

In a sample of lay Catholics from 1967, 37 per cent were under 21 years. Of the adults 29 per cent were Norwegian-born converts, 29 per cent were born in Norway in Catholic families, and 42 per cent were foreign-born Catholics.

It is among the rural and the less educated classes, in the lay religious associations, and in the radical sects that open anti-Catholic prejudice on the personal level is now mainly found. In the lay associations it is a part of the faith in the Lutheran Reformation, and as the associations control much of the clerical structure, in particular missionary activities, the Ecumenical Movement encounters much resistance. Norway was the only member of the World Missionary Council that withdrew when the Council

*Table 3. Proportion of the members of the main dissenting religious bodies by main economic categories in 1960 (in %)*

| | Blue Collar | | White collar: | | | Main Economic Categories | | | |
|---|---|---|---|---|---|---|---|---|---|
| | Primary farming fishing | Second-ary and tertiary | Scientific technical humanities | Other tertiary: Upper echelon | Other tertiary: Lower echelon* | House-wives | Pension-ers | Children and others | Total |
| Total outside Norwegian Church | 4.7 | 23.6 | 5.3 | 9.0 | 2.0 | 21.5 | 5.9 | 28.0 | 100 |
| Roman Catholics | 1.2 | 22.3 | 12.4 | 8.3 | 1.2 | 16.1 | 7.6 | 30.9 | 100 |
| Methodists | 1.0 | 27.7 | 5.5 | 11.6 | 1.9 | 23.9 | 4.9 | 23.5 | 100 |
| Baptists | 6.3 | 25.5 | 3.5 | 7.8 | 1.8 | 25.2 | 6.1 | 23.8 | 100 |
| Adventists | 3.8 | 25.7 | 5.9 | 4.7 | 2.8 | 26.1 | 5.5 | 25.8 | 100 |
| Main Free Lutheran Church | 6.6 | 21.8 | 3.7 | 9.5 | 2.1 | 20.7 | 4.5 | 31.1 | 100 |
| Pentecostalists | 5.5 | 23.3 | 3.2 | 7.0 | 1.8 | 24.0 | 6.4 | 28.8 | 100 |
| Other religions | 4.5 | 23.6 | 4.8 | 9.0 | 2.1 | 22.4 | 6.2 | 27.4 | 100 |
| No religion | 5.0 | 23.7 | 8.4 | 12.4 | 2.4 | 15.0 | 5.7 | 27.4 | 100 |

* The Lower echelon 'White collar' category comprises smaller independent operators like shop-keepers and artisans, who are not, of course, 'white collar' in their dress.
Source: *Folketellingen*, 1950, pp. 34–35; *1960*, pp. 30–31.

became affiliated to the World Council of Churches in 1962. Although the Norwegian Church is officially a member of the World Council of Churches, participation is limited to individuals within the liberal clerical group. The possibility that W.C.C. may join the Roman church, or vice versa, is still an efficient deterrent for a broader participation in its activities.

*The members of No Religious Body*

Only a part of the about 22,000 (0.6 per cent of the population in 1960) non-aligned persons are non-believers. Some are persons who have lost faith in organised religion, but retain the basic Christian articles of faith. A formal withdrawal through a visit to the parish priest or a letter asking for a certificate of non-membership is required by the law only for those who want to join some other recognised religious body. Many who get such a certificate in order to join sects like the Baptists, Adventists, Pentecostals or Jehova's Witnesses, may after a few years become unable to keep up the fervour and dedication that their new membership requires. They will become disaffiliated, but may not be positively motivated to go back to their former church, even if they may have returned to its faith.

No nation-wide study has been made of this type of non-alignment but it may sometimes be identified in the Census statistics. In some small municipalities, where a particular sect has a larger membership there is often an unusual number of respondent without membership in a religious body. In larger urban municipalities it is, of course, probable that a greater proportion of the non-aligned are people with a negative reaction to religion in general.

The only organized group in Norway that has as its specific aim the promotion of the interests of non-believers, is the '*Human-etisk Forbund*' Humanist Ethics League with its active youth section, member of the 'International Humanist and Ethical Union'. In 1966, ten years after its founding, the combined membership was only about 1,000. Its most spectacular activity is the organising of a 'Civil confirmation', as an alternative to the very popular religious confirmation. Only a few hundred young people a year participate. Apart from this, it propagates the idea of ethics emancipated from religion, wants a course in the empirical study of religion in the schools instead of the Lutheran confessional instruction now imparted, and it works for the dispensation of persons belonging to no religion from paying the part of their taxes that goes to the support of the State Church – a dispensation already conceded to the members of dissenting religious organisations.

2. Data in this section refers to the Norwegian State Church, unless otherwise stated.

RELIGIOUS PARTICIPATION AND BELIEFS

The general level of religious belief, as measured by various Gallup polls of orthodox Christian doctrines seems to be consistently high compared with other Western nations. The level of church attendance is, on the other hand, exceptionally low but allowance has to be made here for the pattern established when the population was even more scattered and communications far more difficult than they are today. The level of attention to the radio services is probably higher than in other countries, even considering the fact that there is only one radio network, and hence no alternative programmes.

Various polls, one of them given in the end of Table 7, indicate that more than 50 per cent of the population are regular listeners to the Sunday High Mass broadcast. In a 1953 poll 38 per cent were listening every Sunday and 14 per cent every second Sunday. Half of the listeners were sitting attentively still for the full hour, while others combined the listening with some other activities part of the time. About 70 per cent of the population would be occasional listeners, and only 18 per cent 'never' listen. Nearly one third of the population listen daily to the radio's quarter hour morning devotional at 8.15 a.m. [Mathiesen, 1967].

As for the 'rites of passage', 96 per cent of the church members have their children baptised, 80 per cent of the children receive confirmation at the age of 15, 85 per cent of marriages and 95 per cent of funerals are celebrated with religious rites.

Of a Gallup sample of people with children in 1956, 84 per cent stated

*Table 4. Mass attendance in Norwegian dioceses (in %)*

| Diocese of | Total membership attending: Easter Sunday | Total membership attending: Average Sunday High Mass |
|---|---|---|
| Oslo | 4.1 | 2.2 |
| Hamar | 4.1 | 2.0 |
| Tunsberg | 5.3 | 2.7 |
| Agder | 9.8 | 4.1 |
| Stavanger | 7.3 | 2.7 |
| Bergen | 8.6 | 3.6 |
| Nidaros | 4.5 | 2.6 |
| Bodoe | 4.1 | 2.5 |
| Tromsoe | 3.5 | 2.7 |
| Total Norway | 5.8 | 2.7 |

Source: Gunnar Spilling, 1958, pp. 102–110.

that they have taught or intend to teach their children to say their evening prayers, and nearly half the population affirmed that they pray themselves every day. About a third of the respondents in this poll had read in their Bible within the last few weeks and 95 per cent supported religious instruction in the schools.

The percentage of the whole population assisting at the 11 a.m. High Mass on an average Sunday in 1956 was 2.7. In a similar count in April-May 1961 it was 2.8, but this survey has not been further analysed.

Table 4 of the Diocesan percentage illustrates some geographical variation.

*Table 5. Church attendance in Norwegian deaneries by number of people per priest (in %)*

| Deaneries with Number of People per Priest | Population in these Deaneries | Contribution to church attendance | Average Sunday attendance |
|---|---|---|---|
| Under 3,000 | 18 | 27 | 3.8 |
| 3,000–3,499 | 21 | 22 | 2.7 |
| 3,500–3,999 | 18 | 17 | 2.6 |
| 4,000–4,999 | 29 | 24 | 2.2 |
| 5,000 and more | 14 | 10 | 1.9 |
| | 100 | 100 | 2.63 |

Source: Gunnar Spilling, 1958, pp. 102–110.

Table 5 shows that there is a clear negative correlation between the percentage of church-goers in a district and the number of people per priest.

A systematic typology of geographical milieus in Norway correlated with church attendance and proportion of dissenters from the Norwegian Church is presented in Table 6. It is taken from Rokkan and Valen [1964, p. 222] who built on the typologies of the Central Bureau of Statistics and of A. Thormodsaeter, and on material prepared by the present author for the religious indices. The attendance index is the total of average attendances at each local place of worship in the State Church, as found in the nation-wide count of parish service participation by a Committee of the Joint Meeting of the Diocesan Councils in April and May 1956.[3] The percentages indicated in Table 6 are much higher than those in Tables 4 and 5, and give a better

3. This 1956 study and the 1957 nation-wide survey of factors correlated with political behaviour done by Rokkan and Valen, are the only two major Norwegian studies in the field.

*Table 6. Estimated proportions of church-goers and dissenters*

| Region[1] | Electorate 1957 (100%) | Attendance count '56: estimated number of churchgoers in % of electorate | Dissenters in % of electorate |
|---|---|---|---|
| Oslofjord | 710,552 | 6.0 | 6.6 |
| A | 522,885 | 3.8 | 6.7 |
| B | 22,261 | 7.9 | 6.7 |
| C | 98,688 | 12.3 | 6.3 |
| D | 66,718 | 12.8 | 6.6 |
| East Inland | 434,699 | 13.9 | 5.9 |
| A | 95,905 | 5.5 | 9.8 |
| B | 33,460 | 9.7 | 9.3 |
| C | 280,825 | 16.3 | 4.1 |
| D | 10,371 | 19.0 | 11.9 |
| E | 14,148 | 29.8 | 3.6 |
| South | 117,877 | 19.8 | 11.1 |
| A | 41,037 | 13.5 | 13.1 |
| B | 17,329 | 11.5 | 10.7 |
| C | 16,815 | 32.7 | 12.0 |
| D | 31,457 | 20.4 | 9.7 |
| E | 11,239 | 34.5 | 6.5 |
| West | 553,520 | 14.5 | 3.4 |
| A | 218,578 | 4.6 | 5.0 |
| B | 36,255 | 12.9 | 2.6 |
| C | 86,477 | 20.6 | 1.8 |
| D | 169,934 | 20.2 | 3.0 |
| E1 | 18,336 | 36.4 | 1.2 |
| E2 | 27,940 | 25.6 | 1.2 |
| Trøndelag | 208,236 | 14.6 | 2.5 |
| A | 72,759 | 6.9 | 3.5 |
| B | 12,390 | 14.7 | 1.1 |
| C | 78,922 | 18.5 | 1.3 |
| D | 21,928 | 18.8 | 4.0 |
| E1 | 4,128 | 15.4 | 0.6 |
| E2 | 18,109 | 23.4 | 3.0 |
| North | 259,771 | 17.3 | 4.8 |
| A | 47,007 | 5.6 | 4.5 |
| B | 11,814 | 20.8 | 2.3 |
| C | 26,663 | 10.9 | 2.4 |
| D | 83,062 | 16.5 | 6.0 |
| E1 | 24,503 | 26.9 | 3.5 |
| E2 | 66,722 | 24.8 | 5.3 |

1. Types of communes distinguished: A: Cities, towns, suburbs. B: Rural, high density. C: Rural, low density, not periph., inland. D: Rural, low density, not periph., coastal. E: Peripheral; E1: Peripheral, largely inland. E2: Peripheral, largely coastal.
2. Data for one urban unit (849) missing.
Source: S. Rokkan and H. Valen, 1964, p. 222.

*Table 7. Frequencies of attendance at church services and religious meetings in six regions of Norway in 1957**

| Region | Sex of respondent | N (100%) | Reported attendance 1957 (%) (1) | (2) | (3) | Total (1+2+3) | (4) | NA |
|---|---|---|---|---|---|---|---|---|
| Oslofjord | Total | 478 | 6 | 8 | 9 | 24 | 67 | 9 |
| | M | 220 | 4 | 8 | 8 | 20 | 71 | 9 |
| | W | 258 | 8 | 9 | 10 | 27 | 64 | 9 |
| East Inland | Total | 298 | 6 | 12 | 7 | 26 | 69 | 5 |
| | M | 145 | 2 | 10 | 2 | 14 | 79 | 6 |
| | W | 153 | 11 | 14 | 12 | 37 | 59 | 4 |
| South | Total | 97 | 16 | 8 | 13 | 38 | 47 | 14 |
| | M | 46 | 17 | 7 | 9 | 33 | 52 | 15 |
| | W | 51 | 16 | 10 | 18 | 43 | 43 | 14 |
| West | Total | 324 | 10 | 12 | 10 | 32 | 61 | 7 |
| | M | 172 | 10 | 14 | 8 | 32 | 61 | 7 |
| | W | 152 | 10 | 10 | 12 | 32 | 61 | 7 |
| Middle | Total | 221 | 6 | 8 | 8 | 22 | 74 | 5 |
| | M | 112 | 7 | 7 | 3 | 17 | 79 | 5 |
| | W | 109 | 5 | 9 | 14 | 27 | 69 | 4 |
| North | Total | 128 | 7 | 9 | 11 | 27 | 72 | 1 |
| | M | 67 | 9 | 6 | 9 | 24 | 76 | – |
| | W | 61 | 5 | 13 | 13 | 31 | 67 | 2 |

1. Attends church and meetings.
2. Attends church, never meetings.
3. Never church, attends meetings.
4. Never church, never meetings.

The question was: How many times during the last month have you: a) been to church service? b) been to religious meetings? c) listened to a service on the radio? The marginal response distributions were (in %)

| | Never | Occasionally varies | 1–3 times last month | Every Sunday | More frequently | NA other |
|---|---|---|---|---|---|---|
| Church | 76 | 2 | 16.0 | 1.5 | 0.5 | 4 |
| Meetings | 77 | 2 | 13.5 | 1.5 | 1.0 | 4 |
| Radio | 17 | 14 | 20.0 | 30.0 | 12.0 | 8 |

Source: S. Rokkan and H. Valen, 1964, p. 224.

indication of the level of church-going. With the low population density and only one service celebrated by each active priest each Sunday (about 800 High Masses in all on the average Sunday), only about a third of the population in the rural areas would be within reasonable distance of the nearest service on a particular Sunday. The rest would have to wait one or two Sundays until the priest came to their neighbourhood.

Many people in low density population areas may be attracted to the lay association's religious meetings in the neighbourhood oratory; these are more accessible and also offer more intensive social interaction. On the other hand, participation in oratory meetings requires high commitment to a pietist-puritan religiosity that repels many.

From Rokkan and Valen's national survey it would appear that about 10 per cent of the population who would not attend church in the same period, frequent lay oratory meetings once or more during a month. Another 10 per cent attend both meetings and church, and about 10 per cent attend church monthly but no meetings. Table 7 gives the geographical and sex variations.

### RELIGIOSITY AND SEX, ETHNIC GROUPS, GEOGRAPHICAL LOCATION, POLITICAL PARTY AND SOCIAL CLASS

The task here will be to show how the above basic secular categories are each correlated with various religious categories: membership in different associations, degree of assent to various doctrines and participation in religious practices.

There is a definite relationship between social class and the type of religiosity indicated by membership in the lay associations. Table 8 indicates some differences between occupational groups in different districts.

Apart from a few associations that gravitate more towards the clerical-territorial church structure (like one of the two nation-wide University and High-school Student Associations), the great majority of the lay associations are only functional to the rural populations, the more recent immigrants to the towns and recent arrivals in the middle class. The traditional unionised working class and the professional, economic and cultural élites, or upper middle classes, have interests that fall outside the framework of the lay associations, and a liberal attitude that is foreign to their fundamentalism.

This liberal attitude may easily be confused with, or develop into, an anti-transcendental agnosticism or atheism, but it may also be an expression of a deeper and more secure religious faith than the one that is dependent on the leadership of the lay associations. In 1954 the whole nation took part in a debate on the existence of Hell, initiated by the liberal Bishop of Hamar, Kr.

*Table 8. Membership in religious associations by occupational groups in the two contrasting divisions of the country (in %)*

| Region | Occupation | Location | Sex | N (100%) | Member State Church | Member of religious association: Mission Society | Other in State Church | Dissenter | NA |
|---|---|---|---|---|---|---|---|---|---|
| East, Trøndelag, North | Worker | Total | M | 281 | 90 | 4 | 3 | 2 | 1 |
| | | | W | 283 | 82 | 9 | 6 | 5 | 1 |
| | | Urban | M | 111 | 91 | 1 | 3 | 3 | 2 |
| | | | W | 119 | 83 | 4 | 7 | 6 | – |
| | | Rural | M | 170 | 88 | 6 | 3 | 2 | 1 |
| | | | W | 164 | 81 | 10 | 5 | 4 | – |
| | Smallholder, farmer | | M | 87 | 92 | 5 | – | 2 | – |
| | | | W | 111 | 60 | 31 | 3 | 5 | – |
| | Middle class | | M | 169 | 88 | 5 | 4 | 4 | – |
| | | | W | 167 | 81 | 7 | 5 | 5 | 1 |
| South, West | Worker | Total | M | 92 | 91 | 3 | 4 | 1 | – |
| | | | W | 86 | 74 | 13 | 8 | 5 | – |
| | | Urban | M | 34 | 94 | – | 6 | – | – |
| | | | W | 43 | 88 | 2 | 9 | – | – |
| | | Rural | M | 58 | 90 | 5 | 3 | 2 | – |
| | | | W | 43 | 60 | 23 | 7 | 9 | – |
| | Smallholder farmer | | M | 56 | 82 | 13 | – | 5 | – |
| | | | W | 55 | 45 | 45 | 3 | 5 | 2 |
| | Middle class | | M | 69 | 84 | 9 | 1 | 4 | 1 |
| | | | W | 59 | 76 | 15 | 4 | 5 | – |

Source: S. Rokkan and H. Valen, 1964, p. 225.

Schjelderup, as a mild protest against a fire and brimstone radio sermon of the fundamentalist theologian Professor Hallesby. This debate did not so much reveal a deep doctrinal split in the Norwegian Church as the existence among the faithful of two distinct personality types based on different social milieux. Upon complaints from the Fundamentalists, the Government ruled that Bishop Schjelderup had not disqualified himself as a bishop by his liberal doctrine on Hell, but it based its ruling on a verdict obtained from the University Professors of Theology, thus avoiding the popish role of being a final arbiter in doctrinal controversies.

The form of Christianity institutionalized in the lay associations is marked by an aggressive self-confidence. This has generated a profound 'status' uncertainty in those who subscribe to forms of religiosity characterized more by the mystical 'via negativa' than by positive affirmation. Among the latter there is a tendency to doubt the right to call themselves 'Christian', or 'Personal Christian', the terms used by the lay association members to describe themselves. This special semantic situation is the basis for the answers given to the Gallup poll question: 'Do you consider yourself to be a personal Christian'? Only 26 per cent of a sample of adult Norwegians answered 'yes'; 21 per cent answered 'perhaps', and 49 per cent, who may simply have conceded the monopoly on the term 'Christian' to the association members, answered 'no' [Mathiesen, 1967].

Table 7 indicates that for church attendance in the West, Middle and South of Norway, and for meetings in the North, Norway provides an exception to the common tendency in Western Christianity for women to practice more than men. Table 8 demonstrates the same phenomenon at least in relation to membership of the State Church and not of associations.

However, geographical differences are equally striking. There has been some attempt to explain these in terms of ethnic groups. In the far North we find a distinct racial group of about 20,000 Lapps. Together with a number of the surrounding Norwegians, some of whom have Finnish blood, they subscribe to a peculiar form of Lutheranism, named after *Laestadius*, a Swedish Lutheran priest, who started a revival among the Lapps in the middle of the last century. The official church at first refused to recognize this communitarian and ecstatic revival as Lutheran. The Lapps were nearly driven into a schism, when in about 1870 the wise Bishop Skaar changed this atmosphere of distrust and defined *Laestadianism* as 'the heart of Lutheranism'. Their religion has transformed the economic situation among the Lapps mainly by saving them from drinking. It has also made them unreceptive to radical non-Lutheran sects.

The rest of the population appear to be very homogeneous. There has, in fact, been very little influx of foreigners since the Bronze Age arrival of the Germanic Northerners. Anthropometrical research has, however, revealed that there is a significantly higher incidence in Western Norway of a possibly pre-Germanic type, with a higher skull index, darker hair and brown eyes. What interests us is that an attempt has been made to associate this type with a religious personality type, that does indeed dominate Western Norway. Such people are characterized by an affinity to Pietism and Puritanism, a high membership score in the lay associations and a certain lack of liberal tolerance which makes them supporters of the Christian People's Party to further religion and suppress vice [Hansen, 1899].

A concentration of all these phenomena may indeed be observed in Western Norway, but they are also found elsewhere, where they correlate far less. Geographical factors, and socio-cultural factors connected with geography would seem to have a higher explicative value.

From this point of view Norway may be seen as a country of considerable contrasts. The South and West is the home of the fjord farmers, fishers-farmers and other smaller isolated agriculturalists. In the North and Middle districts large-scale fishing is the rule. While in the East and Troendelagen there are much larger scale farming operations. In contrast to the equalitarian communities of the South and West, this has brought about a proletariat of farm and forest day-labourers.

The Puritan inner-directedness and the lay spirit of independence in relation to the clergy may be connected with the characteristics of the fjord farmer and others in the South and West. Here only the nuclear family can be the operational unit and an unusual degree of resourcefulness and initiative is therefore needed. The children have to be taught independence, as they all, save the one who will take over the farm, will have to create their own future elsewhere. The extraordinary nature of Western Norway was analysed in the sociological school of Le Play as the place where the nuclear family system started and the Faustian spirit of Europe was born [cf. Bureau, 1906]. The characteristic religiosity of the fishing families in the West may also be a function of the great dangers and incertitude of small boat fishing.

Regional differences are also clearly evident when one looks at the relationship between religion and politics. Stein Rokkan and Henry Valen suggest that

> the rural communities of the East, the Troendelag and the North have tended to be much more hierarchical and have offered much stronger incentives to class politics than the equalitarian communities so frequently found in the South and the West [Rokkan and Valen, 1964, p. 175].

The West is indeed the stronghold of the Christian Peoples Party, which has explicit religious aims. From a local Western party in 1933, it was launched as a national party in 1945. Its share of the electorate was 9.3 per cent in 1961 and 7.8 per cent in 1965. Apart from a few pockets in Eastern and Northern Norway its strength is still in the West where it may reach 35 per cent of the vote in the most peripheral island fishing communities.

In an electoral study in the Stavanger area prior to the 1957 elections, Henry Valen and Daniel Katz asked both voters and party leaders which issues they regarded as important in the forthcoming elections; 55 per cent of the Christian People's Party's voters (and 74 per cent of its leaders) mentioned moral and religious issues. Only 4 per cent of the Liberal and Agrarian voters (5 per cent of the leaders) and none of the Labor and Conservative voters and leaders mentioned such issues [Valen and Katz, 1966, p. 243).

While the Christian People's Party thus attracts nearly all those who have not accepted a secular concept of politics, it only appeals to 25 per cent of the regular church attenders. In a sample of 1,017 adults 187 voters declared that they attended church regularly; 15 per cent of these church-goers declared their intention of voting Labor, 23 per cent Liberal, 25 per cent Christian, 14 per cent Agrarian, and 10 per cent Conservative [Valen and Katz, 1966, p. 167]. The Labor party is the only party in which church-goers are strongly under-represented.

The following table indicates the effect of geographical location and membership of the religious lay associations on a worker's voting behaviour.

*Table 9. Relation between party preference and membership in religious associations for workers in East and West*

| Region | Lay Association | N | % Political Party Vote | | | | |
|---|---|---|---|---|---|---|---|
| | | | Socialist | Conservative | Middle parties | Undecided or N.A. | Christian People's Party |
| East, North and Trøndelag | Member | 74 | 43 | 8 | 19 | 30 | 55 |
| | Non-member | 486 | 67 | 6 | 6 | 21 | 36 |
| West and South | Member | 30 | 33 | 7 | 27 | 33 | 63 |
| | Non-member | 148 | 50 | 6 | 17 | 27 | 29 |

Source: S. Rokkan and H. Valen, 1964, p. 229.

While it is clear from Table 9 that workers in all categories express a clear preference for the Socialist Party, religious and regional differences still remain striking. Regardless of membership in the lay associations residence in the East (Treendelagen and the North) is correlated with a higher Socialist vote than in the West (and South). Nevertheless within both regions religious differences are at least equally, and in the East more, significant: 24 per cent more workers who are not members of the lay associations vote Socialist in the East, while 17 per cent more of them vote Socialist in the West.

It is also clear that a high proportion of the lay association worker members who do not vote Socialist see the Christian People's Party as the main alternative – particularly so in the West as one would expect.

Nevetheless, it should be emphasized that the labour movement is supported by many religious people. In spite of its Marxism it has never promoted any antireligious movement. During its thirty years in power it loyally furthered the interest of the State Church. At present the State Church system is under attack from the New Left Party, and from the youth sections of the Labor party and the Liberal party, but this is a policy that meets with approval from a great many church members too.

REFERENCES AND BIBLIOGRAPHY

Barnes, John Arundel, 'Class and committees in a Norwegian island parish.' *Human Relations*, 7, 1954.

Bolling, Reider, *Norske prester og teologiske kandidater* [Norwegian Clergymen and Bachelors of Divinity]. Oslo, 1958.

Bureau, P., *Le Paysan des Fjords* [The Farmer in the Fjords]. 1906.

Flint, John T., 'The Church in relation to Family Life,' in: T. D. Eliot, *et al.* (eds), *Norway's Families*. Philadelphia, 1960.

—, 'The Secularization of Norwegian Society.' *Comparative Studies in Society and History* 6, 1963/64.

Hansen, Andreas M., *Norsk Folkepsykologi* [Psychology of the Norwegian People]. Oslo, 1899.

Jonassen, Chr. T., 'The Protestant Ethnic and the Spirit of Capitalism in Norway.' *American Sociological Review*, 1947.

Mannsaaker, D., *Det norske presteskapet i det 19. aarh.* [The Norwegian Clergy in the Nineteenth Century]. Oslo, 1954.

Matheisen, Thomas, 'Religionen i Norge' [Religion in Norway], in: Wilhelm Aubert *et al.*, *Det Norske Samfunn: en sosiologisk beskrivelse* [Norwegian Society: a sociological description]. Oslo, 1967.

Molland, Einar, *Fra Hans Nielsen Havge til Eivind Berggrav: hovedlinjer i Norges kirkehistorie i det 19. og. 20.* [From Hans Nielsen Hauge to Eivind Berggrav; main currents in Nineteenth and Twentieth Century Norwegian Church History]. Oslo, 1951.

Polland, Sonja, 'Prestetradisjon og presterekruttering 1720–1955' [Clergy Culture and Clergy Recruitment, 1720–1955]. *Tidskrift for samfunnsforskning* [Review of Social Research], Oslo, 1962.

Rokkan, S., and Valen, H., 'Regional contrasts in Norwegian Politics,' in: E. Allardt and Y. Littunen (eds.), *Cleavages, Ideologies and Party Systems*. Helsinki, 1964.

Spilling, Gunnar, 'Vi mobiliserer for sekt kirkesoekning' [We mobilize for increased Church Service Participation], in *Aarbok for den Norske Kirke* [Yearbook of the Norwegian Church]. Oslo, 1958.

Valen H., and Kats, D., *Political Parties in Norway*. Oslo, 1966.

Vogt, E. D., *The Catholic Church in the North*. Bergen, 1962.

JOZEF MAJKA*

# Poland

It is impossible to understand the place of religion in Polish society, the character of religiosity and even the social and religious situation today, without taking into account the thousand year old religious and cultural tradition of Poland and the relationship between political development and Christian civilization.

Although the beginnings of Christianity date back several decades earlier,[1] the year 966 marks the official acceptance of Christianity – an acceptance which flowed not from preceding evangelization but from an essentially political act – the marriage of the Polish prince Mieszko to a Czech princess. Mieszko's son Boleslaw, received his crown from the pope and became one of the European rulers of the day [Grabski, 1966]. Neither the organizational framework not the doctrinal force of the old Slav religions was very substantial; Christianity met with only weak resistance. The short-lasting reaction, the product of political chaos, if anything, showed up the superficial nature of original Christianity and, in the long run contributed to its strengthening by provoking a reorganization of the religious structure of the country.

* Jozef Majka was born in Suchorzów, District of Rzeszów, Poland, in 1918. Studied theology at the University of Cracow, and social sciences at the Catholic University of Lublin. Professor at the Mayor Seminary of Tarnów (1950–1970), Lecturer of catholic social doctrine and sociology of religion, Director of the Institute of Sociology of Religion at the Catholic University of Lublin, and Rector of the Pontifical Faculty of Theology of Wroclaw. Member of the Committee of Studies, the Pastoral Commitee, the Commitee 'Justitia et Pax', and the Commitee for Vocations of the Polish Episcopate, National Secretary for Non-believers. Member of the editorial commitee of *Roczniki Filozoficzne* (Annals of Philosophy), *Concilium*, *Colloquium Salutis*, and *Diakonia – Der Seelsorger*. Directed several socio-religious researches. His scientific interest is divided between catholic social doctrine and sociology of religion and the application of both in pastoral care. His major works include *The Problem of Wages in the Light of Personalism*, *Interest and Usury in Catholic Moral Teaching*, commentaries on the encyclicals 'Mater et Magistra', 'Pacem in Terris', and 'Populorum Progressio', *Sociology of the Parish*, and more than 130 articles.

1. Archeological discoveries in Wislica support the traditional version of the so-called *Legenda Pannonska* [Wartolowska, 1963, pp. 31–44].

During the period of political fragmentation of Poland from the twelfth to fourteenth centuries, the Church was sufficiently strong and cohesive to become the main force of national unity. Throughout the remainder of the Piast dynasty it continued to play an important role in consolidating political unity and guiding cultural progress into the mainstream of Western civilization, as is evident, for example, by the foundation in Krakov of the Jagiellonian University by the last of the Piast rulers (1364).

Union with Lithuania changed the religious situation in the new, and greatly enlarged state, in two ways. On the one hand, it strengthened Catholicism in numbers and political prestige; on the other, by the admission of a larger Orthodox Ruthenian minority, it contributed to the religious differentiation of the new state. Efforts to unite Orthodoxy and Catholicism were only partly successful (1596), and from the fourteenth century significant numbers of Jews and, later on, a substantial Moslem minority, mainly of Tartar origin, contributed further to religious heterogeneity.

At the time of the Reformation Poland found herself in a unique situation. The attitude of tolerance displayed by the authorities gave Poland the reputation of an *asylum haereticorum* in other Catholic countries, yet tolerance was not conducive to sharp religious conflicts and the country remained predominantly Catholic. Lutheran and Calvinist influence was never firmly grounded or widespread and the Polish Arians (known also as Socyans) rapidly became extinct. Thus in spite of the Orthodox influences coming from the East and the strength of Reformation amongst the remaining neighbours (Sweden, Prussia, Bohemia) Poland and her ethnically pure Polish and Lithuanian population remained faithful to Catholicism.

During the Enlightenment religiosity declined but, because so many of those responsible for the introduction of these new ideas were in fact Catholic clergy, the rationalist and deist philosophies of the period had less impact in Poland than in the countries of Western Europe. Polish romanticism was later to neutralize these influences. Represented mainly in the works of the leading poets (Mickiewicz, Slowacki, Krasinski, Norwid) this romanticism was permeated by the spirit of religious and nationalistic messianism appropriate to a period in which non-Catholic Russia and Prussia attacked Polish independence. Nationalistic and religious elements were combined here (Mickiewicz was one of the founders of a Catholic order for men) and contributed to the maintenance of loyalty to Catholicism.

If the influence of the Reformation and the Enlightenment weakened the development of Catholic reform in Poland, loss of independence made the bishops, who had espoused the Council of Trent's reforms, even less concerned about seeking political or court careers and free to concentrate on clerical education and pastoral duties.

The general revival of European Catholicism in the second half of the nineteenth century left a distinct imprint on the Polish society. On the one hand, the anti-Polish and anti-Catholic policies of the occupying powers (e.g. the *Kulturkampf* in the Prussian occupation zone, the political repression after the 1863- Rising and the attempt to liquidate the Uniate Church in the Russian occupation zone) hampered the development and deepening of Catholicism. On the other hand, persecution strengthened religious convictions and made the Church into the one force of social unity capable of strengthening national culture and the moral rebirth of the people. This revival of Catholicism was reflected not only in resistance to persecution but also in frequent national manifestations, pilgrimages, popular mission activities and in the revival of monastic life. In particular the many new religious orders for women aided the social and pastoral work of the diocesan clergy. The mechanism of this religious revival has aroused the interest of both historians and sociologists but its evaluation necessitates further study [Gorski, 1957, pp. 267–283; Urban. 1966, pp. 1–430; Majka, 1966, pp. 117–137].

Nevertheless when Poland regained her independence in 1918 she was neither ethnically nor religiously a homogeneous country. All denominations, and especially Catholicism, entered the period of independence (1918–1939) with serious organizational and cultural weaknesses due to the pressure of the occupying powers. By the 1925 Concordat between the Polish Government and the Holy See the ecclesiastical organization of the four different Catholic rites[2] was reorganized. The status of other denominations was also legally defined and their organizational structures made to conform to the existing legislation. A special legal measure was enforced to make the Orthodox Church independent of the Moscow Patriarchate [Markiewicz, 1967, p. 49]. The state also gave financial assistance to the different denominations: 89 per cent of the total aid went to the Catholic Church while the remaining 11 per cent was shared among the other denominations [*M.R.S.*, 1939]. Table 1 shows denominational composition in 1934.

The Catholic Church with its superiority in numbers (75 per cent of population) and priviliged legal status [Articles 114 and 115 of the Constitutional Law of the Polish Republic of 17 March 1921; Piekarski, 1967, p. 49.] showed considerable organizational dynamism and social vitality. The theological and general Catholic education systems (the Catholic University of Lublin, four theological faculties in State Universities, secondary, technical and primary schools) were quickly reorganized; charitable activities, the Catholic Press and other Catholic organizations expanded and in 1931 were

2. The four Catholic rites were: a) the Latin Rite: 5 metropolitan Sees and 21 dioceses; b) the Greek Ukrainian Rite; 1 metropolitan see, 3 dioceses and 1 administration; c) the Armenian Rite: 1 Archdiocese; and d) the Byzantine-Slovanic Rite: 1 apostolic visitor. [Pirozynski and Szczech, 1938; *M.R.S.* 1939, p. 353].

*Table 1. Denominational composition in Poland in 1934*

| Denomination | | N | % |
|---|---|---|---|
| Catholics | | 24,029,500 | 75.2 |
| *Latin rite* | 20,670,100 | | |
| *Greek rite* | 3,336,200 | | |
| *Armenian rite* | 5,200 | | |
| *Eastern-Byzantine rite* | 18,000 | | |
| Polish Orthodox | | 3,762,500 | 11.8 |
| Lutheran | | 835,200 | 2.6 |
| Other Christian denominations | | 145,400 | 0.5 |
| Jewish | | 3,113,900 | 9.8 |
| Other non-Christian religions | | 6,800 | 0.0 |
| Undefined | | 45,700 | 0.1 |
| Total | | 32,547,000 | 100.0 |

Source: Pirozynski, 1935, pp. 12–13; *M.R.S.*, 1939, pp. 25–26.

grouped under Catholic Action [Pirozynski and Szczech, 1938, pp. 65ff; Urban, 1966, pp. 431–545; Mystek, 1966; Strzeszewski and Majka, 1966]. Thus the church played an important part not only in religious life but also in the cultural and social regeneration of Polish society. The religiosity of the inter-war period was the subject of various studies mainly concerned with institutional structures, especially parishes [Mirek, 1928], Catholic Action [Zdaniewicz, 1958], charitable works [Majka, 1966, pp. 117–137], social work more broadly conceived [Strzeszewski and J. Majka, 1966], and the issue of vocations to priestly and religious orders [Majka, 1967, pp. 48–57]. All these studies demonstrated a significant deepening of religiosity due to such factors as increase in the number of clergy, extension of religious education, institutional growth of the church and, above all, the shaping of a new religious culture in which all the humanistic values could be integrated.

The 1939–45 war brought a marked increase of religiosity despite restrictions in pastoral work and public worship and severe material or institutional losses. A 1948 survey of these losses has not yet been fully analysed.[3] However, it is clear that 25 per cent of the pre-war members of the clergy perished at the hands of the Gestapo or in concentration camps and, even in rural dioceses, about one third of all church buildings were destroyed. In some

3. This survey was carried out by M. Pirozynski and after his death it was handed for further analysis to the Department of Sociology of Religion, Catholic University of Lublin.

cities (Warszawa, Wroclaw, Gdansk) the situation was much worse and only a few churches were spared.

During the war there was a noticeable increase in the prestige of the clergy due to their patriotic devotion, and refusal to accept class based discrimination between people. This together with the great leveling of social differences in the war situation produced greater social solidarity and drew people closer to Christianity. After the war the unprecedented extension of the charitable work of the church [Majka, 1967, pp. 377–396; Lisowski, 1965] continued. This also aided pastoral work and favoured the growth of religiosity. Now when charitable work on this scale is no longer necessary, pastoral activity continues with increasing vitality [Majka, 1966; pp. 217–225].

## DENOMINATIONAL STRUCTURE

A precise account of Poland's denominational structure is not possible because there are no official denominational statistics and the question on religion was not included in post war population censuses. We have to rely, therefore, on estimates based on sample surveys as well as some statistical information collected by the non-Catholic denominations. There are some data published nearly every year by the individual Catholic dioceses giving the numbers of clergy and parishes as well as numbers of the faithful in each parish. These statistics, however, frequently greatly underestimate the number of adherents, especially in cities where the discrepancy may be of the order of 10 to 40 per cent below the actual figure.[4]

The sample surveys conducted by the Public Opinion Centre of the Polish Radio show that approximately 95 per cent of the population adhere to some religious denomination. The number of persons in non-Catholic denominations is quite small, and does not exceed 250,000. It can be estimated, therefore, that in the population of 32 million in Poland today more than 30 million are Catholics, belonging mainly to the Latin Rite. The number of Greek Rite Catholics is small and they are to be found mainly in Western and Northern Poland. Amongst the remaining denominations the most numerous one is the Lutheran Church (approximately 110,000), the Polish National Catholic Church (60,000) and the Orthodox Church. The Mariawit Sect numbers about 20,000, while the other Christian denominations (the Reformed Church, the Methodists, Baptists, Seventh Day Adventists,

4. The discrepancies can be accounted for in two ways. First, the scale of taxes imposed on the parish priests varies with the number of the faithful. Secondly, the rapid migration to the cities makes it difficult for the parish priests to estimate the size of their flocks.

and Jehovah's Witnesses) do not number more than 10,000 each; some have fewer than 5,000 members [Markiewicz, 1967). Some 30,000 Polish people of Jewish extraction have either been baptized or declare themselve indifferent.

The present denomination structure is clearly radically different to the pre-war situation, as shown in Table 1. Several factors explain this change. (a) The shift of the eastern frontier and the evacuation of the Ukrainian population to the U.S.S.R. brought about a decrease in the numbers of Catholics belonging to Eastern Rites and greatly reduced the number of adherents of the Orthodox Church. (b) The Jewish population was virtually liquidated by the Nazis. (c) the evacuation of the German minority from Poland, carried out during the war, contributed to a decrease in adherents of the Lutheran Churches. Hence the Western Territories (east of the Oder and the Neisse) have now a virtually uniform Catholic population. A small number of Lutherans can be found in Masuria, and in the Cieszyn District of Silesia and in Warsaw.

## RELIGIOUS PARTICIPATION AND BELIEFS

Since 95 per cent of the population of Poland affirm attachment to the Roman Catholic Church we shall be concerned mainly with the religiosity of Catholics. Poland has a reputation as a country in which the churches are full and religious practices often assume the form of public manifestations. Statistics support this picture. Baptism for the children of Catholic parents is almost universal, even among those who do not, for various reasons, marry in church. Baptismal records show that compared with fifty years ago when the sacrament was administered on the day of birth or on the following day, the tendency now is to delay. Yet, it is not easy to draw from this fact any conclusions about the level of religiosity, particularly when the low level of infant mortality removes the danger of a child dying without Baptism, and when even today it is customary for the mother to take her baby to church as she is leaving the obstetrics ward.

Another practice which is almost universal is the First Communion. This is a more difficult practice because it must be preceded by a long period of instruction. The importance of this is illustrated by the greatly increased attendance at the catechism classes of children at the age for First Communion. Thus in a study of the industrial centre of Nowa Huta the attendance at primary school catechism classes was best in grades two and three, whilst in the more senior grades it was not as satisfactory [Karsznia, 1962]. Further, it is clear that in individual families the occasion is becoming increasingly more festive. This applies to the essentially religious aspect (often the whole family receives Communion together) as well as the social aspect (e.g. special dress for the child, reception for the family and friends, etc.).

The matter of church marriage is more complicated. Most people have a religious ceremony; only about 10 per 10,000 persons do not. The latter, however, may not lack religiosity, they may simply wish to avoid or delay a public declaration of loyalty to the church which a religious ceremony entails. In some cases such people later contract a church marriage privately, in some remote spot whenever a suitable opportunity arises. A marital impediment, especially when one party is divorced, is a much more common reason for civil marriage. Although the incidence of divorce (c. 5 per 10,000 in 1960) is about half the incidence of civil marriage, it is similar to that of other countries with a similar structure, although appreciably higher in the large cities and industrial centres.[5] One should emphasize, however, that very many couples married outside the Church, remarry within it as soon as any impediments are removed. This is therefore an important feature of their attitude to religion.

It is also very rare for the person on his death bed or his family to refuse a Christian burial. If a small number of persons do not follow this practice, it is generally because Canon Law prohibits it as in the case of *peccatores publici*, e.g. persons living in concubinage, or because social organisations arrange a secular burial for their leading members.

Thus Civil marriage is the only one of these 'rites of passage' in which there is a significant departure from church norms. This is particularly significant because many Catholics maintain that the Church should be less strict in its demands in this matter. Such views are even voiced by people whose loyalty to the Church and personal devotion to the faith could not be doubted [Majka, 1963; Sajdok, 1964].

We do not have complete data from the whole of Poland on compulsory practices such as Sunday mass and Easter duty (i.e. Holy Communion during Eastertide), but in several dioceses estimates have been made which enable us to give an approximate picture. Sunday Masses are usually crowded. However, despite the increased number of masses, the number of churches in Poland is still completely inadequate particularly in industrial centres. Hence, full churches do not mean that all Catholics fulfil the precept of Sunday Mass. Estimates of Sunday attendance in several rural dioceses have shown that in some parishes the proportion of Sunday Mass attenders varies between 40 and 50 per cent. The average attendance is relatively high. In the greater majority of parishes (about 80 per cent) the number of persons at Sunday masses amounted to from 65 to 80 per cent

5. It is highly characteristic that in Warsaw divorce is five times higher than the national average and ten times higher than in agricultural provinces. The number in Warsaw is also much in excess of that of other cities [*R.S.*, 1968; Borkowicz, 1964].

of those bound by this duty. There is a small number of parishes in which this proportion is lower but there also are parishes where it is considerably higher. There are even instances when the number exceeds 100 per cent because the faithful come not only to the morning but also to the afternoon mass in place of Vespers. Moreover, the averages for the rural dioceses or the rural parts of mixed dioceses are high, amounting to between 70 to 75 per cent.[6] In the cities, mass attendance is somewhat lower, but recent surveys have shown that it varies from 35 to 50 per cent.[7]

Information concerning the second compulsory duty, Communion at Easter time, is equally scanty. The diocesan offices have data but they have not been fully analysed. From survey data it seems that the numbers fulfilling this precept are somewhat higher than the figures for Sunday Mass attendance. The explanation is relatively easy. The practice of going to Confession and Communion in Advent and during Lent has a long tradition. Moreover the great majority of parishes hold Lenten missions and retreats followed by Confession for those also who rarely go to church on Sundays. It can be assumed that the total number of those who go to Confession and Communion at least once a year at Easter amounts to 85 per cent of those who are bound to do so. This proportion is considerably higher in some districts although lower in the cities.[8]

In spite of such a high proportion of those who fulfil the Easter duty the annual number of Communions for individual Catholics is relatively low. In some parishes it does not exceed 10 per cent and rarely is it as high as 15. There are even rural parishes in which the average is only half this number. We must also take into account that the number of communicants is considerably inflated by primary[9] and secondary school[10] children who are

6. The data relates to the following dioceses: Tarnow (estimates by Fr. H. Kietlinski), Sandomierz (Rev. I. Wojciechowski), Gniezno (Rev. F. Welc), Warsaw (excluding the metropolitan area Rev. F. Olszewski) and several parishes in other dioceses.

7. The study was conducted by Rev. Taras.

8. It is assumed here that the total number of persons who are bound to receive Communion at Easter is approximately the same as the number bound to come to Mass on Sundays. Although the age at which Communion is received can be sometimes higher than 7, there are nevertheless in Poland additional causes that can give dispensation from Sunday Mass, e.g. illness, distance, etc. Our estimates are based on the surveys that have been carried out by the Department of Religious Sociology at the Catholic University in Lublin and also in the dioceses of Gniezno, Tarnow, Wroclaw, Olsztyn and others.

9. In Nowa Huta 41.5 per cent of children attending catechism classes received monthly Communion [Karsznia, 1962:68].

10. In Lublin 13 per cent of the secondary school sample received monthly Communion. In other cities the proportion is higher [Pyclik, 1960: 5].

exhorted by the catechists to go to Confession once a month and reminded about it continuously. In view of this, the global picture which emerges is not indicative of an intensive eucharistic life among adult Catholics. Pastoral emphases on Communion on the first Friday of each month is an attempt to develop the quality of eucharistic life. Only a small group of Catholics communicate daily or weekly, although, despite lack of pastoral emphasis, this practice is slowly being adopted by the intelligentsia.

All this does not necessarily imply that the eucharistic cult is weak or neglected. It tends to assume other forms, e.g. adoration rather than communion. Particularly in cities visits to church by young people on the way to school, workers on the way to factories and offices and housewives going shopping are relatively frequent. Special paraliturgical services such as the May, June or October devotions, evening Benedictions, Saturday devotions to Our Lady Queen of Poland or the so called perpetual novena, some of which attract large crowds, link exposition of the Blessed Sacrament or, at least Benediction, to Marian devotion. To understand the nature of religiosity in Poland one must fully realise the closeness of the link between the devotion to Our Lady and the eucharistic cult.

One practice which is virtually universal and, in the opinion of the people, absolutely compulsory is that of Lenten Missions. Most people, a proportion higher than those who attend Sunday mass, attend Lenten mission every year (and some also during Advent).

In addition to the paraliturgical practices organized by the clergy, there are also many traditional practices which are led by the laiety though occasionally with a participating priest. These include May devotions, hymn singing at wayside chapels and shrines, all kinds of votive devotions and especially pilgrimages. The pilgrimage movement in Poland is essentially, though not exclusively, Marian in character. On the feast days of Our Lady, as many as 100,000 people make their way to Czestochowa, the main shrine, and on special occasions the number of pilgrims reaches half a million. The pilgrimage movement is so universal that in some dioceses there is not a single parish which does not organise a pilgrimage every year.[11]

The problem of religious vocations in Poland merits special attention. The number of secular clergy is relatively small and inadequate; in 1960 there were 12,795 priests engaged in pastoral duties and the average ratio of faith-

11. This is shown for example in the map of pilgrimages in the Tarnow diocese which has been prepared by Fr. W. Witkowski, C.S.S.R. The nation-wide spread of the sources of pilgrimages that head for Czestochowa during the week preceding the feast of Our Lady on 15 August, is illustrated in a map prepared by Tereliza Braun in the Polish Academy of Sciences. There is also a study by Rev. W. Piwowarski [1964, pp. 115–198] who describes the unique character of the rural votive pilgrimages in Warmia which are called 'losiery'.

ful per priest was 1/2,291. Moreover, the clergy are unequally distributed. While in the Tarnow diocese in 1960 there was one priest for every 1,318 faithful, in the Lodz diocese the ratio was 1/3,511. In only five dioceses was this ratio less than 1/2,000 while in three dioceses it was in excess of 1/3,000[12]

The total number of members of religious orders for men in Poland in 1961 was over eight thousand (8,103) out of which half (4,097) were ordained priests. Hence, in comparison with the secular clergy the number of priests in religious orders is relatively small, though it has increased in recent decades at a faster rate than that of the diocesan clergy and many orders have taken charge of parishes. There was a marked rise in the number of priestly vocations between the end of World War II and 1956, but since then numbers have declined.

The rise in religiosity, particularly among certain groups of the population during the postwar period, the cumulative effect of the war-time lag on the number of late vocations, and the extension of secondary education to rural youth are social factors relevant to the increase in priestly vocations. It is too early yet to say whether the current decline is a temporary phase or the beginning of a long term change. [Zdaniewicz, 1960, pp. 525–534; Wawro, 1961; Majka, 1967, pp. 48–57].

Vocations among women in Poland increased from the inter war period until 1956, without the fluctuations, during and after the war, characteristic of male vocations. Currently there are 29,512 nuns in some 100 religious orders, most of which are engaged in an active apostolate.

A feature of the religious practices of the Polish laiety is their close association with the clergy, the relative ease with which people submit to the control of the clergy, and the high prestige of the priest in society as evidenced by several studies [Lisowski, 1962; Piwowarski, 1962; 1964]. Even the traditional practices many of which are part of folk-lore do not take place without the consent of the priest and his participation. When the initiative regarding religious practice comes from the faithful, it is always carried out in consultation with the pastor and in any case with the consciousness of his approval. This influence and control of the clergy over religious practice is the result of constant and organized pastoral care. This is also a characteristic feature of the catechetic spiritual formation of Polish Catholics. Its manifestations can be seen in the fact that all major pastoral 'actions' undertaken by the Church find a ready response amongst the faithful.

12. The distribution of priests in the various dioceses is illustrated in a map prepared by Rev. T. Makowski. This ratio was of course a lot worse during the years immediately after World War II.

RELIGIOSITY AND SOCIO-CULTURAL FACTORS IN THE PAST

A full account of the religiosity of yesterday would present some difficulty since there have been very few sociological studies in the past. Some early ones, e.g. those of L. Krzywicki, S. Czarnowski and F. Znaniecki although marred by the lack of modern standards of methodological rigour do give a partial picture, particularly of the religiosity of the Polish peasantry. Moreover, recent sociological research based on historical material, including some of the author's as yet unpublished work, provide supplementary material.

The Polish gentry was traditionally and institutionally religious. This religiosity, mainly Catholic in character, constituted an element not only of their life style as a class but also of their social position and role as the owners of large estates and the patrons of parish churches. As such they had a certain voice in the choice of parish priests and therefore helped to maintain social order through their influence on the clergy. This does not mean that their religiosity was interest-oriented or even purely traditional; some sections of the gentry played an important part in the process of religious revival before World War I and during the inter-war period members of the gentry were particularly active in Catholic Action and in such pioneer organizations as *Odrodzenie* and the Association of Polish Catholic Intelligentsia [Strzeszewski and Majka, 1966].

The intelligentsia as a social class was not homogeneous in its religiosity. On the one hand, some were greatly influenced by the philosophy of positivism and neopositivism. The latter was particularly responsible for shaping the outlook of university graduates and indirectly of people with secondary education. Indeed, at the beginning of this century a university graduate or a student had to be (in a sense in principle and because of the pressure of his social environment) a non-believer [Turowski, 1937]. There was a shock reaction in these circles when the first priest was appointed to a university chair and when the first Catholic organizations (such as the sodalities and *Odrodzenie*) were set up among the students [Strzeszewski and Majka, 1966]. On the other hand, deeply patriotic, even messianic romanticism was influential among the intelligentsia and there was a strong movement towards deepening the religious basis of this outlook, as for example in the highly dynamic *Eleusis* movement which played an important part in forming [Pawlowski, 1962] the religious foundation of the Polish Scout movement.

The religiosity of the Polish cities varied according to the composition of the population and the dynamics of social and economic change. In the small towns of former Galicia and the Russian occupation zone, crafts and commerce were in the hands of the Jews while the Polish inhabitants derived their livelihood mainly from agriculture. The Jews preserved their cultural and religious separateness. There was a traditional religiosity intent upon all the minutia of ritual prescriptions but the religiosity of the Polish population of these towns was not much different from that of the peasantry.

In the urban districts of the Prussian occupation zone and particularly in the district of Poznan the towns had a predominantly Polish population and displayed much economic and social dynamism in resisting the pressures of German occupation. The Catholic clergy were the main leaders and this gave them tremendous social prestige and made it easier to extend their religious influence. For this reason the religiosity of the Poznan district was deepened and consolidated earlier than in other parts of Poland and retained its exemplary position during the inter-war period when the city became the See of the Primate of Poland, the headquarters of Catholic Action and the centre of pastoral and social work in the whole of the Polish Church.

There was yet a different pattern in the towns which developed during the first phase of industrialization (end of nineteenth and beginning of twentieth centuries) particularly in Upper Silesia and some parts of the former Congress Kingdom (e.g. the Dabrowa Coal Basin, Warsaw, Lodz). The rapid industrialization of Silesia coincided with the active political, social and pastoral role of a clergy attempting to meet the spiritual needs of the rapidly increasing population. In spite of the difficulties (e.g. German colonization, Jewish settlement, the *Kulturkampf*) this work produced totally unexpected results and gave lie to the thesis that industrialization and urbanisation will invariably bring about a decline in religiosity. It seems that in an industrialized working class district it was possible not only to maintain a high level of religious practice and to extend religious organization, but also to create new working class religious traditions which persisted in spite of later difficulties and political pressures [Bigdon, 1968].

In the former Russian zone of occupation, where the occupant deliberately maintained low standards of priestly education, the situation was not so advantageous and consequently there was a marked progress towards the dechristianization of major working class centres. In total, however, the differences between the urban and rural religiosity are not so very great.

Several Polish sociologists of the inter-war period attempted a characterization of rural religiosity. Among these one should mention, in the first place, Stefan Czarnowski whose studies, published as collected works some twenty years after his death [1956], owe much to the influence of Durkheim and his pupils (M. Mauss and H. Hubert). This is why for Czarnowski, religion is above all an element of folk culture. He stresses that 'religious phenomena are a separate category of facts' [Czarnowski, 1956, Vol. II, p. 235] but that in 'religious facts there is manifested not only the influence but also the active co-operation of the social group as a whole'. Hence religious facts are 'social facts, while the representations on which they depend are collective representations' [Czarnowski, 1956, Vol. II, p. 238]. This means that for Czarnowski religion is an element of social culture, created by a given solid collectivity, more precisely by several collectivities, because 'culture is in its essence an inter-group phenomenon' [Czarnowski, 1956, Vol. I, pp. 19ff.]. The two concepts – religious culture and the religion of a given social group – are interchangeable [Czarnowski, 1956, Vol. I, p. 88; Majka, 1963, p. 456; 1967, pp. 227ff.].

When studying the religious culture of the Polish peasantry at the beginning of this century Czarnowski's [1956 Vol. I: 38–107] theoretical viewpoint led to a stress on the spontaneous reciprocal adaption between religion (in this case Catholicism) and the group which produces it. Polish peasant Catholicism is seen as a unique phenomenon with several characteristic features:

a. This religiosity is a form of religious nationalism which is *sui generis* and consists of a fusion of the elements of Polish national feeling and Catholicism – hence the belief that every Pole is a Catholic and that a Catholic who is not a Pole is a poor Catholic *(Dajczkatolik)*.

b. The second characteristic feature is its social, communal character. The connection with the local group is expressed through communal participation in religious worship and with the regional and national community, through the ties of religious consciousness with regional and national shrines as well as souvenirs brought from pilgrimages.

c. Rural religiosity is intimately connected with the daily round which it permeates:

> In this way every single moment of the peasant's life, from his birth to death, all his activities in the home and on the farm, his cares and his joys, his family homestead, his kin and the village as a whole – every single aspect of his life is protected by the Mother of God, Our Lady of Czestochowa, before whose shrine there take place religious manifestations of the faithful of the whole nation [Czarnowski, 1956, Vol. 1, pp. 88–107].

The character of the religious cult itself and its content are also connected with the family life and the agricultural cycle.

d. This Catholicism is still sensual and practical. There are few instances of mysticism, fewer theoretical disputes or philosophical discussions. Realism is the keynote and all religious representations such as images of the Saints, while the moral elements play a minor part. Sensualism is expressed in a vigorous cult of the images, connected particularly with definite places and the tendency to dramatization.

e. Finally, rural religiosity is traditional and full of ritual; any attempt to introduce changes produces violent reaction for it would undermine the forms of social interaction.

> The peasant until recently would feel a loss of his identity and of his membership of a certain collectivity, with specific functions in it, if he had not scrupulously fulfilled those religious functions which are traditional for this collectivity [Czarnowski, 1956, Vol. 1, p. 106].

Though undoubtedly interesting, the documentation, limited to selected examples, is inadequate. Czarnowski's work was published at the time (1937) when important changes had begun to take place in the religiosity of rural Poland. He seemed to perceive them when he wrote:

> Rural Poland, during the last thirty years, and particularly since the war [i. e. World War I] is undergoing a spiritual ferment. This process is accelerating all the time, reaching deeper and deeper, and is of course closely connected with the transformations in the whole nation. The changes that take place seem to foreshadow significant and far-reaching transformation in the form of religious life both in the direction of separating it from the rest of commercial life and in the matter of deepening its ethical and doctrinal content [Czarnowski, 1956, Vol. 1, p. 107].

Czarnowski's characterization, moreover, is unidimensional. He does not perceive any geographical differentials which could have been observed at the time he wrote his essay, nor does he show any traces of religious stratification. Czarnowski's comments resemble in several respects earlier pronouncements by L. Krzywicki who also was influenced by Durkheim's school though more so by historical materialism. Krzywicki conducted studies of the religiosity of the district of Zmudz [1906] but also wrote an essay on Pilgrimage to the shrine of Czestochowa in which he gives a Marxist interpretation [1923, pp. 147–164].

An interesting assessment of Polish peasant religiosity has been given by the authors of the well known book on the Polish peasant, W.I. Thomas and F. Znaniecki [1928]. They distinguish four religious types among the peasants, which may separately, or in combination, correspond to separate human groups or to four stages in the development of religiosity. [Thomas and Znaniecki, 1958, p. 206].

a. The first type represents a specific religious-magical attitude, characterized by a tendency toward animism, a feeling of solidarity with nature and a devotional attitude towards it. Individualization of even the most common objects, ascribing to the animals ability to understand and morally appraise the human being, paying special attention to certain places, objects and animals, and respect for some persons and dislike or fear of others, are all manifestations of this frame of mind. Certain elements of religion are inseparably mixed here with magic. There is also some interplay with aesthetic perception though, on this point, the authors are not very convincing.

b. The second system of religious beliefs is based upon the admission of a world of spirits within, beside or above natural objects. There are good spirits that help man, and evil spirits, that may harm him. Several examples of these are given by the authors; the water spirits *(Boginki)* the midday woman *(Poludnica)*, cloud-beings *(Planetniki)* and a horrid old woman *(Jedza)* who eats children. Most of these beliefs were introduced with Christian dogmas concerning apparition of the angels, devils and souls of the dead. The authors argue that the belief in spirits contains some religious elements, but that the practices connected with it are in essence, magical; hence Christian religious practices may be perceived by some as a form of magic.

c. The third type, based on the idea of a moral unity of the human society under the leadership of the priest, is purely Christian and contains no magical or pagan elements. The parish is a kind of great family whose members are united by a community of moral interests and this is manifested in active participation in divine service, celebrations of feast days, pilgrimages and a special devotion to the Virgin Mary and some saints. On such occasions a group demonstrates consciousness of its unity not only by the mere fact of its presence in one place, but also by its community of interests and attitudes.

d. Religion, as a mystical connection between the individual and God expressed by attitudes of love, personal subordination, desire for personal perfection and eternal life with God, is little developed among the peasants. The peasant is a practical man: religion remains interwoven with his practical interests, while mysticism requires precisely a liberation from those interest. Manifestations of mysticism can be observed, however, in emergencies and times of crisis. This type is also to be found among the peasant women who migrated [Thomas and Znaniecki, 1958, p. 206].

## RELIGIOSITY AND SOCIO-CULTURAL FACTORS IN THE PRESENT

Studies of structural differences in Polish religiosity have only just begun, but some results may be reported.

'The opening up' of country areas to contact with the cities, and the accessability of mass communication media, has contributed to the change in the religious profile of the rural population. The characteristics given by Czarnowski, Thomas and Znaniecki as well as the traditional distinction between rural and urban religiosity no longer correspond to reality – indeed they were never completely proved. No radical rural-urban differences in religious practices can be observed either in quantity or quality.

Nor is it possible in Poland today to talk about the de-Christianization of suburban areas of the cities. The studies carried out in one of the suburbs of Cracow, one which has been badly neglected in religious and moral terms, have shown that the laiety play an active part in the setting up and development of new parishes [Lis, 1963].

Although a full analysis of the religiosity of different age groups, would require more detailed studies, it is possible on present data to reconstruct a general picture. The introduction of compulsory school attendance (both in law and in fact) has contributed to an extension of the Church's influence among children. Catechism classes were provided at first at school, and later, after the teaching of religion in schools was prohibited, in after-school classes in churches and chapels. In spite of initial difficulties of an organizational nature and difficult conditions under which classes are being held in large cities and new industrial centres,[13] attendance has been good. Nearly all primary and a very high proportion of secondary school children have been included in the programme.[14] The situation is worse in some large cities where less than 50 per cent of secondary school children have been in-

13. The attendance at catechism classes from all primary schools in Nowa Huta was as follows:

| *Grade* | *% of children who enrolled* | *% attending* |
|---|---|---|
| I | 78.0 | 62.0 |
| II | 92.2 | 90.2 |
| III | 80.5 | 70.5 |
| IV | 78.2 | 63.5 |
| V | 75.8 | 68.1 |
| VI | 78.6 | 61.9 |
| VII | 74.9 | 53.1 |

The percentages are based on the total number of children in all primary schools in Nowa Huta [Karsznis, 1962, supplement].

14. As an example we can cite some data from a rural diocese (Tarnow) with an efficient system of catechetical instruction. The following percentages of the total school population in the various categories of schools were enrolled for catechism classes: primary schools – 98 per cent; secondary schools – 94 per cent; technical schools – 86 per cent (Fr. P. Bednarczyk's analysis of the statistics kept by the diocesan office).

cluded in catechism classes. There is correspondingly good attendance at Sunday Masses and monthly Holy Communion.[15]

The religious practices of adolescents do not differ very much from those of primary grades though the impact of the environment on their religiosity is much greater; the standard of practice of urban youth is a lot lower than that of rural youth. Also, the boys are less regular in practice than girls. The studies carried out in two middle-sized cities have shown that the basic religious practices were observed by approximately three-quarters of all male students and nearly all girl students attending secondary schools. Monthly Confession is less frequent than among primary school children (4 per cent of boys, 17 per cent of girls) but the proportion of those who never go to Confession is also very small (3 per cent).[16]

The religiosity of school leavers is not as well documented. Surveys undertaken by the Centre for Public Opinion Research of the Polish Radio show that 78.2 per cent of respondents consider themselves Catholics and 4.3 per cent as atheists; 70 per cent have never had any doubt about the basic religious practices; 75.4 per cent consider that it is their duty to bring up their children in faith and 76.4 per cent agree with the statement that it is not correct to sacrifice one's religious convictions for those whom one loves. On the other hand, only 26.7 per cent are not in favour of abortion and 41.8 per cent condemn this practice but only under certain circumstances [Skorzynska, 1960, p. 14].

Religiosity of university students presents a somewhat different picture. Surveys conducted over a period of three years among the students of Warsaw University seem to suggest that 70 per cent of students is loyal to the faith and Church, although about half do not practise regularly [Pawelczynska, 1961, p. 107]. Dissent from the moral norms of the church is even greater. The surveys carried out among female students in Lublin (excluding the students of the Catholic University) show that about three-quarters of them reject, at least in hypothetical terms, the Christian model of the family.[17]

A more detailed analysis of the relationship between religiosity and occupational structure is not possible with existing data. In particular little is known about the religiosity of the intelligentsia, and especially about an

15. In Nowa Huta, which is probably not a good example, owing to the industrial character of the town, 82.5 per cent of all children attends Mass on Sundays and a further 12.6 per cent three times a month [Karsznis, 1962, pp. 67ff.].

16. These studies were conducted a few years ago by Rev. W. Pyclik and Rev. F. Gawlik.

17. The following characteristics of the Christian model of family were included in the questionnaire Survey conducted by K. Sajdok; insolubility of marriage, premarital chastity, faithfulness in marriage, rejection of neo-malthusian principles, prohibition of abortion.

ever increasing number of the 'technical intelligentsia'. All we have at our disposal are some inital and not wholly representative items of information concerning the religious attitudes of teachers and university professors.

The studies in Lodz (i.e. in a city traditionally dominated by the working classes and Socialist supporters) have shown that 60.3 per cent of male teachers and 63.2 per cent of women teachers take part in religious practices; teachers with secondary school education are more religious (62 per cent) than those who have a university degree or at least some university experience (58.1 per cent). Younger teachers (aged between 18 and 24) have a higher proportion of persons who practice (75.2 per cent) than older teachers (50 years and over) among whom only 49.6 per cent admitted to practice [Wedrychowicz, 1961, pp. 49ff].

A survey of university staffs found that 54 per cent of respondents admit some ties with the church and 55 per cent maintain some practices of religion. More than a third declared an indifferent attitude to religion, while 7.7 per cent are prepared to combat it [Nowakowska, 1961]. However, due to a low response rate (1,366 persons in a sample of 5,000) and the fragmentary way the findings have been published, the validity of these data cannot be established.

Among the intelligentsia several groups can be distinguished:

a. First, there are the survivors of the older intelligentsia, elderly people who were brought up in an atmosphere of religious patriotism, and in this sense can be said to derive their religiosity from the *Eleusis* movement [Pawlowski, 1962]. These people are loyal to the church and orthodox in doctrinal matters but, while sympathetic to the Christian cultural tradition and its moral discipline are, in fact, not very close to the church and largely ignorant of her theological and particularly social teaching. This type of religiosity has to be distinguished from the political Catholicism of the people who are ideologically close to the former National Democratic Party.
b. There are an increasing number of Catholics who attempt to understand the teachings of the Gospels in their entirety and to live wholly within Christian culture. Their religiosity extends beyond the conventional practices, and being often more zealous than the clergy, this sometimes leads to a peculiar form of anticlericalism. The Catholic organizations (especially youth organizations) of the inter-war period[18] and today in particular the adult catechetical movement, provide the roots of this ideological formation.

18. We have in mind here the student youth organisations such as *Odrodzenie*, the *Sodalities*, *Inventus Christiana*, etc.

c. The latter group blend into a large group whose religiosity is traditional. They have stronger ties with the Church as an institution than with Christianity as a body of moral precepts and teachings, some of which they occasionally question or misunderstand.
d. The rapidly growing 'technical intelligentsia' forms another group about whose religiosity little is known. It seems to be traditional in character, and characterized by observance and basic religious practices, though how it will develop cannot be predicted.
e. A small but significant proportion (10–20 per cent) of the intelligentsia, 'the Catholics with a baptismal certificate', are members of the church in name only. They are not hostile to the church but because of their social position temporal preoccupation or rejection of the moral precepts of the church, they remain apart.
f. There is also a small group of humanists and positivists, mainly represented by the older generation, who while not in principle hostile to religion, consider it as a pseudo-problem, and are indifferent to all religious questions.
g. Finally there are the convinced atheists who are often greatly interested in the matters of religion and the church. They could be divided into two groups: the philosophical atheists who feel unable to reconcile their personal outlook with religion and the social atheists who consider the church as an anti-humanistic institution or an alien political force. This is a relatively small group which does not constitute a large proportion (less than 1 per cent) of the Polish intelligentsia.

## CONCLUSION

It would be difficult to give an unambiguous answer on the prospects for religiosity in Poland without oversimplification. We are still in a period of transition which is full of difficulties and dangers. We hear a great deal about the laicization of life in Poland, but at the same time it would be difficult to deny that there exists a distinct and powerful drive for the manifestation of the people's religious convictions. The traditional functions of religion, which are so apparent in the rural communities, are less in evidence in urban communities, but there is no realization in the minds of the people of any dysfunctional properties of Christianity. To the contrary, one can safely argue that there is a growing awareness of new functional effects of Christianity in the life of a modern, urbanized society and, in particular, in the life of the Polish society today. This explains the growing interest in Christianity among the circles of the intelligentsia, where, until recently, criticism of religion was considered a norm of behaviour.

This phenomenon is undoubtedly linked with the general rise in living standards and a growing interest in spiritual culture. Until recently the French worker rejected religion because he maintained that the Church in its alliance with the rich, was an obstacle in his fight for better living conditions. This was a social obstacle to the acceptance of Christianity as an idea of the Kingdom of God. The Polish peasant was attached to religion because it entered his daily existence and helped him in his fight for better living conditions; this removed an obstacle to acceptance of the Church's teaching and the graces of salvation. Today when the fight for a daily existence is moved to a more remote plane, the questions concerning the purpose of life and the bases of existence assume greater importance. The point of contact with Christianity is more direct while its social and economic conditions lose in importance.

The social function of religion – moral, social, educational and humanistic – assume a different meaning. Religiosity itself becomes less institutional, less formalized and more 'Gospel-oriented'. We have put the latter term in quotation marks to emphasise that this form of Christianity need not be highly authentic; indeed it can perhaps be a search for authenticity. This search may involve some criticism and may even border on heresy. But this, however, need not mean questioning the role of the Church or a formal act of leaving the Church; the search is a way of pleading for new and more effective forms.

An associated factor is a change in the motivation of religious practices and forms of behaviour. The motivation which could perhaps be described as cosmological, and which involves a daily and direct dependence on God, is being shifted to a second plane. In its place is a new form of motivation which relies on the motives of perfection, salvation and mysticism. In the secondary, social motivation of religious practice there is also a shift away from socio-cultural (customs, association with the local or national culture) to socio-religious motivation which emanates from the consciousness of belonging to a religious community in association with the church [Majka, 1967].

The whole picture of religiosity in Poland is still traditional, but in it we can discern certain factors of change. Whether these are the elements of a new picture or the symptoms of de-christianization cannot be answered in terms of an easy over-simplification. Each of these factors of change requires separate analysis, so that the symptoms of de-christianization are not confused with the symptoms of the rise in religiosity.

REFERENCES AND SELECTED BIBLIOGRAPHY

Bigdon, R., *Religijnosc mieszkancow Bytomia w dobie industrializacji; Na przykladzie parafii NMP w Bytomiu od polowy XIX wieku de pierwszej wojny swiatowej* [The Religiosity of the People of Bytom during the Era of Industrialization: as shown in the Parish of St Mary's from the Middle of the 19th Century to World War I]. Unpublished. Ph.D. thesis. Lublin, Catholic University of Lublin, 1968.

Borkowicz, W., 'Rozwod po polsku' [Divorce in Poland]. *Polityka* 8, 1964.

Ciupak, E., 'Religijnosc Warszawiakow' [Religiosity of Inhabitants of Warsaw]. *Argumenty* 8, 1964.

Czarnowski, C., *Dziela* [Collected Works]. Vols. I-II. Warszawa, P.W.N., 1956.

Gorski, K., 'Genealogia religijnosci polskiej w XX wieku' [Genealogy of Polish Religiosity in the 20th Century]. *Znak*, 9, 1957.

—, *Od religijnosci do mistyki* [From religion to mysticism]. Lublin, Catholic University of Lublin, 1962.

Grabski, A. F., *Boleslaw Chrobry* [Boleslaw Chrobry]. Warsaw, P.W.N., 1966.

Karsznia, Father Niward, *Srodowisko spoleczne a religijnosc dzieci*. Unpublished Master's thesis. Lublin, Catholic University of Lublin, 1962.

Krzywicki, L., *Zmudz starozytna* [Ancient Zmudz]. Warsaw, 1906.

—, 'Do Jasnej Gory' [To Jasna Gora (Our Lady Shrine of Czestochowa)]. *Studia Socjologiczne* (Warsaw), I, 1923, pp. 147–164.

Lis, S., *Formowanie sie parafii podmiejskiej i jej przemiany* [The Formation of a Suburban Parish and its Transformations]. Unpublished Master's thesis. Lublin, Catholic University of Lublin, 1963.

Lisowski, S., *Akcja Charytatywna a duszpasterstwo; Na przykladzie koscielnej akcji dobroczynnej w latach 1945–1949* [Charitable Works and Pastoral Work; using as an Example the Church's Work in 1945–49]. Unpublished Ph.D. thesis. Lublin, Catholic University of Lublin, 1965.

—, *Zagadnienie dystansu spolecznego miedzy inteligencja a duchowienstwem* [The problem of Social Distance Between the Laity and Clergy]. Unpublished Master's thesis. Lublin, Catholic University of Lublin, 1962.

Majka, Rev. J., *Postawy religijne pracownikow nauki* [Religious Attitudes of Scientific Workers]. Lublin 1963a (Typescript).

—, 'La sociologie de la religion en Pologne' [The Sociology of Religion in Poland]. *Social Compass* 10, 1963b.

—, 'Koscielna dzialalnosc dobroczynna w Polsce w XIX i pierwszej polowie XX wieku' [Charitable Work of the Church in Poland in the 19th and the First Half of the 20th Century]. *Zeszyty Naukowe*, (Catholic University of Lublin), IX (1–2), 1966a.

—, 'Duszpasterstwo polskie na przelomie Tysiaclecia' [Pastoral Work in Poland on the Eve of the Second Millennium]. *Homo Dei* 35, 1966b.

—, 'Caritas and Postwar Reconstruction', in: Zatko, J. J. (ed.), *The Valley of Silence*. London, Notre Dame, 1967a.

—, 'Sociology of Religion in Poland', in: Zatko, J. J. (ed.), *The Valley of Silence*. London, Notre Dame, 1967b.

—, 'Socjografia powolan kaplanskich w Polsce' [The Sociography of Priestly Vocations in Poland]. *Ateneum Kaplanskie* 70, 1967c.

—, 'Gdzie jestesmy' [Where Do We Stand]. *Tygodnik Powszechny*, 21 (42), 1967d.

—, 'The Character of Polish Catholicism'. *Social Compass* 15, 1968, pp. 185–208.

*Maly Rocznik Statystyczny 1939 (M.R.S.)* [Concise Statistical Yearbook for 1939]. Warsaw, G.U.S.

Markiewicz, S., *Wspolczesne chrzescijanstwo w Polsce* [Contemporary Christianity in Poland]. Warsaw, Ksiazka i Wiedza, 1967.

Mirek, F., *Elementy spoleczne parafii rzymsko-katolickiej* [Social Elements of a Roman Catholic Parish]. Poznan, Wyd. Poznanskie, 1928.

Myslek, W., *Kosciol Katolicki w Polsce w Latach 1918–1939* [The Catholic Church in Poland, 1918–1939]. Warsaw, Ksiazka i Wiedza, 1966.

Nowakowska, I., 'Swiatopoglad pracownikow nauki' [The Outlook of the Man of Learning]. *Argumenty*, 5 (32), 1961.

Pawelczynska, 'Les attitudes des étudiants varsoviens envers la religion', [The Attitude of Warsaw Students Towards Religion]. *Archives de sociologie des religions*, 12, 1961.

—, *Dynamika przemian religijnych na wsi* [The dynamics of religious changes in the country]. Warsaw, P.W.N., 1966.

Pawlowski, T., *Zalozenia programowe i dzialalnosc speleczna Zwiazku Filaretow 'Eleusis'* [The Programme and Social Activity of the Filaret Society 'Eleusis']. Unpublished Master's thesis. Lublin, Catholic University of Lublin, 1962.

Piekarski, S., *Wyznania religijne w Polsce, Warszawa 1927* [Religious Denominations in Poland]. Warsaw, Wyd. Prawnicze, 1927.

Pirozynski, M. and Szczech. S., *Rocznik Statystyczny Kosciola Katolickiego w Polsce 1937* [Statistical Yearbook of the Catholic Church in Poland 1937]. Lublin, Catholic University of Lublin, 1938.

Pirozynski, M., *Statystyka Kosciola Katolickiego w Polsce* [Statistics of the Catholic Church in Poland]. Lublin, Catholic University of Lublin, 1935.

Piwowarski, W., *Ksieza w opinii parafian wiejskich* [Clergy in the Opinion of Their Urban Parishioners]. Lublin, 1962 (Typescript).

—, 'Ksieza w opinii parafian miejskich'. *Wiez*, 7 (5), 1964.

—, 'Typologia religijna katolikow poludniowej Warmii' [Religious Typology of Catholics in Southern Warmia]. *Studia Warminskie*, (1), 1964b.

—, 'La Pratique religieuse dans les villes polonaises au cour de vingt dernières années' [Religious practice in Polish towns during the past twenty years]. *Social Compass*, 15, pp. 277–284, 1968.

Pyclik, W., *Religijnosc miejskiej mlodziezy licealnej* [Religiosity of Senior Secondary School Students]. Lublin, Catholic University of Lublin, 1960 (Typescript).

*Rocznik Statystyczny (R.S.)* [Statistical Yearbook]. Warsaw, G.U.S., 1945ff.

Sajdok, K., *Stosunek mlodziezy do chrzescijanskiego modelu rodziny* [The Attitude of Youth to the Christian Model of the Family]. Unpublished M.A. thesis Lublin, Catholic University of Lublin, 1964.

Skorzynska, Zofia, and Szaniawska, M. (eds.), *Swiatopoglad mlodziezy a przynaleznosc do organizacji mlodziezowych* [The Outlook of Youth and the Membership of Youth Organizations]. Public Opinion Research Bureau of the Polish Radio, 1960.

Strzeszewski, C. and J. Majka, *Mysl i dzialalnosc spoleczna Kosciola w Polsce w dwudziestoleciu miedzywojennym* [Social Thought and Social Work of the Church in Poland during the Inter-war Period]. Lublin, 1966 (Typescript).

Taras, P., *Spoleczne uwarunkowania i motywy wstapienia do zakonnego seminarium duchownego* [Social background and motives of enrolment in monastic seminaries]. Poznan, Pallottinum, 1969.

Thomas, W. I. and F. Znaniecki, *Polish Peasant in Europe and America.* New York, Macmillan, 1958.

Turowski, K., 'Renesans katolicyzmu mlodego pokolenia polskiego' [The Renaissance of Catholicism among Poland's Youth]. *Przeglad Powszechny,* 1937.

Urban, W., *Ostatni etap dziejow Kosciola w Polsce przed nowym Tysiacleciem, 1815–1965* [The Last Phase of the History of the Church in Poland before the Next Millennium, 1815–1965]. Rome, Hosianum, 1966.

Wartolowska, Z., 'Osada i grod w Wislicy' [The Settlement and Castle in Wislica] *Odkrycia w Wislicy* (Warsaw), 1963.

Wawro, *Powolania kaplanskie a srodowisko spoleczne* [Religious Vocations and the Social Environment]. Lublin 1961 (Typescript).

Wedrychowicz, A., 'Przyczynek do badan nad udzialem nauczycieli lodzkich w praktykach religijnych' [A Contribution to the Study of Religious Practice by the Teachers of Lodz]. *Euhemer,* 5 (6), 1961.

Zatko, J. J. (ed.), *The Valley of Silence.* London, Notre Dame, 1967.

Zdaniewicz, W., *Wskazania Piusa XI w liscie 'Quae nobis' a ich realizacja w Polsce* [The Teachings of Pius XI in his Encyclical '*Quae nobis*' and their Implementation in Poland]. Unpublished Ph.D. thesis. Lublin, Catholic University of Lublin, 1958.

—, 'Zagadnienie kryzysu powolan kleryckich w zakonach meskich w Polsce' [The Problem of Religious Vocations in the Male Orders in Poland]. *Homo Dei,* XXIX, 1960.

AUGUSTO QUERIDO

# Portugal

## RELIGIOUS PRACTICE

In this study[1] of conformity amongst Portuguese Catholics, we will use the terminology which has been proposed by Gabriel Le Bras. According to him

> the overwhelming majority of Christians can be graded into three categories: the seasonal, the observant or the devout conformists, according to whether they accept (or their family decides to accept) the solemn, periodical or exceptional acts [Le Bras, 1955, p. 400].

We do not possess even approximate figures of 'devout'. This is indeed the type which is most difficult to approach because the 'practices' which characterize its members are the most personal and therefore least visible. It is known that nuclei of very fervent young Catholics have been formed in academic circles and in the pilot parishes of Lisbon. One of these nuclei of 'devout', who are enthusiasts for biblical and liturgical revival, intimate groups, film clubs and Christian democracy, is formed by the supporters of the journal *Encontro*.

We know of only three dioceses which have made comprehensive surveys of the observers of Sunday duty: Lisbon, Portalegre and Faro. The results of the census of Lisbon have been published in a special issue of the periodical *Novellae Olivarum* [1956] by the founder of the sociology of Catholicism in Portugal, Abbé Falcao. The rate of observance for the entire diocese, which embraces part of the districts of Santarém and Setubal, was 17.2 per cent. It was almost the same as for the city of Lisbon: of the men, 9.4 per cent practised, of the women 20.3 per cent and of the children (7–14 years) 30.4 per cent. Among the rural population of the diocese the percentage of those practising ranged from 38 per cent in the extreme north to 1.2 per cent of the men and 5.8 per cent of the women and children in a parish of the 'Leziras' on the shore of the Tagus.

1. This article first appeared in the *Archives de Sociologie des Religions*, VII, Jan.-June, 1959.

The results of the census of Faro, in the extreme south of Portugal, have been published by the bishop of that diocese, Mgr Francisco Rendeiro, in the periodical *Lumen* [Nov. 1953]. The total percentage of practising people was 15 per cent for the town of Faro and 8 per cent for the entire diocese.

The surveys which were carried out by all the clergy of the diocese of Portalegre, under the direction of Canon Boulard, show that the diocese falls into two zones: the most observant zone to the north of the Tagus and the less observant zone to the south. The existence of these large non-observant rural areas to the south of the Tagus is borne out by the three surveys.

This study particularly emphasizes 'periodic conformity', as we have found in the statistics of the registry office an index of periodic conformity which is established quite firmly and covers the entire country: the rate of Catholic marriages. The value of this index is due to the original regulation about marriage in Portugal which was established by the Concordat of 7 May 1940 between the Holy See and the Republic of Portugal. Article 22 of the Concordat states that:

> the State of Portugal recognizes the civil consequences of marriages which are celebrated according to canonical laws, with the condition that the act of marriage is also entered in the civil registers of the relevant offices...

The value of this conformity is particularly enhanced by the fact that by choosing canonical marriage the Portuguese automatically renounce the right to divorce. Indeed, according to Article 24 of the same Concordat:

> in accordance with the essential nature of Catholic marriage, it is understood that, by the very fact of celebrating canonical marriage, the spouses renounce the legal right to ask for divorce, which right cannot be applied by the civil tribunals to Catholic marriages.

Figure 1, which has been constructed on the basis of the rate of Catholic marriages for the period 1949–54, gives us a quite accurate picture of the extent to which Portuguese Catholics conform. The country is clearly divided into two parts by the Tagus River. A more detailed analysis would lead us to distinguish a still transitional area located on both sides of this religious boundary. This hypothesis is confirmed very well by surveys carried out in Lisbon and Portalegre on Sunday observers. These two dioceses cover in fact almost the whole of that transitional area and show rates of observance which are lower than those of the dioceses in the north but higher than those of the southern dioceses.

*Figure 1*
*Percentage of Catholic marriages in relation to the total number of marriages, 1949–1953*

*Figure 2*
*Birth rates, 1951–1955*

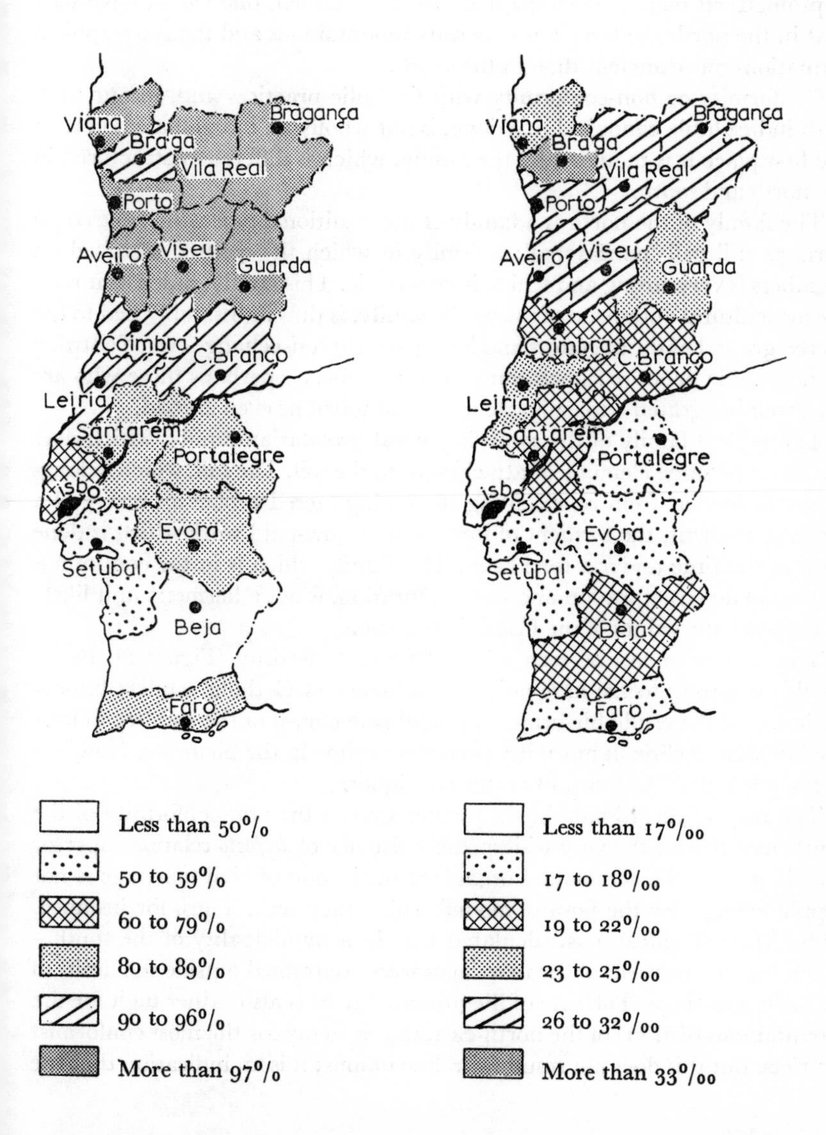

## DEMOGRAPHIC AND ECONOMIC FACTORS IN THE DISTRIBUTION OF RELIGIOUS PRACTICES

Our sole aim here is to gather elements for an explanation of this behavioural difference between the north and south. We have therefore prepared a whole series of maps, giving economic and demographic data, on which these two Portugals are always clearly delimited. If a geological and a hypsometrical map of Portugal had also been added, one would have seen that in the north the terrain is generally mountainous and the geographical formations more ancient than in the south.

Conformity or non-conformity with Catholic practices and, in our case, with indissoluble canonical marriage, is not wholly an individual choice. In the first place it is moulded by the family, which is differently structured in the north and south.

The family of the north is a family of the traditional type which one could perhaps still call 'patriarchal': a family in which the control exercised on members is very strong and which is very static. This family, based as it is on the agricultural enterprise of the whole family, is thus indissolubly tied to the sacred ground of the ancestors and is prepared to resist change even if a strong demographic pressure impels some of its members – perhaps those who are least well integrated – to emigrate to coastal towns or even abroad.

The typical family of the south is a rural proletarian family, which does not have the same element of attachment to the soil. The soil, which belongs to the *Senhor*, far from representing something sacred evokes an image of a place of torment, the torment of intermittent, low-paid work which is done most of the time under a torrid sun. This family which is in the continuous process of de-structuration and re-structuration, is not a hermetic unit likely to conserve the values of the Catholic tradition.

That this is so can be seen with reference to fertility (Figure 2). But it would be wrong to see here only the influence of Catholic values; the co-variation of the crude birthrate and deathrate curves of the country follows the law that decline in mortality precedes decline in the birthrate. Now it is in the north that the mortality rates are higher.

The map of illegitimate births further stresses the non-conformity of the south, as it reveals the very widespread existence of *de facto* relationships: for certain groups the ceremonial organized institution of civil marriage is not supple enough for the family 'model' which they seek. Thus, for instance, Abbe Manuel Falcao has calculated that in a municipality of the south – Odemira – 80 per cent of the marriages were contracted outside the limits of Catholic marriage. The rate of illegitimate births is also rather high for the mountainous districts of the north-east, that is to say for the most conformist districts. But this does not result from free unions; it is an indication that the

*Figure 3.*
*Rate of illegitimate births, 1951–1955 (per 1,000 live births)*

*Figure 4.*
*Demographic growth rate, 1900–1950*

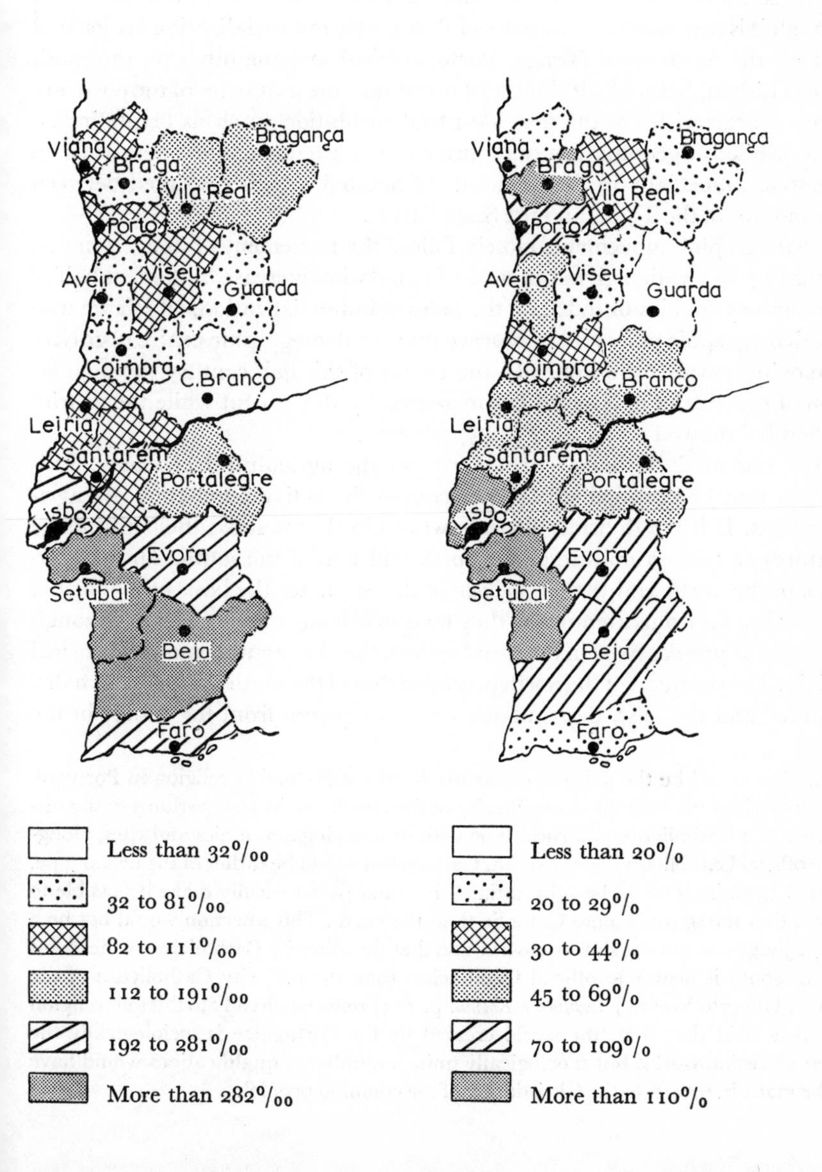

Catholic group does not always succeed in imposing its morality on the isolated populations in the mountains. It must be added that it is also these north-eastern districts which have the highest homicide rates in the country.[2]

The framework of the family interpenetrates the economic framework: on one hand it is based on the system of production and distribution, on the other hand it conditions the movement of the whole economy. The economy of the south is, taken as a whole, more dynamic than that of the north. Although it is true that the two poles of Portuguese industrialization are located one on the north coast (Braga, Porto, Aveiro) and the other on the south coast (Lisbon, Setubal), it should be noted that the industries of the north are those characteristic of the first industrial revolution (such as textile industries) while burgeoning heavy industry shows a tendency to concentrate in the south, especially in the peninsula of Setubal, which is located between the mouths of the Tagus and the Sado Rivers.

Demographic movements closely follow the movement of the economy. Thus Figure 4 which gives the rates of population increase in the first half of the century enables us to locate the poles of industrialization, which are also the demographic poles and to observe that the demographic centre of gravity is moving towards the south. In the course of this half century the population of the district of Guarda has increased by 16 per cent while the district of Setubal showed an increase of 137 per cent.

But our analysis bears particularly on the agricultural economy. It is known that in Portugal still 47 per cent of the active population are agriculturists. It is the division of land-ownership that bestows their distinctive features on the agriculture of the north and that of the south. The *minifundium* of the north and the *latifundium* of the south are the basis of a policy of waste; but far from attenuating they tend to become more marked. Although they are at present fixed in the social system, they have a well known historical origin. The conquest of the north preceded that of the south by one and a half a century and the oast, depopulated areas conquered from the Moors in the

2. This would be the point of departure for the study of folk religion in Portugal. An analysis of the content of conformity of the North would lead perhaps to the discovery of a Catholicism of a rural type with its own dogmas, ethics and rites, alongside official Catholicism. In the south, Catholicism would be rather of the urban type. If that hypothesis could be substantiated it would paradoxically make it possible to assert that the south is more Catholic than the north. This assertion would not be a value judgment but the simple observation that the minority Catholicism of the towns in the south is nearer to official Catholicism than the majority Catholicism of the north. Gilberto Freyre [*Aventura e Rotina*. p. 173] referred already to this folk religion when he said that that 'the world created by the Portuguese is sociologically the most Christian world. But theologically quite a number of qualifications would have to be made in regard to the Christianity of the common people'.

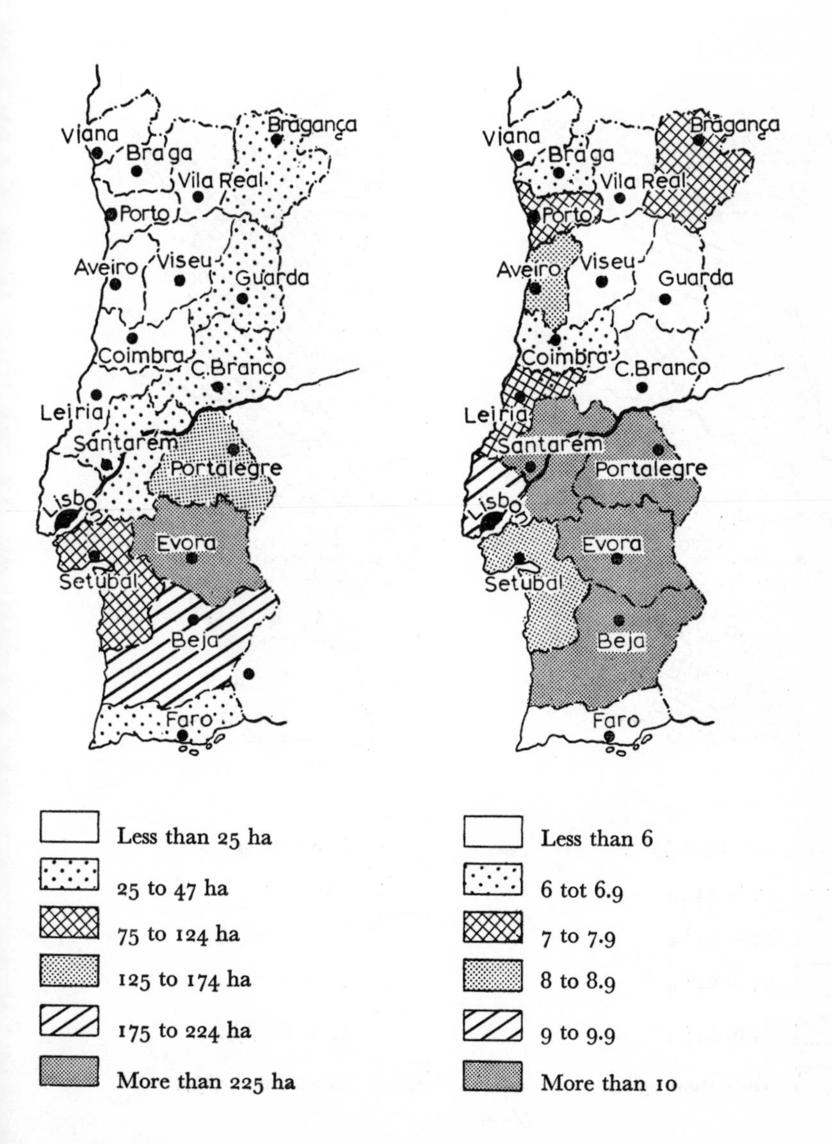


*Figure 5.*
*Size of holdings, average number of hectares per owner*

*Figure 6.*
*Value of agricultural production per person active in agriculture (per 1,000 escudes)*

*Figure 7.*
*Percentage of wage earning agricultural workers in the population which is active in agriculture*

*Figure 8.*
*Mortality rates*

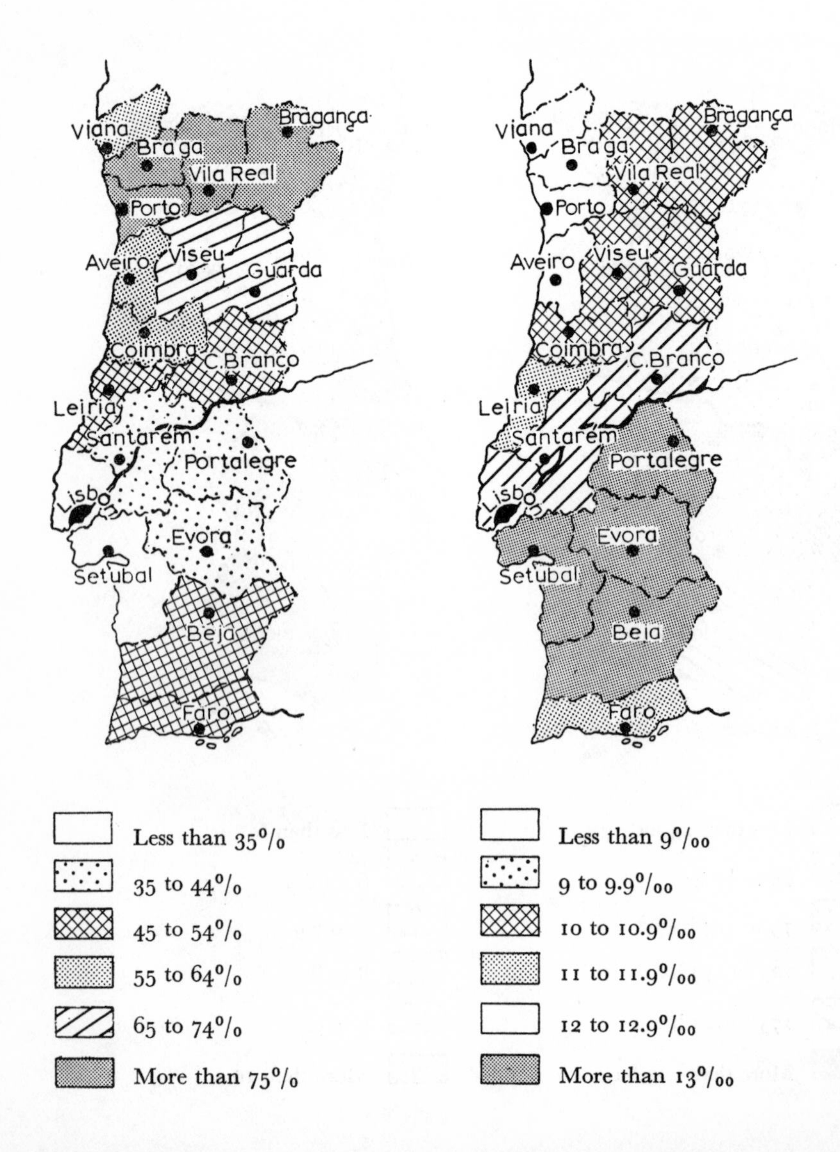

south were divided between the crown, the nobility and the military orders. It is this which lies at the origin of the concentration of property (shown in Figure 5).[3] Agriculture in the north is based on the family while that of the south is capitalistic. While the former uses only primitive equipment, the latter is considerably more mechanized and industrialized.[4]

The question of whether the north or the south have a higher standard of living is often discussed in Portugal. The mortality rate of the north certainly has its origin in very defective medical facilities and in very backward hygiene practices. This all forms part and parcel of a climate of social stagnation. The system by which income is distributed also varies between the two halves of the country. In the family enterprise typical of the north, the family provides the capital and the labour force; but in the end the family may consume the total production, which essentially serves only to cover its subsistence requirements. In the south the overwhelming majority of the active population (82 per cent of the district of Evora) has no other source of income than an average salary of 20 escudes for men and 10 escudes for women.

If seasonal unemployment is added, and it can last for half the year, one has the explanation for the existence in the south of a rural subproletariat, in which class consciousness can only accelerate. It is here we touch upon the richest element for a sociological explanation of non-conformity among Portuguese Catholics. A discontent social class tends to reject all the values of the society of which it forms a part and which it identifies with the values of the dominant class. If the total society is Catholic at least sociologically, then Catholicism is rejected.

This is why we think collective behaviour patterns of conformity or non-conformity in regard to Portuguese Catholicism can only be explained by the collective attitudes towards the Portuguese nation, or rather towards a certain conception of the Portuguese nation.

3. The *minifundium* and the *latifundium* are common, at the same latitude, to the whole Iberian Peninsula. A study of the entire peninsula would make it possible to ascertain whether this parallelism affects all aspects of social life.

4. In the northeastern district of the Vila Real, for example, there were only two tractors in 1950 for 191,000 persons active in agriculture. The north as a whole had 234 tractors while the total number of active agriculturalists was 2,096,000. This means that there was one tractor per 8,900 active agriculturalists. The south had 2,884 tractors for a total population of 1,110,000 active agriculturalists. In other words there was one tractor for every 380 persons. Such a difference in equipment is of course not without influence on the value of agricultural output and on social dynamics.

SELECTED BIBLIOGRAPHY

Andrade, Raimundo, 'Sociologie Religiosa e Apostolado' [Religious Sociology and the Apostolate]. *Lumen*, XX (2), 1956, 121–136.

Birot, Pierre, *Le Portugal. Etude de géographie regionale* [Portugal. A Study of Regional Geography]. Paris, A. Colin, 1950.

Carmo, Francisco, 'Notas de Sociologia Religiosa' [Notes on the Sociology of Religion]. *Lumen*, XVII (9–10), 1953, pp. 530–550.

Dumont, Rene, 'Revolution dans les campagnes chinoises' [Revolution in the Chinese Countryside]. Chap. 17, in: *L'Europe meridionale sera-t-elle bientôt dépassée, au Portugal ou en Gréce*? [Will Southern Europe soon be surpassed in Portugal or in Greece?]. Paris, Ed. du Seuil, 1957.

Freyre, Gilberto, *Aventura e Rotira* [Adventure and Routine]. No publishing details available.

Le Bras, Gabriel, *Etudes de Sociologie Religieuse* [Studies of religious sociology]. Vol. II. Paris, P.U.F., 1955.

Martins, Antonio, 'Données statistiques sur les vocations sacerdotales au Portugal' [Statistical data concerning Priestly Callings in Portugal], in: *Vocation de la Sociologie. Sociologie des Vocations* [The Vocation of Sociology. Sociology of Vocations]. Tournai, Casterman, 1958.

—, 'Dados para uma sociografia das vacocoes sacerdotais na diocese de Vila Real' [Data for a Sociography of Sacerdotal Callings in the Diocese of Vila Real]. *Lumen* XXII (6), 1958, pp. 443–464.

Montalvao Machado, J. T., *Como nascen e morrem os portugueses* [How the Portuguese are Born and Die]. Demography study. Lisbon, Gomes and Rodrigues, 1956.

Moura, Francisco Pereira de, Pinto, Luis Maria Teixeira, Nunes, Manuel Jacinto, 'Estrutura da economia portuguesa: agricultura, industria, comercio externo' [The Structure of the Portuguese Economy: Agriculture, Industry, Foreign Commerce]. *Revista do Centro de Estudos economicos* [Periodical for the Centre for Economic Studies], 13, 1953, pp. 7–163.

Nabais, J. Antonio, *A vocacoa a luz da psicologia moderna* [The Religious Calling in the Light of Modern Psychology]. Porto, Tavares Martins, 1953.

Pinto, Manuel. 'Problemas de Sociologia Religiosa e os padres da Missao de Franca' [Problems of the Sociology of Religion and the Fathers of the French Mission]. *Broteria* LX (7) 1955, pp. 5–24.

—, 'Portugal 1957'. *Informations Catholiques Internationales*, 42, 15 February 1957, pp. 13–24.

EDWARD HIGGINS*

# South Africa

## INTRODUCTION

In South Africa sociology as an academic discipline was only established in the 1930s. It was precisely at this time that South Africa was experiencing the impact of the great depression in general and her own poor White problem in particular. Consequently, a strong social welfare element appears in much of the early sociology taught at South African universities as well as in the research carried out. However, in recent years, sociological research has broadened its base and certain studies more properly sociological have been undertaken; some of these are in the field of the sociology of religion.

Most of the research in the sphere of the sociology of religion has been fragmentary or tangential in that it deals with one or other racial group or religious group or is confined to a particular locality. No overall depth research in the sociology of religion has been carried out in South Africa. The research that has been done is more descriptive than analytical, more empirical than theoretical. However, there are signs of a more sociologically mature approach to research in the sociology of religion in the undertakings of some of the younger sociologists.

Consequently, this chapter will concentrate on the demographic aspects as the raw data for these are to be found in the census which is taken every ten years in South Africa. In addion, some attention will be devoted to research already carried out in South Africa in the sociology of religion; refer-

* Edward Higgins was born in Cape Town, South Africa, in 1923. He was educated at St. Paul's College, Washington D.C., and the University of the Witwatersrand. He has been a lecturer at Pius XII College, Lesotho (Basutoland), Rhodes University, Grahamstown, and the University of Natal, Durban. He has also been a school teacher in Johannesburg. He is now Senior Lecturer and Acting Head of the Sociology Department at Rhodes University, Grahamstown. He has published many articles and reviews in the fields of religion, demography, and the sociology of religion.

This chapter was already in print before the results of the latest (1970) census were published. The religious breakdown of the 1970 census has not yet been published.

ence will also be made to the relevant research in progress at the present time.[1]

In many ways the varied composition of South African society is a fascinating one for sociological research. The population of the Republic of South Africa which covers 471,445 square miles of the southern portion of the African continent is composed of four main ethnic groups, viz., the Whites (descendants of early Dutch, French, British and German settlers), the Coloured (a non-White people of mixed racial descent), the Asiatics (chiefly Indian – the descendants of nineteenth century migrant Indian labourers) and the Bantu (the descendants of various negroid tribes who moved southwards about the same time as the White settlers moved northwards, viz., mid-eighteenth century).

The Whites are divided into two main language groups, English- and Afrikaans-speaking – in addition these linguistic divisions are fairly coterminous with religious differences. The Coloureds are what many sociologists would describe as a marginal group, i.e. in pigmentation non-White yet culture-wise western. Like the Whites, the Coloured group is predominantly Christian *vis-a-vis* religious affiliation. The Asiatics constitute a predominantly non-Christian group; they are mainly Hindu with about one-fifth being Muslim. The Bantu are composed of different tribal and linguistic groups and, from the viewpoint of Christian religious affiliation, occupy a mid-position between the Whites and Coloureds on the one hand and the Asiatics on the other.

*Table 1. Numerical and percentage distribution of population of South Africa by race, 1960 and 1966*

| Race | 1960 N | 1960 % | 1966 N | 1966 % |
|---|---|---|---|---|
| White | 3,080,159 | 19.3 | 3,491,500 | 18.9 |
| Coloured | 1,509,053 | 9.4 | 1,812,800 | 9.8 |
| Asiatic | 477,047 | 3.0 | 576,500 | 3.1 |
| Bantu | 10,927,922 | 68.3 | 12,584,000 | 68.2 |
| Total | 15,994,181 | 100.0 | 18,464,800 | 100.0 |

Source: The 1960 figures represent the revised final figures for the 1960 census made available by the Bureau of Census, Pretoria. These figures do not always coincide with the totals appearing in other Bureau publications; this is due to the method of computer processing of the data. The 1966 figures appear in *Statistical Yearbook*, 1966; compiled by Bureau of Statistics, Pretoria, p. 41.

1. This is necessarily incomplete as not all university departments and individual sociologists have responded to the writer's request for information. In addition, in South Africa a good deal of social science research is never published.

The numerical and percentage distributions of the total population as at 1960 and mid-1966 appear in Table 1.
The above table indicates that in the nineteen-sixties the Bantu comprised the largest population group in South Africa – approximately two-thirds of the total population, while the Whites account for somewhat less than one-fifth; the Asiatics constituted a very small minority while nearly every tenth person in South Africa is Coloured.

## RELIGIOUS DEMOGRAPHY

That South Africa is, culturally speaking, a heterogeneous country is evident from the following table.

*Table 2. Percentage distribution of total population of South Africa by religious affiliation, by race as at 1960 census*

| Religious affiliation | Total population | Race | | | |
|---|---|---|---|---|---|
| | | White | Coloured | Asiatic | Bantu |
| Christian | 73.4 | 94.2 | 90.8 | 7.5 | 67.9 |
| Jewish | 0.7 | 3.7 | – | – | – |
| Hindu | 2.0 | – | – | 68.5 | – |
| Islam | 1.2 | – | 6.1 | 20.7 | – |
| Other and unspecified | 22.7 | 2.1 | 3.1 | 3.3 | 32.1 |
| Total | 100.0 | 100.0 | 100.0 | 100.0 | 100.0 |

Source: All raw data pertaining to religious affiliation is available in *Population census 6th September*, 1960, Volume 3, 'Religion', Bureau of Statistics, Republic of South Africa.

In terms of religious affiliation, the South African is quite largely Christian with nearly three-quarters of the total population belonging to one or other Christian denomination. In the case of both the White and Coloured groups nine out of every ten persons are Christians as are two-thirds of the Bantu population. The Asiatics are mainly Hindu with a sizeable (one-fifth) Moslem minority plus a tiny Christian minority. As persons with no religious affiliation at all form a negligible proportion of the total population, they are not listed separately in Table 2 but are grouped with 'Other and Unspecified'. Only among the Bantu is a significant proportion of 'non-religious' persons encountered, viz., 27.4 per cent. These are mainly persons who have not been evangelized by Christian missionaries. Some of these 'non-religious' persons are given to ancestors worship; in fact, South African anthropologists contend that there has been a post-war resurgence in ancestor worship among the Bantu.

Figure 1 represents diagrammatically the proportion of Christians in the four main population groups as well as for the total population.

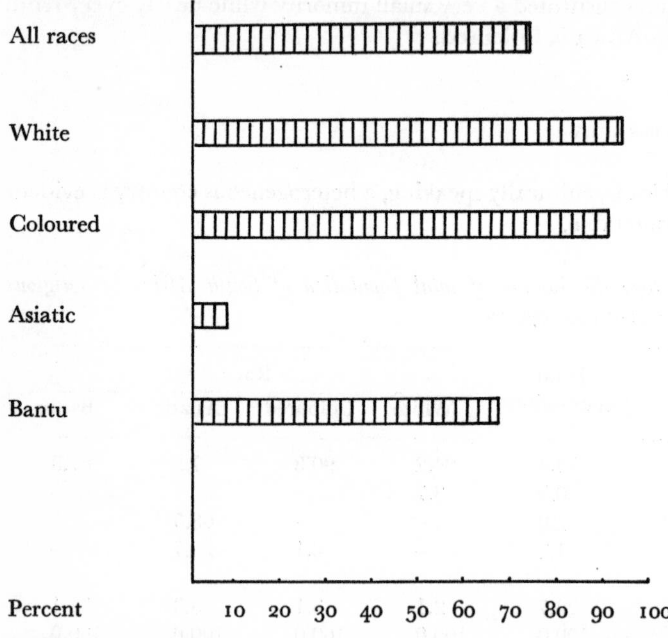


*Figure 1. Percent Christian of total population, by race as at 1960 census*

All the major Christian denominations are to be found in South Africa. Among the Whites the numerically strongest group is the Dutch Reformed Church which actually consists of three separate Calvinist churches whose members are Afrikaans-speaking.[2] Approximately three-fifths of the White population as well as nearly nine-tenths of the Coloureds reported Afrikaans as their home language at the 1960 census.

In addition to the usual Christian denominations found in the western world, South African Bantu Christians have founded many indigeneous churches in the last few decades; some of these churches are breakaway

2. These three churches are: – Nederduits Gereformeerde Kerk (Dutch Neo-Calvinist Church) Gereformeerde Kerk (Neo-Calvinist Church) and the Nederduits Hervormde Kerk (Dutch Reformed Church). At the 1960 census the membership of these three churches for all races was as follows: N.G. Kerk 2,289,128; Geref. Kerk 124,655 and the N.H. Kerk 216,419.

movements from established denominations while others are entirely new creations. This phenomenon is not, of course, confined to South Africa but is encountered in other parts of the African continent as well. Some anthropological research has been done and is being done on the Bantu Separatist Church movement in South Africa. (Reference to this will be found in the bibliography at the end of the chapter). *En passant*, we may note that some anthropologists regard this phenomenon as a partial substitute for enfeebled kin groups in the face of westernization, urbanization and industrialization. The South African census classifies all these churches as Separatist churches. These groups tend to fit Troeltsch's well-known sect typology in certain respects [Troeltsch, 1949].

Table 3 depicts the percentage distribution of all Christians in terms of denomination and race.

*Table 3. Percentage distribution of all Christians, by race, by denomination, as at 1960 census*

| Denomination | All Christians | Race | | | |
|---|---|---|---|---|---|
| | | White | Coloured | Asiatic | Bantu |
| | (N= 11,727,479) | (N= 2,899,756) | (N= 1,371,702) | (N= 35,962) | (N= 7,420,059) |
| Afrikaans churches | 22.4 | 55.7 | 32.8 | – | 7.6 |
| Anglican | 12.0 | 13.3 | 19.0 | 16.7 | 10.0 |
| Methodist | 14.6 | 9.2 | 8.5 | 6.9 | 17.8 |
| Presbyterian | 2.7 | 3.8 | 0.5 | – | 2.8 |
| Congregational | 2.5 | 0.5 | 10.2 | – | 1.9 |
| Lutheran | 5.5 | 1.2 | 5.4 | – | 7.3 |
| Roman Catholic | 9.2 | 6.6 | 8.7 | 28.7 | 10.2 |
| Separatist churches | 19.7 | – | – | – | 31.2 |
| Other | 11.4 | 9.7 | 14.9 | 47.7 | 11.2 |
| Total | 100.0 | 100.0 | 100.0 | 100.0 | 100.0 |

From the above table it will be observed that among White Christians, the Afrikaans churches account for more than half of the White Christian membership, while just less than one-third of the Bantu Christians belong to one or other Separatist church. As regards overall Christian church membership, it will be noted that nine out of every ten South African Christians are Protestants. It will also be seen that Asiatics are disproportionately overrepresented among the sects.

*Table 4. Percentage distribution of major Christian denominations by racial composition as at 1960 census*

| Christian denomination | Race | | | | |
|---|---|---|---|---|---|
| | White | Coloured | Asiatic | Bantu | Total |
| Afrikaans Churches N=2,630,202 | 61.4 | 17.1 | – | 21.5 | 100.0 |
| Anglican N=1,403,399 | 27.4 | 18.6 | 0.4 | 53.6 | 100.0 |
| Methodist N=1,707,293 | 15.6 | 6.9 | 0.1 | 77.4 | 100.0 |
| Presbyterian N=321,387 | 34.6 | 1.9 | – | 63.5 | 100.0 |
| Congregational N=291,690 | 5.3 | 48.0 | – | 46.7 | 100.0 |
| Lutheran N=650,666 | 5.2 | 11.4 | – | 83.4 | 100.0 |
| Roman Catholic N=1,076,523 | 17.9 | 11.0 | 1.0 | 70.2 | 100.0 |
| Other N=1,135,058 | 18.6 | 18.8 | 1.7 | 60.9 | 100.0 |
| All Christians N=11,727,479 | 24.7 | 11.7 | 0.3 | 63.3 | 100.0 |
| Total Population N=15,994,181 | 19.3 | 9.4 | 3.0 | 68.3 | 100.0 |

Interesting differences appear in Table 4 which gives the racial composition of the major Christian denominations. Table 4 shows a reasonably close correspondence between the racial composition of the total Christian population and that of the total population of South Africa. However, quite striking differences in racial composition are evident between the various denominations. White over-representation is found to a considerable degree in the Afrikaans churches and to a lesser extent among Presbyterians and Anglicans. Apart from the Separatist churches, which are entirely Bantu and not listed in the above table, Bantu over-representation occurs among Methodist and Lutheran Christians. Coloured Christians are greatly over-represented in the Congregational Church, and to a much lesser extent, in the Afrikaans and Anglican Churches and among the sects. Of all the churches, the Roman Catholic comes closest to reflecting the country's racial composition in its membership. These differences are largely the result of historical and territorial factors.

South Africa's four main ethnic groups differ in the degree of urbanisation they manifest. For instance, the Whites and Asiatics are somewhat more urbanized than the Coloured group while two-thirds of the Bantu are classified as rural. Rural-urban differences are to be found in all the Christian denominations in South Africa as will be seen in Table 5.

*Table 5. Percentage urban, all Christians, by denomination and race as at 1960 census*

| Denomination | All Christians | Race | | | |
|---|---|---|---|---|---|
| | | White | Coloured | Asiatic | Bantu |
| Afrikaans churches | 62.1 | 75.7 | 46.6 | – | 35.3 |
| Anglican | 64.4 | 91.7 | 82.2 | 95.8 | 44.1 |
| Methodist | 48.0 | 91.9 | 68.4 | 87.1 | 37.2 |
| Presbyterian | 59.4 | 93.8 | 62.7 | – | 40.5 |
| Congregational | 48.8 | 93.3 | 62.9 | – | 29.2 |
| Lutheran | 40.7 | 76.9 | 67.1 | – | 34.8 |
| Roman Catholic | 58.9 | 94.2 | 82.3 | 93.5 | 45.8 |
| Separatist churches | 37.9 | – | – | – | 37.9 |
| Total population | (46.7) | 83.6 | 68.3 | 83.2 | 31.8 |

With reference to all Christians the Anglican and Afrikaans Churches are the most urban while the Lutheran and Separatist Churches manifest a greater degree of rural membership. Among the Whites the Afrikaans and Lutheran Churches are less urban than the other denominations. All non-White Anglicans and Catholics are disproportionately urban. This is partly explained by the fact that these two religious bodies were comparative late-comers to the rural mission fields which are still largely non-White.

To obtain some idea of the growth of the various religious groups in South Africa we now compare membership in the census year 1921 with that of the latest 1960 census. In 1921 just over half (51.3 per cent) of the total population was Christian while the relevant proportion for 1960 was nearly three-quarters (73.4 per cent). This increase has been due mainly to the evangelization of the Bantu rather than to mere natural increase on the part of South African Christians. While 34.2 per cent of the Bantu were Christians at the 1921 census 67.9 per cent of them were classified as Christians at the time of the 1960 census. Between these two census years the proportion of Jews, Hindus and Moslems has remained constant.

During the period 1921–1960 all Christian denominations gained numerically from this Bantu movement toward Christianity, none more so than the Separatist churches. This latter group was not even listed as such in the 1921

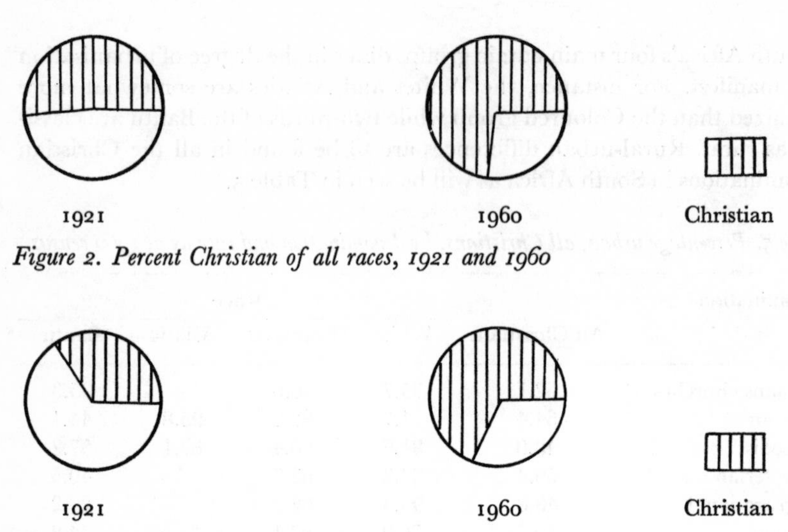


*Figure 2. Percent Christian of all races, 1921 and 1960*

1921
1960
Christian

*Figure 3. Percent Christian of Bantu, 1921 and 1960*

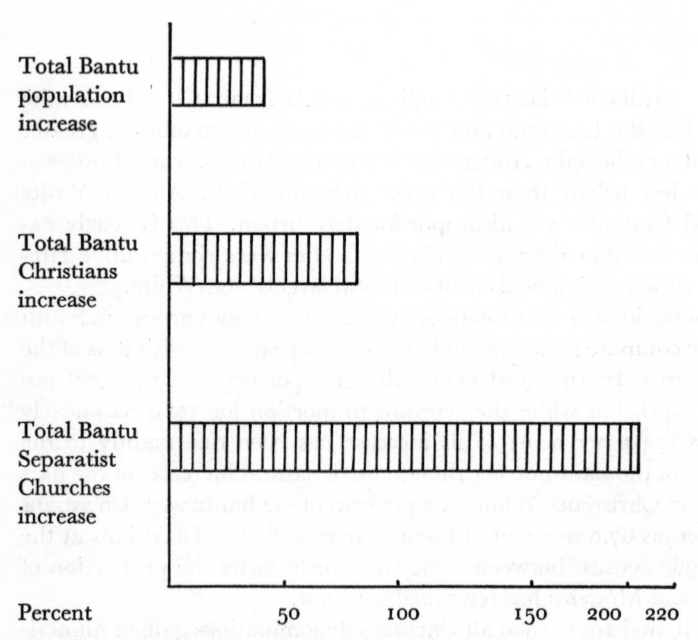


*Figure 4. Percent increase 1946–1960 of total Bantu population, Bantu Christian, and membership of Bantu separatist churches*

census. *Vis-a-vis* the total Christian population, all Christian denominations except the Roman Catholic and certain sects show a proportionate decline mostly at the expense of the Separatist churches. In 1921 Roman Catholics comprised 4.0 per cent of the total Christian population whereas by 1960 this proportion had increased to 9.2 per cent. In 1960 the Separatist churches accounted for 19.7 per cent of the total Christian church membership. In 1921 the sects (listed as 'other') comprised 4.0 per cent of all Christians, in 1960 they accounted for 11.4 per cent. The sects have gained among Whites, Coloured and Asiatics.

Figures 2 and 3 represent the percentage growth of all Christians and Bantu Christians from 1921 to 1960.

Clearly, the most striking socio-religious phenomenon in South Africa has been the rapid growth of the Separatist Church movement among the Bantu. This phenomenon has been the subject of intensive research among the anthropologists and references to their work appears in the bibliography at the end of the chapter. This phenomenal growth is apparent in Figure 4

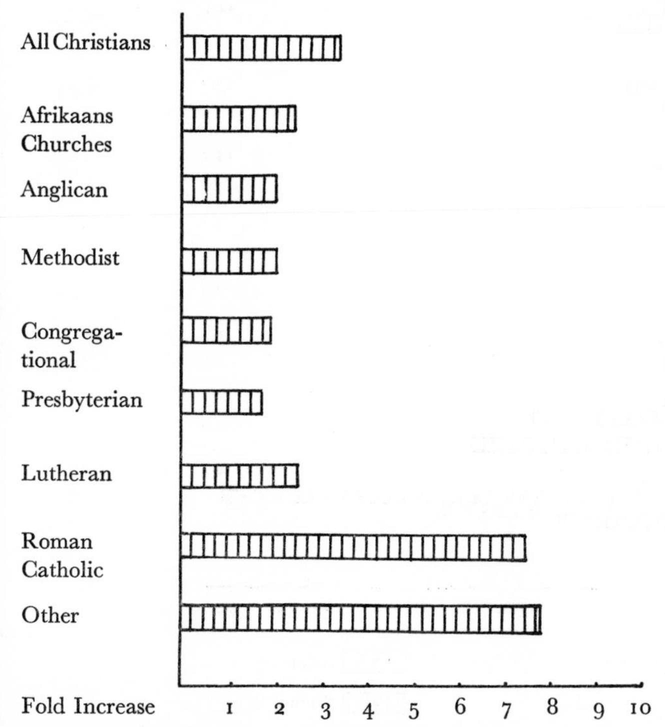


*Figure 5. Times increase in membership of major christian denominations of all races, 1921–1960*

which compares the increase of Bantu Christians as well as the relevant increase on the part of the Bantu Separatist churches.

It has already been mentioned that all Christian denominations experienced an increase in membership from 1921 to 1960. This is portrayed in Figure 5 which shows that the total Christian population increased more than threefold while the Roman Catholic Church and the sects both experienced an almost eightfold increase in membership.

The increase in Christian church membership between the years 1921 and 1960 has not always been racially even. This will be seen in Figure 5. Parti-

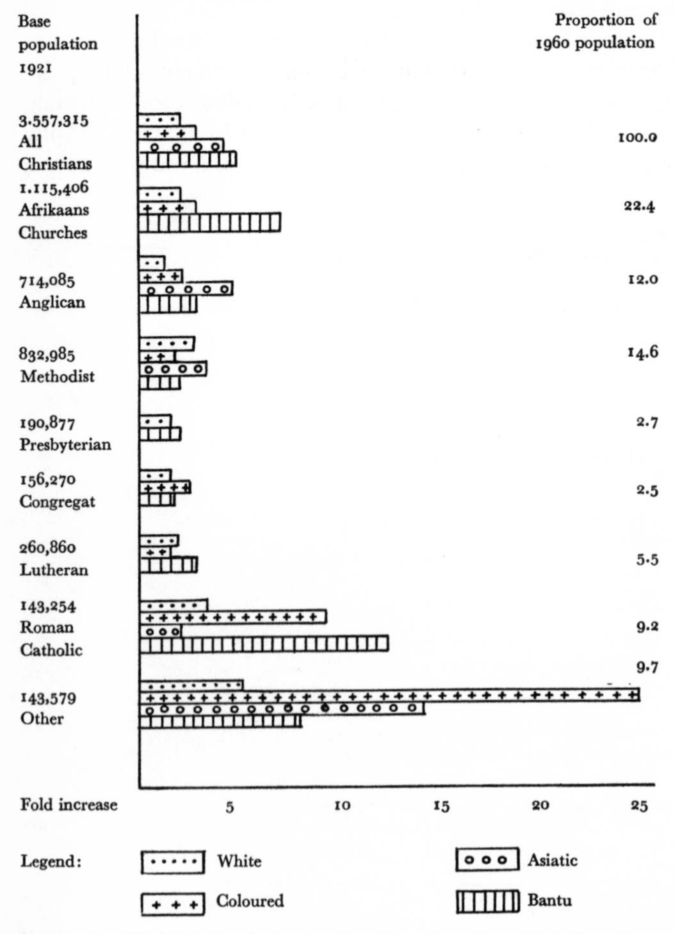


*Figure 6. Times increase in membership of major Christian denominations by race, 1921–1960*

cularly noticeable is the increase in Bantu membership on the part of the Afrikaans and Roman Catholic churches together with the increase in Coloured adherents on the part of the Roman Catholic Church and the various sects (see Figure 6).

The racial composition of some Christian denominations has changed over the period 1921–1960. Proportionately, a considerable change in racial composition has come over the Roman Catholic Church – a marked increase in non-White membership; a lesser increase in non-White membership has occurred in the Afrikaans and Anglican Churches; a slight increase in non-White membership is evidenced on the part of the Presbyterian and Lutheran Churches. Table 6 reflects the change in racial composition of the Roman Catholic Church over the years 1921–1960.

*Table 6. Numerical and percentage racial composition of Roman Catholic Church: 1921 and 1960*

| Race | Roman Catholic Church | | | |
|---|---|---|---|---|
| | 1921 | | 1960 | |
| | N | % | N | % |
| White | 61,246 | 42.7 | 192,234 | 17.9 |
| Coloured | 13,410 | 9.4 | 118,900 | 11.0 |
| Asiatic | 5,419 | 1.0 | 10,316 | 0.9 |
| Bantu | 63,179 | 44.1 | 755,073 | 70.2 |
| Total | 143,254 | 100.0 | 1,076,523 | 100.0 |

According to the above table, a notable switch in the racial composition of the Roman Catholic Church has occurred over the last four decades. According to the 1921 census the Roman Catholic Church in South Africa was disproportionately White vis-a-vis the total population whereas by 1960 this religious body had come to reflect in a far more accurate manner the general racial composition of the country more closely than any other religious body. This change cannot be attributed to natural increase but was due largely to missionary effort among the non-White population but more particularly among the Bantu. After World War I quite a number of German Catholic missionaries from former German territories as well as certain British possessions were obliged to leave their mission fields: these missionaries were accordingly given mission territories in South Africa. This factor plus a world-wide increase in missionary activity during the pontificate of Pope Pius XI (1922–1939) explains the notable Roman Catholic gain in non-White membership absolutely and proportionately between 1921 and 1960.

## RELIGIOUS PARTICIPATION AND BELIEF

With regard to religion, the South African census only records reported religious affiliation. In a considerable number of cases, this indicates nothing more than nominal adherence; it certainly does not indicate religious commitment. In South Africa we have no study even resembling Lenski's *The Religious Factor* [1961] either in depth or extent. The published work which we have about degree of religiosity, church attendance and so forth is scattered in a number of studies, all of which are confined to small populations such as one racial group in a given town or a sample of University students.

## COMPLETED RESEARCH

As far as South African Christians are concerned Catholics and Afrikaans-speaking Protestants generally record a higher church attendance than other denominations. A typical pattern appears in the following table. This is based on data gathered in a fertility survey of 1,022 White married women conducted in Johannesburg in 1957–58 [Higgins, 1964]. (At that time the total population of Johannesburg was 884,007 of whom 359,477 were Whites).

*Table 7. Percentage distribution of all respondents reporting religious affiliation by church attendance of respondent*

| Church attendance of respondent | All respondents | Religion of Respondent | | | |
|---|---|---|---|---|---|
| | | Afrikaans Protestant | English Protestant | Jewish | Catholic |
| Often | 38 | 57 | 33 | 18 | 54 |
| Seldom | 46 | 37 | 48 | 60 | 33 |
| Never | 16 | 6 | 19 | 22 | 13 |
| Total | 100 | 100 | 100 | 100 | 100 |

With regard to the above table it should be noted that the respondents themselves defined the attendance categories and consequently some exaggeration is possible.

In a study conducted by the author at Rhodes University with a sample of 397 students (approximately one-third of the universe) it was found that only 13.1 per cent of the students had not attended church or synagogue during the five month period prior to the survey [Higgins, 1965]. The mean church attendance of the majority who reported church/synagogue attendance during the preceding five months appears in Table 8.

*Table 8. Church/Synagogue attendance of Rhodes university students*

| Religious affiliation | N | Mean number of attendances during five months prior to the Survey |
|---|---|---|
| Anglican | 123 | 10.6 |
| Methodist | 72 | 13.3 |
| Presbyterian | 46 | 13.2 |
| Roman Catholic | 31 | 18.2 |
| Jewish | 18 | 12.3 |
| Dutch Reformed | 18 | 14.5 |
| Baptist | 8 | 18.6 |
| Other | 19 | 11.3 |
| No religion | 3 | 4.2 |
| Total | 338 | 12.7 |

It is evident that Catholic and Baptist students attended church far more regularly than the average student in this sample as well as students belonging to other religious groups.

In a study of some community patterns in the White population (6,727) of King William's Town, H. L. Watts asked a sample of White adults how often they usually went to church. He reports as follows:

> 'A total of 38 per cent of the sample stated that they go to church weekly; 27 per cent, or about one-quarter, more or less monthly; and 16 per cent sometimes. A tenth said that they never go to church. Thus if the replies of the informants can be taken at their face value, about two-thirds go to church monthly, or more often. However, as a certain amount of guilt is sometimes associated with non-church-going, it may well be that these figures are over-estimated. They suggest, nevertheless, that the religious institutions of the town are moderately well supported' [Watts, 1966, p. 89].

It is clear from the census material presented in this chapter that the majority of South Africans admit to some church affiliation, however, tenuous. However, South Africa has not completely escaped the secularization trend which has become so apparent in the contemporary world. Some years ago P. W. Venter [1957] conducted a sociological investigation into the phenomenon of churchlessness[3] among Afrikaans-speaking South Africans. The

3. The English word 'churchlessness' does not quite correspond to the Afrikaans 'onkerksheid' which actually means having no virtual contact with any denomination or religious body and yet admitting to some formal religious affiliation.

empirical part is based on a study of the three Afrikaans churches in certain major urban and rural areas of the Transvaal. Venter discovered definite evidence of some churchlessness among Afrikaans-speaking persons, particularly the younger generation, despite reported formal adherence to one of the three Afrikaans churches.

D. P. van Zyl [1966] has made a religious sociographic study of 464 youths between the ages of 15 and 25 belonging to an urban congregation of the Nederduits Gereformeerde Kerk (N. G. Kerk) in Pretoria. This study concerns itself with delineating the main religious, moral and economic problems of the youth in question as well as with the general feeling of alienation most of them experience in an urban environment. Van Zyl concludes that the church youth movement sponsored by the N. G. Kerk comes closest to an ideal club or organization for urban youth in that it meets nearly all their requirements.

Certain studies not dealing directly with religion, nevertheless refer to the religious variable in analysing their data. One example of this is to be found in H. J. Lever's study [1966] of social distance among White high school children in Johannesburg. According to Lever:

> 'Religion was not found to be an important factor differentiating the attitudes of pupils in the Afrikaans schools. There were no significant differences in the attitudes of Dutch Reformed and Apostolic pupils in these schools in relation to any of the nine respondee groups. With one exception, namely in the case of attitude towards Natives, there was no important difference in the ethnic attitudes of Anglicans, Presbyterians and Methodists in the English-medium schools. Roman Catholics differed from members of the other Christian faiths by expressing a more unfavourable attitude towards English-speaking South Africans, Afrikaans-speaking South Africans, Hollanders and the British. Since a number of pupils were of Italian or Portugese origin, the sample of Roman Catholics may be considered a heterogeneous one. Jews were relatively favourable towards Natives, Coloureds, and Indians and relatively unfavourable towards Germans' [Lever, 1966, pp. 342–343].

Religion, by itself, can be a misleading variable. In a sample study of the students of Rhodes University, Grahamstown, conducted in 1965, religious denomination did not appear an important variable in the shaping of ethnic and political attitudes [Higgins, 1965]. Of far greater significance was degree of commitment to the religious institution. Time and again, this commitment cut across denominational boundaries. As far as the religious role-complex of the students was concerned, what really counted – especially in attitude formation – was religious commitment rather than mere religious identification. A similar phenomenon was encountered in a study of students at the University of Natal in 1966 [Higgins, 1967].

In the Calvinist tradition Sunday observance constitutes a matter of great importance. From a religious point of view, the Calvinist tradition in South Africa is both the oldest, the strongest and the most influential and this partly explains why, broadly speaking, South African society is more repressive when compared with other Western countries which may be described as more permissive. Traces of eighteenth and nineteenth century Sabbatarian legislation still exist in South African law today.

A few years ago C. J. Alant [1965] conducted a survey on Sunday observance in a sample of 50 N. G. Kerk congregations in the province of the Transvaal. By means of interviews Alant obtained evidence which suggests that the traditional patriarchal form of Sunday observance – which flourished in the pre-industrial Transvaal – is slowly being discarded. This process is more rapid in the cities than the rural areas; furthermore, it is particularly noticeable among persons aged sixteen – forty-five years as well as among those in the professional-executive occupational category. These age and occupational groups appear as bearers of a new pattern of Sunday observance and celebration. Alant regards this changing phenomenon as a transitional stage which is characterized by amorphousness and confusion. He found no indication of any change in those central religious values upon which Sunday observance is based.

In a nation-wide survey of a stratified sample of 2,229 White families belonging to the three Afrikaans churches conducted in 1952 as part of a detailed study of family life, Cronjé [1958] concluded that the religious life and religious inclination cannot be accurately evaluated in terms of one single criterion only. Cronjé found that the individual's religious and church life formed a complex unity which reflected itself in varying degrees in life's myriad activities.

Depending on many factors, religion can manifest an integrative and cohesive role or one which is divisive and dysfunctional. In a study of a sample of 209 Coloureds in Stellenbosch (a prominent educational centre in the Western Cape with a then Coloured population of 7,158), W. B. van Wyk [1954] found that those respondents who were active Church members were, in certain respects, better adjusted to their life situation than were those who had no religious affiliation at all. In addition, the former were more well-disposed towards the Whites than the latter. According to Van Wyk, active Church members were happier and fuller social beings than those who had no religion at all.

In 1959 W. H. Keyter [1964] made a study of church patterns in the Coloured community of Paarl (a Western Cape town with a total population in 1960 of 66,594 of whom 38,995 were Coloured). This researcher applied the social system theory of Parsons to one section of the Coloured community of Paarl. Keyter found evidence of a highly differential church pattern particularly among Protestants and he argues that this is due chiefly to socio-cultural factors rather than to purely personal or doctrinal differences. The creation of new sects was especially due to socio-cultural factors. Keyter contends that race attitudes, demographic growth, industrialisation as well as internal ecological processes have been the main socio-cultural factors leading to the development of different socio-religious systems within the overall ecclesiastical pattern. This study shows, in particular, the influence of ecological factors on the physical aspects of the differential church pattern, in that different churches and sects are not haphazardly grouped but distributed and located in a definite and patterned manner.

Church membership among Coloureds in seven towns in the South-western part of the Cape Province was studied by W. J. Smit [1950]. This was an exploratory study of a demographic nature which showed that the Coloured population in these areas was overwhelmingly Christian. Smit found that most churches do not increase their membership by winning converts; increase in numbers is due mainly to natural increase.

Apart from these studies, W. J. van der Merwe [1964] has written a descriptive historical and demographic outline of religion among the Coloured people.

The Bantu Separatist Church movement has been fairly comprehensively studied by anthropologists while the Coloured group (predominantly Christian) have been studied by sociologists. The Asiatics have not been studied to any notable degree in a socio-religious context. However, in 1962 Theresa Currin [1962] made an interesting study of the Indian Catholic community of Durban with special emphasis on the sociological aspects of conversion. *Inter alia*, Currin makes this interesting observation:

> Fortuitously, where the Hindu converts of Durban are concerned, the Catholic structure is, through its own history of urban development, potentially functional for these persons. But it seems to be relatively unsuccessful in its missionary field of the younger adult generation because its theodicy is still rooted in the emotional needs of other times and past cultural complexes' [Currin, 1962, p. 221].

Recently H. J. W. Rocher made a study of a selected group of Tamil-speaking Hindus in South Africa in which he found evidence suggesting:

> that a gradual decline in traditional thought and practices is taking place... The social influence of western culture, with which the Hindus are in very close contact appears to be playing an important contribu-

> tory role in the process of deviation from traditional Hindu thought and practices [Rocher, 1966, p. 46].

Content analysis represents one data-gathering technique which has been rarely employed by South African sociologists. One such study, entitled 'A Study of Socio-Religious Phenomena as reflected in the Daily Press of Cape Town' was conducted by Monica Bedford [1966] during 1965–1966. In a personal communication to the author she states:

> All articles in a sample of the Press having any religious interest were classified as to whether the religious interest was primary or secondary, and in the latter case, as to whether the primary interest was political, educational, personal etc. These were correlated with age, sex and ethnic groups, with conflict, co-operation, competition and so on. The primary religious articles were also analysed in terms of Talcott Parsons' pattern variables and social systems.

In her study Monica Bedford found that:

> in Cape Town society, as reflected in its daily press, religion embraces only a small portion of social life (2½ per cent as compared with politics, 23 per cent, and personalities, 12 per cent); nevertheless it pervades a very large variety of other aspects of everyday life... Analysis according to Parsons' pattern variables showed the social systems represented by the press items to be predominantly facing the adaptation problem, although this did not apply to the non-White groups.

The Sociology Department of Pretoria University has completed a nation-wide survey on youth and its attitude to church and religion, as well as the actual religious life of young people. The findings will be published in four volumes late in 1967.

## RESEARCH IN PROGRESS

At the present moment a certain number of studies in the field of the sociology of religion are in progress.[4] These studies are all being conducted under the aegis of the sociology departments of the various South African universities.

T. J. Basson is engaged on a sociological study aimed at discovering the reasons why the Bantu join the N.G. Kerk.

S. F. Kotze has undertaken a theoretical as well as an empirical study

4. Details of these studies are listed at the end of the Bibliography.

among the Coloured population with a view to determining this hypothesised marginality in terms of the religiousness of the Coloured people.

Sheila Brown is busy with an interesting theoretical and empirical study concerning the sporadic integration between the family and the Christian religion in the Bantu community at Rwarwa. Her major hypothesis is that the degree of Christianisation results from an all-embracing acculturation process rather than from a restricted process of doctrinal conversion by means of pure theological missionary activity.

C. J. Alant has just commenced a sociological study of the image held by the average member of the N.G. Kerk of the office of clergyman. Dr. Alant suggests that the church member has changed his view of the N. G. Kerk clergyman as a 'man of God'.

At Rhodes University, Grahamstown, Beryl Wright is nearing the completion of an empirical project which centres around the hypothesis that there is a discernible relation between the members of various religious orders (churches and 'sects') and moral discrimination in attitudes and values.

C. S. Steenkamp is presently occupied with a sociological study of religiosity in the community. He is concentrating on the need for, as well as the consciousness and manifestation of religiousness.

The Department of Sociology at Pretoria University is currently conducting a survey on the adjustment of Roman Catholic students at Pretoria University. This study seeks to determine precisely what adjustment problems Roman Catholic students experience. In addition, the survey hopes to gather data which will enable a comparison to be made vis-a-vis university adjustment between religiously-committed Roman Catholic students and those who are only nominally associated with the Roman Catholic Church. Furthermore, comparisons will be drawn between students who attended Roman Catholic schools and those who were educated at State schools.

F. H. Boot, an anthropologist at the University of South Africa has completed the fieldwork part of a study of the process of acculturation in the religious sphere among the Mkhwanazi tribe. This group includes pagans, members of certain separatist churches, as well as other Christians. In this study special attention is paid to doctrine, ritual and group leaders as well as the relationships between these groups and the role that they play in the socio-cultural life of the tribe as a whole.

Another anthropologist, B. A. Pauw, of the University of South Africa, is preparing a book on belief and ritual among Xhosa (a Bantu tribe) Christians, both rural and urban, in the context of social and cultural change.

South Africa with its racial and religious heterogeneity undoubtedly presents an exciting field for research in the sociology of religion. For a variety of reasons, as far as research goes, this branch of sociology has not taken root in equal measure at the various South African universities and university colleges (there are sixteen). However, a South African Sociologist, F. A. Maritz [1959] has made an eloquent and forceful plea for greater endeavours in this important branch of our discipline.

## SELECTED BIBLIOGRAPHY


Alant, C. J., 'n *Sosiologiese Studie van Sondagviering in die Nederduitse Gereformeerde Kerk van Transvaal* [A sociological study of spending of the Sabbath in the Dutch Neo-Calvinist Church of the Transvaal]. Unpublished D. Litt. and Phil. thesis. Pretoria, University of South Africa, 1965.

Bedford, Monica, *A Study of Socio-Religious Phenomena as Reflected in the Daily Press of Cape Town.* Unpublished study. University of Cape Town, 1966.

Brandell-Syrier, Mia, *Black Woman in Search of God.* London, Lutterworth Press, 1962.

Cilliers, S. P., *Wes-Kaapland, 'n Sosio-Ekonomiese Studie* [The Western Cape: A Socio-Economic Study]. Stellenbosch, Kosmo-Uitgewery, 1964.

Cronje, G., ed., *Kerk en Huisgesin: Die huidige en godsdienstige lewe van die Afrikaner* [Church and Family: The Religious Life of the Afrikaner today]. Cape Town-Pretoria, N.G. Kerk Uitgewers, 1958.

Currin, Theresa E. V., *The Indian in Durban: An Exploratory Study of the Roman Catholic Indian Minority, with Special Emphasis on the Sociological Aspects of Conversion.* Unpublished M. Soc. Sc. dissertation. Durban, University of Natal, 1962.

Du Plessis, J. S., 'Die oorsake van separatisme in die sendingvelde van Suid-Afrika' [The Cause of Separatism in the Mission Fields of South Africa]. *Op die Horison* (Stellenbosch), 1939.

Eberhardt, Jacqueline, 'Messianisme en Afrique du Sud' [Messianism in South Africa]. *Archives de Sociologie des Religions,* 4, 1957.

Fernandez, James, W., 'African Religious Movements – Types and Dynamics.' *The Journal of Modern African Studies,* 2, (4), 1964.

Gous, A. G. S., *Die Jeug. 'n Godsdienssosiologiese Studie van die blanke jeugdiges in die Republiek van Suid-Afrika tussen die ouderdomme van 16 en 25 jaar (aspekte van hul godsdienstige –, Kerklike – en liefdeslewe)* [Youth: A Religious sociological study of white youth in the Republic of South Africa, between the ages of 16 and 25 (aspects of their religious, church and love-life)]. Unpublished D. Phil. thesis. University of Pretoria 1966.

Higgins, E., 'Differential Fertility outlook and Patterns among Major Religious Groups in Johannesburg.' *Social Compass,* 11 (1), 1964.

—, *A Survey of some Religious attitudes of a Sample of Rhodes University Students.* Unpublished report. Grahamstown, Rhodes University, 1965.

—, *Socio-Religious Types and Economic Attitudes: A Sample Survey of Full-time Students at Howard College, University of Natal.* Unpublished monograph. Durban, University of Natal, 1967.

Hunter, Monica, *Reaction to Conquest.* London, Oxford University Press, 2nd edition, 1961.

Jabavu, D. D. T., *An African Independent Church*. Lovedale, 1942.
Keyter, W. H., *Die Kerklike Patroon in 'n Kleurlinggemeenskap* [Church Patterns in a Coloured Community]. Unpublished M. A. dissertation. University of Stellenbosch, 1959.
Kuper, L., Watts, Hilstan, and Davies, Ronald, *Durban: A Study in Racial Ecology* Jonathan Cape – London, 1958.
Lever, H. J., *A Comparative Study of Social Distance among various groups of the White High School Population of Johannesburg*. Unpublished Ph. D. thesis. Johannesburg, University of the Witwatersrand, 1966.
Loram, C., 'The Separatist Church Movement.' *International Review of Missions*, 1926.
Le Roux, du P., C., *The Ramakrishna Movement in South Africa: A Socio-Religious Study*. Unpublished Ph. D. thesis. University of Stellenbosch, 1965.
Maritz, F. A., *Die Aard en die taak van die Godsdienssosiologie* [The Nature and the Purpose of the Sociology of Religion]. Unpublished M. A. dissertation. University of Pretoria, 1959.
Mayer, Philip. *Townsmen or Tribesmen: Conservatism and the Process of Urbanization in a South African Town*. Cape Town, O.U.P., 1963.
—, 'Some forms of Religious Organization in a South African City', in: *Urbanization in African Social Change: Proceedings of the Inaugural Seminar held in the Centre of African Studies, University of Edinburgh, 5–7th January*, 1963. Edinburgh, Edinburgh University Press, 1963.
Norton, G. R., 'The Emergence of New Religious Organizations in South Africa.' *Journal of the Royal African Society*, 1940.
Pauw, B. A., *Religion in a Tswana Chiefdom*. O.U.P., London, 1960.
—, 'African Christians and their Ancestors', in: Hayward Victor E. W. (ed.), *African Independent Church Movements*. Research Pamphlets No 11. London, Edinburgh House Press, 1963.
—, *The Second Generation. III: Xhosa in Town*. Cape Town, O.U.P., 1963.
—, 'Patterns of Christianization among the Tswana and the Xhosa-speaking Peoples, in: *African Systems of Thought*. Studies presented and discussed at the Third International African Seminar in Salisbury, December 1960. London, O.U.P., 1965.
Rocher, H. J. W., 'A Study of the Theory and Practice of the Hindu Religious Tradition among a Selected Group of Tamil-speaking Hindus in South Africa: A Sociological Approach.' *Journal of the University College* (Durban) I (2), November 1966.
Schapera, I. (ed.), *Western Civilization and the Natives of South Africa*. London, Routledge, 1934.
Schlosser, Katesa, *Eingeborenenkirchen in Süd- und Süd-westafrika* [Native Churches in South and South-West Africa]. Kiel, Walter G. Mühlau, 1958.
Shepherd, R. H. W., 'The Separatist Churches of South Africa.' *International Review of Missions*, 1937.
Smit, W. J., '*Kerkverband in Suid-wes Kaapland*' [Church Affiliation in South West Cape]. Unpublished M.A. dissertation. University of Stellenbosch, 1950.
Sundkler, Bengt, G. M., 'Separatisme en die Sending' [Separatism and Mission]. *Op die Horison* (Stellenbosch), 1940.
—, 'Black Man's Church.' *Libertas* (Johannesburg), 1945.

—, *Bantu Prophets in South Africa*. 2nd edition. London, O.U.P., 1961.

—, 'Chief and Prophet in Zululand and Swaziland' in: *African Systems of Thought*. Studies presented and discussed at the Third International African Seminar in Salisbury, December 1960. London, O.U.P., 1965.

University of Natal, *The Baumanville Community*. Durban, University of Natal, Institute for Social Research, 1955.

Van Antwerpen, C. M., *Die Separatistiese Kerklike Beweging onder die Bantoe van Suid-Afrika* [The Separatist Church Movement of the Bantu in South Africa]. Unpublished M.A. dissertation. University of Cape Town, 1938.

Van der Merwe, W. J., 'Godsdiens' [Religion], in: Theron, E., and Swart, M. J. (eds.), *Die Kleurling Bevolking van Suid-Afrika* [The Coloured Population of South Africa]. Stellenbosch–Grahamstown, Universiteits-uitgewers en – boekhandelaars, 1964.

Van Wyk, W. B., *Die Godsdienstige Lewe van die Kleurlinge op Stellenbosch* [The Religious Life of the Coloured People in Stellenbosch]. Unpublished M.A. dissertation. University of Stellenbosch, 1954.

Van Zyl, D. P., *Godsdienssosiografiese Studie van die Jeug in die gemeente Burgerspark met die Kerkjeugveriniging as agtergrond'* [A Religious Sociography of Youth in the Burgerspark parish against the background of the Church-Youth Association]. Deo Gloria, 1966.

Venter, P. W., *Onkerksheid: 'n Sosiaal-Historiese en Godsdiens-Sosiologiese Ondersoek* [Churchlessness: A Socio-historical and Religious-sociological Investigation]. Pretoria, Haum, 1957.

Vilakazi, Absolom, *Zulu Transformations*. Pietermaritzburg, University of Natal Press, 1962.

Watts, H. L., *South African Town*. Grahamstown, Rhodes University, Institute of Social and Economic Research, Occasional paper No 8, 1966.

Wilson, Monica, and Mafeje, Archie, *Langa: A study of Social Groups in an African Township*. Cape Town, O.U.P., 1963.

*Research in progress 1968*

Alant, C. J., *'n Sosiologiese Studie van die 'beeld' wat die gemeentelid in die Nederduitse Gereformeerde Kerk van die Amp van die Predikant het* [A Sociological Study of the Image of the Office of the Minister held by the Membership of the Nederduits Gereformeerde Kerk]. Pretoria, University of South Africa.

Basson, T. J., *'n Sosiologiese Studie van die N.G. Kerk met besondere verwysing na die N.G. Kerk in Afrika, Gemeente Zola Johannesburg* [A Sociological Study of the N.G. Kerk with particular reference to the N.G. Kerk in Africa, Zola Parish, Johannesburg]. Pretoria University of South Africa.

Boot, F. H., *Akkulturasie op religieuse gebied by die Abakwamkhwanazi* [Religious Assimilation of the Abakwamkhwanazi]. Pretoria, University of South Africa.

Brown, Sheila, *A Sociological Study of the Influence of the Church in the Bantu Community at Rwarwa, with special reference to the structure of the family*. Pretoria, University of South Africa.

Kotze, S. F., *Die Begrip Marginale Mens* [The Concept of Marginal Man]. Pretoria, University of South Africa.

Steenkamp, C. S., *Religieusiteit in die Samelewing: 'n Sosiologiese ondersoek na die behoefte aan en die bewussyn en manifestasie van Godsdienstigheid* [Religiosity in Society: A Sociological Investigation about the need for and the consciousness and manifestation of religiosity]. University of Pretoria.

Wright, Beryl, *A Study of Religious orders and Personal and Group Attitudes and Values*. Grahamstown, Rhodes University.

PAULINA ALMERICH*

# Spain

## HISTORICAL INTRODUCTION

Despite polemical emphasis on traditional Spanish Catholic unity, it is, in fact, true that Spain was one of the first countries to show that peaceful coexistence of three different religions was possible. Between the Arab invasions in the eighth century and the expulsion of the Jews and Moriscos (Moors converted to Christianity) at the end of the fifteenth century, Christians, Jews and Moriscos lived together peacefully in the Hispanic cities of Castile and Aragon, under laws which protected them equally.[1] If disturbances occurred, the causes were economic rather than religious.

However, the decline of feudalism and the strengthening of the power of the Crown led the Catholic Monarchs, Isabella and Ferdinand, and their immediate successors, to find a focus of loyalty which transcended political differences inherent in an artificial union of states with different cultures, customs, languages and laws. Such a focal point could only be religion: the Catholic faith professed by the great majority of the people of Castile, Navarre and Aragon-Catalonia. This alone offered a solid and effective bulwark necessary for the founding of a powerful monarchy.

Yet unity based on religious grounds was not a great achievement. Someone as unbiased as the Marquis of Lozoya, states:

> Religious and racial plurality was the basis of the mediaeval development of Spain. Thus measures adopted at first by the Catholic mon-

* Paulina Almerich has a Licenciada en Letras from the University of Barcelona. She has taken part in numerous studies of the sociology of religion undertaken by the Centre for the Study of Applied Sociology (1958–1962) and later, with the Institute of Sociology and Pastoral Applications (I.S.P.A.). She has headed the Publications section of I.S.P.A. She has collaborated in the publication of many articles.

1. During the reign of Ferdinand and Isabella the total population of Aragon-Catalonia was 960,000, distributed between various socio-religious groups according to the following percentages; Old Christians 69.2; Converts 3.1; Jews 3.1; Moriscos 24.5. The equivalent percentages for these groups in the population of Castille (7,000,000) were 91.5, 3.1, 2.4 and 2.8 respectively [Contreras, 1967, III, p. 102].

> archs and then by Phillip II, were bound to affect adversely the racial and economic evolution of Spain [Contreras, 1967, III, p. 108].

In fact, binding the country within limited spiritual boundaries resulted in a great impoverishment, not only economic and social, but spiritual as well. On the other hand, it allowed Spain to overcome the great religious crisis of the seventeenth century and spared her the religious wars suffered elsewhere in Europe.

Of course it cannot be stated dogmatically that the ideas of the Reformation did not penetrate into Spain. They did, and they had some influence among small groups of the intellectual élite. In the ferment of the Universities of Valladolid, Toledo and Seville especially, important heretical groups were formed, which the Inquisition undertook to annihilate or drive out of the country. Among those who escaped was the notable Cipriano de Valera to whom we owe the famous Protestant Bible [Desumbila, 1965, IV, 75].

Despite the existence of these fragmentary groups, and because of the harsh penalties exacted by the Inquisition, the religious scene in Spain was, for four centuries, solidly uniform; the term 'Spanish' was almost a synonym for 'Catholic'. The absolutist policy of the Bourbons strengthened these tendencies; political unity needed to shelter under a symbol meaningful to the simple and fiery Spanish people.

The first liberal parliament which came into being after the suppression of the Tribunal of the Inquisition was the first Cortes of Cadiz (1812). It took the first step towards the recognition of dissenting Christians, i.e. Protestants. However, the prohibition against practising any religion but Catholicism remained. Real toleration was not won until the revolution of 1868 and then only by extending to Spanish Protestants the law which allowed foreigners resident in the country to practise their religion. This was equivalent to allowing Spaniards to practise a 'foreign' religion. Thus Protestants and other non-Catholic Spaniards began to take their place in national life, thanks to the political favour shown them by a less religious section of the community. Sociologically they were regarded as an appendix to foreigners.

In the wake of this religious freedom, the great Protestant denominations of the world came into Spain with their missionaries. From this period date the first chapels and communities of Plymouth Brethren, Baptists, Methodists, Congregationalists, etc.

The first authentic Spanish Protestants were usually religious people, ex-Catholics who for various reasons joined the Protestant ranks.[2] The principal

2. The principal Protestant groups in Spain were first established in the following areas: Granada, Málaga, 1863; Seville (Cabrera), 1868; Valencia, Alicante, 1860/70; Mahon, Villacarlos, 1868; Majorca, Barcelona, 1869; Zaragoza (Matamoros) 1860;

groups were clustered in Andalusia, shielded by their proximity to Gibraltar.

The necessity to unite in one church soon became obvious to the dissenters. An attempt was made by a Spaniard, Juan B. Cabrera, a former member of a Catholic teaching order, who founded the Spanish Reformed Church in 1868. Unfortunately, public worship by non-Catholics was prohibited under the new Constitution of the Bourbon Restoration which remained in force until the Republican régime of 1931 to 1936.

In 1880 the young Reformed Church was split by disagreement as to whether its structure should be Episcopalian or Presbyterian. This split gave birth to the *Inglesia Española Reformada Episcopal* – IERE, (Spanish Reformed Episcopalian Church) whose first bishop was Cabrera, and to the *Inglesia Evangelica Española* (Spanish Evangelical Church). The Latter eventually absorbed the various foreign missions of the evangelical type, and unified them into one ecclesiastical body [Desumbila, 1965, 77].

Because these reformed churches were always, or nearly always, clandestine organizations, they had little influence on the religious life of the nation. Their work was reduced, in most cases, to aggressive proselytism, especially among the more needy classes and, in the suburbs of the larger cities, among the discontended, socially non-integrated and dissatisfied populations.

At present, ostensibly under order from the Second Vatican Council, but in reality under pressure from various foreign countries (e.g. U.S.A.), the Spanish State has adopted a Law of Religious Freedom guaranteeing the existence of, and the right to practise, non-Catholic faiths. However, while this appears to be a positive step, the Law has been rejected by the majority of Churches because it continues to put them in an inferior position, similar to that of any private association in which the State has a right to intervene.

## DEMOGRAPHIC DATA

At present, the overwhelming majority of Spaniards are Catholic. Non-Catholics amount to approximately 0.1 per cent of the total population and most of these are of foreign origin. However, there is developing in their ranks a noticeable proportion of Spaniards, descended from the first Protestants of the last century. One of the aims of current Spanish Protestantism is to demonstrate that it is possible to be a good Protestant and a good Spaniard at the same time [Estruch, 1968, p. 127].

Madrid, 1870/71; Asturias, Santander, 1870; Parts of Barcelona, 1871; Logrono, San Sebastian, 1872; Salamanca, 1875; Valladolid, Bilbao, Reus, Galicia, 1876 [Estruch, 1968].

It is very difficult to obtain valid statistics about non-Catholics because, as they are not officially recognised and their groups are dispersed, we are forced to rely on data supplied by the government, and this is not always reliable. Moreover, except for a recently published degree thesis by Juan Estruch, a member of IERE, there are neither statistics nor reliable studies on which to lean.

According to Estruch's study there are in Spain nine Protestant denominations, various minor sects, Jews, Mohammedans (especially in Madrid), and one Oriental sect (Bah-hai). Their numbers are shown below.

*Table 1. Non-Catholics in Spain, 1961 and 1967*

| Religious denominations | Estimates 1961[a] | | 1967[b] |
|---|---|---|---|
| | Minimum | Maximum | |
| Spanish Evangelical Church | 2,544 | 3,062 | 3,800 |
| Episcopal Reformed Church of Spain | 558 | 697 | 1,000 |
| Baptist Union of Spain | 3,472 | 4,060 | 5,400 |
| Federation of Independent Evangelical Churches of Spain | 1,006 | 1,163 | 3,100 |
| Spanish Christian Mission | 488 | 693 | |
| Plymouth Brethren | 5,013 | 5,849 | 6,000 |
| Pentacostalists | 218 | 281 | 3,500 |
| Independent Baptists | 517 | 665 | 2,000 |
| Quakers | 52 | 75 | n.a. |
| Adventists | 1,329 | 1,707 | 5,200 |
| Jehova Witnesses | 635 | 857 | n.a. |
| Bah-hai | 141 | 195 | n.a. |
| Hebrew | 3,600 | 3,600 | n.a. |
| Orthodox schismatics | 150 | 200 | n.a. |
| Total | 19,723 | 23.004 | 30,000 |

Source: a. Estruch, 1968, pp. 38–39.
b. Data from *Comisión Defensa Evangelica* 1967 (Commission for Evangelical Defence)

Protestants are not evenly distributed throughout the country. Estruch calculated that one third of the members of the first eight groups of Table 1 were concentrated in Catalonia. Only in the provinces of Andalusia, Galicia, Old Castile (Madrid) and Valencia did the number of Protestants exceed 1,000, and none of these Protestant populations exceeded 2,500 [Estruch, 1968, pp. 43–83].

The disproportion between Catholics and non-Catholics is so enormous that the difficulty of establishing a comparison is self-evident. Data is available only from the already cited work of Juan Estruch. A comparison of sex and marital status is shown in Table 2.

*Table 2. Sex and marital status of Catholics and Protestants (in %)*

| | Catholic[a] | Protestant[b] |
|---|---|---|
| Males | 48.5 | 33.8 |
| Females | 51.5 | 66.2 |
| Total | 100.0 | 100.0 |
| Single | 51.3 | 65.3 |
| Married | 42.1 | 28.0 |
| Widowed | 6.3 | 5.6 |

Sources: a. *Anvario Estadísticode Espana* (Statistical Year Book of Spain), 1966.
b. Estruch, 1968, pp. 113–115.

*Table 3. Composition by age (in %)*

| Age | Catholics[a] | Age | Protestants[b] |
|---|---|---|---|
| 0–4 years | 9.9 | | |
| 5–9 years | 8.8 | | |
| 10–14 years | 8.6 | 0–19 years | 29.6 |
| 15–24 years | 14.9 | | |
| 25–34 years | 15.6 | | |
| 35–44 years | 13.7 | 20–59 years | 64.8 |
| 45–54 years | 11.2 | | |
| 55–64 years | 9.0 | 60 and over years | 5.6 |
| 65 and over years | 8.1 | | |

Source: a. *Statistical Yearbook of Spain*, 1966.
b. Estruch, 1968, p. 113.

A comparison of the figures in Table 3 is not really possible. However, it does show a slight tendency for more Protestants to be middle-aged than Catholics. There are proportionally more Catholics in the younger age groups, perhaps because Protestants tend to be urban dwellers and families in the cities tend to be smaller.

Table 4 shows an apparent educational superiority of the Protestant population over the Catholic, but the reader must take into account that the Protestant sample refers only to one church (Spanish Episcopal Church, IERE) and only to Barcelona. Generally Protestants belong to the middle and lower classes, and include a high proportion of labourers; most Protestant converts are from the poorest migrant populations.

*Table 4. Level of education by denomination in Barcelona (in %)*

| | Catholic | Protestant* |
|---|---|---|
| Illiterate | 13.78 | 0.9 |
| Primary education | 76.13 | 74.5 |
| Secondary and technical studies | 9.97 | 20.5 |
| Tertiary education | 0.10 | 3.6 |

* Protestant population of the Spanish Episcopal Church only.
Source: Estruch, 1968, p. 122.

Unfortunately, we do not possess statistics related to the socio-professional distribution of non-Catholics and are therefore unable to make detailed comparisons. We only know that in Barcelona, 56,3 per cent of the adult Protestant population are employed, a figure very close to that of 52.5 per cent for the Catholic population.

Catholic families are, on the average, larger than Protestant families. In Barcelona, the Catholic family has an average of 3.9 members whereas the Protestant family has an average of 2.9.

Although it should be noted that there is a certain proportion of mixed marriage in Spain the following totals for 1966, and the percentage of total marriages (given in brackets) is an indication of its relative unimportance: mixed Religion, 194 (0.8%); different rites, 66 (0.02) and civil marriage, 41 (0.01) [Guia de la Inglesia en España, 1966]. Spanish migration to Northern Europe and the presence of Americans in Spain helps account for these mixed marriages, but because of the enormous numerical disproportion between Catholics and non-Catholics, the phenomenon is not widespread. Non-Catholics appear more interested than Catholics in avoiding mixed marriages, for to them it is a matter of survival. If a non-Catholic marries a Catholic, the Catholic Church insists that the progeny be brought up in the Catholic faith. Also, there is a tendency for young Protestants, when marrying a Catholic, to go over to the Catholic Church.

As there are such a small number of Protestants in Spain, they do not have much influence on religious life as a whole. Nevertheless, their proselytizing work is remarkable, particularly in the more squalid suburban areas of the big cities and in certain rural districts. Increasing membership of non-Catholic faiths, especially among Protestant groups, is due more to conversion than to natural increase. Conversions are usually achieved through crusading among migrants, newly settled in cities and industrial areas, who tend to feel lost and disoriented and to whom help, not entirely disinterested help, is offered. Such prospective converts, in general, have been either indifferent to religion or come from regions where, due to the scarcity of priests or to isolation, the standards of religious practice are poor.

In the Spanish Evangelical Church in 1965, conversions accounted for 28.8 per thousand members. Nevertheless, conversions from Catholicism to Protestantism have not reached appreciable numbers in comparison with the number of Catholics. However, in the future effective propaganda by Protestants could attract large numbers of those who are only nominally Catholic.

## RELIGIOUS PARTICIPATION AND BELIEF

Unfortunately there have been no studies on religious practice in Spain of a general character or following a common methodology to facilitate comparisons. There are several local studies, limited to definite cities or dioceses, or to a simple recording of Mass attendance or consultations with parish priests. There are detailed studies such as those ordered by dignitaries of the Church in preparation for general missions, or with the aim of parish reconstruction or simply to determine the extent of the problems they have to face. In other cases, studies have been commissioned by a group of parish priests for the purpose of preparing a combined pastoral report on the region. Consequently the available data are irregular and in some cases have to be taken only as pointers needing modification by future, more scientific studies.

To date, the fullest and most precise work on the Spanish scene is the *Análisis sociológico del catolicismo español* (Sociological Analysis of Spanish Catholicism) by Dr R. Duocastella and others [Duocastella, 1967b] from which much of the data presented below is taken. More recent is a book by D. J. M. Vazquez *Realidades socioreligiosas de España* (Socio-religious Factors in Spain) which follows step by step the areas studied by Duocastella and tries to add new data, some of which, unfortunately, is not as reliable as could be desired [Vazquez, 1967].

Largely as a result of the historical upheavals to which we referred, there is a profound diversity of outlook, custom, standards of practice, and even religious concept among the various regions of Spain. Hence, the findings of any one local or regional study cannot be generalised to the whole of Spain.

Nevertheless, some features of the national pattern can be identified. While the northern regions are, in general, more regular in practice and more attached to traditional religion, if sometimes of a negative and sombre character, southern religion is more folkloric, more popular, noisy, and brilliant, but also more superficial. There, the processions of Holy Week and colourful pilgrimages are evidence of a very naive and simple, yet distorted faith.

Secondly, the generalization that the economic situation (especially in the more industrial regions) is a stronger determinant of religious practice than the traditional religious climate of an area seems to hold true. Hence, an industrial town in the north will be less religious than other northern areas and more like industrial centres in other regions traditionally less religious.

Thirdly, there are significant urban rural differences. The known data on Sunday Communion appear to suggest that the larger the proportion of Sunday attendants the smaller the proportion of Sunday communicants. Rural areas have the highest proportion of Sunday attendance, and in conjunction with their low rate of Sunday communion this suggests a social rather than a personal religion. Urban areas represent a tendency in the opposite direction – a lower proportion attending Sunday Mass, but a more equivalent proportion of communicants. In rural areas, in contrast to urban areas, the proportion participating in Easter observance is greater than the proportion attending Sunday Mass. This again suggests that the social and legalistic rather than the personal and individualistic aspects of religion are more characteristic of rural areas. It should, however, again be emphasized that data on this subject is relatively scarce. These generalizations are advanced on the basis of collating various regional and parish studies carried out, not always by experts, over the last twenty-five years. Tables 6 to 11 at the end of this chapter provide recent data illustrative of regional variation.

Data on the practices of Protestant communities are scarce and unreliable. However, the study by Estruch gives church attendance rates of 50 to 92 per cent for the Episcopal community of Barcelona [Estruch, 1968, p. 141]. It is logical that there should be a high standard of practice among them, thanks to their greater internal cohesion and deep conviction. Because of the smallness of their communities and the consequent high extent of social contact, they are more likely to be scrupulous in their religious practices. Estruch gives also percentages of practising Episcopalians; 68.5 in 1957 and 67.5 in 1965 [Estruch, 1968, p. 142].

Family prayer is one of the practices which has changed as a result of urbanization and industrialization. There is no doubt that city life, much more complex than rural, makes it difficult for a sense of family unity to exist. Work in the fields which has to be carried out according to the natural rhythms of light and dark, leaves much more free time at night which the family can use for community prayer – in Spain usually the Rosary. But city life, with its many demands – long hours of exhausting work, children's schooling, teenagers' studies, the many entertainments available – is an almost insurmountable obstacle to the reciting of a prayer as long as the Rosary. Hence, this is one of the aspects of religious life most affected by the changes sweeping through Spain.

For this reason, the majority of studies carried out on family prayer are not restricted to the Rosary, as before, but include any type of prayer said by the whole family at the same time, or at least by a greater part of the family. According to this criterion, the latest studies include as 'family prayer' the saying of grace at meals and, in some cases, the prayers which parents say with small children at bed-time and which are the first religious instruction received by a child. Table 5 is derived from various recent studies and gives a comparison of prayer habits and Mass attendance.

*Table 5. Family prayer and Bible ownership related to mass attendance*

| Region | Daily family prayer | | Bible ownership | |
|---|---|---|---|---|
| | % of population | % of regular Mass attenders | % of population | % of regular Mass attenders |
| Vitoria (township)[1] | 19.0 | 33.3 | | |
| Vitoria (rest of diocese)[1] | 28.6 | | | |
| Tarrasa (Cátalonia)[2] | | | 8.6 | 54.1 |
| Mining basin Nalon (Asturias)[3] | 0.3 | 18.8 | | |
| Mining basin Mieres (Asturias)[4] | | 47.0 | | |
| Salamanca (capital)[5] | 29.6 | 54.1 | 23.9 | 43.6 |
| Granada (Capital)[6] | 13.9 | 36.0 | 13.1 | 34.1 |
| Ciudad Real (capital)[7] | | 27.8 | | |
| Miranda de Ebro (Industrial Region)[8] | | | | |
| Diocese Alicante-Orihuela[9] | 11.0 | | | |
| Diocese Menorca[10] | 17.9 | 54.08 | 13.9 | 41.9 |
| Average | 17.1 | 36.6 | | |

Sources: Various regional studies: 1. Duocastella, 1967; 2. Duocastella, 1968; 3. I.S.P.A., 1967c; 4. I.S.P.A., 1968; 5. Duocastella, 1968; 6. Ocana, 1967; 7. Romo 1967; 8. Caballero and Aguiano, 9. Office of Statistics, 1962 and 1965; 10. Current study in charge of I.S.P.A.

Reading or possessing the Bible does not have the same meaning for Catholics as prayer or attendance at Mass, partly due to the semi-prohibition by the Church on the people directly reading the Holy Scriptures. Hence, Bible reading was regarded as if it were 'sinful', and in some regions a Catholic who showed excessive interest in the Bible was even looked upon with distrust, as such reading was considered tacitly to be a trait exclusive to Protestants. However, the Second Vatican Council has encouraged Catholics to nourish their faith by reading the Holy Scriptures and hence the Bible has become very popular, as shown by Table 5. Luxury editions have been printed, one after another, and many Catholics are attracted, if not to its study, at least to its ownership, because of the beauty of the editions. We could say that at present the Bible is 'in fashion'; and the more attractive the illustrations the better. This is not so with Protestants, for whom it is the primary book and source of spiritual guidance.

Like family prayer, baptism has undergone a great change in the past fifty years. At the beginning of the century, up until about 1920, the supernatural nature of the sacrament prevailed above all other considerations, and, as a symbol of God's grace, it was esteemed and appreciated. Therefore, the newly born were baptized as early as possible. It used to be common practice in Spain for babies to be baptised within 24 hours of birth. For example, in the rural area of Vitoria, in 1900, 84 per cent of babies were baptized within four days of their birth, compared with 20 per cent in 1950. In the mining basin of Nalòn, the proportion has dropped from 54.4 per cent to 6.6 per cent in the same period.

The delay in baptism has several causes. The principal one is social; the desire for as many friends and relatives as possible to take part, and the more modern custom of celebrating it in a hired hall with the mother present. The spiritual meaning has been eclipsed by the social. There has also been a drop in the infant mortality rate (from 11.2 per thousand in 1900 to 6.1 per thousand in 1965). These advances in medicine and hygiene give a much wider margin of security, allowing for a greater delay before baptism.

Unfortunately, this subject has been barely studied in our country and, where it has been investigated, it has only been a minor element in general studies of religious practice. In the diocese of Barcelona, Duocastella has given it particular attention, and has collated data from other studies. For the most part this has not been published, although details have been given to interested persons outside Spain.

## RELIGION AND PROFESSION, SOCIAL CLASS AND EDUCATION

This subject has received a lot of attention from students of the sociology of religion in Spain, although not always with a high degree of scientific accuracy. As a general rule, even the most rigorous studies have come up against the problem of deriving a meaningful grouping of professions, the only basis on which comparative work is possible. This obstacle is difficult to overcome. At present there is a tendency to adopt the official census classification, although this has the severe disadvantage of not categorizing within professions.

At any rate, despite this lack of uniformity, the various studies carried out provide a fairly accurate picture. The overall impression is that, in addition to the estrangement of the great proportion of workers from the Church, the intellectual classes are being lost, and even middle class adherence is breaking down, mainly because their religiosity is less a matter of vital need than of convenience born of the erroneous identification of Catholicism and conservatism.

Naturally, it is necessary to point out once more that religious practices of various categories and socio-professional groups are greatly affected by the religious climate of an area. Workers or labourers in the Basque Country practice more than those in the Levante or Andalusia; but there are similarities, for example between working-class practice in the mining-industrial region of Asturia and in the industrial area of Catalonia.

Tables 6–11 show church attendance by occupation for six different areas. The tables have been selected from the most recent studies with the dual purpose of illustrating both general class differentials and specific regional variations in Spanish religious practice.

*Table 6. Occupation and attendance at mass in the mining basin of Nalòn**

| Occupation (those over 15 years) | Attending Mass each Sunday in % |
|---|---|
| Higher technicians | 66.6 |
| Students – university and equivalent | 33.4 |
| Public servants (civil service, police, army) | 27.6 |
| Liberal professionals | 21.7 |
| Domestic servants | 21.3 |
| Clerks | 17.6 |
| Shopkeepers, tradesmen | 14.9 |
| Students of professions | 14.0 |
| Working women | 12.3 |
| Farmers | 8.6 |
| Miners (surface) | 5.9 |
| Retired pensioners | 5.0 |
| Miscellaneous workers | 4.9 |
| Metal workers | 4.1 |
| Transport workers | 1.9 |
| Miners (underground) | 1.9 |

* The northern mining basin of the Nalòn in Asturias is an area which, in the course of considerable social and political unrest, has been influenced to a large extent by socialism and communism.
Source: Duocastella, 1967c.

*Table 7. Occupation and attendance at mass in Metaro**

| Occupation | Attending Mass each Sunday in % |
|---|---|
| Big industrialists | 80.8 |
| Students, primary | 68.0 |
| Students, secondary and above | 65.9 |
| Clerks | 54.0 |
| Supervisors, foremen | 53.0 |
| Liberal professions | 51.3 |
| Army ranks | 51.0 |
| Shop assistants | 38.0 |
| Merchants | 36.0 |
| Public servants | 36.0 |
| Landowners | 28.2 |
| Housemaids | 26.8 |
| Small industrialists | 25.0 |
| Retired pensoners | 18.6 |
| Municipal public servants | 17.0 |
| Unemployed | 17.0 |
| Tradesmen | 14.0 |
| Farm labourers | 5.0 |
| Industrial labourers | 5.0 |
| Fishermen | 3.2 |

* Metaro is an industrial town of 36,000 inhabitants, dependent primarily upon the knitting industry. It is located on the Mediterranean coast, approximately 20 miles from Barcelona. Source: Duocastella, 1960, p. 248.

*Table 8. Occupation and mass attendance in the diocese of Albacete**

| Occupation | Attending Mass each Sunday in % |
|---|---|
| Liberal professions, technicians | 66.3 |
| Employers | 24.6 |
| Tradesmen | 20.0 |
| Labourers | 11.6 |

* This is a depressed rural area between the centre of Spain and Andalusia. Catholicism is generally less fervent here than in the north. The average cultural level is low. There is scarcely any industry; although some wines are grown in the region of La Mancha; there is much emigration. Source: *Oficina Sociologica pastoral del Obispado. Cumplimiento dominical en la Diöcesis de Albacete*, 1967.

*Table 9. Occupation and Mass Attendance in the diocese of Vitoria**

| Occupation | Attending Mass each Sunday in % | |
|---|---|---|
| | Capital city | Rural area |
| Property owners (large and small) | 100.0 | 89.5 |
| Students over 14 years | 100.0 | 91.4 |
| Domestic servants | 100.0 | 85.0 |
| Liberal professions | 90.2 | 90.0 |
| Administrators, clerks | 86.3 | 78.0 |
| Those with private income | 66.4 | 36.0 |
| Retired pensioners | 65.5 | 88.8 |
| Housewives | 62.9 | 89.0 |
| Public servants | 56.0 | 84.5 |
| Higher technicians, managers | 55.1 | 89.0 |
| Tradesmen, transport workers | 51.6 | 75.1 |
| Students, under 14 years | 44.9 | 90.2 |
| Unskilled workers | 29.2 | 81.2 |
| Unemployed | 19.4 | 30.5 |
| Total | 58.9 | 86.1 |

* Vitoria is a diocese in the Basque region where religious practice is very high. The city has begun to be industrialised, a fact which will lead to a modification of the high indices. It is significant that in most categories the rural zone has higher rate of religious practice. Source: Duocastella, 1965, p. 162.

*Table 10. Occupation and mass attendance in Gerona**

| Occupation | Attending Mass each Sunday in % |
|---|---|
| Liberal professions | 66.5 |
| Students | 58.0 |
| Clerks | 54.5 |
| Public services | 51.6 |
| Commercial employees | 49.3 |
| Domestic servants | 42.3 |
| Housewives | 41.9 |
| Industrialists, artisans | 35.7 |
| Merchants | 28.8 |
| Farmers | 24.1 |
| Industrial Workers | 14.5 |
| Retired | 12.9 |

* Gerona is a city in Catalonia near the French border. Source: *Oficina de sociologia del Obispado Gerona*, 1967.

*Table 11. Occupation and mass attendance in the diocese of Salamanca**

| Occupation | Attending Mass each Sunday in % |
|---|---|
| Higher technicians | 94.6 |
| Priests and other religious | 86.9 |
| Students | 84.6 |
| Farmers | 75.9 |
| Housewives | 71.9 |
| Liberal professions | 65.9 |
| Shop assistants | 58.5 |
| University professors, school masters | 54.6 |
| Industrialists and businessmen | 52.9 |
| Employees (and waiters and servants) | 51.8 |
| Apprentices | 51.6 |
| Public servants | 49.8 |
| Police | 47.5 |
| Domestic servants | 42.5 |
| Merchants | 41.3 |
| Retired, pensioners and those with private income | 34.1 |
| Tradesmen | 31.3 |
| Artisans and craftsmen | 27.7 |
| Transport workers | 22.8 |
| Building and other labourers | 11.5 |

Source: Duocastella, 1968.
* This is a Castilian city with a great Catholic and university tradition.

In each of these six studies the lowest rate of Sunday Mass attendance is among working class men, while the highest rate occurs in the upper middle class strata among the property owners, big industrialists and higher technicians. The rate of attendance among members of the liberal professions, roughly indicative of the intelligentsia, falls somewhere between the two.

However, what is most striking is the considerable variation within the same class, between different areas. Thus, working class practice varies from the extremely low 1.9 per cent in the Nalón basin to 29.2 per cent (or the extremely high 81.2 per cent, if we include unskilled rural workers) in Vitoria. There is a comparable variation of about 33 per cent between the highest rates of attendance in these six areas. An explanation of these differences involves the points made earlier – church attendance tends to be greater in the north than the south; greater in rural rather than urban areas; and is significantly affected by industrialization.

## RELATIONSHIP BETWEEN RELIGION, POLITICS AND ECONOMY

The nature of the Spanish political régime prevents any investigation of this topic. The régime has leant on religion to secure support from the majority of the nation who are sincerely religious, and above all, from the ruling classes. A real dictatorship has been imposed, without even a glimmer of genuine freedom of expression; all the laws of freedom of the press are nullified when put into practice. To do any research on this topic would constitute a crime against the country.

If, by chance, any studies do exist, they have been conveniently framed according to state directions, and no guarantee of scientific honesty and credibility is offered by studies with predetermined findings.

What can be said is that the identification of religion and Francoism has done tremendous harm to the Church and to the Catholic faith. In the minds of many people rejection of the political régime also means rejection of Catholicism.

## OTHER SIGNIFICANT STUDIES IN THE SOCIOLOGY OF RELIGION

The Bibliography provides a sample of other work carried out in Spain in the Sociology of Religion. Studies of the clergy, their attitudes, work, problems, training and the nature and number of vocations have received much attention. The religious behaviour of Spanish youth has also been the subject of a number of specific studies, but general studies on youth also offer useful religious data.

In connection with religion and social change, migration and tourism have been of particular interest to Spanish scholars. Migration, especially from the poorer agricultural areas of the south to northern urban and industrial cities and, indeed, to other countries of Europe, is an important feature of Spanish socio-economic life. A number of studies have investigated the influence of population movement on religious life. Tourism, newly developed as a major industry, is also having its impact, and in recent years has received considerable attention from sociologists.

## SELECTED BIBLIOGRAPHY

### *General works*

Almerich, P., 'The Present Position of Religious Sociology in Spain.' *Social Compass*, XII (4–5), 1965.

Arzobispado de Madrid-Alcalá [Arch diocese of Madrid, Alcalá], *Nuevas estructuras pastorales en la diócesis de Madrid-Alcalá* [New Pastoral Structures in the Diocese of Madrid-Alcalá]. Madrid, Office of the Archbishop, 1965.

Arin, A., 'El lado social de la práctica religiosa' [The Social Side of Religious Practice]. *Vida Neuva*, 408, 1964.

Caballero, G., 'Valoración sociológico-pastoral de la práctica religiosa dominical' [Sociologico-Pastoral Assessment of Sunday Religious Practice]. *Pentecostés*, 13, 1966.

Caritas Española, *Actitudes religiosas del desarrollo económico* [Economic Development and Religious Attitudes]. Madrid, Caritas Española, 1962.

Contreras, Juan de, Marquis de Lozoya, *Historia de España* [History of Spain]. Pomplona, Salvat Editores, 1967.

Duocastella, R., *Como estudiar una parroquia* [How to Study a Parish]. Barcelona, I.S.P.A., 1967a.

Duocastella, R., *et al.*, *Análisis Sociológico del Catolicismo Español* [A Sociological Analysis of Spanish Catholicism]. Barcelona, I.S.P.A., 1967b.

Rodriguez, Osuna J., *La nueva estructura parroquial de Madrid* [New Parish Structure of Madrid]. Madrid, Instituto de Estudios Madrileños [Institute of Madrid Studies]. I, 1966.

Seminario Derecho Político [School of Political Law], 'Encuesta sobre el impacto religioso en la sociedad laica de Salamanca' [Research into the Impact of Religion on Lay Society in Salamanca]. *Boletin Informativo* (University of Salamanca) 1955.

*Non-Catholics*

Castro, Adolfo de, *Historia de los Protestantes españoles* [History of the Spanish Protestants]. Cadiz, Press and Library of the Medical Review, 1851.

Desumbila, José, *El ecumenismo en España* [Ecumenism in Spain]. Estela-Barcelona, I.S.P.A., 1965.

Estruch, Juan, *Ecumenismo, actitud espiritual* [Ecumenism – the Spiritual Attitude]. Barcelona, I.S.P.A., Nova Terra 1965.

—, *Los protestantes en España* [The Protestants in Spain]. Barcelona, I.S.P.A., Nova Terra, 1968.

Hughey, David J., *Historia de los Bautistas en España* (translated from the English) [History of the Baptists in Spain]. Barcelona, Junta Bautista de Publicaciones, 1964.

—, *Religious Freedom in Spain; Its Ebb and Flow*. London, Carey Kingsgate Press, 1955.

Jofre, Fernandez, E., *Las relaciones entre judíos y católicos en España, hoy* [Relations between Jews and Catholics in Spain Today] Unpublished. Madrid, 1966.

Ventura, Jordi, *Els heretges catalans* [Catalan Heretics]. Barcelona, Ed. Selecta, 1963.

*Religion and occupation*

Bayés, R., *Los ingenieros, la sociedad y la religión* [Engineers, Society and Religion]. Barcelona, Ed. Fontanella, 1965.

Brugarola, M., S. J., *Sociología rural católica* [Catholic Rural Sociology]. Madrid, Fomento Social, 1950.

Duocastella, R., 'La práctica religiosa y las clases sociales' [Religious Practice and Social Classes]. *Arbor*, 38, 1957.

—, *Sociologia Religiosa y Pastoral de Conjunto de la Diocesis de Salamanca* [Current Study of the City and Diocese of Salamanca]. Barcelona, (I.S.P.A.), 1968.

—, *Sociología religiosa de una ciudad industrial; Metaro* [Religious Sociology of an Industrial City, Mataro]. Barcelona, I.S.P.A., 1960.

Duocastella, R., *et al.*, *Sociología y pastoral de una diocesis Vítoria* [Sociology and Pastoral Work in the Diocese of Vitoria]. Barcelona, I.S.P.A., Nova Terra, 1965l

—, *Sociología religíosa de la ciudad de Tarrasa* [Religious Sociology of the City of Tarrasa]. Barcelona, I.S.P.A., 1968.

Hermandades Obreros de Acción Catholic (H.O.A.C.) [Catholic Action Workers Brotherhood], 'Encuesta sobre 15,000 obreros sobre asistencia a misa dominical' [Research on Sunday Mass Attendance among 15,000 Workers]. *Esprit*, February 1964.

Instituto de Sociologia y Pastoral Aplicadas (I.S.P.A.) [Institute of Applied Sociology and Pastoral Study], *Sociología religiosa y b storal de conjunto de las cuencas del Lena-Caudal-Aller* [Religious and Pastoral Sociology of the Combined Basins of Lena-Caudal-Aller]. Barcelona, I.S.P.A., 1968a.

Negre, P., S. J., 'La práctica religiosa obrera y su motivación' [Workers' Religious Practice and its Motivation]. *Anales de Sociología*, 1, Barcelona, 1966.

—, 'Criterios de descristianización en la clase obrera' [Criteria of de-Christianization of the Working Class]. *Mundo Social* (Zaragoza), 15 October 1966.

Romo, P. Alfonso, Caballero, B., Sanchez Aguiano, M., *Estudio sociológico pastoral de una ciudad* [Pastoral Sociology of a City]. Madrid, Perpetuo Socorro – Ciudad Real 1967.

Sánchez, Ocana, *Estudio socio-religioso de Granada* [Socio-Religious Description of Granada] (typescript). Granada, 1967.

*Religion, politics and economic life*

Aliene Urosa, J., 'Diferencias regionales de renta en la economía espanola' [Regional Differences of Income in the Spanish Economy]. *Revista Internacional de Sociología*, 87, Madrid, 1964.

Dominguez, R., and Tenzanos, J. F., 'Una encuesta socio-politica a los universitarios de Madrid' [Socio-political Inquiry into the University Population of Madrid]. *Cuadernos para el Dialogo*, No. extra 1968.

Fuenmayor, Amadeo de, '*Estado y Religión*' [The State and Religion]. *Revista de Estudios Políticos* (Madrid) 152 (III–IV), 1967.

*Religion and youth*

Duocastella, R., 'Resultados de una encuesta sobre la juventud' [Result of a Survey on Youth] in *Pastoral de la Juventud*. Madrid, P.P.C., 1967d.

Ellecuria, I., 'La juventud religiosa actual' [Present Day Religious Youth]. *Hechos y Dichos*, 67 (11), 1967.

García Salve, F., S J., 'La juventud, qué piensa de la Iglesia?' [Youth – What does it think of the Church?]. *Vida Nueva*, 13 J7ly 1967.

Gutierrez Comas, M. C., 'La religiosidad de la juventud universitaria femenina' [Religiosity of Female University Students]. *Eidos*, 22, June 1965.

Mencia Fuente, E.F.S.C., 'La religiosidad de nuestros jóvenes en un momento crítico' [Religiosity of our Youth at a Critical Moment]. Madrid, C.S.I.C. (Instituto San Jose de Calasanz), 1962.

Miguel, A. de, 'Religiosidad y clericalismo en los jóvenes españoles' [Religiosity and Clericalism among Young Spaniards]. *Revista del Instituto de la Juventud*, 8, December 1966.

Sánchez Terán Salvador, 'Estudio Sociológico sobre la descristianización de la juventud actual' [Sociological Study of the de-Christianisation of Present Day Youth]. *Pastoral de la juventud*, Madrid, P.P.C., 1967.

Tenzanos, J. F., and Dominguez, R. A., 'Los universitarios y la religión [University Students and Religion]. *El Ciervo*, 124, 1965.

Vazques, Jesus, M., O. P., *Encuesta socioreligiosa de la Juventud* [Socio-religious Research into Youth]. Unpublished. Madrid, 1960.

*Religious calling*

Abaitua, C., *Aspecto sociológico de las vocaciones en la diócesis de Vitoria y Pamplona* [Sociological aspects of Callings in the Diocese of Victoria and Pamplona]. Vitoria, Surge, 1958.

Arimón, C., *La enseñanza media en los seminarios de Espana* [Secondary Education in the Seminaries of Spain]. Barcelona, 1935.

Fernándes, Aguilar M., and Garcia Sanchez, A., *Notas para un estudio sociológico del clero Málaga* [Notes for a Sociological Study of the Clergy in Malaga]. Unpublished. Madrid, 1966.

Guerrero, J., 'Emigración de los religiosos a la ciudad' [Migration of the Religious to the Cities]. *Razón y Fe*, 1954.

Vazques, J. M., *Estudio sobre las vocaciones sacerdotales en Galicia* [Study of Priestly Vocations in Calicia]. Unpublished. Madrid, 1963.

—, *Estudio sobre las activida des de los religiosos españoles sin parroquia en las grandes ciudades* [Study of Activities of the Spanish Religious without a Parish in the Great Cities]. Unpublished. Madrid, 1965.

—, *Estudio sobre la mentalidad de los sacerdotes de la zona Huete-Cuenca* [Study of the Outlook of Priests in the Region of Huete-Cuenca]. Unpublished. Madrid, 1966.

*Migration*

Abaitua, C., *Las migraciones interiores, un nuevo capítulo en la pastoral contemporanea* [Internal Migration, a New Chapter in Contemporary Pastoral Work]. Vitoria, Surge, 1958.

Comisión Española de Emigración [Spanish Commission on Emigration], 'Influencia de la emigración española en la vida religiosa de España' [Influence of Spanish Emigration on Religious life in Spain]. *Boletín Informativo*, 114, 1967.

Diaz Mozas, J. M., 'Problemas que plantea la migración interior. Un quehacer político de urgencia' [Problems Posed by Internal Migration. An urgent Political Task]. *Ecclesia*, 1/18, 1958.

Duocastella, R., 'Problémes d'adaptation dans le cas de migrations interieures' [Problems of Adaptation in Internal Migrations]. *Population*, January-March, 1957.

—, 'Estudio de las migraciones internas en España [Study of Internal Migration in Spain]. *Documentación Social*, 4, Madrid, 1958.

—, 'Fenómenos de aculturación religiosa de la immigración en Cataluña' [Phenomena of Religious Acculturation of Immigrants in Catalonia]. Barcelona, Consejo Superior Investigaciones Cientifices, *Estudios Geográficos*, 1965.

—, 'Impliciones de los factores en el campo de la pastoral' [Implications of Sociological Factors in the Pastoral Field]. *Pastoral Misionera*, 1, January-February, 1965.

Perez de San Román, J. Pastoral de migración, [Pastoral Work and Migration]. *Palabra*, December, 1965.

Vazques, J. M., *Sociologia religiosa de las migraciones* [Religious Sociology of Migration]. Madrid, Valle de los Caidos, 1964.

*Tourism*

Bennassar, Bartolomé, *Turismo y Pastoral* [Tourism and Pastoral Work]. Barcelona, Estela, 1967.

Casco, J., *Atención pastoral a trabajadores y empleados inmigrados para el servicio del turismo* [Pastoral Attention to Workers and Employees who Immigrated for Tourist Services]. Malaga, Conferencias Pastorales Nacionales de Turismo, 1964.

Duocastella, R., *Sociologia y Pastoral del turismo* [Sociology and Pastoral Study of Tourism]. (roneoed) Barcelona, 1966.

Izarra, Prieto, J., *La pastoral del turismo en España* [Pastoral Work Related to Tourism]. Revised edition, unpublished. Madrid, 1965.

Llompart, G., *Perspectivas religiosas del turismo en Mallorca* [Religious Perspectives of Tourism in Majorca]. Majorca, Secrenarindo Diocesano de Turismo, 1964.

Vazques, J. M., O. P., *Estudio socio-religioso de la Costa Brava en relación con el turismo* [Socio-religious Study of the Costa Brava with relation to Tourism]. Madrid, Ministry of Information and Tourism, 1963.

—, *Turismo y Pastoral* [Tourism and Pastoral Work]. Madrid, Instituto de Estudios Políticos [Institute of Political Studies], 1966.

BERNDT GUSTAFSSON*

# Sweden

## INTRODUCTION

A pluralist community like that of twentieth century Sweden contains a variety of religious associations and groups, in marked contrast to the older rural society, where religious behaviour was rather homogeneous. Yet it is a peculiar characteristic of the Nordic countries that the old idea of a national church (i.e. the church identified with the whole people) has survived. In Sweden only 1.75 per cent of the adult population were not members of the National Church on 1st November, 1965.[1] The majority of Free-Church members still nominally also belong to the Swedish National Church.[2]

However, since the nineteenth century there has been a gradual change in the legal status of the National Church – a change which marks the emancipation of society from the church. The Local Government Act of 1862 initiated the first stage in this process; parishes and municipalities were separated. The parish priest, however, remained entitled to participate in the deliberations and decisions of the municipal council and when in 1918 Public

* Berndt Gustafsson was born in 1920 in Rogberga, Sweden. He holds the position of Assistant Professor at the University of Lund, and has been Director of The Stockholm Institute of Sociology of Religion since its foundation in 1962. He has a Ph.D. in Sociology and a D.D. in Church History. Major publications include *Kyrkan och socialdemokratien 1881–1890* [Church and Social Democracy 1881–1890], Lund, 1953, *Svensk kyrkohistoria* (Church History of Sweden), Stockholm, 1957, *Svensk kyrkogeografi* [Religious Geography of Sweden], Lund, 1957, *Religionssociologi* [Sociology of Religion], Stockholm, 1965.

1. According to data from parish registries 0.67 per cent left the Church of Sweden from 1 January 1952 to 31 December 1966. The withdrawal rate was highest in 1952, and 1957–8. At present it is about 3,000 per year (0.3 per cent). The number of withdrawals have been highest in the top socio-economic category and in the younger generation. The cities show a higher proportion of non-members (greater Stockholm 2.92, greater Gothenburg 2.92; the Malmö-Lund area 1.92). This figure is increasing, more because of immigration than because of withdrawals.

2. On the average, only about 10 per cent of Free Church members have left the Church of Sweden (Baptists, Methodists and members of *Svenska Missionsförbundet* (Swedish Mission Association) are above this average, Pentecostalists far below).

Assistance Boards and in 1924 Childrens Welfare Boards were introduced he was to be a member. The former position was abolished in 1956, but the latter continues.

The emancipation of the schools began later, but has progressed faster. Even after 1862 the schools belonged to the parish and were managed by the parochial vestry chaired by the vicar. Diocesan Chapters governed the primary and high schools of the diocese. Gradually between 1904 and 1930 these powers were transferred to the civil authority.

An important phase in the emancipation of society from the National Church commenced with the Religious Freedom Act of 1951; something like equality of status was given to all religious associations, membership in the Church of Sweden acquired a more voluntary character, and the Constitution was amended so that only the cabinet minister responsible for ecclesiastical matters, in stead of the whole Cabinet, had to be a member of the Church of Sweden. The peculiar status of the National Church is now mainly that it is maintained by the State. Further changes in the remaining organizational links between the State and the Church of Sweden may be expected from the parliamentary commission which, since 1958, has been working on the future relations between church and state.

As this emancipation of society from the church progressed, religious traditions have continuously receded. In 1900 an average of 17 per cent of the population went to the Sunday Morning Service in the Church of Sweden; in 1950 it had dropped to 3.0 per cent; in 1965 to 2.7 per cent (to this should be added fairly strong Free Church attendance figures, but even these have declined since 1950). Since the turn of the century a new significant difference has emerged between the church as a worshipping community and the church as an official institution: many utilize the church only for religious services such as Baptism, Confirmation, weddings and burial.

## RELIGIOUS ASSOCIATIONS

### *Types of religious organizations*

In this description the now classical typology of *church*, *denomination* and *sect* or *particular church* will be used in a modified form. However, it must be recognised that the pure types no longer exist and that since 1951 all religious associations in Sweden have had more or less the same legal status.

*The church.* The *church* is characterized by the domination of a territorial region by which it is in turn influenced. To some extent the *church's* norms and patterns of activity have their sources in society as a whole (although they are often related to an older stage of the society) for a *church* tries to make differences between its own and society's norm-systems as small as possible. It is culturally and ideologically open and inclusive. It gives room to modernism and conservatism (e.g. Schartavanism), liberalism; and fundamentalism (Bible Friends), high and low church tendencies[3] while endeavouring to leave its mark on the whole of society, with respect to religion and morality. Child baptism is a further characteristic: membership is more often constituted by membership of a family and citizenship than by a voluntary act.

The Church of Sweden, with its territorial organisation covering the whole country and encompassing 98 per cent of the population, traditionally represents the *church* type. Although the 1951 Act made great changes in its status, and voluntary membership has since been further emphasised,[4] territorial monopoly still plays an important part in ecclesiastical thinking. Nevertheless the Church of Sweden has become more similar to a *denomination*, and is in most places in competition with other associations.

The Free-Churches, primarily the Swedish Mission Association and the Methodist Church, also combine elements of the *church* and the *denomination*. These exhibit *church*-type features such as child baptism[5] and a certain openness to generally accepted modes of conduct. Their authority to conduct wedding services (since 1951) and burial services, implies official recognition and by participation in public matters they are becoming somewhat more *church*-like. Free-Church ministers have also authority to act as official mediators in marital disputes.

From an international point of view, the Roman Catholic Church forms a variant of the church type, and Catholicism in Sweden also has some of the features characterizing the sociological *church*. But it is not particularly influenced by Swedish traditions and environment. Only about one-fifth of its 8,000 members are Swedish citizens, although the proportion has been increasing.[6] In Sweden it comes close to being a *particular church*[7] – as it is in the

3. Low Church organizations attach less importance to priesthood and liturgy and aim more towards a free exercise of faith among the laity, although inside the church framework. In contrast, High-Churchness stresses liturgy and priesthood.

4. Since 1 January 1964 the rules for leaving the Church of Sweden have also been simplified, only a written explanation being required. It is no longer necessary to make a personal appearance at the parish registry.

5. Child baptism in the Swedish Mission Association is only an option.

6. The Catholic church grew from 5,200 in 1940, 16,550 in 1950, 29,200 in 1960 to 40,000 in 1966. In 1960 the number of Swedish citizens among its adherents was 6,000 and in 1966 8,000.

7. The concept of a 'sect' has not only a theologically negative connotation but conveys also the idea of low social prestige. Some sociologists of religion prefer to

U.S.A. according to Yinger [1957]. It also has authority to conduct weddings and burials.

*The denomination.* On the whole the Free-Churches are to be regarded as *denominations* in the American style. The characteristic features of a *denomination:* free competition in one and the same region, voluntary membership, and independence from the state, explain much of the variation of religious social structure in the country districts of central Sweden. In the *denomination* religious discipline is more rigorous than in the *church*, but more formal and conventional than in the *particular church*. A *denomination* is supported by broad sections of the people, who want to change society in accordance with their norms, in preference to adjusting to it. Child baptism may occur, but is not considered to constitute membership. Entry is gained only at a more mature age, and is based on a personal declaration of faith.

The numerical strength of various denominations of today's Sweden is shown in Table 1. It is evident that the position of the largest denominations in society has somewhat weakened since the 1930's. At the same time some religious movements, the Swedish Alliance Mission, Örebro Mission Society, and Holiness Union have changed their character. They have become *denominations* and not infrequently have attracted members from older denominations (e.g. Örebro Mission Society from the Swedish Mission Association). This reflects a tendency towards complete denominationalism which is characteristic of religion in Sweden today.

*Particular churches.* Like the *denomination*, the *particular church* is characterised by voluntary membership, for adults only. Religious discipline is strict, and charismatic leadership is of greater importance than hierarchical and formal leadership. The *Particular church* is based on groups in society in conflict with current values and styles of life of society as a whole.

The most typical *particular church* in Sweden in this century is the Pentecostalist Movement, which having almost doubled its membership between 1930 and 1960, is now slightly receding. Now that entry age (baptismal age) has become lower (not infrequently under ten years) it has become more like a *church;* free competition is still repudiated, and the movement persists in rejecting denominationalism. Nevertheless, its situation, in fact, is *denominational*, although its many local *particular churches* do not belong to a common organization. The Pentecostalist Movement is ideologically closer to fundamentalism than any other Swedish Free Church and is in this respect exclusive.

refer to an association's *own* definition of its type and purpose. Here the term 'sect' will be replaced by the expression *Särkyrka* (particular church) in view of the claim of these associations to be 'the true church'.

*Table 1. Numerical strength of the free churches**

| | Number of members | | | | % of population in 1965 |
|---|---|---|---|---|---|
| | 1900 | 1930 | 1960 | 1965 | |
| Swedish Mission Association | 80,000 | 113,721 | 96,731 | 92,626 | 1.2 |
| Swedish Alliance Mission | – | – | 14,948 | 14,042 | 0.2 |
| Swedish Baptist Association | 40,759 | 63,399 | 32,540 | 29,360 | 0.4 |
| Free Baptists | 5,000 | 5,000 | 1,500 | 1,246 | 0.02 |
| Örebro Mission Society | – | – | 20,000 | 19,542 | 0.3 |
| Holiness Union | – | – | 5,623 | 4,828 | 0.06 |
| The Methodist Church | 17,268 | 15,648 | 11,249 | 9,977 | 0.1 |
| Swedish Salvation Army | – | 1,500 | 1,600 | 1,600 | 0.5 |

* All these associations regard themselves as Free-Churches, but the Pentecost movement with 1.2 per cent of the population is usually also included with the Free Churches proper.

A typical *particular church* with strong fundamentalist features, although based on an ideology very different to that of other associations, is the Jehova's Witnesses body (8,600 members in 1960; 11,000 in 1965) largely recruited from denominations in which they were ill-fitted. Another growing *particular church* is the Church of Christ of the Latter Day Saints (the Mormons) which today numbers 4,000 members as against 2,000 in 1944. The Adventists, who are similar to the Free Churches except for their Saturday Sabbath, have increased their membership slightly (1950: 3,434 members – 1965: 3,800).

*Religious movements which are intra-church or without formal organization.* Organizations of this type have in common the voluntary character of membership and the free activity of faith. Their spread and importance has decreased in today's society; some have already undergone a transformation into *denominations*. The Baptist Örebro Mission Society and the Holiness Union, for example, were previously non-denominational and only loosely connected to the Baptist Church; the Swedish Alliance Mission was previously low-church. Other organizations, such as the Evangelical National Society and the Bible Friends used to show denominational tendencies, but do not do so any more. The latter, with the East Smaland Mission Society are organizations within the Church.

Independent of the churches, but often in informal liaison with the Free Churches, is the Salvation Army, from which a *denomination*, the Swedish Salvation Army, separated in 1905. The former, in contrast to the latter, does not administer sacraments of Baptism and Holy Communion. Weddings and burials are conducted in the Salvation Army although many salvationists are still buried according to the ritual of the Church of Sweden.

Organizations like *K.F.U.M.* (Y.M.C.A.) and *K.F.U.K.* (Y.W.C.A.), since 1966 merged into one national organization, are interdenominational. In 1966 they hay 78,000 participants.

*Loosely organized religious movements.* Nowadays Laestadianism is the primary example of this type of movement. The great popular religious revival in the nineteenth century gave birth to fairly unorganized movements, but via intra-church organization they developed into *denominations*. In Laestadianism the original character of a movement was preserved, with a minimum of organization and with the 'meeting' as the cohesive bond, but otherwise members worshipped in the Church of Sweden, and were the 'keenest communicants' of northern Sweden in the Church of Sweden.

### *Group structure*

Until the middle of the nineteenth century in Sweden the identity between the National Church and society remained. It was eliminated with the growth of modern society, but the congregations remained in principle, extended neighbourhood groups comprising all inhabitants of the district. In this sense membership was to a large extent compulsory, and exceptions could occur only on certain conditions. During the nineteenth century the worshipping congregations of the Church of Sweden became more and more voluntary groups, entry into which was a matter of individual choice. Today, especially since the 1951 Act, they are completely voluntary and parishes have in principle ceased to be identical with neighbourhoods. The situation in the Free Churches is similar but with a higher threshold of qualification: admission to Holy Communion is limited to believers.

The sub-groups of congregations vary with different associations. The Free Churches encourage small groups, prayer cells, prayer groups, circles and evangelical teams which have strong interaction and bring about strong integration [Goffman, 1956; Zetterberg, 1950]. Particularly in the Pentecostalist Movement prayer groups, rarely of more than 20–25 persons, are important instruments for social control.

Pluralistic sub-groups, i.e. groups without limitations as to size, generally serve to recruit new members to the congregation and to integrate it on the local level. They are characterized by voluntary membership, not infrequently by lowered religious membership requirements and links with natural social groups, primarily age groups. It is in *denominations* where adults only are eligible for membership that junior and youth societies mainly occur. A *particular church* like the Pentecostalist Movement, however, has no pluralistic sub-groups of this kind but has, like the other associations, a very large number of Sunday School groups.

Qua recruitment groups pluralistic groups appear rather closed and interrelated. According to an investigation by Hans Zetterberg, in 1949, nobody had become a member of the Youth of the Swedish Mission Association without having belonged to a Sunday School, Confirmation class, or junior society of this denomination, and 80 per cent had reached membership via all these channels [Zetterberg, 1950]. Pluralistic groups have become increasingly differentiated according to religious organization during this century and this is partly related to their recruitment function.[8]

*Leadership and membership influence*

Leadership in religious organizations is mainly of two kinds, formal and charismatic. Formal leadership implies leading the external organization, negotiations, and administrative meetings, while charismatic leadership[9] is linked to the tasks of worship, propagating the faith, and care of souls.

Personal charisma is of most importance for leadership in the Pentecostalist Movement and associations close to it, such as the Holiness Union and

8. The Swedish Mission Association, for example, has S.M.U. (Svenska Missionsförbundets Ungdom, S.M.'s Youth), S.M.J. (Svenska Missionsförbundets Juniores, S.M.'s Junior Work) and *Våra Flickor* (Our Girls), and *Våra Pojkar* (Our Boys). However, separate denominational clubs for teen-age boys and girls have disappeared with the dissolution of ubiquitous sex barriers in modern society (e.g. mens' and womens' pews/side of the church) [*Svenska Missionsförbundet*, 1956]. Most numerous, and occurring in most churches, are women's sewing circles (membership in 1959: Church of Sweden: 131,851: Low- and Free-Church organizations and the Salvation Army: 64,884). Special societies for men have emerged in the Church of Sweden (the Church Brethren, 1965, 22,500 members). This is related to low male recruitment to groups of religious activity, and the absence of any formal lay organization.

9. Max Weber, who introduced the term charisma (gift of grace) distinguished between personal charisma and the charisma of office. Leadership based on personal charisma is sometimes simply called charismatic leadership, while leadership endowed through consecration into an office would then be named hierarchical. In the present account these will both be called charismatic.

the Örebro Mission Society. In the Pentecostalist Movement 'baptism in the Holy Ghost', often combined with speaking with tongues, is an important condition for any kind of leadership. Personal charisma is far from unimportant in the other Free-Churches ('to be anointed', 'to have the Spirit', 'to have the gift'), but when formalized rituals gain in importance its influence is diminished in favour of the charisma of the office, as in the Swedish Mission Association.

In the Church of Sweden leadership is more connected with *the office conferred by consecration.* Even in associations where personal charisma is dominant, charisma of office, conveyed by consecration, dedication, etc., has gained in importance. In Low-Church organizations within the church, finally, personal charisma is stressed with the requirement for 'converted' clergy; the charisma of office is rejected.

In most intra-church religious movements, formal leadership is separated from charismatic leadership, and is bestowed on laymen. Although the ministers have strengthened their position, lay members still have a great influence in most Free-Churches. This applies in particular to the Swedish Mission Association and Swedish Baptist Association, where local congregations appoint their own preachers and have extensive autonomy, which partly extends to matters of cult and doctrine. None of these congregations are obliged to use their official manuals for conducting worship and other religious services.

Among the Pentecostalists members' influence has become less because of leader-dominance, both locally and nation-wide.[10] In the Methodist Church and the Salvation Army members' influence is also limited.[11]

In the Church of Sweden, finally, lay people now have more influence: they have a majority in the General Synod, and since 1964 have been entitled to vote in episcopal elections although the right of parishes to elect their clergy has been somewhat limited in favour of the Cabinet and Diocesan Chapters (Clergy Elections Act 1957). Parishes exercise considerable autonomy through vestries and parish councils of which the minister is no longer *ex officio* chairman (Parish Government Act 1963).

10. In matters of cult and doctrine, the preachers, primarily Lewi Pethrus, have played a decisive part. In matters of church discipline members' influence is now and then indirect, because of the institution of 'elders'. In the Pentecostalist Movement, however, there is no central authority, so members' influence is mainly confined to their local congregation, which also appoints its own preachers.

11. At the annual conference of the Methodist Church the bishop appoints the ministers and allocates the parishes to them. In the Salvation Army, members' influence is very small, due to the military type of organization.

*The social basis of religious associations*

*Urban-rural differences.* Table 2 indicates that Church of Sweden worshippers live in the country, to a greater extent than do Free-Church worshippers, whose distribution varies little between country and densely populated areas. However, in the latter the Swedish Mission Association and the Pentecostalist Movement have a higher rate of church attendance than the Free Churches.

*Table 2. Church-going frequency in the Church of Sweden and the Free Churches by population density and economic character*

| | The average number of church attendances on Sundays and Church Holidays in 1965, in % of the population | | | | | | | | |
|---|---|---|---|---|---|---|---|---|---|
| | *According to population density** | | | | | | | | |
| | A | B | C | D | E | F | G | H | Total |
| Church of Sweden | 8.5 | 7.7 | 6.6 | 4.8 | 4.2 | 2.8 | 1.9 | 1.4 | 3.2 |
| Free Churches | 2.4 | 2.7 | 2.4 | 2.8 | 2.6 | 2.3 | 1.8 | 1.4 | 2.1 |
| Total | 10.9 | 10.4 | 9.0 | 7.6 | 6.8 | 5.1 | 3.8 | 2.8 | 5.3 |

| | *According to the proportion in agricultural employment*** | | | | | | |
|---|---|---|---|---|---|---|---|
| | 0 | 1 | 2 | 3 | 4 | 5 | 6–7 |
| Church of Sweden | 1.8 | 3.1 | 4.7 | 5.0 | 5.8 | 6.7 | 7.8 |
| Free Churches | 1.8 | 2.0 | 2.6 | 3.0 | 3.1 | 2.0 | 2.8 |
| Total | 3.6 | 5.1 | 7.3 | 8.0 | 8.9 | 8.7 | 10.6 |

*A = Sparsely populated areas.
H = Densely populated areas.
**0 = 0.0–9.9% employed in agriculture.
1 = 10.0–19.9% employed in agriculture.
2 = 20.0–29.9% employed in agriculture, etc.
Source: The Stockholm Institute of the Sociology of Religion.

The Swedish Baptist Association and the Örebro Mission Society are, as shown by Table 3, evenly distributed in areas of different population density; members of Holiness Union are found mainly in sparsely, members of the Methodist Church mainly in densely populated areas. Table 4 shows that of the various communities, the Swedish Mission Association and the Swedish Alliance Mission are the most urban, the Baptist communities somewhat more urban than rural, and the Lutheran communities, like the Church of Sweden the most rural.

*Table 3. Membership of religious associations in the municipalities of Sweden 1965 (per thousand of the population)*

| | According to population density* | | | | | | | |
|---|---|---|---|---|---|---|---|---|
| | A | B | C | D | E | F | G | H |
| Evangelical National Society | 2 | 5 | 9 | 8 | 10 | 4 | 2 | 1 |
| Swedish Mission Association | 18 | 22 | 16 | 18 | 15 | 14 | 9 | 6 |
| Swedish Baptist Association | 4 | 4 | 3 | 4 | 5 | 5 | 4 | 4 |
| Örebro Mission Society Society | 2 | 4 | 3 | 3 | 3 | 2 | 3 | 0.7 |
| Holiness Union | 0.8 | 3 | 1 | 2 | 0.7 | 0.3 | 0.2 | 0.3 |
| Pentecost Movement | 15 | 14 | 13 | 15 | 14 | 14 | 10 | 9 |
| The Methodist Church | 9.3 | – | 0.3 | 0.3 | 0.3 | 1 | 2 | 2 |
| Swedish Alliance Mission | 7 | 1 | 3 | 5 | 2 | 2 | 0.5 | 0.2 |

*A = Sparsely populated areas.
H = Densely populated areas.
Source: The Stockholm Institute of the Sociology of Religion.

*Table 4. Membership of religious associations in town and country 1950 and 1959*

| | Religious Association's membership in % | | | |
|---|---|---|---|---|
| | 1950 | | 1959 | |
| | Town | Country | Town | Country |
| Evangelical National Society | 24 | 76 | 21 | 79 |
| Salvation Army | – | – | 79 | 21 |
| Holiness Union | 6 | 94 | 12 | 88 |
| The Methodist Church | 76 | 24 | 80 | 20 |
| Swedish Alliance Mission | 14 | 86 | 7 | 93 |
| Swedish Baptist Association | 52 | 48 | 54 | 46 |
| Swedish Mission Association | 36 | 64 | 36 | 64 |
| Örebro Mission Society | 54 | 46 | 55 | 45 |
| Pentecost Movement | 53 | 47 | 58 | 42 |
| Total Free-Church Associations | – | – | 47 | 53 |

*Social class.* Table 5 shows that in the worshipping congregations of the Church of Sweden the middle-class is clearly over-represented; the working-class clearly under-represented and the wealthy are neither.

*Table 5. Attendance in the Church of Sweden and the Free-Churches by socio-economic status, 1955 (in %)**

| Socio-economic Category | Attendance | | |
|---|---|---|---|
| | Church of Sweden | Free-Churches | Normal population |
| I – Upper | 6 | 1 | 5 |
| II – Middle | 59 | 53 | 42 |
| III – Lower | 35 | 46 | 53 |
| Total | 100 | 100 | 100 |

* These data refer to adults over 18 going to church at least twice a month.
Source: B. Gustafsson, 1958.

If casual attenders are included, the proportion of wealthy people in particular increases. As the figures above show, the middle classes are over-represented in the Free Churches as well, although less markedly, and the working class proportion is greater, but not at level with the average for the population. The wealthy, on the contrary, are clearly under-represented.

According to the 1930 census and later investigations the middle-class is most dominant in the Swedish Mission Association and the Swedish Baptist Association; the working-class element is largest in the Salvation Army and the Pentecostalist Movement, although it is over-represented only in the Salvation Army.

*Sex.* Table 6 shows that women are over-represented both in the Church of Sweden and the Free Churches.

*Table 6. Attendance in the Church of Sweden and the Free-Churches by sex, 1955 (in %)*

| | Attendance | | |
|---|---|---|---|
| | Church of Sweden | Free-Churches | Normal population |
| Men | 43 | 41 | 49 |
| Women | 57 | 59 | 51 |
| Total | 100 (n=453) | 100 (n=235) | 100 |

Source: B. Gustafsson, 1958.

There are more female than male church-goers in all age-groups. The sex difference is least, and rather insignificant, in the age groups 26–35, probably because married women with small children have less opportunity to attend services. If church-goers are divided into casual and regular attenders as in Table 7, an interesting difference can be seen between the Church of Sweden and the Free Churches. It is evident that attendance of male church-goers is more sporadic and attendance of female church-goers is more regular in the Church of Sweden, while the opposite holds for the Free Churches.

*Table 7. Regular and irregular attendance in the Church of Sweden and the Free-Churches, 1966 (in %)*

| | Church of Sweden | | Free-Churches | |
|---|---|---|---|---|
| Attenders: | Occasional | Regular | Occasional | regular |
| Men | 46 | 38 | 36 | 44 |
| Women | 54 | 62 | 64 | 56 |
| Total | 100 (n=288) | 100 (n=163) | 100 (n=79) | 100 (n=158) |

Source: The Stockholm Institute of the Sociology of Religion.

With respect to formal membership, the proportion of women is rarely less than 60 per cent of the total membership (see Table 8).
Wherever it is possible to compare with the 1930 census, it appears that the proportion of women has generally increased.

*Table 8. Female members of religious associations (% of total membership)*

| | Female members | |
|---|---|---|
| | 1930 | 1959 |
| Evangelical National Society | – | 64 |
| Salvation Army | 68 | 76 |
| Swedish Salvation Army | – | 73 |
| Holiness Union | – | 60 |
| The Methodist Church | 66 | 72 |
| Swedish Alliance Mission | – | 59 |
| Swedish Baptist Association | 65 | 67 |
| Swedish Mission Association | 61 | 64 |
| Örebro Mission Society | – | 65 |
| Pentecost Movement | 64 | 64 |

Sources: Census 1930; The *Swedish Official Reports*, 1963, p. 39.

*Age.* Table 9 shows that older age-groups are highly over-represented, and constitute almost half of all church-goers.

*Table 9. Church attendance in the Church of Sweden and the Free-Churches (in %)*

| | Attendance | | |
|---|---|---|---|
| Age | Church of Sweden | Free-Churches | Normal population |
| 18–25 | 8 | 7 | 13 |
| 26–35 | 12 | 18 | 21 |
| 36–45 | 12 | 17 | 22 |
| 46–55 | 21 | 19 | 19 |
| 56– | 47 | 39 | 25 |
| Total | 100 | 100 | 100 |

Source: B. Gustafsson, 1958.

In the Church of Sweden the age selection is, however, less representative of the population than in the Free Churches taken as a whole. If the groups of 'casuals' and 'regulars' are compared, the difference with respect to the Church of Sweden worshippers is that the age-groups under 35 predominate somewhat among the 'casuals', and those over 56 among the 'regulars'. The Free Churches show a marked increase among their 'casuals' from the age groups 26–45, and a corresponding decrease of these ages among their more regular church-goers.

The inner structure of the Free Churches is obviously more homogeneous. There are, however, great differences between different Free Churches. Almost two-thirds of the Methodist membership is over 50; only in the Holiness Union, the Pentecostalist Movement and the Örebro Mission Society are more than half of the members younger than 50. Also, a considerable 'senilization' has taken place since 1930 as can be seen from Table 10.

*Recruitment – Religious mobility*

Those communities whose age structure is top-heavy also show a decline in membership, mainly since the 1930's. In these associations, the trend is towards internal recruitment, and efforts to use the family, and not just youth associations as the basis for recruitment have become more conscious. The association strives to be a 'family church', and the *denomination* tends to become a *church.*

Recruitment from without has mainly occurred in the Pentecostalist Movement, but there also internal recruitment has become more important.

*Table 10. Age composition in the various religious associations in 1930 and 1959*

| | | –25 years | 26–50 years | 51–years |
|---|---|---|---|---|
| Evangelical National Society | 1959 | 9 | 37 | 54 |
| Free Baptists | 1959 | 11 | 31 | 58 |
| Salvation Army | 1930 | 21 | 52 | 27 |
| | 1959 | 11 | 37 | 52 |
| Holiness Union | 1959 | 17 | 40 | 43 |
| The Methodist Church | 1930 | 14 | 37 | 49 |
| | 1959 | 6 | 30 | 64 |
| Swedish Alliance Mission | 1959 | 11 | 36 | 53 |
| Swedish Baptist Association | 1930 | 14 | 45 | 41 |
| | 1959 | 9 | 31 | 60 |
| Swedish Salvation Army | 1959 | 7 | 38 | 55 |
| Swedish Mission Association | 1930 | 12 | 41 | 46 |
| | 1959 | 9 | 35 | 56 |
| Örebro Mission Society | 1959 | 14 | 37 | 49 |
| Pentecost Movement | 1930 | 18 | 57 | 25 |
| | 1959 | 20 | 36 | 44 |
| Total Free-Church Associations | 1959 | 12 | 35 | 53 |

Sources: 1930 Census data; *Swedish Official Reports*, 1963, p. 39.

To a large extent, people have come to the Pentecostalist Movement from other churches (in particular from the Bible Friends, the Swedish Mission Association, and the Salvation Army) yet this religious mobility has been largely within the Free Church configuration.

Within the leadership there used to be a limited migration from the Church of Sweden to the Free Churches, but today the situation is reversed. On the whole, mobility has been greatest in the 'Baptist' movements (the Pentecostalists, Bible Friends, Örebro Mission Society, and Holiness Union). Full denominationalism – the consolidation of independent churches and their free competition – with the anti-denominationalism of the largest Baptist community and, previously, of the Örebro Mission Society and the Holiness, have influenced the mobility.

The number of converts to the Roman Church has increased slightly in Sweden in latter years, but is still only a little above a hundred per year (1960, 116 conversions). Between 1940 and 1960, 2,746 Swedes joined, most of them women in lower middle age, and with completed secondary education. A reverse trend is also noticeable, in that children of Catholic immigrants gradually join the Church of Sweden as a part of their becoming assimilated into Swedish society.

*Interdenominational relations*

*Ecumenical efforts towards Unity.* The period up to World War I was one of increasing denominational divisiveness. New *denominations* or *particular churches* emerged from several communities, the most recent being the Pentecostalist Movement, which began as a *particular church* in 1913. By 1918, however, the trend to differentiation was already being overtaken by efforts towards unity, but between the Free Churches and mainly internationally.

Opposition to the privileged State Church is part of the background to unity efforts in the Free Churches and only recently has the emphasis been on co-operation.[12] Plans for a federated Swedish Free Church, introduced in 1948 but not yet realised, can be seen as a step in the development towards greater solidarity between the denominations. The Pentecostalist Movement remains outside, but there have been moves towards greater unity between the Baptist movements.

International ecumenism did not have a national counterpart until 1932, when the Swedish Ecumenical Council was organized to promote co-operation between the Church of Sweden and the Free Churches. Its activities have largely concerned reconstruction of Christian norms on social issues, and the defence of common interests, such as the place of 'Christianity' in school curricula, and the role of the Sabbath. Ecumenism was an expression of group cohesion against non-Christian groups. Only at the end of the 1950's was a local ecumenical committee appointed to probe into interdenominational relations.

*Interdenominational tensions.* The 1951 Act and consequent statutes have led to a relaxation in the relations between Church and Free Churches although some basis for antagonism remains primarily for ideological reasons (on Baptism, 'membership church' versus 'national church') but also because of the official monopoly of the Church of Sweden. Nevertheless, the Free Churches would defend the freedom of the National Church to decide on its faith against what is regarded as unjustified governmental interference, and many appreciate its position as a bulwark against a feared secularization.

Interdenominational tensions in this century have mainly been caused by

12. *Frikyrkliga Samarbetskommitten* (the Committee for Free Church Co-operation), formed in 1918, now called *Frikyrkeradet* (the Council of Free Churches), has a brief to watch and promote common Free Church interests, not least in matters of church politics. Gradually, and in particular after the new Religious Freedom Act of 1951, its task has been to promote mutual co-operation. This co-operation has found expression in various ways; in an organisation for adult education, an institute for further theological training of ministers, and a Free Church broadcasting committee.

the competitive system inherent in full denominationalism. Such tensions still arise,[13] particularly between older churches and those which have become denominations more recently and which consequently attempt to expand their organization and membership, for example, between the Swedish Baptist Association and the Örebro Mission Society ('Stockholm Baptism' and 'Örebro Baptism'), and in the Jönköping province between the Swedish Mission Association and the new denomination, the Swedish Alliance Mission.

Local competition has increased because of the Free Church interpretation of the concept of religious community in the 1951 Act. It is interpreted as implying that a person can belong to one community only; many members of local Free Church congregations have belonged to two or three associations or organizations and have been faced with a choice between them.

### RELIGIOUS PARTICIPATION

As Table 11 shows, regular Sunday attendance is not characteristic of the Swedish National Church although about half the Free Church members are regular Sunday worshippers.

*Table 11. Church attendance in the Church of Sweden and the Free-Churches (in %)*

| Number of visits during one month | Church of Sweden | | Free-Churches | |
|---|---|---|---|---|
| | 1955/56 (N=451) | 1963/64 (N=1,427) | 1955/56 (N=237) | 1963/64 (N=697) |
| 1 | 64 | 50 | 33 | 26 |
| 2 | 22 | 20 | 25 | 15 |
| 3 | 6 | 8 | 12 | 12 |
| 4 | 8 | 14 | 30 | 47 |

In Sweden a general high rate of religious participation occurs only in relation to those services which approximate to the 'rites of passage': Baptism is received by 87 per cent of all children under one year of age; Confirmation by 88 per cent of those who qualify i.e. baptized fourteen-year-olds; weddings by 92 per cent; and burial services by 96 per cent.

13. A quite new tension arose in the fifties in the Baptist compound because of the Maranata break-away from the Pentecostalist Movement. Its inception was not unrelated to a certain formalisation of Pentecostalist meetings and organizations.

Rare or isolated attendances at religious services indicate that many have a merely cultic[14] type relationship with the National Church. Thus 11 per cent of church-goers in Lund in 1961 attended only in connection with a family ritual [Gustafsson, 1963, p. 26] and in one Stockholm suburb 82 per cent had not been in church for four to five months in 1966; 57 per cent not for a year or more.

With divine services on radio and T.V. a new kind of cult has emerged. In 1963–64 57 per cent of the population said that they had listened to a radio service or devotional on some occasion during one month; 38 per cent had watched T.V. A minor investigation in Stockholm showed, however, that for only one-third of the audience did this involve worship in the proper sense. The size of the audience is also decreasing (a November Sunday in 1958, 28 per cent; in 1963; 9 per cent [Sjöden, 1967, p. 55; Gustafsson, 1963; Religionssociologiska Institutet, 1967, p. 9].

There are a few other phenomena – the general customs of lighting candles on graves, particularly on All Saint's Day, church visits on the first Sunday of Advent and the rush to sermons of certain preachers – which do have, despite other differences, such an affinity to the classical cult that it could be said to have a *secularized* counterpart today.

Despite this general low rate of religious participation the attendance of children at Sunday School is quite high. The number of Sunday School children was, in 1962, for the whole country, 407,265 (35 per cent of all children between four to fourteen years old), of which 135,963 belonged to the Church of Sweden Sunday Schools (12 per cent of all children of Sunday School age). In the cities, however, the children under eight tend to be a majority in Sunday Schools, and the proportion of Sunday School children then decreases for each year (in the whole of Sweden the age distribution was, in 1962: 4–7 years 44 per cent, 8–10 years 34 per cent, 11–14 years 22 per cent).

As might be expected there are considerable regional differences in Sweden with respect to attendance and Communion frequency. To a large extent these differences reflect the regional strength of the Free-Churches and Intra-Church organisations. In a wide area south-east of a borderline from Dalsland to south-east Smaland (with the exception mainly of the Gothenburg area and the southernmost parts of the country) Sunday attendance is comparatively frequent (in north Halland and in the Ulricehamm district it is above 10 per cent). This diagonal line across southern Sweden is also known to be an old cultural borderline, and a border between different

14. In the *cult* it is the individual rather than the communal aspect of religious practice which is paramount. The *cult* participants come voluntarily, and there is a minimum of group discipline. Leadership is often charismatic.

dialects. Within this area there are several districts,[15] (often called old-church districts) which have preserved older traditons through the church revivals of the nineteenth centurty; the Free-Churches are strong in other districts[16] and in northern Skane the low church organizations of Bible Friends and Evangelical National Society are also firmly entrenched. High Church tendencies are not limited in the same way to (rural) districts.

North of the above-mentioned borderline from Dalsland to south-east Smaland, in the area extending to and including middle Norrland[17] there is a lesser degree of church activity (less than 5 per cent of the population go to church on an ordinary Sunday or festival day, and in some areas, e.g. Stockholm, Bergslagen and Medelpad, less than 2.5 per cent go). Accordingly, it is in middle Sweden that the Free-Churches have most adherents.[18]

Middle and upper Norrland is of old, a Low-Church region. Its Low-Church character is expressed in the rather high figures for church-going in the Church of Sweden. The Evangelical National Society is the leading association from the Skule mountain in the south to Lulea in the north (4.4 per cent of the population of the province of Västerbotten), while in the far north Laestadianism dominates in the Torne valley (in some places 10 per cent of the population belong), and in northern Lapland. Of the Free Churches primarily only the Pentecostalists (in southern and middle Lapland) and the Swedish Mission Association (in Västerbotten) have any greater strength in this area.

15. The main districts are: the Bjäre peninsula, East Göinge, Värend, Västbo, southern Västergötland, the Västergötland plains, the West Coast north of Varberg, and southern Dalsland.

16. Free Church districts occur mainly around Hässleholm, in Sunnerbo, northern Sjuhäradsbygden and the isles of Bohuslän.

17. This area includes north-east Götaland, Svealand and southern and middle Norrland.

18. The Swedish Mission Association (1.2 per cent of the population), still reaches its highest figures in northern Uppland, Värmland, central Västergötland, and the Jönköping province (often more than 5 per cent). The Swedish Baptist Association (0.4 per cent of the population in 1965) have greatest strength in the Jönköping district, where sometimes very high figures are reached (sometimes over 20 per cent). All these cases are predominantly non-urban. The Methodist church (0.1 per cent of the population) is on the whole centred in urban communities, except in Karlskoga bergslag, while its daughter organisation, the Salvation Army (0.5 per cent of the population in 1965) has some influence in country districts only in Dalecarlia and Jämtland. The Swedish Alliance Mission is a typical country district movement, now a Free Church but confined mainly to the Jönköping county and the adjacent areas of Skaraborg county (where 4 per cent of the population belongs to it); so is the Low Church East Smaland Mission Society.

*Influence of social environment on religious life*

*Urbanization.* Until the middle of the nineteenth century town and country were uniform with regard to religion. Then old-Lutheranism began to dissolve under the influence of an expanding population and later of urbanization. In small country parishes (with less than 1,500 inhabitants) the older forms of church life tended to survive, with preservation of religious uniformity, but in high density areas new religious groupings emerged. In the cities organizational units grew; many functions of the church became bureaucratized and new methods were tried to influence people, first by the Free Churches, and then, to some extent, by the National Church; informal preaching to mass meetings, and various proselytising sub-groups developed. Greater religious differentiation is characteristic of the modern city and particularly in the National Church considerable rarefication takes place. Rooted of old in a rural environment, where it still has an excess of clergy and churches, its position in the modern city is considerably altered.

However, Table 12 shows that the difference between town and country was less in 1963–64 than in 1955–56. Church-going frequence has increased somewhat in the bigger cities, but decreased in country areas.

*Table 12. Rural and urban church-going in the Church of Sweden and the Free Churches (% of population)*

| | Those who attend at least once a month | | | |
|---|---|---|---|---|
| | Church of Sweden | | Free-Churches | |
| | 1955–56 | 1963–64 | 1955–56 | 1963–64 |
| Bigger cities | 9 | 13 | 3 | 5 |
| Other cities | 15 | 15 | 10 | 8 |
| Townships, villages | 17 | 17 | 14 | 10 |
| Country areas | 27 | 22 | 12 | 10 |

Source: The Swedish Institute of Public Opinion Research.

In urban areas there are relatively fewer occasional worshippers; urbanisation effects a contraction of the religious sector of the community, but also an increase in its intensity and closedness. Among the Free Churches urbanization has strongly influenced the forms of activity, giving more scope for high pressure evangelization and thereby for the free competition inherent in denominationalism.

Urbanization has also led to transition between the Free Churches, so that the biggest Baptist movement, Pentecostalism, has surpassed the Swedish Mission Association in the cities, although the Swedish Mission Association is still in the lead in rural areas.

*Table 13. Membership in the Free-Churches in urban and rural areas (pro mille of the population)*

| | Town | | | | Country | | | |
|---|---|---|---|---|---|---|---|---|
| | 1930 | 1950 | 1960 | 1965 | 1930 | 1950 | 1960 | 1965 |
| Evangelical National Society | – | – | 2 | 2 | – | – | 9 | 7 |
| Swedish Mission Association | 14 | 11 | 9 | 9 | 18 | 18 | 17 | 15 |
| Swedish Baptist Association | 9 | 6 | 5 | 4 | 9 | 5 | 4 | 3 |
| Örebro Mission Society | – | – | 3 | 3 | – | – | 2 | 2 |
| Holiness Union | – | – | 0.2 | 0.2 | – | – | 1 | 1 |
| Pentecostalist Movement | 5 | 14 | 14 | 12 | 6 | 11 | 11 | 11 |
| The Methodist Church | 4 | 3 | 2 | 2 | 1 | 1 | 1 | 0.5 |
| Salvation Army | – | – | 8 | – | – | – | 2 | – |
| Swedish Alliance Mission | – | – | 0.3 | 0.5 | – | – | 4 | 5 |
| All Free Church Associations | – | – | 43 | 38 | – | – | 52 | 48 |

Religious life in Pentecostalism is characterised by high emotional intensity combined with a high qualification threshold, and because of this urbanization has resulted in increased intensity within a more sharply demarcated religious section.

*Changes in rural areas.* The depopulation of the countryside has considerably changed the structure of religious life. Membership of various congregations has dwindled; some of the smaller ones can no longer support their minister or preacher; some have dissolved. The number of mergers between small country congregations has increased. The 1962 Act made possible joint parish Divine Services in the Church of Sweden. Increased centralization of communications and of economic and social life have also led to a centralisation of religious activities in cities and townships. Associations without any organized activity in the countryside (and which have thus been able to concentrate their activities in cities and townships) have benefitted most.

*The industrial environment.* The very early industrial locations were rather closed and religiously strongly conformist. When patriarchal relations between employers and workers were replaced by conflicts of interest the church, in the class-norm of the working class and the eyes of the Social Democratic Movement, appeared as an instrument of the upper classes and an obstacle to working-class advancement [Gustafsson, 1953].

Around the turn of the century (and in the Sundsvall area earlier) industrial environments, by now socially heterogeneous, became secularized. With the differentiation of separate socio-cultural classes, the middle class predominated in church activities although for a time the Free Churches, for example, the Methodist Church, Mission Union and Free Baptists and the Salvation Army were closer to the cultural environment of industrial workers [*Svensk geografisk arsbok*, 1952]. Gradually, however, the class-norm of the working class resulted more in religious uniformity, and the connection with the Free Churches weakened; they became more middle-class. Thus the industrial environment produced isolation from any participation in worship, and at the same time a stronger formal connection with the State Church than any other environment [Segerstedt and Lundquist, 1955].

*Ethnic environments.* In spite of the ethnic homogeneity in Sweden, special ethnic environments have had a great influence on the structure of religious life in some areas. In the north, Laestadianism was long confined to Finnish speaking areas which still remain its central base. Older Laestadianism contains many Finnish cultural traditions. In Lapland *samic* ecstacy has been held to explain the occurrence of ecstatic movements like *Laestadianismen* and *Pingströrelsen.* Post-war immigration from Central and Southern Europe[19] has given Roman Catholicism a strong foothold in the bigger cities, in some industrial towns such as Oskarström, Västeras and some townships of Bergslagen.

The immigrants gradually adjust themselves to the Swedish level of religiosity.[20] In smaller, comparatively uniform, industrial townships (e.g. Oskarström), the religious community is best preserved, and is often the last

19. There are also Scandinavian, Eastern European and Middle Eastern immigrants in Sweden. Finnish Lutherans, decidedly the largest immigrant group, long preserve their religious tradition but find the transition to the Church of Sweden comparatively least difficult.

20. Investigations among Hungarian refugees showed that in 1959, 15 per cent felt that their religious needs were not satisfied; in 1963 the figure was 11 per cent. In 1957, 26 per cent said they had no religious needs; the 1963 figure was 30 per cent [Lundquist-Busch, 1966, p. 91]. In 1959, 58 per cent, in 1963, 59 per cent felt that their religious needs were satisfied. Among Italians in Greater Stockholm in 1966, the corresponding figure was 57 per cent, while 21 per cent expressed dissatisfaction with opportunities to practise their religion in Sweden [Ershammar, 1966].

remnant of the country of origin's traditions. In bigger towns and cities immigrant religious activity gradually decreases. After three years about half go to church less often than they used to in their country of origin. About 20 per cent are estimated to cease all formal religious activity quite quickly [Ershammar, 1966].

In many places – mainly where the service is conducted in Swedish – the Catholic Church contributes to the Swedification but also to the general adjustment of immigrants. Without the church probably more immigrants would leave. For a number of immigrant nationalities; Italians, Croats, Serbs, Slovenians, Poles, Spaniards and Hungarians, the Catholic Church provides clergy who speak and conduct services in their language. Greek Orthodox immigrants are often more scattered and are cared for by both the Catholic and State Church.[21]

## RELIGIOUS ASSOCIATIONS AND POLITICS

A connection between the Free Churches and liberalism has been supposed to exist for some generations [Svärd, 1954; Hultquist and Freeman, 1954]. The connection was fairly strong even in the fifties: the liberals had twice as many sympathizers among Free Church church-goers as they had among those outside the Free Churches. But the conservative and centre parties also had a stronger connection with the former than with the latter. The social democrats were clearly under-represented in the Free Church compound.

However, in the latest elections, 1964 and 1966 (Table 12) [Religionssociologiska Institutet, 1966a, p. 10] and probably also in earlier elections in the sixties, the centre party has been significantly stronger than the liberal party in purely rural areas, though not in densely populated and city areas. In electoral districts with many Free-Church members the conservatives also appear to have improved their position. In these districts the social democrats have become even more under-represented.

Few data are available for individual Free Churches. Still, in the 1964 and 1966 elections the Evangelical National Society appears to have inclined towards the conservative and centre parties, and the Swedish Mission Association and the Swedish Baptist Association towards the liberals. The

21. In 1967 the number of Greek Orthodox was estimated to be 21,000, of which 7,000 were Greeks, 7,000 Yugoslavs, 3,000, Finns, 3,000 Estonians and 1,000 Russians. For the care of their souls the Orthodox Church co-operates with the Catholic, but where the Orthodox form only small populational islets, they would often use the Church of Sweden for Baptism, Confirmation and Communion, without giving up their Orthodox faith.

Swedish Alliance Mission, a rurally dominated movement was notably inclined towards the liberals. In the Pentecostalist Movement rural districts the centre party was under-represented, and the new party, Christian Democrats *(Kristlig Demokratisk Samling)* was strongly over-represented; otherwise there was little deviation from the average (This applies also to Social Democrats).

In the old society, the Church of Sweden played a major role politically, and the clerical estate was one of the four Estates of Parliament. After the parliamentary reform 1865–66 the Church became essentially a political pressure group with a conservative bias, determined by its older Old-Lutheran view of society.[22] It seems still possible to talk about a political conservative norm in the National Church. The conservative party, and today especially the centre party, is stronger in districts with high church-going frequency; in these districts labour, Communists and even Christian Democrats are weaker.

Groups within the Church of Sweden and the Free Churches did not emerge as pressure groups in parliamentary politics until the 1950's. When they did emerge it was only in connection with general elections (K.S.A. – Christian Community Responsibility) and then mainly to have 'Christian' candidates nominated. As with ecumenism a growing feeling of solidarity against a non-Christian world was an important motivation, but while ecumenism tends to a liberal ideology, this political activity rests on conservative, partly fundamentalist, attitudes.

Encouraged by the success of a petition in favour of retaining the *status quo* of Christianity as a secondary school subject in 1963, some groups, mainly Pentecostalist and *Kyrklig Samling* (The Church Union), (a Church of Sweden movement against the admission of women to the clergy, ideologically and socio-ethnically conservative) formed a new political party, the Christian Democrats. In the 1964 elections about half the Pentecostalists would have cast their votes for it, giving it a third of its total number of votes [Gustafsson, 1967]. In the 1966 elections the party incurred losses in the Pentecostalist districts, perhaps due to despondency about the prospects of the party.

## RELIGION AND ECONOMICS

Evidence concerning the connection between revivalism and the spirit of

22. The old Lutheran doctrine of the three estates – the teaching, defending, and nourishing estates – was a basic constituent in the ideology of the old society. Hence the Church also exercised a strong influence in the sphere of political ideology.

*Table 14. Elections of provincial councillors in 1966 in comparison with the parliamentary elections in 1964 by population density of electoral districts (communes) and proportion of Free Church members*

| Degree of population density | Proportion of Free-Church association members (%) | | % party distribution of valid votes* | | | | | | | | Number of valid votes |
|---|---|---|---|---|---|---|---|---|---|---|---|
| | | | H | C | F | S | K | K.D.S. | MiS | BoS | |
| A | –4.9 | 1966 | 15.5 | 38.3 | 11.6 | 27.6 | 2.4 | 1.1 | 3.4 | – | 59533 |
| | | 1964 | 15.0 | 35.1 | 10.8 | 31.0 | 2.2 | 1.4 | 1.4 | 3.4 | 60278 |
| | 5.0–9.9 | 1966 | 14.5 | 41.3 | 12.1 | 28.0 | 2.2 | 2.0 | – | – | 26128 |
| | | 1964 | 13.9 | 39.3 | 11.7 | 31.3 | 1.7 | 2.1 | – | – | 21754 |
| | 10.0– | 1966 | 16.3 | 42.3 | 15.6 | 18.5 | 0.9 | 6.5 | – | – | 9332 |
| | | 1964 | 14.7 | 36.8 | 15.3 | 25.5 | 1.3 | 6.3 | | | 13215 |
| C | –4.9 | 1966 | 15.0 | 34.7 | 10.1 | 33.6 | 3.6 | 1.4 | 1.7 | – | 268972 |
| | | 1964 | 13.6 | 33.5 | 10.5 | 37.6 | 2.4 | 1.0 | 1.3 | – | 271877 |
| | 5.0–9.9 | 1966 | 12.4 | 30.5 | 11.6 | 34.0 | 3.0 | 2.7 | 5.8 | – | 82663 |
| | | 1964 | 11.5 | 28.8 | 13.1 | 37.2 | 2.4 | 3.0 | 3.9 | – | 95267 |
| | 10.0– | 1966 | 13.2 | 27.4 | 15.8 | 30.7 | 3.7 | 4.6 | 4.8 | – | 59931 |
| | | 1964 | 11.8 | 27.6 | 16.5 | 34.5 | 3.1 | 5.1 | 1.4 | – | 63868 |
| E | –4.9 | 1966 | 14.4 | 20.0 | 12.1 | 45.5 | 5.4 | 1.3 | 1.3 | – | 253858 |
| | | 1964 | 12.2 | 18.3 | 11.8 | 52.2 | 5.3 | 1.1 | 0.1 | – | 217125 |
| | 5.0–9.9 | 1966 | 14.8 | 27.6 | 10.6 | 39.4 | 4.1 | 2.0 | 1.4 | – | 122474 |
| | | 1964 | 12.2 | 20.1 | 13.7 | 47.2 | 4.2 | 2.5 | – | – | 96239 |
| | 10.0– | 1966 | 11.7 | 23.0 | 14.2 | 41.3 | 4.6 | 4.2 | 1.0 | – | 48550 |
| | | 1964 | 11.2 | 21.1 | 14.3 | 46.5 | 3.6 | 3.3 | – | – | 47652 |
| G | –4.9 | 1966 | 12.8 | 6.0 | 17.9 | 46.2 | 7.3 | 1.4 | 1.7 | 6.7 | 1308796 |
| | | 1964 | 12.6 | 4.6 | 19.0 | 52.0 | 5.8 | 1.1 | 0.2 | 4.8 | 1250421 |
| | 5.0–9.9 | 1966 | 15.1 | 12.5 | 17.3 | 45.9 | 5.8 | 2.2 | 1.3 | – | 271883 |
| | | 1964 | 14.2 | 6.9 | 18.5 | 53.2 | 4.7 | 2.2 | – | – | 306997 |
| | 10.0– | 1966 | 15.4 | 11.9 | 21.7 | 40.2 | 4.7 | 3.8 | – | 2.3 | 39872 |
| | | 1964 | 13.0 | 8.7 | 22.4 | 47.2 | 3.9 | 4.9 | – | – | 33367 |

* H — Conservatives; C — Centre; F — Liberals; S — Social Democrats; K — Communists; K.D.S. — Christian De-

*Table 15. Elections of provincial councillors in 1966 in comparison with the parliamentary elections of 1964 by population density of electoral districts (communes) and frequency of sunday worship in the Church of Sweden.*

| Degree of population density | Church of Sweden Sunday attendance (% of the population) | | % party distribution of valid votes | | | | | | | | Number of valid votes |
|---|---|---|---|---|---|---|---|---|---|---|---|
| | | | H | C | F | S | K | K.D.S. | MiS | BoS | |
| A | –4.9 | 1966 | 10.1 | 36.2 | 9.5 | 37.1 | 5.2 | 1.8 | – | – | 22864 |
| | | 1964 | 8.5 | 30.0 | 9.7 | 42.8 | 6.2 | 2.7 | – | | 22535 |
| | 5.0–9.9 | 1966 | 15.8 | 40.5 | 14.2 | 24.1 | 1.4 | 2.3 | 1.7 | | 48858 |
| | | 1964 | 15.1 | 38.5 | 13.1 | 27.7 | 1.3 | 2.6 | 1.7 | | 49669 |
| | 10.0– | 1966 | 19.3 | 40.6 | 10.6 | 22.3 | 1.0 | 1.0 | 5.2 | | 22271 |
| | | 1964 | 19.4 | 38.7 | 10.1 | 25.1 | 0.8 | 1.1 | 4.8 | – | 23418 |
| C | –4.9 | 1966 | 10.9 | 29.6 | 11.4 | 40.2 | 4.7 | 2.1 | 1.2 | – | 153881 |
| | | 1964 | 9.9 | 28.5 | 11.9 | 43.9 | 3.8 | 1.9 | – | – | 164425 |
| | 5.0–9.9 | 1966 | 15.3 | 33.2 | 11.1 | 30.4 | 2.9 | 2.2 | 4.9 | – | 205462 |
| | | 1964 | 13.5 | 31.2 | 12.3 | 35.0 | 2.0 | 2.2 | 3.9 | – | 208341 |
| | 10.0– | 1966 | 10.9 | 40.9 | 10.9 | 23.9 | 2.4 | 1.9 | 0.2 | – | 46874 |
| | | 1964 | 10.1 | 41.8 | 11.0 | 25.6 | 1.0 | 1.6 | – | – | 58246 |
| E | –4.9 | 1966 | 13.0 | 21.4 | 11.1 | 45.2 | 5.7 | 1.9 | 1.7 | – | 300095 |
| | | 1964 | 11.3 | 18.2 | 12.3 | 50.9 | 5.4 | 1.8 | 0.1 | – | 270106 |
| | 5.0–9.9 | 1966 | 17.1 | 25.3 | 13.7 | 38.6 | 3.1 | 1.8 | 0.3 | – | 101039 |
| | | 1964 | 14.2 | 22.0 | 13.6 | 45.4 | 3.0 | 1.9 | – | – | 88282 |
| | 10.0– | 1966 | 23.9 | 21.9 | 18.2 | 32.8 | 2.1 | 1.1 | – | – | 2659 |
| | | 1964 | 22.1 | 20.9 | 17.9 | 36.2 | 1.7 | 1.1 | – | – | 2620 |
| G | –4.9 | 1966 | 13.1 | 7.1 | 17.9 | 46.1 | 7.1 | 1.5 | 1.6 | 5.6 | 1624575 |
| | | 1964 | 12.9 | 5.1 | 18.9 | 52.2 | 5.2 | 1.4 | 0.1 | 3.8 | 1566796 |
| | 5.0–9.9 | 1966 | 16.9 | 14.1 | 21.1 | 43.1 | 2.3 | 2.5 | – | 3.3 | 27442 |
| | | 1964 | 14.9 | 10.0 | 21.1 | 48.9 | 2.0 | 3.2 | – | – | 23989 |

small-scale private enterprise in Sweden is ambiguous.[23] However, the significance of a spirit of social co-operation as an important environmental factor has been indicated in relation to the small-scale industry in Västbo, Jönköping province [William-Olsson, 1950].

A connection between thrift and ascetic religiosity[24] occurs not only in Free Church districts but also in strongly Church of Sweden districts, e.g. on the West Coast. Several trust funds in Gothenburg emanate from *Schartavan* (Old Lutheran) piety and style of life [Malmeström, 1950]. A peculiar connection between exclusive group spirit and economic initiative occurs in the Pentecostalist Movement, which has founded its own bank, *Allmänna Spar- och Kreditkassan* (General Savings and Credit). Its aim is to keep savings away from a 'circulation which supports cinemas, theatres, and other amusement establishments' and instead to find an avenue for financing its own activities.

Large financial reserves, based on donations, occur in all communities. Tithes are an additional source in the Pentecostalist Movement and some minor communities like the Seventh Day Adventists. In 1959 the free communities collected 80 million kronor (280 kronor per member). There clearly is a connection between religious attitude and thrift and economic care [Tawney, 1956], but the effect of this on private accumulation of capital and economic initiative is uncertain.

## RELIGION AND THE TEMPERANCE MOVEMENT. OTHER POPULAR MOVEMENTS AND CULTURAL PATTERNS

The religious communities have for a long time had a complex relationship to the temperance movement. The oldest temperance movement, one not committed to absolute abstinence, had a religious basis and was supported

23. From the middle of the last century many people in private enterprise joined the religious popular movements. However, this may have been due less to an original connection between private enterprise and revivalism than to the general weakened position of the church. The basic demand for freedom from governmental tutelage does form a common denominator between Free Church thinking and economic and political liberalism. The connection between religion and economic life sought to be most obvious in small-industry districts, such as the provinces of Jönköping and Närke, where many industrialists in fact do belong to the Free Churches. A major industry such as *Oscaria* in Örebro could once be described as a Free Church Baptist family company, but this could well be due more to uniformity of religious geography.

24. Long ago, the parliamentary commission on emigration drew attention to the large number of savings accounts in Smaland and Närke.

by the revivalist movements. It was opposed by many in the Church, but its aims were shared by the Free Churches, which still form something like a separate temperance movement, dedicated to personal abstinence. Free Church members only rarely joined the main temperance organisations, Blue Ribbon and White Ribbon,[25] yet the Free Church following has been much greater than the Church following: of the former, 16 per cent belonged to a temperance society in 1955; of the latter only 8 per cent belonged. There is an absolutist group norm in the Free Churches, but except for the Low Church, not in the Church of Sweden. The geographical distribution of temperance organizations [Lindman, 1943] displays a connection between high membership of temperance organizations and support for the Low and Free Church.[26]

The fact that the Low Church and the Free Churches both adopt personal abstinence as an important norm and requirement for membership, and keep a distance from the temperance movement, testifies to the tendency of these communities to become closed multi-purpose groups. The Church in virtue of its stronger specialization and concentration on one aim is a more open group. But even here the degree of openness has decreased particularly in the field of adult education.[27] The National Church, the Free Churches and other religious associations have separate organizations for adult education clearly demarcated from other cultural popular movements.

In the Church of Sweden a variety of ways of life are tolerated. Schar-

25. *De kristna samfundens nykterhetsrörelse* (the Temperance Movement of Christian Associations) formed in 1920, is interdenominational and acts like an ordinary pressure group, mainly inside the associations; at the moment it tends to concern itself not only with temperance but with social problems in general. It reflects a tendency towards a more closed norm-foundation than in society as a whole.

26. The prohibition referendum in 1922 disclosed great similarities between religious and temperance geography. There was a majority in favour of prohibition in Norrland (Low Church in the North, Free Churches further South), in Värmland, Närke and Northern and Middle Uppland where the Swedish Mission Association and the Bible Friends are influential, in the Jönköping province and in the Kristianstad district. Enquiries by the 1944 parliamentary commission on temperance [S.O.U., 1961, p. 43] showed that the number of absolutists was greatest in the Jönköping province, and in Central and Northern Sweden, and least in South-west Sweden, and in Stockholm and adjoining parts of Uppland and Södermanland. Liquor sale figures and the number of liquor pass-books in South West Sweden, where the Church of Sweden is comparatively influential, was not only higher than the Free Church Jönköping province and Low-church Central and Northern Norrland, but also than all other parts of the country except Greater Stockholm.

27. The Church of Sweden Education Association (originally called *Sveriges Kyrkliga Bildningsförbund*, now named *Sveriges Kyrkliga Studieförbund*), was founded in 1930. The Free Church Education Association followed in 1947.

tavans, and other old-church groups have, however, preserved an ancient cultural pattern, which has its roots in rural conditions, and in which not only modern forms of entertainment but also modern fiction and fashions are rejected, and in which the sabbath is strictly observed. Low-church groups often reject the use of cosmetics as well as alcohol and tobacco (although smoking is allowed in Bible Friends); in some cases (West-Laestadianism) neither sartorial elegance (e.g. wearing of a tie), nor well-appointed homes are accepted.

The *particular churches* display the most conspicuously exclusive way of life. The Pentecostalists, for example, have also repudiated lotteries, football pools, necklaces, and hair permanents, although this way of life (which was not unrelated to the recruitment of members, and which partly determined it) is now breaking up. But the repudiation of the 'world' is still essential to the movement and a cause of grave personal conflicts in the younger generation. Contraceptives used to be rejected, but are today accepted, in bigger cities, for intramarital use.

The exclusive way of life of Pentecostalism has counterparts elsewhere, but some Free Churches do tolerate cinema and theatre-going, mainly in the cities, where social control, in particular informal social control, cannot easily be exercised. These ways of life correspond to the group character of different communities: the *church* being more open, the *particular church* more closed, the *denomination* half-open. Their mores also serve as membership and in their integrative function play a decisive part in forming the structure of religious life [Gustafsson, 1952; Fur, 1952]. The religious mobility towards Pentecostalism should be seen against the background of its more exclusive cultural pattern, and the threat, felt by many, from a non-Christian environment.

## INTEGRATIVE AND DISINTEGRATIVE FUNCTIONS OF RELIGION

In older Swedish society the National Church was in many respects a cohesive force because of its norm system and exercise of social control. For some centuries, religious unity was 'first and foremost in the constitution of the realm'. In its encounter with the new society the Church fulfilled this integrative function by adopting a conservative attitude; it regarded its dominating position in society as a necessary condition for the continued existence of the old society. In this way the Church had a disintegrative influence on the new society and the tensions between it and new movements, such as the labour movement, sometimes gave rise to open social conflicts [Gustafsson, 1953].

The Free Churches, on the other hand, by virtue of their democratic organisation and commitments, contributed to the formation of the new society, and to the disintegration of the old [Johansson, 1952]. Gradually their integrative influence waned, and in the present situation their influence on society and its various environments is too varied and often too specifically religious to be described in terms of integration and disintegration. Today these findings of religion are only of relevance with respect to the family and neighbourhood contexts in which religion can dominate more than in the wider social milieu.

*The family*

In patriarchal times the function of religion in the family was highly developed; family religious rituals, mainly family prayers and home devotions, had a strongly integrative effect. With the dissolution of the older family type, religious interaction in the family is no more a common custom. It was to be limited to the mother-child relationship, except in strongly religious homes. Among communities like the Pentecostalists and in some old-church districts, the family has marked religious functions while the Free Churches have endeavoured to restore family religious life.

Religious life and death rituals – marriage, funeral, Baptism and Confirmation – owe their popularity to the integrative function within the family and kinship group. In the absence of general religious uniformity today the emancipation of young adults from dependence on their parents and home background often implies that religion has an immediate disintegrative effect on family life. But this is not always so; where children take over the parent's religious attitudes and way of life, family community is strengthened.

Generally, believers appear to be more family-centred, and one could guess that those types of religion, whose norm-systems are concerned with interpersonal relations, tend to integrate the family. The effect of a religious attitude is more noticeable in men; independent of religious interest most women are more strongly family-directed. However, Table 16 shows that even in women, family directedness increases somewhat with stronger religiosity.

Some family uniformity in religious attitudes is a necessary condition for the integrative function of religion in the family [Karlsson, 1951; Hultgren and Stoltz, 1956]. Where spouses' religious attitudes differ, religion can give rise to maladjustment, though rarely gravely so. Mixed marriages are rare, in contrast to the situation in the U.S.A., but they are likely to become more frequent with the increase of religious differentiation. Marriages between Catholics and Lutherans are increasing in number.

*Table 16. Relationship between interest in religion and family life among men and women in 1955*

| Religious interest | Interest in family life | | | |
|---|---|---|---|---|
| | Men | | Women | |
| | Strong % | N | Strong % | N |
| Weak | 58 | 371 | 71 | 211 |
| Medium | 74 | 470 | 83 | 481 |
| Strong | 73 | 56 | 86 | 99 |

Source: B. Gustafsson, 1958.

*The neighbourhood*

Religion used to have a cohesive effect on neighbourhood groups. The co-ordination of work and holidays in the villages rested, to a certain extent, on the church's effort to set standards for neighbour relations ('good friends, faithful neighbours'). Although neighbourhood groups, both natural and religious, have disappeared, the religious groups arising from revivalist movements have often remained linked to neighbourhood groups; what often happened was only that the parish church, as the place of worship for the neighbourhood, with a special pew for each village, was replaced by a meeting-house in the immediate vicinity. The spatial distribution of meeting places of different associations, would in many places still show the function of the meetinghouse as a neighbourhood-centre. The meeting places of different associations are in close proximity only in cities and townships. In the provinces, therefore, religious life has not infrequently preserved its neighbourhood-integrating effect; in urban and semi-urban areas its differentiation has sometimes been disintegrative. In modern society, religious life creates social cohesion only in more limited neighbourhood environments.

*Norm conflicts*

An increasing number of persons from a religious background are, probably, experiencing a conflict between inherited norms and those of friends, schools and society. This can be partly a matter of tension between different cultural patterns. Also, older norms are weakening, particularly in the larger associations. There remains mainly the requirement of premarital sexual abstinence. It is unknown how often religious adolescents violate this norm, but sometimes at least one out of three do [Karlsson, 1964]. This can give rise to guilt-feelings, personality stress, and even open conflicts. Religious sexual taboos may also create other anxiety and guiltfeelings. The most severe conflicts will occur in adolescents from small *particular churches* with firm systems of norms and rigorously controlled behaviour.

There may also exist a gap between older methods of moral teaching in which morality is seen as a collection of authoritarian commands, and a more recent, group-directed formation of morals, which is more like a trial-and-error-process. There appears to be a typical *lag* in those representatives of religion who still regard morality as an authoritarian norm rather than a self-experienced truth.

The tension between religion and science can be also experienced as a conflict. Some associations seek to harmonize religion and science (Roman Catholicism, the Church of Sweden, to some extent also Methodism and movements influenced by it); others – movements of a marginal kind – appear to profit from a dramatization of the tension. This is sometimes due to a feeling of being, generally, an outsider to modern society.

## REFERENCES AND BIBLIOGRAPHY

Ershammar, M., *Personlig anpassning hos grekiska och italienska immigranter med särskild hänsyn till religiösa faktorer* [Personal Adjustment in Greek and Italian Immigrants, with special reference to Religious Factors]. Stockholm, (mimeo.), 1966.

Fur, G., 'Frikyrklighet och socialgeografiska regioner i Småland' [The Free Churches and Social-Geographical Regions in Småland]. *Svensk geografisk årsbok* [Swedish Yearbook of Geography], Lund, 1952.

Goffman, E., *The Presentation of Self in Every-Day Life*. Edinburgh, 1956.

Gustafsson, B., 'Religion och fördomar' [Religion and Prejudice]. *Våra Fördomar* [Our Prejudices], Lund, 1952.

—, *Socialdemokratien och kyrkan 1881–1890* [Social Democracy and the Church 1881–1890]. Stockholm, 1953a.

—, 'Kyrkan och arbetarrörelsen' [The Church and the Labour Movement]. *Härnösands stift i ord och bild* [The Härnösand Diocese in Words and Pictures]. Stockholm, 1953b.

—, *Svensk kyrkogeografi* [Swedish Church Geography]. Lund, 1957.

—, *Kristen i 50-talets Sverige* [The Christian in Sweden of the 50's]. Stockholm, The Swedish Institute for Public Opinion Research, 1958.

—, 'The Lund Inquiry,' in: *Statens offentliga utredningar* [The Swedish Official Reports]. No. 26. Stockholm, 1963a.

—, *The Stockholm Inquiry: Aktivitetsnivåer vid lyssnande till radiogudstjänster* [Divine Service Broadcasts: Levels of Audience Activity]. Stockholm, The Stockholm Institute of Sociology of Religion (mimeo.), 1963.

Gustafsson, G., *Religion och politik* [Religion and Politics]. Lund, University of Lund, (Department of Sociology), (mimeo.), 1967.

Hultgren, S., and Stoltz, I., *Äktenskapet och lyckan* [Marriage and Happiness]. Stockholm, 1956.

Hultquist, N., and Freeman, L., *Väckelserörelser och partibildningar* [Revival Movements and Party Formations]. Jönköping, 1954.

Johansson, H., *Folkrörelserna och det demokratisk statsskicket i Sverige* [The Popular Movements and the Democratic Form of Government in Sweden]. Lund, 1952.
—, *Folkrörelserna* [The Popular Movements]. Stockholm, 1954.
Karlsson, G., *Adaptability and Communication in Marriage.* Uppsala, 1951.
—, 'Sexuella vanor och attityder bland folkhögskole-elever' [Sexual Habits and Attitudes in Folk High School Pupils]. *Sociologisk forskning* I, 1964.
Lundman, E., *Nykterhetens geografi* [The Geography of Temperance/Sobriety]. Tirfing, 1943.
Lundquist, A., Bursh, Karin, *Främling i Sverige* [Stranger in Sweden]. Uppsala, 1966.
Malmeström, E., 'Ur stiftets bygdesociologi' [From the Rural Sociology of the Diocese]. *Göteborgs stift i ord och bild* [The Gothenburg Diocese in Words and Pictures]. Stockholm, 1950.
Statens Offentliga Utredningar [The Swedish Government Official Reports], *Kyrkor och trossamfund i Sverige* [Churches and Religious Associations in Sweden]. Report No. 39. Stockholm, 1963.
*Svenska Kyrkans Arsbok* [The Church of Sweden Yearbook]. Stockholm, 1967.
Svenska Missionsförbundet [Swedish Mission Association], *Ungdomen Kommer* [The Adolescents are Coming]. Stockholm, 1956.
Religionssociologiska Institutet i Stockholm [The Stockholm Institute of the Sociology of Religion]. *Smärre Meddelanden* [Minor Bulletins], No. 2, 1963; (mimeo, revision of S.I.F.O. data) No. 3. Stockholm, 1964.
—, *Religiös kommuntyp och politisk förskjutning i valet 1966* [Types of Religion in Election Districts and Political Changes in the 1966 Election]. No. 10. Stockholm, 1966.
—, *The Enquiry in a Stockholm Suburb*, Forskningsrapporter [Research Reports]. No. 7. Stockholm, 1967.
*Religions statistik för Stockholms Stad 1963* [Religious Statistics for the City of Stockholm]. Stockholm, 1964.
Segerstedt, T. T., and Lundquist, A., *Människan i industrisamhället* [Man in Industrial Society]. Stockholm, 1955.
Sjödén, B., *Etermediernas Publik* [The Audiences of Broadcasting Media]. Stockholm, 1957.
*Statistisk Arsbok* [Yearbook of Official Statistics]. Stockholm, yearly.
Svärd, Lydia, *Väckelserörelsernas folk i Andra kammaren 1867–1911* [The People of the Revival Movements in the Second Chamber, *i.e.* the Lower House of the Riksdag]. Stockholm, 1954.
Tawney, R. H., 'Religion and Economic Life'. *The Times Literary Supplement*, 6 January, 1956.
Temperance Commission of 1944, *Statistiska undersökningar kring alkoholfrågan* [Statistical Enquiries on the Liquor Problem]. Statens offentliga utredningar [Swedish Government Official Reports], No. 43, Stockholm, 1951.
Thörnberg, E. H., *Folkrörelser och samhällsliv i Sverige* [Popular Movements and Social Life in Sweden]. Stockholm, 1952.
William-Olssen, W., 'Ett småindustriområde' [A Light Industry Region]. *Hantverk och Kultur* [Crafts and Culture], (Stockholm) 1950.
Zetterberg, Hans, 'Enquiry', *Svensk Veckotidning* [The Swedish Weekly]. 1950.

ROLAND J. CAMPICHE*

# Switzerland

## HISTORICAL INTRODUCTION TO THE ORGANIZATION OF THE SWISS CHURCHES

Switzerland came into existence in 1291 as a result of the alliance of three cantons which were under Austrian rule. However, it did not assume its present form – a confederation of twenty-two more or less autonomous cantons with a central authority – until 1848. In the course of the centuries and until 1815, nineteen cantons and states attached themselves to the league of the three original ones. The religious history of these cantons and states until the sixteenth century was closely linked with the history of the bishoprics to which they belonged. But after the Reformation one witnesses a radical change in the situation. Starting in such cities as Zurich, Basel, Bern and Geneva the Reformation spread to the territories which belonged to those cities, while the rural cantons remained faithful to Rome. Henceforth, Switzerland was not only divided into territories which differed markedly in respect to language and customs and which remained, until the establishment of a federal government, very independent of one another, but in addition it became divided into two confessional blocs. This new division increased tensions within a Confederation which had established its unity only with difficulty. In 1847, this unity was even further endangered when, during a swift and restrained war, the Protestant cantons brought the Catholic cantons, which had united themselves into a separate alliance, back to the bosom of the Confederacy.

The Protestant Church built its organizational structure parallel to the political structure of the country. Thus until the beginning of the present century, reformed cantonal churches had very strong ties with the state. Thereafter, church and state were separated in most Protestant cantons while, in the Catholic ones, church and state continued to collaborate

* Roland J. Campiche was born in La tour de Peilz, Switzerland in 1937. He is at present senior researcher at the Swiss National Foundation for Scientific Research and professor at the University of Lausanne. He has previously been pastor in Lausanne and Geneva. He is currently engaged in establishing *L'Institut romand de sociologie de la religion*. Publications include *Urbanisation et vie religieuse* [Urbanization and Religious Life], 1968.

closely. In the latter, schools were denominational. The establishment of closer ties between the cantonal churches is also characteristic of the twentieth century. These churches, generally led by a Synod and a Synodal council, federated in 1920 and co-ordinated their missionary efforts through the establishment of a Swiss council of missions in 1945. These new organs embraced the cantonal churches as well as the free churches, which had originated in the nineteenth century as a result of the combined effect of the Revival and the conflicts which – particularly in French-speaking Switzerland – arose from opposition to the Protestant churches and the cantonal governments. Since World War II, two of the three free churches of the French speaking part of Switzerland have united with the cantonal churches. The Revival also led to the appearance of a certain number of sects. It is, however, not possible to describe here their organization and their ties with the established churches.

The Roman Catholic church lost the majority of its faithful at the time of the Reformation. Several bishoprics, from which the bishops had been removed had to be reorganized. That reorganization was ratified by the Concordat, signed in 1828, between the Federal Diet and Pope Leo XII. The territory was divided into small national dioceses of which there are nowadays six. Although geographically the bishoprics are not always coterminous with the cantons, each canton has its vicar-general. The Conference of Swiss Bishops assures the unity of Helvetian Catholicism. Its activity has gained considerably in scope, especially during recent years, as pastoral planning is established. After the first Vatican Council the Catholic Church in Switzerland underwent, as in many other European countries, a new Schism, which gave rise to the *Eglise catholique chrétienne* (Catholic Christian Church) – the third church recognized by the state.

Calvin and Zwingli unambiguously marked off Protestantism from Catholicism. Dogmatic counter positions were taken by the Council of Trent. The adoption of these positions explains the difficulties of interdenominational relations in Switzerland. Ecumenical dialogue is timid and does not give rise to institutional forms. However, ecumenical commissions convene in order to study certain circumscribed problems, such as that of mixed marriages or underdeveloped countries. However, a collaboration of Christian Churches is gradually taking the place of an often precarious interdenominational peace, preparing the way for the establishment of a Swiss Christian Council [Heussi and Peter, 1967; Pfister, 1964].

## DENOMINATIONAL STRUCTURE

After having constituted a clear majority since the Reformation, Protestants will soon form only half of the population of Switzerland; the Catholic minority has increased considerably as a result of the excess of births over deaths and particularly of foreign immigration. [B.F.S., *Annuaire statistique de la Suisse*. The annual reports are also the source of statistical data in the following section].

*Table 1. Resident population of Switzerland according to religion**

| | Protestant | Catholic | Catholic Christian Church | Jews | Others or without religion |
|---|---|---|---|---|---|
| 1860 | 1,478,591 | 1,021,821 | | | 10,082 |
| | (58.9) | (40.7) | | | (0.4) |
| 1910 | 2,107,814 | 1,593,538 | | 18,462 | 33,479 |
| | (56.1) | (42.5) | | (0.5) | (0.9) |
| 1960 | 2,861,522 | 2,463,214 | 29,754 | 19,984 | 54,587 |
| | (52.7) | (45.4) | (0.5) | (0.5) | (1.0) |

* Figures in brackets represent percentages.

Not only is the proportion of Protestants residing in Switzerland diminishing, but also the proportion of Swiss Protestant citizens. Thus, if in 1900, 61.6 per cent of all Swiss nationals were Protestant and 38 per cent Catholic, in 1960, 57 per cent were Protestant and 41.4 per cent Roman Catholic. Since 1871, which is the first year for which we have data, fertility has been decreasing in Switzerland.

*Table 2. Fertility of marriages per 1,000 married women aged 15 to 44 years*

| Years | Towns | Remainder of Switzerland | Switzerland |
|---|---|---|---|
| 1899/02 | 215 | 280 | 267 |
| 1909/12 | 151 | 243 | 221 |
| 1919/22 | 109 | 211 | 184 |
| 1929/32 | 88 | 170 | 148 |
| 1940/43 | 99 | ? | 143 |

This decline is particularly marked in the industrial areas and in the cities with a Protestant majority where young Catholic and Protestant couples have adopted the same habits in respect to the number of children. [Campiche, 1968, p. 54]. It is less strong in the agricultural regions, particularly in those which have a Catholic majority, where, to give an example, fertility remained stationary between 1871 and 1920. It is noteworthy that since 1956 the number of live-births to Catholic families has exceeded the number of Protestant live-births as a result of the presence of numerous young foreign workers whose fertility is distinctly higher than that of Swiss Catholics.

The foreigners residing in Switzerland – in 1960, 11 per cent, and in August 1964, 18 per cent of the total population – are increasingly more predominantly Roman Catholic (68.9 per cent in 1900, 80.2 per cent in 1960). Among them the number of men decidedly exceeds the number of women. This results in a perfect equilibrium in the distribution of sexes for the Catholic population residing in Switzerland. Among Protestants, because female foreigners outnumber male foreigners, the male population is in a minority (48 per cent in 1960). Particularly in the urban Protestant cantons the influx of foreigners had led to a marked increase in the proportion of Catholics. In 1960 they constituted nearly a third of the Catholic population of the canton of Zurich and over a quarter of that of the canton of Vaud.

These same foreigners also contribute, in large measure, to the increase of mixed marriages in Switzerland. Thus in 1960, 10,757 male Catholic foreigners married Catholics and 5,742 married Protestants. Against this, 5,422 male Protestant foreigners married Protestants and 1,069 married Roman Catholics. Among the totality of married couples living together between 1880 and 1950, one notes a slow but continuous increase in mixed marriages.

If we consider the religious affiliation of newly-weds over four years, selected

*Table 3. Religion of couples living together 1880 and 1950**

| | Protestant men married to wives who are: | | | | Catholic men married to wives who are: | | | |
|---|---|---|---|---|---|---|---|---|
| | Prot. | Cath. | Jew | Other or no church membership | Prot. | Cath. | Jew | Other or no church membership |
| 1880 | 244,220 | 9,985 | 18 | 98 | 12,250 | 155,077 | 5 | 20 |
| | (96) | (4) | (0.04) | | (7) | (93) | (0.01) | |
| 1950 | 542,531 | 59,829 | 249 | 1,823 | 47,859 | 312,450 | 99 | 675 |
| | (90.1) | (9.6) | (0.03) | | (13) | (86.8) | (0.2) | |

* Figures in brackets represent percentages.

from among the last decades, we see that the increase in mixed marriages shows a tendency to accelerate (Table 4).

*Table 4. Newly-weds according to religion 1942–1966*

| | Protestant men married to wives who are: | | | | Catholic men married to wives who are: | | | | Total of mixed marriages | |
|---|---|---|---|---|---|---|---|---|---|---|
| | Prot. | Cath. | Jews & others | | Cath. | Prot. | Jews & others | | | |
| | % | % | % | N | % | % | % | N | % | N |
| 1942 | 83.7 | 16.0 | 0.3 | 22,345 | 79.9 | 20.0 | 0.1 | 14,049 | 18 | 6,579 |
| 1950 | 78.0 | 21.0 | 0.4 | 21,394 | 81.6 | 18.2 | 0.2 | 15,253 | 20 | 7,359 |
| 1960 | 75.4 | 24.2 | 0.4 | 20,438 | 81.5 | 18.2 | 0.3 | 20,556 | 22 | 8,863 |
| 1966 | 76.5 | 23.0 | 0.5 | 21,256 | 77.4 | 22.1 | 0.5 | 22,144 | 23 | 9,997 |

Particularly noticeable is the increase in the number of Protestant males who marry Catholic women (1945: 16 per cent, 1960: 24 per cent). Those mixed unions are especially frequent in the cities and the persons concerned are often those who are most urbanized [Campiche, 1968, pp. 99ff]. A socio-graphical survey in Geneva, which deals with the main vertical villages (new city sectors of high-rise buildings) shows that about 40 per cent of the couples of which one spouse is Protestant are, in fact, mixed couples. A similar observation was made in Küsnacht on the outskirts of Zurich [Schaer and Bäumle, 1968, p. 31] where it was found that half of all the couples of which one spouse is Catholic, constitute denominationally heterogeneous marriages. As a final remark on mixed marriages, we mention the observation which was made in Lausanne, that not only the urban environment favours this type of union, but also that the children from mixed marriages, married someone with a different religious affiliation with noticeably higher frequency than did children not from mixed marriages [Campiche, 1968, p. 100].

## RELIGIOUS PARTICIPATION AND BELIEFS

The great majority of Swiss respect the solemn acts of religious life. In a Lausanne study 99 per cent of the people questioned were baptised, 96 per cent were confirmed or had renewed their baptismal vows, and 91 per cent of marriages were celebrated in the church. Those who do not contract a religious marriage are either couples of mixed denomination or persons contracting a second marriage [Campiche, 1967, p. 100]. Yet if the majority of the Swiss are 'seasonal conformists' 27 per cent have given up all regular church attendance (34 per cent of Protestants, 18 per cent of Catholics).

The only study [Boltansky, 1966, pp. 62ff.] which gives data concerning religious practice for the whole country shows that it fluctuates according to region, denominational composition of the canton, or size of the habitat. Thus one finds that attendance at religious services or the mass and the density of sacerdotal and religious vocations remains considerable in the mountainous cantons where the majority of the population is generally Catholic, while it falls off noticeably in the urban cantons with a Protestant majority.

*Table 5. Religious practice in Switzerland (1962) according to individual religion and the predominant religion of the canton of residence (in %)*

| Cantons | Practising | | Not practising | |
|---|---|---|---|---|
| | Prot. | Cath. | Prot. | Cath. |
| With Prot. majority | 64 | 75 | 36 | 25 |
| With Cath. majority | 79 | 87 | 21 | 13 |
| Mixed | 70 | 87 | 30 | 13 |
| Prot. N=638 Cath. N=512 | | | | |

Source: Boltansky, 1966, p. 179.

A Sunday survey of church attendance of Catholics in French speaking Switzerland is particularly revealing [A.C.R., 1962, map 7]. One finds that in 1958 more than 85 per cent of the Catholics of the high valleys attend Mass on Sunday, while in the towns which are located in the Catholic cantons 20 and 30 per cent of the Catholics attend Mass. This percentage drops to between 15 and 20 per cent in the urban areas with a Protestant majority. According to a survey conducted on Sunday in Geneva the rate of practice

*Table 6. Church attendance according to the size of the habitat*

| Size of the habitat | Attend church | Do not attend church |
|---|---|---|
| | % | % |
| – 1,000 (N=257) | 85 | 15 |
| 1,000– 10,000 (N=534) | 76 | 24 |
| 10,000–100,000 (N=190) | 63 | 37 |
| Over 100,000 (N=219) | 43 | 57 |

Source: Boltansky, 1966, p. 179.

for Protestants is between 6 and 7 per cent [Perret, 1963]. Table 6 indicates that these findings are also valid for the whole of Switzerland.
Although the studies which we have just cited give us an idea of the rate of Sunday practice and of the percentage of those who attend church, we do not know very much about the intensity of such practice. The figures below which concern the inhabitants of a sector of Lausanne will serve to balance the limited information conveyed by the Sunday surveys and the too gross distinction between those who attend church and those who do not.

*Table 7. Frequency of church attendance on sunday in Sévelin-Lausanne in 1965 (in %)*

| Population | Those who attend | | | | | |
|---|---|---|---|---|---|---|
| | Every Sunday | 2–3 times a month | Once a month | A few times a year | Never | Cannot |
| Total population (N=441) | 16 | 13 | 10 | 36 | 22 | 3 |
| Protestants (N=248) | 3 | 14 | 9 | 44 | 26 | 4 |
| Catholics (N=171) | 30 | 9 | 13 | 29 | 18 | 1 |
| Members of Sects (N=22) | 56 | 39 | – | 5 | – | – |

Source: Campiche, 1968, p. 102.

Frequency of taking Communion varies according to the same variables found to be significant in relation to church attendance. One finds, however, that, according to the earlier mentioned surveys taken in French speaking Switzerland, Protestants and Sectarians who attend church at least once a week take Communion more frequently than Catholics who attend Mass every Sunday and that the difference between Protestants and Catholics in regard to worship is now decidedly less important. A survey conducted in the Bernese Jura has for instance revealed that 45.75 per cent of respondents take Communion as often as possible. [Commission jurassienne..., 1966]. It seems that Protestants are less held back than in the past by an anti-sacramental suspicion.

Individual practice has not been the subject of numerous studies, for example, there is only one study of the frequency of Confession among Catholics [Campiche, 1968, pp. 123ff.]. A survey in Neuchâtel among the Protestants and one in Lausanne among inhabitants selected randomly in a sector of the city show, as in Table 8, that the majority of the members of sects and a minority of the Protestants read the Bible.

*Table 8. Frequency of bible reading (in %)*

| | Denomination | Read the Bible | | | |
|---|---|---|---|---|---|
| | | Regularly | Occasionally | Never | No reply |
| Neuchâtel 1963 | Protestants (N=300) | 25 | 50 | 25 | – |
| Lausanne 1965 | Total population (N=441) | 15 | 28 | 56 | 1 |
| | Protestants (N=248) | 18 | 36 | 45 | 1 |
| | Catholics (N=171) | 5 | 16 | 78 | 1 |
| | Members of Sects (N=22) | 83 | 17 | – | – |

Source: Campiche, 1968, p. 125f.; Bugnon, 1964. (Results based on the study of 300 registered Protestants).

To conclude we must note that religious worship is diminishing constantly in the cities. Nevertheless, rather than a diminution of practice one should speak of its deplacement and the appearance of a new category of those who practise at home. For instance it has been found in Lausanne that the majority of the population continues to pray (51 per cent daily) and that those who do not go to a place of worship often listen to the religious service on the radio or television. According to this survey, approximately two-thirds of those who did not go to church either prayed at home or followed the service or the Mass on the radio [Campiche, 1968, pp. 125ff, 189].

In Switzerland no opinion poll has been conducted to find out whether the inhabitants believe in God ... Nevertheless the information which has been collected [Campiche, 1968, pp. 151ff; Boltanski, 1966, pp. 51, 67; Favarger, 1967–68] concerning conceptions of the task of the church and the role of the pastor or priest is revealing. Only a minority is able to give a definition of the task of the church which corresponds with the teaching of the church. What the majority of the Swiss want is a consoling church which is the guarantor of morality; the activities of the clergy should be consonant with this conception. No allowance whatsoever is made for the prophetic mission of the church. It seems

> as if it did not have, or no longer had, the power to call forth from the people particular attitudes towards existence in its totality, as if the religious sphere had become autonomous at the very time when the ethical principles which had sprung from the dogma, but were detached

> from it, were finding wider and wider acceptance, as if the religious laws and canons served only to regulate the practice of the believer in his relations with the sacred and with religion itself [Boltanski, 1966, pp. 51ff.].

According to an investigation conducted in Geneva among eighty-five public opinion leaders with an average amount of influence on the propagation of ideas, leaders who belonged predominantly to the scientific professions – we are moving towards a post-Christian Humanism, a religious conception which has become devoid of its Christian substance in order to make way for an Eastern mysticism, for a religious syncretism, for a pronounced moralism [Favarger, 1967–68]. This tendency however, which was found among people who have a very stereotyped picture of the church, is not necessarily valid for the whole population and must merely be retained as a hypothesis concerning the evolution of attitudes towards church and religion.

On the level of ethics and attitudes in daily life, it should be noted that although Catholics and Protestants have different patterns of behaviour on the practical level and in their behaviour towards the parochial community, they are in agreement in recognising in religion a line of conduct, in defending a rational asceticism, and in promoting a spirit of work. One finds for instance that under the influence of the Protestant majority the Catholic clergy even goes further than the Calvinists in extolling strictness and puritanism. The Catholic clergy has succeeded in creating an amalgam of religious values and the national values first defined by the Protestants. Paradoxically, this seems to assure a better transmission of these values, which are generally received, accepted and internalised without their origin being perceived. This ethic appears therefore more as the fruit of a cultural heritage than as a revealed gift [Boltanski, 1966, pp. 50ff; Campiche, 1968, pp. 175ff.].

### VARIABLES INFLUENCING RELIGIOUS LIFE AND BEHAVIOUR

All the studies to be reviewed here show that religious practice decreases markedly, especially among Protestants, after the age of twenty or twenty-five, then remains stationary at a low level until the age of forty, rises slightly thereafter and, generally at the age of sixty-five, diminishes again among Protestants, while increasing a little among Catholics.

Confronted with a variable such as civil status, religious practice undergoes important variations. The Sunday congregations consist predominantly of unmarried minors, of married people of the same denomination and of widowed persons. Spouses of mixed unions and divorced people have an extremely low rate of religious practice (in Geneva, 1.5 per cent for divorced males and 3.4 per cent for divorced females against 5.4 per cent and 6.4 per cent respectively for married Protestant males and females).

Among social classes the workers usually have the lowest rate of practice: 27.3 per cent of the skilled Catholic workmen in Lausanne and 15.1 per cent of the Catholic unskilled workers attended Mass on the day of the survey, against 68.9 per cent of the executives [A.C.R., 1962, p. 21]; in Sion, where the inhabitants, as in the canton, are over 90 per cent Catholic, the percentages are 15, 31 and 60 respectively. In Geneva 2.5 per cent of the Protestant workmen and labourers attended the service on the day of the survey, against 3.81 per cent of the executives [Perret, 1963]. The same conclusion is reached by the earlier mentioned surveys made in Neuchâtel, Küsnacht, Sevelin-Lausanne or Morges [Cf. Bridel, 1967]. However, even if the worker very frequently views the church as an alien institution in which he does not easily find his place, even if he considers it to be bound up with the propertied classes and too much involved in politics [Cf. Commission des Communautés, 1967, a survey covering about 150 Catholics] one cannot speak in Switzerland of a total rupture between labour and the churches.

One finds, however, that on the whole the members of the middle classes constitute the majority of the faithful of the churches, while employees of the hotel trade, the independents (crafsmen, tradesmen), the small employees and the labourers maintain an attitude of reserve. This statement is particularly true for the urban environment where one finds that below and above a certain income threshold religious practice decreases. This statement, however, applies less well to the rural Catholics cantons. There a high rate of religious practice is found when the occupational spectrum is narrow, and a low average rate of religious practice where the occupational spectrum becomes broader. Unfortunately we have no comparable data concerning the rural Protestant areas.

The same observation with respect to the economic threshold can be made with respect to comparison of religious practice of men and women; and the difference is greater in the regions where only the minority attend church. Those who are not employed for gain are represented in the Sunday congregations out of proportion to their real numerical importance; in Geneva for instance, they constitute 59.2 per cent of those attending, while they represent only 46.8 per cent of the total Protestant population [Perret, 1963, p. 96].

Church attendance, or better, the regularity of church attendance increases with length of formal education. In addition to this, persons who have had the benefit of a long formal education are more inclined to define the task of the Church in terms which correspond with its teachings. These persons also integrate the Gospel more easily into their private lives [Perret, 1963, p. 67; Campiche, 1968, pp. 106, 166, 172]. There is a strong relationship between religious life and the rate of religious practice on the one hand, and secondary education on the other. It appears therefore that the variations in the rate of practice and attitudes are very closely related to a mode of existence, influenced by profession, income and level of education.

These variables, age, civil status, income, class, sex, education, etc. do not suffice to explain fully the differences in behaviour or in rates of practice which are found in Switzerland. Integration into the social environment also plays an important role, especially with Protestants. Although village dwellers conform, as one would expect, more readily to social and religious practices than city dwellers, one finds that city dwellers, who are well integrated in their daily environment and who participate actively in social and political life have maintained much closer contacts with their church and have a greater respect for its teaching than those who suffer from the anonymity of urban life, whose work is far from where they live and who have very dispersed social relations. This observation applies especially to Protestants, as it seems that, in regard to church attendance particularly, Catholics are less affected by the absence of tight-knit social structures in the cities. This becomes understandable in our view if one takes the different ecclesiologies of the two Christian denominations into consideration. Protestants manifest, in effect, a greater attachment to the parish community and, in contrast with Catholics, rarely attend church without having established contact with it. This can be seen from the following table concerning Sevelin-Lausanne.

*Table 9. Frequency of church attendance according to whether contact has been established with the parish (in %)*

| Parish contact and denomination | Frequency of Church attendance | | | | | |
|---|---|---|---|---|---|---|
| | Every Sunday | 2–3 times per month | Monthly | A few times a year | Never | Not able |
| *Protestant* | | | | | | |
| Contact established | 100* | 97 | 83 | 61 | 45 | 50* |
| No contact | – | 3 | 17 | 39 | 55 | 50* |
| *Catholic* | | | | | | |
| Contact established | 80 | 63 | 55 | 42 | 43 | 50* |
| No contact | 20 | 37 | 45 | 58 | 57 | 50* |

* Given as indication.

Source: Campiche, 1968, p. 134.

In a country where in 1960 23 per cent of the active population are people who work outside their residential area, where horizontal and vertical mobility is intense, community life will inevitably be weakened. The degree to which religious life is affected depends, however, on the type of mobility. Commuting threatens religious life when it has been established a long time [Cf. A.C.R., 1962, p. 16]. So also do long commuting stretches and frequent changes of residence within a locality [Cf. Campiche, 1968, p. 31]. External mobility (before establishment in a locality), as well as social mobility and week-end mobility [Maret, *et al.*, 1961]. does not weaken religious life – on the contrary. We give these examples in order to show that, although the rates of religious practice vary considerably with the size of the habitat, as we have seen in the previous paragraph, certain features of urban life affect it more particularly than do others. [For a development of this point see Campiche, 1968].

In a country where, from the industrial revolution onwards there has been a massive influx of rural Catholics into the Protestant cities, one observes the appearance of new population strata with different traditions and mentalities. However, the most striking feature at the moment is the growing interpenetration of the Catholic and the Protestant population as a result of mixed marriages. They are contracted principally by city-dwellers, employees and workmen, who have grown up in the Protestant cities [Campiche, 1968, pp. 99ff.]. All the studies bearing on religious practice or religious attitudes which have been mentioned in the course of this chapter, agree in showing that the spouses of mixed unions give up participating in religious services to a higher degree than the parochial community as a whole and that they are the least interested in what the church or the Gospel teaches in respect to daily life. To this must be added that even if they practise, they confess and take Communion less frequently than spouses of denominationally homogeneous marriages. This can be seen from Table 10 concerning the Catholics of Küsnacht.

*Table 10. Frequency of communion and type of marriage (in %)*

| Denomination of spouse | Frequency of communion of Catholics | | | | | |
|---|---|---|---|---|---|---|
| | Very frequent | Quite frequent | Few times a year | Once a year | Never | No reply |
| Catholic | 13 | 36 | 30 | 13 | 3 | 5 |
| Non-Catholic | – | 38 | 33 | 10 | 11 | 8 |

Source: Schaer and Baumle, 1968, Table 41.

## RELIGION POLITICS AND ECONOMICS

Due to the almost total absence of studies which attempt to demonstrate relationships between the political or economic spheres and religion in Switzerland, we will only make some brief remarks. Let us begin by pointing out that such relationships exist. The activity of a Christian social conservative Catholic party proves this. The Protestants have no party, except in Zurich where there is a small Evangelical party. But one can say with confidence that Protestantism is tied more or less strongly according to the canton, with the bourgeois, radical and liberal parties or those of the peasants, artisans and members of the middle class. One finds indeed that according to a comparison which was made in Lausanne between frequency of worship and marked preference for a political party, regular church-goers very frequently choose the radical and liberal parties, while the great majority of the Catholics are members of the Christian Social Party [Cf. Campiche, 1968, p. 115].

Luc Boltanski, in his analysis of 'Swiss Happiness', notes that denominational membership plays a role on the political and economic level. He remarks, for instance, that 'the Catholics complain that all the important posts are held by Protestants' [Boltanski, 1966, p. 49]. Saving and thrift, which have been elevated to national virtues, and which are recognized as the fruits of Protestant asceticism, are not without influence on the economic behaviour of the Swiss citizen [Boltanski, 1966, p. 55].

Although relationships evidently exist between the political or economic sphere and religion – those who attend church participate generally in political life, they vote regularly in contrast to those who are indifferent in religious matters – it does not seem that this relationship is recognized by the average Swiss. Even if he attends religious services he generally replies negatively to the question: 'Does the Gospel or the teaching of the church influence your decisions in the political or economic sphere?' This denial of any interference of religion in public life is also confirmed by his attitude towards the clergy, to whom half of the people questioned denied the right to play a role even in local political life [Cf. Campiche, 1968, pp. 160ff, 173ff]. It seems thus, that the relationship between these spheres exists because religion has penetrated culture, but it is only perceived at the latter level.

## OTHER STUDIES IN THE SOCIOLOGY OF RELIGION

Several studies, some of which are completed, some still in progress, concern the priest or the pastor and the image which the layman has of him.

From the Catholic side, a longitudinal and regional study has been made of priestly vocations [*Cf.* A.C.R., 1962, p. 17; Wagner, 1968]. A sociographical analysis of the clergy has been attempted as preparatory stage, before beginning a sociological study of the image of the priest among youth. These studies show the decline of priestly callings in Switzerland during the last decades and indicate clearly the increasing average age of the Catholic clergy of whom 48 per cent are over 37 and 31 per cent over sixty-two years of age [A.C.R., 1962, p. 13]. Two studies [Frauenfelder, *et al.*, 1967; Campiche, 1968, 151ff] have aimed at showing the activities of the pastor which the layman considers most important. Ulrich Locher and René Riesen [1968] have tried to sketch a picture of the pastor based on thirty-six interviews of Bernese pastors. That pilot study will be taken up again and completed. It is noteworthy that most of the persons questioned have retained the traditional activities. The sermon takes the first place according to the survey, which was conducted at Oberwinterthur among the Protestants [Frauenfelder, *et al*', 1967, pp. 107, 143, 150]. This is followed immediately by the cure of souls and work among the young. According to another survey, this time among Catholics and Protestants of Lausanne, visits take the first place, followed by the formation of the young and the sermon. It is interesting to note that Catholics and Protestants agree in designating the same activities and that by both the designation of preaching is almost equally rare. We can conclude from these two studies that the priest and pastor occupy an important place in the life of the inhabitants of the areas considered and that the relations between the individual and the church are usually reduced to the relations between the parishioner and the priest or pastor.

Among other studies which are in progress we should mention Herman van de Spijker's study of religious life in the Catholic parish of Rapperswil [Publication expected 1969–70] which is based on a survey of the type which the Germans call *Pastoralsoziologie* (Pastoral Sociology). The institute for *Kirchensoziologische Forschung und Beratung* (Research in the field of Church Sociology and Counselling) of Zurich intends to conduct studies of the parish analysis type.

The author is at present conducting a study which is more allied to basic research. The theme is social change and community. The goal is to discover the influence of the evolution of social relationships on the formation of the social and religious community. Because in the urban environment the community is no longer there where the people live, one tries to find out whether the community is reconstituted elsewhere and if so how, or whether we live in a society in which relationships are reduced to personal contact and the bond with the Church does not depend on community life. This study is being conducted within the framework of the creation of the *Institut romand de sociologie de la religion* (Publication expected in 1971–72).

CONCLUSION

Sociology of religion is an altogether new science in Switzerland; only two universities, Zurich and Lausanne, at present gives courses in this field. Most of the studies mentioned in this chapter fall in the category of applied research. Nevertheless, an effort has recently been made on the national level with the foundation of the A.S.S.O.R.E.L. [*Association suisse de sociologie de la religion* (Swiss Association of the Sociology of Religion)]. This association tries to unify research criteria and to provide a theoretical framework for studies, so that their results will permit the progress of basic research.

One could ask why the sociology of religion has developed so late in Switzerland. In waiting for a more thorough study of the question, a tentative explanation can be made if one considers the situation of this country. The unity of the Swiss has always risen around a consensus, which was generally achieved with difficulty, but which was then fiercely defended. Anything that could menace it has to be avoided. As a result of what it would reveal about the relationship between Protestants and Catholics and the drastic religious changes which are taking place in this country the sociology of religion could endanger a certain image which the Swiss have made of themselves. However, nowadays the pressure of social change is so strong that even the churches are beginning to accept the idea of letting themselves be analysed and confide to one or other sociological institute the task of making surveys. Such surveys have multiplied so rapidly during the last decade that one can expect that it will soon be possible to make a synthesis of them.

SELECTED BIBLIOGRAPHY

The bibliography which follows will not be as selective as that for other countries due to the state of sociology of religion in Switzerland. In order to facilitate the task of the investigator works are classified and the results of surveys are partly commented upon. The reader will find that some attempt has been made to distinguish the sociological approach to Protestantism from the sociological approach to Catholicism and to define the role of sociology in regard to the church.

*Works of a purely theoretical nature*

Bridel, Laurent, 'Les critères de l'appartenance au protestantisme' [Criteria of belonging to Protestantism]. *Bulletin du Centre protestant d'études* (Geneva) 3, 1964.
Attempt to define a sociological approach which goes beyond statistics, sociography and social morphology and which takes account of the characteristic features of Protestantism.

Campiche, Roland J., 'L'église face à l'aménagement du territoire' [The Church faces the Disposal of Church lands]. *Cahiers Protestants (Lausanne)*, 5–6, 1968.

Perret, Edmond, 'La sociologie religieuse, introduction et bibliographie '[Religious Sociology, Introduction and Bibliography]. *Bulletin du Centre protestant d'études* (Geneva) 2, 1961.
Introduction to religious sociology, definition of its aim and delimitation of its field of application.

Stucki, Pierre-André, 'L'idée d'une sociologie normative de l'Eglise' [The Concept of a Normative Sociology of the Church]. *Bulletin du Centre protestant d'études* (Geneva) 4, 1965.
Attempt by a philosopher to show the critical function of sociology in respect to the Church, based on the ideas of the theologian E. Brunner.

*Works including empirical research*

Boltanski, Luc, *Le bonheur Suisse* [Swiss Happiness]. Paris, *Ed. de Minuit*, 1966.
Contains an excellent chapter on Religion and integration, written on the basis of a survey which has covered the entire country (1962). The aim of the remainder of the work, which is sometimes very subjective, is to define the Swiss national character.

Bucher J., Juillan D., Zimmermann E., *Paroisse et quartier*, Université de Genève, 1971.

Campiche, Roland J., *Urbanisation et vie religieuse, une analyse sociologique de l'influence de l'urbanisation sur la vie et le comportement religieux des habitants du secteur lausannois de Sévelin* [Urbanization and Religious Life. A Sociological Analysis of the Influence of Urbanization on the Religious Life and Behaviour of the Inhabitants of Sévelin-Lausanne]. Lausanne, Payot, 1968.
Systematic comparison of different features of urban life with religious variables based on a survey which made use of the stratified random sampling method.

*Reports of surveys*

Action Catholique Romande (A.C.R.) [Catholic Action of French Speaking Switzerland], *Diocèses de Suisse romande, aspects sociologiques et religieux* [The Dioceses of French Speaking Switzerland, Sociological and Religious Aspects]. Lausanne, 1962.
Map of Catholic practice made according to the method of Canon Boulard. The results for the towns and cities were obtained by Sunday surveys, whilst those for the countryside, which are less precise, have been transmitted by the clergy – an interesting general view.

Bridel, L., *La planification des équipements paroissiaux, exemple de la paroisse reformeé de Morges* [The Planning of Parish Buildings, an Example of the Reformed Parish of Morges]. Lausanne, Documents de l'aménagement régional No. 4, 1967.
Results and interpretation of two Sunday surveys made with a two year interval. Numerous tables and comparisons.

Favarger, R., *Etude sur les attitudes et les tendances actuelles à l'égard de l'Eglise et de la religion* [Study of Attitudes and Modern Tendencies with regard to the Church and Religion]. Geneva, (roneo) 1967–68.
Results and interpretation of a survey made of 85 persons, for the most part university educated people, selected randomly. This opinion poll has a prospective and indicatory value.

Frauenfelder, S., Hofmann, U., and Solenthaler, J., *Gemeindeglieder nehmen Stellung zum Kirchlichen Zentrum* [Church Members Take a Stand Regarding the Church-centre]. Zurich Schule für Soziale Arbeit [Zurich School of Social Work]. (roneo), 1967.
Empirical study which aims at describing the style of life of the inhabitants of Oberwinterthur, their religious practice, social life and needs. Interviews of 126 Protestants selected at random and six group interviews.

Perret, Edmond, La pratique du culte à Genève, enquête sociologique [Sociological Investigations of Religious Worship in Geneva]. *Bulletin du Centre protestant d'études* (Geneva) 2–3, 1963.
Commentaries on and presentation of a Sunday survey which embraced the totality of the practising Protestants of the canton of Geneva surveyed on the same Sunday.

Schaer, A., and Bäumle, M., *Pastoral planung der Pfarrei Küsnacht* [Pastoral planning of the Küsnacht Parish]. Zurich, K.F.B., 1968.
Study of the *Gemeindeanalyse* (Parish analysis), type. Historical and demographic study, Sunday consultations and results of some interviews.

Wagner, A., 'Die Schweizerische Priesterfrage. Untersuchung zum Nachwuchsproblem beim Priesterberuf katholischer Konfession' [The Problem of the Priesthood in Switzerland. A Survey of the Recruitment of Catholic Priests]. *Bulletin der Arbeitsstelle für Pastoralplanung* (Zurich).
Sociographical analysis of the Swiss clergy and study of the development of priestly callings through time and according to bishoprics.

REFERENCES NOT SUPPLIED IN THE SELECTED BIBLIOGRAPHY

Bugnon, Claude, *Enquête sur la pratique du culte à Neuchâtel* [A Study of Religious Worship in Neuchâtel] (mimeographed). 1964.

Bureau Fédéral de Statistique (B.F.S.) [Federal Office of Statistics], *Annuaire statistique de la Suisse* [Annual Statistics of Switzerland], edited by Birkhäuser. Basel.

Commission des communautés, *Mission du Grand Fribourg – Rapport général de la commission des communautés* [The Greater Fribourg Mission – General Report of the Communities' Commission]. Fribourg, (roneo) 1967.

Commission jurassienne d'évangélisation, groupe d'études sociologiques [The Jura Evangelization Commission, Sociological Studies Group], *La pratique de la Sainte-Cène, Saint-Imier* [Observance of the Holy Communion, Saint Imier] (mimeo.). January 1966.

Heussi, K., and Peter, E., *Précis de l'historie de l'Eglise* [Summary of the History of the Church]. Neuchâtel, Delachaux and Niestlé, 1967.

Locher, U., and Riessen, R., *Materialen und Hypothesen zum Berufsabbild des Pfarrers* [Data and Hypotheses concerning the Professional Image of the Clergy]. St. Stephan, (roneo), 1968.

Maret, G., *et al.*, *Enquête sur la semaine de 5 jours* [Enquiry on the Five-day Week]. Geneva, (roneo) 1961.

Pfister, R., *Kirchengeschichte der Schweiz* [Church History of Switzerland]. Zurich, Zwingli Verlag, 1964.

Van de Spijker, A. M. J. M. Herman, *Befragte Gemeinde*. Rapperswil, Katholisches Pfarrambt, 1970.

DAVID MOBERG*

# U.S.A.

Conventional American religious histories begin with immigrants from Europe. In fact, however, the aboriginal Indians who have inhabited the North American continent since prehistoric times had their own religions. These continue to exist in modified forms, especially in the culture islands known as Indian Reservations, alongside Christianity, Judaism, Buddhism, and other imported socio-religious systems in the United States.

The primitive religions of the American Indians represent a wide variety of beliefs, practices, and patterns of social organization; indeed, nearly all the basic types of primitive religion are represented among them. Driver's brief survey, for instance, refers to the Ghost Dance and Peyote religions, the magic and medicine men of the Navaho, the forgiving ceremony of the Green Corn Dance among the Creeks, the Vision Quest of the Sanpoil, and the possessional shamanism of the Eskimo [Driver, 1961, Chap. 23]. Some of these primitive religions have not only lingered on to the present day but actually are experiencing growth and a revival of interest and significance [Norbeck, 1961, pp. 235, 251–253]. Nevertheless, the majority of contemporary American Indians have adopted various forms of Christianity or of secularism as their religion whether they remain on reservations, reside in urban slums, or are assimilated into the white population.

* David Moberg, was born in 1922 in Montevideo, U.S.A. He holds the position of Professor of Sociology and Chairman of the Department of Sociology, Marquette University, Wisconsin. He has been editor of the *Journal of the American Scientific Affiliation*, 1962–64, an associate editor of the *Sociological Quarterly* and on the committees of the Midwest Sociological Society, the Religious Research Association, the American Scientific Affiliation, Society for the Scientific Study of Religion and the Minnesota Conference on Social Work Education. He is currently editor of the *Review of Religious Research* and a member of the Honour Societies, Alpha Kappa Delta and Pi Gamma Mu. He has written many articles in the fields of the sociology of religion and social gerontology. Major books include *The Church as a Social Institution*, 1962, *The Church and the Older Person* (with Robert M. Gray), 1962, *Inasmuch: Christian Social Responsibility in the Twentieth Century*, 1965.

## HISTORICAL INTRODUCTION AND THE DENOMINATIONAL SPECTRUM

The dominant religious groups of America were imported with the European settlers from Europe who immigrated during and since the seventeenth century. The Episcopal Church sprang up out of Anglicanism. Roman Catholicism still bears internal differences related to the Irish, German, Italian, French, and other national origins of its people and priests. Lutheranism of Northern Europe was reflected in the existence of nearly 300 distinct denominational bodies in the mid-nineteenth century, reduced through successive mergers to 10 in 1967. Methodist religious leaders from England brought the sparks of Wesleyan revivalism to the American colonies where they lit the flames of religious fervour and spread rapidly, especially during the nineteenth century. Presbyterian and Reformed bodies were initially transplanted from Scotland, the Netherlands, Switzerland, and other Calvinist regions of Europe. Eastern Orthodox Churches came with immigrants from Eastern and Southeastern Europe and the Middle East. Mennonites and Brethren groups from Northern and Central Europe and Russia formed culture islands in scattered rural areas. Jews streamed from the various nations of Europe, coming in especially large numbers during anti-Semitic pogroms. Buddhists, Hindus, and Muslims migrated from the Orient, Near East, and Africa.

Each of these imported religions became acculturated, in varying degrees, to the new social environment. Many of them had been established or state churches, but in the pluralistic religious environment of America they were forced to change their methods, modify their traditional programs of activities, adjust their social philosophies, and adapt their organizational structures. In numerous and often significant ways American Catholics, Jews, and Protestants became different from their counterparts in other nations [Moberg, 1962, pp. 54–57, 455–458].

Among the most important denominations in America are several that originated in the pluralism, paradoxes, and problems of American life. The very heterogeneity of the population, together with accompanying social conditions on the early frontier and the concomitant westward movement of the population, contributed to a high degree of religious liberty. Freedom of speech, the press, and the right to assemble also helped to spawn, spread, and swell the membership of new religious groups. Most prominent of these are the Baptists, Disciples of Christ, Mormons, and Pentecostal-Holiness Churches [Mead, 1965].

Historical roots of the Baptists can be traced to the Anabaptist movement of earlier centuries, but as specific associations they can be traced to John Smyth and Thomas Helwys in the Netherlands and England during the first decade of the seventeenth century. Their American origin, however, is relatively independent of the European background. Roger Williams and John Clarke established Baptist churches in Rhode Island in 1639 and 1641 as bastions of religious liberty in the face of persecution from the established Puritan theocracy in the neighboring Massachusetts Bay Colony [Moore, 1965]. Their early growth was slow, but they have become the largest denominational family among American Protestants.

Baptist bodies, known as conventions, conferences, associations, etc., have varying degrees of social distance from each other and in 1965 ranged in size from the 10,770,573 members in the Southern Baptist Convention (with congregations in all 50 states) to the 70 on record for the Independent Baptist Church of America [Jacquet, 1967, p. 199]. Democratic church polity, independence of each local congregation, individualistic theology that stresses the importance of personal Christian faith, and insistence upon freedom of thought in the interpretation of the Bible, especially the New Testament, as the sole guide to faith and conduct have led to a wide variety of theological perspectives, congregational programs, and worship patterns [Armstrong and Armstrong, 1967].

Despite their name, Baptists place much less emphasis upon baptism than many other Christian denominations, for they believe that it is not a sacrament that confers saving merit but only an ordinance that gives public witness to personal faith in obedience to the will of Jesus Christ. The greatest of the numerous cleavages that have occurred in their history was the separation of northern from southern Baptists when the Southern Baptist Convention was formed in 1845. Theological issues and even controversies over slavery were less significant in this division than other sociological and psychological factors linked with differences between the cultures of the North and the South [Hill and Torbet, 1964].

The Disciples of Christ are even more purely American in origin and growth. Beginning with the work of Rev. Thomas Campbell, a Presbyterian clergyman who formed a new religious association in 1809 for purpose of restoring the New Testament polity and ideal, his movement was closely related to that of the 'Christian Churches' that had arisen out of three separate protest movements of the preceding two decades. Congregational in polity, believing in the Bible as the only rule of faith and life, and celebrating the Lord's Supper each Sunday 'not as a sacrament, but as a memorial feast' open to every sincere follower of Christ, their organizational system and tenets of faith fitted American cultural conditions during the western frontier movement well, and they remain consistent with America's democratic way of life.

The Latter-day Saints, better known as Mormons, began as a laymen's movement and remains that to a higher degree than any other large denomination. Their churches were founded by Joseph Smith in New York State in 1830 after he testified he had received a series of heavenly visions and an angel's revelation on golden plates which he translated as the *Book of Mormon*, a work held equal to the Bible.

Persecution drove the Mormons to Ohio, Missouri, Illinois, and eventually the desert valley of the Great Salt Lake in what is now Utah. There in great hardship and courage they created a self-existent community. Their belief that women could not be saved unless they were married encouraged polygamous marriages, a practice abolished by federal law in 1890. Baptism for the dead, a hierarchical progression of priestly roles and statuses for men, the sending out of thousands of pairs of young men annually as missionaries to all parts of the world on appointments without any salary, close bonds of association in local congregations (called *wards*, which in turn are grouped into *stakes*), and a strong program of social welfare under church auspices all help to account for the remarkable growth of Mormonism in American society.

Pentecostal churches are distinguished from others chiefly by ecstatic experiences interpreted as the work or manifestation of the Holy Spirit. Glossolalia ('speaking in tongues'), faith healing, rhythmical body movements accompanying instrumental and vocal music, ejaculatory responses during preaching, and other emotional expressions are characteristic of most of them, although in varying forms and degrees. Divided into numerous independent bodies, the largest of which is the Assemblies of God with 572,123 members and a Sunday school enrollment of 1,012,932 in 1965, they are almost entirely a product of the twentieth century. Much of their membership consists of lower class people who have been subtly rejected by congregations of the major denominations. They bear a wide variety of names, and there is some disagreement as to whether several Churches of God and holiness groups should be considered parts of the same category. Many elements characteristic of their worship are also found in lower class Negro congregations which are identified publicly as Baptist or Methodist.

Glossolalia, faith healing, and associated ecstatic spiritual experiences are currently appearing in isolated middle class Lutheran, Presbyterian, Episcopal, and other congregations [Stagg, Hinson and Oates, 1967]. Whether these will be able to remain within their denominations or will withdraw, either voluntarily or under pressure, to join existing Pentecostal groups or to form new ones remains to be seen [Sadler, 1964].

## DENOMINATIONAL STRUCTURE, PARTICIPATION AND BELIEFS

### *American religious statistics*

The best single source of current statistics on memberships reported by denominational bodies in the U.S. and Canada is the annual *Yearbook of American Churches* [Jacquet, 1967]. Its 1967 edition reported that 64.3 per cent of the United States population were church members as of 1965. This compares to estimated percentages of 16 in 1850, 22 in 1890, 43 in 1910, 47 in 1930, 49 in 1940, 57 in 1950, and 63 in 1960. The greatest increases in membership strength occurred from 1890 to 1910 as a result of the Moody revivals and at mid-twentieth century when a large number of social conditions both within churches and in society at large coalesced to bring people into church membership in somewhat larger proportions than in earlier decades [Moberg, 1962, pp. 38–43]. This can be seen as basically a continuation of trends of a century or more, however [Lipset, 1959].

When one considers the voluntary nature of church membership in America and the fact that the vast majority of Protestants (the dominant religious group) do not count children in their membership until after confirmation, believer's baptism, or an equivalent rite of passage typically occurring at ages 10–15, the fact that nearly two-thirds of the total population are included in church membership statistics is remarkable. If 'non-member' children in church-related families were added to those statistics, the total church constituency would very likely approximate 80 per cent of the national population.

Membership is not the same as either religious self-identification or church participation, however. In 1957 the U.S. Bureau of the Census took a sample survey of the religious preferences of civilian persons aged 14 years and over. Its basic question 'What is your religion?' was answered on a voluntary basis because compulsory cooperation could be interpreted as a violation of the religious liberty provisions of the U.S. Constitution. Cooperation was nevertheless greater than on many questions conventionally asked, only 0.9 per cent not reporting their religious preference (Table 1). The total of all who gave no report plus agnostics, atheists, and those who professed to have no religion is only 3.6 per cent. In other words, about 964 persons of every 1,000 claimed to have some religion [Bureau of the Census, 1958].

Church attendance records give a different impression. Occasional public opinion polls of the American Institute of Public Opinion have asked adults whether they attended church or synagogue services during the week preceding the interview. In 1939 an affirmative response was given by 41 per cent. A low of 36 per cent was reached in 1942, and a high of 49 per cent in

*Table 1. Religious preference of persons 14 years and over, U.S. civilian population, March 1957*

| Religion | Number of persons | | % of population | |
|---|---|---|---|---|
| Protestant | | 78,952,000 | | 66.2 |
| Baptist | 23,525,000 | | 19.7 | |
| Methodist | 16,676,000 | | 14.0 | |
| Lutheran | 8,417,000 | | 7.1 | |
| Presbyterian | 6,656,000 | | 5.6 | |
| Other Protestant | 23,678,000 | | 19.8 | |
| Roman Catholic | | 30,669,000 | | 25.7 |
| Jewish | | 3,868,000 | | 3.2 |
| Other religion a | | 1,545,000 | | 1.3 |
| No religion b | | 3,195,000 | | 2.7 |
| Religion not reported | | 1,104,000 | | 0.9 |
| Total | | 119,333,000 | | 100.0 |

a. Eastern Orthodox, Polish Catholic, Old Catholic, Buddhist, Moslem, etc.
b. Includes atheists and agnostics.
Source: Bureau of the Census, 1958.

1955 and 1958. Since 1958 the figure dropped gradually to 44 per cent in 1965 [Jacquet, 1967, p. 220], but it was back to 45 per cent in 1967 [*New York Times*, 25 Dec. 1967, p. 13]. Such data are not fully comparable, however, for some years' figures are based upon December and April surveys; attendance patterns tend to be higher among Christians during the Christmas and Easter seasons, so the variations by year may be as much a reflection of the week in which the polls were taken as of actual behaviour of people.

In all Christian groups, with the possible exception of Latter-day Saints, women are more likely to be church members than men. They participate in church activities more frequently than men and are more likely to accept the traditional beliefs of their religious groups. Cultural rather than biological factors seem to be primary sources of these sex differences [Moberg, 1962, pp. 396–401]. Once established, however, they tend to be self-perpetuating, for church programs are planned chiefly to serve the interests and needs of those already in the church rather than in terms of what might attract persons not there. (This tendency may pertain even more to socio-economic differences, such as the variations in social class composition from one church congregation to another.)

Age differences in attendance patterns are evident in a number of studies, but the precise patterns vary with the religious group, the community or region investigated, and other socio-cultural variables. The most consistent pattern is an attendance slump during the late teens and twenties, but any other broad generalizations would be misleading [Lazerwitz, 1962; Fichter, 1954, pp. 83–93; Salisbury, 1964, pp. 88–89; Glock, Ringer and Babbie, 1967, pp. 45–58].

In a study of 790 Catholic, Jewish and Congregational Protestant children aged 5 to 14 years, Elkind found strong evidence that religious identity grows during childhood in a regular sequence of stages related to age. From an early global, undifferentiated impression of their religious denomination as a kind of family name, they moved into a period of concrete conceptions of their religious identity. Only after ages 10 to 12 did they display an abstract conception of their religious identity which saw their denomination as involving such non-observable qualities as belief, faith, and intelligence. It was concluded that until adolescence the child knows more than he understands about his religious identity, and this is why religious conversions occur most frequently in adolescence and the Jewish barmitzvah is at age 13 [Elkind, 1964].

American church attendance patterns differ significantly by religion. Among Catholics attendance rates are much higher than among Protestants; theological differences in the religious significance of participation contribute to these variations. Participation in the Mass is a sacrament for Catholics; among most Protestants Holy Communion is typically celebrated only once a month and even then it is interpreted as only an ordinance with symbolic meanings but no saving grace. In terms of the subjectively interpreted meanings of participation in worship services, it is conceivable that once- or twice-a-month attendance at church services by a Protestant is the socio-psychological equivalent of weekly attendance by a Catholic. Jews have the lowest attendance patterns of all the major groups; this too can be related to theological doctrines.

The relative strength of Protestants and Catholics has been shifting very gradually in recent decades. It is estimated that in 1790 only one per cent of the white population was Catholic. European immigration, especially from Germany and Ireland, rapidly increased that proportion during the nineteenth century. With the 'new immigration' of southern and eastern Europeans after 1890, the proportionate as well as total number of Catholics swelled even more. Relatively systematic and comparable statistics have been kept since 1926; the relative proportions (in %) of the total population in selected years since that date are as follows [Jacquet, 1967, pp. 217, 219]:

| | *1926* | *1940* | *1950* | *1960* | *1965* |
|---|---|---|---|---|---|
| Protestants | 27.0 | 28.7 | 33.8 | 35.4 | 35.6 |
| Catholics | 16.0 | 16.1 | 18.9 | 23.3 | 23.8 |
| All religions | 45.0 | 49.0 | 57.0 | 63.0 | 64.3 |

The major religious groups reporting statistics to the 1967 edition of the *Yearbook of American Churches* are summarized in Table 2. Christian religions obviously dominate American religious life. The statistics of the groups are

*Table 2. Church membership statistics for major religious groupings, United States, 1965.*

| Religious group | Number of churches | Membership N | Membership % | Membership % of population |
|---|---|---|---|---|
| Protestant | 296,406 | 69,088,183 | 55.4 | 35.6 |
| Roman Catholic | 23,668 | 46,246,175 | 37.1 | 23.8 |
| Jewish Congregations | 4,079 | 5,600,000 | 4.5 | 2.9 |
| Eastern Churches | 1,529 | 3,172,163 | 2.5 | 1.6 |
| Old Catholic, Polish National Catholic, and Armenian Church | 321 | 483,901 | 0.4 | 0.2 |
| Buddhist | 93 | 92,000 | 0.07 | 0.0 |
| Total | 326,096 | 124,682,422 | 100.0 | 64.3 |

Source: Jacquet, *Yearbook of American Churches*, 1967.

not strictly comparable, however. Eastern Churches include all persons who are part of each respective nationality or cultural group (Greek, Russian, Syrian, and other Orthodox bodies). The number of Jews represents an estimate of all Jewish persons who are associated with an Orthodox, Conservative, or Reform congregation. Roman Catholics, Lutherans, and Episcopalians include all baptized persons, and most other Protestants reckon only full members, chiefly aged 13 and over [Jacquet, 1967, p. 196].

The statistics of Table 2 are not a complete summary of all religious groups in the United States. The Church of Christ, Scientist, refuses to report, believing enumeration of members is sinful. In the U.S. Census of Religious Bodies of 1936 it was credited with 268,915 members and an additional 139,758 Sunday school pupils aged 5 to 20 years. There is no reason to believe that it has failed to keep pace with American population growth.

Also omitted are Hindus and Muslims, who have an estimated fifteen to twenty places of worship including a mosque in Washington, D.C. Reports come from a total of only 251 religious bodies, but it has been estimated that there are at least 400 small sects in America, scores of which have not reported their statistics to the *Yearbook of American Churches* [Clark, 1949]. Numerous additional people participate in churches without being members [Cuber, 1940].

These omissions may be counterbalanced by duplications, failures to keep records up to date, and other defects which inflate membership reports. Allowing for the errors in both directions, it is conceivable that the reported total membership figures are not far from the actual proportion of the population that is included on church rolls. Of course, mere membership and attendance statistics are only extremely crude indicators of the religious commitments of any population.

*Denominationalism and ecumenism*

Comments are often made on the great diversity of American religion. Protestants, especially, include a wide variety of doctrinal positions, patterns of organisational structure, programs of activities, and relationships to the rest of society. Their major groupings are summarised in Table 3.

*Table 3. Protestant religious bodies reporting membership statistics, United States, 1965*

| Major group or Family | Number of denominations | Number of churches | Number of members |
|---|---|---|---|
| Baptist | 29 | 93,916 | 23,812,119 |
| Methodist | 21 | 55,222 | 13,287,081 |
| Lutheran | 10 | 17,591 | 8,794,106 |
| Presbyterian | 9 | 14,556 | 4,420,566 |
| Disciples and Churches of Christ | 2 | 26,581 | 4,268,471 |
| Latter Day Saints | 5 | 5,277 | 1,963,008 |
| Churches of God | 10 | 9,857 | 530,630 |
| Reformed | 6 | 1,644 | 523,945 |
| Adventist | 4 | 3,684 | 402,517 |
| Pentecostal Assemblies | 12 | 5,317 | 379,540 |
| Brethren (German Baptists) | 4 | 1,442 | 245,548 |
| Mennonite | 12 | 1,771 | 175,511 |
| Spiritualists | 3 | 432 | 172,184 |
| Friends | 8 | 1,102 | 127,523 |
| Evangelistic Associations | 10 | 619 | 72,383 |
| Moravian | 2 | 206 | 68,669 |
| Churches of the Living God | 2 | 383 | 47,670 |
| Old Catholic Churches | 5 | 103 | 37,530 |
| United Brethren | 2 | 324 | 23,116 |
| All others | 66 | 56,379 | 9,736,066 |
| Total | 222 | 296,406 | 69,088,183 |

Source: Jacquet, *Yearbook of American Churches*, 1967.

Some Protestants look upon denominational differences as a 'scandal' which violates Christ's will that all his followers should be united. For doctrinal, pragmatic, and idealistic reasons they seek unity. Others view denominational structures as simply facets of the division of labor which facilitates fulfilling Christ's will more effectively than would be the case if all were united into one vast bureaucratic unit. They see the divisions as functional, not dysfunctional. Actually, both functional and dysfunctional consequences are associated with both denominationalism and ecumenism. Proponents of the ecumenical movement are attempting to maximise its functional consequences and mininize dysfunctions, while opponents' opinions rest upon accentuating the opposite.

Possibly the most prominent organization representing ecumenical and co-operative ventures among Protestant and Orthodox Christians is the National Council of the Churches of Christ in the U.S.A. formed in 1950 as a merger of the Federal Council of Churches and fifteen other national agencies. Its current membership consists of thirty constituent bodies with a total membership of 41,946,590 [Jacquet, 1967, p. 214]. This represents about 33.6 per cent of the church membership of the United States.

The largest 'conservative evangelical' interdenominational body is the National Association of Evangelicals (N.A.E.). It was founded in 1942 as a 'vehicle through which all believers in the Lord Jesus Christ may become united and articulate in relation to matters of common interest and concern'. A January 1967 news release of its Church News Service claimed N.A.E. had forty-three member denominations with two and a half million members and a 'service constituency' of over ten million people. It is closely related to the larger but more loosely organized National Sunday School Association formed in 1946 to restore an evangelistic emphasis and a stress upon the Bible as the primary textbook in Protestant Sunday church schools.

A large number of denominational bodies have merged. Perhaps the most mergers have occurred among Lutherans who declined from nearly three hundred denominations in the mid-nineteenth century to ten in 1967. The most notable recent merger was the formation of the United Church of Christ in 1961 which united the Congregational-Christian and Evangelical and Reformed Churches, each of which was the product of an earlier merger (in 1931 and 1934, respectively). Representing a successful merger of groups that differed both doctrinally and organizationally, this was one source of the Consultation on Church Union (C.O.C.U.) which is now exploring the possibilities and problems of a proposed merger of several major Protestant denominations.

Involved in the C.O.C.U. discussions in 1967 were ten denominations with a combined membership of about 25,500,000. (They are the Episcopal Church, Methodist Church, United Church of Christ, United Presbyterian

Church, African Methodist Church, African Methodist Episcopal Zion, Southern Presbyterian, Disciples of Christ, Evangelical United Brethren, and Christian Methodist Episcopal Churches.) Problems of organizational structure, the ordination and appointment of clergy, apathetic contentment with the *status quo* of denominationalism by most church members, and certain doctrinal matters appear to be the chief barriers to successful merger, but it is anticipated that a major united church may be formed by the early 1970's. Now as in the past it appears that social forces are a more basic influence upon both denominationalism and ecumenism than strictly theological factors as such [Niebuhr, 1957; Muelder, 1956; Kerr, 1958; Lee, 1960].

Critics of the ecumenical movement prefer 'spiritual unity' over organizational unity. They claim implicitly that the two are incompatible and see ecumenism as leading toward the founding of a great 'Super-Church' which will reduce religious liberty, cause churches to strive for goals of the organization *per se* and thus lose sight of their basic spiritual tasks, and put pressure upon church congregations and members to support social, political, and economic positions which the critics believe to be inconsistent with Christian values [Lowell, 1967; Murch, 1967]. The greatest recent thunderbolt against the movement was dropped in 1967 by ecumenical-minded Methodist Theologian Paul Ramsey who contended that the 'social action curia' of the World and National Councils of Churches has reduced ecumenical ethics to a partisan political movement. His conclusions were based upon personal observation of the W.C.C. 1966 Conference on Church and Society in Geneva in which 410 delegates rushed out 118 'conclusions' about specific issues on the basis of perfunctory debate and voting that involved no more than half of the persons attending. Professor Ramsey said that detailed resolutions on church and society are 'jurisdictionally beyond the competence of churchmen' [Ramsey, 1967]. His book stirred up a storm of discussion both for and against his theses.

The coexistence of increasing denominationalism and rising ecumenism in American Protestantism has been explained sociologically as adaptations to pluralistic competition. Ecumenicity is based socially upon the class specificity of the mainline Protestant churches, economic inflation, and the development of an autonomous denominational bureaucracy. These three factors force the churches to rationalise their competition, thus releasing pressures toward 'cartelization'. Denominationalism is based in the necessity to differentiate 'products' as the cartelization increases [Berger, 1963].

Ecumenical relationships are also developing rapidly between Catholics and Protestants and, in many cities, Jews and Christians. The tremendous impact of Vatican Council II is increasingly felt in Catholic parishes, colleges, universities, and other agencies and institutions as they open their doors to fellowship with other Christians and even to the stimulating 'breath of fresh air' of non-Christian perspectives that challenge them to think through their faith, practices, and structures [Brown, 1967].

In Judaism, too, evidence of both 'denominationalism' and 'ecumenism' is present. In the American setting of religious voluntarism and pluralism Judaism developed into three major denominational groups: Orthodoxy, Conservatism, and Reform. Alongside of these, Reconstructionism is gaining self-consciousness and separate identity. Within Conservatism are a right, left, and center and within Orthodoxy traditionalists, ultra-traditionalists, and the 'modern Orthodox'. These subdivisions of viewpoint and organizational life are not greatly different from incipient denominations that so often have emerged as new religious bodies among Protestants. Yet an increasing 'Jewish religion-in-general' permeates all of these groups. The mid-twentieth century growth in the institutional strength of Judaism reflects a strong identification of the Jewish religion with the American culture as well as a renewed emphasis upon Jewishness. Three forms of organized, institutionalized religious life are open to the private option of American Jews; 'American Judaism is itself a 'triple melting pot'' [Rosenberg, 1964. pp. 185–254; quotation on p. 233].

Least noticed but perhaps the most significant of all ecumenical activities are small groups that have sprung up relatively spontaneously in all parts of the nation during the past decade. Centering upon Bible study, prayer, and the sharing of personal experiences of faith, these cut across all denominational and faith lines within Christendom, often bringing together people who are Catholics, liturgical and informal Protestants, and even rather thoroughgoing secularists who are attracted by the feeling that 'these Christian friends seem to have something; it won't hurt me to find out what it's all about'. Lay oriented and led by laymen, usually without formal connections with any church, some of these use materials produced by Christian Outreach as a guide to Bible study [Coleman, 1960]. Experiences of many people with these groups are reported in a semipopular magazine, *Faith at Work*. Informal personal experiences of participants in such groups may be contributing far more to breaking down denominational boundaries between Christians than the formal efforts of denominational and ecumenical leaders.

## RELIGION: ETHNIC, RACIAL, AND SOCIAL CLASS CHARACTERISTICS

Differences in the composition of church membership by social class, national origin, and race are evident both within and between American religious bodies. Roman Catholicism, ostensibly committed to a territorial system of parishes, has long had national parishes with jurisdiction over ethnic groups scattered among other parishes [Houtart, 1955]. Residential movements of the population which have broken up cultural islands within cities have created many problems in the relationships between these parishes, and there have been many attempts to integrate members of divergent ethnic backgrounds, but the distinctions between these parishes remain strong in most large cities. Many Catholic parishes are known informally as German, Irish, French, Polish, Italian, or Slovakian.

Religious differences linked with nationality similarly remain a source of a plurality of religious bodies within the Baptist, Lutheran, Reformed, and other denominational categories. Jewish congregations have been divided on the basis of the European nationality backgrounds of their members, but the distinctions between the Ashkenazim and Sephardim are now almost totally supplanted by the Orthodox, Conservative, and Reform distinctions previously mentioned. Yet despite the importance of ethnicity in religion, there has been relatively little direct research on the subject [Rossi, 1964].

Negro religion is especially variegated. Free Negroes had their own churches before the Civil War; after it, the newly emancipated slaves preferred to have their own churches over inferior status in white congregations during the Reconstruction Era, so Negro religious institutions developed alongside of but independent from white churches. As the dominant social institution in the typical Negro community, the church has played a significant role in numerous aspects of corporate life [Frazier, 1964]. Since 1955 it has taken on the new task of serving as a basic training ground and staging area for the protest movement in the fight for equal opportunities and freedom of the black people. As a result, ministers seem to be regaining the position of ascendancy in the Negro community that they temporarily had been losing to other professions [Pope, 1964].

As of 1964 an estimated 94 per cent of the Negro Protestants were in Negro denominations, just as had been the case twenty years earlier. A significant difference was appearing, however, on the very level of church life often supposed to be the most intransigent in regard to race relations – the local congregation. As early as 1950 to 1954 a study in three denominations revealed that 28 per cent of the churches replying, or 10 per cent of all congregations involved, had some interracial character; this compared to less than 2 per cent at the end of World War II [Pope, 1964].

Societal patterns of residential concentration and segregation, economic deficiencies, and shortcomings of church doctrines may be overcome in time as most Christian churches continue to refuse to practice or to condone discrimination and segregation. Nevertheless, Washington's opinion that fulfillment of Christian ideals can occur only when the Negro takes the offensive, closing his own houses of worship, demanding assimilation into the larger Christian community, and changing unauthentic Christian communities from within, may have a high degree of validity [Washington Jr.,

1964]. Perhaps the dangerous potential of sectarian groups like the Black Muslims can only thus be overcome [Lincoln, 1961].

Many Protestant denominations are primarily Negro in their membership. These include the National Baptists, Progressive Baptists, African Methodist Episcopal, and several holiness groups. Many congregations of other denominations also consist chiefly of Negro members. In the Methodist Church continuation of the 'Central Jurisdiction', a Negro unit which overlaps the predominantly white geographical jurisdictions, has been a source of embarrassment to denominational leaders and theologians who have been working for full racial integration of white and Negro people in society [Culver, 1953; Wogaman, 1960].

A great deal has been said and done by Catholics, Jews and Protestants of most denominations to promote the civil rights of minorities [Dirks, 1965: 132–141]. Religious leaders have been the most important positive influence upon the public conscience supporting the civil rights movement [Fichter, 1965]. Many efforts also have been expended to integrate Negro and white church congregations, but ethnic patterns of worship and other activities, vested interests of minority group pastors and denominational executives who fear loss of position or prestige, differences in the personal and social interests and needs of the people, and long-ingrained prejudices in both racial groups combine to perpetuate and at times even to accentuate the divisions. Most Negroes hence continue to be segregated in their worship, although increasing numbers are affiliating themselves with predominantly white parishes and congregations, especially as they rise into the middle classes. It remains true that 'for the masses of Negroes, the Negro church continues to be a refuge, though increasingly less of a refuge, in a hostile white world' [Frazier, 1964, p. 81].

As long as most congregations of the main Protestant denominations remain middle-class institutions which cannot assimilate lower-class whites, it is highly unrealistic to assume that they can assimilate Negroes who bear both the traditional onus of racial discrimination and the stigma of being members, for the most part, of the lower social classes [Moberg, 1960]. In other words, social class is an even more basic source of contemporary Protestant organizational differentiation than race.

A large number of studies have touched upon the subject of social class and religion. As a result, we know that people from the more prosperous occupational groups are more likely to be church members, participants, and lay leaders in their congregations than persons from lower socio-economic levels. New sects, on the whole, draw a disproportionately large fraction of their membership from the lower classes, so some interpreters have referred to them as 'refuges of the disinherited'. Although fewer lower class people are church members, those who are spend proportionately more of their total voluntary organization activity time in church than others do, and their rate of giving as a percentage of their total income is higher.

Churchlike and sectlike patterns of belief and behaviour are associated with social class differences. The first of these perspectives reinforces 'secular' values and pursuits, while the second represents an effort to modify or to withdraw from them. When friction appears in religious denominations and congregations, it often results from or includes components of tensions between these orientations. Demerath's research on Protestants revealed that 'the church is indeed a point of friction. The concomitance of churchlike and sectlike functions carries a tension which often leads to conflict and may go to actual dissolution' [Demerath, 1965, p. 183].

On the other hand, the tension between these two polarities may be an asset for the organization's endurance, for churchlike pressures to accommodate secular society threaten to bring about the demise of a church, while sectlike pressures to become withdrawn in sectarian insularity threaten the loss of contact with 'secular reality'. Each tendency curbs the other, so their co-existence amounts to a division of labor in which the 'successful functions in one direction complement successful functions in the other' [Demerath, 1965, p. 185]. The conflict clarifies competing demands, sharpens objectives, and produces a force for change in a continual process of dynamic adaptation. The Roman Catholic Church is a case in point of a peculiar mixture of churchlike and sectlike qualities which have contributed to its strength through diversity [Demerath, 1965, pp. 182–189].

Occupational achievement and the aspirations of youth for their future are related to these intertwined racial, religious, and social class differences to such a degree that it is difficult to unravel the relative importance of each. Considerable evidence supports the hypothesis that the Protestant ethic is influential in America, for in general white Protestants hold a larger proportion of the most influential positions in industry and business than Catholics. Yet there also is contrary evidence, for when some degree of control is introduced over other socio-economic factors, the differences tend to disappear. Even this is not invariably true, however; when Lenski limited his comparisons of data from the Detroit area to third-generation Americans reared in the North, differences between the socio-religious groups became more pronounced than they were for the total sample, the Jews and white Protestants being most clearly identified with the competitive individualism of the middle-class Protestant ethic and spirit of capitalism, and the Catholics and Negro Protestants being more collectivistic and security-oriented [Lenski, 1961, pp. 75–102]. Yet Catholic students in a Protestant university were found to adhere to the 'Protestant ethic' more closely than the Protestants [Wagner, Doyle, and Fisher, 1959].

The relatively small number of Roman Catholics in scientific and scholarly occupations [O'Dea, 1958] may be due more to historical and cultural factors (especially the relatively late arrival of the national groups from which most Catholics are offspring) than to theological differences between the religions. The traditional members of the American upper class are W.A.S.P.'s – white Anglo-Saxon Protestants – who have begun to lose their early preeminence over Jews and Catholics in the numerous power structures and status hierarchies of the nation only since the early part of this century, especially since 1929 [Baltzell, 1964]. Greeley's analysis of N.O.R.C. survey data of a national sample of 1961 graduates of 135 American colleges and universities finds that if Catholics differ from the various Protestant groups, it is in the fact that they are ahead in plans for graduate studies, near the top in academic inclinations, and more likely to enter the arts and sciences in graduate school. (Jews are far ahead of the other two major faiths.) He concludes that this represents a change from the earlier intellectual lag of Catholics and believes that a 'permanent moratorium' should be placed upon use of the expression, 'the Protestant ethic' [Greeley, 1963].

Although more specific details of this complex subject must await further research, there is clear evidence that ethnic factors as well as social class continue to be important sources of divergent religious and political orientations and attitudes in American Catholicism [Abramson and Noll, 1966].

## RELIGION AND SOCIO-POLITICAL AND ECONOMIC ISSUES

Relationships between political and religious institutions have been a significant factor in American history ever since the colonial period. Religious toleration, in the modern sense, was unknown to Europe at that time. Religious dissenters who came to the American wilderness for refuge were themselves intolerant, with notable exceptions, of those whose religious views disagreed with their own. Anglican or Puritan (Congregational) churches were firmly established in Virginia, the Carolinas, Massachusetts, Connecticut, and New Hampshire. New York, New Jersey, Maryland, and Georgia had a shifting or uncertain pattern of 'co-operation' between church and state which was close to an establishment of religion. Only in Rhode Island, Pennsylvania, and Delaware was there a large measure of religious liberty and a complete or almost complete lack of an establishment.

By the American Revolution the principle of tolerating dissenting religious beliefs had gained considerable force [Butts, 1960]. As a result, the 'Bill of Rights' added to the federal Constitution to go into effect in 1791 included in its very first item the provision that 'Congress shall make no law respecting an establishment of religion, or prohibiting the free exercise thereof', as well as the related freedoms of speech, the press, assembly, and petition for redress of grievances. Thus separation of church and state and religious liberty were built into the federal guarantees of civil rights from the earliest days of the new nation [Marnell, 1964; Bates, 1945; Bates, 1959].

Despite federal provisions, however, religious establishments were not discontinued in all states until November 1833 when, following internal church dissension between Trinitarians and Unitarians, increasing religious diversity in the population, and court cases by which other religious groups fought compulsory worship and church taxes, the voters of Massachusetts abolished their establishment [Marnell, 1964, pp. 102–112]. This however, was not the end of political tensions relating to religious issues.

During the nineteenth century, and into the twentieth, Protestant intolerance of Catholics and in many communities vice versa, efforts to enforce Sabbath observance, problems relevant to religion in public schools and other institutions, questions of the enforcement of religiously based moral standards by legislation, divergent applications of ethico-religious principles to basic issues of social welfare and other political action, and numerous other problems have appeared frequently [Blau, 1964; Odegard, 1960; Stokes, 1950]. Because the different church groupings have different social characteristics, historical experiences, and religious values, their practical positions on political, economic, and social issues often differ. Catholics and Jews are most likely to vote for candidates of the Democratic Party, and most white Protestants outside the South strongly favor Republican candidates. This is not basically a result of ethnic factors; only social class seems to be as strong an influence as religion upon party support. Religion is today, as in the past, a main source of party cleavage and political tone [Lipset, 1964]. It has a significant, even if at times indirect and subtle, influence upon government and politics [Roucek, 1963].

During the past two decades a series of decisions by the U.S. Supreme Court pertinent to church-state relationships have attracted considerable attention in public debate and the mass media of communications. These have supported the use of public funds for bus transportation of parochial school pupils, struck down the requirement of a declaration of belief in God as a prerequisite to holding public office, prohibited the recitation of a prayer in public school classes, prevented released time religious education programs using public school classrooms, exempted a Seventh Day Adventist from the requirement of being willing to take a job requiring work on Saturday in order to be eligible for unemployment compensation coverage, permitted American Indians to continue using peyote as a part of the 'honest practice' of their religion despite narcotic laws normally prohibiting the use of that drug, and continued to uphold the governmental provision of religious services through chaplaincy and other programs to persons withdrawn from ordinary opportunities for worship and pastoral care as 'neutralizing aids' that balance out restrictions upon religious freedom that would otherwise result from the government's secular activities. These and other related cases have been interpreted by many critics as representing a reduction of religious liberty by 'taking God out of the schools' or 'forcing secularism upon the population'. Actually they are better interpreted as expanding religious freedom and creating a political-legal structure favorable to a mature, healthy, religious pluralism that reflects an active commitment to the separation of church and state and full religious liberty for people of all religions and of none [Katz and Southerland, 1967].

The responsibility for religious education has been shifted increasingly away from public schools and to the churches and families of the nation. This is a continuation of the trend toward establishment of a 'secular state' in which no religion can serve as a state church, religious liberty is upheld in deed as well as in word, and free public school education supplants the sectarian schools that dominated earlier periods of American history [Wood, 1967; Carlson, 1964].

The secularization of government in the United States did not result in the removal of religious considerations from politics. Churches and their agencies work actively in support of many public issues and against others through lobbying, educational influences upon their members (a major part of the electorate), resolutions about pending and proposed legislation, use of the mass media of communications to promote their views on public affairs, and others efforts. Despite the news headlines and other attention some of these effort occasionally receive, Political Scientist Stedman's comment is apropos: 'No large American church has ever really mastered the techniques of translating what national spokesmen say into local action within a short enough period of time to make any marked political difference' [Stedman, 1964, p. 145]. Nevertheless, religiously-linked differences in patterns of political orientation suggest the possibility that a subtle religious influence operates throughout much of American political life as citizens' political consciences are touched directly or indirectly by the teachings of their churches [Lenski, 1961, pp. 121–191; Hadden, 1963]. The orientation of interests and values is an important variable influencing responses to crises and change [Neal, 1965].

A study of data collected from Episcopalians in 1952 concluded that church involvement is essentially irrelevant to 'political permissiveness', defined as the willingness of a parishioner to have his church concern itself with political and economic problems [Glock, Ringer and Babbie, 1967, pp. 113–136]. Yet church lobbying and religious pressures by churchmen on laymen who in turn influenced their congressmen seem to have had a determining influence in the passage of the Civil Rights Act of 1964. The consciences of church people of all major faiths, who comprise much of the electorate, had been influenced gradually over preceding decades by sermons, books, articles, tracts, and the passage and publication of church resolutions on pertinent topics. A very active program of efforts to influence clergymen and small groups of laymen throughout the nation to exert active pressure on their congressmen was launched by a number of church bodies [Dirks, 1965, pp. 142–149]. The defeat of Barry Goldwater, Republican candidate for the presidency in 1964, similarly was partly the result of opposition from many clergy and other churchmen [Dirks, 1965, pp. 150–155].

On any political issue, however, the churches tend to be divided. Even within a local parish or congregation there are typically both Republicans and Democrats, political liberals and conservatives, and other contrasting perspectives. As a result, the clergy and denominational leaders often feel their hands are tied with regard to political-social issues; if they take a specific stand, they are in danger of alienating members upon whom they depend for a livelihood. Furthermore, once alienated, the individual may no longer be subject to the influence of his church, so any hope of gradually exerting a modifying influence upon this positions may be lost. This became very evident in the conflicts over racial integration in many communities as pressures were brought toward implementing more fully the provisions and implications of the federal Constitution for the civil rights of Negroes. Even ministers whose professional reference system favored integration were neutralized, and their self-reference systems became confused under pressures from their congregations' values [Campbell and Pettigrew, 1959].

*Liberalism and conservatism*

The intermingling of conservatism and liberalism within a group is complicated by the numerous dimensions, types, and indicators used to identify those positions. Wiley's study of 1,190 summer school students in a Jesuit university revealed a tendency for religious liberals to be politically liberal and religious conservatives to be politically conservative, but the relationship was imperfect. Among the laity of the sample the relationship measured by Goodman and Kruskal's gamma was only .16; among nuns it was .41 and among priests .49. Among the priests and nuns of the study, liberalism was more complete – carrying over to political as well as ecclesiastical matters – than among the laity, for whom no simple liberal syndrome encompassed both types of matters. There possibly are at least two types of religious liberalism – progressivism, which was the focus of this investigation, and doctrinal heterodoxy. These types may be related to the class structure in opposite ways, progressivism representing a middle and upper class response and heterodoxy a reaction more characteristic of the lower or working class [Wiley, 1967].

The inconsistent findings of relationships between liberalism and conservatism [Buss, 1964; Lipset, 1960, pp. 97–130, 298–301; Henriot, 1966] probably relate to the fact that these are such complex phenomena that they do not comprise unitary or homogeneous dimensions of personality and group orientations in modern complex society. One study of only five types of liberalism-conservatism (economic, aesthetic, political, religious, and social) revealed all possible variations and combinations in a sample of only 246 male students [Kerr, 1952]. Lenski found very little relationship between political liberalism and doctrinal heterodoxy in his analysis of data from the Detroit Area Study [Lenski, 1961, pp. 187–191].

To a degree these conclusions are related also to studies of voting behaviour. Protestants in the United States are generally more inclined to vote for candidates of the Republican Party, except in the South where Democrats have been so strongly entrenched, while Catholics and Jews are more likely to vote for Democratic candidates [Greer, 1961; Berelson, Lazarsfeld, and McPhee, 1954, pp. 59–73; Guysenir, 1958; Rischin, 1960; Lamanna and Stephenson, 1964; Lanphier, 1967]. To some extent this may reflect differences in relative position in the occupational and social status structure, for voting patterns also reflect differences in social class, but even within the same occupational groups differences associated with religion are apparent [Glantz, 1959; Lipset, 1964, pp. 83–117].

Johnson's studies of Protestant church members in Eugene, Oregon, and Tallahassee, Florida, found that persons active in 'fundamentalist churches' are inclined toward a Republican position in politics, while those in 'liberal' churches are more inclined toward the Democratic side. He believes that the churches have a 'muting effect' on the political views of their members. Upper and middle class Protestants, who on the basis of social class are most likely to be Republicans, also are the most likely to be in the 'liberal' churches which support Democratic views. Lower and lower-middle class people are more likely to be inclined toward the Democratic position and also to comprise the membership of 'fundamentalist' churches, the leaders and pastors of which tend to support Republican viewpoints [Johnson, 1962, 1964].

An attempt to test the validity of these relationships in a midwestern rural county, however, resulted in different conclusions. Catholics there, as in most other communities, were predominantly Democratic in their party preference, but no significant differences were found between the 'liberal' and 'fundamentalist' Protestants. These exceptions to Johnson's findings may result from problems of definition and identification of key classifications and variables, or they may be due to inherent problems of research on 'the religious factor', which draws one inevitably into complex issues of theology as well as of research design [Anderson, 1966].

Relationships between religion and extremist politics are related to liberalism-conservatism in very complex interlocking patterns. The far left, especially as represented by the American Communist Party, has never been very strong among churchmen [Roy, 1960, 1964]. The tendency of many socially concerned clergymen to promote 'liberal' economic and political causes, however, contributes both to liberalism and to a backlash of right-wing extremism. National controversy over racial integration, the war on poverty, religion in public schools, tax support of church-related institutions, international relations, monetary policies and inflation, and other issues have contributed to the growth of the 'radical right'. Sectarian segments within both Protestantism and Catholicism have been among the leaders of this political movement. Anti-Semitism is often one orientation of these organizations; it is readily identified with anti-Negro and either anti-Catholic or anti-Protestant perspectives, as well as with almost anything feared by insecure people who are 'have-nots' or 'haves' who fear the possible loss of their privileges and possessions. The interweaving of political, economic, psychological, social welfare, religious, educational, military defense, and other themes in the propagandistic activities of the right wing seems puzzling until one realizes that

> What the right wing is fighting ... is essentially 'modernity' – that complex of attitudes that might be defined most simply as the belief in rational assessment, rather than established custom, for the evaluation of social change – and what it seeks to defend is its fading dominance, exercised once through the institutions of small-town America over the control of social change [Bell, 1964, p. 16].

As a result, the religious segment of the right wing tends to be dominated by fundamentalists opposed to everything they conceive to be associated with any form of modernism or liberalism, but it also includes theological liberals who support the conservatism of *Christian Economics* and the recently defunct *Faith and Freedom* of Spiritual Mobilization. Using the mass media of communications relatively effectively and spending millions of dollars annually in its campaigns, the radical right was a major force behind the candidacy of Senator Goldwater for the presidency of the United States in 1964. Its efforts to destroy the civil rights movement and to oppose social legislation of all forms can no longer be ignored in American politics [Epstein and Forster, 1967; Forster and Epstein, 1964; Redekop, 1967].

*Prejudice and bigotry*

The linkage of bigotry with religion sporadically wins attention in behavioral science research. Numerous and contradictory findings have resulted, some showing religious faith or behavior positively correlated with prejudice and others finding it negatively related. Regional differences undoubtedly are an intervening variable [Maranell, 1967]. Different definitions, indicators, and scales to measure prejudice, as well as differences between divergent samples of the population, are undoubtedly part of the reason for these inconsistencies. There is evidence that Christian religious education has contributed to anti-Semitism through certain interpretations of the crucifixion of Jesus Christ by biased lesson materials and teachers whose attitudes towards Jews spill over into their Sunday school work [Olson, 1962]. On the other hand, there also is considerable evidence of lesson materials and educational efforts designed to break down prejudice and promote intergroup tolerance, if not also respect [Eakin and Eakin, 1953]. Christian leaders and educators have been saying a great deal about the need to promote the civil and religious liberties for all people, including minorities; if they have failed, it is on the level of tangible deeds to support their doctrines [Littell, 1963]. While a minority of religious leaders march with the right wing in support of traditional patterns of racial and cultural relations, the majority have arrayed themselves on the side of integration, equality, and social justice in a pluralistic society.

Vanecko's recent research using National Opinion Research Center data from a probability sample of 2,071 adult Catholics in the United States supports the conclusion of Gordon Allport [1960] that external or institutional religiosity based on the religious group as a source of security and a resolution of ambiguity is associated with anti-Negro and anti-Jewish prejudice, while internal or interiorized religiosity, which involves attachment to an ethical system prescribing love for all men, is associated with tolerance. The association of the open mind with tolerance and the closed mind with prejudice, as implied by Rokeach [1960], is similarly supported in the same study, but the conclusions of Glock and Stark [1966] that dogmatism or orthodoxy is related to anti-Semitism are contradicted. Different dimensions of religious behaviour seem to be involved in these divergent studies; prejudice is a very complex multidimensional phenomenon that cannot be studied adequately with unidimensional assumptions and measures [Vanecko, 1966, 1967]. The fallacy of doing so is very likely a major source of the inconsistencies of research findings relating religion to prejudice and bigotry.

Social cross-pressures may be one of the sources of ethnic, political, religious, and other attitude inconsistency [Olsen, 1962]. When the focus of concern is religious matters, a failure by behavioural scientists to understand intricate implications and profound ramifications of the faith of their subjects as the subjects themselves interpret it may also be a source of what a non-member sees as an inconsistency, but it may not be interpreted as such by the person nor by the members of his group. 'Pictures in the mind' are of great significance in the study and interpretation of religious phenomena.

## SPECIAL AREAS OF STUDY IN THE SOCIOLOGY OF RELIGION

### *Religious education and Youth*

The effects of parochial school education have only begun to receive systematic evaluation. Among American Catholics parochial schools have become an important device for maintaining group identity, especially among certain ethnic groups [Rossi and Rossi, 1961]. An intensive study of Catholic schools in a midwestern city, however, failed to reveal significant differences between their pupils and Catholics in the public schools except in areas directly related to religion. Those in parochial schools were more likely to have only Catholics as best friends, had attitudes more favorable toward Negroes, refugees, and foreign aid, were more orderly and less likely to get into trouble with juvenile court authorities, and were more apt to interpret historical events religiously [Fichter, 1958].

A NORC survey of 2,753 Catholics aged 23 to 57 selected through a multistage area probability sample for interviewing during the winter of 1963–64, together with additional data from other selected groups, suggests that parochial schools are far less influential than many of their supporters and opponents have thought them to be [Greeley and Rossi, 1966]. Similar conclusions grow out of Johnstone's study of Lutheran parochial education. Since the 'ideal' Lutheran parents are more likely than others to send their children to parochial schools, those who already are the most religiously inclined are the most likely to become enrolled in a parochial school. Except for a few youths from religiously 'marginal' families, the family rather than school appears to be the basic factor in the greater church participation by parochial school youth. The conclusion that Lutheran parochial schools tend to serve those who least need to be served while neglecting those in greatest need of Christian education seems to apply to Catholics as well [Johnstone, 1966; Greeley and Rossi, 1966, pp. XII].

Surprisingly little research has been done by sociologists on religion and youth, but some data are available from related disciplines. Strommen's four-year study of three thousand Lutheran high school youth, for example, revealed that the ideas adult church leaders have about the concerns and interests of youth in their congregations are not valid. The problems of youth vary by community and congregation. Bible study programs and other church activities often do not seem meaningful to youth. Religious concepts like forgiveness used in them are understood by only a fraction of the young people. There is a relationship between adults in a congregation and the relative health of its young people; where adults show greatest sensitivity to the problems of youth, the youths are the most healthful, and vice versa [Strommen, 1963].

Study of paragraphs written in a ninth-grade English class in answer to questions pertinent to religion revealed six types of recurrent religious experiences in which these adolescents felt closest to God. In order of frequency, these were labelled church, solitary, anxiety and fear, worry, prayer, and moral action experiences. Differences between boys and girls can be explained along cultural lines, but interesting differences between honor and average students also appeared. Acute religious experiences in which they felt especially close to God reflected appreciation, meditation, lamentation, religious initiation ceremonies, and revelation. The report of this study concluded with the author's opinion that personal religion 'apparently remains an important force in the adolescent's life during the very period in which institutional religion is losing its hold on his interest and participation' [Elkind and Elkind, 1962].

Freshmen in a Jewish religious college experience special difficulty in areas of social and recreational activities, health and physical development, and adjustment to school work, probably because of a combination of academic overloading and concern and the traditional Jewish emphasis on verbal learning [Levinson, 1959]. Many other studies of religion and religious development in children and youth have been made by psychologists [Van Dyke and Pierce-Jones, 1963].

### *Dimensions of religiosity*

The inadequacies of using but one or two simple indicators as a basis for the analysis of the role or influence of religion in human affairs has long been recognized as a serious deficiency. One of the most significant recent contributions to religious research therefore was Glock's spelling out of five 'dimensions of religiosity'. His differentiation of the experiential dimension (emotions, perceptions, feelings, and sensations defined as involving some communication with God, ultimate reality, or transcendental authority), the ideological dimension (religious beliefs), the ritualistic dimension (religious practices), the intellectual or cognitive dimension (religious information and knowledge), and the consequential dimension (the secular effects of the other four dimensions on the individual) provides an excellent framework for studying religion and assessing religiosity [Glock and Stark, 1965].

These five dimensions do not, however, cover every aspect of Christianity, and for other religions as well they probably fall short of exhaustively covering 'all of the many and diverse manifestations of religiosity prescribed by the different religions of the world', as Glock believes they do. The transcendental man-God relationship of the chief western religions tends to be treated under this typology as if it is only a figment of men's imaginations or a subsidiary dependent variable rather than an independent or causal variable in human behavior. This is irksome to theologians and religiously oriented people whose personal religious experiences, institutional vested interests, and theologically based ideologies seem threatened by a narrowly empirical approach. It has therefore been suggested that, although we may be able to study nothing more than the five dimensions empirically at the present time, there is a spiritual component of religiosity that can be neither proved nor disproved scientifically. It can be explored currently by behavioural scientists only through the methods of introspective psychology and *verstehende* sociology, so great humility should accompany its investigation [Moberg, 1967]. Meanwhile, however, Glock's typological approach to dimensions of religiosity is making a significant contribution to a number of research projects.

## SUMMARY AND CONCLUSION

This survey has sketched only a few representative descriptive aspects of religion in the United States. We have seen that pre-historical and colonial influences are still evident and that the diversity of institutional forms, belief systems, and action patterns present in American churches, sects, and cults are products of the interaction of cultural importations brought by a wide range of ethnic groups and unusual features of the socio-cultural and geographical environment in which they were brought into contact with each other. Religious liberty, the separation of church and state, and other civil liberties were major factors both causing and resulting from religious and ethnic pluralism.

Despite the lack of an established church, if not because of it, interest in religion is at a relatively high level in the U.S.A. Nearly two-thirds of the total population and close to four-fifths of the adults are church members. About 45 per cent of all adults attend church during a typical week, with many more attending at less frequent intervals. In this situation both denominationalism and ecumenism seem to be advancing. Racial, ethnic, and social class differences continue to be important sources of diversity within as well as between religious groups from the congregational or parish level all the way up to national inter-denominational associations.

Religion is an important factor in American political life, and it is related in varying degrees and often a subtle manner to all other institutions as well. This contributes to controversies over religion in the public schools, tax funds to subsidise various aspects of church-related schools, the nature and effectiveness of religious education, and the impact of religious commitments upon personal and social life. The lack of consensus on such issues reflects the multiplicity of opinions and paucity of facts about them, a paucity which is contributing to increasing interest in the sociology of religion, religious research, and related disciplines. Growing sophistication of research methodologies is one of the wholesome by-products.

The complexity of religious behaviour *ipso facto* is complicated by the realities of American pluralistic society. Where people are exposed to a wide range of political, religious, and other alternatives in an atmosphere of liberty that emphasizes voluntary choices, diversity is multiplied and complex subjects are made even more complicated. When rapid social change is an additional feature, the resulting inconsistencies of institutional life are likely to break down traditional interpretations related to such political issues as church-state relationships and lead even the most adamant advocates of church-state separation into relationships that appear, on the surface at least, to compromise their convictions [Peterson, 1967]. The coexistence of a wide variety of philosophies of church-state relationships in America can be seen as both a product and a source of religious liberty and religious pluralism [Moberg, 1965; Sanders, 1964; Stroup, 1967].

The pluralism of American religious life and the accompanying complexity of social and institutional patterns of religion help to explain the diversity of findings from research dealing with relationships between religion and other aspects of personal and institutional life. There is, nevertheless, a strong conviction on the part of many scholars that underlying the apparent diversity of American religion is a single basic American culture religion centered around 'the American Way of Life' as 'the operative faith' of the American people. This common denominator is evident in the three major religious branches of Catholicism, Protestantism, and Judaism; each can be seen as a different representation of the one great American religion with its generalized ideas of doing good and especially of upholding a democratic way of life [Herberg, 1955].

A 'civil religion' with 'simple dogmas of ... the existence of God, the life to come, the reward of virtue and the punishment of vice, and the exclusion of religious intolerance' [Bellah, 1967, p. 5] has been evident to some degree throughout the major crises of American history. Bellah contents that it is not the worship of the American nation but a heritage that is seen as a light unto all nations. Awareness of the significance of the American political experiment for the whole world is related to an eschatological hope that its civil religion will serve as an example and source of a world-wide civil religion with a similar motivating spirit of fulfilling the obligation to carry out God's will on earth [Bellah, 1967].

While the unity and consensus implied by the concept of a 'tripartite American culture religion' or an 'American civil religion' may easily be overemphasised, the American religious pattern may be interpreted as one of interacting conspiracies. This viewpoint defines 'conspiracy' as 'unison, concord, unanimity in opinion and feeling, a *breathing together*'. The American conspiracy has four chief camps – Protestant, Catholic, Jewish, and secularist – in each of which are additional subdivisions. Although there is an underlying consensus that tolerance is essential, tensions and conflict between these groups have been characteristic. The arms are only gradually being replaced by argument and discussion out of which full civic unity coexistent with religious pluralism can come [Murray, 1964].

In many communities social interaction between people takes place within rather than between the major religious groups. Despite similarities of social and occupational status, interaction with others in formal and leisure time activities tends to be limited to persons of one's own religious group. Religious issues tend to lurk in the background of many larger civic affairs even when the existence of religious divisions is stoutly denied. Religiously mixed marriages are also considered undesirable and kept at a minimum in the 'open ghetto' system of many residential suburbs [Greeley, 1962].

Critics of religion are numerous in American society. Secularized values of activism, universalism, and individualism have been identified with the American culture religion [Nottingham, 1954, pp. 73–74]. Churches have been admonished to adjust to the transition from an age in which Christendom dominated American society to a new era of urban secularity [Cox, 1965]. Secularization of attitudes and behavior appears to be a dominant factor underlying changing relationships between religion and society, and 'the tension between religion and secularization remains one of the significant sources of conflict in the western world today' [O'Dea, 1966, p. 90].

There has been little solid empirical research to test the degree to which secularization characterizes Americans. Interviews with a sample of 211 husbands and wives in St Paul, Minnesota, to gather information about family religious practices in their present and childhood homes revealed no significant differences between the generations [Moberg, 1958b]. A study of influences contributing to the voluntary act of joining Baptist churches revealed a large number of social, religious, and personal factors. The majority of these were basically sacred' or mixed 'sacred and secular' rather than purely 'secular' reasons, according to the independent classification of the motives and influences by a panel of judges, but the study nevertheless led to the hypothesis that one basic factor contributing to the rapid growth of

American church membership in the 1950's was the increasing secularization of American society [Moberg, 1958a].

A questionnaire study of values and motives for participation in parish activities in a Catholic Church in the Bronx, New York, found that 70 per cent of the motives involved 'giving to God' (adoration, reparation, thanksgiving), 15 per cent 'giving to the Church', 40 per cent praying for spiritual or temporal blessings, and only 5 per cent attending due to relatives or friends. This reveals a very heavy emphasis upon 'spiritual' motivations for participating in church activities and raises doubt about the validity of philosophical discussions which emphasise the importance of secularization in American religious life [Schuyler, 1958]. On the other hand, human motivations are extremely complex. Responses that are verbalized in answer to open-ended questions may be those which respondents feel are desired or expected and may hence represent a parroting back of ideas previously suggested as 'the correct reasons' by parents, the clergy, or other authority figures. They may also represent face-saving rationalizations.

Despite indications of creeping secularization, religious values and perspectives may remain as important to the American people as they have been in the past. In the first place, their past religiosity often has been distorted and overemphasized. Secondly, the indicators used to identify what is alleged to be secularization may reflect technological modifications in culture patterns that are not integrally linked with either a religious or a non-religious worldview. Thirdly, a decline in institutionalized aspects of religion, such as control over other institutions by church hierarchies, may occur independently of changes in the influence of religious beliefs upon the mentality and behavior of the individual persons who are the 'atoms' comprising society and its institutions. Fourthly, as we have seen, religion continues to play a very important role, even if often a subtle and latent one, for many people and in every major sphere of American public and private life.

The diversity, complexity, and fluidity of American pluralistic religion make all attempts to generalize about its overall nature very hazardous. Changes in outward forms of religiosity may occur without any major shifts in the interiorized meanings of religion. Religious practices may increase while personal faith, devotion, and piety decrease, or outward practice may decrease while religious motivations expand to pervade more fully all aspects of personal and social behaviour. In these complexities lie vast opportunities for social and behavioural scientists interested in religious research!

## SELECTED BIBLIOGRAPHY

### *Resources for study*

American sociology and its sister disciplines have produced several textbook-type surveys of the sociology of religion [Wach, 1944; Nottingham, 1954; Yinger, 1957; Hoult, 1958; Benson, 1960; Vernon, 1962; Yinger, 1963; Schneider, 1964; Knudten, 1967] which draw much of their content from American culture and research.

In addition to these, several basic resources are oriented directly and without apology around American religion [Sklare, 1958; Lambert, 1960; Moberg, 1962; Salisbury, 1964; Graubard, 1967].

The most prolific sources of research reports and specialized studies are the various periodicals devoted to religious research. Foremost among these are the *Review of Religious Research*, *Sociological Analysis*, and the *Journal for the Scientific Study of Religion*, but *Ministry Studies*, *Religious Education*, *Information Service* of the National Council of Churches, and other specialized journals also are helpful. Articles reporting on religious studies in America often appear in *Social Compass* and *Archives de Sociologie des Religions*, and the general sociological journals occasionally publish them. Many of these are abstracted in *Sociological Abstracts*.

Two very helpful bibliographical works [Berkowitz and Johnson, 1967; Menges and Dittes, 1965], together with the books, journals, and other references cited in this chapser, can help inquisitive readers discover much of the tremendous wealth in American monographs and other specialised studies available in the form of books, journal articles, research reports, and other reference materials. A mere attempt to list the references to these would comprise a full-length book, so this bibliography at best represents a miniscule sample of what is available in and from American sociology of religion and other closely related disciplines.

Abramson, Harold J. and Noll, C. Edward, 'Religion, Ethnicity, and Social Change.' *Review of Religious Research*, 8 (1), pp. 11–26, Fall 1966.

Allport, Gordon, *Personality and Social Encounter*. Boston, Beacon Press, 1960.

Anderson, Donald N., 'Ascetic Protestantism and Political Preference.' *Review of Religious Research*, 7 (3), pp. 167–171, Spring 1966.

Armstrong, O. K., and Armstrong, M. M., *The Indomitable Baptists*. Garden City (N.Y.), Doubleday, 1967.

Baltzell, E. Digby, *The Protestant Establishment: Aristocracy and Caste in America*. New York, Random House, 1964.

Bates, M. Searle, *Religious Liberty: An Inquiry*. New York, Harper and Brothers, 1945.

—, 'Religious Liberty – Church and State.' *Occasional Bulletin* (Missionary Research Library), 10 (6), 1–19, 15 July, 1959.

Bell, Daniel, 'The Dispossessed (1962),' in: Daniel Bell (ed.), *The Radical Right.* Garden City (N.Y.), Anchor Books, 1964.

Bellah, Robert N., 'Civil Religion in America.' *Daedalus,* 96 (1), pp. 1–21, Winter 1967.

Benson, Purnell H., *Religion in Contemporary Culture: A Study of Religion Through Social Science.* New York, Harper and Row, 1960.

Berelson, Bernard R., Lazarsfeld, Paul F. and McPhee, Wiliam N., *Voting: A Study of Opinion Formation in a Presidential Campaign.* Chicago, University of Chicago Press, 1954.

Berger, Peter L., 'A Market Model for the Analysis of Ecumenicity.' *Social Research,* 30 (1), 77–94, Spring 1963.

Berkowitz, Morris I. and Johnson, J. Edmund, *Social Scientific Studies of Religion: A Bibliography.* Pittsburgh, University of Pittsburgh Press, 1967.

Birnbaum, Norman and Lenzer, Gertrud, *Sociology and Religion: A Book of Readings.* Englewood Cliffs (N.J.), Prentice-Hall, 1969.

Blau, Joseph L., Editor, *Cornerstones of Religious Freedom in America.* New York, Harper and Row, revised Torchbook edition, 1964.

Brown, Robert McAfee, *The Ecumenical Revolution: An Interpretation of the Catholic-Protestant Dialogue.* Garden City (N.Y.), Doubleday, 1967.

Bureau of the Census, 'Religion Reported by the Civilian Population of the United States: March 1957.' *Current Population Reports: Population Characteristics.* Series P-20, No. 79, 2 February, 1958.

Buss, Martin J., 'Comment on Hadden's "An Analysis of Some Factors Associated with Religion and Political Affiliation".' *Journal for the Scientific Study of Religion,* 3 (2), pp. 245–246, Spring, 1964.

Butts, R. Freeman, 'What "Establishment of Religion" meant in Colonial America', in: Peter H. Odegard (ed.), *Religion and Politics.* Dobbs Ferry, N.Y., Oceana Publications Inc., 1960, 10–17.

Campbell, Ernest Q. and Pettigrew, Thomas F., 'Racial and Moral Crisis: The Role of Little Rock Ministers.' *American Journal of Sociology,* 64 (5), 509–516, March 1959.

Carlson, C. Emanuel, 'Should Government Legislate Prayer.' *Bethel* (Bethel College and Seminary), 46 (7), pp. 1–11, June 1964.

Clark, Elmer T., *The Small Sects in America.* New York, Abingdon Press, revised edition, 1949.

Coleman, Lyman, *Growth by Groups.* Huntingdon Valley (Pa.), Christian Outreach, 1960.

Cox, Harvey, *The Secular City: Secularization and Urbanization in Theological Perspective.* New York, Macmillan, 1965.

Cuber, John F., 'Marginal Church Participants.' *Sociology and Social Research,* 25 (1), pp. 57–62, September-October 1940.

Culver, Dwight W., *Negro Segregation in the Methodist Church.* New Haven, Yale University Press, 1953.

Cutler, Donald R. (ed.), *The Religious Situation: 1968.* Boston, Beacon Press, 1968.

Demerath, Nicholas J., *Social Class in American Protestantism.* Chicago, Rand McNally, 1965.

—, and Hammond, Phillip E., *Religion in Social Context: Tradition and Transition.* New-York, Random House, 1969.

Dirks, Lee E., *Religion in Action: How America's Faiths are Meeting New Challenges.* Silver Spring (Md.), The National Observer, 1965.

Driver, Harold E., *Indians of North America.* Chicago, University of Chicago Press, 1961.

Eakin, Frank and Eakin, Mildred Moody. *Sunday School Fights Prejudice.* New York, Macmillan, 1953.

Elkind, David, 'Age Changes in the Meaning of Religious Identity.' *Review of Religious Research,* 6 (1), pp. 36–40, Fall 1964.

—, and Elkind, Sally, 'Varieties of Religious Experience in Young Adolescents.' *Journal for the Scientific Study of Religion,* 2 (1). pp. 102–112, Fall 1962.

Epstein, Benjamin R. and Forster, Arnold. *The Radical Right: Report on the John Birch Society and Its Allies.* New York, Random House, 1967.

Fichter, Joseph H., S. J., *Social Relations in the Urban Parish.* Chicago, University of Chicago Press, 1954.

—, *Parochial School: A Sociological Study.* Notre Dame (Ind.), University of Notre Dame Press, 1958.

—, 'American Religion and the Negro'. *Daedalus,* 94 (4), pp. 1085–1106, Fall 1965.

Forster, Arnold and Epstein, Benjamin R., *Danger on the Right.* New York, Random House, 1964.

Frazier, E. Franklin, *The Negro Church in America.* New York, Schocken Books, 1964.

Gallup, George H., Jr. and Davies, John O., *Gallup Opinion Index: Special Report on Religion,* Princeton (N.J.), American Institute of Public Opinion, 1969.

Glantz, Oscar, 'Protestant and Catholic Voting Behavior in a Metropolitan Area.' *Public Opinion Quarterly,* 23, (1), pp. 73–82, Spring 1959.

Gleason, Philip, Editor, *Contemporary Catholicism in the United States.* Notre Dame (Ind.), University of Notre Dame Press, 1969.

Glock, Charles Y., Ringer, Benjamin B. and Babbie, Earl R., *To Comfort and to Challenge: A Dilemma of the Contemporary Church.* Berkeley, University of California Press, 1967.

Glock, Charles Y. and Stark, Rodney, *Christian Beliefs and Anti-Semitism.* New York, Harper and Row, 1966.

—, *Religion and Society in Tension.* Chicago, Rand McNally, 1965.

Goldstein, Sidney and Goldscheider, Calvin, *Jewish Americans: Three Generations in a Jewish Community.* Englewood Cliffs (N.J.), Prentice-Hall, 1968.

Graubard, Stephen R. (ed.), 'Religion in America' (special issue). *Daedalus,* 96 (1). Winter 1967.

Greeley, Andrew M., 'Some Aspects of Interaction Between Religious Groups in an Upper Middle Class Roman Catholic Parish.' *Social Compass,* 9, (1–2), pp. 39–61, 1962.

—, *Religion and Career: A Study of College Graduates.* New York, Sheed and Ward, 1963.

—, and Rossi, Peter H., *The Education of Catholic Americans.* Chicago, Aldine, 1966.

Greer, Scott, 'Catholic Voters and the Democratic Party.' *Public Opinion Quarterly,* 25, (4), pp. 611–625, Winter 1961.

Guysenir, Maurice G., 'Jewish Vote in Chicago.' *Jewish Social Studies,* 20 (4).

Hadden, Jeffrey K., 'An Analysis of Some Factors Associated with Religion and Political Affiliation.' *Journal for the Scientific Study of Religion*, 2, (2), pp. 209–216, Spring 1963.

Hadden, Jeffrey K., *The Gathering Storm in the Churches: The Widening Gap Between Clergy and Laymen*. Garden City (N.Y.), Doubleday 1969.

Henriot, Peter J., S. J., 'The Coincidence of Political and Religious Attitudes.' *Review of Religious Research*, 8 (1), pp. 50–58, Fall 1966.

Herberg, Will, *Protestant–Catholic–Jew: An Essay in American Religious Sociology*. Garden City (N.Y.), Doubleday, 1955'

Hill, Samuel S., Jr. and Torbet, Robert G., *Baptists North and South*. Philadelphia, Judson Press, 1964.

Hough, Joseph C., Jr., *Black Power and White Protestants: A Christian Response to the New Negro Pluralism*. New York, Oxford University Press, 1968.

Hoult, Thomas Ford, *The Sociology of Religion*. New York, Holt, Rinehart and Winston, 1958.

Houtart, Francois, 'A Sociological Study of the Evolution of the American Catholics.' *Social Compass*, 2, (5–6), pp. 189–216, 1955.

Jacquet, Constant H., Jr. (ed.), *Yearbook of American Churches (Edition for 1967)*. New York, National Council of the Churches of Christ in the U.S.A., 1967.

Johnson, Benton, 'Ascetic Protestantism and Political Preference.' *Public Opinion Quarterly*, 26 (1), pp. 35–46, Spring 1962.

—, 'Ascetic Protestantism and Political Preference in the Deep South.' *American Journal of Sociology*, 69 (4), pp. 359–366, January 1964.

Johnstone, Ronald L., *The Effectiveness of Lutheran Elementary and Secondary Schools as Agencies of Christian Education*. St Louis (Mo.), Concordia Seminary, 1966.

Katz, Wilber, G. and Southerland, Harold P., 'Religious Pluralism and the Supreme Court.' *Daedalus*, 96 (1), pp. 180–192, Winter 1967.

Kerr, Hugh T., *What Divides Protestants Today*. New York, Association Press, 1958.

Kerr, Willard A., 'Untangling the Liberalism-Conservatism Continuum.' *Journal of Social Psychology*, 35 (1), pp. 111–125, February 1952.

Knudten, Richard D., Editor, *The Sociology of Religion: An Anthology*. New York, Appleton-Century-Crofts, 1967.

Lamanna, Richard A. and Stephenson, John B., 'Religious Prejudice and Intended Voting Behavior.' *Sociological Analysis*, 25 (2), pp. 121–125, Summer 1964.

Lambert, Richard D., Editor, 'Religion in American Society.' *Annals of The American Academy of Political and Social Science*, Vol. 332, November 1960.

Lanphier, C. Michael, 'Voting of Catholics: The IPP Revisited.' *Sociological Analysis*, 28 (1), pp. 1–13, Spring 1967.

Lazerwitz, Bernard, 'Membership in Voluntary Associations and Frequency of Church Attendance.' *Journal for the Scientific Study of Religion*, 2 (1), pp. 74–84, Fall, 1962.

Lee, Robert, *The Social Sources of Church Unity*. New York, Abingdon Press, 1960.

Lenski, Gerhard, *The Religious Factor: A Sociolagical Study of Religion's Impact on Politics, Economics, and Family Life*. Garden City (N.Y.), Doubleday 1961.

Levinson, Boris M., 'The Problems of Jewish Religious Youth.' *Genetic Psychology Monographs*. 60, pp. 309–348, November 1959.

Lincoln, C. Eric, *The Black Muslims in America.* Boston, Beacon Press, 1961.
Lipset, Seymour M., 'Religion in America: What Religious Revival?.' *Review of Religious Research*, 1 (1), pp. 17–24. Summer 1959.
—, *Political Man.* Garden City (N.Y.), Doubleday, 1960.
—, 'Religion and Politics in the American Past and Present,' in: Robert Lee and Martin E. Marty (eds.), *Religion and Social Conflict.* New York, Oxford University Press, 1964.
Littell, Franklin H., 'Religion and Race: The Historical Perspective', in: Mathew Ahmann (ed.), *Race Challenge to Religion.* Chicago, Henry Regnery, 1963.
Lowell, C. Stanley. *The Ecumenical Mirage.* Grand Rapids (Mich.), Baker Book House, 1967.
Maranell, Gary M., 'An Examination of Some Religious and Political Attitude Correlates of Bigotry.' *Social Forces*, 45 (3), pp. 356–362, March 1967.
Marnell, William H., *The First Amendment: The History of Religious Freedom in America.* Garden City (N.Y.), Doubleday, 1964.
Marty, Martin E., Rosenberg, Stuart E. and Greeley, Andrew M., *What Do We Believe?: The Stance of Religion in America.* New York, Meredith Press, 1968.
Mead, Frank S., *Handbook of Denominations in the United States.* New York, Abingdon Press, 4th edition, 1965.
Menges, Robert J. and Dittes, James E., *Psychological Studies of Clergymen: Abstracts of Research.* New York, Thomas Nelson and Sons, 1965.
Moberg, David O., 'Die Säkularisierung und das Wachstum der Kirchen in den Vereinigten Staaten.' *Kölner Zeitschrift für Soziologie und Sozialpsychologie*, 10 (3), pp. 430–438, 1958a.
—, 'Religious Practices in the Family', in: Nels Anderson (ed.), *Recherches sur la Famille (Studies of the Family)*, Vol. III, pp. 213–223. Göttingen, Vandenhoeck und Ruprecht, 1958b.
—, 'Social Class and the Churches.' *Information Service*, 37 (12), pp. 6–8, 14 June 1958c.
—, 'Does Social Class Shape the Church?' *Review of Religious Research*, 1 (3), 110–115, Winter 1960.
—, *The Church as a Social Institution.* Englewood Cliffs (N.J.), Prentice-Hall, 1962.
—, 'Religious Pluralism in the United States of America', in: Joachim Matthes (ed.), *Religious Pluralism and Social Structure (International Yearbook for the Sociology of Religion)*, Vol. I, pp. 69–112. Köln – Opladen (West Germany), Westdeutscher Verlag, 1965.
—, 'The Encounter of Scientific and Religious Values Pertinent to Man's Spiritual Nature.' *Sociological Analysis*, 28(1), pp. 22–23, Spring 1967.
Moore, LeRoy, 'Roger Williams as an Enduring Symbol for Baptists.' *A Journal of Church and State*, 7 (2), pp. 181–189, Spring 1965.
Muelder, Walter G., 'Institutional Factors Affecting Unity and Disunity.' *The Ecumenical Review*, 8 (2), pp. 113–126, January 1956.
Murch, James DeForest, *The Protestant Revolt.* Arlington (Va.), Crestwood Books, 1967.
Murray, John Courtney, 'America's Four Conspiracies', in: Earl Raab (ed.), *Religious Conflict in America.* Garden City (N.Y.), Doubleday and Co., 1964.

Neal, Sister Marie Augusta, S.N.D., *Values and Interests in Social Change*. Englewood Cliffs (N.J.), Prentice-Hall, 1965.

Niebuhr, H. Richard, *The Social Sources of Denominationalism*. Cleveland, The World Publishing Co., Meridian Books edition, 1957.

Norbeck, Edward, *Religion in Primitive Society*. New York, Harper and Row, 1961.

Nottingham, Elizabeth K., *Religion and Society*. New York, Random House, 1954.

O'Dea, Thomas F., *American Catholic Dilemma: An Inquiry into the Intellectual Life*. New York, Sheed and Ward, 1958.

O'Dea, Thomas F., *The Sociology of Religion*. Englewood Cliffs (N.J.), Prentice-Hall, 1966.

Odegard, Peter H. (ed.), *Religion and Politics*. Dobbs Ferry (N.Y.), Oceana Publications, The Eagleton Institution of Politics at Rutgers, The State University, 1960.

Olsen, Marvin E., 'Liberal-Conservative Attitude Crystallisation.' *Sociological Quarterly*, 3 (1), pp. 17–26, January 1962.

Olson, Bernhard E., *Faith and Prejudice*. New Haven (Conn.), Yale University Press, 1962.

Peterson, Walfred H., *An Initial Sketch of Church-State Relations Affecting Southern Baptist Churches and Institutions*. Washington (D.C.), 1967. Baptist Joint Committee on Public Affairs, 1967.

Pope, Liston, 'The Negro and Religion in America.' *Review of Religious Research*, 5 (3), pp. 142–152, Spring 1964.

'The Radical Right.' *Information Service*, 43 (16), pp. 1–12, 10 October, 1964.

Ramsey, Paul, *Who Speaks for the Church?* New York, Abingdon Press, 1967.

Redekop, John H., *The American Far Right: A Case Study of Billy James Hargis and Christian Crusade*. Grand Rapids (Mich.), Wm. B. Eerdmans Publishing Co., 1967.

Rischin, Moses, *Our Own Kind: Voting by Race, Creed, or National Origin*. Santa Barbara (Cal.), Center for the Study of Democratic Institutions, 1960.

Rokeach, Milton, *The Open and Closed Mind*. New York, Basic Books, 1960.

Rosenberg, Stuart E., *The Search for Jewish Identity in America*. Garden City (N.Y.), Doubleday, Anchor Books edition, 1965.

Rossi, Peter H., 'New Directions for Race Relations Research in the Sixties'. *Review of Religious Research*, 5 (3), pp. 125–132, Spring 1964.

—, and Rossi, Alice S., 'Some Effects of Parochial School Education in America.' *Daedalus*, 90 (2), pp. 300–328, Spring 1961.

Roucek, Joseph S., 'The Role of Religion in American Politics.' *Journal of Human Relations*. 11 (3), pp. 350–362, Spring 1963.

Roy, Ralph Lord, *Communism and the Churches*. New York, Harcourt, Brace and Co., 1960.

—, 'Conflict from the Communist Left and the Radical Right', in: Robert Lee and Martin E. Marty (eds.), *Religion and Social Conflict*. New York, Oxford University Press, 1964.

Sadler, A. W., 'Glossolalia and Possession: An Appeal to the Episcopal Study Commission.' *Journal for the Scientific Study of Religion*, 4 (1), pp. 84–90, October 1964.

Salisbury, W. Seward, *Religion in American Culture: A Sociological Interpretation.* Homewood (Ill.), Dorsey Press, 1964.

Sanders, Thomas G., *Protestant Concepts of Church and State.* New York, Holt, Rinehart and Winston, 1964.

Schneider, Louis, Editor, *Religion, Culture and Society: A Reader in the Sociology of Religion.* New York, John Wiley and Sons, 1964.

Schuyler, Joseph B., 'Religious Behavior in a Northern Parish: A Study of Motivating Values.' *American Catholic Sociological Review,* 19 (2), pp. 134–144, June 1958.

Sklare, Marshall (ed.), *The Jews: Social Patterns of an American Group.* Glencoe (Ill.), The Free Press, 1958.

Stagg. Frank, Hinson, E. Glenn and Oates, Wayne E., *Glossolalia: Tongue Speaking in Biblical, Historical, and Psychological Perspective.* Nashville (Tenn.), Abingdon Press, 1967.

Stark, Rodney and Glock, Charles Y., *American Piety: The Nature of Religious Commitment.* Berkeley, University of California Press, 1968.

Stedman, Murray S., Jr. *Religion and Politics in America.* New York, Harcourt, Brace and World, 1964.

Stokes, Anson Phelps, *Church and State in the United States,* 3 vols. New York, Harper and Brothers, 1964.

Strommen, Merton P., *Profiles of Church Youth,* St Louis, Concordia Press, 1963.

Stroup, Herbert, *Church and State in Confrontation.* New York, Seabury Press, 1967.

Van Dyke, P. and Pierce-Jones, J., 'The Psychology of Religion of Middle and Late Adolescence: A Review of Empirical Research.' *Religious Education,* 58 (6), pp. 529–537, November-December 1963.

Vanecko, James J., 'Religious Behavior and Prejudice: Some Dimensions and Specifications of the Relationship.' *Review of Religious Research,* 8 (1), pp. 27–37, Fall 1966.

Vanecko, James J., 'Types of Religious Behavior and Levels of Prejudice.' *Sociological Analysis,* 28 (3), pp. 111–122, Fall 1967.

Vernon, Glenn M., *Sociology of Religion.* New York, McGraw-Hill 1962.

Wach, Joachim, *Sociology of Religion.* Chicago, University of Chicago Press, 1944.

Wagner, Helmut R., Doyle, Kathryn and Fisher, Victor, 'Religious Background and Higher Education.' *American Sociological Review,* 24 (6), pp. 852–856, December 1959.

Washington, Joseph R., Jr., *Black Religion: The Negro and Christianity in the United States.* Boston, Beacon Press, 1964.

Whitley, Oliver Read, *The Church: Mirror or Window? Images of the Church in American Society.* St Louis (Mo.), The Bethany Press, 1969.

Wiley, Norbert, 'Religious and Political Liberalism among Catholics.' *Sociological Analysis,* 28 (3), pp. 142–148, Fall 1967.

Wogaman, J. Philip, *Methodism's Challenge in Race Relations.* Washington (D.C.), Public Affairs Press, 1960.

Wood, James E., Jr., 'Editorial: Religion and America's Public Schools.' *A Journal of Church and State,* 9 (1), pp. 5–16, Winter 1967.

Yinger, J. Milton, *Religion, Society and the Individual.* New York, Macmillan, 1957.

—, *Sociology Looks at Religion.* New York, Macmillan 1963.

WILLIAM C. FLETCHER*

# U.S.S.R.

## INTRODUCTION: THE STATE OF SOVIET SOCIOLOGY OF RELIGION

Sociological analysis of religion in the U.S.S.R. is one of the more frustrating aspects of Soviet area studies. Only occasional efforts have been made in the field in the West[1] while among Soviet scholars the sociological study of religion on any scientifically convincing basis is a new and relatively weak plant springing up within the past ten years.

Prior to the initiation of the still continuing antireligious campaign in the late fifties,[2] Soviet attempts to analyse religion as a social phenomenon were, with rare exceptions, confined within the boundaries prescribed by the general social theory of Marxist-Leninist dialectics [e.g. Iaroslavskii, 1957]. The necessity to superimpose a preconceived theoretical structure on social analysis of religion usually resulted in less of a sociological study than of a philosophical treatment and, indeed, as the assertion of dogmatic dialectical materialism became less and less descriptive of the development of Soviet

* William Fletcher was born in Oakland, California in 1932, and has retained his American citizenship. He obtained a B.A. from the University of California, Los Angeles, a B.D. from the California Baptist Theological Seminary, and a Ph.D. from the University of Southern California. He is currently Director of the *Centre de Recherches et d'Etude des Institutions Religieuses*, Geneva, Switzerland. Publications include *Christianity in the Soviet Union: an annotated Bibliography*, 1963; *A Study in Survival: The Church in Russia*. 1927–43, 1968; *Nikolai*, 1968; *Religion and the Search for New Ideals in the U.S.S.R.* (with Antony J. Stroven), 1967, and *Religion and the Soviet State: a Dilemma of Power* (with Max Hayward), 1969.

1. The sociologist Nicholas S. Timasheff, emeritus at Fordham University, and, more recently, the ethnographer Stephen P. Dunn of Ohio State University, have made significant contributions in this field.

2. The current antireligious campaign is briefly reviewed by the author [Fletcher, 1968, pp. 7–10], while fuller treatment of various aspects of the campaign may be found in an earlier work in [Fletcher and Stover, 1967]. The effect of the campaign on the Russian Baptists receives detailed treatment in Bourdeaux, [1968]. Numerous studies of the current campaign have appeared in scholarly and general periodicals, notably the *Bulletin of the Institute for the Study of the U.S.S.R.* (Munich) and *Problems of Communism* (Washington, D.C.).

society, the attempt to fit religion into the scheme often fell from a philosophical to a merely casuistical level [e.g. Khudiakov, 1958, 1960]. This pattern of dogmatic analysis continues to hamper the development of Soviet sociology on religion, and in terms of number of adepts and mass of published material, maintains a vast predominance over the relatively recent attempt to develop the sociology of religion as an independent science, objectively grounded in concrete, verifiable experimentation [For examples, see bibliography].

In large measure the deficiency of attention to religion by Western sociological study and the weakness of Soviet fledgeling efforts in this field may be traced to a common source: lack of data. Religion remains an exceedingly delicate area in the view of Soviet officialdom and, especially during the current decade of tension, no great attempts are made by Soviet official circles to disseminate data except in certain exceedingly limited areas which are adjudged necessary for properly equipping antireligious workers [See, e.g. *Kazakhstanskaia Pravda*, 31 July 1968]. Official treatment of religion during the periods of tension has always fallen far short of the legal statutes propagated by state and Party [e.g. Bourdeaux and Struve, 1968]. This discrepancy between the promise in the laws and the actuality in the administration of religious affairs cannot but embarrass the regime, and, therefore, any attempt to gain a valid understanding of the situation is made exceedingly difficult by the existing blockade of information.

For these reasons, this chapter will not attempt the rather tedious task of surveying in detail what few attempts have been made to analyse religion in the U.S.S.R. from the viewpoint of sociological methodology. Instead, this chapter will confine itself to a review of one of the basic tools of accurate sociological research – the compilation of statistics on religion – followed by a brief review of representative trends in contemporary Soviet scholarship in this field.

Obviously, reliable statistics on the number of churches, clergy, and members of extant religious organizations are a pre-requisite to any attempt to derive a scientifically valid sociological analysis of this subject and, indeed, without such basic knowledge, there is almost no possibility of drawing accurate generalizations from the various other tools of sociological research such as field studies and the like. [3] In order to keep this study within manageable proportions, only the predominant religion in the U.S.S.R. – the Russian Orthodox Church – will be included in this survey. As will quickly become apparent in the treatment which follows, the study will serve less to

3. Field studies, questionnaires, interviews, systematic observation and the like are relatively new phenomena in the study of religion in the USSR, and will be reviewed briefly below. Such studies by Western observers are most difficult, and relatively infrequent; [see, e.g., Fletcher, 1963, pp. 9–11].

illuminate the actual sociological situation of religion in the country, than to illustrate, by a case study approach, the chaotic nature of the discipline of Sociology of Religion as applied to the U.S.S.R. If basic statistical knowledge of the Russian Orthodox Church is unreliable and deficient, the same applies in equal or even greater degree, with regard to demographic analysis for the country as a whole and for discrete religious denominations, for concrete elaboration of religious participation and beliefs, for economic indices amongst religious believers and, indeed, for nearly every other relevant area of concern to the sociologist of religion.

### RUSSIAN ORTHODOX CONGREGATIONS

Before the Revolution the Russian Orthodox Church had 54,174 churches and 23,592 chapels [*Ezhegodnik Rossii za*, 1914, p. 99; *Cf.* Iudin, 1962; 1963, p.117, where the figure of 78,767 is given for the eve of the Revolution]. These data are official figures published by the Russian Orthodox Church at the time and may be considered fairly exact. As such they represent the last reliable figures which have been published.

One can speculate that World War I resulted in some adjustment in the number of churches. Some churches were doubtless damaged, destroyed, or even put out of operation entirely in those areas of the Russian Empire in which the battle raged. Far more important were the territorial losses suffered by the nation during the closing months of the war. In addition, the period of the Provisional Government in Russia (February to October, 1917) may have been a time in which certain superfluous churches were closed down due to the decreasing intimacy of church-state relations under the Provisional Government.[4] The result was that by the end of 1917 the figures cited above had become unreliable and should be revised downward by some unknown degree. One Western commentator places the number at 40,474 [Sheen, 1948, p. 179] but, as will become apparent below, this figure may be somewhat smaller than was the actual case.

For the next four years Russia was in the throes of Civil War. Considering the brutality of that war and the degree to which it was not limited to men at arms but spread over into the general population in disputed areas, with

4. While the Church seemed enthusiastically in favour of a continuation of its intimate relationship with the state, the latter appeared to be in doubt about the matter [Spinka, 1927, pp. 73–76]. This period probably witnessed the closure of churches or chapels maintained for the royal entourage, (which were rendered superfluous by the abdication of the Tsar), as well as any churches which may have been kept open through oversight or sheer inertia on the part of the tsarist bureaucracy.

massive destruction of property, the church may be assumed to have suffered considerably along with the population [For treatment of the Civil War, see Chamberlin, 1952, Vol. II; Pipes, 1954]. It should be noted that the Soviet regime harboured deep suspicions that the Church was directly involved in resisting Red forces in the Civil War [Emhardt, 1939, pp. 242–250]. In the waning days of the Civil War, the church came under attack by the state, which was ideologically committed to atheism, and churches were being closed either punitively (on counter-revolutionary charges) [McCullagh, 1924], or on general principles.

Much more precipitate were the losses caused by the famous 'Living Church Adventure'. This was a schismatic movement begun in 1922 and, with the enthusiastic blessing of the state, it gained extraordinary power during its initial months [The best treatment remains that of Emhardt, 1929]. After the release of Patriarch Tikhon from confinement in 1923 and the withdrawal of state support over the next few years, the Living Church declined and eventually disappeared.[5] However, at the height of its power, the Living Church controlled a large proportion of the formerly Orthodox church buildings. According to one Soviet historian, the Living Church controlled more than half of all the parishes in 1923 [Okulov, 1966;]. Walter Kolarz [1962, p. 40] states that the Living Church controlled 12,593 parishes, while N. F. Platonov, a Living Church Metropolitan who defected to atheism in 1938, wrote in his memoirs that a total of almost 15,000 parishes went over to the schismatics [Titov, 1967, p. 116]. As late as 1929 it was estimated that the Living Church retained control over 35 per cent of the total number of Orthodox parishes [Spinka, 1936, p. 78]. Numerous bishops and priests had been expelled in order to make room for the Living Church, [McCullagh, 1924, XVII] and, although the populace as a whole remained loyal to the Patriarchal Church, these parishes were infrequently returned to the jurisdiction of the Mother Church even with the waning of the schism [Pol'skii, 1957, pp. 190–191]. Therefore, the Russian Orthodox Church must be presumed to have suffered a serious loss in the number of its churches during the early and middle twenties.

According to the *Statistical Review* published by the People's Commissariat of Domestic Affairs, in 1925 there were 28,381 Russian Orthodox congregations in 48 of the 87 administrative districts in the country [Spinka, 1927, p. 305]. One might be tempted to extrapolate a total figure of some 52,000 from this partial number, but such temptation naturally should be resisted for, without knowing the relative size, demographic constitution, and reli-

5. The surviving clerics of the Living Church repented and rejoined the Orthodox Church immediately after the conclusion of the agreement between Church and State in 1943, even though, for all practical purposes, the movement was defunct long before [Kolarz, 1962, pp. 38–42, 52].

gious tradition of the reporting districts as against those which were silent, one can say nothing at all about the total number on the basis of this figure. The estimate of 39,000 churches remaining open in 1925 [Curtiss, 1953, p. 223] is probably somewhat more reliable.

The collectivization campaign which was waged vigorously from 1928 to 1932 [Baykov, 1946; Hindus, 1933] was a period of rapid decline in the number of remaining churches in the U.S.S.R. In part this was due to the simple practice of making the village church a casuality when the village was re-organized into a collective farm [Fletcher, 1965, pp. 46–48]. However, a vigorous anti-religions campaign was also waged during these years. New laws of an exceedingly restrictive nature were applied against religion in 1929 [Gidulianov, 1929] and many churches could be closed legally as a consequence [Fletcher, 1965, p. 61]. A great many other churches were closed by simple fiat or on the most gossamer of pretexts [Fletcher, 1965, p. 61]. In 1929 alone, 1,440 churches were closed [Conquest, 1968, p. 21][6] and in 1930, midway through the campaign, Metropolitan Sergii, then the leader of the Church (in absence of the other successors to the late Patriarch Tikhon, all of whom were in prison) estimated that 30,000 Russian Orthodox churches remained [*Izvestiia*, 19 February 1930].

From 1932 until the Great Purges, the pressure against religion was considerably relaxed. However, at no time during that period did the regime abandon its commitments to atheism, and it seems most unlikely that any significant number of churches re-opened during that period. Indeed, it is probable that closure of churches continued spasmodically during this period. According to Spinka, [1936, p. 107], only 40 per cent of the Orthodox churches were still functioning in 1936.

The church came under intense attack during the Great Purges in 1937 and 1938 [On these see Timasheff, 1946; Deutscher, 1949] and while no reliable data are available it is estimated that some 10,000 churches were closed during these years [Timasheff, 1942, p. 53].

It is at this point that official figures begin to obfuscate an already obscure picture. In 1937, officials of the atheist campaign said that there were 30,000 religious associations of all sorts; [Iaroslavskii, 1937, p. 107] this figure was twice repeated in 1938 [*Krasnaia Zvezda*, 22 July 1938; *Izvestiia*, 5 February 1938] and was given again in 1941 [*Soviet War News*, as cited in Timasheff, 1942, p. 92, note 16]. In 1939, however, another state publication gave the figure of 20,000 [Antireligioznik, June 1939].

6. Other estimates seem to corroborate this rate of closings. W. C. White, [1930, p. 67], stated that some 2,000 churches were closed during the year 1928–29, while Paul Miliukov, [1942, p. 203] derived from Soviet sources the figure of 740 churches closed in the first six months of 1929 which, it was said, was equal to the entire year of 1928.

World War II brought a radical change in the approach of the regime toward religion. Antireligious propaganda was quickly abandoned and efforts began to be made to enlist the church in support of the war effort. In the field of statistics there may have been a tendency towards more reliability in the published number of Russian Orthodox churches open, but the picture is far from clear. The Soviet government officially listed the number of Russian Orthodox churches open in 1941 at 4,225 [Timasheff, 1942]. Despite its plausibility [Davis, 1960], this figure may be somewhat inflated,[7] for twenty years later an anti-religious source stated that 'in 1941 there were *nearly* 4,000 Orthodox churches' [Veschikov, 1962, p. 60 – author's italics]. Independent estimates by Western observes reduce the figure to 3,200 [Konstantinov, 1965, p. 17], 1,500 [Hutten, 1967, p. 13], or even 100 churches remaining [Bourdeaux, 1965, p. 58].

With the initiation of the unwritten agreement between state and church in 1943, the statistical picture, which had been obscure enough already, became hopelessly confused. A curious form of detente replaces the earlier bitter struggle between church and state, and the church was allowed a limited degree of freedom of action within the U.S.S.R. in return for its collaboration in areas which the state considered useful [For the concordat of 1943, see Fletcher, 1965, pp. 112–114]. Chief amongst these areas was the field of foreign relations.[8] In order for the services rendered by the church to have maximum impact abroad, however, it was incumbent upon the regime to claim tolerance toward religion for itself and great vigour for the church. For this reason, the statistics given by church or state officials after World War II appear to have been grossly inflated, and, while any single statement as to the number of churches operating at a giving time may be impressive enough, when several of these statements are collated (more or less at random) the result becomes ludicrous.[9]

From the beginning of World War II until at least 1947, there was an impressive resurgence of religion in the U.S.S.R. and the number of active

7. Inasmuch as the same source gives the total number of functioning religious congregations as 30,000 – and Russian Orthodoxy is the predominant religion in the U.S.S.R. – one can only wonder what the other 25,775 were, and, consequently, how reliable these data really are.

8. For the Church's role in post-war international relations, see Fletcher [1968, pp. 54–84, 96–134]. Valuable, if hostile treatments are available also in Spinka [1956, pp. 101–154,] and Alexeev [1955].

9. Nathaniel Davis [1960], devoted considerable care and attention to the tedious process of compiling statistical reports in Western works, based on official and semi-official statements in the U.S.S.R. during the post-war period. A goodly proportion of the figures presented below were located by Dr. Davis, and hearty gratitude is due to him for this service to the study of religion in the U.S.S.R.

churches rose sharply [Murav'ev and Dmitriev, 1961, p. 64]. This was due not only to the virtual abandonment of the antireligious campaign[10] but also to the fact that because of the exigencies of the war, social and police control over the towns and villages was much less efficient and believers could re-organize shattered parishes with relative impunity. In addition, the policy of the German occupational forces had generally encouraged – or at least permitted – re-opening of churches [For German policy, see Fireside, 1968] (as many as 10,000) [Titov, 1967, p. 118], and as the Red Army began to liberate these provinces the U.S.S.R. inherited a considerable number of churches [Veschikov, 1962, p. 8; Kolarz, 1962, p. 78; Bogolepov, 1958, p. 53][11]. The period of relative relaxation continued for the two years following the war.

It is extremely difficult, however, to determine from statements during those years just how great the revival was. G. Karpov,[12] who was the head of the Council for the Affairs of the Russian Orthodox Church from its inception in 1943 [Wolin and Slusser, 1957, p. 23] until 1960, [*Izvestiia* 21 February 1960] and hence was the highest instance of official state policy on religion, gave what was probably the least inflated figure which would appear for a decade and a half, when he stated in 1945 that there were 16,000 churches [*New York Times*, 7 June 1945]. Metropolitan Nikolai, however, who was the leading church official in foreign affairs, gave the figure of 30,000 in 1945 [*New York Times*, 28 November 1945],[13] while other figures deriving from the Patriarchate during this period were 20,000

10. The leading antireligious periodicals had been withdrawn in 1941 [*New York Times*, 1 October 1941, and 7 October 1941]. The hiatus was short-lived, however, for by 1944 antireligious propaganda was resumed under the name of 'scientific educational propaganda' [Curtiss, 1953, pp. 302–303, and Dallin, 1956, pp. 282–283]. Such propaganda efforts were to remain sporadic and desultory until the mid-fifties, however.

11. An unknown number of churches were also inherited by the Russian Orthodox Church as a result of the acquisition of new areas such as Transcarpathia and the Baltic States during the U.S.S.R.'s territorial expansion [See, e.g., *Zhurnal Moskovskoi Patriarkhii*, April, 1945].

12. Karpov was one of the casualties of the rising antireligious campaign, for he had been identified with the earlier policy of limited detente between Church and State. His replacement by V. Kuroedov signaled the re-introduction of rigid policy against the churches thereafter [Fletcher, 1968, p. 193].

13. It may be noted that this figure repeats what had apparently been the 'Party Line' immediately before the war (see above), and hence may represent confusion on Nikolai's part as to just what figures the government expected him to give; or, more subtly, an attempt to claim for Orthodoxy what the government had earlier considered an acceptable number for churches of all denominations, with an eye toward gaining subsequent permission to translate this claim into fact.

[Lonsdale, 1952, p. 138; *Reforme*, 31 August 1946], 22,000 [Spinka, 1956, p. 119] and 25,000 [Strohm, 1947, p. 175]. Similarly, figures given in 1947 were 25,000 [Fontanieu, 1955, p. 60] and 29,000 [Curtiss, 1953, p. 305].

From late 1947 until Stalin's death early in 1953, the regime returned to a much stricter policy toward society, beginning with the *Zhdanovshchina* [Wolfe, 1956] and culminating in the famous Doctor's Plot which was aborted by Stalin's death [*Meditsinskii Rabotnik*, No. 4, 1953; *Klinicheskaia Meditsina*, No. 2, 1953]. This was a period of great tension within Soviet society, with extreme sanctions and restrictions applied against many areas of life. It is not known to what extent the internal life of the Russian Orthodox Church felt these restrictions, although there was a resurgence of anti-religious propaganda [Konstantinov, 1956, p. 47] and other religious groups – notably Jews [*Londen Times*, 26 February 1957] and illegal religious denominations [Mitrokhin, 1961, p. 160] – were severely repressed. In particular, no data have yet been compiled regarding the question of whether Russian Orthodox Churches were closed during this period and, if so, how many. Indeed, the Church may have experienced a net growth during this period, for in 1948, when the Uniates were abolished and forcibly attached to Orthodoxy in the Western Ukraine, the Russian Orthodox Church fell to the bulk of some 3,000 previously Uniate parishes [*Zhurnal Moskovskoi Patriarkhii*, No. 10, October 1948]. These acquisitions are not reflected in the statistical data.

Again the figures given for the number of churches operating during these years appear to be without any discernible pattern whatsoever. According to Karpov, there were 22,000 churches early in 1949. [Antonii, 1960, p. 35] In 1950, 20,000 churches were claimed [Tobias, 1956, pp. 225–271]. In 1951 there were (variously) 20,000 buildings and 30,000 congregations, [Tobias, 1956, p. 276] more than 20,000 [*Soviet News*, 21 August 1951] and 25,000 [MavEoin and Zombory, 1951, p. 11]. In 1952 there were 22,000 [Lamont, 1962, p. 152] 24–25,000 [*Newsweek*, 17 January 1952] and 25,000 [Timasheff, 1955, p. 233].

From the death of Stalin until the consolidation of Khrushchev's power in the latter part of the decade, a period of considerable relaxation of religion during these years was felt throughout Soviet society, [Parker, 1962, p. 1187; Bogolepov, 1958, p. 53; Guins, 1956, p. 255] and church life was sufficiently vigorous to acquire a momentum which lasted well into the antireligious campaign which was initiated between 1957 and 1960 [e.g. *Komsomol'skaia Pravda*, 31 January 1962; *Cf.* Khrushchev's opening address at the XXII Party Congress, *Pravda*, 18 October 1961]. Predictably, however, no reflection of this religious revival appeared in the statistics on the number of Russian Orthodox Churches, for in 1954 the same figures of 20,000 [Horsely, 1954] 25,000 [*La Documentation Française*, October 1954] and 25,000 [*News-*

*week*, 18 October 1954] were given. In 1955, Metropolitan Nikolai twice gave the figure of 20,000, [Jackson, 1956, p. 64; Evans, 1955, p. 2] a figure which was repeated by another Patriarchate source, [Guins, 1956: 225] and 22,000 was also given [Guins, 1956, p. 225]. The same two figures appeared the following year. [Anderson, 1956, p. 480; Steinberg, 1968: 1464]. In an unusual departure from precedent the *Journal of the Moscow Patriarchate* printed the figure of 22,000 for 1957 [*Zhurnal Moskovskoi Patriarkhii*, August 1957], while the following year a Patriarchate official claimed 25,000 churches.

The thaw was coming to an end by the later fifties and, particularly for religion, chill winds began to blow. As early as 1954, there was an indication that Khrushchev was no particular friend of religion [*Pravda*, 11 November 1954; for commentary, see Embree, 1959, pp. 106–107; Kellen, 19961, p. 131], and between 1957 and 1960, the resumption of pre-war acerbity toward religion gradually became evident in the regime's actions.[14] By 1960, the antireligious campaign had become general, and for the next four years at least the church was destined to suffer a radical decline in the number of still functioning parishes. Nevertheless, the statistical claims of the Moscow Patriarchate remained constant: 20,000 in 1960, [Hindus, 1961, p. 107] and the same figure as its official size upon entry to the World Council of Churches in 1961 [*Time*, 5 May 1961; *Cf. Time*, 16 February 1962]. Even two years later one Western visitor was told by Patriarchate officials that there were 'around 50 million members in perhaps 23,000 churches' and, in what appears in retrospect to be a burst of credulity, he added, 'These numbers, be it noted, are based on reports made by the clergy on the numbers of believers in their parishes, not on actual membership rolls' [Foltz, 1964, p. 56]. Harrison Salisbury in 1962 was told that there were 20,000 churches, [*Time*, 16 February 1962] and the same figure for 1962 was later repeated by a Soviet scholar, who, with some candour, noted that 'these data are very exaggerated' [Veschikov, 962, p. 3].

The crescendo of the campaign against the churches very quickly made such figures untenable. The obvious discrepancies between the various figures given over the preceding fifteen years makes their credibility highly suspect. It seemed more and more obvious that the figures given were 'round figures' bearing little relationship, if any, to the concrete situation within the Russian

14. The current antireligious campaign is so massive an effort that it took several years for it to reach its full proportions. Consequently, it is hardly possible to point to a specific date as its beginning. As early as 1957 some of the more extreme forms of illegal religion began to feel the pressure. By 1959 the campaign had become general [Struve, 1967, pp. 294–295], and at the end of that year and the beginning of 1960 the Russian Orthodox Church came under the full-scale attack that lesser denominations had already been experiencing [See Fletcher, 1968, pp. 185–202].

Orthodox Church at any given point in time. Particularly as the antireligious press began more and more frequently to give instances of sizable numbers of churches closed [e.g. *Komsomol'skaia Pravda*, 14 June 1961; *Kommunist Moldavii*, July 1961; *Pravda*, 7 October 1963], the figures ranging from 20,000 upwards, which Patriarchal officials had been giving with such bland assurance for the preceding period, became quite absurd.

Indeed, the figures themselves became a source of embarrassment, for the increased communication with the West which resulted from the entry of the Russian Orthodox Church into the World Council of Churches, together with the increasing candour of Soviet atheist writers and with the boldness of the new generation of disaffected religious believers and the ensuing avalanche of letters, protests, and documents sent to the West through clandestine means, the actual situation of the Church could not long be hidden from outside observers. By 1962, the number of active churches within Russian Orthodoxy was, according to an atheist scholar, 11,500, [Iudin, 1962, p. 117] a figure which was shortly thereafter confirmed informally by church officials ['Testimony of Paul B. Anderson', in: *Recent Developments in the Soviet Bloc*, 1964, p. 99]. Two years later informed Western observers were estimating that the number had declined to 10,000 [Struve, 1967, p. 300] or even fewer [*Commonweal*, 15 November 1963]. When these figures are compared with the status quo ante of the fifties, as inevitably they must be compared, the result can be a source of considerable embarrassment to the Soviet regime's claim of justice, equity, etc., in its official religious policy. If the figures from the earlier period were themselves inflated, the resulting comparison will be even less pleasant for the official image of the state. In terms of actual loss of churches, the antireligious campaign of the sixties is exceeded, if at all, only by the very worst excesses of the pre-war period, which is still roundly condemned in the Soviet Union as the period of the 'personality cult' [For an interesting variant of interpretation of the 'personality cult' as regards religion, see *Nauka i Religiia*, April, 1962]. In percentile terms the decline in the number of open churches between 1960 and 1964 may even exceed the losses suffered during equivalent four-year periods between 1917 and 1939. If, however, the most exaggerated figures claimed during the post-war years are used as the basis for comparison, these factors are multiplied accordingly.

Perhaps because of this consideration, and also because of the increasing independence of Soviet scholars of religion and atheism, there have been recent indications that the earlier figures, despite their official sources, were badly inflated. According to an article in the major antireligious journal in 1962:

> In 1941 there were nearly 4,000 Orthodox Churches. In 1948 there were more than 15,000. Most of these churches were opened in the oc-

> cupied territories where the clergy collaborated with the Nazis. However, some of the new Orthodox Churches were registered on the free (unoccupied) Soviet territory.

Since 1948, few new churches have been opened [Veschikov, 1962, p. 8].

This would seem to be a more accurate estimate, particularly when compared with the similar figure given by Karpov in 1945.

By this point in the discussion it should seem obvious that it is futile to expect to derive any accurate statistical assessment of the church from official statements. In fact, one is reduced to the frustrating and annoying disciplines of Soviet Studies in general – if not sheer Kremlinology – in evaluating the statistical aspects of Soviet religious life [Fletcher, 1965, pp. 8–11]. In this case, it seems apparent that official figures have been fabricated out of whole cloth, or have been unjustifiably inflated (whether consciously or not is irrelevant to this discussion), and do not by any means reflect the dynamics of the situation at any point.

There have been a few attempts to account for this obvious inaccuracy in statistics. In reply to a question concerning the number of churches in 1963, Archpriest Borovoy answered:

> That's hard to say, because when religious life is on the upsurge in one part of Russia and new churches are being built, it begins to wane in other parts and the churches are closed. It goes up and down [Jung, 1963, p. 275].

Certainly a similar phenomenon obtains in almost any church in any country, but such fluctuations need not, of course, preclude the compilation of statistical records. The answer does not seem quite so evasive, however, if one presumes that Borovoy was possibly refering to actual – as against officially registered – religious congregations. This number does fluctuate widely and, indeed, is probably quite unknown. According to one atheist scholar:

> Withdrawal of registered statistics frequently results in a mere increase in the number of unregistered but functioning religious societies and groups. Consequently, the copying of figures from one column into another cannot be passed off as an indication of the success of atheistic efforts [Valentinov, 1961, p. 51].

A more sophisticated attempt to avoid the demand for statistical data was made by Karpov himself, when he stated that the very attempt to gather such statistics would be an infringement of religious freedom. [Evans, 1955, p. 8]. This is a specious answer, for, according to the laws of 1929 (which remain in force) 'the number of religious societies and also of groups of believers in the boundaries of the existing territories is [to be] made by the organs which register religious unions' [Gidulianov, 1959, quoting Decree 8, April, 1929]. At the time of its promulgation, the organs referred to in the law were within the O.G.P.U. In 1932, a certain 'commission for consideration of religious questions' was formed [Gidulianov, 1959, quoting Decree 8, April, 1929], and with the creation of the 'Council for the Affairs of the Russian Orthodox Church' under the Council of Ministers of the U.S.S.R. in 1943, the law would become applicable to that council, of which, as has been noted, Karpov was the head. Furthermore, for any church legally to function in the U.S.S.R. it must be granted registration status by the Council and while it has been fashionable for some time to deride the visible inefficiency of the Soviet bureaucracy, to suggest that any governmental council is unable to maintain records concerning registration permits issued by itself strains the imagination.

Obviously then, the imprecision of data concerning the number of Orthodox Churches derives from governmental policy of withholding that data. For so long as this policy continues, attempts to derive satisfactory sociological data will be badly crippled. Walter Kolarz, for example, attempted to delineate the regional and ethnographic distribution of churches and religious groups in the U.S.S.R. in 1960 and 1961 [Kolarz, 1962, p. 82]. Because of the impossibility of securing detailed data, his conclusions, while generally adequate, are far from reliable in terms of their accuracy. Nathaniel Davis made an ingenious attempt to overcome this lack in his doctoral dissertation in 1960, in which he compiled an exhaustive list of local churches mentioned in the *Journal of the Moscow Patriarchate* since 1944, classified them according to frequency of appearance and then, by applying the methodologies of statistical analysis, attempted to determine on this basis how many churches had appeared zero times in the *Journal* [Davis, 1960, Appendix I]. His conclusions, however, seem disproportionately low, which may have been due to a mistaken assumption that the *Journal of the Moscow Patriarchate* would name local churches on a random basis. According to Walter Kolarz,

> News about religious life outside the places visited by foreign travellers is scant. The Church itself does not wish to boast about the fervour of believers in various parts of the country, for this might lead to an immediate increase of antireligious propaganda in the areas concerned. Only very rarely, and almost inadvertently, does the *Journal of the Moscow Patriarchate* give some details about how the Orthodox faith is kept alive even in the more distant places of European Russia, or perhaps there more than anywhere else [Kolarz, 1962, p. 82].

RUSSIAN ORTHODOX BELIEVERS AND RELIGIOUS PARTICIPATION

If data concerning the actual functioning churches in the country are inadequate, the situation with regard to the total number of Russian Orthodox believers is all but impossible to fathom in a statistical manner. In part, this is due to the repressive atmosphere surrounding religious life in the U.S.S.R., for the sanctions applied against those who openly belong to a religous organization would tend to discourage a great number of people from admitting such adherence. Confusing the matter still further is the tradition of the Russian Orthodox Church as the established Church of Russia before the Revolution. The earlier practice – which is still continued to a large measure [*Komsomol'skaia Pravda*, 17 June 1961; *Literaturnaia Gazeta*, 28 November 1961; *Krasnaia Zveda*, 28 December 1958] – of enrolling all new-born infants into the church through the sacrament of Baptism makes it almost impossible to delineate the boundaries of church membership in any meaningful way, particularly after the disestablishment of the Church. Therefore, attempts to determine the number of adherents to Russian Orthodoxy have always been approximate at best and, indeed, often represent no more than sheer speculation.

At the time of the Revolution, the Russian Orthodox Church was estimated to have 117 million adherents [Spinka, 1956, p. 17]. This figure is far from reliable, for, prior to the Revolution, there was every incentive for the parish priest to exaggerate the number of loyal Orthodox in his parish and to underestimate those in his area who adhered to competing denominations [For an excellent study of this phenomenon see Conybeare, 1921, p. 102]. In any event the casualities of World War I, the diminished size of the Russian Empire at the end of the war, and the manifold casualities suffered during the Civil War and subsequently, would render such a figure meaningless.

In 1937, the Soviet government included a question concerning religious beliefs in its general census. Ostensibly because of falsification and negligence on the part of census takers, that census was declared invalid and its results never published [Curtiss, 1953, p. 283]. In subsequent months, however, unverified reports, apparently based on the census, leaked out and it was estimated that some 56 per cent of the population answered the question on religious belief in the affirmative [Timasheff, 1942, p. 65; as amended in 1955, p. 232]. Atheist propagandists estimated the number of believers at 80 million in 1937 and at 90 million in 1940 [Casey, 1946, 80]. Even were these figures based on the aborted census, however, the total religious population of the U.S.S.R. may have been considerably higher due to the natural tendency in such a time of tension to conceal one's personal religious belief even from the census taker [Braun, 1959, p. 38]. On the other hand. Lenin's widow pointed out that the tradition of religious adherence as a sign of social respectability may have induced some to answer the question affirmatively even though they had long since ceased any meaningful participation in religion [*Izvestiia*, 27 April 1937].

More recent estimates have shown even less reliance on concrete evidence and have varied widely. In 1957, the church officials estimated that 50 per cent of the population (ca. 100 million) were Christians and the Western observer to whom this was told thought it too modest [Schakovskoy, 1959, p. 256]. Nathaniel Davis, in his dissertation in 1960, estimated that three or four million Russians may go to church on a given Sunday [Davis, 1960, p. 400], while other estimates of that year ranged from 20 to 30 million as based on sales of candles in the Russian Orthodox Churches [Shaw, 1958, p. 433], to 25 per cent of the population (ca. 50 million) [Bailey, 1958, p. 304]. The estimate based on candle sales (20 to 30 million) was repeated in 1959 [Kolarz, 1959, p. 199], while a second estimate from that year placed the figure at 50 million [Blake, 1959, p. 114]. On its entry into the World Council of Churches, the Moscow Patriarchate repeatedly claimed to represent two-thirds of the Soviet population (ca. 140 million), while World Council leaders were willing to estimate the membership of the Russian Church at 30 million [*Soviet Affairs Amalysis Service*, No. 17, 1961–1962, pp. 2–3]. More conservative estimates on the part of the Patriarchate that year, placed the figures at 40 to 50 million people regularly or irregularly attending services [Hindus, 1961, p. 107]. A curious sidelight that year was the claim that sales of candles in the churches had increased from 12 tons in 1959 to 18 tons in 1961 [Parker, 1962, p. 1187], a claim which seems rather difficult to believe in view of the acceleration of antireligious pressures during those years. In 1962, Martin Niemöller quoted a state official as saying that 65 per cent (130 million) of the Russian people belonged to the church [*New York Times*, 6 July 1962], and as has been noted above, the following year the claim of 50 million was again repeated [Foltz, 1964]. On 24 October 1968 *Ecumenical Press Service* reported that the representative of the Exarch of Western Europe had stated that between 40 and 60 million Russians are practising the Orthodox faith more or less regularly.

Obviously such figures are somewhat less than credible, and certainly are quite useless for any scientifically oriented sociological study. The figures, particularly in the recent period, seem to vary not according to the waxing or waning of religious sentiments in the country, but rather according to the dictates of political expediency at given moments, the expansiveness of the guess made by the particular official being interviewed, or even sheer whimsy. Barring a reversal of the regime's hesitancy to include religious questions in its census-taking procedures since 1937, and, furthermore, in view of the continuing policy of withholding such statistical information, it seems quite unlikely that more accurate bases for sociological study will be available to either Western sociologists or to Soviet scholars themselves in the foreseeable future.

## CURRENT SOVIET STUDIES IN THE SOCIOLOGY OF RELIGION

In view of this lack of data, Soviet sociologists, in attempting to develop a new field in Soviet research and scholarship, have been reduced to marginal studies on the periphery of the sociology of religion. They have not yet acquired the basic tools necessary for generalized sociological study, and, while their efforts have been intelligent, vigorous and exceedingly respectable, they remain ancillary to a more general understanding of the sociological factors operating in the religious life of the U.S.S.R.

Some few investigations have been made concerning discrete aspects of religious observance. Thus, for example, in one locality,

> In families whose heads are employed in state institutions only 21 per cent of the families have icons; families of workers and business employees, 30 per cent; and of collective farmers, 47 per cent. We are not talking about pensioners and unemployed, among whom the major part (60 and 75 per cent respectively) adorn the red corners of their huts with icons. Thus the huts of collective farmers are one-and-a-half to two times more 'saturated' with icons than other families of workers and employees. To some degree this is due to the greater mean age of the collective farmers. For example, the mean age of heads of families employed in business and state institutions is 40 and 42.8 respectively, while that of collective farmers is 46.2. The lower educational level of the collective farmers also enters in, of course [Arutiunian, 1966, p. 60].

Similarly, it was discovered in one Jewish community in Riga that 50 per cent of the dead were given religious funerals in 1963 and 1964, 25 per cent were given religious funerals modified somewhat by new (secular) funeral traditions, and only 25 per cent were given secular funerals [Gorodnik, 1966, p. 53].

Some research has been done on occupational data concerning religious people. This is not a new phenomenon – one such study was made in 1931 ['In the mirror of the foreign press' January 1967, p. 35] – but it has been given much greater emphasis during the past decade. For example, in one region of the Ukraine, 69,2 per cent of the Baptists were discovered to be pensioners, housewives or dependents, while 61 per cent in a neighbouring region were similarly unemployed, and only 36 per cent of the Baptist community in a third region were employed in industry [Dobrotvor and Pastukh 1967, pp. 64–71].

More complex problems which are being analysed by Soviet scholars include research into motivations concerning religion. In one survey among believers,

> Some of them say that religion answers the questions posed in their minds; to the others it 'promises salvation of their soul'; to a third group it offers an aesthetic satisfaction; the fourth group believe in God on the basis of moral and ethical consideration; the fifth group believes 'just in case'; and the sixth group refers to tradition. In no instance have we met with any expressions for reasons of faith in God which would reach beyond the framework of one of the six afore-mentioned motives [Dulman, 1966, pp. 19–23].

Attempts have also been made to develop the interview in depth as a means of acquiring sociological data [Prikhodko, 1967, pp. 62–64].

As yet there have been no attempts to conduct sociological surveys on anything approaching a nationwide basis. Some very promising beginnings have been made, but these have all been confined to local areas and it is difficult to determine whether one can generalize upon such studies. As a few examples, several studies were made between 1962 and 1966 on county-wide bases, and while some data were acquired on such matters as church attendance on a given Sunday, insufficient information was given to allow generalization [Iablokov, 1967, pp. 27–36]. In another study, using questionnaires followed by interviews,

> Although an absolute majority of the 177 questioned either do not acknowledge God at all (65 people) or answered 'don't know' to the question of his existence, do not pray at home and pay hardly any attention to the church, even so 58 people consider themselves to be believers – and this, of course, is not an insignificant number.
>
> The survey showed that a proportion of the inhabitants of Porech'e observe religious rites and customs merely in conformity to habit or tradition. Here are some statistics. To the question 'In order to be a moral and good person, is it essential to have one's children baptized?' 109 of those interviewed answered 'No', 12 said 'Don't know' and 56 'Yes'. On inviting a priest to a funeral, 95 said 'No', 10 'Don't know' and 72 'Yes'. An absolute majority of those questioned, 128 people, do not consider it shameful to work on religious feast days, while some believe this to be sinful. 137 do not believe it necessary to attend church but 34 disagree [Safronov, 1967, pp. 66–71].

In a study conducted among 832 peasants, 1,058 skilled workers, and 1,036 professional people in one area, it was discovered that among the peasants 8 per cent considered themselves convinced believers and 4 per cent merely observed church rituals. Among the skilled the figures were 1 per cent in both categories, and the same results were obtained among the professional people [Krasilov, 1966]. In another village, 9 per cent were believers, 8 per cent were vacillating, 58.9 per cent were indifferent to religion, and 24.1 per cent were convinced atheists [Simush, 1966, pp. 125–126]. Studies conducted in predominantly Catholic Lithuania indicated that 81 per cent of all children were baptized, 64.8 per cent of marriages were religious celebrated, and 79 per cent of all funerals were religious in 1958, while corresponding figures for 1964 were 58.3 per cent, 38 per cent and 60.8 per cent, respectively [Pomerantsev, 1966, pp. 2–7]. A similar survey of 300 Jews in Birobidzhan revealed that only 8 considered themselves believers [Vinokur, 1967, pp. 41–43].

Some attempts have been made to escape the dilemma of studies confined to a single area. One such comparison dealt with a collective farm in a rich agricultural area at which only a low percentage fulfilled Orthodox rites, as against a similar collective in a poor area where a high percentage was observed. This particular study failed to mention that the rich collective farm chosen, in Khazakhstan, was in a predominantly Moslem area [Kapparov and Cherniak, 1967, pp. 65–72].

Soviet sociologists of religion have had somewhat better success in dealing with religious groups which are geographically, ethnographically or linguistically identifiable. Naturally, such studies do not cover religious groups which have been obsorbed, assimilated or dispersed within the Soviet populace, and are confined to minority religions instead. Studies of this sort have been conducted among Jews, Moslems, Baltic Churches, and others [Kapparov and Cherniak, 1967. pp. 65–72; Pomerantsev, 1966, pp. 2–7; Dorzhenov, 1967, pp. 50–52].

Finally, fairly complete sociological studies have been devoted to certain discreet religious minorities which are sufficiently small to allow more comprehensive treatment. Such studies are carried out particularly on those groups which the state feels are especially pernicious. Perhaps the best example of this kind of study was that devoted to the True Orthodox Church, a clandestine variant of Russian Orthodoxy [Academy of Sciences of the U.S.S.R., 1961, pp. 144–188].

In general, however, such results of Soviet Sociology of Religion as are available to the Western observer consist primarily of general reports [e.g. Beliaev, *et al.*, 1966]. Much data is suppressed within even the most scholarly reports, and other specifics are presented so generally as to defy evaluation. In particular, questions of methodology, upon which the entire validity of any questionnaire, interview, or survey procedure depends, are, with rare exception, undisclosed [Klibanov 1967].

The result is that the Sociology of Religion remains an immature discipline within the U.S.S.R. Interesting points of data are occasionally available, but on the whole there is no possibility at present for deriving a substantial, generalized picture in this field. Some encouragement may be taken from the seriousness of the efforts within the Soviet academic community within the last few years, but on the whole it would seem that this will remain a deficient and largely neglected field for the foreseeable future.

## SELECTED BIBLIOGRAPHY


Academy of Sciences of the U.S.S.R., *Voprosy istorii religii i ateizma*, [Problems of the History of Religion and Atheism]. 12 Vols. Moscow, Academy Press, 1961.

Alexeev, Wassilij, *The Foreign Policy of the Moscow Patriarchate*, 1939–1953 [in Russian] Research Programme on the U.S.S.R. New York, 1955.

Anderson, Paul B, 'Churchmen Visit Russia.' *Christian Century*, 73, 18 April, 1956.

Antonii, Bishop of Los Angeles, *O polozhenii tserkvi v sovetskoi rossii i o dukhovnoi zhizni russkago naroda* [The Position of the Church in Soviet Russia and the Spiritual Life of the Russian People]. Jordanville (N.Y.), Holy Trinity Monastery, 1960.

Arutiunian, Iu. V., 'The Social Structure of the Rural Population'. *Voprosy Filosofii*, 5, May 1966.

Bailey, S. D., 'Religious Boom in Russia.' *Christian Century*, 75, 12 March, 1958.

Baykov, Alexander, *The Development of the Soviet Economic System.* Cambridge (Mass.), Harvard University Press, 1946.

Beliaev, E. G., *et al.* 'All-Union Symposium, of Sociologists.' *Voprosy Filosofii*, pp. 156–165, October 1966.

Blake, Patricia, 'Alliance with the Unholy.' *Life*, 14 September 1959.

Bogolepov, Aleksandr A., *Tserkov' pod vlast'iu kommunizma* [The Church under the Rule of Communism]. Munich, Institute for the Study of the U.S.S.R., 1958.

Bourdeaux, Michael, *Religious Ferment in Russia.* London, Macmillan, 1968.

—, *Opium of the People.* London, Faber and Faber, 1965.

—, and Struve, Nikita, *U.S.S.R.: Dibattito Nella Comunita Cristiana* [U.S.S.R.: Debate within the Christian Community]. Milan, Russia Christiana, 1968.

Braun, Leopold L., *Religion in Russia, from Lenin to Khrushchev: An Uncensored Account.* Patterson (N. J.), St Anthony's Guild Press, 1959.

Casey, Robert P., *Religion in Russia.* New York, Harper, 1946.

Chamberlin, W. H., *The Russian Revolution.* New York, Macmillan, 1952.

Conquest, Robert (ed.), *Religion in the U.S.S.R.* London, Bodley Head, 1968.

Conybeare, Frederick, C., *Russian Dissenters.* Cambridge (Mass.), Harvard University Press, 1921.

Curtiss, John S., *The Russian Church and the Soviet State, 1917–1950.* Boston, Little, Brown, and Co., 1953.

Dallin, David J., *The Changing World of Soviet Russia.* New Haven (Conn.), Yale University Press, 1956.
Davis, Nathaniel, *Religion and Communist Government in the Soviet Union and Eastern Europe:* (Unpublished Ph. D. dissertation. Cambridge (Mass.), Fletcher School of Law and Diplomacy, 1960.
Deutscher, Isaac, *Stalin: A Political Biography.* New York, Oxford University Press, 1949.
Dobrotvor, V. and Pastukh, M., 'Scientific Atheistic Upbringing and the Vanquishing of Religious Survival.' *Kommunist Ukrainy*, September 1967.
Dorzhenov, S , 'Am I a Muslim?.' *Nauka i Religiia*, April 1967.
Duluman, E., 'Motives of Religiosity.' *Liudina i Svit*, July 1966.
Emhardt, William C., *Religion in Soviet Russia.* London, Morehouse, 1929.
Evans, Stanley G., *The Russian Church To-day.* London, Zeno Publishers, 1955.
*Ezhegodnik Rossii za 1914* (Annual of Russia for 1914). St Petersburg, 1914.
Fedorenko, F., *Sekty, ikh vera i dela* (The Sects, Their Faith and Actions). Moscow, Political Literature Press, 1965.
Fireside, Harvey F., *The Russian Orthodox Church under German Occupation in World War II* Unpublished Ph. D. dissertation. New York, New School for Social Research, 1968.
Fletcher, William C., *Nikolai: Portrait of a Dilemma.* New York, Macmillan, 1968.
—, 'Soviet Society and Religion:A Trip Report.' *Communist Affairs*, June-August 1963.
—, *A Study in Survival: The Church in Russia, 1927–1943.* New York, Macmillan, 1965.
Foltz, Charles, Jr., 'Religion in Russia Today: A First-Hand Report.' *U.S. News and World Report*, 10 February 1964.
Fontanieu, P., 'Le Problème Religieux en U.S.S.R.' [The religious problem in the U.S.S.R.]. *Christianisme Sociale*, January-February 1955.
Gerodnik, G., 'An Atheist's Principles'. *Nauka i Religiia*, November, 1966.
Gidulianov, Pavel V. (ed.), *Otdelenie tserkvi ot gosudarstva. Polnyi sbornik dekretov R.S.F.S.R. i S.S.S.R., instruktsii, tsirkuliarov, i t. d.*
The Separation of Church from State. A Full Collection of Decrees of the R.S.F.S.R. and the U.S.S.R., Instruction, Circulars, etc.]. Moscow, State Publishing House for Juridical Literature, 1959.
Guins, George C., *Communism on the Decline.* The Hague, Martinus Nijhoff, 1959.
Hindus, Maurice G., *The Great Offensive.* New York, Smith and Haas, 1933.
—, *House Without a Roof.* Garden City (N. Y.), Doubleday, 1961.
Horsely, A. A., in: *Sunday Times* (London), 12 December 1954.
Hutten, Kurt, *Iron Curtain Christians.* Translated by Walter G. Tillmans. Minneapolis (Minn.), Augsburg Publishing House 1967.
Iablokov, I. N., 'An Experiment of Concrete Research into Religious Adherence.' *Vestnik Moskovskogo Universiteta*, 4, July-August, 1967.
Iaroslavskii, Emel'ian, 'Church and State.' *Pravda*, 15 September 1937.
—, *O Religii* [On Religion]. Moscow, State Publishing House for Political Literature, 1957.
Iudin, N. I., *Pravda o Petersburgskikh 'Sviatyniakh'* [The Truth about the Petersburg 'Shrines']. Leningrad, Leningrad Publishing House, 1962. (Translation in *Religion in Communist Dominated Areas*, edited by Paul B. Anderson. New York,

National Council of Churches, II (15), 24 June 1963).

Jackson, Joseph H., *The Eternal Flame: The Story of a Preaching Mission in Russia.* Philadelphia (Penn.), Christian Education Press, 1956.

Jung, E. M., 'Table-talk with the Russian Observers: Failure of the Greek Orthodox to send Observers to the First Session of the Council.' *Catholic World,* 196, February 1963.

Kapparov, D. A. and Cherniak, V. A., 'Why and in What Conditions Religious Survivals Persist.' *Voprosy Filosofii,* June 1967.

Kellen, Konrad, *Khrushchev: A Political Portrait.* New York, Praeger, 1961.

Khudiakov, S. N., *Vsegda budet sushchestvovat' religiia* [Will Religion Always Exist]. Moscow, 'Znanie' Press, 1958.

—, *Znanie i vera v boga* [Knowledge and Belief in God]. Moscow, 'Znanie' Press, 1960.

Klibanov, A. I. (ed.), *Konkretnye issledovaniia sovremennykh religioznykh verovanii; metodika, organizatsiia, rezul'taty* [Concrete Research on Contemporary Religious Beliefs; (Methodology, Organization, Results)]. Moskow, 'Mysl' Press, 1967.

Kolarz, Walter, *Religion in the Soviet Union.* London, Macmillan, 1962.

—, 'Religious Believers in Soviet Russia.' *Listener,* 29 January 1959.

Konstantinov, Dmitrii, *Religious persecution in U.S.S.R. London* (Canada), S.B.O.N.R., 1965.

—, *Pravoslavnaia molodezh' v bor'be za tserkov' v S.S.S.R.* [Orthodox Youth in the Struggle for the Church in the U.S.S.R.]. Munich, Institute for the Study of the U.S.S.R., 1956.

Krasilov, A., 'A Sociologist's Notes: Personality and Religion.' *Sel'skaia Zhizn',* 25 November 1966.

Lamont, Corliss, *Soviet Civilization.* New York, Philosophical Library, 1952.

Lonsdale, Kathleen (ed.), *Quakers Visit Russia.* London, East-West Relations Group of the Friends' Peace Committee, 1952.

—, *Reforme,* 31 August 1946.

MacEoin, Gary and Zombory, Akos, *The Communist War on Religion.* New York, Devin-Adair, 1951.

Miliukov, Paul, *Outlines of Russian Culture.* Philadelphia (Penn.), University of Pennsylvania Press, 1942.

Mitrokhin, L. N., 'Reaktsionnaia deiatel'nost' 'Istinno-Pravoslavnoi Tserkvi' na Tambovshchine' [The Reactionary Activity of the 'True Orthodox Church' in the Tambov Area], in: Academy of Sciences of the U.S.S.R., *Sovremennoe sektantstvo* [Contemporary Sectarianism]. Vol. IX of the series, *Voprosy istorii religii i ateizma* [Problems of the history of Religion and Atheism]. Moscow, Academy Press, 1961.

Murav'ev, E. F. and Dmitriev, Iu. V., 'Concreteness in Studying and Overcoming Religious Survivals.' *Voprosy Filosofii,* March 1961. (Translations of this article are available in *Current Digest of the Soviet Press,* XIII (20), 14 June 1961, p. 3–7 and *Soviet Review,* July 1961, pp. 41–56).

McCullagh, Francis, *The Bolshevik Persecution of Christianity.* New York, Dutton, 1924.

Okulov, A. F. (ed.), *Voprosy nauchnogo ateizma* [Problems of Scientific Atheism]. Moscow, 'Mysl'' Press, 1966.
Oleshchuk, F., 'Tasks of antireligious propaganda.' *Pod Znamenem Marksizma*, April 1937.
Parker, E. C., 'East-West Ecumenical Contacts.' *Christian Century*, 30 October 1962.
Pipes, Richard, *The Formation of the Soviet Union*. Cambridge (Mass.), Harvard University Press, 1954.
Pol'skii, Mikhail, *Novye mucheniki rossiskie* [Modern Russian Martyrs]. Jordanville (N.Y.), Holy Trinity Monastery, 1957.
Pomerantsev, V., 'Yesterday and today.' *Nauka i Religiia*, April 1966.
Prikhodko, R., 'What is the Testimony of Sociological Studies?' *Liudina i Svit*, March 1967.
—, 'The Russian Orthodox Church and the Soviet Leadership.' *Soviet Affairs Analysis Service*, 17, 1961–62.
Safronov, Iu, 'What the Answers Showed.' *Kommunist Belorussi*, March 1967.
Schakovskoy, Zinaida, *The Privilege Was Mine*. New York, Putnam, 1959.
Shaw, M., 'Impressions of the Russian Orthodox Church.' *International Review of Missions*, 47, October 1958.
Sheen, Fulton J., *Communism and the Conscience of the West*. Indianapolis (Ind.), Bobbs-Merrill, 1948.
Simush, P., 'Cultural Life in One Belorussian Village.' *Politicheskoe Samoobrazovanie*, July 1966.
Spinka, Mathew, *The Church and the Russian Revolution*. New York, Macmillan, 1927.
—, *The Church in Soviet Russia*. New York, Oxford University Press, 1956.
—, *Christianity Confronts Communism*. New York, Harper, 1936.
Steinberg, S. H. (ed.), *The Statesman's Yearbook*. 1968.
Strohm, John L., *Just Tell the Truth*. New York, Scribner's, 1947.
Struve, Nikita, *Christians in Contemporary Russia*. Translated by Lancelot Sheppard and A. Manson. London, Harvill Press, 1967.
'Testimony of Paul B. Anderson', in: *Recent Developments in the Soviet Bloc*, edited by U.S. Government, House Committee on Foreign Affairs, Washington, D.C., U.S. Government Printing Office, 1964.
Timasheff, Nicholas S., *The Great Retreat*. New York, Dutton, 1946.
—, *Religion in Soviet Russia, 1917–1942*. New York, Sheed and Ward, 1942.
—, 'Urbanization, Operation Antireligion and the Decline of Religion in the U.S.S.R.' *American Slavic and East European Review*, XIV (2), April 1955.
Titov, V. E., *Pravoslavie* [Orthodoxy]. Moscow, Political Literature Press, 1967.
Tobias, Robert, *Communist Christian Encounter in East Europe*. Indianapolis (Ind.), School of Religion Press, Butler University, 1956.
Valentinov, A., 'Soviet Legislation on Cults.' *Nauka i Religiia*, October 1961. Translated in *Joint Publications Research Service* 11797, 'Translations on Religion in the USSR', 8, 29 December 1961.
Veschikov, A., 'Milestones of a Great Journey.' *Nauka i Religiia*, November 1962.
Vinokur, A., 'Eclipse of an Ancient Faith.' *Nauka i Religiia*, January 1967. Translation in *Religion in Communist Dominated Areas*, 149, 24 December 1962.

White, 'The Triple-Barred Cross.' *Scribner's Magazine*, LXXXVIII, July 1930.
Wolfe, Bertram D., *Six Keys to the Soviet System.* Boston, Beacon, 1956.
Wolin, Simon and Slusser, Robert M., *The Soviet Secret Police.* New York, Praeger, 1957.

ANTE FIAMENGO*

# Yugoslavia

## INTRODUCTION

Two main problems dominate the sociology of religion: the influence of the social environment on religious beliefs and the influence of religious conceptions on the social environment. If this the dialectical relationship between the environment and religious conceptions, in the causalgenetic as well as the functional sense, constitutes the essence of the sociology of religion, it should not be overlooked that the environment in itself remains very complex. There is a place for speaking of a social and a natural environment. The notion of social environment also includes several distinct factors: the economic structure of the society, the social structure, the family environment, the cultural configuration etc. Each of these categories is again subdivided into still smaller categories or distinct factors. But this detailed analysis is not the object of the present discussion.

The analysis of the interaction of religious beliefs and technological changes calls for more specific explanations. The technological factor represents one of the constituent elements of the forces of production. It cannot be treated separately from the nature of social relations, that is to say from the nature of the social system, because the process of technological change itself is intimately connected with the transformations of social systems through time. It is from this perspective that we will examine the nature of religious beliefs in Yugoslavia in relation to changes in the social structure, including the technological changes which have taken place since World War II.

During World War II at the very time that the Yugoslavian peoples were fighting for national liberation they also achieved a social revolution: the

* Ante Fiamengo was born in 1912 at Komiza, Yugoslavia. He graduated from the University of Belgrade in 1940. He is presently dean of the Faculty of Political Science and the University of Zagreb. He has been awarded a medal for his work in Yugoslavia, and has held scholarships given by the French Government and the Ford Foundation. Major publications include articles and booklets on both philosophy and religion, as well as books on sociology.

This article is reproduced with the author's permission from the *Archives de Sociologie des Religions*, Vol. 15, 1963, pp. 101–111.

transformation of a capitalist social structure into a socialist one. This change has rapidly given rise to abrupt economic, technological, cultural, psychological and ideological changes.

As a result of the very low level of industrial development to which it was heir, the principal task of the new socialist community of Yugoslavian peoples was to revive the backward technology and economy and to transform Yugoslavia into an industrial country. In this context the development of heavy industry was crucial because this was the only effective means of rapidly putting an end to the backward technological state.

The dynamism of the social economy is most pronounced in the development of production equipment, that is to say in the development of the technological factor.

*Table 1. Index of industrial production*

| | 1939 | 1946 | 1947 | 1948 | 1949 | 1950 | 1951 |
|---|---|---|---|---|---|---|---|
| Production equipment | 100 | 121 | 241 | 352 | 462 | 510 | 534 |
| Capital equipment | 100 | 76 | 113 | 138 | 154 | 160 | 153 |
| Consumer goods | 100 | 84 | 130 | 165 | 171 | 165 | 162 |
| | **1952** | **1953** | **1954** | **1955** | **1956** | **1957** | **1958** |
| Production equipment | 582 | 757 | 785 | 917 | 971 | 1127 | 1375 |
| Capital equipment | 156 | 169 | 193 | 228 | 255 | 292 | 323 |
| Consumer goods | 142 | 160 | 184 | 207 | 230 | 279 | 306 |

Source: Index of the Federal Institute of Statistics, Yugoslavia, No. 4, 1960, p.5.

*Table 2. Number of workers employed in industry*

| Year | N | Year | N | Year | N |
|---|---|---|---|---|---|
| 1918 | 152,811 | 1954 | 717.000 | 1958 | 970,000 |
| 1938 | 197,000 | 1955 | 800,000 | 1959 | 1,031,000 |
| 1952 | 615,000 | 1956 | 835,000 | 1960 | 1,103,000 |
| 1953 | 634,000 | 1957 | 900,000 | 1961 | 1,154,000 |

Source: Index of the Federal Institute of Statistics, Yugoslavia, No. 2, 1932, p. 44.

The average rate of annual increase in industrial production during the period 1947–56 rose to 9.6 per cent, and in the period 1957–1961 the planned rate was 11 or 12 per cent, but during certain years it rose as high as 13 per cent.

*Table 3. Population structure*

| Year | Population (in millions) | Agricultural population % |
|---|---|---|
| 1921 | 12.5 | 78.9 |
| 1931 | 14.5 | 76.6 |
| 1953 | 17.0 | 61.0 |
| 1956 | 17.8 | 58.1 |
| 1961 | 18.5 | 51.0 |

The rapid progress of industrial development in Yugoslavia has influenced the change in the structure of the population; there has been a marked rise in the number of workers employed in industry, and between 1931 and 1961 the proportion engaged in agriculture fell from 76.6 per cent to 51.0 per cent. This has been followed by an increase in the number of schools and related staff.

## THE IMPACT OF INDUSTRIAL PROGRESS AND TECHNOLOGICAL DEVELOPMENT ON CHANGES IN RELIGIOUS BELIEFS [1]

Yugoslavia is a social entity comprised of several nations and several religions. Table 4 shows the proportion of Yugoslav nationals of different religious beliefs.

Given that religious affiliation has been mentioned only in the census of 1953, some detailed clarification of the data provided by this census must be given. These data will be compared with the results which were later obtained in some special surveys of students, secondary school teachers and workers. [2]

The results of the population census of 1953 will be presented under the following headings: a) the attitude of the nationalities towards religion;

1. Data concerning church-attendance are lacking.

2. These surveys were:

a. Survey of students of the University of Sarajevo (1957);
b. Survey of Yugoslav students (1959);
c. Survey of secondary school teachers of Sarajevo (1961);
d. Survey of the workers' communes of 8 undertakings in the territory of Bosna-Hercegovina (1961).

*Table 4. Religious affiliation in Yugoslavia 1921–53*

| | | Census of: | |
|---|---|---|---|
| | 31.1.1921 | 31.3.1931 | 31.3.1953 |
| Orthodox | 5,602,227 | 6,785,501 | 6,984,686 |
| Roman Catholics | 4,735,154 | 5,217,847 | 5,370,760 |
| Greek Catholics | 41,597 | – | – |
| Protestants | 216,847 | 231,161 | 157,702 |
| Muslims | 1,337,687 | 1,561,166 | 2,090,380 |
| Jews | 64,159 | – | – |
| Others | 17,636 | – | 68,908 |
| No religious affiliation | 2,016 | – | – |
| Atheists | – | – | 2,127,875 |
| Remainder | – | 138,355 | 136,262 |
| Total | 12,017,323 | 13,934,020 | 16,936,573 |

Source: Census data.

b) religion and the male and female population; c) the attitude of the different age-groups towards religious phenomenon, and d) attitudes of the towns and their corresponding districts towards religion.

Table 5 provides the following results in respect to religion:

1) For Yugoslavia as a whole the average percentage of atheists is 12.6. This is exceeded by: the Montenegrins (32.5 per cent), the Serbs and the Macedonians (15.8 per cent).
2) Below that general average, we find the Slav people of other nationalities, the Slovenes (10.3 per cent), the Croats (10.1 per cent), the unclassified Yugoslavs (4 per cent) and the other non-Slavonic nationalities; the two latter nationalities are comprised chiefly of Muslims.
3) The percentage of atheists is higher in the nationalities of Orthodox faith; it is significantly lower among the Catholic nationalities and is minimal in the Islamic social group.
4) The percentage of declared female atheists is lower than that of male atheists for all nationalities.[3]

3. Using the formula proposed by J. Maitre [1963] for the declaration of 'non-atheism' (which implies, in fact, affiliation to a religion) the coefficient of secular dimorphism is L = 1.76.

*Table 5. Atheism in Yugoslavia according to sex*

| Nationality | Sex | Population total | N | % |
|---|---|---|---|---|
| Serbian | Total | 7,065,923 | 1,119,432 | 15.8 |
| | Male | 3,455,302 | 695,286 | 20.1 |
| | Female | 3,610,621 | 424,146 | 11.8 |
| Croat | Total | 3,975,550 | 407,311 | 10.1 |
| | Male | 1,876,261 | 253,415 | 13.6 |
| | Female | 2,099,289 | 153,796 | 7.7 |
| Slovene | Total | 1,487,100 | 153,206 | 10.3 |
| | Male | 697,603 | 90,049 | 13.0 |
| | Female | 789,497 | 63,157 | 8.0 |
| Montenegrin | Total | 466,093 | 184,710 | 39.5 |
| | Male | 225,892 | 104,532 | 47.0 |
| | Female | 240,201 | 80,378 | 33.0 |
| Macedonian | Total | 893,247 | 141,372 | 15.8 |
| | Male | 454,277 | 87,593 | 19.2 |
| | Female | 438,970 | 53,779 | 12.2 |
| Yugoslav, unclassified | Total | 998,698 | 39,393 | 4.0 |
| | Male | 481,777 | 26,420 | 5.5 |
| | Female | 516,921 | 12,973 | 2.5 |
| Slav, of other nationalities | Total | 235,992 | 24,528 | 10.3 |
| | Male | 114,134 | 14,950 | 13.2 |
| | Female | 121,858 | 9,578 | 7.9 |
| Non-Slav, of other nationalities | Total | 1,813,970 | 58,028 | 3.3 |
| | Male | 899,349 | 39,202 | 4.4 |
| | Female | 914,621 | 18,821 | 2.2 |
| Total | Total | 16,936,573 | 2,127,875 | 12.6 |
| | Male | 8,204,595 | 1,311,247 | 16.0 |
| | Female | 8,731,978 | 816,628 | 9.4 |

Source: Census data, 1953.

The data in Table 6 show that the greatest number of declared atheists is found in the 20–34 year age-group (almost half of the total number of atheists). A noticeable decrease in the percentage of declared atheists is evident in the older age-groups.

The explanation is twofold: the younger social groups are seized by the desire to realize their ideals in the practice of life and are therefore not very much concerned about the perspectives of life after death. Secondly, these

*Table 6. Relationship between age-groups and religious groups**

| Age groups | Population | | Atheists | | |
|---|---|---|---|---|---|
| | N (in thousands) | % | N (in thousands) | % (of the population of the same group) | % (of the total number of atheists) |
| 0–6 years | 2,754 | 16.3 | 383 | 13.9 | 18.4 |
| 7–14 years | 2,422 | 14.3 | 214 | 8.8 | 10.3 |
| 15–19 years | 1,753 | 10.4 | 239 | 13.7 | 11.4 |
| 20–34 years | 4,221 | 24.9 | 911 | 21.6 | 43.7 |
| 35–49 years | 2,805 | 16.6 | 243 | 8.7 | 11.6 |
| 50–64 | 1,963 | 11.6 | 77 | 3.9 | 3.7 |
| 65 years and over | 1,005 | 5.9 | 18 | 1.8 | 0.9 |
| Total | 16,923 | 100.0 | 2,085 | 12.3 | 100.0 |

* According to the 1953 Census the total population of Yugoslavia was 16, 936, 573, the number of atheists was 2, 127, 875 (12.6 per cent). We have a slight difference in Table 5 for two reasons: (1) the statistical data were obtained by sampling; (2) the figures are expressed here in thousands.

groups are engaged in the production process and are thus connected with the technology which provides man with the means to dominate natural phenomena and to subject them to his own needs. The older age groups are less engaged in this process.

The relationship between religious beliefs and social and technological phenomena is shown particularly well by the distribution of declared atheists and believers in the rural and urban populations.

The considerable disproportion between the number of declared atheists in the towns and the surrounding rural areas cannot be explained by a single cause but is the result of several factors. We would like to stress some of the most important of these.

The population which is concentrated in the towns is connected with a more advanced form of production (which gives less support to religious phenomena) than the population involved in agricultural production. Secondly, the level of education, which is higher in the urban population, has certainly influenced the attitude to religion. Thirdly, the institutions and officers necessary for the organized activity of the churches are relatively stronger in the rural than the urban environment.

*Table 7. Population of declared atheists in the towns and in the surrounding rural areas*

| | Town | | | District | | |
|---|---|---|---|---|---|---|
| | Total | Atheists N | Atheists % | Total | Atheists N | Atheists % |
| Serbia | | | | | | |
| 1. Belgrade | 470,172 | 138,785 | 29.5 | 86,781 | 7,158 | 8.2 |
| 2. Nish | 60,704 | 18,815 | 31.0 | 95,519 | 1,044 | 1.1 |
| 3. Kragujevac | 40,612 | 15,652 | 38.5 | 45,980 | 2,295 | 5.0 |
| Croatia | | | | | | |
| 1. Zagreb | 350,829 | 67,291 | 19.2 | 57,213 | 3,018 | 5.3 |
| 2. Pula | 28,572 | 12,119 | 42.4 | 39,911 | 5,874 | 14.7 |
| 3. Split | 75,640 | 26,154 | 34.6 | 67,325 | 9,988 | 14.8 |
| Slovenia | | | | | | |
| 1. Ljubljana | 138,981 | 33,786 | 24.3 | 119,873 | 8,693 | 7.3 |
| 2. Maribor | 77,387 | 17,040 | 22.0 | 105,994 | 5,257 | 5.0 |
| Bosna-Hercegovina | | | | | | |
| 1. Sarajevo | 136,283 | 38,341 | 28.1 | 61,637 | 7,856 | 12.7 |
| 2. Mostar | 31,680 | 12,607 | 39.8 | 40,592 | 1,791 | 4.4 |
| 3. Zenica | 28,981 | 6,769 | 23.4 | 58,152 | 1,320 | 3.5 |
| Montenegro | | | | | | |
| 1. Titograd | 16,031 | 10,213 | 63.7 | 56,031 | 21,920 | 39.1 |
| Macedonia | | | | | | |
| 1. Skopje | 122,143 | 33,974 | 27.8 | 91,443 | 3,872 | 4.2 |

## THREE OPINION SURVEYS

It is interesting to examine the number of declared atheists and believers in a few special surveys conducted among three different social groups: students, secondary school teachers and workmen.

Among 1,109 students questioned at the University of Sarajevo in May 1957 [Fisera, 1961], forty-two students declared themselves believers (3.8 per cent), 466 students classified themselves as indifferent (42 per cent) and 381 as atheists (52.5 per cent). The proportion of atheists in this social group is thus considerably higher than that in the corresponding age-group in the 1953 Yugoslav census.

In a student survey conducted in all Yugoslav Universities 2,967 students (that is to say 76.3 per cent) of a total of 3,889 students questioned declared themselves atheists. Table 8 gives a more precise and differentiated picture of the attitudes of the students in different academic centres. It is based on replies to the question 'What is your attitude towards religion?'

*Table 8. Attitudes towards religion among students of several university cities*

| | Belgrade | | Zagreb | | Ljubijana | | Sarajevo | | Skopje | | Total | |
|---|---|---|---|---|---|---|---|---|---|---|---|---|
| | N | % | N | % | N | % | N | % | N | % | N | % |
| Practising believers | 28 | 1.6 | 43 | 4.5 | 24 | 8.0 | 8 | 2.0 | 9 | 1.9 | 112 | 2.9 |
| Believers who do not practise | 58 | 3.2 | 77 | 8.0 | 7 | 2.4 | 14 | 3.6 | 20 | 4.3 | 176 | 4.5 |
| Believers who practise periodically | 76 | 4.3 | 88 | 9.2 | 21 | 7.0 | 15 | 3.8 | 9 | 1.9 | 209 | 5.4 |
| Unbelievers who practise periodically | 343 | 19.3 | 117 | 15.3 | 38 | 12.8 | 29 | 7.5 | 59 | 12.6 | 616 | 15.8 |
| Unbelievers who do not practise | 485 | 27.2 | 238 | 24.9 | 85 | 28.6 | 87 | 22.5 | 120 | 25.7 | 1015 | 26.1 |
| Resolute opponents of religion | 767 | 43.0 | 349 | 36.5 | 113 | 38.0 | 226 | 58.6 | 243 | 52.0 | 1698 | 43.7 |
| No answer or unknown | 25 | 1.4 | 14 | 1.6 | 9 | 3.2 | 8 | 2.0 | 7 | 0.6 | 63 | 1.6 |
| Total | 1782 | 100 | 956 | 100 | 297 | 100 | 387 | 100 | 467 | 100 | 3889 | 100 |

Table 8 shows the different trends in the attitudes of the students: the lowest percentage is in the group of students who believe and who are practising; the percentage is very low for the group who believe but who do not practise and for those who believe and practise periodically. The percentage increases abruptly in the group who do not believe but who practice periodically. The number of students in the group of non-practising unbelievers is very high; while finally almost half the general total declared themselves to

*Table 9. Attitude of secondary school teachers towards religion*

| | Male | Female | Total |
|---|---|---|---|
| *Your attitude* | | | |
| Profoundly religious | – | – | – |
| Religious | – | 3 | 3 |
| Religious but without conviction | 2 | 1 | 3 |
| Indifferent | 18 | 21 | 39 |
| Atheist, but not consistent | 5 | 8 | 13 |
| Consistent Atheist | 54 | 19 | 73 |
| Unknown – No answer | 7 | 2 | 9 |
| *The attitude of your parents* | | | |
| Profoundly religious | 4 | 4 | 8 |
| Religious | 20 | 16 | 36 |
| Religious but without conviction | 11 | 7 | 18 |
| Indifferent | 13 | 15 | 28 |
| Atheist, but not consistent | 4 | 3 | 7 |
| Consistent Atheist | 4 | 4 | 8 |
| Unknown – No answer | 30 | 5 | 35 |
| *What is according to you the influence of technological changes on religious beliefs?* | | | |
| Very strong | 23 | 12 | 35 |
| Considerable | 49 | 9 | 58 |
| None | 2 | 1 | 3 |
| I don't know | 9 | 19 | 28 |
| Unknown – No answer | 3 | 13 | 16 |
| *What in your opinion is the influence of socio-economic changes on religious beliefs?* | | | |
| Very strong | 35 | 16 | 51 |
| Considerable | 45 | 13 | 58 |
| None | 1 | 3 | 4 |
| I don't know | 2 | 6 | 8 |
| Unknown – No answer | 3 | 16 | 19 |

be determined enemies of religion (43.7 per cent). The two last categories (69.8 per cent) cover for the most part the group of atheist students (76.3 per cent).

Similar trends are shown in the replies of secondary school teachers who were questioned in November 1961. Three questions are of capital importance for the clarification of our problem: the attitude of the persons questioned and of their parents to religion; the influence of technological changes on religious beliefs and the influence of socio-economic changes on the transformation of religious life.

On the basis of the data given by Table 9 several conclusions can be drawn. The percentage of 'consistent atheists' is considerably higher for males than for females (63 per cent against 39 per cent). According to the statements of secondary schoolteachers the percentage of atheists among their parents is insignificant. Two categories predominate among their parents: believers and those who are indifferent. This group considers that the influence of socio-economic changes is somewhat greater than the influence of technological changes, but this difference is hardly significant.

The survey concerning 'The functioning of workers' self-management in some undertakings in Bosnia-Hercegovina' is of special interest.[4] Three questions were dedicated to religion: What is your attitude towards religion? Do you attend places of worship? If you are not attached to religion what has made you adopt this attitude? We will confine ourselves mainly to two aspects: attitude towards religion according to qualification (Table 9) and the motifs which have induced the persons questioned to adopt the atheist position (Table 10).

The attitudes of the different categories of workers show some quite clear tendencies. The highest percentage of declared atheists (those without any religious attachments) is found in the category of skilled (56.3 per cent) or highly skilled workers (55.5 per cent); this is followed by the category of semi-skilled workers (40 per cent) while in the category of unskilled workers the percentage is lower (30.7 per cent). Similarly with church-attendance, the highest percentage of declared non-practising people (those who never visit a place of worship) is in the category of highly skilled (72.4 per cent) or skilled workers (69.2 per cent); it is considerably lower in the category of semi-skilled workers (53.1 per cent) and minimal in the category of unskilled workers (44.9 per cent).

These trends confirm an indirect relationship between the technological element and religion. That is to say, in the category of highly skilled workers, a category of people who are more intimately connected with the more high-

4. The survey was conducted in eight undertakings on the basis of a sample of 10 per cent of the workers. The total number of persons questioned was 1,669.

*Table 10. Professional qualification and attitude to religion*

| Qualification | Total | Attitude Towards Religion | | | | | | | | Church Attendance | | | | | | | |
|---|---|---|---|---|---|---|---|---|---|---|---|---|---|---|---|---|---|
| | | I value religion | | I do not value religion very much | | I do not value religion at all | | Un-known | | Regular attend-ance | | Period-ical attend-ance | | No church attend-ance | | Un-known | |
| | | N | % | N | % | N | % | N | % | N | % | N | % | N | % | N | % |
| Highly skilled | 155 | 22 | 14.2 | 43 | 27.7 | 86 | 55.5 | 4 | 2.6 | 5 | 3.2 | 34 | 21.9 | 112 | 72.3 | 4 | 2.6 |
| Skilled | 568 | 92 | 16.2 | 135 | 23.8 | 320 | 56.3 | 21 | 3.7 | 33 | 5.8 | 121 | 21.3 | 392 | 69.0 | 22 | 3.9 |
| Semi-skilled | 465 | 139 | 29.9 | 133 | 28.6 | 186 | 40.0 | 7 | 1.5 | 51 | 11.0 | 157 | 33.8 | 247 | 53.1 | 10 | 2.1 |
| Unskilled | 254 | 85 | 33.5 | 84 | 33.1 | 78 | 30.7 | 7 | 2.9 | 24 | 9.4 | 108 | 42.5 | 114 | 44.9 | 8 | 3.2 |
| Tertiary education | 15 | – | – | 2 | – | 13 | – | – | – | – | – | 1 | – | 14 | – | – | – |
| Technical education | 2 | – | – | 1 | – | 1 | – | – | – | – | – | – | – | 2 | – | – | – |
| Secondary schooling | 93 | 6 | 6.5 | 14 | 15.1 | 73 | 78.4 | – | – | 3 | 3.2 | 4 | 4.3 | 86 | 92.5 | – | – |
| Primary schooling | 104 | 5 | 4.8 | 22 | 21.2 | 75 | 72.1 | – | – | – | – | 8 | 7.7 | 95 | 91.3 | 1 | – |
| Casual employees | 11 | 1 | – | 6 | – | 4 | – | – | – | 1 | – | 3 | – | 7 | – | – | – |
| Unknown | 2 | 1 | – | – | – | 1 | – | – | – | – | – | 1 | – | 1 | – | – | – |
| Total | 1669 | 351 | 21.1 | 440 | 26.5 | 837 | 50.0 | 41 | 2.5 | 117 | 7.0 | 437 | 26.2 | 1070 | 64.1 | 45 | 2.7 |

*Table 11. Professional qualifications and motives for religious abstention*

| Qualification | Total | | Motives which have led to non-belief | | | | | | | | | | |
|---|---|---|---|---|---|---|---|---|---|---|---|---|---|
| | | | Education at home | Education at school | Contacts with people who do not value religion | Ideological Political training | Reading | Opinion that life and work depends on man and not on supernatural forces | | Process of work at the place of employment | Other motives | Not known | |
| | N | % | N | N | N | N | N | N | % | N | N | N | % |
| Highly skilled | 86 | 100 | 3 | 1 | 4 | 10 | 4 | 33 | 38.3 | 1 | 1 | 29 | 33.7 |
| Skilled | 320 | 100 | 16 | 21 | 33 | 33 | 17 | 106 | 33.1 | 7 | 1 | 86 | 26.9 |
| Semi-skilled | 186 | 100 | 13 | 8 | 27 | 12 | 11 | 42 | 22.6 | 9 | 12 | 52 | 28.0 |
| Unskilled | 78 | 100 | 5 | 1 | 8 | 4 | 4 | 24 | 30.8 | – | 2 | 30 | 38.4 |
| Tertiary education | 13 | 100 | – | 1 | – | 1 | – | 7 | 53.8 | – | – | 4 | 30.8 |
| Technical education | 1 | 100 | – | – | – | – | – | 1 | – | – | – | – | – |
| Secondary schooling | 73 | 100 | 2 | 4 | 6 | 12 | 2 | 28 | 38.4 | – | 1 | 18 | 24.7 |
| Primary schlling | 75 | 100 | 7 | 5 | 5 | 10 | 4 | 28 | 37.3 | – | – | 16 | 21.4 |
| Casual employees | 4 | 100 | – | – | – | – | – | 2 | – | 2 | – | – | – |
| Unknown | 1 | 100 | – | – | – | – | – | – | – | – | – | 1 | – |
| Total | 839 | 100 | 46 | 41 | 83 | 82 | 42 | 271 | | 19 | 17 | 236 | |

ly developed technological sector, one notices a decline in attachments to religion in its ideological as well as in its practical aspects.

The analysis of the responses of the declared atheists on the motives that they consider to have induced them to that attitude (Table 11) reveal the following trends: of nine given factors the opinion that human life and work depend solely on man and not on supernatural forces ranks first (32.5 per cent), followed by the factor of 'contact with other persons who do not value religion' (9.9 per cent) and 'political-ideological traning' (9.8 per cent). The other factors range between 5.5 and 1.9 per cent. However, the 21.1 per cent non-response should be pointed out.

## REFERENCES AND SELECTED BIBLIOGRAPHY

Fisera, J. and Fiamengo, A, 'Religion et opinions chez les étudiants de l'Université Sarejevo' [Religion and Attitudes among the Students of the University of Sarajevo]. *Archives de Sociologie des Religions*, 12, 1961, pp. 145–155.

Maitre, J., 'Représentations logarithmiques de phénoménes religieux' [Logarithmic Representation of Religious Phenomena]. *Revue française de sociologie*, IV (1), 1963.

Official Information Service of Belgrade, *La situation de l'Eglise Catholique romaine en Yougoslavie* [The Situation of the Roman Catholic Church in Belgrade]. Reference R.N. 334/61–F.

—, *La situation de l'Eglise en R.P.F.Y.* [The Situation of the Church in the Peoples Federal Republic of Yugoslavia]. Reference R.N. 318/61–F.

# Index of Names

# Index of Subjects

# Contents

RELIGION AND REASON I
*Method and Theory*
*in the Study and Interpretation of Religion*

# Category Formation and the History of Religions

*by Robert D. Baird (University of Iowa)*

This study is concerned with the discipline of the *history of religions* and more particularly with its fundamental concepts of 'religion', of 'history' and of 'understanding'. The author pleads for a functional-definitional method as opposed to what he calls the essential-intuitional one.

In the three central chapters of this book, Professor Baird analyzes and discusses some prevailing definitions of the concepts of *religion, history* and *understanding*. He offers in each case a suitable functional definition and develops his arguments consistently. In the case of the category of 'understanding' the author wants to distinguish four levels of understanding: in this connection the work of Bronislaw Malinowski (functional understanding), Mircea Eliade (phenomenological understanding), Wilfred Cantwell Smith (personal understanding), Hendrik Kraemer, Hans Küng and Sarvepalli Radhakrishnan (normative understanding) is discussed.

In the concluding chapter some concepts which are inadequate according to the author, are rejected: 'Religions' in the plural, 'syncretism' and 'transhistorical structures'. The concept of 'religion' in the singular is considered to be an adequate primary category.

The present study is one of the first attempts to clarify systematically, on the basis of logical analysis, the fundamental categories used in the history of religions. It differentiates the specific method of this discipline, on the one hand, from other fields of historical study, and, on the other hand, from other disciplines in the study of religion. A new definition of the history of religions is offered, which opens new avenues for the discipline.

Robert D. Baird is Associate Professor of History of Religions at the University of Iowa. He started teaching at the University of Omaha in 1962 and obtained his Ph.D. degree in religion at the University of Iowa in 1964. His work concentrates on religion in India and on methodology of the history of religions.

# Category Formation and the History of Religions